Linux: The Complete Reference, Fifth Edition

Richard Petersen

McGraw-Hill/Osborne
New York Chicago San Francisco
Lisbon London Madrid Mexico City
Milan New Delhi San Juan
Seoul Singapore Sydney Toronto

McGraw-Hill/Osborne
2600 Tenth Street
Berkeley, California 94710
U.S.A.

To arrange bulk purchase discounts for sales promotions, premiums, or fund-raisers, please contact **McGraw-Hill/**Osborne at the above address. For information on translations or book distributors outside the U.S.A., please see the International Contact Information page immediately following the index of this book.

Linux: The Complete Reference, Fifth Edition

1234567890 DOC DOC 0198765432

Book p/n 0-07-222506-8 and DVD p/n 0-07-222507-6
parts of ISBN 0-07-222505-X

Publisher
Brandon A. Nordin

Vice President & Associate Publisher
Scott Rogers

Acquisitions Editor
Francis Kelly

Senior Project Editor
Carolyn Welch

Acquisitions Coordinator
Emma Acker

Technical Editor
Dean Henrichsmeyer

Copy Editor
Lunaea Weatherstone

Proofreader
Robin Small

Indexer
Claire Splan

Computer Designers
Apollo Publishing Services,
Kathleen Fay Edwards

Illustrators
Michael Mueller, Lyssa Wald

Series Design
Peter F. Hancik

This book was composed with Corel VENTURA™ Publisher.

About the Author

Richard Petersen holds a M.L.I.S. in Library and Information Studies. He currently teaches Unix and C/C++ courses at the University of California, Berkeley.

About the Technical Editor

Dean Henrichsmeyer has been using Linux since 1995. He has a B.S. in Computer Science and has been an active member of the Linux community, presenting at Linux focused tradeshows such as LinuxWorld Conference and Expo and Atlanta Linux Showcase. He's managed high profile community Web sites such as Themes.org and Linux.com. For the past three years, he's worked as a site director for VA Research, now known as VA Software Corporation. Dean has also edited *Red Hat Linux: The Complete Reference, Second Edition,* available from McGraw-Hill/Osborne.

To my brothers,
George, Robert, and Mark

Contents

Part IV
Clients and Applications

Part V

Servers

Acknowledgments

I would like to thank all those at McGraw-Hill/Osborne who made this book a reality, particularly Francis Kelly, acquisitions editor, for his continued encouragement and support of such a complex project. I would also like to thank Jane Brownlow for her help on previous editions; Dean Henrichsmeyer, technical editor, whose analysis and suggestions proved very insightful and helpful; Emma Acker, editorial assistant, who provided needed resources and helpful advice; Lunaea Weatherstone, copy editor, for excellent editing as well as insightful comments; and senior project editor Carolyn Welch, who incorporated the many features found in this book and coordinated the intricate task of generating the final version. Thanks also to Scott Rogers who initiated the project.

Special thanks to Linus Torvalds, the creator of Linux, and to those who continue to develop Linux as an open, professional, and effective operating system accessible to anyone. Thanks also to the academic community without whose special dedication Unix would not be the flexible and versatile operating system it is today. I would also like to thank professors and students at the University of California, Berkeley, for their experience and support in developing new and different ways of understanding operating system technologies.

I would also like to thank my parents, George and Cecelia, and my brothers, George, Robert, and Mark, for their support and encouragement with such a difficult project. Also Valerie and Marylou and my nieces and nephews, Aleina, Larisa, Justin, Christopher, and Dylan, for their support and deadline reminders.

Introduction

The Linux operating system has become one of the major Linux distributions, bringing to the PC all the power and flexibility of a Unix workstation as well as a complete set of Internet applications and a fully functional desktop interface. This book is designed not only to be a complete reference on Linux, but also provides clear and detailed explanations of Linux features. No prior knowledge of Unix is assumed; Linux is an operating system anyone can use.

This book identifies six major Linux topics: basic setup, environments and applications, the Internet, servers, administration, and network administration. These topics are integrated into the different ways Linux is used as a desktop workstation, network workstation, server, and administrative platform. The section on the Desktop workstation covers environments and applications. As a network workstation, Internet applications are added. For servers, the configuration and setup of various Internet servers are discussed. The Administrative section introduces you to different system and network administration topics like configuring the kernel, accessing files systems, and setting up firewalls.

The first two sections of the book are designed to cover tasks you would need to perform to get your system up and running. After an introduction to the working environment, including both Gnome and KDE desktops, you learn how to quickly update your system, access CD-ROMs, and set up your printer. The various automatic update tools make software updates nearly automatic, letting you update the software on your system, including applications, all at once, with just a couple of mouse clicks. Internet access can be set up for modems, DSL, and Ethernet networks with easy-to-use GUI tools that guide you every step of the way. Security is a primary concern for any networked system. This section shows you how to implement basic protection methods such as encryption, intrusion detection, and firewalls. Many people now use Linux to set up a home or local business network. The steps involved to implement a basic network can now be carried out using simple software tools. All these topics are covered in greater detail later in the book.

Gnome and the K Desktop Environment (KDE) have become standard desktop graphical user interfaces (GUI) for Linux, noted for their power, flexibility, and ease-of-use. These are complete desktop environments that are more flexible than either Windows or the Mac/OS. They support standard desktop features such as menus, taskbars, and drag-and-drop operations. But they also provide virtual desktops, panel applets and menus, and Internet capable file managers. KDE and Gnome have become the standard GUI interface for Linux systems. You can install both, run applications from one to the other, and easily switch from one to the other. Both Gnome and KDE were designed with software development in mind, providing a firm foundation that has encouraged the development of a massive number of new applications for these interfaces. They have become integrated components of Linux, with applications and tools for every kind of task and operation. Instead of treating Gnome and KDE as separate entities, Gnome and KDE tools and applications are presented throughout the book. For example, Gnome and KDE mail clients are discussed in the chapter on Internet mailers, along with other mail clients. Gnome and KDE FTP clients, editors, graphic tools, administration tools, among others are also covered in those respective chapters.

Linux is also a fully functional Unix operating system. It has all the standard features of a powerful Unix system, including a complete set of Unix shells such as BASH, TCSH, and the Z-shell. Those familiar with the Unix interface can use any of these shells, with the same Unix commands, filters, and configuration features.

For the Internet, Linux has become a platform for very powerful Internet applications. You can use the Internet, and, with Linux, become a part of it, creating your own Web and FTP sites. Other users can access your Linux systems, several at the same time, using different services. You can also use very powerful Gnome, KDE, and Unix clients for mail and news. Linux systems are not limited to the Internet. You can use it on any local intranet, setting up an ftp or Web site for your network. Most available Linux distributions come equipped with a variety of fully functional FTP and Web servers already installed and ready to use. All you need to do is add the files you want onto your site.

Linux has the same level of administration features that you find on standard Unix systems as well as several user-friendly GUI configuration tools that make any administration task a simple matter of choosing items on a menu or clicking a checkbox. It has the same multiuser and multitasking capabilities. You can set up accounts for different users and each can access your system at the same time. Each user can have several programs running concurrently. With Linux you can control access, set up network connections, and install new devices. Many distributions like Red Hat, SuSE, Mandrake, and Caldera include very powerful and easy-to-use window-based configuration tools for tasks like configuring your printers and setting up your network connections. You can also use comprehensive configuration tools like Linuxconf and Webmin. Although you can use this book for any Linux distribution, particular attention is given to Mandrake, Red Hat, SuSE, Debian, and Caldera.

A wide array of applications operates on Linux. Many personal versions of commercial applications are available for Linux free of charge such as WordPerfect and Sybase database. You can download them directly from the Internet. Numerous Gnome and KDE applications are continually released through their respective Web sites. The GNU public licensed software provides professional level applications such as programming development tools, editors and word processors, as well as numerous specialized applications such as those for graphics and sound. A massive amount of software is available at online Linux sites where you can download applications and then easily install them onto your system.

Since this book is really five books in one—an Internet book, a Gnome and KDE book, a Server book, and Networking book, and an Administration book—how you choose to use it depends upon how you want to use your Linux system. Almost all Linux operations can be carried out using either the Gnome or KDE interface. You need to use the Linux command line interface very little, if at all. You can focus on the Gnome and KDE chapters and their corresponding tools and applications in the different chapters throughout the book. On the other hand, if you want to delve deeper into the Unix aspects of Linux, you can check out the Shell chapters and the corresponding shell-based applications in other chapters. If you only want to use Linux for its Internet services, then concentrate on the Internet clients and servers, most of which are already installed for you. If you want to use Linux as a multiuser system servicing many users or integrate it into a local network, you can use the detailed system, file, and network administration information provided in the administration chapters. None of these tasks are in any way exclusive. If you are working in a business environment, you will probably make use of all three aspects. Single users may concentrate more on the desktops and the Internet features, whereas administrators may make more use of the Unix-like features.

Part I of this book provides an introduction to Linux along with a listing of Linux resources, including software repositories, documentation sites, newsgroups, and Linux news and development sites. The next chapter covers the streamlined installation procedure for most distributions, which takes about 30 minutes. The installation programs from distributions like Red Hat, SuSE, Caldera, and Mandrake provide excellent commentary, describing each step in detail. In this section you also learn the essentials of using both Gnome and KDE, along with the basics of working on the shell command line.

Part II is designed to help you start using Linux quickly. System configuration tasks like mounting CD-ROMs and adding new user accounts are presented with the easiest methods, without much of the complex detail described in the administration chapters that is unnecessary for basic operations. Basic network configuration tasks are discussed such as setting up a connection to an Internet Service Provider (ISP) over a modem, and entering ISP network information such as nameserver and gateway addresses. Then a brief discussion of network security methods shows you how to quickly set up simple protection for a single system connected to the Internet, as well as where to find out more if you have more complex security requirements. Finally, you learn how to set up a small local network that could even include Windows systems. You see how each host should be connected and configured, and how to create a gateway, connecting local hosts to the Internet. You learn to quickly configure and run services such as Domain Name Service, Samba, Sendmail, and a Web site.

Part III deals with Linux as a Desktop Workstation. Here you are introduced to the different kinds of user environments and applications available for Linux, starting with KDE and Gnome. Different features such as applets, the Panel, and configuration tools are described in detail. With either of these interfaces, you can run all your applications using icons, menus, and windows. At any time, you can open up a terminal window through which you can enter standard Linux commands on a command line. You can also choose to use just the standard Unix command line interface to run any of the standard Unix commands. Next, the BASH shell and its various file, directory, and filter commands are examined. The remaining chapters in this section discuss the applications available for Linux, beginning with Office suites like KOffice and Star Office. The different database management systems available are also discussed along with the Web site locations where you can download them. Several different text editors are also available, including several Gnome and KDE editors, as well as the Vim (enhanced VI), gvim (graphical Vi), and GNU Emacs editors.

Part IV incorporates the added features of Linux as a Network Workstation. Here, the book discusses in detail the many Internet applications you can use on your Linux system. Linux automatically installs mail, news, FTP, and Web browser applications, as well as FTP and Web servers. Both KDE and Gnome come with a full set of mail, news, FTP clients, and Web browsers. There are also many independent mail clients, newsreaders, and Internet tools you can easily install from your desktop.

Part V discusses Internet servers you can run on Linux, including FTP, Web, and DNS servers. Internet servers have become integrated components of most Linux systems. Both the standard wu-ftpd FTP server and the newer ProFTPD server with its directive format are presented. ProFTPD covers features like guest and virtual FTP sites. The Apache Web server chapter covers standard configuration directives like those for automatic indexing as well as the newer virtual host directives. Configuration files and features for the Domain Name System (DNS) and its BIND server are examined in detail along with features like virtual domains and IP aliases. With Linux you can easily set up your own Domain Name server for a home or small local network. Both sendmail and POP mail servers are covered. The INN news server, the Squid proxy server, and the ht:/DIG and WAIS search servers are also examined.

Part VI discusses system administration topics including managing users and software, and file system, device, kernel, and X window administration. There are detailed descriptions of the configuration files used in administration tasks and how to make entries in them. First, basic system administration tasks are covered such as selecting runlevels, monitoring your system, and scheduling shutdowns. Then, aspects of setting up and controlling users and groups are discussed. Presentations include both the GUI tools you can use for these tasks and the underlying configurations files and commands. Software installation has been simplified with package management systems like the Red Hat Package Manager (RPM) and the Advanced Package Tool (APT). There are GUI tools like Kpackage and GnomeRPM you can use to easily install and uninstall software, much as you would with the Windows install wizard. Next, different file system tasks are covered such as mounting file systems, selecting device names, and accessing Windows files. Device configuration covers topics such as device files, installing printers, and using the kernel modules to support new devices. Using, updating, and configuring the Linux kernel with its modules is covered in detail along with procedures for installing new kernels. X window system topics cover the XFree86 servers, window manager configuration, X window system startup methods like the display manger, and X window system configuration commands.

Part VII covers Network administration dealing with topics such as configuring remote file system access and setting up firewalls. The various network file system interfaces and services like NFS for Unix, NIS, and NetaTALK for AppleTalk networks are presented. The chapter on Samba shows how to access Windows file systems and printers. Then the different aspects of network administration are discussed such as network connections and routes, Domain Name services, Hostname designations, IP virtual hosts, and IP masquerading. Network security topics cover firewalls and encryption using netfilter (iptables) to protect your system, the Secure Shell (SSH) to provide secure remote transmissions, and Kerberos to provide secure authentication (the older ipchains firewall system is also covered).

Finally, there is an appendix covering what is available on the DVD-ROM included with this book.

Part I

Introduction

The Complete Reference

Chapter 1

Introduction to Linux

Linux is a fast, stable, and open-source operating system for PC computers and workstations that features profressional-level Internet services, extensive development tools, fully functional graphical user interfaces (GUI), and a massive number of applications ranging from office suites to multimedia applications. Linux was developed in the early 1990s by Linus Torvald, along with other programmers around the world. As an operating system, Linux performs many of the same functions as Unix, Macintosh, Windows, and Windows NT. However, Linux is distinguished by its power and flexibility. Most PC operating systems, such as Windows, began their development within the confines of small, restricted personal computers, which have only recently become more versatile machines. Such operating systems are constantly being upgraded to keep up with the ever-changing capabilities of PC hardware. Linux, on the other hand, was developed in a different context. Linux is a PC version of the Unix operating system that has been used for decades on mainframes and minicomputers, and is currently the system of choice for network servers and workstations. Linux brings the speed, efficiency, and flexibility of Unix to your PC, taking advantage of all the capabilities that personal computers can now provide.

Technically, Linux consists of the operating system program, referred to as the *kernel*. But it has always been distributed with a massive number of software applications, ranging from network servers and security programs to office applications and development tools. Linux evolved during the open source software movement, when independent programmers joined together to provide free quality software to any user. Linux has become the premier platform for open source software, much of it developed by the Free Software Foundation's GNU project. Many of these applications are bundled as part of standard Linux distributions. Currently, thousands of open source applications are available for Linux from sites like SourceForge's **sourceforge.net**, KDE's **apps.kde.com**, and Gnome's **www.gnome.org**.

Along with Linux's operating system capabilities come powerful networking features, including support for Internet, intranets, Windows, and AppleTalk networking. As a standard, Linux is distributed with fast, efficient, and stable Internet servers, such as the Web, FTP, and DNS servers, along with domain name, proxy, news, and mail servers. In other words, Linux has everything you need to set up, support, and maintain a fully functional network.

With both Gnome and K Desktop, Linux also provides GUI interfaces with that same level of flexibility and power. Unlike Windows and the Mac, you can choose the interface you want and then customize it further, adding panels, applets, virtual desktops, and menus, all with full drag-and-drop capabilities and Internet-aware tools. On your desktop, a file manager window can access any Internet site, enabling you to display Web pages and download files with a few simple mouse operations. To print a file, simply drag it to a printer icon.

Linux does all this at a great price. Linux is free, including the network servers and GUI desktops. Unlike the official Unix operating system, Linux is distributed freely under a GNU General Public License as specified by the Free Software Foundation, making it available to anyone who wants to use it. GNU stands for "Gnu's Not Unix" and is a project initiated and managed by the Free Software Foundation to provide free software to users, programmers, and developers. Linux is copyrighted, and it is not public domain. However, a GNU public license has much the same effect as being in the public domain. The GNU public license is designed to ensure Linux remains free and, at the same time, standardized. Only one official Linux exists. Linux is technically the operating system kernel, the core operation. In addition, Linux is commonly bundled with an extensive set of software available under the GNU public license, including environments, programming languages, Internet tools, and text editors. People sometimes have the mistaken impression that Linux is somehow less than a professional operating system because it is free. Linux is, in fact, a PC and workstation version of Unix. Many consider it far more stable and much more powerful than Windows. This power and stability have made Linux an operating system of choice as a network server.

To appreciate Linux completely, you need to understand the special context in which the Unix operating system was developed. Unix, unlike most other operating systems, was developed in a research and academic environment. In universities, research laboratories, data centers, and enterprises, Unix is the system most often used. Its development paralleled the entire computer and communications revolution over the past several decades. Computer professionals often developed new computer technologies on Unix, such as those developed for the Internet. Although a sophisticated system, Unix was designed from the beginning to be flexible. The Unix system itself can be easily modified to create different versions. In fact, many different vendors maintain different official versions of Unix. IBM, Sun, and Hewlett-Packard all sell and maintain their own versions of Unix. The unique demands of research programs often require that Unix be tailored to their own special needs. This inherent flexibility in the Unix design in no way detracts from its quality. In fact, this flexibility attests to the ruggedness of Unix, allowing it to adapt to practically any environment. This is the context in which Linux was developed. Linux is, in this sense, one other version of Unix—a version for the PC. The development of Linux by computer professionals working in a research-like environment reflects the way Unix versions have usually been developed. Linux is publicly licensed and free—and reflects the deep roots Unix has in academic institutions, with their sense of public service and support. Linux is a top-rate operating system accessible to everyone, free of charge.

As a way of introducing Linux, this chapter discusses Linux as an operating system, the history of Linux and Unix, the overall design of Linux, and Linux distributions. This chapter also discusses online resources for documentation, software, and newsgroups, plus Web sites with the latest news and articles on Linux. Web and FTP site listings are placed in tables at the end of this chapter for easy reference. Here, you can find sites for different distributions, Linux publications, software repositories, and Linux development, as well as for office suites and commercial databases.

Operating Systems and Linux

An *operating system* is a program that manages computer hardware and software for the user. Operating systems were originally designed to perform repetitive hardware tasks. These tasks centered around managing files, running programs, and receiving commands from the user. You interact with an operating system through a user interface. This user interface allows the operating system to receive and interpret instructions sent by the user. You only need to send an instruction to the operating system to perform a task, such as reading a file or printing a document. An operating system's user interface can be as simple as entering commands on a line or as complex as selecting menus and icons on a desktop.

An operating system also manages software applications. To perform different tasks, such as editing documents or performing calculations, you need specific software applications. An *editor* is an example of a software application that enables you to edit a document, making changes and adding new text. The editor itself is a program consisting of instructions to be executed by the computer. To use the program, it must first be loaded into computer memory, and then its instructions are executed. The operating system controls the loading and execution of all programs, including any software applications. When you want to use an editor, simply instruct the operating system to load the editor application and execute it.

File management, program management, and user interaction are traditional features common to all operating systems. Linux, like all versions of Unix, adds two more features. Linux is a multiuser and multitasking system. As a multitasking system, you can ask the system to perform several tasks at the same time. While one task is being done, you can work on another. For example, you can edit a file while another file is being printed. You do not have to wait for the other file to finish printing before you edit. As a multiuser system, several users can log in to the system at the same time, each interacting with the system through his or her own terminal.

Operating systems were originally designed to support hardware efficiency. When computers were first developed, their capabilities were limited and the operating system had to make the most of them. In this respect, operating systems were designed with the hardware in mind, not the user. Operating systems tended to be rigid and inflexible, forcing the user to conform to the demands of hardware efficiency.

Linux, on the other hand, is designed to be flexible, reflecting its Unix roots. As a version of Unix, Linux shares the same flexibility designed for Unix, a flexibility stemming from Unix's research origins. The Unix operating system was developed by Ken Thompson at AT&T Bell Laboratories in the late 1960s and early 1970s. The Unix system incorporated many new developments in operating system design. Originally, Unix was designed as an operating system for researchers. One major goal was to create a system that could support the researchers' changing demands. To do this, Thompson had to design a system that could deal with many different kinds of tasks. Flexibility became more important than hardware efficiency. Like Unix, Linux has the advantage of being able to deal with the variety of tasks any user may face.

This flexibility allows Linux to be an operating system that is accessible to the user. The user is not confined to limited and rigid interactions with the operating system. Instead, the operating system is thought of as providing a set of highly effective tools available to the user. This user-oriented philosophy means you can configure and program the system to meet your specific needs. With Linux, the operating system becomes an operating environment.

History of Linux and Unix

As a version of Unix, the history of Linux naturally begins with Unix. The story begins in the late 1960s when a concerted effort to develop new operating system techniques occurred. In 1968, a consortium of researchers from General Electric, AT&T Bell Laboratories, and the Massachusetts Institute of Technology carried out a special operating system research project called MULTICS (MULTiplexed Information Computing System). MULTICS incorporated many new concepts in multitasking, file management, and user interaction. In 1969, Ken Thompson, Dennis Ritchie, and the researchers at AT&T Bell Laboratories developed the UNIX operating system, incorporating many of the features of the MULTICS research project. They tailored the system for the needs of a research environment, designing it to run on minicomputers. From its inception, Unix was an affordable and efficient multiuser and multitasking operating system.

The Unix system became popular at Bell Labs as more and more researchers started using the system. In 1973, Dennis Ritchie collaborated with Ken Thompson to rewrite the programming code for the Unix system in the C programming language. Dennis Ritchie, a fellow researcher at Bell Labs, developed the C programming language as a flexible tool for program development. One of the advantages of C is that it can directly access the hardware architecture of a computer with a generalized set of programming commands. Up until this time, an operating system had to be specially rewritten in a hardware-specific assembly language for each type of computer. The C programming language allowed Dennis Ritchie and Ken Thompson to write only one version of the Unix operating system, which could then be compiled by C compilers on different computers. In effect, the Unix operating system became transportable, able to run on a variety of different computers with little or no reprogramming.

Unix gradually grew from one person's tailored design to a standard software product distributed by many different vendors, such as Novell and IBM. Initially, Unix was treated as a research product. The first versions of Unix were distributed free to the computer science departments of many noted universities. Throughout the 1970s, Bell Labs began issuing official versions of Unix and licensing the systems to different users. One of these users was the Computer Science department of the University of California, Berkeley. Berkeley added many new features to the system that later became standard. In 1975, Berkeley released its own version of Unix, known by its distribution arm, Berkeley Software Distribution (BSD). This BSD version of Unix became a major contender to the AT&T Bell Labs version. Other independently developed versions of Unix sprouted up. In 1980, Microsoft developed a PC version of Unix called Xenix. AT&T developed several research versions of Unix and, in 1983, it released the first commercial version, called System 3. This was later followed by System V, which became a supported commercial software product. You can find more information on Unix in *UNIX: The Complete Reference*, written by the Unix experts at AT&T labs, Kenneth Rosen, Doug Host, James Farber, and Richard Rosinski.

At the same time, the BSD version of Unix was developing through several releases. In the late 1970s, BSD Unix became the basis of a research project by the Department of Defense's Advanced Research Projects Agency (DARPA). As a result, in 1983, Berkeley released a powerful version of Unix called BSD release 4.2. This release included sophisticated file management as well as networking features based on TCP/IP network protocols—the same protocols now used for the Internet. BSD release 4.2 was widely distributed and adopted by many vendors, such as Sun Microsystems.

The proliferation of different versions of Unix led to a need for a Unix standard. Software developers had no way of knowing on what versions of Unix their programs would actually run. In the mid-1980s, two competing standards emerged, one based on the AT&T version of Unix and the other based on the BSD version. In bookstores today, you can find many different books on Unix for one or the other version. Some specify System V Unix, while others focus on BSD Unix.

AT&T moved Unix to a new organization, called Unix System Laboratories, which could focus on developing a standard system, integrating the different major versions of Unix. In 1991, Unix System Laboratories developed System V release 4, which incorporated almost all the features found in System V release 3, BSD release 4.3, SunOS, and Xenix. In response to System V release 4, several other companies, such as IBM and Hewlett-Packard, established the Open Software Foundation (OSF) to create their own standard version of Unix. Two commercial standard versions of Unix existed then—the OSF version and System V release 4. In 1993, AT&T sold off its interest in Unix to Novell. Unix Systems Laboratories became part of Novell's UNIX Systems Group. Novell issued its own versions of Unix based on System V release 4, called UnixWare, designed to interact with Novell's NetWare system. Unix Systems Laboratories is currently owned by Caldera and is distributed as OpenUnix. With Solaris, Sun has introduced System V release 4 onto its Sun systems. Two competing GUIs for Unix, called Motif and OpenLook, were superseded by a desktop standard called the Common Desktop Environment (CDE), which has since been incorporated into OpenMotif, an open source version of Motif also for use on Linux.

Throughout much of its development, Unix remained a large and demanding operating system requiring a workstation or minicomputer to be effective. Several versions of Unix were designed primarily for the workstation environment. SunOS was developed for Sun workstations and AIX was designed for IBM workstations. As personal computers became more powerful, however, efforts were made to develop a PC version of Unix. Xenix and System V/386 are commercial versions of Unix designed for IBM-compatible PCs. AUX is a Unix version that runs on the Macintosh. A testament to Unix's inherent portability is that it can be found on almost any type of computer: workstations, minicomputers, and even supercomputers. This inherent portability made an effective PC version of Unix possible.

Linux was originally designed specifically for Intel-based personal computers. Linux started out as a personal project of a computer science student named Linus Torvald at the University of Helsinki. At that time, students were making use of a program called *Minix,* which highlighted different Unix features. Minix was created by Professor Andrew Tannebaum and widely distributed over the Internet to students around the world. Linus's intention was to create an effective PC version of Unix for Minix users. He called it Linux, and in 1991, Linus released version 0.11. Linux was widely distributed over the Internet and, in the following years, other programmers refined and added to it, incorporating most of the applications and features now found in standard Unix systems. All the major window managers have been ported to Linux. Linux has all the Internet utilities, such as FTP file transfer support, Web browsers, and remote connections with PPP. It also has a full set of program development utilities, such as C++ compilers and debuggers. Given all its features, the Linux operating system remains small, stable, and fast. In its simplest format, Linux can run effectively on only 2MB of memory.

Although Linux has developed in the free and open environment of the Internet, it adheres to official Unix standards. Because of the proliferation of Unix versions in the previous decades, the Institute of Electrical and Electronics Engineers (IEEE) developed an independent Unix standard for the American National Standards Institute (ANSI). This new ANSI-standard Unix is called the Portable Operating System Interface for Computer Environments (POSIX). The standard defines how a Unix-like system needs to operate, specifying details such as system calls and interfaces. POSIX defines a universal standard to which all Unix versions must adhere. Most popular versions of Unix are now POSIX-compliant. Linux was developed from the beginning according to the POSIX standard. Linux also adheres to the Linux file system standard (FSSTND), which specifies the location of files and directories in the Linux file structure. See **www.pathname.com/fhs** for more details.

Linux Overview

Like Unix, Linux can generally be divided into three major components: the kernel, the environment, and the file structure. The *kernel* is the core program that runs programs and manages hardware devices, such as disks and printers. The *environment* provides an interface for the user. It receives commands from the user and sends those commands to the kernel for execution. The *file structure* organizes the way files are stored on a storage device, such as a disk. Files are organized into directories. Each directory may contain any number of subdirectories, each holding files. Together, the kernel, the environment, and the file structure form the basic operating system structure. With these three, you can run programs, manage files, and interact with the system.

An environment provides an interface between the kernel and the user. It can be described as an interpreter. Such an interface interprets commands entered by the user and sends them to the kernel. Linux provides several kinds of environments: desktops, window managers, and command line shells. Each user on a Linux system has his or her own user interface. Users can tailor their environments to their own special needs, whether they be shells, window managers, or desktops. In this sense, for the user, the operating system functions more as an operating environment, which the user can control.

The shell interface is simple and usually consists of a prompt at which you type a command, and then press ENTER. In a sense, you are typing the command on a line; this line is often referred to as the *command line*. You will find the commands entered on the command line can become quite complex. Over the years, several different kinds of shells have been developed and, currently, three major shells exist: Bourne, Korn, and C shell. The *Bourne shell* was developed at Bell Labs for System V. The *C shell* was developed for the BSD version of Unix. The *Korn shell* is a further enhancement of the Bourne shell. Current versions of Unix, including Linux, incorporate all three shells, enabling you to choose the one you prefer. However, Linux uses enhanced or public domain versions of these shells: the Bourne Again shell, the TC shell, and the Public Domain Korn shell. When you start your Linux system, you are placed in the Bourne Again shell, an updated version of the Bourne shell. From there, you can switch to other shells as you choose.

As an alternative to a command line interface, Linux provides both desktops and window managers. These GUI based on the X Window System developed for Unix by the Open Group consortium (**www.opengroup.org**). A *window manager* is a reduced version of an integrated desktop, supporting only window operations, but it still enables you to run any application. A desktop provides a complete GUI, much like Windows and the Mac. You have windows, icons, and menus, all managed through mouse controls. Currently, two desktops are freely available and both are included with most distributions of Linux: Gnome and KDE.

In Linux, files are organized into directories, much as they are in Windows. The entire Linux file system is one large interconnected set of directories, each containing files. Some directories are standard directories reserved for system use. You can create your own directories for your own files, as well as easily move files from one directory to another. You can even move entire directories, and share directories and files with other users on your system. With Linux, you can also set permissions on directories and files, allowing others to access them or restricting access to you alone. The directories of each user are, in fact, ultimately connected to the directories of other users. Directories are organized into a hierarchical tree structure, beginning with an initial root directory. All other directories are ultimately derived from this first root directory.

With the K Desktop Environment (KDE) and the GNU Network Object Model Environment (Gnome), Linux provides a completely integrated GUI interface. You can perform all your Linux operations entirely from either interface. Both rely on an underlying X Window System, which means as long as they are both installed on your system, applications from one can run on the other desktop. You can run KDE programs like the KDE mailer or the newsreader on the Gnome desktop. Check their Web sites at **www.gnome.org** and **www.kde.org** for more information.

Note *Ximian currently maintains an enchanced version of Gnome called Ximian Gnome at www.ximian.com.*

Open Source Software

Linux was developed as a cooperative effort over the Internet, so no company or institution controls Linux. Software developed for Linux reflects this background. Development often takes place when Linux users decide to work on a project together. When completed, the software is posted at an Internet site, and any Linux user can then access the site and download the software. The potential for Linux-based software is explosive. Linux software development has always operated in an Internet environment and it is global in scope, enlisting programmers from around the world. The only thing you need to start a Linux-based software project is a Web site.

Most Linux software is developed as open source software. This means that the source code for an application is freely distributed along with the application. Programmers over the Internet can make their own contributions to a software's development, modifying and correcting the source code. Linux is considered open source. Its source code is included in all its distributions and is freely available on the Internet. Many major software development efforts are also open source projects, such as the KDE and Gnome desktops, along with most of their applications. Netscape Communicator Web browser package has also become open source, with all its source code free available. The OpenOffice office suite supported by Sun is an open source project based on the former StarOffice office suite. Many of the open source applications that run on Linux have located their Web sites at Source Forge (**sourceforge.net**). SourceForge is a hosting site designed specifically to support open source projects. You can find more information about the open source movement and recent developments at Linuxcare (**www.linuxcare.com**) and at **www.opensource.org**.

Open source software is protected by public licenses. These prevent commercial companies from taking control of open source software by adding a few modifications of their own, copyrighting those changes, and selling the software as their own product. The most popular public license is the GNU Public License provided by the Free Software Foundation. This is the license that Linux is distributed under. The GNU Public License retains copyright, freely licensing the software with the requirement that the software and any modifications made to it are always freely available. Other public licenses have also been created to support the demands of different kinds of open source project. The Lesser GNU Public License (LGPL) lets commercial applications use GNU licensed software libraries. Netscape made its Netscape Communicator software available under a Netscape Public License (NPL) that covers modifications made directly to the Netscape source code. Additions made to Netscape are covered under the Mozilla Public License. The QT Public License (QPL) lets open source developers use the QT libraries essential to the KDE desktop. You can find a complete listing at **www.opensource.org**.

Linux is currently copyrighted under a GNU public license provided by the Free Software Foundation, and is often referred to as GNU software (see **www.gnu.org**). GNU software is distributed free, provided it is freely distributed to others. GNU software has proven both reliable and effective. Many of the popular Linux utilities, such as C compilers, shells, and editors, are all GNU software applications. Installed with your Linux distribution are the GNU C++ and Lisp compilers, Vi and Emacs editors, BASH and TCSH shells, as well as Tax and Ghostscript document formatters. In addition, there are many open source software projects that are licensed under the GNU Public License (GPL). Many of these software applications are available at different Internet sites, and these are listed in Table 1-1. Chapters 4 and 28 describe in detail the process of downloading software applications from Internet sites and installing them on your system.

Under the terms of the GNU General Public License, the original author retains the copyright, although anyone can modify the software and redistribute it, provided the source code is included. Also, no restriction exists on selling the software or giving it away free. One distributor could charge for the software, while another one could provide it free of charge.

Lately, major software companies are also developing Linux versions of their most popular applications. A Linux version of Sun's Java Software Development Kit (SDK) is also available through **www.blackdown.org**. Corel has developed a Linux version of WordPerfect, while Oracle provides a Linux version of its Oracle database. (At present, there are no plans in the works for Microsoft applications.)

Linux Software

A great deal of Linux software is currently available from online sources. You can download applications for desktops, Internet servers, office suites, and programming packages, among others. Several centralized repositories make it easy to locate an application and find information about it. Of particular note are **sourceforge.net**, **freshmeat.net**, **rpmfind.net**, **apps.kde.com,** and **linuxapps.com**.

Software packages are distributed in compressed archives, in RPM packages, or APT (Advanced Package Tool) packages. RPM (Red Hat Package Manager) packages are those archived using the Red Hat Package Manager, and are used extensively in many distributions including SuSE, Caldera, Mandrake, and Red Hat. APT packages were developed for the Debian distribution. Compressed archives have an extension such as **.tar.gz** or **.tar.bz2**, whereas RPM packages have an **.rpm** extension, and APT packages have a **.deb** extension. Whenever possible, you should try to download software from a distribution's FTP site, but you could also download the source version and compile it directly on your system. This has become a simple process, almost as simple as installing the compiled versions (see Chapters 4 and 28).

Linux Internet sites that provide extensive software archives have mirror sites, such as **www.kernel.org**, that hold the new Linux kernels. Most distributions also have a large number of mirror sites from which you can download updates for software packages they distribute. If you have trouble connecting to a main FTP site, try one of its mirrors.

The following tables list different sites for Linux software. Repositories and archives for Linux software are listed in Table 1-1, along with several specialized sites, such as those for commercial and game software. When downloading software packages, always check to see if versions are packaged for your particular distribution. Many sites provide packages for the different popular distributions, such as SuSE, Mandrake, Red Hat, Caldera, and Debian. For others, first check the distribution FTP sites for a particular package. **rpmfind.net, freshmeat.net**, **sourceforge.net**, and **www.linuxapps.com** are also good places for locating packages for particular distributions.

URL	Internet Site
sourceforge.net	Source Forge, open source software development sites for Linux applications and software repository
www.linuxapps.com	Linux software repository
www.gnu.org	GNU archive
freshmeat.net	New Linux software
rpmfind.net	RPM package repository
apps.kde.org	KDE applications
www.gnome.org	Gnome applications
filewatcher.org	Linux FTP site watcher
www.opensound.com	Open sound system drivers
www.blackdown.org	Web site for Linux Java
www.fokus.gmd.de/linux	Woven goods for Linux
metalab.unc.edu	Mirror site for Linux software and distributions
www.linux.com	Linux software
www.happypenguin.org/	Linux Game Tome
www.linuxgames.com	Linux games
www.linuxquake.com	Quake
www.linuxlinks.com	Linux links
www.linuxdoc.org/links.html	Linux links

Table 1-1. *Linux Software Archives, Repositories, and Links*

Linux Office and Database Software

Many professional-level databases and office suites are now available for Linux. These include Oracle and IBM databases as well as the OpenOffice and KOffice office suites. Table 1-2 lists sites for office suites and databases. Many of these sites provide free personal versions of their software for Linux and others are entirely free. You can download from them directly and install on your Linux system.

Internet Servers

One of the most important features of Linux, as well as all Unix systems, is its set of Internet clients and servers. The Internet was designed and developed on Unix

URL	Databases
www.oracle.com	Oracle database
www.sybase.com	Sybase database
www.software.ibm.com/data/db2/linux	IBM database
www.informix.com/linux	Informix database
www.mysql.com	MySQL database
www.ispras.ru/~kml/gss	GNU SQL database
www.postgresql.org	PostgreSQL database
www.fship.com/free.html	Flagship (interface for xBase database files)
koffice.kde.org	Katabase (KOffice desktop database)
gaby.netpedia.net	Gaby (Gnome desktop personal database)
Office Software	
koffice.kde.org	KOffice
linux.corel.com	WordPerfect
www.sun.com/staroffice	StarOffice
www.openoffice.org	OpenOffice
www.gnome.org/gw.html	Gnome Workshop Project

Table 1-2. *Database and Office Software*

systems, and Internet clients and servers, such as those for FTP and the Web, were first implemented on BSD versions of Unix. DARPANET, the precursor to the Internet, was set up to link Unix systems at different universities across the nation. Linux contains a full set of Internet clients and servers including mail, news, FTP, and Web, as well as proxy clients and servers. Sites for Internet server software available for Linux are listed in Table 1-3. Most of these are already included with a Linux distribution, including the Red Hat DVD-ROM included with this book; however, you can obtain news, documentation, and recent releases directly from the server's Web sites.

Development Resources

Linux has always provided strong support for programming languages and tools. All distributions include the GNU C and C++ compiler (gcc). Most distributions come with full development support for the KDE and Gnome desktops, letting you create your own Gnome and KDE applications. You can also download the Linux version of the Java Software Development Kit for creating Java programs. Perl and Tcl/TK versions of Linux are also included with most distributions. You can download current versions from their Web sites. Table 1-4 lists different sites of interest for Linux programming.

URL	Servers
www.apache.org	Apache Web server
www.proftpd.org	ProFTPD FTP server
www.isc.org	Internet Software Consortium: BIND, INN, and DHCPD
www.sendmail.org	Sendmail mail server
www.squid.org	Squid proxy server
www.samba.org	Samba SMB (Windows network) server
www.eudora.com/free/qpop.html	Qpopper POP3 mail server
netfilter.samba.org	IP tables firewall server
netfilter.samba.org/ipchains	IP chains firewall server
www.ssh.com	Secure Shell encryption
web.mit.edu/kerberos/www	Kerberos network authentication protocol
www.openssh.com	Open Secure Shell (free version of SSH)

Table 1-3. *Network Servers and Security*

URL	Internet Sites
www.linuxprogramming.org	Linux programming resources
www.gnu.org	Linux compilers and tools (gcc)
dev.scriptics.com	Tcl Developers Xchange, Tcl/TK products
java.sun.com	Sun Java Web site
www.perl.com	Perl Web site with Perl software
www.blackdown.org	Sun's Java Software Development Kit for Linux
developer.gnome.org	Gnome developers Web site
www.openprojects.nu	Open Projects Network
developer.kde.org	Developer's library for KDE
www.linuxcare.org	Linux open source software support

Table 1-4. *Linux Programming*

Online Information Sources

Extensive online resources are available on almost any Linux topic. The tables in this chapter list sites where you can obtain software, display documentation, and read articles on the latest developments. Many Linux Web sites provide news, articles, and information about Linux. Several are based on popular Linux magazines, such as **www.linuxjournal.com** and **www.linuxgazette.com**. Others operate as Web portals for Linux, such as **www.linux.com**, **www.linuxworld.org**, and **www.linux.org**. Some specialize in a particular area, such as **linuxheadquarters.org** for guides on Linux software and **www.linuxgames.com** for the latest games ported for Linux. Currently, many Linux Web sites provide news, information, and articles on Linux developments, as well as documentation, software links, and other resources. These are listed in Table 1-5.

URL	Internet Site
www.linuxdoc.org	Web site for Linux Documentation Project
www.lwn.net	Linux Weekly News

Table 1-5. *Linux Information and News Sites*

URL	Internet Site
www.linux.com	Linux.com
www.linuxtoday.com	Linux Today
www.linuxplanet.com	Linux Planet
www.linuxpower.org	Linux Power
www.linuxfocus.org	Linux Focus
www.linuxworld.org	Linux World
www.linuxmall.com	Linux Mall
www.linuxjournal.com	Linux Journal
www.linuxgazette.com	Linux Gazette
www.linuxmagazine.com	Linux Magazine
www.linux.org	Linux Online
www.li.org	Linux International Web site
www.linux.org.uk	Linux European Web site
linuxheadquarters.com	Linux guides and software
slashdot.org	Linux forum
webwatcher.org	Linux Web site watcher
www.opensource.org	Open source information

Table 1-5. *Linux Information and News Sites* (continued)

You can find other sites through resource pages that hold links to other Web sites—for example, the Linux Web site on the World Wide Web at **www.linuxdoc.org/links.html**.

Documentation

Linux documentation has also been developed over the Internet. Much of the documentation currently available for Linux can be downloaded from Internet FTP sites. A special Linux project called the Linux Documentation Project (LDP), headed by Matt Welsh, has developed a complete set of Linux manuals. The documentation is available at the LDP home site at **www.linuxdoc.org**. Linux documentation guides provided by the LDP are listed in Table 1-6, along with their Internet sites.

Sites	**Web Sites**
www.linuxdoc.org	LDP Web site
ftp.linuxdoc.org	LDP FTP site
Guides	**Document Format**
Linux Installation and Getting Started Guide	DVI, PostScript, LaTeX, PDF, and HTML
Linux User's Guide	DVI, PostScript, HTML, LaTeX, and PDF
Linux System Administrator's Guide	PostScript, PDF, LaTeX, and HTML
Linux Network Administrator's Guide	DVI, PostScript, PDF, and HTML
Linux Programmer's Guide	DVI, PostScript, PDF, LaTeX, and HTML
The Linux Kernel	HTML, LaTeX, DVI, and PostScript
Linux Kernel Hacker's Guide	DVI, PostScript, and HTML
Linux HOWTOs	HTML, PostScript, SGML, and DVI
Linux FAQs	HTML, PostScript, and DVI
Linux Man Pages	Man page format

Table 1-6. *Linux Documentation Project*

An extensive number of mirrors are maintained for the Linux Documentation Project. You can link to any of them through a variety of sources, such as the LDP home site **www.linuxdoc.org** and **www.linuxjournal.org**. The documentation includes a user's guide, an introduction, and administration guides. These are available in text, PostScript, or Web page format. You can also find briefer explanations, in what are referred to as HOW-TO documents. HOW-TO documents are available for different subjects, such as installation, printing, and e-mail. The documents are available at Linux FTP sites, usually in the directory **/pub/Linux/doc/HOW-TO**.

You can find a listing of different Linux information sites in the file **META-FAQ** located at Linux FTP sites, usually in the directory **/pub/Linux/doc**. On the same site and directory, you can also download the Linux Software Map (LSM). This is a listing of most of the software currently available for Linux.

In addition to FTP sites, Linux Usenet newsgroups are also available. Through your Internet connection, you can access Linux newsgroups to read the comments of other Linux users and to post messages of your own. Several Linux newsgroups exist, each beginning with **comp.os.linux**. One of particular interest to the beginner is **comp.os.linux.help**, where you can post questions. Table 1-7 lists some of the Usenet Linux newsgroups you can check out, particularly for posting questions.

Distribution FTP and Web sites, such as **www.redhat.com** and **www.mandrake.com,** provide extensive Linux documentation and software. The **www.gnome.org** site holds software and documentation for the Gnome desktop, while **apps.kde.com** holds software and documentation for the KDE desktop.

Most of the standard Linux software and documentation currently available is already included on your distribution CD-ROM. HOW-TO documents are all accessible in HTML format, so you can view them easily with your Web browser, though you may need to access Linux Internet sites directly for current information and software.

Newsgroup	Title
comp.os.linux.announce	Announcements of Linux developments
comp.os.linux.devlopment.apps	For programmers developing Linux applications
comp.os.linux.devlopment.system	For programmers working on the Linux operating system
comp.os.linux.hardware	Linux hardware specifications
comp.os.linux.admin	System administration questions
comp.os.linux.misc	Special questions and issues
comp.os.linux.setup	Installation problems
comp.os.linux.answers	Answers to command problems
comp.os.linux.help	Questions and answers for particular problems
comp.os.linux.networking	Linux network questions and issues
linux.dev.*group*	There are an extensive number of development newsgroups beginning with **linux.dev**, such as **linux.dev.admin** and **linux.dev.doc**.

Table 1-7. *Usenet Newsgroups*

Linux Distributions

Although there is only one standard version of Linux, there are actually several different distributions. Different companies and groups have packaged Linux and Linux software in slightly different ways. Each company or group then releases the Linux package, usually on a CD-ROM. Later releases may include updated versions of programs or new software. Some of the more popular distributions are Red Hat, Mandrake, Caldera, SuSE, and Debian. The Linux kernel is, of course, centrally distributed through **www.kernel.org**. All distributions use this same kernel, although it may be configured differently.

Linux has spawned a great variety of distributions. Many aim to provide a comprehensive solution providing support for any and all tasks. These include distributions like SuSE, Red Hat, and Mandrake. Others have been developed for more specialized tasks or to support certain features. Distributions like Slackware provide a more bare-boned but fast operating system, and Debian provides cutting edge developments. Many distributions provide more specialized versions, usually bundled with commercial applications such as databases or secure servers. Currently, **www.distrowatch.com** lists 87 Linux distributions. Check this site for details about current distributions. Table 1-8 lists the Web sites for several of the more popular

URL	Internet Site
www.redhat.com	Red Hat Linux
www.mandrake.com	Mandrake
www.suse.com	SuSE Linux
www.caldera.com	OpenLinux (Caldera)
www.debian.org	Debian Linux
www.infomagic.com	Infomagic
www.turbolinux.com	Turbo Linux
www.slackware.com	Slackware Linux Project
www.linuxiso.com	Web site for downloading CD-ROM ISO images of Linux distributions
www.distrowatch.com	Web site with detailed information about Linux distributions.
www.kernel.org	The Linux Kernel

Table 1-8. *Linux Distributions and Kernel Sites*

Linux distributions. The FTP sites for these distributions use the prefix **ftp** instead of **www**, as in **ftp.redhat.com**. Also listed here are Linux kernel sites where the newest releases of the official Linux kernel are provided. These sites have corresponding FTP sites where you can download updates and new releases.

Red Hat Linux

Red Hat Linux is currently the most popular Linux distribution. As a company, Red Hat provides software and services to implement and support professional and commercial Linux systems. Red Hat freely distributes its version of Linux under the GNU Public License. Red Hat generates income by providing professional level support, consulting, and training services. The Red Hat Certified Engineers (RHCE) training and certification program is designed to provided reliable and highly capable administrators and developers to maintain and customize professional-level Red Hat systems. Red Hat originated the RPM package system used on several distributions, which automatically installs and removes software packages. See **www.redhat.com** for more information, including extensive documentation such as Red Hat manuals, FAQs, and links to other Linux sites.

Red Hat maintains an extensive library of Linux documentation that is freely accessible online. On its Web site, you can link to its support page, which lists the complete set of Red Hat manuals, all in Web page format for easy viewing with any Web browser. These include the Reference Guide, the Getting Started Guide, and the Installation Guide. Tip, HOW-TO, and FAQ documents are also provided. All the Red Hat documentation is freely available under the GNU public license.

Red Hat offers several commercial products and services for business and e-commerce solutions. These are bundled products where Red Hat Linux is combined with other commercial and noncommercial applications to provide solutions for business. Each is accompanied with extensive support to guarantee effective implementation and ongoing reliability.

Mandrake

Mandrake Linux is another popular Linux distribution with many of the same features as Red Hat. It focuses on providing up-to-date enhancements and an easy-to-use installation and GUI configuration. For software installation, it uses RPM packages. You can learn more about Mandrake at **www.mandrake.com**.

SuSE

Originally a German language-based distribution, SuSE has become very popular throughout Europe and is currently one of the fastest growing distributions worldwide. Its current distribution includes both KDE and Gnome. Its distributions include WordPerfect, OpenOffice, and KOffice. For software installation, it uses RPM packages. For more information, see **www.suse.com**.

Unlike other distributions, SuSE does not provide any CD-ROM images for downloading. Instead, you have to download the entire distributions (almost 2GB) to a hard disk and then follow instructions for installing with several install floppies.

Debian

Debian Linux is an entirely noncommercial project, maintained by hundreds of volunteer programmers. It is a GNU project that intends to maintain Linux's grass roots orientation. Its aim is to enhance Linux with new and improved applications and implementations. Debian is supported by O'Reilly & Associates and VA Linux. Currently, Debian supports Alpha, Intel, Macintosh 68K, and Sparc platforms. For more information, see **www.debian.org**. Debian Linux features a sophisticated package management and update system called the Advance Management Tool, instead of RPM packages. Several Web sites provide current information and support, such as **www.debianplanet.org**, **www.debianhelp.org**, and **www.debianworld.org** (French).

Caldera

Caldera OpenLinux is designed for corporate commercial use. OpenLinux system and software packages include all the GNU software packages, as well as the X Window System managers, Internet servers, WordPerfect, and the K Desktop. However, it does not presently include Gnome. It is POSIX compliant, adhering to Unix standards. Caldera distributes its OpenLinux system free of charge.

Caldera has organized its OpenLinux distribution into several different packages, each geared to different markets. These include the eDesktop package, which is designed for basic workstation operations, and the eServer package, which is designed for Linux servers. The eDesktop, included with this book, provides workstation software such as the KDE Desktop. The eServer installs server software such as the mail, FTP, and DNS servers. For software installation, it uses RPM packages. See the Caldera Web site at **www.caldera.com** for more information.

Caldera also offers a line of commercial and proprietary Linux packages. Such proprietary, licensed software packages are not freely distributable. They include such products as the Novell NetWare client. Recently, Caldera merged with The Santa Cruz Operation (SCO) to acquire Unix and distributes a version of Unix called OpenUnix.

Slackware

Slackware is available from numerous Internet sites, and you can order the CD from Walnut Creek Software. It includes both Gnome and KDE. The Slackware distribution takes special care to remain as closely Unix compliant as possible. Though it does not have the kind of distribution administrative tools found in other distributions, Slackware is noted for its speed and efficiency. For software installation, it uses RPM packages. See **www.slackware.com** for more information.

TurboLinux

TurboLinux provides English, Chinese, and Japanese versions of Linux. It includes several of its own packages, such as TurboPkg, for automatically updating applications and the TurboDesk desktop. Like Red Hat, it supports RPM packages. It is currently widely distributed in East Asia. See **www.turbolinux.com** for more information.

Chapter 2

Installing Linux

This chapter describes the basic installation procedure for Linux. Installation includes the Linux operating system, a great many Linux applications, and a complete set of network servers. In addition, configuration for your different hardware devices as well as Internet connections and different users is implemented. Different Linux distributions usually have their own installation programs. Linux installation programs are designed to be efficient and brief, while installing as many features as possible.

Note *Your Linux distribution will provide a detailed installation manual at its Web site. The manual will normally consist of Web pages you can view using any browser. They will include detailed figures and step-by-step descriptions. Checking this manual before you install is strongly recommended. This chapter presents a basic checklist that is not as detailed as an installation manual.*

Installing Linux involves several steps. First, you need to determine whether your computer meets the basic hardware requirements. These days, most Intel-based PC computers do. Most distributions support several methods for installing Linux. You can install from a local source such as a CD-ROM or a hard disk, or from a network or Internet source. In addition, you can start the installation process by booting from your CD-ROM, from a DOS system, or from boot disks that can then use the CD-ROM or hard disk repository. Your distribution documentation will cover each of these methods in detail.

Once the installation program begins, you simply follow the instructions, screen by screen. Most of the time, you only need to make simple selections or provide yes and no answers. The installation program progresses through several phases. First, you create Linux partitions on your hard drive, and then you install the software packages. After that, you can configure your network connection and then your X Window System for graphical user interface support. Both the X Window System and network configurations can be performed independently at a later time.

Once your system is installed, you are ready to start it and log in. Normally you will log in using a graphical login, selecting the desktop you want and entering your username and password. Alternatively, you can log in to a simple command line interface. From the command line, you can then invoke a desktop such as Gnome or KDE that provides you with a full graphical user interface.

Hardware, Software, and Information Requirements

Before installing Linux, you must ensure that your computer meets certain minimum hardware requirements. You also need to have certain specific information ready concerning your monitor, video card, mouse, and CD-ROM drive. All the requirements are presented in detail in the following sections. Be sure to read them carefully before you begin installation. During the installation program, you need to provide responses based on the configuration of your computer.

Hardware Requirements

Listed here are the minimum hardware requirements for installing a standard installation of the Linux system on an Intel-based PC:

- A 32-bit Intel-based personal computer. At least an Intel or compatible 80386, 80486, or Pentium class microprocessor is required.
- A 3 1/2-inch floppy disk drive. (If you have a bootable CD-ROM or other means of installing Linux, you don't really need a floppy drive. However, to install Linux from the DVD-ROM included with this book, you will have to create a bootable floppy disk first.)
- Normally at least 64MB RAM. (Linux can run on as little as 12MB RAM.)
- At least 2GB free hard disk space for a standard installation, including applications (keep in mind that Linux can run on far less on a minimum installation, as little as 100MB and 16MB swap); 3 to 6 GB or more is recommended for a full installation (all applications). You need about 3GB to install all the software packages on most distribution CD-ROMs. The standard installation of basic software packages normally takes 2GB, plus 64 to 512 MB for swap space, depending on the amount of RAM memory you have. If you have less than 1GB, you can elect to perform a minimum install, installing only the Linux kernel without most of the applications. You could later install the applications you want, one at a time.
- A 3 1/2-inch, DOS-formatted, high-density (HD) floppy disk drive, to be used to create an install disk (if you are installing from a floppy). If you install directly from a CD-ROM, you will not need the floppy disk.
- A CD-ROM drive.

Software Requirements

There are only a few software requirements. If you intend to install using the floppy disks, you need an operating system from which you can create the disks. The Windows operating system is required to enable you to prepare your installation disks. Using a Windows system, you can access the CD-ROM and a program to create your installation disks.

These days, Linux is usually run on its own hard drive, though it can also be run in a different partition on a hard drive that also contains a separate partition for a different operations system such as Windows.

If you have already installed Windows on your hard drive and configured it to take up the entire hard drive, you would resize its partition to free up unused space. The freed space could then be used for a Linux partition. To do this on Windows, you need either the defrag and fips utilities or disk management software like Partition Magic or GNU Parted. The fips utility is provided on most Linux distribution CD-ROMs under the **dosutils** directory. This utility essentially frees space by reducing the size of your current extended or primary partition. Defrag and fdisk are standard Windows utilities. Defrag is used with fips to defragment your hard disk before fips partitions it. This collects all files currently on the partition into one area, leaving all the free space grouped in one large chunk. If you are installing on a new empty hard drive and you want to use part of it for Windows, you can use fdisk to set up your Windows partitions. All these tasks can also be carried out using GNU Parted and Partition Magic.

Information Requirements

Part of adapting a powerful operating system like Linux to the PC entails making the most efficient use of the computer hardware at hand. In almost all configurations, your Linux installation process will automatically detect and configure your hardware components. Sometimes, however, particularly with older or very recent hardware, your installer may not be able to correctly identify a component. If you should have such components, such as a new model monitor or video card, you should first check their manuals and take note of certain configuration settings.

You will also need to determine how you want to use hardware resources, for example, how much of your hard disk you want to devote to Linux.

CD-ROM, Hard Disk, and Mouse Information

For some older SCSI CD-ROM drives, you need the manufacturer's name and model.

Decide how much of your hard drive (in megabytes) you want to dedicate to your Linux system. If you are sharing with Windows, decide how much you want for Windows and how much for Linux.

Decide how much space you want for your swap partition. Your swap partition should be about the same as your RAM memory, but can work with as little as 64MB. The size of the swap partition was expanded with the 2.4 kernel. Your swap partition is used by Linux as an extension of your computer's RAM.

Find the make and model of the mouse you are using. Linux supports serial, USB, PS/2, IMPS/2, and bus mice. Most mice are supported, including Microsoft, Logitech, and Mouse Systems.

Know what time zone you are in and to what time zone your hardware clock is set. This can be either Greenwich Mean Time (GMT) or your local time zone.

Know which kind of port your mouse is using, such as PS/2, USB, or serial port. Most systems now use a PS/2 port. For a serial port mouse, you will need to know which port it is connected to: COM1, COM2, or none.

Video and Monitor Information

Although most monitors and video cards are automatically configured during installation, you might still need to provide the manufacturer's make and model, in case the detection is wrong. Find out the manufacturer for your monitor and its model, such as Iiyama VisionMaster or Hitachi CM828. Do the same for your video card—for example, Matrox Millennium G400 or ATI XPERT@Play (you can find a complete list of supported cards at **www.xfree86.org**). This should be listed on the manuals or registration information provided with your computer. For some of the most recent monitors and video cards, and some older, uncommon ones, you may need to provide certain hardware specifications. Having this information on hand, if possible, is advisable, just in case. At the end of the installation process, you are presented with lists of video cards and monitors from which to choose your own. These lists are extensive. In case your card or monitor is not on the list, however, you need to provide certain hardware information about them. If the configuration should fail, you can always do it later using an X Window System configuration utility such as Xconfigurator and XF86Setup. Of particular importance is the monitor information, including the vertical and horizontal refresh rates.

Video Card Information You should also know the following video card information, though the chipset is most likely not necessary:

- What is the make and model of your video card?
- What chipset does your video card use?
- How much memory is on your video card?

Monitor Information What is the manufacturer and model of your monitor? Linux supports an extensive list of monitors, covering almost all current ones. Your monitor will be automatically detected and selected. If the detection is wrong, you can find it and select it from the list. If, however, your monitor is not on this list, you may need to provide the following information. Be sure this information is correct. If you enter a horizontal or vertical refresh rate that is too high, you can seriously damage older monitors. Newer ones will just shut down. You can choose a generic profile or you can enter information for a custom profile. To do that, you need the following information:

- The horizontal refresh rate in Hz
- The vertical refresh rate in Hz

Network Configuration Information

Except for deciding your hostname, you will most likely not have to provide any configuration information. Most networks today provide network information automatically by a DHCP server. In this case, you will only need your system's hostname. Most local networks, cable, and DSL connections now use DHCP to automatically configure hosts. During the installation process, you may be given the option of either automatically configuring your network connection (DHCP) or entering the network information manually.

You can also put configuration off until a later time and use network configuration utilities provided by your distribution to perform network configuration. All you need to do during installation is provide a hostname.

If you decide to manually configure your network connection, you will need the following information, usually obtainable from your network administrator:

- A name for your computer (this is called a hostname). Your computer will be identified by this name on the Internet. Do not use "localhost," which is reserved for special use by your system. The hostname should be a simple alphabetic word; it can include numbers, but not punctuation such as periods and backslashes. A computer's name is made up of its hostname and domain name, so turtle.mytrek.com has the hostname turtle and the domain name mytrek.com.
- Your domain name.
- The Internet Protocol (IP) address assigned to your machine. Every host on the Internet is assigned an IP address. This address is a set of four numbers, separated by periods, which uniquely identifies a single location on the Internet, allowing information from other locations to reach that computer.
- Your network IP address. This address is usually similar to the IP address, but with one or more zeros at the end.
- The netmask. This is usually 255.255.255.0 for class C IP addresses. If, however, you are part of a large network, check with your network administrator.
- The broadcast address for your network, if available. Usually, your broadcast address is the same as your IP address with the number 255 used for the last number.
- The gateway IP address for your network, if you have a gateway.
- The IP address of any name servers your network uses.
- The NIS domain and IP address if your network uses an NIS server.
- The Samba server if your network is connected to a Windows network.

Creating the Boot Disks

If you are installing Red Hat using the DVD-ROM included with this book, you will need to create and use boot floppy disks as describe here. However, if, instead, you are using a set of CD-ROM disks to install Linux, and your computer is fairly new, it most likely has the ability to boot from your CD-ROM. You can download or purchase CD-ROMs from any distribution including Mandrake, SuSE, and even Red Hat. In this case, you can just use your CD-ROM as your installation disk and skip this section. (You may need to configure your BIOS to boot from your CD-ROM.) If you cannot boot from your CD-ROM, you will have to create floppy install disks as described here.

You create the install disk from either Windows, DOS, or Linux. On Windows you can use use either the Windows **rawritewin** or the MS-DOS **rawrite** program. On MS-DOS you use **rawrite**. Install disk images exist for local installation (**boot.img**), installing from a network source such as a Web site (**netimage.img**) and installing with PCMCIA support (**pcmcia.img**). The actual names used will vary with each distribution. Mandrake and Red Hat use this set of names, whereas Caldera uses **intall144.img** and SuSE uses **install.img**.

Note *If you are installing from the Red Hat DVD-ROM included with this book, you will need a DVD-ROM drive on your computer to read the DVD-ROM disk, and floppy drive to install Red Hat from the DVD-ROM. On either a Windows, DOS, or Linux system you will need to create an install floppy disk with the **images/boot.img** file on the DVD-ROM (unless you are performing a network or hard disk installation).*

On Windows, to use the **rawritewin** program to create a floppy install disk, first insert the CD-ROM into your CD-ROM drive (if you are installing from the DVD-ROM disk included with this book, you would use your DVD-ROM drive instead). Change to your CD-ROM drive. Once you have changed to the CD-ROM drive, you then need to change to the **\dosutils** directory. On Mandrake and SuSE, the **rawritewin** command is in the **dosutils** directory, whereas on Red Hat it is in the **dosutils\rawritewin** directory. Just double-click it to start it. It is very easy to create a boot disk with **rawritewin**. Just run it from on Windows and use its interface to select the floppy disk image you want. On the CD-ROM included with this book, the install disk images are **boot.img**, **pcmia.img**, and **netboot.img**. The image file you want for a CD-ROM installation is the **boot.img** file located on your CD-ROM in the images directory, **images/boot.img**. Be sure that your floppy drive is correctly listed. The default will be **A:**. Then place a blank floppy in your floppy drive and click Write.

For **rawrite**, which you have to use on MS-DOS, at your DOS prompt, change to your CD-ROM drive, using whatever the letter that drive may be. For example, if your CD-ROM drive is the E drive, just type **e:** and press ENTER. Once you have changed to the CD-ROM drive, you then need to change to the **\images** directory. On the CD-ROM included with this book, the install disk images are **boot.img**, **pcmia.img**, and **netboot.img**. The **rawritewin** command is in the **dosutils** directory.

The **rawrite** comand has to be run at a DOS prompt. Enter the full path for the **rawrite** command including the CD-ROM or DVD-ROM drive letter such as **e:\dosutils\rawrite**. The **rawrite** command first prompts you for the name of the disk image file you want to copy. Enter the full name of the install image file (in this example, **boot.img**). The command then asks you to enter the letter of the floppy drive where you put your floppy disk. On many systems, this is the A drive.

```
E:\> cd images
E:\col\launch\floppy > e:\dosutils\rawrite
```

```
Enter source file name: boot.img
Enter destination drive (A or B) and press ENTER: a
```

Press ENTER to confirm that you have a blank floppy disk in the drive. **rawrite** will then copy the image file to your floppy disk, creating your install disk. When it finishes, remove your disk from the floppy drive. This is the disk that the installation procedure (described later) refers to as the *install diskette*. If you need to create a network boot disk, use **netimage.img** instead. For PCMCIA support, use **pcmcia.img**.

To create floppy disks on a Linux or Unix system, you use the **dd** command and specify the boot image file to use along with the name of the floppy device and the size of the floppy disk. You will first need to mount the CD-ROM, then change to its mount directory. On most Linux systems, the first floppy disk drive is at **/dev/fd0** and its size is usually 1400 for a 1.4 floppy disk. With the **if** option you specify the image file to use, the **of** option indicates the floppy device name, and the **bs** option specifies the block size.

```
dd if=images/boot.img of=dev/fd0  bs=1440k
```

Installing Linux

Installing Linux involves several processes, beginning with creating Linux partitions, and then loading the Linux software, configuring your X Window System interface, installing the Linux Loader (LILO) that will boot your system, and creating new user accounts. The installation program used on all major Linux distributions is a screen-based program that takes you through all these processes, step by step, as one continuous procedure. You can use either your mouse or the keyboard to make selections. When you finish with a screen, click the Next button at the bottom to move to the next screen. If you need to move back to the previous screen, click the Back button. You can also use the TAB, the arrow keys, SPACEBAR, and ENTER to make selections. You have little to do other than make selections and choose options. Some screens provide a list of options from which you make a selection. In a few cases, you are asked for information you should already have if you followed the steps earlier in this chapter. You are now ready to begin installation. The steps for each part of the procedure are delineated in the following sections. This should not take more than an hour.

Starting the Installation Program

If you followed the instructions in the first part of the chapter, you have freed space on your hard drive, and created your install and module disks. Now you are ready to create your Linux partitions. To do this, you need to boot your computer using the install disk you made earlier. When you start your computer, the installation program will begin and, during the installation, you can create your Linux partitions.

You can start the installation using one of several methods. If your computer can boot from the CD-ROM, you can start the installation directly from the CD-ROM. Just place the CD-ROM in the CD-ROM drive before you start your computer. After turning on your computer, the installation program will start up.

Note *To boot from a CD-ROM, you may first have to change the boot sequence setting in your computer's BIOS so that the computer will try to boot first from the CD-ROM. This requires some technical ability and knowledge of how to set your motherboard's BIOS configuration.*

If you have a DOS system installed on your hard drive, you can start up DOS and then use the **autoboot.bat** command in the **dosutils** directory to start the installation, as shown here. You have to execute this command from a DOS system, not the Windows DOS window. Only DOS can be running for this command to work.

```
e:\dosutils\autoboot.bat
```

If neither of these options is feasible for you, you can use the install floppy disk (see the previous section on creating a boot disk). This is perhaps the most fail-safe method of installing Linux. Insert the Linux install disk into your floppy drive and reboot your computer. Performing a cold boot is best: turn off the computer completely and then turn it on again with the install disk in the floppy drive.

The installation program will start, presenting you with an Introduction screen. After a moment, the following prompt will appear at the bottom of your screen:

```
boot:
```

Press ENTER. (If necessary, you can enter boot parameters as described in the installation manual.) Configuration information will fill your screen as the installation program attempts to detect your hardware components automatically.

Your system then detects your hardware, providing any configuration specifications that may be needed. For example, if you have an IDE CD-Write drive, it will be configured automatically as a SCSI drive so that CD Writing software can make use of it (see Chapter 4). If you are installing from a floppy disk, it will detect your CD-ROM. If for some reason it cannot do so, your system will ask you to select yours from a list. If you still have difficulty, you may have to specify the CD-ROM at the boot prompt.

```
Boot: linux hdx=cdrom
```

Replace the *x* with one of the following letters, depending on the interface the unit is connected to, and whether it is configured as master or a slave:

- a First IDE controller master
- b First IDE controller slave
- c Second IDE controller master
- d Second IDE controller slave

As each screen appears in the installation, default entries will be already selected, usually by the auto-probing capability of the installation program. Selected entries will appear highlighted. If these entries are correct, you can simply click the Next button to accept them and go on to the next screen.

Linux Installation

The installation screens are structured differently depending on the distribution you are installing. All installers will display a help panel explaining each step in detail. Hardware components will be automatically detected and displayed as you progress. During installation you will be able to perform administrative tasks such as configure your network connections, create users, and set the time. Keep in mind that such administrative tasks can also be performed after installation. Several tasks are critical to the install process, such as setting up your Linux partitions and selecting packages to install. Also, X Window System configuration is needed if you want to use GUI interfaces such as KDE or Gnome. Toward the end of the installation you will be asked to create a boot disk. Be sure to make one. Should anything go wrong with your boot loader, you will still be able to boot Linux using the install disk.

Partitions

Early on, most installers will ask you to set up and designate the Linux partitions you want to use on your hard drive. Most provide an automatic partitioning option if you just want to use your entire hard drive. If you are sharing your hard disk with a Windows system, you can set up a Linux partition in your drive's free space. Mandrake, Red Hat, Caldera, and SuSE all provide a very detailed and graphic-oriented partitioning tool for setting up your partitions.

You are advised to set up at least two Linux partitions: a swap partition and a root partition. The *root partition* is where the Linux system and application files are installed. If you are sharing a large hard drive with other systems, such as Windows, you can install the Linux root partition anywhere on the hard drive.

Except for the swap partition, when setting up a Linux partition you must specify a mountpoint. A *mountpoint* is a directory where the files on that partition are connected to the overall Linux file structure for your system. The mountpoint for your root partition is the root directory, represented by a single slash, **/**. The mountpoint for your boot partition is the path **/boot**. For a user's partition, it would be **/home**.

When creating a new partition, you must specify its size, though you can have the partition automatically expand to the available free space on your hard drive. The size of the swap partition should be the same size as your RAM memory, with a recommended minimum size of 64MB. With 256MB of RAM, you could use a 256MB swap partition. If you have a large amount of RAM, you can make the swap partition the same size. If your disk space is limited, you should make your swap size at least 64MB.

Be sure enough space is available for it on your hard drive. If not, you will receive an Unallocated Requested Partition message. You can free space by deleting unwanted partitions already set up or edit the new partition's entry and change its requested size. Check the entry for your hard drive in the Drive Summaries pane to find out how much free space is available on your hard drive.

To create the new partition, you will need to provide the mountpoint, the size (in megabytes), the file system type, and the hard disk on which you want to create the partition. For the size, you can select the Grow To Fill Disk option to have the partition automatically expand to the size of the remaining free space on the disk. For file system type, select ext3, the Linux native type for standard Linux partitions, and select the Linux swap type for your swap partition.

You also have the option of creating software RAID disks. First create partitions and select as their type Software RAID (see Chapter 11 for more details on RAID). Once you have created your partitions, you can create a RAID disk. Click the Make RAID button and then select the partitions you previously created that you want to make up the RAID disk, choosing also the type of RAID disk.

If you are formatting any old Linux partitions that still have data on them, a dialog box will appear listing them and asking you to confirm that you want to format them (new Linux partitions that you created will automatically be formatted). If you already have a Linux system, you will most likely have several Linux partitions already. Some of these may be used for just the system software, such as the boot and root partitions. These should be formatted. Others may have extensive user files, such as a **/home** partition that normally holds user home directories and all the files they have created. You should *not* format such partitions.

Boot Loaders

Once your partitions are prepared, you install a boot loader. You can choose either the Linux Loader (LILO) or the Grand Unified Bootloader (GRUB). GRUB is now the default boot loader for many distributions. You use a boot loader to start Linux from your hard drive. You can also use it to start any other operating system you may have installed on your computer, such as Windows. You have two choices for where to install the boot loader: the Master Boot Record (MBR) or the root partition. The recommended place is the MBR. You also can specify a label for the Linux system (usually **linux**), decide whether it is to be the default system (if you have more than one operating system), and specify any kernel parameters your system may require for Linux. On the screen there are usually options for creating a boot disk, selecting either the GRUB or LILO boot loaders, or *not* installing a boot loader.

Installing Software

You can then select the packages you want to install on your system. Most distributions let you choose a set of pre-determined collections tailored to Workstations or to Servers. You can also select all the packages, or choose a custom installation. On the custom installation you can select groups of packages, like those for Gnome, KDE, different servers like Web or FTP servers, games, editors, and development support which includes compilers and debuggers.

You will also have the options to select individual software packages, though you will need to know the names of packages you want. Many software packages require that other software packages also be installed. This is called a *dependency*. Should you not have these already selected for installation, they will be displayed showing the packages you need to install.

The packages are then installed, showing each package as it is installed and the progress of the installation. Most distributions now use several CD-ROMs to install Linux. You will be prompted when to install the next CD-ROM. The current one will automatically be ejected for you (for the Red Hat DVD-ROM included with this book, the DVD-ROM will also be ejected as if it were a CD-ROM. Just reinsert the same DVD-ROM. The DVD-ROM functions as all three Red Hat CD-ROMs). When the installation finishes, a post-install process with complete. You are then usually given the option to create a boot disk. You can use this disk to access your Linux system should your hard disk boot somehow fail.

Note *If you are installing from the Red Hat DVD-ROM, during the software package installation, you will be prompted to insert the second and later, possibly the third CD-ROM. Just reinsert the same DVD-ROM disk. The single Red Hat DVD-ROM with this book is recognized as all three Red Hat CD-ROMs in the Red Hat distribution. The disk will be automatically ejected, just reinsert it.*

Finishing Installation

Once your installation is finished, your system will reboot. If you chose GRUB as your boot loader, a GRUB menu will be displayed listing Linux and other operating systems you specified, such as Windows. Use the arrow keys to move to the Linux entry, if it is not already there, and press ENTER. If you chose LILO as your boot loader, a command line boot prompt is displayed. If you set up Linux as your default operating system, just press ENTER or do nothing. Linux will then start up. If Linux is not your default, enter the label you gave it when configuring LILO (usually **linux**). If you booted from a CD, your CD will be ejected before rebooting. If you booted directly from the CD-ROM, you may want to change your boot sequence in your BIOS back to your floppy drive.

When your system restarts, the login prompt or the login screen will appear, depending on whether you chose to have the X Window System start up automatically. You can then log in to your Linux system using a login name and a password for any of the users you have set up. If you log in as the root user, you can perform administrative operations, such as installing new software or creating more users. To log in as the root user, enter **root** at the login prompt and the root user password at the password prompt.

If you want copies of your boot disk in case you lose or damage the one you made during installation, you can create more with the **mkbootdisk** command. Enter this command in a terminal window or at the command line, and specify the version number of the kernel, as shown here:

```
mkbootdisk 2.4.18-0
```

You can also create boot disks from the Gnome desktop using the **qmkbootdisk** tool, accessible from the Gnome system menu. This tool also lets you specify different kernels to boot (see Chapter 31). The current kernel will already be selected.

When you finish, you can shut down your system. If you are using a command line interface, use the command **halt**. From Gnome or KDE, you can elect to shut down the entire system. If the system should freeze on you for any reason, you can hold down the CTRL and ALT keys and press DEL (CTRL-ALT-DEL) to safely shut it down. Never just turn it off.

Chapter 3

Interface Basics

To start using Linux, you must know how to access your Linux system and, once you are on the system, how to execute commands and run applications. Accessing Linux involves more than just turning on your computer. Once Linux is running, you have to log in to the system using a predetermined username and password. Once on the system, you can start executing commands and running applications. You can then interact with your Linux system using either a command line interface or a graphical user interface (GUI). The Linux systems use GUI interfaces such as Gnome and KDE with which you can use windows, menus, and icons to interact with your system. Most distributions allow you to use a graphical login. A simple window appears with menus for selecting login options and text boxes for entering your username and password.

Obtaining information quickly about Linux commands and utilities while logged in to the system is easy. Linux has several online utilities that provide information and help. You can access an online manual that describes each command or obtain help that provides more detailed explanations of different Linux features. A complete set of manuals provided by the Linux Documentation Project is on your system and available for you to browse through or print. Both the Gnome and KDE desktops provide help systems that give you easy access to desktop, system, and application help files.

Note *To make effective use of your Linux system, you must know how to configure certain features. Administrative operations such as adding users, specifying network settings, accessing CD-ROM drives, and installing software can now be performed with user-friendly system tools as well as the original command line utilities.*

User Accounts

You never directly access a Linux system. Instead, Linux sets up an interface called a *shell* through which you can interact. A Linux system can actually set up and operate several user shells at once, accommodating several users simultaneously. In fact, you can have many users working off the same computer running a Linux system. Each particular user appears to be the only one working on the system, as if Linux can set up several virtual computers and each user can then work on their own virtual computer. Such virtual computers are actually individually managed interfaces whereby each user interacts with the Linux system.

These user shells are frequently referred to as *accounts*. Unix, which Linux is based on, was first used on large minicomputers and mainframes that could accommodate hundreds of users at the same time. Using one of many terminals connected to the computer, users could log in to the Unix system using their usernames and passwords. All of this activity was managed by system administrators. To gain access to the system, you needed to have a user account set up for you. This was commonly known as "opening an account." A system administrator created the account on the Unix system, assigning a username and password for it. You then used your account to log in and use the system.

Each account is identified by a username with access protected by a password. Of course, you can access any account if you know its username and password. On your Linux system, you can create several accounts, logging into different ones as you choose. Other people can access your Linux system, making use of usernames and passwords you provide for them. They have their own accounts on your system. Recall that in Chapter 2 on installing Linux, you created a username and password for yourself. These are what you use to access Linux regularly. When you created the username and password, you were actually creating a new user account for yourself.

Note *You can, in fact, create other new user accounts using special system administration tools. These tools become available to you when you log in as the root user. The* root user *is a special user account reserved for system administration tasks, such as creating users and installing new software. Basic system administration operations are discussed briefly in Chapter 5, but they are discussed in detail in Chapters 25–37. For now, you only need your regular username and password.*

Accessing Your Linux System

To access and use your Linux system, you must carefully follow required startup and shutdown procedures. You do not simply turn off and turn on your computer. If you have installed a boot loader, either GRUB or LILO, when you turn on or reset your computer, the boot loader first decides what operating system to load and run. GRUB will display a menu of operating systems to choose, whereas LILO will display a command line prompt, as shown here.

```
LILO: linux
```

If, instead, you wait a moment or press the ENTER key, the boot loader loads the default operating system. If there is a Windows system listed, you can choose to run that instead.

You can think of your Linux operating system as operating on two different levels, one running on top of the other. The first level is when you start your Linux system, and where the system loads and runs. It has control of your computer and all its peripherals. You still are not able to interact with it, however. After Linux starts, it displays a login prompt, waiting for a user to come along and log in to the system to start using it. To gain access to Linux, you have to log in first.

You can think of logging in and using Linux as the next level. Now you can issue commands instructing Linux to perform tasks. You can use utilities and programs such as editors or compilers, or even games. Depending on a choice you made during installation, however, you may either be interacting with the system using a simple command line interface or using the desktop directly. There are both command line login prompts and graphical login windows. In the case of most Linux distributions, if you choose to use a graphical interface at the end of the installation, you are presented with a graphical login window at which you enter your username and password. If you choose not to use the graphical interface, you are presented with a simple command line prompt to enter your username.

The Display Manager: GDM and KDM

With the graphical login, your X Window System starts up immediately and displays a login window with boxes for a username and a password. When you enter your username and password, and then click the OK or GO button, your default GUI starts up. On Mandrake and Red Hat, this is usually Gnome.

For Mandrake and Red Hat, graphical logins are handled by the Gnome Display Manager (GDM). The GDM manages the login interface along with authenticating a user password and username, and then starting up a selected desktop. If problems ever occur using the X Window System display of the GUI interface, you can force a shutdown of the X Window System and the GUI with the CTRL-ALT-BACKSPACE keys. For GUI logins, it will restart the X Window System, returning you to the login screen. Also, from the GDM, you can shift to the command line interface with the CTRL-ALT-F1 keys, and then shift back to the X Window System with the CTRL-ALT-F7 keys.

When the GDM starts up, it shows a login window with a box for login. Three menus are at the top of the window, labeled Session, Language, and System. To log in, enter your username in the Login box and press ENTER. Then you are prompted to enter your password. Do so, and then press ENTER. By default, the Gnome desktop is then started up.

When you log out from the desktop, you return to the GDM login window. To shut down your Linux system, click the System menu to display the entries Reboot or Halt. Select Halt to shut down your system. Alternatively, you can also shut down when you log out from Gnome. Gnome will display a logout screen with the options to logout, shutdown, or reboot. Logout is the default, but selecting Shutdown will also shut down your system. Selecting Reboot will shut down and restart your system. (You can also open a terminal window and enter the **`shutdown`**, **`halt`**, or **`reboot`** commands as described in the next section. **`halt`** will log out and shut down your system.)

From the Session menu, you can select the desktop or window manager you want to start up. Here you can select KDE to start up the K Desktop instead of Gnome, among others. The Language menu lists a variety of different languages that Linux supports. Choose one to change the language interface.

On systems like SuSE and Caldera that use the KDE Display Manager, the login window also shows boxes for Login and Password. To log in, enter your username and password and then click Go. Your GUI starts up. When you log out of your GUI, you return to the KDM login screen. To shut down the system, click Shutdown to display a Shutdown dialog box from which you can choose to shut down, restart the X server, or shift to the console mode (command line interface).

You can use the Sessions drop-down menu to select the GUI to use. On OpenLinux, there is only an entry for KDE. KDM also displays icons for different users defined on the system at the top of its login window. You can click a user's icon to have that user's name automatically entered in the login box. The root user has the image of a conductor. To log in as root, just click it and you will see the word "root" appear in the login box. Then enter the root user password in the Password box.

If you log in as the root user to the KDE desktop, you can then use the KDM Configuration Manager to configure the KDM interface. Here you can select what background picture to use, the color of the login window, the icons to use for particular users, and the logo you want displayed. The Sessions panel lets you select what GUIs you want to access, provided they are installed on your system. GDM also provides a configuration manager similar to KDM's.

Accessing Linux from the Command Line Interface

For the command line interface, you are initially given a login prompt. The system is now running and waiting for a user to log in and use it. You can enter your username and password to use the system. The login prompt is preceded by the hostname you gave your system. In this example, the hostname is **turtle**. When you finish using Linux, you first log out. Linux then displays exactly the same login prompt, waiting for you or another user to log in again. This is the equivalent of the login window provided by the GDM. You can then log into another account.

```
Red hat Linux release 7.3
Kernel 2.4.18-3 on i686

turtle login:
```

If you want to turn off your computer, you must first shut down Linux. If you don't shut down Linux, you could require Linux to perform a lengthy systems check when it starts up again. You shut down your system in either of two ways. First, log in to an account and then enter the **halt** command. This command will log you out and shut down the system.

```
$ halt
```

Alternatively, you can use the **shutdown** command with the **-h** option. With the **-r** option, it shuts down the system and then reboots it. In the next example, the system is shut down after five minutes. To shut down the system immediately, you can use **+0** or the word **now** (see Chapter 25 for more details).

```
# shutdown -h now
```

Note *Shutting down involves a series of important actions, such as unmounting file systems and shutting down any servers. Never simply turn off the computer.*

You can also reboot your system from the login prompt. Logging out does *not* shut down the system: it is still running and has control of your machine. To shut down and reboot your system, hold down the CTRL and ALT keys, and then press the DEL key (CTRL-ALT-DEL). Your system will go through the standard shutdown procedure and then reboot your computer. At this point it is safe to turn off your computer if you wish, or just let the system restart.

When you shut down, you will see several messages as Linux shuts itself down. It is not finished until you see the "System is halted" message. If you are rebooting, Linux will shut down and then reboot your system, at which time you can turn it off if you wish. The following steps include all the startup and shutdown procedures for the command line interface:

1. Boot your computer.
2. At the boot loader, make sure the entry for your Linux system is selected and press ENTER. (Or press ENTER if Linux is your default.)
3. After a few messages, the login prompt appears, and you can log in to the system and use it.
4. When you finish working in an account, you can log out. The login prompt then reappears, and you can log in to another account.
5. If you are finished working on Linux and want to shut it down, enter the **halt** command while still logged into your account (**shutdown -r** will reboot).
6. At the login prompt, you can also shut down and reboot the system with CTRL-ALT-DEL. The system first shuts down and then restarts, at which time you can turn off your computer or just let the system start up again.

Once you log in to an account, you can enter and execute commands. Logging in to your Linux account involves two steps: entering your username and then your password. You already know what the login prompt looks like. Type in the user name for your user account. If you make a mistake, you can erase characters with the BACKSPACE key. In the next example, the user enters the username **richlp** and is then prompted to enter the password:

```
Red hat Linux release 7.3
Kernel 2.4.18-3 on i686

turtle login: richlp
Password:
```

When you type in your password, it does not appear on the screen. This is to protect your password from being seen by others. If you enter either the username or password, incorrectly, the system will respond with the error message "Login incorrect" and will ask for your username again, starting the login process over. You can then reenter your username and password.

Once you enter your username and password correctly, you are logged in to the system. Your command line prompt is displayed, waiting for you to enter a command. Notice the command line prompt is a dollar sign (**$**), not a sharp sign (**#**). The **$** is the prompt for regular users, whereas the **#** is the prompt solely for the root user. In this version of Linux, your prompt is preceded by the hostname and the directory you are in. Both are bounded by a set of brackets.

```
[turtle /home/richlp]$
```

To end your session, issue the **logout** or **exit** command. This returns you to the login prompt, and Linux waits for another user to log in.

```
[turtle /home/richlp]$ logout
```

Once logged in to the system, you have the option of starting an X Window System GUI, such as Gnome or KDE, and using it to interact with your Linux system. In Linux, the command **startx** starts the X Window System along with a GUI, which then enables you to interact with the system using windows, menus, and icons. The **startx** command starts the GUI desktop by default. Once you shut down the GUI interface, you will return to your command line interface, still logged in.

On Red Hat, you can use the **switchdesk** command, while in your desktop, to switch between Gnome or KDE. You make your selection and then quit the desktop to return to the command line interface. When you start up the GUI again, the desktop you selected is used.

Gnome Desktop

The Gnome desktop display, shown in Figure 3-1, initially displays a panel at the bottom of the screen, as well as any icons for folders and Web pages initially set up by your distribution. You see several Web page icons and a folder for your home directory. The panel at the bottom of the screen contains icons for starting applications, such as Mozilla (the Mozilla logo) and the Help system (the question mark logo). You can start applications using the main menu, which you display by clicking the Gnome icon (the image of a bare footprint), located on the left side of the panel.

When you click the folder for your home directory on your desktop or select the File Manager entry on the main menu, a file manager window opens showing your home directory. You can display files in your home directory and use the up arrow button to move to the parent directory. Back and Forward buttons move through previously displayed directories. In the location window, you can enter the pathname for a directory to move directly to it. The file manager is also Internet-aware. You can use it to access remote FTP directories and to display or download their files (though it cannot display Web pages).

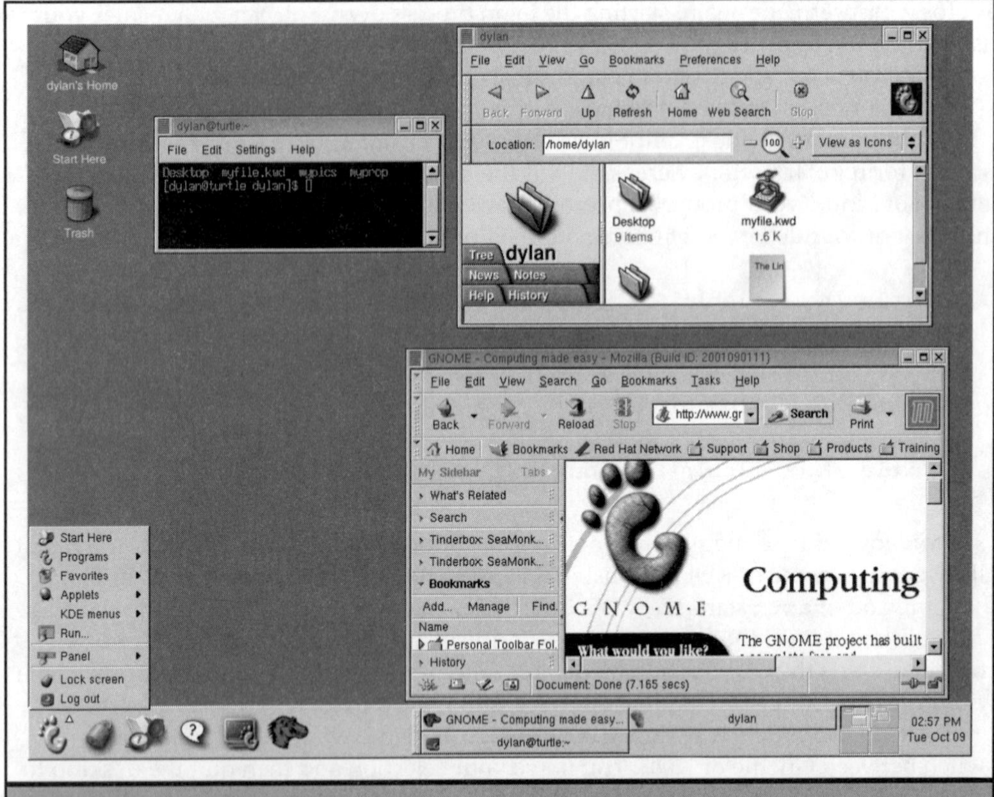

Figure 3-1. *The Gnome desktop*

To move a window, left-click and drag its title bar or right-click its other borders. Each window supports Maximize, Minimize, and Close buttons, as well as a Stick Pin button. Double-clicking the title bar will "shade" a window, reducing it to only its title bar. You can redisplay the window with another double-click. The desktop supports full drag-and-drop capabilities. You can drag folders, icons, and applications to the desktop or other file manager windows open to other folders. The move operation is the default drag operation. To copy files, click and drag, then press the CTRL key before releasing the mouse button. To create links, hold down the SHIFT key when you click and drag. In most cases, you would use links for desktop icons.

The panel also contains a pager for desktop areas, which appears as four squares. Clicking a square moves you to that area. You can think of the desktop work area as being four times larger than your monitor screen, and you can use the pager to display different parts. You can configure your Gnome interface, setting features such as the background, by using the Gnome Control Center. (The Gnome Control Center is accessible on Red Hat from the Preferences window in the Start-Here window. Click the image of a compass with a map on the panel to open the Start-Here window.) To configure system settings such as adding users, installing printers, and setting up network connections, open the System menu.

To quit the Gnome desktop, select Log Out at the bottom of the main menu. If you entered from a login window, you are then logged out of your account and returned to the login window. If you started Gnome from the command line, you are returned to the command line prompt, still logged into your account.

The K Desktop Environment (KDE)

The K Desktop Environment (KDE), shown in Figure 3-2, initially displays a panel at the bottom of the screen, as well as any icons for folders and Web pages initially set up by your distribution. In the upper-left corner, you can see a row of icons with labels like Autostart, Trash, and Printer. When a user starts KDE for the first time, the KDE

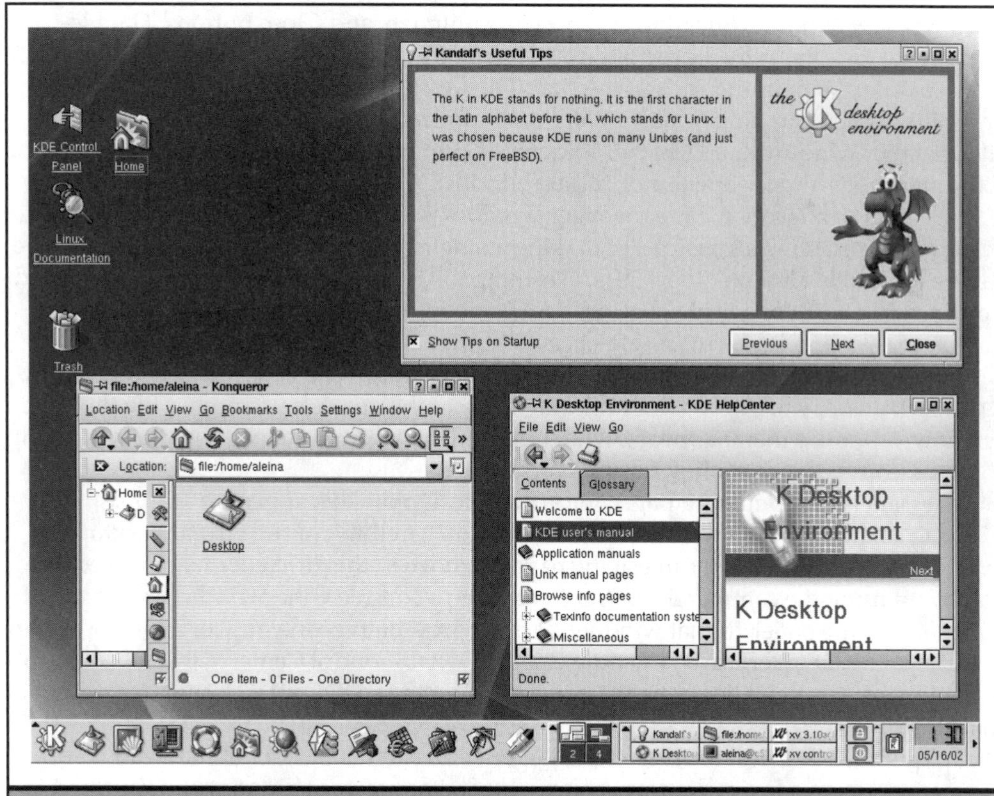

Figure 3-2. *The K Desktop Environment*

Setup Wizard is run, displaying a series of four windows advising you to set up icons for KDE Web pages, as well as CD-ROM and printer icons. Initially, the KDE Wizard enables you to choose a theme, such as a Windows, KDE standard, or Mac theme. You can change this later if you want. The next windows ask if you want to add icons for your CD-ROM and printer, and links to certain Web sites, such as the KDE Web site.

You can start applications using the main menu, which you display by clicking the button in the panel with the large *K* on a cogwheel. This button is located on the left side of the panel. When you click the folder for your home directory on your panel (the icon of a folder with a house on it) or select the File Manager entry on the main menu, a file manager window opens, showing your home directory. You can display files in your home directory and use the up arrow button to move to the parent directory. Back and Forward buttons move through previously displayed directories. In the location window, you can enter the pathname for a directory to move directly to it. The file manager is also Internet-aware and a fully functional Web browser. You can use it to access remote Web and FTP sites, displaying Web pages or downloading files from an FTP site.

To move a window, click and drag its title bar or click and drag its other borders. Each window supports Stick Pin, Maximize, Minimize, and Close buttons. Double-clicking the title bar reduces the window to only its title bar (known as shading), which can redisplay with another double-click. The desktop supports full drag-and-drop capabilities. You can drag folders, icons, and applications to the desktop or to another file manager window open to other folders. Clicking the cogwheel in the right corner of a file manager window opens a duplicate window.

Selection of an icon in a file manager window is different than in other GUIs. To select an item, CTRL-click instead of making a single left-click. The single left-click is the same as a double-click on other GUIs, executing the item or opening it with its associated application. So, if you single-click on a folder icon, you open the folder (as opposed simply to selecting it). If you single-click a file, you start up the application using that file. To select items, be sure to CTRL-click them. To deselect a selected item, be sure to CTRL-click again. When you click and drag a file to the desktop or another file manager window, a pop-up menu appears, which then enables you to choose whether you want to move, copy, or create a link for the item.

The panel also contains a pager for virtual desktops. This appears as four squares. Clicking a square moves you to that desktop. You can think of the virtual desktops as separate desktops, and you can use the pager to move to the different ones. To execute a command using the command line interface, open a console window. Click the image of a monitor on the panel. In that window, at the **$** prompt, type in your command. You can modify your KDE interface at any time using the KDE Control Center. Click the image of a monitor with a circuit board on the panel or select the KDE Control Center from the main menu.

To quit the KDE desktop, select the Logout entry at the bottom of the main menu. If you entered from a login window, you are logged out of your account and returned to the login window. If you started KDE from the command line, you are returned to the command line prompt, still logged in to your account.

Command Line Interface

When using the command line interface, you are given a simple prompt at which you type in your command. Even with a GUI, you sometimes need to execute commands on a command line. Linux commands make extensive use of options and arguments. Be careful to place your arguments and options in their correct order on the command line. The format for a Linux command is the command name followed by options, and then by arguments, as shown here:

```
$ command-name options arguments
```

An *option* is a one-letter code preceded by a hyphen, which modifies the type of action the command takes. Options and arguments may or may not be optional, depending on the command. For example, the **ls** command can take an option, **-s.** The **ls** command displays a listing of files in your directory, and the **-s** option adds the size of each file in blocks. You enter the command and its option on the command line as follows:

```
$ ls -s
```

An *argument* is data the command may need to execute its task. In many cases, this is a filename. An argument is entered as a word on the command line after any options. For example, to display the contents of a file, you can use the **more** command with the file's name as its argument. The **more** command used with the filename **mydata** would be entered on the command line as follows:

```
$ more mydata
```

The command line is actually a buffer of text you can edit. Before you press ENTER, you can perform editing commands on the existing text. The editing capabilities provide a way to correct mistakes you may make when typing in a command and its options. The BACKSPACE and DEL keys let you erase the character you just typed in. With this character-erasing capability, you can BACKSPACE over the entire line if you want, erasing what you entered. CTRL-U erases the whole line and enables you to start over again at the prompt.

You can use the UP ARROW *to redisplay your previously executed command. You can then re-execute that command, or you can edit it and execute the modified command. This is helpful when you have to repeat certain operations over and over, such as editing the same file. This is also helpful when you've already executed a command you entered incorrectly.*

Help

A great deal of help is already installed on your system, as well as accessible from online sources. Both the Gnome and KDE desktops feature Help systems that use a browser-like interface to display help files. To start KDE Help, click the Book icon in the panel. Here, you can select from the KDE manual, the Linux Man pages, or the GNU info pages. KDE Help features browser capabilities, including bookmarks and history lists for documents you view (see Figure 3-2).

To start the Gnome Help browser, click the icon with the question mark (?) in the panel. You can then choose from the Gnome user guide, Man pages, and info pages. The Gnome Help browser and KDE Help Center also feature bookmarks and history lists.

Both Gnome and KDE, along with other applications, such as Linuxconf, also provide context-sensitive help. Each KDE and Gnome application features detailed manuals that are displayed using their respective Help browsers. Also, system administrative tools like the Mandrake Control Center, the SuSE YaST Control Center, and Red Hat administrative tools, along with Linuxconf and Webmin feature detailed explantions for each task.

Note *Extensive help is provided online. Most distribution desktops display Web page icons for support pages, including online manuals and tutorials.*

On your system, the **/usr/share/doc** directory contains documentation files installed by each application. Within each directory, you can usually find HOW-TO documents for that application.

You can also access the online manual for Linux commands from the command line interface using the **man** command. Enter **man** with the command on which you want information. The following example asks for information on the **ls** command:

```
$ man ls
```

Pressing either the SPACEBAR or the F key advances you to the next page. Pressing the B key moves you back a page. When you finish, press the Q key to quit the man utility and return to the command line. You activate a search by pressing either the slash (/) or question mark (?). The / searches forward and the ? searches backward. When you press the /, a line opens at the bottom of your screen, and you then enter a word to search for. Press ENTER to activate the search. You can repeat the same search by pressing the N key. You needn't reenter the pattern.

You can also use either the Gnome or KDE Help systems to display Man pages.

Online Documentation

When you start up your browser, a default Web page lists links for documentation both on your own system and at your distribution Web site. To use your distribution Web site, you first must be connected to the Internet. However, your CD-ROM and your system contain extensive documentation showing you how to use the desktop and take you through a detailed explanation of Linux applications. Other documentation provides detailed tutorials on different Linux topics.

The **/usr/share/doc** directory contains the online documentation for many Linux applications, including subdirectories with the names of installed Linux applications that contain documentation, such as **readme** files. You can access the complete set of HOW-TO text files in the **/usr/share/doc/HOWTO** directory. The HOW-TO series contains detailed documentation on all Linux topics from hardware installation to network configuration. In addition, **/usr/share/doc/HOWTO/HTML** holds documentation in the form of Web pages you display with a Web browser. You can use the following URL on a Web browser, such as Netscape, to view the documents:

```
file:/usr/share/doc/HOWTO/HTML
```

Online documentation for GNU applications, such as the gcc compiler and the Emacs editor, also exists. You can access this documentation by entering the command **`info.`** This brings up a special screen listing different GNU applications. The info interface has its own set of commands. You can learn more about it by entering **`info info`**. Typing **`m`** opens a line at the bottom of the screen where you can enter the first few letters of the application. Pressing ENTER brings up the info file on that application.

Note *You can also display info documents using either the Gnome or KDE Help browsers.*

Part II

Basic Setup

The Complete Reference

Chapter 4

System Configuration

To make effective use of your Linux system, you must know how to configure certain features. Administrative operations such as adding users, accessing CD-ROM drives, and installing software can now be performed with user-friendly system tools. This chapter discusses basic system administration operations that you need to get your system up and running, as well as to perform basic maintenance such as adding new users or printers.

There are three basic system configuration tasks that you most likely will have to deal with: user management, file system access, and printer setup. You can manage users, adding new ones and removing others. File systems such as floppy disks, CD-ROMs, or other hard drives can be attached to your system at specific directories. You can also add different kinds of printers. All of these tasks you were asked to perform during installation. You can make changes or additions easily using the administration tools described in this chapter.

When logged in as the root user, you can also perform certain configuration operations from the command line. You can manually access system configuration files, editing them and making entries yourself. For example, the domain name server entries are kept in the **/etc/resolv.conf** file. You can edit this file and type in the addresses.

Configuration tools are only accessible by the root user. You will first need to log in using **root** *as your username and providing the root password you specified during installation.*

Most configuration operations can be performed using administrative tools provided by your Linux distribution (see Table 4-1). Most can be used either on a desktop like Gnome or KDE, or on a shell command line. These tools cover a variety of tasks such as user and file management, network configuration, and printer installation

Administration Tools	Description
Mandrake Control Center	Mandrake administrative tools
YaST Control Center	SuSE administrative tools, YaST2
System Settings	Red Hat window for accessing administrative tools
Text Mode Setup utility (Setuptool)	Red Hat command line configuration tools
Linuxconf	Linuxconf administrative system **www.solucorp.qc.ca/linuxconf**
Webmin	Web-based administrative system **www.webmin.com**

Table 4-1. *Administrative tools*

(network configuration is covered in Chapter 5). Each distribution has its own set of tools, designed for their own implementation of Linux. For example, users on Mandrake can be managed by Mandrake's UserDrake tool, whereas on Red Hat you would use the Red Hat User Manager. For any given distribution, most of these tools are accessible from a centralized interface, such as the Mandrake Control Center or YaST Control Center on SuSE. Red Hat provides a directory window labeled System Settings from which you can access different administrative tools easily.

In addition to the distribution-specific tools, you can also use certain distribution independent tools. Some of these are designed for use on either Gnome or KDE, and perform a specific task, such as KUser, a KDE tool that manages users. Others are designed to manage all administrative tasks, from network configuration to server management. Linuxconf and Webmin fall into this category. With either you can administer your entire system. Some distributions also make use of these comprehensive administrative systems. Mandrake currently still uses Linuxconf for some tasks, whereas Caldera uses Webmin for all its administrative needs.

All administrative tools are operated as front ends for making entries in Linux configuration files. You can edit these files and make entries directly, if you want. The underlying administration tasks are the same.

Distribution Administrative Tools

Many of the Major Linux distributions include their own administrative tools. These are designed to make it easier to administer administrative tasks. Most tools use simple GUI interfaces, freeing the user from having to edit a collection of different and often confusing configuration files. These tools are distribution-specific and cannot be relied on to work on other distributions. You cannot use the Red Hat User Manager to manage users on SuSE systems reliably.

Mandrake Control Center

Mandrake provides an extensive set of administrative tools noted for their ease of use. You can access them easily from the Mandrake Control Center (see Figure 4-1). Here you can configure your hardware, system features, boot configuration, among others. For basic configuration, you will mostly need the Hardware and System panels. Network configuration is discussed in Chapter 5. In the Hardware panel, you can configure devices such as keyboards, mice, and printers, and your video card. In System panel, you can perform many of the basic administrative tasks such as setting the time and date, and installing software, and managing users. Each task is carried out by a separate tool, usually having "drake" in its name. User management is handled by a tool called UserDrake. Fonts are added by DrakFont. PrinterDrake lets you add and configure printers. With MenuDrake, you can add and remove menu items on your main menu easily.

From the Mandrake Control Center, you can also configure how you want your system to start up. With the BootConfig tool you can select whether you want either a

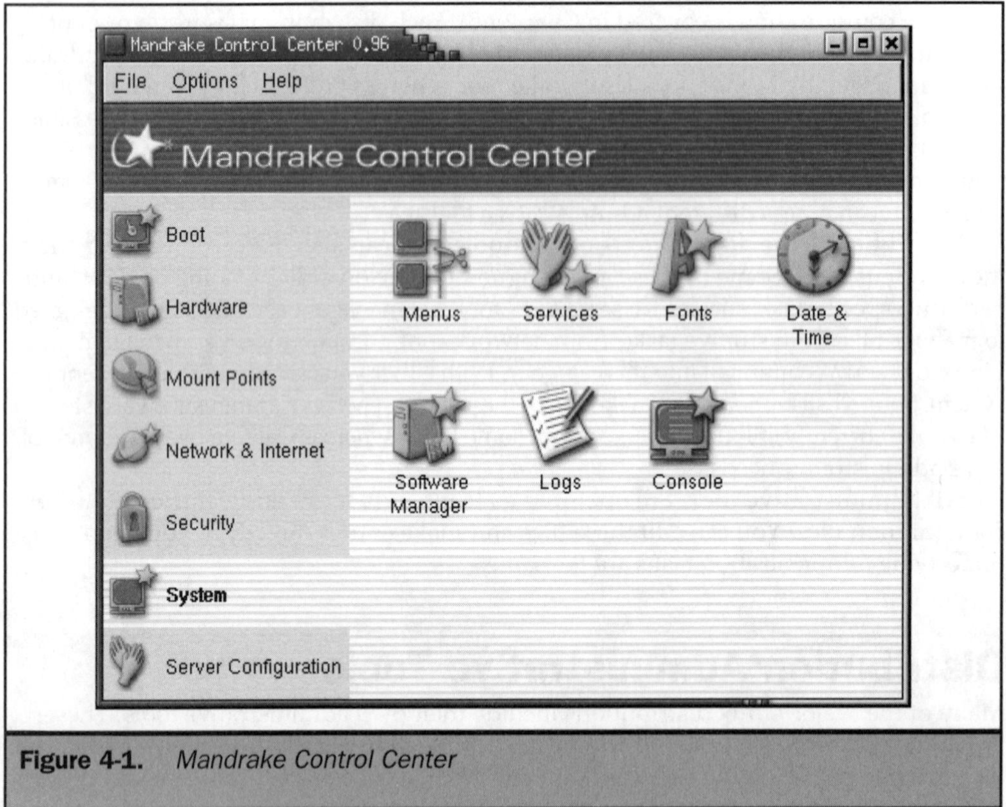

Figure 4-1. *Mandrake Control Center*

graphical or text login, and if you want to automatically log in to a particular account. You can also select and configure different boot loaders, as described in Chapter 26.

To install new hardware, such as sound cards, you can use HardDrake. HardDrake will try to automatically detect and configure your new hardware, as well as let you select and configure the hardware manually. You can also make configuration changes such as setting IRQ entries for sound cards. The HardDrake Wizard will take you step-by-step through the install process. HardDrake does not actually perform the configuration, but invokes GNU configuration tools and modules appropriate for particular hardware. You can also use HardDrake to obtain information about hardware already installed on your system.

In addition, Mandrake also provides tools for selecting your type of mouse, the keyboard language, and adding new partitions. The partition management tool, DiskDrake, operates much like Red Hat's DiskDruid, letting you create, destroy, resize, and modify partitions on your hard disk. You would most likely use DiskDrake to create partitions in a new hard drive. Exercise great care when using DiskDrake. If you make a mistake, you could easily erase your system.

YaST Control Center (SuSE)

On SuSE, you configure your system using the Yet Another System Tool 2 (YaST2). You can run YaST2 as the YaST Control Center on any GUI, such as Gnome and KDE, which will provide you with easy access to all SuSE configuration tools (see Figure 4-2). The Hardware panel lists tools for configuring devices such as printers, graphic cards, your mouse, and sound cards. In the System menu, you can set features such as your keyboard layout, set the time and day, configure your boot loader, or create a boot disk. The Security And User panel lists tools for creating and editing users.

Note *YaST2 replaces the original YaST with SuSE 8.0,*

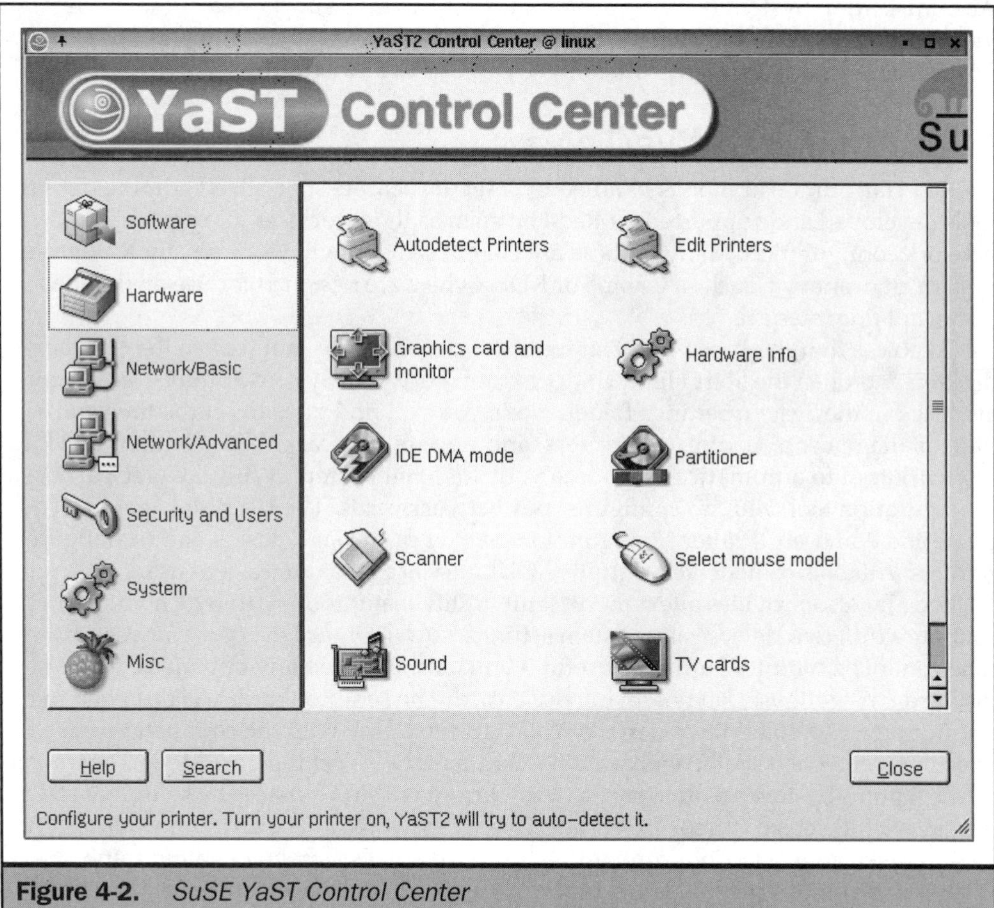

Figure 4-2. *SuSE YaST Control Center*

To run the YaST Control Center on the command line, you enter the command **yast**. Use the arrow keys, TAB, and ENTER to make selections. On the main menu, choose System Administration and press ENTER. This will display a submenu for different configuration options.

To choose whether you want to start the system with the command line or the display manager (KDM), select Login Configuration and make your choice.

SuSE has its own XFree86 configuration tool, called SaX2. SaX2 provides a simple and easy-to-use interface for configuring your mouse, keyboard, video card, and monitor.

Caldera Configuration

On Caldera OpenLinux, you configure your system using either the Caldera Open Administration System (COAS) or Webmin. COAS also supports a cursor-based interface that you can run from the command line by entering the command **coastool**. To configure your X Window System, you can use **lizardx**.

Red Hat Administrative Tools

On Red Hat, administration is handled by a set of separate specialized administrative tools developed and supported by Red Hat such as those for user management and network configuration. Many of these are GUI-based and will work on any X Window System environment, such as Gnome or KDE. Others are designed for use on the shell command line interface.

To access the GUI-based Red Hat tools, you log in as the root user to the Gnome desktop and open the Start Here window (see Figure 4-3). System administrative tools are listed in the System Settings folder. Here, you will find tools to set the time and date, manage users, configure printers, and update software. You use the Red Hat Network tool to automatically update your Red Hat system. With the Network Configuration tool, you can configure your network cards. The User Manager lets you create and edit users. Printer Configuration invokes printconf to install and reconfigure printers. All tools provide very intuitive GUI interfaces that are easy to use.

Red Hat also provides a text mode setup utility (setuptool) with which you can configure different devices and system settings, such as your keyboard, mouse, and time zone. The setuptool utility is useful if you have changed any of your devices—say, installed a new mouse, keyboard, or sound card. The setuptool utility is designed to be run from the command line interface. You start the utility with the command **setup**, which you enter at a shell command line. You can also select the Text Mode Tool menu on the Gnome System menu to run setuptool from within Gnome. The setuptool utility provides a full-screen, cursor-based interface where you can use arrow, TAB, and ENTER keys to make your selections. Initially, setuptool displays a menu of configuration tools from which you can choose. The setuptool utility is actually an interface for running several configuration tools. You can call any of these tools separately using their commands. For example, the **kbdconfig** command starts the keyboard configuration

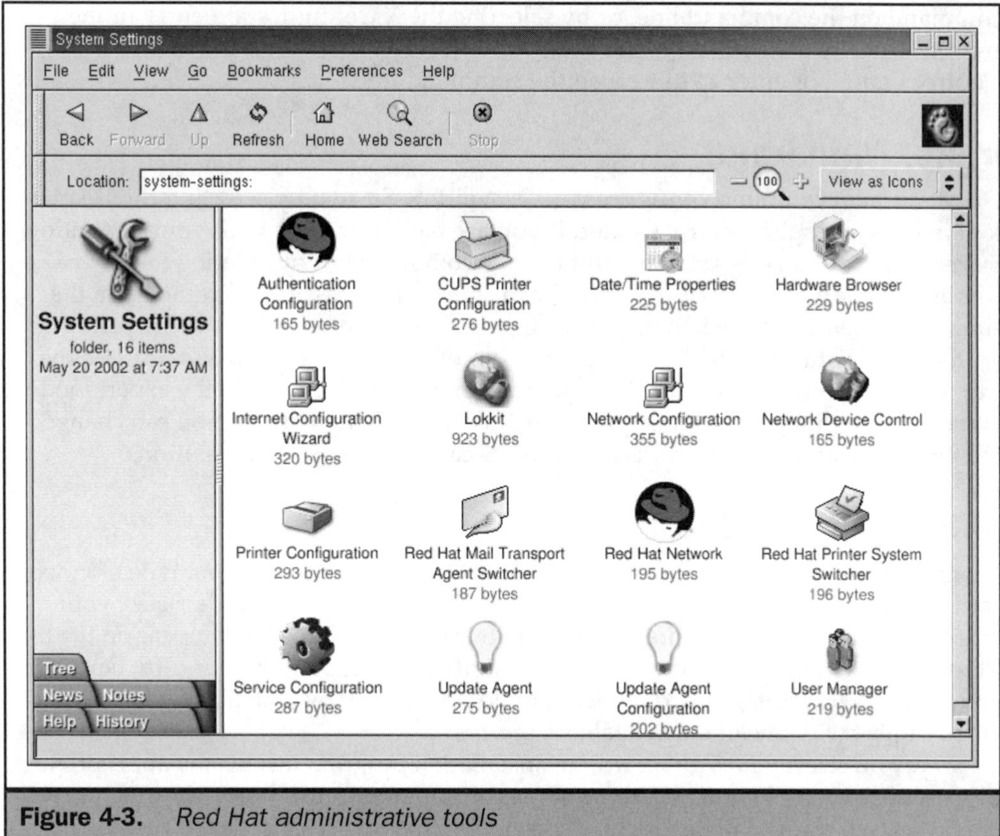

Figure 4-3. *Red Hat administrative tools*

utility that enables you to select the type of keyboard, while the **mouseconfig** command enables you to select the type of mouse.

X Window System Configuration

One important set of utilities are the X Window System configuration tools provided by respective distributions. On Red Hat, you use Xconfigurator; on Mandrake XFdrake and on SuSE, you use SaX2. If you have trouble with your X Window System configuration, you can use one of these utilities to configure it again. These tools are also helpful for updating your X Window System if you change your video card. Simply run the appropriate tool again and select the card. You can run these tools either on the command line, or by selecting them in their respective distribution's control centers. For example, on Red Hat you can run Xconfigurator by entering the **Xconfigurator** command on the command line, or by selecting the X Configuration entry in the setuptool utility's menu. On Mandrake, you can select Display in the Mandrake Control Center, or enter **`XFdrake`** on the command line.

XFdrake: Mandrake

On Mandrake, you can reconfigure your X Window System by selecting the Display tool in the Mandrake Control Center. If you are having trouble with your X Window System, you can run this same tool from a shell command line by entering the **`XFdrake`** command. The XFdrake tool runs in either a simple mode or an expert mode. In the simple mode, you can use it to quickly change your video resolution. You are presented with a panel listing available resolutions from which you can choose. To access the expert mode, you click the More button while in the simple mode. In the expert mode, you can select different hardware for your X Window System. Here, you can change the type of monitor, select a different graphics card, and choose a resolution.

Xconfigurator: Red Hat

Xconfigurator first probes your system in an attempt to determine what type of video card you have. Failing that, Xconfigurator presents a list of video cards. Select your video card from the list and press ENTER. If your video card does not appear on the list, XFree86 may not support it. If you have technical knowledge about your card, however, you may choose Unlisted Card and attempt to configure it by matching your card's video chipset with one of the available X servers.

Once you select your video card, the installation program installs the appropriate XFree86 server, and Xconfigurator presents a list of monitors. If your monitor appears on the list, select it and press ENTER. If it is not on the list, select Custom. This displays a screen where you enter the horizontal sync range and vertical sync range of your monitor (these values are generally available in the documentation that accompanies your monitor or from your monitor's vendor or manufacturer). Be careful to enter the correct horizontal and vertical frequencies. If you enter values that are too high, you may overclock your monitor, which could damage older models. You should not select a monitor similar to your own unless you are certain the monitor you are selecting does not exceed the capabilities of your monitor.

The next screen prompts you for the amount of video memory installed on your video card. If you are not sure, please consult the documentation accompanying your video card. Choosing more memory than is available does not damage your video card, but the XFree86 server may not start correctly if you do.

If the video card you selected has a video clock chip, Xconfigurator presents a list of clock chips. The recommended choice is No Clockchip Setting because, in most cases, XFree86 can automatically detect the proper clock chip.

In the next screen, Xconfigurator prompts you to select the video modes you want to use. These are screen resolutions you may want to use. You can select one or more by moving to it and pressing the SPACEBAR. Xconfigurator then starts the X Window

System and displays a dialog box asking if you can see it. Xconfigurator then generates an X Window System configuration file called **/etc/X11/XF86Config**. This is the file the X Window System uses to start up.

SaX2: SuSE

On SuSE, you can use the SuSE Advanced XF86 Configurator (SAX2) to configure your X Window System. To run SAX2, select the Graphic Card And Monitor entry from the YaST Control Center or run SAX2 from the KDE or Gnome program menu. As with other X Window System configuration tools, SAX2 will automatically try to detect your video card and monitor, though you can make your own selection from an extensive listing. SAX2 will initially detect your mouse and keyboard. On the Graphics Device Setup panel, it will detect and choose a graphics card. You can click the Properties button to open a listing of cards you can manually choose from. On the following Desktop Setup panel, you can manually change properties such as color depth, resolution, and monitor type by clicking the Properties button. The Monitor panel will list a extensive set of monitor models to choose from. If you install a new monitor or video card, you can use SAX2 to update your configuration.

Linuxconf and Webmin

Linuxconf and Webmin are two popular comprehensive administration tools that let you perform almost all your administrative tasks. This offers you the advantage of using just one software program to manage your system.

Linuxconf

Linuxconf is a comprehensive configuration tool for almost all your administrative tasks, including user and file system management, as well as network services. Linuxconf is designed to work on any Linux distribution and is currently compatible with Caldera, Red Hat, SuSE, Slackware, and Debian. Both compressed archive and RPM versions of the software are provided. You can download the current version from the Linuxconf Web site at **www.solucorp.qc.ca/linuxconf**. Here, you can also find documentation and links to any added packages.

Linuxconf provides an extensive set of configuration options, enabling you to configure features such as user accounts and file systems, as well as your Internet servers, dial-up connections, and LILO. The version included with Red Hat does not provide support for servers. You can access the main Linuxconf interface with its entire set of configuration options or use specialized commands that display entries for a particular task, such as configuring user accounts or entering your network settings. The specialized commands include **`userconf`** for user accounts, **`fsconf`** for file systems, and **`netconf`** for networks. In all cases, you need to log in as the root user.

Linuxconf supports three interfaces: an X Window System interface, a cursor-based interface, and a Web interface. The X Window System interface runs under Gnome using gnome-linuxconf to provide Gnome desktop features. You can use the cursor-based interface from a Linux command line, and you needn't be running a GUI. The interface presents a full-screen display on which you can use arrow keys, the TAB key, the SPACEBAR, and the ENTER key to make selections. With the Web-based interface, you use your Web browser to make selections (though this is meant for use on local networks). Use the URL for your system with a **:98** attached, as in **turtle.mytrek.com:98**.

Much of the configuration support for specific components, such as the Apache Web server or Squid, is implemented using modules. You can add or remove modules as you choose. Modules are usually included with the Linuxconf software package. You can then select which modules to load into Linuxconf using the Configure Linuxconf Modules panel in the Control Files And Systems list under Control Panel. This panel shows all the available modules with check boxes you can use to toggle whether a module should be loaded. For example, to add firewall configuration panels to Linuxconf, make sure the firewall module check box is selected. Links to different modules are available on the Linuxconf Web site and most are also kept on the FTP site, **ftp.solucorp.qc.ca/pub/linuxconf/modules**.

Linuxconf enables you to create multiple system configurations that you can load, activating or deactivating features and services. You can have one set of configurations for your office and one for home, or even one for, say, a Web server. A home configuration might have your Web server turned off, whereas a Web server configuration might have it running. If you have Linux running on a portable PC, you could switch networking configurations just by switching Linuxconf system configurations. Different configurations are placed in subdirectories in the **/etc/linuxconf/archive** directory. Their names are the same as those subdirectories. Linuxconf provides two for you by default: Office and Home-Office.

Webmin

Webmin is a Web-based interface for Unix and Linux system administration tasks. You can use any Web browser that supports tables and forms to access Webmin and perform extensive administrative operations. Webmin itself is composed of a simple Web server with CGI Perl programs with which you can directly update system configuration files such as **/etc/passwd**. Webmin is available free of charge under the BSD license. You can find out more about Webmin at **www.webmin.com**.

Webmin is a Web page-based interface that you can run on any Web browser by accessing port 10000 at localhost, **http://localhost:10000**. The initial Webmin page will have panels for different kinds of configuration tasks such as system, hardware, and servers. For basic administration tasks, click the System panel to show icons for different system administration tasks such as managing users and mounting file systems. With Webmin, you can perform all the tasks that the Red Hat tools perform.

For example, on Webmin you can manage users with the Users And Groups page selected from the System page. Here you can add new users, entering their usernames and passwords. Current users are listed, each with the username as a link you can use to display a page for editing the user's account.

Webmin is an extensible application designed to be enhanced by modules that any users can write and plug into their versions. A number of standard modules are provided with Webmin that cover areas such as user account setup, LILO modification, and server configuration. Numerous third-party modules are under development. You can access them at **www.thirdpartymodules.com/webmin**.

Configuring Users

Currently, the easiest and most effective way to add new users on your Linux system is to use user management tools like the Red Hat User Manager, Mandrake's UserDrake, or KDE's KUser. You can also use administrative tools like SuSE's YaST2 or Caldera's COAS. Linuxconf and Webmin also provide strong user management capabilities. In general, a user management tool will display panels for listing both users and groups. A button bar will list various tasks you can perform, including creating new users or groups, editing current ones, or deleting a selected user or group.

Note *SuSE's YaST Control Center provides tools to create and edit users. When creating a user, click the Details button if you want to add specific groups or change the login shell.*

Creating a new user opens a panel with entries for the username, password, and login shell, along with options to create a home directory and a new group for that user. Once you have created a user, you can edit its properties to add or change features. You can also select the groups that the user belongs to, adding or removing group membership.

Instead of using a user management tool, you can use the **useradd** command to add user accounts and the **userdel** command to remove them. These commands operate on a simple command line and let you quickly add and remove users. The following example adds the user **dylan** to the system:

```
$ useradd dylan
```

One common operation performed from the command line is to change a password. Any user can change their own password with the **passwd** command. The command prompts you for your current password. After entering your current password and pressing ENTER, you are then prompted for your new password. After entering the new password, you are asked to reenter it. This is to make sure you actually entered the password you intended to enter. Because password characters are not displayed when you type them, it is easy to make a mistake and to press a wrong key.

```
$ passwd
Old password:
New password:
Retype new password:
$
```

Some distributions provide a GUI password tool to change your password.

Managing CD-ROM, Floppy, and CD-R/RW Drives

Files and directories contained on different hardware devices such as floppy disks, CD-ROMs, and hard disk partitions are called *file systems.* The Linux partition you used to install your Linux system on is called the *root partition.* This is where you mounted the root file system, the root directory indicated with a single slash, **/**. The root partition contains the main file system with a directory tree, starting from the root and spreading out to different systems and user subdirectories. To access files on another file system, such as a CD-ROM disc, you need to attach that file system to your main system. Attaching a file system is called *mounting the file system.* You first set up an empty directory to which you want to mount the file system.

On many distributions, the ***/mnt/cdrom*** *directory is already reserved for mounting CD-ROMs and the* ***/mnt/floppy*** *directory is reserved for floppy disks (on SuSE these are* ***/cdrom*** *and* ***/floppy****). If you have more than one CD-ROM, numbered directories will be added, for example,* ***/mnt/cdrom1*** *for the second CD-ROM.*

Managing CD-ROMs

The Gnome and KDE interfaces also provide a simple method for mounting and unmounting a CD-ROM. Simply insert the CD-ROM into your CD-ROM drive; you then see an icon labeled CD-ROM appear on the desktop. A CD-ROM is automatically mounted. A file manager window also automatically appears, which displays the contents of the CD-ROM. You can also mount and unmount the CD-ROM using a pop-up menu on the CD-ROM icon. Right-click it to display a pop-up menu with options to mount and unmount the CD-ROM, along with other options. Selecting Unmount Volume at the bottom of the pop-up menu will automatically unmount and eject the CD-ROM from your drive. You can access the CD-ROM you placed in your CD drive by double-clicking the CD-ROM icon. Your CD-ROM drive remains locked until you select the Unmount entry that is now displayed on the pop-up menu. If you do not see an icon for your CD-ROM, you must first make it user-mountable.

On Red Hat, you can also perform simple mount and unmount operations using the Disk Management tool accessible from the Gnome System menu. This tool will list all the file systems that can be mounted and will display buttons for mounting or unmounting them.

From any shell command line, you can also easily mount and unmount file systems with the `mount` and `umount` commands. To mount your CD-ROM, you only have to enter the command `mount` and the directory **/mnt/cdrom**. You can then access the contents of the CD-ROM at the **/mnt/cdrom** directory.

```
$ mount /mnt/cdrom
```

When you finish, unmount the CD-ROM with the `umount` command.

```
$ umount /mnt/cdrom
```

You can also manually mount and unmount floppy disks and hard disk partitions. See Chapter 29 for a detailed discussion.

Installing IDE CD-R/RW Drives

If your system has a CD-R/RW drive that uses an IDE interface, it may have been detected during installation. To support CD-R/RW IDE drives, a kernel module called ide-scsi has to be loaded. The installation process may have detected your CD-R/RW and configured your system to automatically load the ide-scsi module. In that case, your CD-R/RW is ready to use. You can check to see if your CD-R/RW drive was configured correctly by entering the following command. Information about your SCSI drives should be displayed.

```
cdrecord -scanbus
```

The same procedures for installing IDE CD-R/RW drives also applies to IDE DVD-R/RW drives as well as to IDE DVD+R/+RW drives.

If configured correctly, there should be an entry in your **/etc/grub.conf** or **/etc/lilo.conf** file that loads the module for your CD-R/RW device. GRUB will add the argument to the command executed from its menu, which you can edit if you want. LILO will contain an append line in the

```
append="hdc=ide-scsi"
```

Note *SCSI CD-R/RW drives will be automatically configured during the install process.*

There are four possible IDE devices on standard PCs, corresponding to the four primary and secondary master and slave IDE ports. The device name used in Linux depends on what IDE port you connected your CD-ROM or CD-R/RW drives to. The primary master IDE port is usually used for an IDE hard drive. The other IDE ports are usually used for CD drive. The primary slave IDE port is hdb, the secondary master is hdc (the most common connection), and the secondary slave is hdd. The above example is for a CD-R/RW drive connected to the secondary master IDE port (hdc).

Many systems will have both a CD-R/RW drive and a regular CD-ROM drive. If you want to copy CD-ROMs directly from the CD-ROM drive to the CD-RW drive, you need to also configure the CD-ROM drive as a SCSI drive. In the following example, there is an IDE CD-ROM drive on the secondary slave port (hdd). In the **/etc/grub.conf** file, you add it right after the **hdc=ide-scsi** entry. For **/etc/lilo.conf**, the append line would have to be modified to include the hdd drive (be sure to execute the `lilo` command after making changes to **lilo.conf**).

```
append="hdc=ide-scsi hdd=ide-scsi"
```

When you restart, your CD-R/RW as well as CD-ROMs should be installed as SCSI drives and can be used by CD write software such as cdrecord and KonCD.

You can also manually specify the ide-scsi module as a kernel parameter when your system boots up. At the `boot:` prompt, enter the following kernel parameter.

```
boot:  linux hdc=ide-scsi
```

Enter as many CD drive entries as you need. For example, if you need to configure both the CD-ROM and the CD-RW, you could enter:

```
boot: linux hdc=ide-scsi hdd=ide-scsi
```

Your CD drives will be configured only until the system is shut down. The next time you boot up, you will have to enter the parameters again if you wish to do CD write tasks.

Note *To write to a CD-R/RW drive, you use the **cdrecord** tool or any of several CD burner applications, like KonCD. To write to a DVD-R/RW drive, you use **dvdrecord**, an enhanced version of cdrecord. For DVD+r/+RW drives, you need to use the dvd+rw tools, such as **growisofs** and **dvd+rw-format**, currently included only in the Debian distribution (check the "DVD+RW/+R for Linux" Web site). See Chapter 29 for more details.*

Printer Configuration

As part of the installation procedure for Linux, you configured a printer connected to your computer. To change configurations or to add a new printer later, you can use a printer configuration tool provided by your distribution. Such a utility enables you to select the appropriate driver for your printer, as well as set print options such as paper size and print resolutions. You can use these utilities to access a printer connected directly to your local computer or a printer on a remote system on your network (see Chapter 30).

A Windows (SMB share) printer is one located on a Windows network. To access an SMB share remote printer, you need to install Samba and have the Server Message Block services enabled using the **smbd** daemon. Printer sharing must, in turn, be enabled on the Windows network. In the printer configuration utility, you need to enter the name of the share, its IP address, the name of the printer's workgroup, and the username and password. The share is the hostname and printer name in the format **\\hostname\printername**. The hostname is the computer where the printer is located, and printer name is the name of the printer as it is known to remote hosts. The username and password can be one for the printer resource itself, or for access by a particular user. You can then use a print client lpr to print a file to the Windows printer. lpr will invoke the Samba client smbclient to send the print job to the Windows printer.

Red Hat Printer Configuration (printconf)

The printconf utility provided on Red Hat distributions is an easy interface for setting up and managing your printers. Using only printconf, you can easily install a printer on your Linux system. You can start printconf by selecting the Printer Configuration entry in the Gnome System menu. The printconf utility enables you to select the appropriate driver for your printer, as well as to set print options such as paper size and print resolutions. Once you have configured your printer with printconf, printconf will generate an entry for it in the **/etc/printcap** file. See the printconf section in the Red Hat Customization Guide for more details.

When you start up printconf, you are presented with a window that lists your installed printers. To add a new printer, click the New button. To edit an installed printer, double-click its entry or select it and click the Edit button. Once you have made your changes, you can click the Apply button to save your changes and restart the printer daemon. If you have more than one printer on your system, you can make one the default by selecting it and then clicking the Default button. The Delete button will remove a printer configuration. You can test your printer with a PostScript, A4, or ASCII test sheet selected from the Test menu.

When you select New, a series of dialogs are displayed where you can enter the printer name, its type, and its driver. You can also edit a printer to change any settings. For editing, a set of four tabbed panes are displayed for the printer name, queue type, driver, and options. For the queue selection, you can specify entries for the printer device and spool directory. The device is the port to which the printer is connected. For the first three parallel ports, these are **lp0**, **lp1**, **lp2**. For serial ports, these are **ttyS0**, **ttyS1**, and **ttyS2**, and so on. From a drop-down menu, you can also specify whether the printer is local or remotely connected through a Linux/Unix, Windows (SMB), or NetWare network.

For the driver selection, you are presented with an expandable tree of printer types. You first select the manufacturer, such as Cannon or Apple, which then expands to a list of particular printer models. Click on yours.

For the options selection, you can specify printer features such as paper size and resolution. When you finish, click OK to close the window. You then see your printer listed in the printconf window. Choose the Quit item from the File menu to quit printconf. You are now ready to print. For a detailed explanation of printer installation, see the **Printing-HOWTO** file in **/usr/share/doc/HOWTO**.

If you manage your printers with printconf, printconf will maintain and overwrite the ***/etc/printcap*** *file as you change and add printers. If you need to create a printcap entry manually, you can place it in the* ***/etc/printcap.local*** *file.*

You can also use printconf to set up a remote printer on Linux, Unix, Microsoft, or Novell networks. When you add a new printer, an edit window opens with a sidebar for selecting printer configuration tasks. For the queue, a pane is displayed with a drop-down menu where you can select whether this is a local, Unix (lpd share), Windows (SMB share), Novell (NDP queue), or JetDirect printer. For a remote Linux or Unix printer, select Unix Printer (lpd share). This displays a dialog box for configuring the remote printer with entries for the server and the queue. For the server, enter the hostname for the system that controls the printer. For the queue, enter the device name on that host for the printer. A Novell (NCP queue) screen will add entries for the user and the password. A Windows (SMB share) will have entries for the share name, host IP address, workgroup, user, and password.

Mandrake Printer Configuration

You can configure printers on Mandrake using the PrinterDrake utility, accessible from the Mandrake Control Center. Select the Printer tool in the Hardware panel. You can run PrinterDrake either in an expert mode or with the Printer Configuration Wizard. With the Printer Configuration Wizard, PrinterDrake will automatically detect and configure a printer connected to your system. It will guide you through the steps of selecting a port, choosing a name, specifying the type of printer, and determining the defaults. Once a printer is added, it will be listed whenever you start PrinterDrake. To reconfigure the printer, you select its name from the list. A panel will then list choices for the printer options, name, type, and connection. You can even test the printer or uninstall it.

For remote printers, you use the Expert mode for PrinterDrake. This displays an initial screen where you can choose the type of remote printer: local, remote lpd (remote

Linux system), network (printer on your network), or Windows (Windows PC on your network), URI (Universal Resource Identifier).

In the expert mode, you can also change the printer's driver, or switch between the printing systems, LPRng and CUPS (see Chapter 30).

SuSE Printer Configuration

From the YaST Control Center, you can install and configure printers easily. There are two icons for printers, Autodetect and Edit. You use Autodetect Printers to install new printers, and Edit Printers to reconfigure installed ones. You click the Configure button to start configurations. In the first screen, you determine the printer type. Here, you can select from Local, LPD (remote Linux/Unix printers), Samba/Windows, and Novell printers. In subsequent panels, you select the connection, name for the printer, model and driver, as well as text output configuration. If you want to later edit a printer, you can start the Edit Printers tool to list all your installed printers. You can then select the one you want, which will display a list of features, including the connection used, name, model, and driver.

Updating Linux with Distribution Update Tools

These tools are distribution specific. New versions of distributions are released every 6 to 12 months. In the meantime, new updates are continually being prepared for particular software packages. These are posted as updates you can download from your distribution FTP site and install on your system. These include new versions of applications, servers, and even the kernel. In the period between major releases, distributions post package updates for software installed from your CD-ROM on its Web sites. Such updates may range from single software packages to whole components—for instance, all the core, application, and development packages issued when a new release of Gnome, KDE, or XFree86 is made available.

Updating your Linux system has become a very simple procedure, using automatic update tools provided by many distributions. With such tools, downloading and installing updates can be accomplished with just a few mouse clicks. Initially, you will need to register with and configure access to a distribution Web site. Once configured, you can update your system securely and automatically. The update tool will provide secure access to officially certified updates, including bug fixes and security advisories.

Mandrake Update

The Mandrake Update tool is part of Mandrake's Software Manager utility. First, make sure that the FTP site for the Update source is defined. Click the Define Sources button to display a list of software package sources, one of which will be update_source. By default, this is set to the Mandrake Update directory on the Mandrake FTP site. You could set this to a mirror site for faster access. Then, from the Software Manager tool bar, click on Mandrake Updates to start the update process.

Mandrake Update will list packages you have installed, and then let you choose the ones you want to upgrade. Initially, you can choose to upgrade bug fixes, security updates, or normal updates. Clicking on a package selects or deselects it. As you select a package, a description, details about it, and the files it uses are displayed in the Brief, Details, and Files panels. Then the packages are downloaded and installed.

SuSE Online Update

The SuSE Online Update will let you automatically download and update software installed on your system. You can select the Online Update tool in Software panel on the YaST Control Center. In the first panel, you select your update mode, either automatic or manual. You then select the installation source. A list of FTP sites is available from a drop-down menu. If you click the Expert button, you can enter an FTP site of your own choosing. SuSE will determine the packages you have installed and download any updates (patches) for them.

Red Hat Network (RHN)

For a Red Hat system, you can use the Red Hat Update Agent to download and install updates with just a few mouse clicks. The Red Hat Update Agent takes advantage of an update service provided by the Red Hat Network (RHN). Registering with and configuring access to the Red Hat Network is a very simple procedure. You can access the RHN either through a Web browser or with the Red Hat Update Agent, installed on your system. With the Red Hat Update Agent, you can automatically locate, download, and install any updates for your Red Hat system. To use the Red Hat Network, however, you first must register using the Red Hat Network Registration client. Once registered, you are then provided with a username and password with which to access the Red Hat Network, where you can set up access to the Software Manager that will automatically download your updates through the Red Hat Update client. To start the Red Hat Network, select its entry in the Gnome System menu.

The first time you use RHN, you will be asked to register. You are asked for your root user password as an added precaution. You will need to specify a username and password, along with any other user information you want to provide. A system profile is then created consisting of your hardware specifications and the packages you want to update. Your system is automatically probed for its hardware configuration. A list of all the RPM packages on your system is generated with all entries selected. These will be the packages that the RHN network will update. You have the option of deselecting those you don't want to update.

You then need to set up access by your system to the Software Manager, identifying your computer by its hostname. This enables access to Red Hat updates. Log in to the Red Hat Network using your username and password, and click on the Systems entry to display the screen for your network. An entry should be there for your registered system. Clicking it displays a screen with information about the status of the system.

Once you have registered and set up access to the Software Manager, you can access the RHN automatically with the Red Hat Update Agent (or manually with a Web browser). Once notified of updates, the Red Hat Update Agent will download and install them for you. To use the Red Hat Update Agent, you first have to configure it. On the Gnome desktop, select the Update Agent Configuration entry on the System menu. This displays the Configuration dialog box, with three tabbed panels: General, Retrieval/Installation, and Package Exceptions. On the General panel, you can enable your HTTP proxy server, should your ISP or local network use one. The Retrieval/Installation panel is where you enter download instructions and the download directory you want to use. The Package Exceptions panel holds the names of any packages you do not want to automatically update.

You are now ready to run the Red Hat Update Agent. Select Update Agent from the Gnome System menu. The first time you use the agent, you are prompted to install Red Hat GPG key. Click Yes to install. The Red Hat Update Agent then lists the possible updates it found. You can select individual packages by clicking the check boxes next to them or click the All check box to select them all.

When you click Next, the packages you selected are downloaded. Information for each package is displayed along with its download progress. Once downloaded, the packages are installed. That's all there is to it.

If you installed Ximian Gnome (see Chapter 9), you can use Ximian's Red Carpet update utility to update your system.

Installing Software Packages

Now that you know how to start Linux and access the root user, you can install any other software packages you may want. Installing software is an administrative function performed by the root user. Unless you chose to install all your packages during your installation, only some of the many applications and utilities available for users on Linux were installed on your system. Many distributions, including Mandrake, SuSE, Caldera, and Red Hat, use the Red Hat Package Manager (RPM) to organize Linux software into packages you can automatically install or remove. Debian has its own package management tool called the Advanced Package Tool (APT) (see Chapter 28). With these tools, you can easily install or remove software from your system. The software packages on your CD-ROMs, as extensive as they are, represent only a small portion of the software packages available for Linux.

You can download additional software from online software sites such as **sourceforge.net**. The **sourceforge.net** site not only distributes software, but also serves as the primary development site for a massive number of open source software projects. Many Linux software projects have migrated to **sourceforge.net** in the last few years.

You can also locate many of the newest Linux applications from **freshmeat.net** or **www.linuxapps.com**. Here, you can link to the original development sites for these applications and download documentation and the recent versions. Table 4-2 lists several Linux software sites. For distributions that support RPM packages like SuSE, Mandrake, and Red Hat, you can find RPM package versions for software on the online repository **rpmfind.net**. Packages here are indexed according to distribution, group, and name. This includes packages for every distribution, including previous versions of those distributions.

Installing Packages with RPM

An RPM software package operates like its own installation program for a software application. A Linux software application often consists of several files that must be installed in different directories. The program itself is most likely placed in a directory called **/usr/bin**, online manual files go in another directory, and library files in yet another directory. In addition, the installation may require modification of certain configuration files on your system. The RPM software packages perform all these tasks for you. Also, if you later decide you don't want a specific application, you can uninstall packages to remove all the files and configuration information from your system (see Chapter 28 for more details).

From a desktop like Gnome or KDE, you can use GUI software management tools to install and remove RPM packages. Some distributions provide their own software management tools. Mandrake provides the Mandrake Software Manager, which operates much like kpackage. SuSE's YaST Control Center's software tools let you install, update, and remove software. Caldera OpenLinux lets you install and remove packages with COAS. You can also manage RPM packages using two distribution

Internet Sites	Description
sourceforge.net	Source Forge open source software repository and development site
www.linuxapps.com	Linux software repository
freshmeat.net	New Linux software
rpmfind.net	RPM package repository
metalab.unc.edu	Mirror site for Linux software and distributions
apps.kde.com	KDE software applications
www.gnome.org	Gnome software applications

Table 4-2. *Linux Software Sites*

independent tools, GnomeRPM or the kpackage utility. GnomeRPM is designed to work on any Gnome desktop, and kpackage is part of the KDE desktop. With all these tools, you can locate packages on your file system. Choose the packages you want to install. Both list packages already installed. You can select them to view their details and file list.

Problems can occur if the package requires that another package be installed or updated first. This is often the case where an application may need an updated version of a shared library. In this case, you will be notified of the problem and asked if you want to proceed. You can cancel at that time, and then locate and install any packages that are required first.

If you do not have access to the desktop or you prefer to work from the command line interface, you can use the **rpm** command to manage and install software packages. The command name stands for the Red Hat Package Manager. This is the command that performs installation, removal, and verification of software packages. Each software package is actually an RPM package, consisting of an archive of software files and information about how to install those files. Each archive resides as a single file with a name that ends with **.rpm**, indicating it is a software package that can be installed by the Red Hat Package Manager.

You can use the **rpm** command either to install or uninstall a package. The **rpm** command uses a set of options to determine what action to take. Table 4-3 lists the set of **rpm** options. The **-i** option installs the specified software package, and the **-U** option updates a package. With an **-e** option, **rpm** uninstalls the package. A **q** placed before an **i** (**-qi**) queries the system to see if a software package is already installed and displays information about the software (**-qpi** queries an uninstalled package file).

Option	Action
-U	Update package
-i	Install package
-e	Remove package
-qi	Display information for an installed package
-ql	Display file list for installed package
-qpi	Display information from an RPM package file (used for uninstalled packages)
-qpl	Display file list from an RPM package file (used for uninstalled packages)

Table 4-3. *rpm Options*

The **--h** option provides a complete list of **rpm** options. The syntax for the **rpm** command is as follows (*rpm-package-name* is the name of the software package you want to install):

```
rpm options rpm-package-name
```

The software package name is usually quite lengthy, including information about version and release date in its name. All end with **.rpm**. In the next example, the user installs the Linuxconf package using the **rpm** command. Notice that the full filename is entered. To list the full name, you can use the **ls** command with the first few characters and an asterisk, **ls webmin***. You can also use the * to match the remainder of the name, as in **webmin-0*.rpm inuxconf-1.16*.rpm**. In most cases, you are installing packages with the **-U** option, update. Even if the package is not already installed, **-U** still installs it.

```
$ rpm -Uvh webmin-0.980-1.noarch.rpm
```

When RPM performs an installation, it first checks for any dependent packages. These are other software packages with programs the application you are installing needs to use. If other dependent packages must be installed first, RPM cancels the installation and lists those packages. You can install those packages and then repeat the installation of the application. In a few situations, such as a major distribution update where packages may be installed out of order, installing without dependency checks is all right. For this, you use the **--nodeps** option. This assumes all the needed packages are being installed, though.

To determine if a package is already installed, use the **-qi** option with **rpm**. The **-q** stands for query. To obtain a list of all the files the package has installed, as well as the directories it installed to, use the **-ql** option.

To query package files, add the **p** option. The **-qpi** option displays information about a package, and **-qpl** lists the files in it. The following example lists all the files in the Webmin package:

```
$ rpm -qpl webmin-0.980-1.noarch.rpm
```

To remove a software package from your system, first use **rpm -qi** to make sure it is actually installed, and then use the **-e** option to uninstall it. As with the **-qi** option, you needn't use the full name of the installed file. You only need the name of the application. In the next example, the user removes the xtetris game from the system:

```
$ rpm -e xtetris
```

An important update you may need to perform is to update the XFree86 packages. If you install a new video card or a monitor, and the current XFree86 package does not support it, chances are the new one should. Simply download those packages from the distribution update sites and install them with the RPM update operation, as shown here:

```
$ rpm -Uvh --nodeps XFree86*rpm
```

Installing Software with Debian

The Debian Linux distribution uses its own software packaging system called the Debian package system. It is much more capable than its RPM counterpart, with the ability to automatically resolve dependencies, installing any other needed packages. Packages are named with the software name, the version number, and the **.deb** extension. For example, Kernel packages bear a name like **kernel-image-2.2.19.deb**.

You can install Debian packages with the Advanced Package Tool (apt-get). The apt-get tool takes two arguments: the command to perform and the name of the package. The command is a term such as **`install`** for installing packages or **`remove`** to uninstall a package. To install the kernel image package, you would use:

```
apt-get install kernel-image-2.2.19.deb
```

Upgrading is a simple matter of using the **`upgrade`** command.

```
apt-get upgrade kernel-image-2.2.19.deb
```

Installing Source Code Applications

Many programs are available for Linux only in source code format. These programs are stored in a compressed archive that you need to decompress and then extract. The resulting source code can then be configured, compiled, and installed on your system. The process has been simplified to the extent that it involves not much more than installing an RPM package. The following example shows how to extract, compile, and install the KonCD program, a CD writer and ripper.

Note *Be sure that you have installed all development packages onto your system. Development packages contain the key components such as the compiler, Gnome and KDE headers and libraries, and preprocessors. You cannot compile source code software without them.*

- First, you locate the software—in this case, from **apps.kde.com**—and then download it to your system. KonCD is downloaded in a file named **koncd-1.0rc2.tar.gz**.

- Then, decompress and extract the file using the **tar** command with the **xvzf** options, as shown here.

  ```
  tar xvzf koncd-1.0rc2.tar.gz
  ```

- This will create a directory with the name of the software, in this case **KonCD-1.0.0**. Change to this directory with the **cd** command.

  ```
  cd koncd-1.0rc2
  ```

- Issue the command **./configure**. This generates a compiler configuration for your particular system.

  ```
  ./configure
  ```

- Compile the software with the **make** command.

  ```
  make
  ```

- Then, install the program with the **make** `install` command.

  ```
  make install
  ```

That's it. Most KDE and Gnome software will also place an entry for the program in the appropriate menus—for example, a KonCD entry will be placed in the KDE Applications menu. You can then run KonCD from the menu entry. You could also open a terminal window and enter the program's name to run it.

The Complete Reference

Chapter 5

Network Configuration

This chapter discusses the network configuration tools available for easily configuring network connections on Linux. Network configuration differs depending on whether you are connected to a local area network (LAN) with an Ethernet card, a DSL or ISDN modem, or using a dial-up ISP connection. You had the opportunity to enter your LAN network settings during the installation process. For a dial-up ISP using a modem, you will have to configure your network connection using a PPP configuration utility provided by distribution network configuration tools such as Mandrake's Draknet or the Red Hat Network Configuration tool, as well as distribution-independent tools like KDE's Kppp and Gnome's GnomePPP or GnOme Dialer. Table 5-1 lists several different network configuration tools.

Network Configuration Tools	Description
Draknet	Mandrake network configuration tool, accessible from the Mandrake Control Center
Red Hat Network Configuration	Red Hat network configuration tool for both modem and network cards
Internet Connection Wizard	Red Hat DSL and ISDN configuration tool
YaST Control Center	SuSE network configuration tools, accessible from the Network panel
netconf	Linuxconf network administration, enter **netconf** command in terminal window
Webmin	Webmin network configuration, access with browser on localhost:10000
isdn-config	ISDN configuration, access on System menu with internet-config
adsl-config	DSL configuration, access on System menu with internet-config
Kppp	K Desktop PPP configuration and connection
GnomePPP	Gnome Desktop PPP configuration and connection
pppd	Point-to-Point Protocol daemon, enter on a command line and use connection script
wvdial	PPP connection, enter on a command line

Table 5-1. *Network Configuration Tools*

LAN

If you are on a network, you may need to obtain certain information to configure your network card. Most networks now support dynamic configuration using the Dynamic Host Configuration Protocol (DHCP). In this case, you need only check the DHCP entry in most network configuration tools. However, if your network does not support DHCP, you will have to provide detailed information about your connection. You can obtain most of your network information from your network administrator or from your ISP (Internet service provider). You will need the following information:

- **The device name for your network interface card (NIC)** This is usually an Ethernet card and has the name eth0 or eth1.
- **Hostname** Your computer will be identified by this name on the Internet. Do not use "localhost"; that name is reserved for special use by your system. The name of the host should be a simple word, which can include numbers, but not punctuation such as periods and backslashes. The hostname includes both the name of the host and its domain. For example, a hostname for a machine could be **turtle**, whose domain is **mytrek.com**, giving it a hostname of **turtle.mytrek.com**.
- **Domain name** This is the name of your network.
- **The Internet Protocol (IP) address assigned to your machine** Every host on the Internet is assigned an IP address. This address is a set of four numbers, separated by periods, which uniquely identifies a single location on the Internet, allowing information from other locations to reach that computer.
- **Your network IP address** This address is usually similar to the IP address, but with one or more zeros at the end.
- **The netmask** This is usually 255.255.255.0 for most networks. If, however, you are part of a large network, check with your network administrator or ISP.
- **The broadcast address for your network, if available (optional)** Usually, your broadcast address is the same as your IP address with the number 255 added at the end.
- **The IP address of your network's gateway computer** This is the computer that connects your local network to a larger one like the Internet.
- **Name servers** The IP address of the name servers your network uses. These enable the use of URLs.
- **NIS domain and IP address for an NIS server** Necessary if your network uses an NIS server (optional).

Red Hat Network Configuration

Red Hat provides an easy-to-use network configuration tool called redhat-config-network which you can use to configure both network interface cards and modems. On the start-here System-Settings window, its icon is labeled Network Configuration, and is referred to as such in this section. The Network Configuration window consists of four tabbed panels: Hardware, Device, Hosts, and DNS (see Figure 5-1). Clicking a tab displays its panel. Basic configuration of your network requires you to specify the hostname and IP address of your own system, the IP addresses of your network's name servers and gateway, the network netmask, and your network devices. Using the Network Configuration tool, you can easily enter all this information. The DNS panel is where you enter your own system's hostname and your network's name server addresses. The Hosts panel lists host IP addresses and their domain names, including those for your own system. On the Devices panel, you add and configure your network interfaces, such as an Ethernet or PPP interface. The Hardware panel is where you list your network hardware devices. If you already configured your network during installation, your entries are already in these panels.

The Hardware panel lists your system's network cards, such as Ethernet network interface cards (NIC), or any modems you have installed.

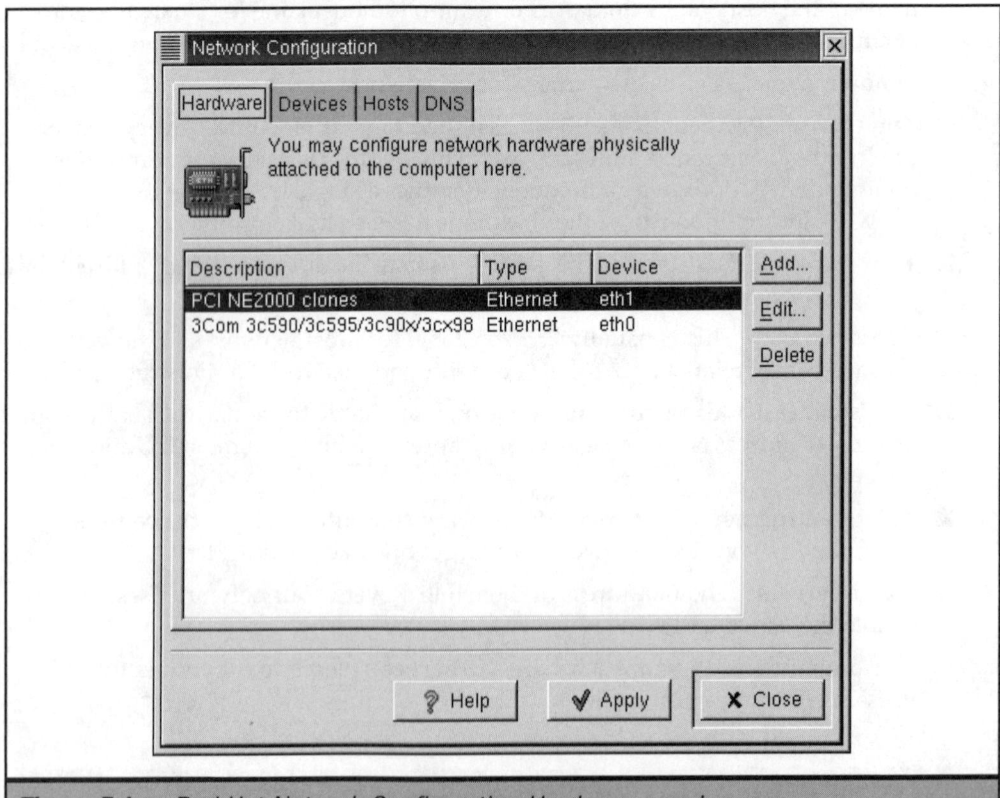

Figure 5-1. *Red Hat Network Configuration Hardware panel*

The DNS panel has two boxes at the top, labeled Hostname and Domain (see Figure 5-2). Here, you enter your system's fully qualified domain name and your network's domain name. For example, **turtle.mytrek.com** is the fully qualified domain name and **mytrek.com** is the domain name. There are boxes for entering the IP addresses for your system's primary, secondary, and tertiary DNS servers. You can then list search domains, with buttons for editing, deleting, or changing the priority of a domain to search. Both the search domain and the name server addresses are saved in the **/etc/resolv.conf** file. The hostname is saved to your **/etc/HOSTNAME** file.

The Hosts panel has a single pane with Add, Edit, and Delete buttons. This panel lists entries that associate hostnames with IP addresses. You can also add aliases (nicknames). The Hosts panel actually displays the contents of the **/etc/hosts** file and saves any entries you make to that file. To add an entry, click the Add button. A window opens with boxes for the hostname, IP address, and nicknames. When you click OK, the entry is added to the

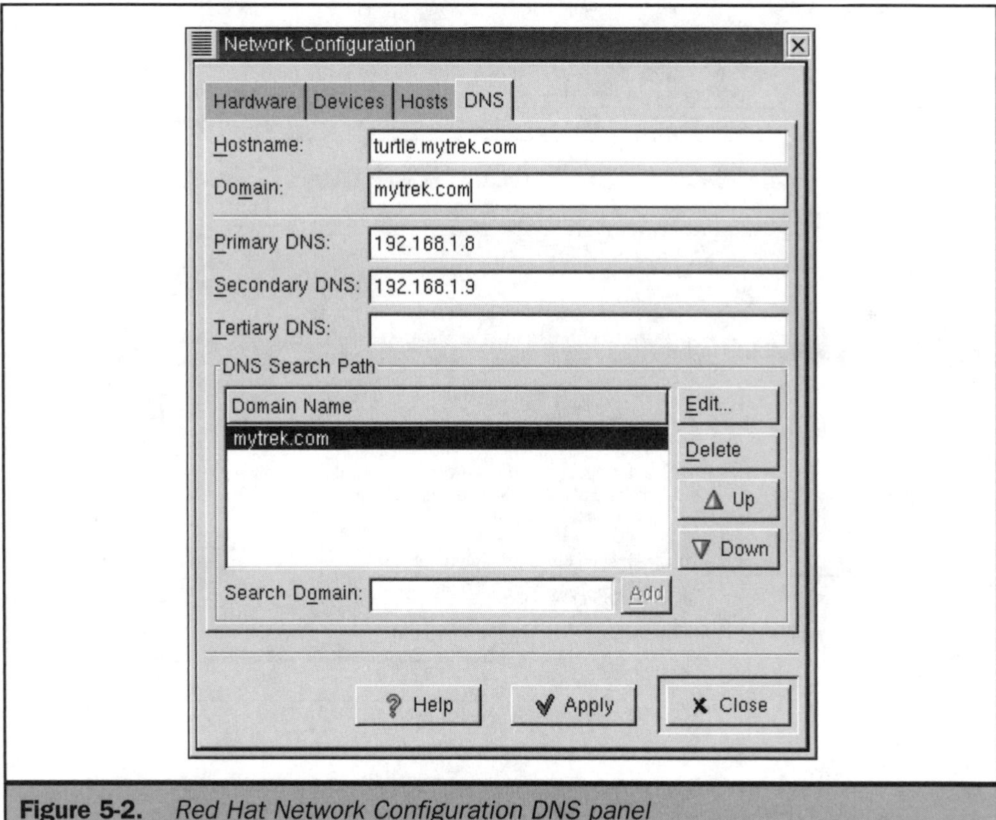

Figure 5-2. *Red Hat Network Configuration DNS panel*

Hosts list. To edit an entry, click the Edit button and a similar window opens, enabling you to change any of the fields. To delete an entry, select it and click the Remove button.

If you are having trouble connecting with an Ethernet device, make sure that the Hosts panel lists your hostname and IP address, not just localhost. If your hostname is not there, add it.

The Devices panel lists configured network devices on your system (see Figure 5-3). Making entries here performs the same function as ifconfig. An entry shows the device

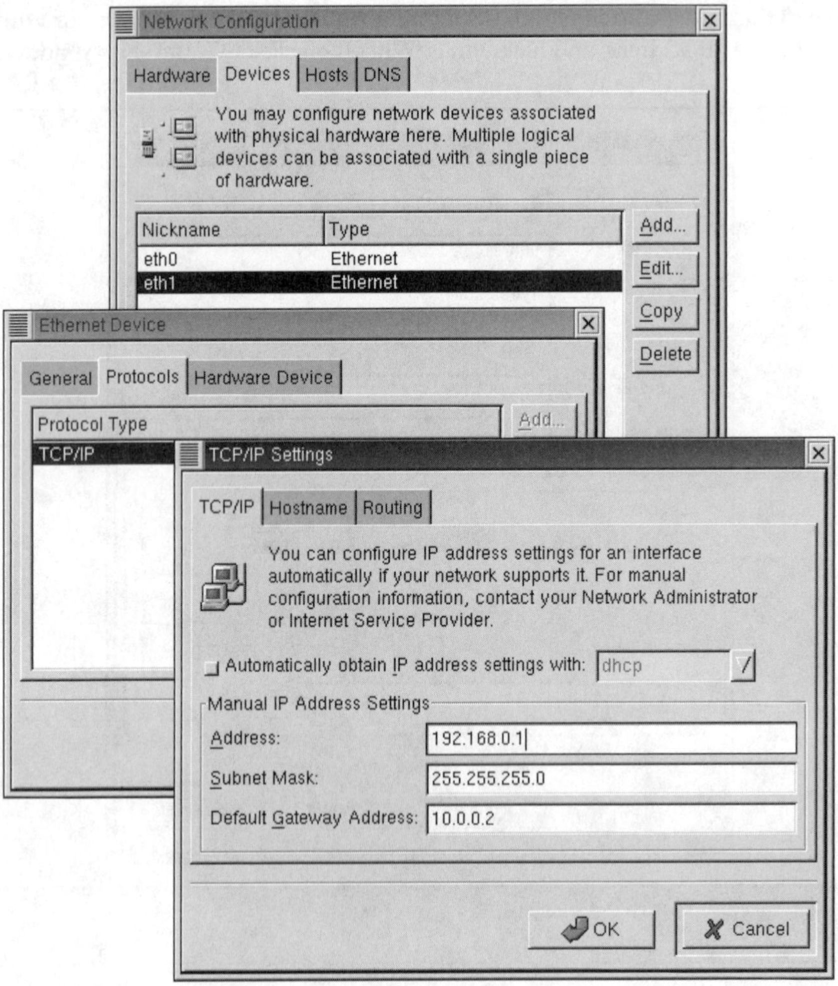

Figure 5-3. *Red Hat Network Configuration devices*

name and its type. Use the Add, Edit, Copy, and Delete buttons to manage the device entries. When you add or edit a device, you open a tabbed panel for configuring it, enabling you to specify its IP address, hostname, gateway, and the hardware device it uses. For example, when you installed Red Hat, any Ethernet network devices you had installed would be listed here. Editing the device opens a configuration window with three tabbed panels: General, Protocols, and Hardware device. The Hardware panel selects a hardware device to use from a list of installed devices. In the General panel, you can set features such as activation at boot time or edit the nickname. The Protocols panel will list the protocols used on this device, usually TCP/IP. Editing the protocol will open a TCP/IP Settings window with tabbed panels for TCP/IP, Hostname, and Routing. Here, you can enter the IP address assigned to the device, along with its netmask and network gateway. In the Hostname, panel you can enter the device's hostname. Should you add a new network device, you will need to use the Devices panel and its Protocol and TCP/IP settings windows to assign the device the IP address, hostname, netmask, and gateway, among other features.

When you finish and are ready to save your configuration, click the Apply button to have your changes take effect. If you want to abandon the changes you made, you can close without saving. You can run Network Configuration at any time to make changes in your network configuration.

You can also use Network Configuration to configure a PPP device for a modem. When you click Add and select Modem as the interface, a Modem Dialup Configuration window opens with several panels, including Provider, Options, and Protocol. Select the Provider panel to display entries for your ISP's dial-up phone number as well as your login name and password. On the Options panel, you can set PPP options. In the Protocol panel's TCP/IP entry, you can elect to have your DNS information, such as your hostname and name servers, obtained automatically from the provider.

Mandrake Network Configuration

You can configure your network connections on Mandrake using the Draknet tool, which provides three options in the Network & Internet panel on the Mandrake Control Center. You can set your network connections, proxy configuration, and Internet connection sharing. For the proxy configuration, you can enter the Internet addresses of any FTP or Web proxies set up by your network administrator or your ISP. Internet connection sharing is used for a local network where the local computers share a single computer's access to the Internet. Mandrake will run a wizard that sets up a simple automatic IP address allocation for the local computers, designating which network cards the Internet-connected computer uses to access the local network and the Internet.

For network connections, Mandrake will list your network hardware, either a modem or network interface card (NIC). During installation you may have already configured your Internet connection. Select the hardware connection you want to configure. You have the choice of using either the wizard or the Expert Mode configuration process. There are buttons for each (see Figure 5-4). The wizard will take you step by step through the configuration. First, it automatically detects your network hardware and then asks what type of connection you want to configure. You have the choice of configuring a modem, ISDN, DSL, cable, or LAN connection. The wizard will have already chosen an appropriate one for you. Make sure it is correct. For a modem connection, you will be prompted to enter information such as the phone number, login ID, password, and DNS addresses for your ISP. For a cable and LAN connection, you will be asked to either enter your IP address or click the DHCP if your IP address is allocated automatically (the usual case). You then enter your hostname. For ISDN and DSL, you will also be asked to enter a phone number and login information.

The Expert Mode configuration will display buttons for configuring your Internet connection and your hardware connection. For example, for an Ethernet card, a window is displayed where you can directly enter all the connection information, such as the IP address, network mask, and whether to activate the connection automatically whenever the system starts up. To specify a gateway, click the Internet connection button.

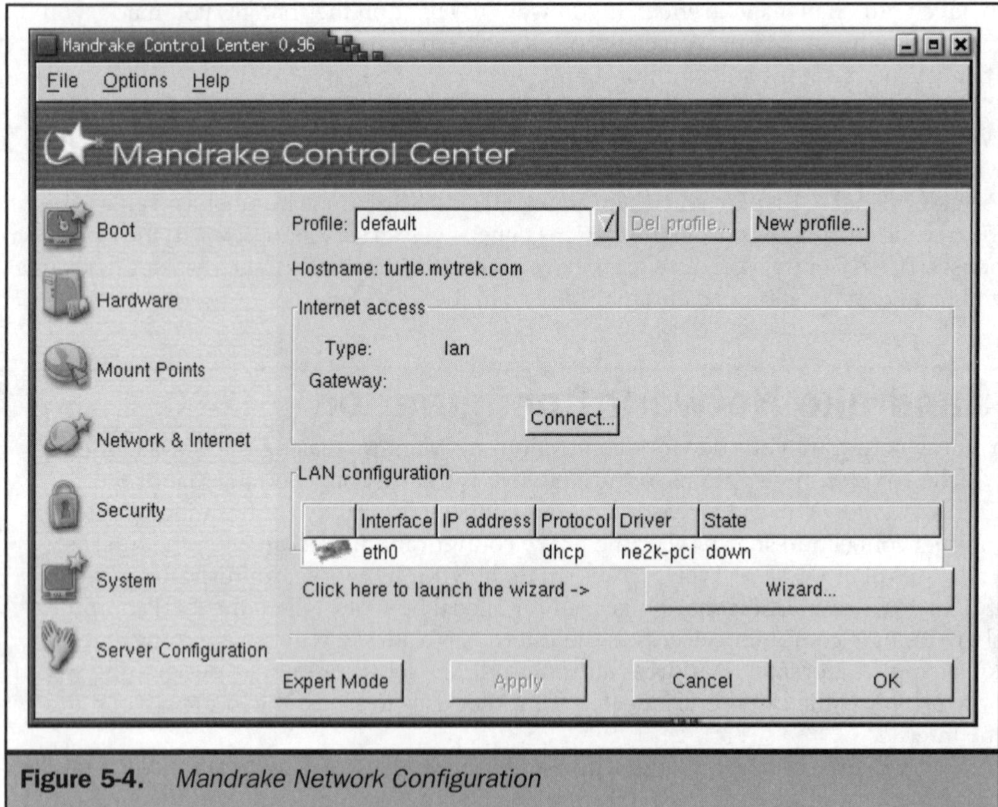

Figure 5-4. *Mandrake Network Configuration*

SuSE Network Configuration

On SuSE, the YaST Control Center provides several tools for configuring your network connections. On the Network/Basic panel, you can choose from modem, DSL, ISDN, and network card configuration tools. To configure your modem connection, you will be prompted for information such as your ISP's phone number, login ID, and password. For your network card, you will need to supply your IP address or specify DHCP for an IP address that is dynamically allocated. In the Network/Advanced panel, you can enter information for a local area network. Here, you can specify the hostname for your system and the DNS servers your network uses. With the Routing tool, you can list your network's gateway, including its IP address and hostname.

Network Configuration with Linuxconf and Webmin

To configure a LAN connection in Linuxconf, start netconf from a terminal window. This displays a window with buttons for various network configuration options. Click the Basic Host Information button to display the Host Configuration window. In the first Adapter panel, you can enter the IP address, network device (usually **eth0**), and the kernel module to use (the drivers for your Ethernet card) along with other data such as the hostname and netmask. Then, in the Network Configurator window, click the Name Server Specification button to display the Resolver Configuration window, where you can enter the IP addresses for the domain name servers on your network. Click the Routers and Gateway button to enter the IP address for the gateway computer.

To use netconf to configure PPP connections, click the PPP/SLIP/PLIP button on the Network Configurator window. A window opens that asks you to choose the type of interface you want. Select PPP. Then a small window opens displaying a ppp0 entry. Double-click it to display the PPP interface window with panels for setting your modem connections, the phone number to dial, and the Expect and Send entries for your login name and password. To activate a connection, click Connect. You can also use dial-up managers like Kppp and GnomePPP to set up and manage your PPP connections.

With Webmin, select the Network Configuration page on the Hardware page. From the Network Configuration page, select the Network Interfaces page to configure your Ethernet device, entering information such as the IP address, the netmask, and the device name. On the Routing and Gateways page, you enter the IP address of your network's gateway, and on the DNS page, you enter your name server addresses. On the Host Address page, you enter the hostname and IP address for your system, along with any others you want.

DSL and ISDN

As with a modem connection, you will need to provide login and password information for DSL and ISDN. In other respects, DSL and ISDN connections operate much like a local area network (LAN), treating a host as an integrated part of a network. As you have seen, most major Linux distributions provide support for configuring DSL and ISDN connections in their own network configuration tools. On Red Hat, you can use the Internet Configuration Wizard to set up a DSL or ISDN connection. On Mandrake, you can use Draknet, accessible from the Mandrake Control Center. For SuSE, the YaST Control Center provides DSL or ISDN configuration tools. Like the distribution tools, the Linuxconf and Webmin administrative systems let you configure DSL and ISDN connections. You can also use independent tools like TkPPPoE, adsl-config, and isdn-config. adsl-config will display a dialog box with entries for entering your login name, password, and the Ethernet interface your DSL modem is attached to. You will also need to enter the IP addresses for the DNS servers provided by your ISP. You can elect to have the connection automatically made up when your system starts up.

adsl-config makes use of the pppoe utility to make your DSL connections. pppoe enables the use of dynamic IP addresses with an ISP over a DSL connection. Many Linux distributions use the Roaring Penguin package of pppoe commands (rp-pppoe). As an alternative to adsl-config, you can use the **adsl-setup** command to configure your DSL connection. adsl has a command line interface and can be run at any shell prompt. As with adsl-config, you are prompted to enter your username, password, Ethernet card, and domain name server addresses. You can also specify basic firewall security levels. You can then establish your DSL connection with the **adsl-start** command, and disconnect with the **adsl-stop** command.

isdn-config will display a dialog box labeled ISDN config, showing four panes labeled Dial, Provider, Hardware, and About. In the Dial pane, you can make a connection to a selected ISP. In the Provider pane, you enter information about your ISP. You use the Hardware pane to configure your ISDN modem.

PPP Connections

As an alternative to hardwired network connections such as Ethernet, you can use a modem with telephone lines to connect to a network. Two protocols can transmit IP communications across the telephone lines. These are the *Serial Line Internet Protocol* (*SLIP*) and the *Point-to-Point Protocol* (*PPP*). SLIP is an older protocol, whereas PPP is newer and has become predominant. Most modem-based connections used by current ISPs use PPP. The SLIP and PPP protocols are specifically designed for users who connect their systems to the Internet over a modem and a telephone line. Usually, a connection is made to an ISP, which then connects the system to the Internet through its own systems.

Most major Linux distributions provide support for configuring PPP connections in the own network configuration tools. On Red Hat, you can use the Red Hat Network

Manager to set up a PPP connection. On Mandrake, you can use Draknet, accessible from the Mandrake Control Center. For SuSE, use its modem configuration tool provided by the YaST Control Center. In addition to the distribution network tools, you can also use the Linuxconf and Webmin administrative systems to set up your PPP connection. There are also PPP configuration tools such as Kppp (described here) and GnomePPP, which are designed for use on any system running either KDE or Gnome. Most of these run on X Window System interfaces like KDE and Gnome. To connect using just the command line, you would use wvdial (described in this chapter) or pppd.

You can use Kppp as a model for using the other PPP tools. During Kppp configuration, you are presented with a set of tabbed panels in which you enter Internet and modem information. Once configured, connecting is simply a matter of clicking a button labeled Connect. The Kppp tool runs fine from the root user, but it needs permission set on certain files to allow use by other users on your system. See the documentation in the **/usr/share/doc/kppp*** directory, which also includes a detailed tutorial you can view with your Web browser.

To configure a connection, click the Setup button. This brings up the Configuration window, which has several panels. One panel appears in the front, with tabs for the others showing at the top. Six panels are in the Configuration window: one for accounts, other panels for device and modem settings, and one for PPP features. Accounts hold your Internet information. You can have more than one account, depending on how many different ISPs you subscribe to (most users have only one). To create an account, click the New button. This brings up a New Accounts window with a set of panels for Internet information. The Dial panel is where you enter connection information, such as the phone number you use to connect to the provider. Be sure to enter a name for the connection, which can be anything you want. The Arguments button brings up another window for entering PPP arguments. These are options for the PPP daemon.

The IP panel is where you enter any local and remote IP addresses, as well as a netmask. Each entry has Dynamic and Static check buttons; the Dynamic check buttons are already set by default. If your ISP gives you dynamic addresses and a netmask, as most do these days, you can leave this panel alone. If, on the other hand, you have a static local or remote address, you must bring up the panel and enter the address. Click the tab labeled DNS to bring up the Domain Name Server panel. Here, you enter the IP addresses of your ISP's domain name servers. Click the box labeled IP Address and type the address. Then click Add to add the address to the list of name servers.

If your ISP requires a specialized login procedure, you may need to create a login script in which you provide the username and password you use to connect to your ISP. To do this, click the Login Script tab to bring up the Script panel. You then see a frame called Edit Script with several buttons and boxes. You need to create a simple script that performs the login tasks using two instructions: send and receive.

After you finish entering the Internet information, click OK to close the New Accounts windows. At the Configure window, click the Device tab to bring up the Device panel. Make sure the modem port is correct. Usually, this is **/dev/*modem***, where *modem* is a link to the actual modem port device. In most cases, you needn't change this. Modem port devices begin with the name **/dev/ttyS** with an attached number from 0 to 3. On your PC, you have four ports from which to choose: 1 through 4. Usually, a modem is connected to either port 2 or port 4. The names for these would be **/dev/ttyS1** and **/dev/ttyS3** (the count is from 0, so port 1 is ttyS0 and port 2 is ttyS1). If you already set up a **modem** alias for the port, you can use **/dev/modem**.

You then need to check the dialing prefix, as well as any special settings you may need for your modem. You can click the Modem panel and then click the Modem Commands button to bring up a window with a long list of boxes with settings for your modem. They should already have default settings entered. The first box is where you enter your modem initialization string, adding such instructions as M0 to turn off the connection sound. The box labeled Dial String is where you enter your dialing prefix. ATDT is the default already entered, which most people use. Check also the Connect Response entry and the Hangup string. The default connect response is CONNECT, which is valid for most ISPs. The *Hangup string* is a standard hang-up instruction for most modems.

After you finish, close the Configuration window by clicking OK. You are then ready to use Kppp. Click the Connect button in the main window. If you have problems, click the Show Log Window button to bring up a window that displays the connection process and any errors that occur. When Kppp makes a connection, it displays the amount of time connected and the speed at which it connected. The Connect button is changed to Disconnect. To end your session, click Disconnect. Clicking Quit ends the Kppp program.

Note *Each individual user can create their own accounts, using the steps described previously. This information is held in a* ***.kppprc*** *file in the user's* ***home*** *directory. In fact, different users could use Kppp to connect to different ISPs.*

Command Line PPP Access: wvdial

If, for some reason, you have been unable to set up a modem connection on your X Window System, you may have to set it up from the command line interface instead of a desktop. For a dial-up PPP connection, you can use the wvdial dialer. wvdial is an intelligent dialer, which not only dials up an ISP service, but also performs login operations, supplying your username and password. wvdial first loads its configuration from the **/etc/wvdial.conf** file. In here, you can place modem and account information, including modem speed and serial device, as well as ISP phone number, username, and password. The **wvdial.conf** file is organized into sections, beginning with a section label enclosed in brackets. A section holds variables for different parameters that are assigned values, such as username = chris. The default section holds default values inherited by other sections, so you needn't repeat them. Table 5-2 lists the wvdial variables.

Variable	Description
Inherits	Explicitly inherit from the specified section. By default, sections inherit from the [Dialer Defaults] section.
Modem	The device wvdial you should use as your modem. The default is **/dev/modem**.
Baud	The speed at which wvdial communicates with your modem. The default is 57,600 baud.
Init1 ... Init9	Specifies the initialization strings to be used by your modem. wvdial can use up to 9. The default is "ATZ" for Init1.
Phone	The phone number you want wvdial to dial.
Area Code	Specifies the area code, if any.
Dial Prefix	Specifies any needed dialing prefix—for example, 70 to disable call waiting or 9 for an outside line.
Dial Command	Specifies the dial operation. The default is "ATDT."
Login	Specifies the username you use at your ISP.
Login Prompt	If your ISP has an unusual login prompt, you can specify it here.
Password	Specifies the password you use at your ISP.
Password Prompt	If your ISP has an unusual password prompt, you can specify it here.
PPPD PATH	If pppd is installed on your Linux system somewhere other than **/usr/sbin/pppd**, you need to specify its location with this option.
Force Address	Specifies a static IP address to use (for ISPs that provide static IP addresses to users).
Remote Name	For PAP or CHAP authentication, you may have to change this to your ISP's authentication name. The default value is *.

Table 5-2. *wvdial Variables*

Variable	Description
Carrier Check	Setting this option to No disables the carrier check by your modem. Used for a modem that reports its carrier line is always down.
Stupid Mode	In Stupid Mode, wvdual does not attempt to interpret any prompts from the terminal server and starts pppd after the modem connects.
New PPPD	Enable this option for use with pppd version 2.3.0 or newer. Instructs pppd to look for a required file **/etc/ppp/peers/wvdial**.
Default Reply	Specifies the default response for prompts that wvdial does not recognize. The default is ppp.
Auto Reconnect	If enabled, wvdial attempts to re-establish a connection automatically if you are randomly disconnected by the other side. This option is on by default.

Table 5-2. *wvdial Variables* (continued)

You can use the wvdialconf utility to create a default **wvdial.conf** file for you automatically. wvdialconf will detect your modem and set default values for basic features. You can then edit the **wvdial.conf** file and modify the Phone, Username, and Password entries with your ISP dial-up information. Remove the preceding semicolon (;) to unquote the entry. Any line beginning with a semicolon is ignored as a comment.

```
$ wvdialconf
```

You can also create a named dialer, such as *myisp* in the following example. This is helpful if you have different ISPs you log in to. The following example shows the **/etc/wvdial.conf** file:

/etc/wvdial.conf

```
[Modem0]
Modem = /dev/ttyS0
Baud = 57600
Init1 = ATZ
SetVolume = 0
Dial Command = ATDT

[Dialer Defaults]
Modem = /dev/ttyS0
Baud = 57600
```

```
Init1 = ATZ
SetVolume = 0
Dial Command = ATDT

[Dialer myisp]
Username = chris
Password = mypassword
Modem = /dev/ttyS0
Phone = 555-5555
Area Code = 555
Baud = 57600
Stupid mode = 0
```


To start wvdial, enter the command **wvdial**, which then reads the connection configuration information from the **/etc/wvdial.conf** file. wvdial dials the ISP and initiates the PPP connection, providing your username and password when requested.

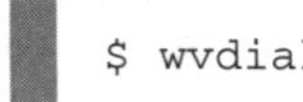

```
$ wvdial
```

You can set up connection configurations for any number of connections in the **/etc/wvdial.conf** file. To select one, enter its label as an argument to the **wvdial** command, as shown here:

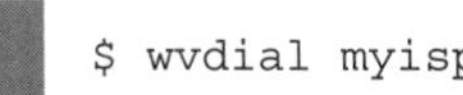

```
$ wvdial myisp
```

Modem Setup

If you have a modem connected to your PC, it is connected to one of four communications ports. The PC names for these ports are COM1, COM2, COM3, and COM4. These ports can also be used for other serial devices, such as a serial mouse (though not for PS/2 mice). Usually, a serial mouse is connected to COM1 and a modem is connected to COM2, though in many cases, your modem may be connected to COM4. Find out which ports your modem and mouse are connected to, because you must know this to access your modem. On the PC, COM1 and COM3 share the same access point to your computer; the same is true of COM2 and COM4. For this reason, if you have a serial mouse connected to COM1, you should not have your modem on COM3. You could find your mouse cutting out whenever you use your modem. If your mouse is on COM1, your modem should either be on COM2 or COM4.

In Linux, you use the serial communication ports for your modem. Serial ports begin with the name **/dev/ttyS,** with an attached number from 0 to 3. (Notice the numbering begins from 0, not 1.) The first port, COM1, is **/dev/ttyS0**, and **/dev/ttyS1** is the second port. The third and fourth ports are **/dev/ttyS2** and **/dev/ttyS3**. In many Linux communication programs, you need to know the port for your modem, which is either **/dev/ttyS1** for COM2 or **/dev/ttyS3** for COM4.

Some communication programs try to access the modem port using only the name **/dev/modem**. This is meant to be an alias for whatever your modem port actually is. If your system has not already set up this alias, you can easily create it using the **ln -s** command.

You can also create an alias on the command line using the **ln** command. The following example creates an alias called **modem** for the COM2 port, **/dev/ttyS1**. If your modem port is **/dev/ttyS3,** use that instead. (You must be logged in as a root user to execute this command.) The following example sets up the **/dev/modem** alias for the second serial port, **/dev/ ttyS1**:

```
# ln -s /dev/ttyS1 /dev/modem
```

Your **/dev/mouse** alias should already be set up for the port it uses. For a serial mouse, this is usually the COM1 port, **/dev/ ttyS0**. If the alias is not set up or if you need to change it, you can use the **ln -s** command. The following example sets up the **/dev/mouse** alias for the first serial port, **/dev/ ttyS0**:

```
# ln -s /dev/ttyS0 /dev/mouse
```

The Complete Reference

Chapter 6

Security Configuration

Once you have installed your Linux system, you should carry out some basic security measures to protect your system from outside attacks. Systems connected to the Internet are open to attempts by outside users to gain unauthorized access. This usually takes the following forms:

- Trying to break into the system
- Having broken in, changing or replacing system files with hacked or corrupt versions
- Attempting to intercept communications from remote users
- Changing or replacing messages sent to or from users
- Pretending to be a valid user

Firewalls, intrusion protection, encryption, data integrity, and authentication are ways of protecting against such attacks (see Chapter 37 also).

- A firewall prevents any direct unauthorized attempts at access.
- Intrusion detection checks the state of your system files to see if they have been tampered with by someone who has broken in.
- Encryption protects transmissions by authorized remote users, providing privacy.
- Integrity checks such as modification digests guarantee that messages and data have not been intercepted and changed or substituted en route.
- Authentication methods such as digital signatures can verify that the user claiming to send a message or access your system is actually that person.

You can use encryption, integrity checks, and authentication to protect both messages you send as e-mail and files you attach. The GNU Privacy Guard encryption package lets you encrypt your e-mail messages or files you want to send, as well as letting you sign them with an encrypted digital signature authenticating that the message was sent by you. The digital signature also includes encrypted modification digest information that provides an integrity check, allowing the recipient to verify that the message received is the original and not one that has been changed or substituted.

You will also need to check the integrity of your system to make sure that it has not already been broken into. With the Tripwire intrusion detection software, you can take a snapshot of your system, taking note of different features for critical files such as size and permissions of configuration files. Later, you can check the current state of those critical files with your previous snapshot version to see if they have changed in any way. If they have, it may be evidence that an intruder has entered your system and is changing files.

A good foundation for your network security is to set up a Linux system to operate as a firewall for your network, protecting it from unauthorized access. You can use a firewall to implement either packet filtering or proxies. *Packet filtering* is simply the process of deciding whether a packet received by the firewall host should be passed on into the local network. It checks the address of the packet and sends the packet on, if it's allowed. The firewall package currently in use is Netfilter (iptables). Older distributions versions releases use an earlier version called ipchains. To implement a firewall, you simply provide a series of rules to govern what kind of access you want to allow on your system. If that system is also a gateway for a private network, the system's firewall capability can effectively protect the network from outside attacks.

Another way to protect access to your system is to provide secure user authentication with encrypted passwords, a Lightweight Directory Access Protocol (LDAP) service, and Pluggable Authentication Modules (PAM). These are discussed in detail in Chapter 30. User authentication can further be controlled for certain services by Kerberos servers, discussed in Chapter 37.

To protect remote connections from hosts outside your network, transmissions can be encrypted. For Linux systems, you can use the Secure Shell (SSH) suite of programs to encrypt any transmissions, preventing them from being read by anyone else. If you don't use SSH, it is best to avoid the standard remote communications tools such as **telnet** and **rcp** (see Chapter 21) for remote access over an unprotected network like the Internet. Outside users may also try to gain unauthorized access through any Internet services you may be hosting, such as a Web site. In such a case, you can set up a proxy to protect your site from attack. For Linux systems, use Squid proxy software to set up a proxy to protect your Web server (see Chapter 24).

This chapter will show you some simple steps you can take to provide a basic level of security. The GNU Privacy Guard encryption and Tripwire intrusion detection software are covered in detail. Netfilter, Squid, and SSH are covered briefly (see Chapters 24 and 37 for a more detailed analysis of these applications). Table 6-1 lists security applications systems.

Applications	Description
GNU Privacy Guard (GPG)	Encryption and digital signatures (Chapter 6) **www.gnupg.org**
Tripwire	Intrusion detection (Chapter 6) **www.tripwire.org**
Netfilter (iptables and ipchains)	Firewall packet filtering (Chapter 37) **netfilter.samba.org**

Table 6-1. *Security Applications*

Applications	Description
Squid	Web proxy server (Chapter 24) **www.squid-chache.org**
SSH	Secure Shell encryption and authentication for remote access (Chapter 37) **www.ssh.org**
Kerberos	User authentication for access to services (Chapter 37) **web.mit.edu/kerberos/www/**
Pluggable Authorization Modules (PAM)	Authentication management and configuration (Chapter 27)
Shadow passwords	Password encryption (Chapter 27)
Lightweight Directory Access Protocol (LDAP)	User management and authorization (Chapter 27) **www.openldap.org**

Table 6-1. *Security Applications* (continued)

Note *Numerous older security applications are also available for Linux such as COPS (Computer Oracle and Password System) to check password security; Tiger, which scans your system for unusual or unprotected files; and SATAN (Security Administration Tool for Analyzing Networks), which checks your system for security holes. Crack is a newer password auditing tool that you can use to check how well your password security performs under dictionary attacks.*

GNU Privacy Guard: Encryption and Authentication

To protect messages that you send by e-mail, most Linux distributions provide GNU Privacy Guard (GnuPG) encryption and authentication. GnuPG is GNU open source software that works much like Pretty Good Privacy (PGP) encryption. With GnuPG, you can both encrypt your messages and digitally sign them—protecting the message and authenticating that it is from you. Currently, KMail and exmh both support GnuPG encryption and authentication. On KMail, you can select the encryption to use on the Security panel in the Options window.

Public-Key Encryption and Digital Signatures

GnuPG makes use of public-key cryptography to encrypt data. Public-key encryption uses two keys to encrypt and decrypt a message, a private key and a public key. The private key you always keep and use to decrypt messages you have received. The public key you make available to those you send messages to. They then use your public key to encrypt any message they want to send to you. The private key decrypts messages, and the public key encrypts them. Each user has private and public keys. Reciprocally, if you want to send messages to another user, you would first obtain the user's public key and use it to encrypt the message you want to send to the user. The user then decrypts the messages with their own private key. In other words, your public key is used by others to encrypt the messages you receive, and you use other users' public keys to send messages to them. Each user on your Linux system can have their own public and private keys. They will use the gpg program to generate them and keep their private key in their own directory.

A digital signature is used to both authenticate a message and provide an integrity check. Authentication guarantees that the message has not been modified—that it is the original message sent by you—and the integrity check verifies that it has not been changed. Though usually combined with encrypted messages to provide a greater level of security, digital signatures can also be used for messages that can be sent in the clear. For example, you would want to know if a public notice of upgrades of a Red Hat release was actually sent by Red Hat, and not by someone trying to spread confusion. Such a message still needs to be authenticated, checked to see if it was actually sent by the sender or, if sent by the original sender, was not somehow changed en route. Verification like this protects against modification or substitution of the message by someone pretending to be the sender.

Digitally signing a message involves generating a checksum value from the contents of the message using an encryption algorithm such as the MD5 modification digest algorithm. This is a unique value that accurately represents the size and contents of your message. Any changes to the message of any kind would generate a different value. Such a value provides a way to check the integrity of the data. The MD5 value is then itself encrypted with your private key. When the user receives your message, they decrypt your digital signature with your public key. The user then generates an MD5 value of the message received and compares it with the MD5 value you sent. If they are the same, the message is authenticated—it is the original message sent by you, not a false one sent by a user pretending to be you. The user can use GnuPG to decrypt and check digital signatures.

Normally, digital signatures are combined with encryption to provide a more secure level of transmission. The message would be encrypted with the recipient's public key, and the digital signature encrypted with your private key. The user would decrypt both the message (with their own private key) and then the signature (with your public key). They would then compare the signature with one the user generates from the message to authenticate it. When GnuPG decodes a message, it will also decode and check a digital signature automatically. Figure 6-1 shows the process for encrypting and digitally signing a message.

GPG operations are carried out with the **gpg** command, which uses both commands and option to perform tasks. Commonly used commands and options are listed in Table 6-2. Some commands and options have a short form that use only one hyphen. Normally two hyphens are used.

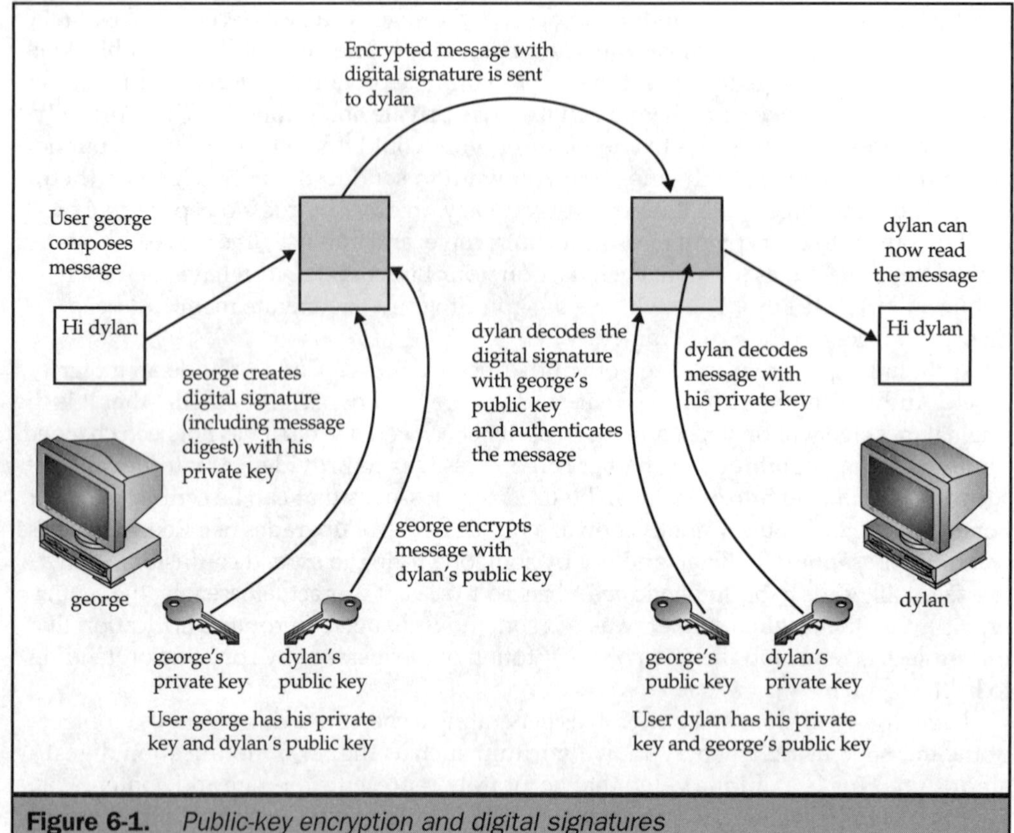

Figure 6-1. *Public-key encryption and digital signatures*

GPG Commands	Description
`-s, --sign`	Signs a document, creating a signature. May be combined with **`--encrypt`**.
`--clearsign`	Creates a clear text signature.
`-b, --detach-sign`	Creates a detached signature.
`-e, --encrypt`	Encrypts data. May be combined with **`--sign`**.

Table 6-2. *GPG Commands and Options*

GPG Commands	Description
`--decrypt` [*file*]	Decrypts file (or stdin if no file is specified) and writes it to stdout (or the file specified with **`--output`**). If the decrypted file is signed, the signature is verified.
`--verify` [[*sigfile*] [*signed-files*]]	Verifies a signed file. The signature can be either contained with the file or be a separate detached signature file.
`--list-keys` [*names*]	Lists all keys from the keyrings or those specified.
`--list-public-keys` [*names*]	Lists all keys from the public keyrings or those specified.
`--list-secret-keys` [*names*]	Lists your private (secret) keys.
`--list-sigs` [*names*]	Lists your keys along with any signatures they have.
`--check-sigs` [*names*]	Lists keys and their signatures and verifies the signatures.
`--fingerprint` [*names*]	Lists fingerprints for specified keys.
`--gen-key`	Generates a new set of private and public keys.
`--edit-key` *name*	Edits your keys. Use commands to perform most key operations such as sign to sign a key or **`passwd`** to change your passphrase.
`--sign-key` *name*	Signs a public key with your private key. Same as **`sign in --edit-key`**.
`--delete-key` *name*	Removes a public key from the public keyring.
`--delete-secret-key` *name*	Removes private and public key from both the secret and public keyrings.
`--gen-revoke`	Generates a revocation certificate for your own key.

Table 6-2. *GPG Commands and Options* (continued)

GPG Commands	Description
`--export` [*names*]	Exports a specified key from your keyring. With no arguments, exports all keys.
`--send-keys` [*names*]	Exports and sends specified keys to a keyserver. The option **`--keyserver`** must be used to give the name of this keyserver.
`--import` [*files*]	Imports keys contained in files into your public keyring.
GPG Options	**Description**
`-a, --armor`	Creates ASCII armored output, ASCII version of encrypted data.
`-o, --output` *file*	Writes output to a specified file.
`--default-key` *name*	Specifies the default private key to use for signatures.
`--keyserver` *site*	The keyserver to look up public keys not on your keyring. Can also specify the site to send your public key to. **`host -l pgp.net	grep www.keys`** will list the keyservers.
`-r, --recipient` *names*	Encrypts data for the specified user, using that user's public key.
`--default-recipient` *names*	Specifies the default recipient to use for encrypting data.

Table 6-2. *GPG Commands and Options* (continued)

GnuPG Setup:gpg

Before you can use GnuPG, you will have to generate your private and public keys. On the command line (terminal window) enter the **gpg** command with the **--gen-key** command. The gpg program will then prompt with different options for creating your private and public keys. You can check the **gpg** Man page for information on using the gpg program.

```
gpg --gen-key
```

You are first asked to select the kind of key you want. Normally, you would just select the default entry, which you can do by pressing the ENTER key. Then you choose the key size, usually the default 1024. You then specify how long the key is to be valid—usually there is no expiration. You will be asked to enter a user ID, comment, and e-mail address. Press ENTER to be prompted for each in turn. These elements identify the key, any of which can be used as the key's name. You use the key name when performing certain GPG tasks such as signing a key or creating a revocation certificate. For example, the following elements create a key for the user richlp with the comment "author" and the e-mail address richlp@turtle.mytrek.com:

```
Richard Petersen (author) <richlp@turtle.mytrek.com>
```

You can use any unique part of a key's identity to reference that key. For example, the string "Richard" would reference the above key, provided there are no other keys that have the string "Richard" in them. "richlp" would also reference the key, as would "author". Where a string matches more than one key, all the matched ones would be referenced.

gpg will then ask you to enter a passphrase, used to protect your private key. Be sure to use a real phrase, including spaces, not just a password. gpg then generates your public and private keys and places them in the **.gnupg** directory. The private keys are kept in a file called **secring.gpg** in your **.gnupg** directory. The public key is placed in the **pubring.gpg** file, to which you can add the public keys of other users. You can list these keys with the **--list-keys** command.

In case you later need to change your keys, you can create a revocation certificate to notify others that the public key is no longer valid. For example, if you forget your password or someone else discovers it, you can use the revocation certificate to tell others that your public key should no longer be used. In the next example, the user creates a revocation certificate for the key richlp and places it in the file **myrevoke.asc**:

```
gpg --output myrevoke.asc --gen-revoke richlp
```

For other users to decrypt your messages, you have to make your public key available to them. They, in turn, have to send you their public keys so that you can decrypt any messages you receive from them. In effect, enabling encrypted communications between users involves all of them exchanging their public keys. The public keys then have to be verified and signed by each user that receives them. The public keys can then be trusted to safely decrypt messages.

If you are sending messages to just a few users, you can manually e-mail them your public key. For general public use, you can post your public key on a keyserver, which anyone can then download and use to decrypt any message they receive from you. The

OpenPGP Public Keyserver is located at **www.keyserver.net**. You can send directly to the keyserver with the **-keyserver** option and **--send-key** command. The **--send-key** command takes as its argument your e-mail address. You only need to send to one keyserver, as it will share your key with other keyservers automatically.

```
gpg --keyserver search.keyserver.net--send-key chris@turtle.mytrek.com
```

If you want to send your key directly to another user, you should generate an armored text version of the key that you can then e-mail. You do this with the **--armor** and **--export** options, using the **--output** option to specify a file to place the key in. The **--armor** option will generate an ASCII text version of the encrypted file so that it can be e-mailed directly, instead of as an attached binary. Files that hold an ASCII encoded version of the encryption normally have the extension **.asc**, by convention. Binary encrypted files normally use the extension **.gpg**. You can then e-mail the file to users you want to send encrypted messages.

```
# gpg --armor --export richlp@turtle.mytrek.com --output richlp.asc
# mail -s 'mypubkey' george@rabbit.mytrek.com < richlp.asc
```

Many companies and institutions post their public key files on their Web sites where they can be downloaded and used to verify encrypted software downloads or official announcements.

Note *Some commands and options for GPG have both a long and short form. For example, the* ***--armor*** *command can be written as* **-a**, ***--output*** *as* **-o**, ***--sign*** *as* **-s**, *and* ***--encrypt*** *as* **-e**. *Most others, like* ***--export***, *have no short form.*

To decode messages from other users, you will need to have their public keys. They can either send them to you or you can download them from a keyserver. Save the message or Web page containing the public key to a file. You will then need to import, verify, and sign the key. Use the file you received to import the public key to your **pubring** file. In the following example, the user imports George's public key, which he has received as the file **georgekey.asc**.

```
gpg --import georgekey.asc
```

All Linux distribution sites have their own public keys available for download. You should, for example, download the Red Hat public key, currently located at **www.redhat.com/about/contact.html**. Click the Public Encryption Key link. From there you can access a page that displays just the public key. You can save this page as a file and use that file to import the Red Hat public key to your keyring. In the following example, the user saved the page showing just the Red Hat public key as **myredhat.asc**, and then imported that file:

```
gpg --import myredhat.asc
```

Note *You can remove any key, including your own private key, with the* **--delete-key** *and* ***--delete-secret-key*** *commands.*

To manually check that a public key file was not modified in transit, you can check its fingerprint. This is a hash value generated from the contents of the key, much like a modification digest. Using the **--fingerprint** option you can generate a hash value from the key you installed, then contact the sender and ask them what the hash value should really be. If they are not the same, you know the key was tampered with in transit.

```
gpg --fingerprint george@rabbit
```

You do not have to check the fingerprint to have gpg operate. This is just an advisable precaution you can perform on your own. The point is that you need to be confident that the key you received is valid. Normally you can accept most keys from public servers or known sites as valid, though it is easy to check their posted fingerprints. Once assured of the key's validity, you can then sign it with your private key. Signing a key notifies gpg that you officially accept the key.

To sign a key, you use the **gpg** command with the **--sign-key** command and the key's name.

```
gpg --sign-key george@rabbit
```

Alternatively, you can edit the key with the **--edit-key** command to start an interactive session in which you can enter the command **sign** to sign the key and **save** to save the change. Signing a key involves accessing your private key, so you will be prompted for your passphrase. When you are finished, leave the interactive session with the **quit** command.

Normally, you would want to post a version of your public key that has been signed by one or more users. You can do the same for other users. Signing a public key provides a way to vouch for the validity of a key. It indicates that someone has already checked it out. Many different users could sign the same public key. For a key that you have received from another user, and that you have verified, you can sign and return the signed version to that user. Once you have signed the key, you can generate a file containing the signed public version. You can then send this file to the user.

```
gpg -a --export george@rabbit --output  georgesig.asc
```

The user would then import the signed key and export it to a keyserver.

*If you want to start over from scratch, you can just erase your **.gnupg** directory, though this is a drastic measure, as you will lose any keys you have collected.*

Using GnuPG

GnuPG encryption is currently supported by KMail and exmh mail clients. You can also use the GNU Privacy Assistant (GPA), a GUI front end, to manage GPG tasks. You can use the **gpg** command to manually encode and decode messages, including digital signatures if you wish. As you perform GPG tasks you will need to reference the keys you have using their key names. Bear in mind that you only need a unique identifying substring to select the key you want. GPG performs a pattern search on the string you specify as the key name in any given command. If the string matches more than one key, all those matching will be selected. In the following example, the Sendmail string selects matches on the identities of two keys.

```
# gpg --list-keys "Sendmail"
pub  1024R/CC374F2D 2000-12-14
            Sendmail Signing Key/2001 <sendmail@Sendmail.ORG>
pub  1024R/E35C5635 1999-12-13
            Sendmail Signing Key/2000 <sendmail@Sendmail.ORG>
```

gpg provides several options for managing secure messages. The **e** option encrypts messages, the **a** option generates an armored text version, and the **s** option adds a digital signature. You will need to specify the recipient's public key, which you should already have imported into your **pubring** file. It is this key that is used to encrypt the message. The recipient will then be able to decode the message with their private key. Use the **--recipient** or **-r** option to specify the name of the recipient key. You can use any unique substring in the user's public key name. The e-mail address usually suffices. You use the **d** option to decode received messages. In the following example, the user encrypts (**e**) and signs (**s**) a file generated in armored text format (**a**). The **-r** option indicates the recipient for the message (whose public key is used to encrypt the message).

```
gpg e -s -a -o myfile.asc -r george@rabbit.mytrek.com myfile
# mail george@rabbit.mytrek.com < myfile.asc
```

You can leave out the ASCII armor option if you want to send or transfer the file as a binary attachment. Without **--armor** or **-a** options, gpg generates an encoded binary file, not an encoded text file. A binary file can only be transmitted through e-mail as an attachment. As noted previously, ASCII armor versions usually have an extension of **.asc**, whereas binary version use **.gpg**.

When the other user receives the file, they can save it to a file named something like **myfile.asc**, and then decode the file with the **-d** option. The **-o** option will specify a file to save the decoded version in. GPG will automatically determine if it is a binary file or an ASCII armor version.

```
gpg -d -o myfile.txt myfile.asc
```

To check the digital signature of the file, you use the **gpg** command with the **--verify** option. This assumes that the sender has signed the file.

```
gpg --verify myfile.asc
```

However, you will need to have the signer's public key to decode and check the digital signature. If you do not, you will receive a message saying that the public key was not found. In this case, you will first have to obtain the signer's public key. You could access a keyserver that you think may have the public key, or request the public key directly from a Web site or from the signer. Then import the key as described previously.

You do not have to encrypt a file to sign it. A digital signature is a separate component. You can either combine the signature with a given file or generate one separately. To combine a signature with a file you generate a new version that incorporates both. Use the **--sign** or **-s** command to generate a version of the document that includes the digital signature. In the following example, the **mydoc** file is digitally signed with **mydoc.gpg** file containing both the original file and the signature.

```
gpg  -o mydoc.gpg  --sign mydoc
```

If, instead, you want to just generate a separate signature file, you use the **--detach-sig** command. This has the advantage of not having to generate a complete copy of the original file. That file remains untouched.The signature file usually has an extension like **.sig**. In the following example, the user creates a signature file called **mydoc2.sig** for the **mydoc2** file.

```
gpg -o mydoc2.sig --detach-sig mydoc2
```

To verify the file using a detached signature, the recipient user specifies both the signature file and the original file.

```
gpg --verify mydoc2.sig  mydoc2
```

You could also generate a clear sign signature to be used in text files. A clear sign signature is a text version of the signature that can be attached to a text file. The text file can be further edited by any text editor. Use the **--clearsign** option to create a clear sign signature. The following example creates a clear signed version of a text file called **mynotice.txt**.

```
gpg -o mysignotice.txt --clearsign mynotice.txt
```

*Numerous GUI front ends and filters are available for GnuPG at **www.gnupg.org**. GPA (GNU Privacy Assistant) provides a Gnome-based front end to easily encrypt and decrypt files. You can select files to encode, choose the recipients (public keys to use), and add a digital signature if you wish. You can also use GPA to decode encoded files you receive. You can manage your collection of public keys, the keys in your keyring file.*

*Steganography is a form of encryption that hides data in other kinds of objects, such as images. You can use JPEG Hide and Seek software (JPHS) to encode and retrieve data in a JPEG image (jphide and jpseek). See **linux01.gwdg.de/~alatham/stego.html** for more details.*

Checking Software Package Digital Signatures

One very effective use for digital signatures is to verify that a software package has not been tampered with. It is possible that a software package could be intercepted in transmission and some of its system-level files changed or substituted. Software packages from your distribution, as well as those by reputable GNU and Linux projects, are digitally signed. The signature provides modification digest information with which to check the integrity of the package. The digital signature may be included with the package file or posted as a separate file. You use the **gpg** command with the **--verify** option to check the digital signature for a file.

First, however, you will need to make sure that you have the signer's public key. The digital signature was encrypted with the software distributor's private key. That distributor is the signer. Once you have that signer's public key, you can check any data you receive from them. In the case of a software distributor, once you have their public key, you can check any software they distribute. To obtain the public key, you can check a keyserver or, more likely, check their Web site. As noted previously, you can download the Red Hat public key from the Red Hat Web site at **www.redhat.com/about/contact.html**. Once you have downloaded the public key, you can add to your keyring with the **--import** option, specifying the name you gave to the downloaded key file (in this case, **myredhat.asc**):

```
# gpg --import redhat.asc
gpg: key CBA29BF9: public key imported
gpg: Total number processed: 1
gpg: imported: 1 (RSA: 1)
```

To download from a keyserver instead, you use the **--keyserver** option and the keyserver name.

You can use the --**fingerprint** option to check a key's validity if you wish. If you are confident that the key is valid, you can then sign it with the **--sign-key** command. In the following example, the user signs the Red Hat key, using the string "Red Hat" in the key's name to reference it. The user is also asked to enter his passphrase to allow use of his private key to sign the Red Hat public key.

```
# gpg --sign-key "Red Hat"
pub  1024R/CBA29BF9  created: 1996-02-20 expires: never  trust: -/q
(1). Red Hat Software, Inc. <redhat@redhat.com>
pub  1024R/CBA29BF9  created: 1996-02-20 expires: never  trust: -/q
 Fingerprint: 6D 9C BA DF D9 60 52 06  23 46 75 4E 73 4C FB 50
 Red Hat Software, Inc. <redhat@redhat.com>

Are you really sure that you want to sign this key
with your key: "Richard Petersen (author) <richlp@turtle.mytrek.com>"
Really sign? yes
You need a passphrase to unlock the secret key for
user: "Richard Petersen (author) <richlp@turtle.mytrek.com>"
1024-bit DSA key, ID 73F0A73C, created 2001-09-26
Enter passphrase:
#
```

Once you have the public key, you can check any RPM software packages for Red Hat with the **rpm** command and **-K** option. The following example checks the validity of the xcdroast and balsa software packages:

```
# rpm -K xcdroast-0.98alpha9-1.i386.rpm
xcdroast-0.98alpha9-1.i386.rpm: md5 OK
# rpm -K balsa-1.1.7-1.i386.rpm
balsa-1.1.7-1.i386.rpm: md5 OK
```

Many software packages in the form of compressed archives, **.tar.gz** or **tar.bz2**, will provide signatures in separate files that end with either the **.asc** or **.sig** extension. To check these, you use the **gpg** command with the **--verify** option. For example, the most recent sendmail package is distributed in the form of a compressed archive, **.tar.gz**. Its digital signature is provided in a separate **.sig** file. First you would download and install the public key for sendmail software obtained from the Sendmail Web site.

```
# gpg --import sendmail.asc
```

You should then sign the Sendmail public key that you just imported. In this example, the e-mail address was used for the key name.

```
gpg --sign-key sendmail@Sendmail.ORG
```

You could also check the fingerprint of the key for added verification.

You would then download both the compressed archive and the digital signature files. Decompress the **.gz** file to the **.tar** file with **gunzip**. Then, with the **gpg** command and the **--verify** option, use the digital signature in the **.sig** file to check the authenticity and integrity of the software compressed archive.

```
# gpg --verify sendmail.8.12.0.tar.sig sendmail.8.12.0.tar
gpg: Signature made Fri 07 Sep 2001 07:21:30 PM PDT using RSA key ID CC374F2D
gpg: Good signature from "Sendmail Signing Key/2001 <sendmail@Sendmail.ORG>"
```

You could also just specify the signature file and gpg will automatically search for and select a file of the same name, but without the **.sig** or **.asc** extension.

```
# gpg --verify sendmail.8.12.0.tar.sig
```

In the future, when you download any software from the Sendmail site that uses this key, you just have to perform the **--verify** operation. Bear in mind, though, that different software packages from the same site may use different keys. You would have to make sure that you have imported and signed the appropriate key for the software you are checking.

Intrusion Detection: Tripwire

When someone breaks into a system, they will usually try to gain control by making their own changes to system administration files, such as password files. They could create their own user and password information, allowing them access at any time, or simply change the root user password. They could also replace entire programs, such as the login program, with their own version. One method of detecting such actions is to use an integrity checking tool like Tripwire to detect any changes to system administration files. An integrity checking tool works by first creating a database of unique identifiers for each file or program to be checked. These can include features such as permissions and file size, but also, more importantly, checksum numbers generated by encryption algorithms from the file's contents. For example, in Tripwire, the default identifiers are checksum numbers created by algorithms like the MD5 modification digest algorithm and Snefru (Xerox secure hash algorithm). An encrypted value that provides such a unique identification of a file is known as a signature. In effect, a signature provides an accurate snapshot of the contents of a file. Files and programs are then periodically checked by generating their identifiers again and matching them with those in the database. Tripwire will generate signatures of the current files and programs and match them against the values previously generated for its database. Any differences are noted as changes to the file, and Tripwire then notifies you of the changes.

Note *AIDE (Advanced Intrusion Detection Environment) is an alternative to Tripwire. It provides easy configuration and detailed reporting.*

The Linux version of Tripwire is freely available as an open source product distributed under the GPL license. Tripwire also provides commercial versions for other operating systems. You can find out more about Tripwire at **www.tripwire.com**, and download the most recent release from **www.tripwire.org**. Detailed documentation is provided in a series of Man pages. **tripwire** discusses the `tripwire` command and its options. **twpolicy** describes in detail how Tripwire rules and directives work in the **twpol.txt** file. **twconfig** covers the configuration variables set in **twcfg.txt**. **twfiles** lists the different directories that Tripwire uses, such as the **/var/lib/tripwire/report** directory that holds Tripwire check results. **twadmin** describes the usage of the `twadmin` command to create and display the policy (**tw.pol**) and configuration (**tw.cfg**) files.

You should install Tripwire when your system is in a secure state—as in not connected to any network. If Tripwire is installed as part of the standard installation, you should remain disconnected from a network after the installation while you configure and initialize Tripwire. Using Tripwire is a continual process of checking the Tripwire database for changes, making any configuration or policy changes that may be needed, and reinitializing the Tripwire database to reflect valid changes. The commands and files used in the installation of Tripwire are listed in Table 6-3.

You can also check your log files for any suspicious activity. See Chapter 25 for a discussion on system logs. ***/var/log/messages*** *in particular is helpful for checking for critical events such as user logins, FTP connections, and superuser logins.*

Tripwire Configuration

To first use Tripwire, you will have to generate a configuration file and a policy file. These files are generated by the **twinstall.sh** script. If you just want to use the standard configuration, you can generate the files immediately by running the **twinstall.sh** script.

Commands and Files	Description
`tripwire`	Initializes and performs integrity checking
`twadmin`	Administers Tripwire configuration and policy files, as well as Tripwire encryption keys
`twprint`	Prints and displays Tripwire database and reports
`siggen`	Generates new passphrases
twinstall.sh	Generates keys and encrypted configuration and policy files
/etc/tripwire/tw.cfg	Encrypted Tripwire configuration file
/etc/tripwire/tw.pol	Encrypted Tripwire policy file
/etc/tripwire/twcfg.txt	Plain text Tripwire configuration file
/etc/tripwire/twpol.txt	Plain text Tripwire policy file
/var/lib/tripwire/report	Holds Tripwire reports
/var/lib/tripwire	Holds Tripwire databases

Table 6-3. *Tripwire Commands and Files*

If you want to customize your configuration and policy files, you will have to first modify their editable versions in the **/etc/tripwire** directory. There are two versions of these files. One is a **.txt** file that you can edit to customize your configuration, and the other is generated by **twinstall.sh** script using the **.txt** file. The configuration file specifies the Tripwire application directories and files, such as the directory where the Tripwire database is placed and reports are stored. **twcfg.txt** is the editable version of the configuration file. This file will already include the standard administrative files. You can edit this file to add any files of your own. The policy file holds the files, programs, and directories that you want Tripwire to check. The **twpol.txt** file is its editable version. You can edit this file to add or change policies to fit your system's particular needs. Once you have made the changes you want to the **twcfg.txt** and **twpol.txt files**, you can then use the **twinstall.sh** script to generate **the tw.cfg** and **tw.pol** files. These are the actual configuration and policy files that Tripwire uses, and, for security reasons, should never be touched.

The Tripwire policy file holds rules used to determine what files and programs to monitor and how they are checked. Rules consist of an object and a property mask. An object is either a directory or file and its entry in the rule consists of the full pathname for that file or directory. The property mask is a list of the object's properties to be checked, such as the size, permissions, or a checksum value like MD5. The object and property mask are separated by a **->** symbol, and the entire rule is terminated by a semicolon. You can only have one rule per object. The property mask is a series of single-character codes denoting different file and directory features, such as **p** for permissions, **s** for size, **t** for type, and **M** for MD5 value. You can specify whether a property is to be checked or not with the **+** and **-** signs. **+p** says to check an object's permissions, **-p** says not to. See the **twpolicy** Man page for a complete listing of the property codes. In the next example, the **/chris/myfile** object will have its permissions and size checked:

```
/chris/myfile -> +ps;
```

Tripwire also defines several built-in variables that hold standard property sets for different types of objects. For example, **ReadOnly** lists standard properties for a file or directory that should have read-only access. The **Dynamic** built-in is used for monitoring files that tend to change. It will check properties such as permissions and users that tend not to change, ignoring those that do, such as size and MD5 values. **IgnoreAll** will simply check to see if a file exists or not, ignoring all other properties. **IgnoreNone** will apply all properties to a file. This can be used to provide a high level of security.

```
/usr/bin -> ReadOnly;
/usr/sbin/slogin -> IgnoreNone
/usr/chris/mydoc -> Dynamic
```

You can further qualify rules with attributes such as **severity** to indicate the severity of a violation or **emailto**, in which you can specify an e-mail address to which a message is to be sent in case of a violation. Attributes are entered within parentheses following the rule. Separate several attributes with commas.

```
/chris/myfile -> +ps (emailto = chris@turtle.mytrek.com);
/usr/bin -> ReadOnly (severity = 70, emailto =
admin@turtle.mytrek.com);
```

You can also group rules together and apply the same attributes to them all. In this case, the rules are encased in braces and the attributes are listed in preceding parentheses. With this feature, you can avoid having to repeat attributes for several files. Also, you can easily add an attribute for several files at once. In the following example, the **/chris/myfile** and **/chris/myproject** directories are both assigned attributes for an e-mail address and a severity level:

```
(
severity = 70,
emailto = chris@turtle.mytrek.com
```

```
)
{
/chris/myfile -> +ps;
/chris/myproject -> +sM;
}
```

There are four attributes: **rulename**, **emailto**, **severity**, and **recurse**. The **rulename** attribute is often used to group rules under a title that will then be used in the Tripwire reports to list any violations in that group. The **recurse** attribute specifies if property checks for a directory are also applied to its subdirectories. The default is true, and a false value will not check any files in the directory. In the following example, **rulename** gives the name **Chris Important Files** to the rules listed in the previous example. Be sure to separate attributes with commas. Also the files and subdirectories in the **/chris/myproject** directory are not checked.

```
(
rulename = "Chris Important Files",
severity = 70,
emailto = chris@turtle.mytrek.com
)
{
/chris/myfile -> +ps;
/chris/myproject -> +sM (recurse = false);
}
```

Tripwire also supports directives in which you can define variables or rules for certain hosts or file systems, as well as global variables. This allows an administrator to create a single policy file to be used on different hosts (see the **twpolicy** Man page for more details). A directive begins with **@@section**. On a standard policy file, you will have a directive for the global variables, **GLOBALS**, and one for the Linux file system, **FS**. The **GLOBALS** section defines locations of Tripwire files and directories. The **FS** section sets the variables used for different property sets, such as **SEC_INVARIANT** that is assigned the properties **+tpug** to check type, permissions, user, and group. This is used for files and directories that should not be changed. You will find the following entry in the **twpol.txt** file:

```
SEC_INVARIANT = +tpug ;
```

A variable is evaluated by encasing it in parentheses and preceding it with the **$** operator. **$(SEC_INVARIANT)** would be used as the property mask in different rules. The following example says that the **/home** directory itself should never be changed (those under it can be changed, **recurse** = 0):

```
/home -> $(SEC_INVARIANT) (recurse = 0) ;
```

Even the built-in variables are also assigned to variables, some with certain qualifications. In the following example, the properties for **ReadOnly** are assigned to the **SecBin** variable:

```
SEC_BIN = $(ReadOnly) ; # Binaries that should not change
```

The most widely used variable is **Sec_Crit**, which is set to all the properties with **IgnoreNone**, with the SHA (**S**) and Havel (**H**) checksum values and the timestamp (**a**) property removed:

```
SEC_CRIT = $(IgnoreNone)-SHa ; # Critical files that cannot change
```

Dynamic is used for configuration files, and **Growing** for log files, as shown here:

```
SEC_CONFIG = $(Dynamic) ; # Config files
SEC_LOG = $(Growing) ; # Files that grow
```

In addition, variables are set for security values. These include **SIG_LOW, SIG_MED**, and **SIG_HIGH** for noncritical, moderately critical, and severely critical violations. The following example is a segment of the **twpol.txt** file, showing the rules for kernel administrative programs:

```
################################### #
# # #
# Kernel Administration Programs # #
# ##
###################################

(
 rulename = "Kernel Administration Programs",
 severity = $(SIG_HI)
)
{
 /sbin/adjtimex -> $(SEC_CRIT) ;
 /sbin/ctrlaltdel -> $(SEC_CRIT) ;
 /sbin/depmod -> $(SEC_CRIT) ;
 /sbin/insmod -> $(SEC_CRIT) ;
 /sbin/insmod.static -> $(SEC_CRIT) ;
 /sbin/insmod_ksymoops_clean -> $(SEC_CRIT) ;
 /sbin/klogd -> $(SEC_CRIT) ;
 /sbin/ldconfig -> $(SEC_CRIT) ;
 /sbin/minilogd -> $(SEC_CRIT) ;
 /sbin/modinfo -> $(SEC_CRIT) ;
```

```
 /sbin/sysctl -> $(SEC_CRIT) ;
}
```

E-mail entries are usually not included in the attributes for different rule groups. If you want Tripwire to notify you by e-mail when a certain violation occurs, you will have to edit the **twpol.txt** file and insert **emailto** attributes into the attribute list for those rule groups. For example, for the previous example you could have Tripwire notify the admin user when a kernel program is violated. Be sure to place a comma at the end of the preceding attribute—in this case, the **severity** attribute:

```
(
rulename = "Kernel Administration Programs",
 severity = $(SIG_HI),
 emailto=admin@turtle.mytrek.com
)
```

The Tripwire configuration file, **twcfg.txt**, is often already set up for your distribution's Linux installation. It will contain a number of Tripwire variables that you can modify if you wish. The **DBFILE** variable holds the directory that contains the database file. **REPORTFILE** specifies the directory where reports are stored. **POLFILE** contains the policy file. **SITEKEYFILE** and **LOCALKEYFILE** specify the location of your local and site key files.

The **twinstall.sh** script will create digitally signed configuration and policy files. To do this, it will prompt you for local and site passphrases. The passphrases are passwords you will need to create a Tripwire database and to access Tripwire reports. You are then prompted to enter the site and local passphrases to generate the configuration and policy files:

```
/etc/tripwire/twinstall.sh
```

twinstall.sh actually runs a **siggen** command to create your passphrases and then the **twadmin** command to create your policy and configuration files. If you later want to change the configuration or policy files, you can run **twadmin** directly, without changing your passphrases. If you want to just change your passphrases, run the **siggen** command. To replace both files and both passphrases, you can just run **twinstall.sh** again.

If you want to make changes to the Tripwire configuration file, you can edit the **/etc/tripwire/twcfg.txt** file and use it with the **twadmin** command to create a new signed **tw.cfg** file, as shown here:

```
twadmin --create-cfgfile /etc/tripwire/twcfg.txt
```

Creating a new policy file is more complicated and is covered in the policy update section.

Using Tripwire

Once the configuration and policy files have been created, you can create the database of signatures for your monitored files and programs by invoking Tripwire with the **`--init`** option. You will initially be prompted to enter your local passphrase, which you specified when you ran **twinstall.sh**:

```
tripwire --init
```


The Tripwire database is kept in **/var/lib/tripwire** and given the name of the host with the extension **.twd**. For example, the Tripwire database for **turtle.mytrek.com** will be **/var/lib/tripwire/turtle.mytrek.com.twd**.

It is recommended, for strong security, to place the Tripwire database on read-only media, like a floppy disk or CD-ROM. You can reconfigure specifying a new Tripwire database directory, or use the **`-d`** *option to manually specify the location of the Tripwire database with your Tripwire commands.*

Now that your database is created, you can use Tripwire to periodically check the integrity of your system. You can do this manually with the **--check** option. You could also set up Tripwire **`--check`** commands as cron jobs to be run automatically at specified times. A Tripwire **`--check`** command will be placed in the **/etc/cron.daily** file and will run Tripwire daily:

```
tripwire --check
```

Tripwire will check all the files listed in your policy file and generate a report. Tripwire reports are placed in files which are named according to the hostname, date, and time of the report, with the extension **.twr**. For example, the report generated on August 12, 2001 at 10:29:54 will have the name **20010812-102954.twr**. These files are kept in the **/var/lib/tripwire/report** directory. The report will list any violations, noting a severity level and indicating whether files were added, removed, or modified.

To view reports, you use the **`twprint`** command with the **--print-report** option. You will have to specify the file you want with the **`-r`** option as well. The report is displayed on the standard input, scrolling down your screen. You can redirect it to a file to save it, or pipe it to the **`more`** or **`less`** commands to view it screen by screen. The following example opens the **20010812-102954.twr** report, piping the output to the **`more`** command:

```
twprint--print-report -r
/var/lib/tripwire/report/20010812-102954.twr | more
```

You can also use **twprint** to query the database for information about particular files. Use the **--print-dbfile** option and the filename:

```
twprint --print-dbfile /etc/passwd
```

As your system changes with files being modified, your Tripwire database can become outdated. You can update the Tripwire database to incorporate those reported violations as correct entries by using the **--update** option. You will have to specify the particular report file that holds the error reports for the valid data.

```
tripwire --update -r /var/lib/tripwire/report/20010812-102954.twr
```

Tripwire will first open the file in an editor, with the violations selected as updates to be incorporated having an [x] in front of their entries. Unselected violations will have empty brackets, [ ]. If you notice any valid violations that are marked for update, you can deselect them by removing the preceding x. When you're finished, save and quit the file with the editor's **save** command (The **EDITOR** variable in the **twcfg.txt** file determines what editor to use—Vi by default). You are then prompted to enter a local passphrase for your local key.

Note *To control the monitoring of files that no longer exist or are newly installed on your system, you will have to change the policy file (see the next section). The update procedure only deals with modification or feature changes.*

Changing Policies

As your system changes over time, you may want to add or remove files that you want to have monitored by Tripwire. The situation becomes aggravated as you install and remove software, adding files not covered by Tripwire and removing those that no longer exist. Tripwire will report any removed files as violations. You can easily add or remove files that Tripwire monitors by inserting or deleting entries in the Tripwire policy file. You can also change the level of checking for different files. You do not edit the Tripwire policy file directly. Instead you edit the text version, **/etc/tripwire/twpol.txt**. If you are removing file missing entries, it is advisable to just comment them out. If you later install the software for them, you will just have to remove the comment. For example, to remove the entries for innd (the INN news server) and for tux (the Tux Web server), just insert a **#** symbol before their entry as shown here:

```
# /var/lock/subsys/innd -> $(SEC_CONFIG) ;
# /var/lock/subsys/tux -> $(SEC_CONFIG) ;
```

Once you have made your changes, you issue the following command to generate a new signed **tw.pol** policy file that Tripwire will actually use. Be sure to specify the text version you are using.

```
twadmin --create-polfile /etc/tripwire/twpol.txt
```

You will then be prompted to enter the site key. A new **tw.pol** file is then generated. You will have to regenerate a new version of the Tripwire database. First remove the old one, and then initialize a new one:

```
rm /var/lib/tripwire/turtle.mytrek.com.twd
tripwire --init
```

Alternatively, you can combine the process by using the **`tripwire`** command with the **`--update-policy`** option to create your policy and update your database:

```
tripwire --update-policy /etc/tripwire/twpol.txt
```

Note *The process of setting up and maintaining a firewall can be complex. To simplify the process, SuSE includes a firewall configuration tool called SuSEfirewall2 which implements IP-Tables firewall rules. Red Hat also has a firewall configuration tool called lokkit, though it implements only the older IP-Chains firewall rules. You can also use the packet-filtering program iptables directly, manually listing your firewall rules. iptables has been developed by the Netfilter Project at **netfilter.samba.org** (see Chapter 37).*

Tip *Linuxconf and Webmin also provide simple firewall, Squid, and SSH configuration.*

Proxies (Squid)

Squid is a proxy-caching server for Web clients, designed to speed Internet access. It implements a proxy-caching service for Web clients that caches Web pages as users make requests and provides security controls for Web site access. Squid is supported and distributed under a GNU Public License by the National Laboratory for Applied Network Research (NLANR) at the University of California, San Diego. The work is based on the Harvest Project. You can obtain current source code versions and online documentation from the Squid home page at **www.squid-chache.org** and the Squid FTP site at **ftp.squid-chache.org**.

Tip *You can also configure Squid using Linuxconf or Webmin.*

To configure Squid to provide security to your Web server, you first define access control lists (ACL) using the **acl** command, in which you create a label for the systems on which you are setting controls. You then use commands such as **http_access** to define these controls. You can define a system, or a group of systems, according to several **acl** options, such as the source IP address, the domain name, or even the time and date. For example, the **src** option is used to define a system or group of systems with a certain source address. To define a **mylan acl** entry for systems in a local network with the addresses 192.168.1.0 through 192.168.1.255, use the following ACL definition:

```
acl mylan src 192.168.1.0/255.255.255.0
```

Once these are defined, you can use an ACL definition in a Squid option to specify a control you want to place on those systems. For example, to allow access by the mylan group of local systems to the Web through the proxy, use an **http_access** option with the **allow** action specifying **mylan** as the **acl** definition to use, as shown here:

```
http_access allow mylan
```

By defining ACLs and using them in Squid options, you can tailor your Web site with the kind of security you want. See Chapter 24 for a more detailed discussion of Squid.

Secure Shell (SSH)

Although a firewall can protect a network from attempts to break into it from the outside, the problem of securing legitimate communications to the network from outside sources still exists. A particular problem is one of users who want to connect to your network remotely. Such connections could be monitored, and information such as passwords and user IDs used when the user logs in to your network could be copied and used later to break in. One solution is to use SSH for remote logins and other kinds of remote connections such as FTP transfers. SSH encrypts any communications between the remote user and a system on your network.

SSH was originally designed to replace remote access operations, such as rlogin, rcp, and Telnet (see Chapter 15) as well as FTP. The ssh-clients package contains corresponding SSH clients to replace these applications. With slogin or ssh, you can log in from a remote host to execute commands and run applications, much as you can with rlogin and rsh. With scp, you can copy files between the remote host and a network host, just as with rcp. With sftp you can transfer FTP files secured by encryption.

Unlike PGP, SSH uses public-key encryption for the authentication process only. Once authenticated, participants agree on a common cipher to use to encrypt transmission. Authentication will verify the identity of the participants. Each user who intends to use SSH to access a remote account first needs to create the public and private keys along with a passphrase to use for the authentication process. A user then sends their public key to the remote account they want to access and installs the public key on that account.

When the user attempts to access the remote account, that account can then use the user's public key to authenticate that the user is who they claim to be. The process assumes that the remote account has set up its own SSH private and public key. For the user to access the remote account, they will have to know the remote account's SSH passphrase. SSH is often used in situations where a user has two or more accounts located on different systems and wants to be able to securely access them from each other. In that case the user already has access to each account and can install SSH on each, giving each its own private and public keys along with their passphrases.

You create SSH public and private keys and select a passphrase with the **ssh-keygen** command. The **ssh-keygen** command prompts you for a passphrase, which it will use as a kind of password to protect your private key. The passphrase should be several words long. The **ssh-keygen** command generates the public key and places it in your **.ssh/identity.pub** file; it places the private key in the **.ssh/identity** file. If you need to change your passphrase, you can do so with the **ssh-keygen** command and the **-p** option. Each user will have their own SSH configuration directory, called **.ssh**, located in their own home directory. The public and private keys, as well as SSH configuration files, are placed here.

Note *The **.ssh/identity** filename used in SSH version 1 may be installed by default on older distribution versions. SSH version 2 uses a different filename, **.ssh/id_dsa**. The authorized keys file is also slightly different, **.ssh/authorized_keys2**.*

A public key is used to identify a user and its host. You use the public key on a remote system to allow that user access. The public key is placed in the remote user account's **.ssh/authorized_keys** file. Remember that the public key is held in the **.ssh/identity.pub** file. If a user wants to log in remotely from a local account to an account on a remote system, they would first place their public key in the **.ssh/authorized_keys** file in the account on the remote system they wants to access. If the user **larisa** on **turtle.mytrek.com** wants to access the **aleina** account on **rabbit.mytrek.com, larisa**'s public key from **/home/larisa/.ssh/identity.pub** first must be placed in **aleina**'s **authorized_keys** file, **/home/aleina/.ssh/authorized_keys**.

With SSH, you can log in from a local site to a remote host on your network and then send commands to be executed on that host. SSH is also capable of supporting X Window System connections. This feature is automatically enabled if you make an SSH connection from an X Window System environment, such as Gnome or KDE. A connection is set up for you between the local X server and the remote X server. The remote host sets up a dummy X server and sends any X Window System data through it to your local system to be processed by your own local X server.

To log in with SSH, you enter the **ssh** command with the address of the remote host, followed by an **-l** option and the login name (username) of the remote account you are logging in to. You will then be prompted for the remote account's SSH passphrase. The following example logs in to the **aleina** user account on the **rabbit.mytrek.com** host:

```
ssh rabbit.mytrek.com -l aleina
```

You use **scp** to copy files from one host to another on a network. Designed to replace **rcp**, **scp** actually uses SSH to transfer data and employs the same authentication and encryption. If authentication requires it, **scp** requests a password or passphrase. Directories and files on remote hosts are specified using the username and the host address before the filename or directory. The username specifies the remote user account that **scp** is accessing, and the host is the remote system where that account is located. You separate the user from the host address with an at sign (**@**), and you separate the host address from the file or directory name with a colon (**:**). The following example copies the file **party** from a user's current directory to the user **aleina**'s **birthday** directory, located on the **rabbit.mytrek.com** host:

```
scp party aleina@rabbit.mytrek.com:/birthday/party
```

Of particular interest is the **-r** option, which enables you to copy whole directories. In the next example, the user copies the entire **reports** directory to the user **justin**'s **projects** directory:

```
scp -r reports justin@rabbit.mytrek.com:/projects
```

Chapter 7

Setting Up a Local Area Network with Linux

Creating a local network of your own involves just a few simple steps. You can set up a system to serve as the main server for your own local area network (LAN), providing services like e-mail, a Web site, or shared printers. You can even connect different types of systems such as those running Windows or the Mac OS. You can also configure your system to serve as a gateway to the Internet, through which all your other systems will connect. In fact, you could have one Internet connection on your gateway that each host on your network could use. A few security precautions allow your system to work as a firewall, protecting your local hosts from outside attacks. You could also set up a very simple configuration to provide Web access only. This chapter will cover the basic concepts for setting up such a network. Later chapters in this book will cover these topics in detail.

Your local area network consists of a collection of host systems connected to the main host running Linux. This main host will be referred to as the *gateway*. The steps for setting up a local network involve the following:

- Setting up and configuring the Ethernet cards on each system. Your gateway should have two Ethernet cards.
- Setting up a proxy server to provide direct Web access (DNS is not required).
- Setting up your DNS server on the gateway (see Chapter 22).
- Configuring your DNS server to allow all other local hosts to access the Internet.
- Setting up firewall protection.
- Enabling up e-mail services (see Chapter 23).
- Setting up local host access to the Internet through DNS (proxy server is not required).
- Sharing printers with Windows hosts (see Chapter 35).
- Setting up a local Web site.

Along with setting up your connections, you will have to run at least one service on the main gateway computer you set up for your network. On Mandrake and Red Hat, you can start and stop a service with the **service** command. On SuSE, you use the appropriate script in the **/etc/rc.d** directory (see the following table). To have the service automatically started, you can use a services management utility provided in most system configuration tools, such as SuSE's YaST or the Mandrake Control Center, as well as specialized tools like System V Init Editor (see Chapter 19). For a simple network, you should have the DNS and Network services running. If you have Windows systems on your network and you want to share printers with them, you will need the Samba service. The Network, Squid, Sendmail, Postfix, DNS, and Samba may have to be restarted as you configure them. You will have to know the names used for the DNS, Sendmail, Postfix, Squid, and Samba server programs to restart them with the service tool. They are shown here. In addition, you will have to add a firewall rule to enable your local hosts to access the Internet through your firewall.

Service Name	Service Program
Domain Name Service (DNS)	named
Samba	smb
Network connections	network
Firewall	iptables
Squid	squid
Sendmail	sendmail
Postfix	postfix

You use the **start**, **stop**, and **restart** arguments to start, stop, and restart a service. To restart the DNS service you would use the following:

```
service named restart
```

Physical Configuration

To set up the physical connections between different computers on your system, you will need to install an Ethernet device on each. Many computers already have an Ethernet card installed or built-in. Most Ethernet configurations use lightweight cables to connect computers, though there are some that are wireless. The computers on a network are referred to as hosts. To connect several hosts together on a network, you will need Ethernet cables for each and a hub that will connect them all together. To connect up a host, connect one end of the cable to its Ethernet card and the other to the hub. A hub will have several plugs, one for each host on your network. For a larger network, you can connect several hubs together.

In the configuration described here, the host running a Linux system will be used as the main server and gateway for the local network. Here, you will install various servers, such as the DNS and Web servers. This host also will function to connect all the local hosts to the Internet (or a larger network). To do this effectively, this gateway/server host will need an Ethernet card and an Internet connection device such as a modem, DSL (digital subscriber line) modem, or another Ethernet card. The type of device you use depends on the type of service that your Internet service provider (ISP) gives you. Some provide only modem connections with which you dial in to connect to the Internet (AOL connections do not work for a LAN). Those that provide DSL connections will use a special DSL modem to allow you connect to the Internet. Both connect to a phone outlet. Cable modems, however, work like Ethernet networks. You need a second Ethernet network card that you connect to the cable modem. This is also the case if you are connecting directly to a larger Ethernet network. The examples in this chapter use a second Ethernet connection.

Note *Another kind of network configuration uses a coaxial cable (thin Ethernet cable) to which hosts connect directly instead of to a hub.*

When you start up your system, Linux will automatically detect your Internet connection device and install the appropriate module for it. For some older Ethernet cards, you may have to perform special configuration tasks, such as making entries in **/etc/modules.conf** with certain parameters.

The wireless LAN device will have an Ethernet name just like an Ethernet card. kmod will automatically detect and load the appropriate modules, listing its alias in the **/etc/modules.conf** file. The Wireless Tools package, described in Chapter 33, provides tools for further configuring wireless connections.

Web Access with Squid

If you only want to provide your hosts Internet Web access, you can do so by just running the Squid server on your gateway host. You will not have to set up and run a DNS server. Squid is a proxy server and can handle the Internet connection between a browser and Internet sites directly. You only have to configure the network connections for each host, providing their IP address. Squid is included with the basic installation.

Note *Squid also provides extensive security options, making it advisable to control Web access through a proxy server like Squid.*

Once installed on the gateway host, you then have to configure Squid to allow access by hosts on your network. Edit the **/etc/squid/squid.conf** file and place the following entries in the **security** section.

```
acl mylan src 192.168.0.0/255.255.255.0
http_access allow mylan
```

The **squid.conf** file is a very large file with default settings commented in detail. An easy way to make your entries is to search for the corresponding localhost entries and add your network ones below them. The acl entry for localhost will begin with **acl localhost**. The entry for access will begin with **http_access allow localhost**. Squid configuration is discussed in detail in Chapter 24. You can also use Linuxconf or Webmin to configure Squid.

Once configured, on Mandrake and Red Hat you can run Squid with the **service** command.

```
service squid start
```

Use **chkconfig** to have Squid start automatically when you boot.

```
chkconfig --level 35  squid on
```

When a user configures their Web browser for Proxy use, they select the Proxy option on their browser configuration, and enter for the proxy server, the IP address of the gateway running Squid and port 3128. On Netscape, select the Proxy entry under Advanced in the Options panel, and then view the manual proxy connections. For example, using the sample network described in this chapter, the Squid proxy server would be running on 192.168.0.1 and use port 3128. So the entry used in Web browsers would be the following for the different servers:

```
192.168.0.1
```

And then use 3128 for the port:

```
3128
```

Now any user on your network with a correctly configured browser can access the Web.

Tip *If you just want to set up Web access through Squid, you can also use DHCP dynamic allocation of IP addresses to automatically configure all your hosts (see Chapter 33). You do not have to manually assign IP addresses to your hosts. On Mandrake, the Internet Connection Sharing tool will set up automatic DHCP for your network.*

DNS Setup

Now that your local network is physically set up, your gateway/server needs to run certain services to allow your hosts to communicate over the network. You first have to configure and run a Domain Name Service (DNS), which will allow all the hosts on your local network to identify each other using a hostname. This involves several steps:

1. Decide on the IP addresses to assign to each local host. Use 192.168.1 as the network address.
2. Decide on the domain name for your local network.
3. Decide on the hostname for each host on your network.
4. Each host has to be configured with its IP address and domain name address.
5. On the gateway/server, configure a DNS server listing each host's IP address and hostname.
6. Start the DNS service.

On Red Hat, the bindconf tool provides an easy way to configure a DNS server.

All hosts on the Internet are identified by their IP addresses. When you send a message to a host on the Internet, you must provide its IP address. Using a sequence of four numbers of an IP address, however, can be difficult. They are hard to remember, and it's easy to make mistakes when typing them. To make identifying a computer on the Internet easier, the DNS was implemented. The DNS establishes a fully qualified domain name address for each IP address. The fully qualified domain name consists of the name of the host and the network (domain) that it belongs to. Whenever you use that name, it is automatically converted to an IP address, which is then used to identify that Internet host. The fully qualified domain name is far easier to use than its corresponding IP address. For example, the name **www.linux.org** has an IP address of 198.182.196.56. A DNS server will translate **www.linux.org** into its IP address, 198.182.196.56.

In Figure 7-1 the user at **rabbit.mytrek.com** wants to connect to the remote host **lizard.mytrek.com**. **rabbit.mytrek.com** first sends a request to the network's DNS server—in this case, **turtle.mytrek.com**—to look up the name **lizard.mytrek.com** and find its IP address. It then returns the IP address for **lizard.mytrek.com**, 192.168.1.3, to the requesting host, **rabbit.mytrek.com**. With the IP address, the user at **rabbit.mytrek.com** can then connect to **lizard.mytrek.com**.

You can then set up domain name services for your network by running a DNS server on one of the machines. This machine becomes your network's DNS server. You can give your machines fully qualified domain names and configure your DNS server to translate the names to their corresponding IP addresses. As shown in Figure 7-2, for

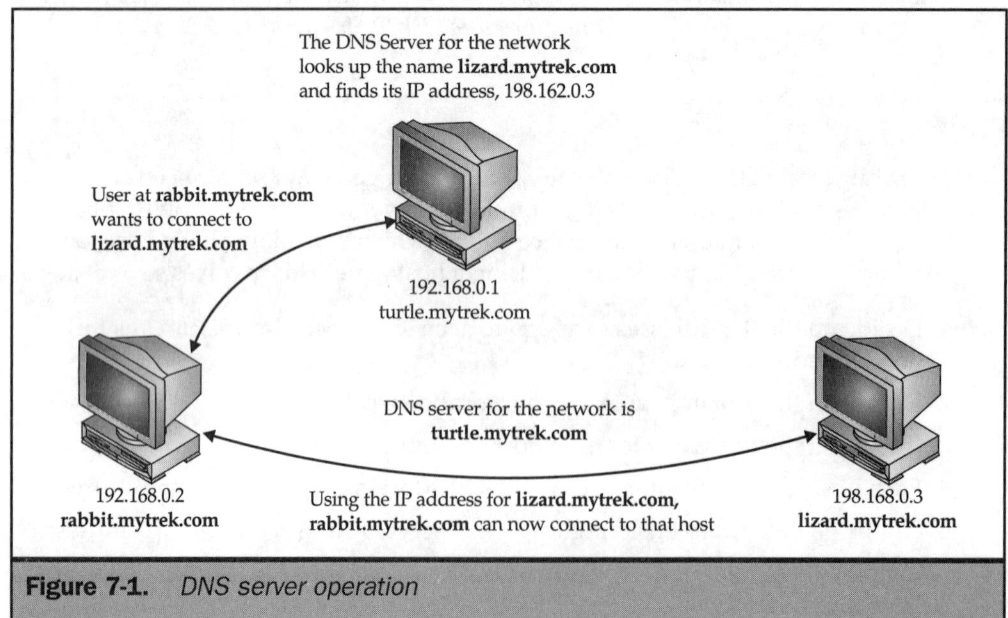

Figure 7-1. *DNS server operation*

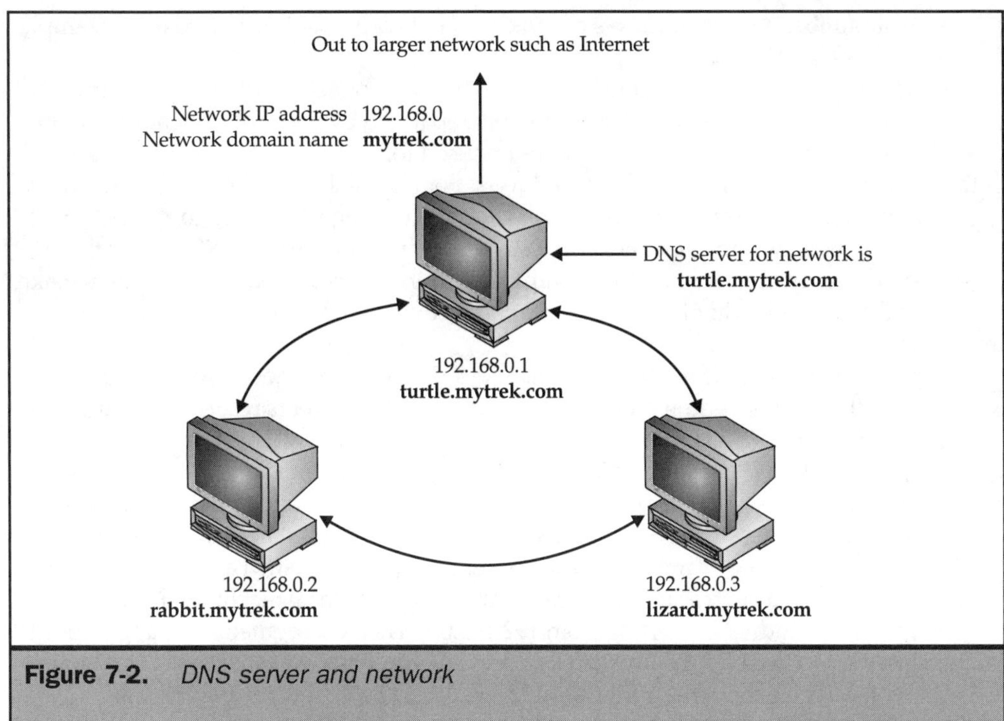

Figure 7-2. *DNS server and network*

example, you could give the machine 192.168.0.1 the name **turtle.mytrek.com**, and the machine 192.168.0.2 the name **rabbit.mytrek.com**. You can also implement Internet services on your network such as FTP, Web, and mail services by setting up servers for them on your machines. You can then configure your DNS server to let users access those services using fully qualified domain names. For example, for the **mytrek.com** network, the Web server could be accessed using the name **www.mytrek.com**.

Note *Instead of a Domain Name Service, you could have the* ***/etc/hosts*** *files in each machine contain the entire list of IP addresses and domain names for all the machines in your network. But, for any changes, you would have to update each machine's* ***/etc/hosts*** *file. You can also use Mandrake or SuSE's Internet Connection Sharing tools to set up DHCP dynamic allocation easily.*

IP Addresses

Most networks, including the Internet, use a set of network protocols called TCP/IP, which stands for Transmission Control Protocol/Internet Protocol. On a TCP/IP network such as the Internet, each computer is given a unique address called an *IP address.* The IP address is used to identify and locate a particular host—a computer connected to the network. It consists of a number, usually four sets of three numbers separated by periods. An example of an IP address is 192.168.0.1.

You will have to assign an IP address to each host on your network. The IP address consists of a number composed of four segments separated by periods. Depending on the type of network, several of the first segments are used for the network address and several of the last segments are used for the host address. For a small local network, the first three segments are the computer's network address and the last segment is the computer's host ID (as used in these examples). For example, in the address 192.168.0.2, 192.168.0 is the network address and 2 is the computer's host ID within that network. Together, they make up an IP address with which the computer can be addressed from anywhere on the Internet.

To set up a DNS server for a local area network (LAN) whose hosts are not directly connected to the Internet, you would use a special set of IP numbers reserved for such non-Internet networks (also known as *private networks* or *intranets*). This is especially true if you are implementing IP masquerading, where only a gateway machine has an Internet address, and the others make use of that one address to connect to the Internet. For a small network (254 hosts or less), these are numbers that have the special network number 192.168.0, as used in these examples. If you are setting up a LAN, such as a small business or home network, you are free to use these numbers for your local machines. For a local network, assign IP addresses starting from 192.168.0.1. The host segment can range from 1 to 254, where 255 is used for the broadcast address. If you have three hosts on your home network, you can give them the addresses 192.168.0.1, 192.168.0.2, and 192.168.0.3.

The network address for such a network would be the first three segments of the IP address, 192.168.0. The network netmask would cover those first three segments, using the number 255.255.255.0. The network netmask is used to determine the host and network parts of an IP address. The broadcast address is used to allow an administrator to contact all hosts at once. You would then use these three IP addresses when configuring a host.

Network IP address	192.168.0.0
Network netmask	255.255.255.0
Host IP addresses	From 192.168.0.1 to 192.168.0.254
Broadcast address	192.168.0.255

In the sample network used in these examples, there are three hosts, each with its own IP addresses and hostnames listed here. The network address, netmask, and broadcast address are the same as those listed above:

```
192.168.0.1
192.168.0.2
192.168.0.3
```

Figure 7-3 shows the format of the sample network with its Ethernet connections and IP addresses, along with their hostnames.

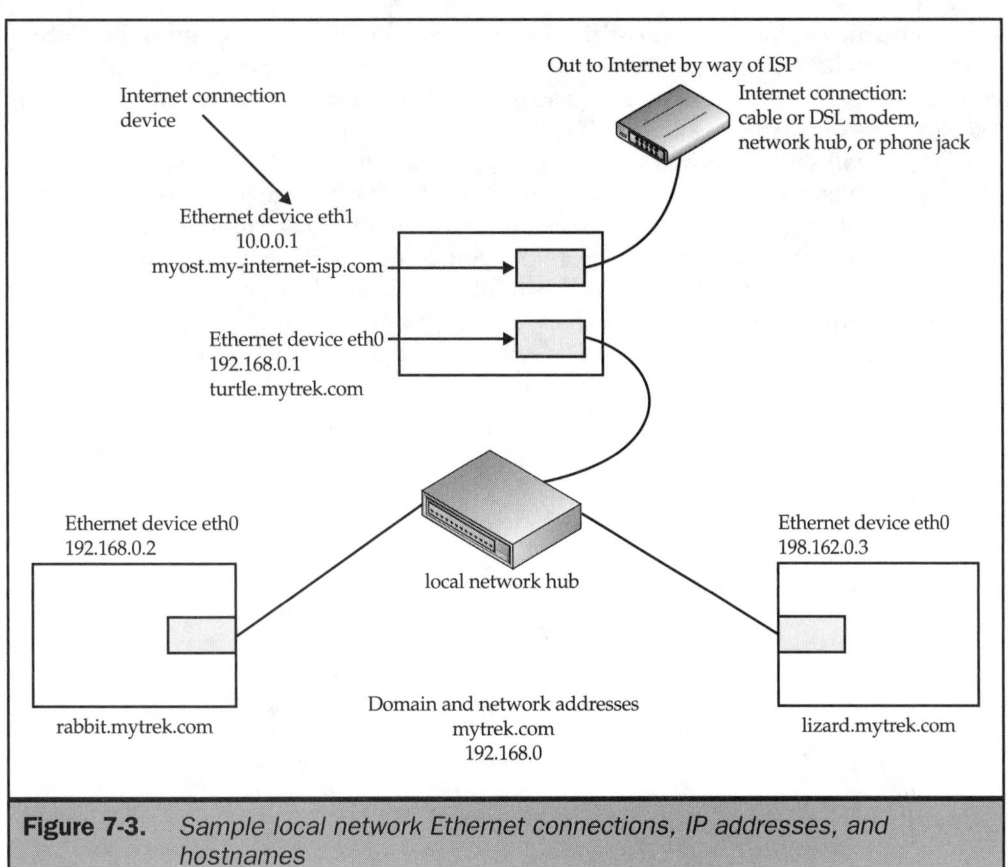

Figure 7-3. *Sample local network Ethernet connections, IP addresses, and hostnames*

Note *See Chapters 22 and 36 for detailed information on IP addresses and DNS server setup.*

Setting Up Your Firewall

To set up your firewall, you use a packet filtering application to check packets of transmissions as they are received. Two different packet filtering programs are used on Linux, ipchains and iptables. ipchains is used on Linux kernel 2.2 and earlier, whereas iptables is used on kernel 2.4 and later. The packet filtering programs use rules to check that packets are valid and can be passed through to your system. Currently there are few applications that can help you automatically set up packet filtering rules. On Red Hat, you can use lokkit, but lokkit only works for the older ipchains rules. On SuSE, you can use SuSEFirewall2 to configure iptables rules, and SuSEFirewall for ipchains. These are invoked directly from the SuSE YaST Control Center. Both Red Hat and Mandrake will save their rules in the **/etc/sysconfig** directory in an ipchains or iptables file. SuSE, instead, keeps its SuSEFirewall2 configuration file there. For both Red Hat and Mandrake you can manually create your rules in a script and then run and save the rules using an iptables service script (see Chapter 37).

The firewall should only run on the gateway. Furthermore, the gateway will have two network connections, one for the local network and an Internet connection device for the Internet. Make sure that the firewall is applied to the device used for the Internet device, not for your local network. On lokkit you do this by making the local network device a trusted device. In the network example used here, the firewall is run on the **eth0** network device (the first Ethernet card), which functions as the gateway. The local network is connected through the **eth1** network device (the second Ethernet card).

Part III

Environments

Chapter 8

The K Desktop Environment: KDE

The *K Desktop Environment* (*KDE*) is a network transparent desktop that includes the standard desktop features, such as a window manager and a file manager, as well as an extensive set of applications that cover most Linux tasks. KDE is an Internet-aware system that includes a full set of integrated network/Internet applications, including a mailer, a newsreader, and a Web browser. The file manager doubles as a Web and FTP client, enabling you to access Internet sites directly from your desktop. KDE aims to provide a level of desktop functionality and ease of use found in MAC/OS and Windows systems, combined with the power and flexibility of the Unix operating system.

Note *KDE version 3.0 has superseded the earlier 2.2 and 1.1 versions of KDE. This chapter describes version 3.0.*

The KDE desktop is developed and distributed by the KDE Project, which is a large open group of hundreds of programmers around the world. KDE is entirely free and open software provided under a GNU Public License and is available free of charge along with its source code. KDE development is managed by a core group: the KDE Core Team. Anyone can apply, though membership is based on merit.

Note *KDE applications are developed using several supporting KDE technologies. These include KIO, which offers seamless and modular access of files and directories across a network. For interprocess communication, KDE uses the Desktop Communications Protocol (DCOP). KParts is the KDE component object model used to embed an application within another, such as a spreadsheet within a word processor. The XML GUI uses XML to generate and place GUI objects such as menus and toolbars. KHTML is an HTML 4.0 rendering and drawing engine.*

Numerous applications written specifically for KDE are easily accessible from the desktop. These include editors, photo and paint image applications, spreadsheets, and office applications. Such applications usually have the letter *k* as part of their name—for example, KWord or KMail. A variety of tools are provided with the KDE desktop. These include calculators, console windows, notepads, and even software package managers. On a system administration level, KDE provides several tools for configuring your system. With KUser, you can manage user accounts, adding new ones or removing old ones. Kppp enables you to connect easily to remote networks with Point-to-Point Protocol (PPP) using a modem. Practically all your Linux tasks can be performed from the KDE desktop. KDE applications also feature a built-in Help application. Choosing the Contents entry in the Help menu starts the KDE Help viewer, which provides a Web page–like interface with links for navigating through the Help documents. KDE version 3.0 includes support for the office application suite KOffice, based on KDE's KParts technology. KOffice includes a presentation application, a spreadsheet, an illustrator, and a word processor, among other components (see Chapter 16 for more details). In addition, an Interactive Development Environment (IDE), called KDevelop, is available to help programmers create KDE-based software.

KDE was initiated by Matthias Ettrich in October 1996, and it has an extensive list of sponsors, including SuSE, Caldera, Red Hat, Mandrake, O'Reilly, DLD, Delix, Live, Linux Verband, and others. KDE is designed to run on any Unix implementation, including Linux, Solaris, HP-UX, and FreeBSD. The official KDE Web site is **www.kde.org**, which provides news updates, download links, and documentation. KDE software packages can be downloaded from the KDE FTP site at **ftp.kde.org** and its mirror sites. Several KDE mailing lists are available for users and developers, including announcements, administration, and other topics. See the KDE Web site to subscribe. A great many software applications are currently available for KDE at **apps.kde.com**. Development support and documentation can be obtained at **developer.kde.org**. Various KDE Web sites are listed in Table 8-1.

Qt

KDE uses as its library of GUI tools the Qt library, developed and supported by Troll Tech (**www.trolltech.com**). Qt is considered one of the best GUI libraries available for Unix/Linux systems. Using Qt has the advantage of relying on a commercially developed and supported GUI library. Also, using the Qt libraries drastically reduces the development time for KDE. Troll Tech provides the Qt libraries as open-source software that is freely distributable. Certain restrictions exist, however: Qt-based (KDE) applications must be free and open sourced, with no modifications made to the Qt libraries. If you develop an application with the Qt libraries and want to sell it, then you have to buy a license from Troll Tech. In other words, the Qt library is free for free applications, but not for commercial ones.

Web Site	Description
www.kde.org	KDE Web site
ftp.kde.org	KDE FTP site
apps.kde.com	KDE software repository
developer.kde.org	KDE developer site
www.trolltech.com	Site for Qt libraries
www.koffice.org	KOffice office suite
kde.themes.org	KDE desktop themes
lists.kde.org	KDE mailing lists

Table 8-1. *KDE Web Sites*

KDE Desktop

One of KDE's aims is to provide users with a consistent integrated desktop, where all applications use GUI interfaces (see Figure 8-1). To this end, KDE provides its own window manager (kwm), file manager (Konqueror), program manager, and desktop panel (Kicker). You can run any other X Window System–compliant application, such as Netscape, in KDE, as well as any Gnome application. In turn, you can also run any KDE application, including the Konqueror file manager, with any other Linux window manager, including Blackbox, Afterstep, and even Enlightenment. You can even run KDE applications in Gnome.

When you start KDE, the KDE panel is displayed at the bottom of the screen. Located on the panel are icons for menus and programs, as well as buttons for different desktop screens. The button for the K Menu shows a large *K* on a cog wheel with a small arrow at the top indicating it is a menu. This button is known as the Application Starter. Click this button to display the menu listing all the applications you can run. The K Menu

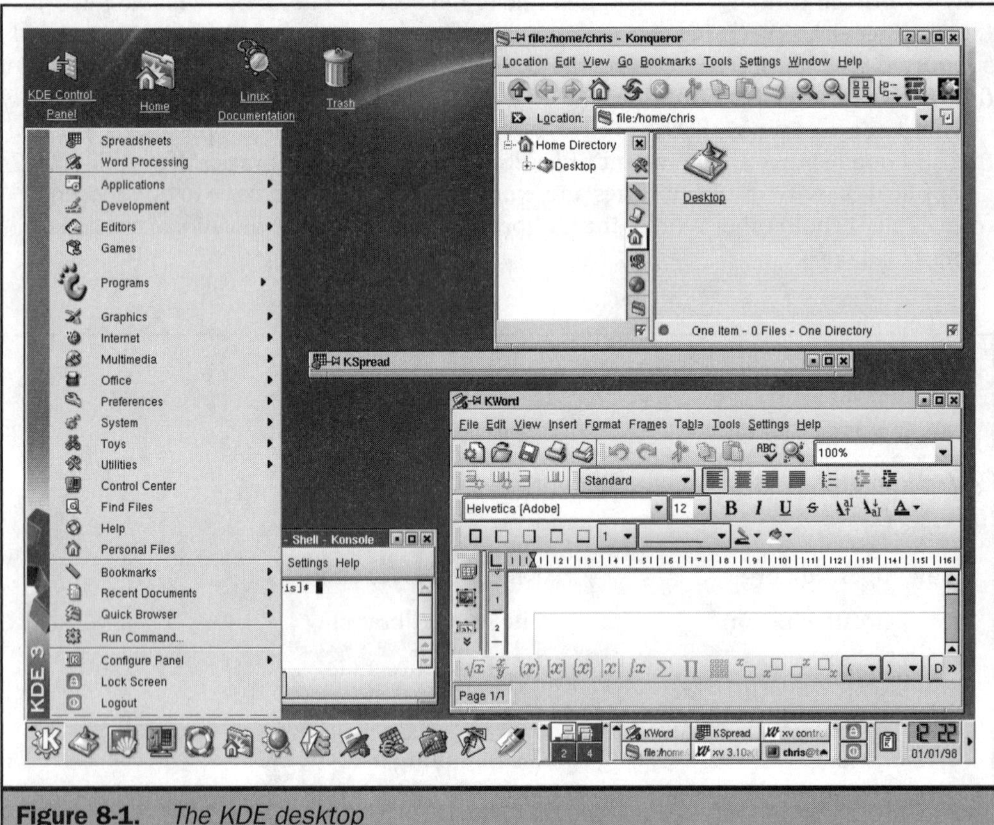

Figure 8-1. *The KDE desktop*

operates somewhat like the Start menu in Windows. The standard KDE applications installed with the KDE can be accessed through this menu. You can find entries for different categories such as Internet, Systems, Multimedia, and Utilities. These submenus list KDE applications you can use. For example, to start the KDE mailer, select the Mail Client entry in the Internet submenu. To quit KDE, you can select the Logout entry in the K Menu, or you can right-click anywhere on the desktop and select the Logout entry from the pop-up menu. You can also click the Logout icon on the KDE panel located below the Lock icon. If you leave any KDE or X11 applications or windows open when you quit, they are automatically restored when you start up again. If you just want to lock your desktop, you can click the Lock icon and your screen saver will appear. To access your desktop, click on the screen and a box appears prompting you for your login password. When you enter the password, your desktop reappears.

Note *You can display a menu for desktop operations across the top of the desktop screen by selecting Enable Desktop Menu from the Desktop pop-up menu displayed when you right-click on the desktop. You can use this menu to create new shortcuts called desktop files for applications and devices, as well as for accessing open windows or changing to different virtual desktops. You can bring up the same set of menus by clicking anywhere on the desktop background.*

A row of icons are displayed along the left side. These include a home directory folder icon labeled Trash, a Printer icon, and floppy and CD-ROM icons. The Trash icon operates like the Recycle Bin in Windows or the trash can on the Mac. Drag items to it to hold them for deletion. To print a document, you can drag it to the Printer icon. You can use the floppy and CD-ROM icons to mount, unmount, and display the contents of CD-ROMs and floppy disks.

Tip *When you use KDE the first time, you are asked to personalize your desktop using KPersonalizer. You can run this program again to change your settings by selecting the Desktop Settings Wizard on the System menu. With KPersonalizer you can select the kind of desktop style you want to use, changing the appearance of your windows and menus.*

The KDE panel displayed across the bottom of the screen initially shows small buttons for the Application Starter, the window list, your home directory, the Help center, a terminal window, and buttons for virtual desktops, among others. The Window List icon looks like several grouped windows. It displays a list of all open windows and the desktop they are on. The Home Directory icon shows a folder with a house. Click it to open a file manager window showing your home directory. The Help Viewer icon is an image of a book. The Terminal Window icon is a picture of two computer monitors. Click this to open a terminal window where you can enter Linux shell commands.

The desktop supports drag-and-drop operations. For example, to print a document, drag it to the Printer icon. You can place any directories on the desktop by simply dragging them from a file manager window to the desktop. The desktop also supports copy-and-paste operations, holding text you copied from one application in a desktop clipboard that you can then use to paste to another application. You can even copy and paste from a Konsole window. For example, you can copy a Web address from a Web page and then paste it into an e-mail message or a word processing document. This feature is supported by the Klipper utility located on the panel.

You can create new directories on the desktop by right-clicking anywhere on the desktop and selecting Create New and then Directory from the pop-up menu. All items that appear on the desktop are located in the **Desktop** directory in your home directory. There you can find the **Trash** directory, along with any others you place on the desktop. To configure your desktop, either click the Desktop icon located on the right of your panel or right-click the desktop and select the Display Properties entry. This displays a window with several tabbed panels for different desktop settings, such as the background or style.

Desktop Files

On the KDE 3.0 desktop, special files called *desktop* files are used to manage a variety of tasks, including device management, Internet connections, program management, and document types. You create a desktop file by right-clicking the desktop and then selecting Create New. From this menu, you choose the type of desktop file you want to create.

The Directory entry lets you create a link to a directory on your system. The CD-ROM and Floppy Device entries each create a desktop file that can mount CD-ROMs or floppy disks on your system. The Text File and HTML File entries are used to reference text files and Web pages on your system. The Link To Application entry is for launching applications. The Link To Location (URL) entry holds a URL address that you can use to access a Web or FTP site.

Given a desktop file that holds an Internet URL address, you can access that site directly by simply clicking the Desktop icon on the desktop. You can also place the desktop file on your desktop or put it in your panel, where it is easily accessible. You can configure the file to display any icon you choose. In effect, you can have an icon on your desktop you can click to immediately access a Web site. When you click the URL desktop file, the file manager starts up in its Web browser mode and will access that address, displaying the Web page. For FTP sites, it performs an anonymous login and displays the remote directory.

To create a URL desktop file, right-click the desktop and select the Create New menu, and then the Link To Location (URL) entry. A window appears that displays a box that prompts you to enter the URL name. You can later edit the desktop file by right-clicking on it and selecting Properties. A desktop dialog box for URL access is then displayed. This dialog box has three tabbed panels: General, Permissions, and URL (see Figure 8-2). On the General panel is the name of your desktop file. It will have as its name the URL address that you entered. You can change this to a more descriptive name if you wish. On the URL panel, you will see a box labeled URL with a URL you entered already in it. You can change it if you want. For example, for KDE themes, the

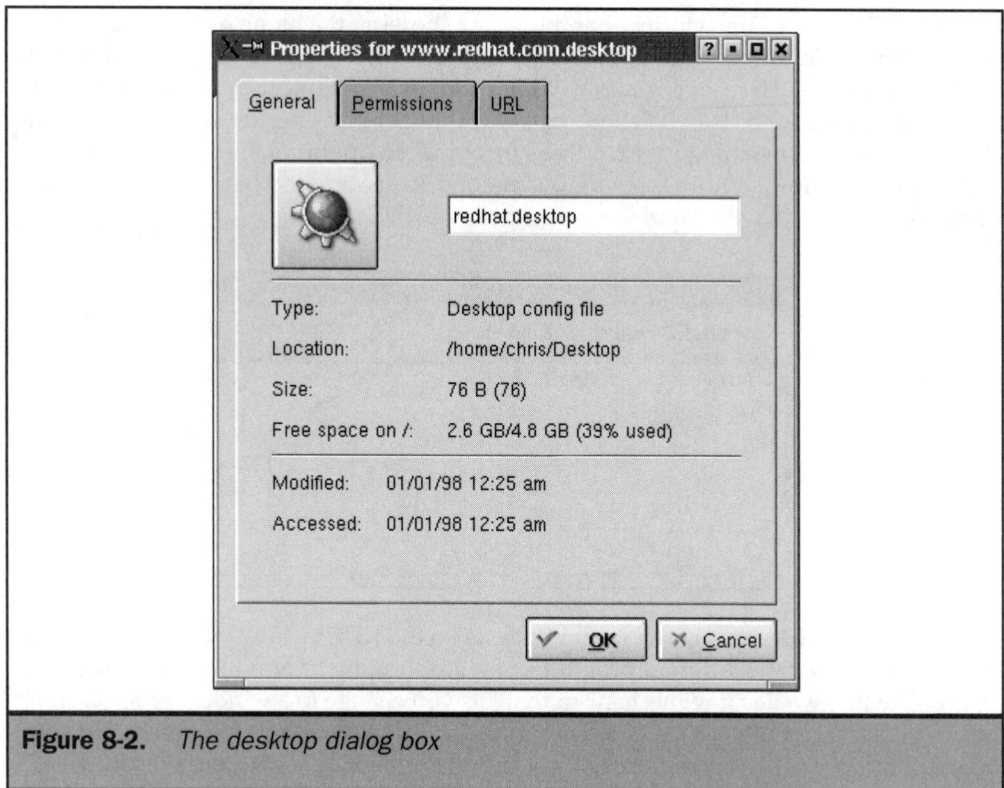

Figure 8-2. *The desktop dialog box*

URL would be **http://kde.themes.org**. Be sure to include the protocol, such as **http://** or **ftp://**. An Icon button on this panel shows the icon that will be displayed for this desktop file on your desktop. The default is a Web World icon. You can change it if you want by clicking the Icon button to open a window that lists icons you can choose from. Click OK when you are finished. The desktop file then appears on your desktop with that icon. Click it to access the Web site. An alternative and easier way to create a URL desktop file is simply to drag a URL from a Web page displayed on the file manager to your desktop. A desktop file is automatically generated with that URL. To change the default icon used, you can right-click the file and choose Properties to display the desktop dialog box. Click the Icon button to choose a new icon.

KDE Windows

A KDE window has the same functionality you find in other window managers and desktops. You can resize the window by clicking and dragging any of its corners or sides. A click-and-drag operation on a side extends the window in that dimension, whereas a corner extends both height and width at the same time. Notice that the corners are slightly enhanced. The top of the window has a title bar showing the name of the window, the program name in the case of applications, and the current directory name for the file manager windows. The active window has the title bar highlighted. To move the window, click this title bar and drag it where you want. Right-clicking the window title bar displays a drop-down menu with entries for window operations, such as closing or resizing the window. Within the window, menus, icons, and toolbars for the particular application are displayed. Here is an example of a KDE window.

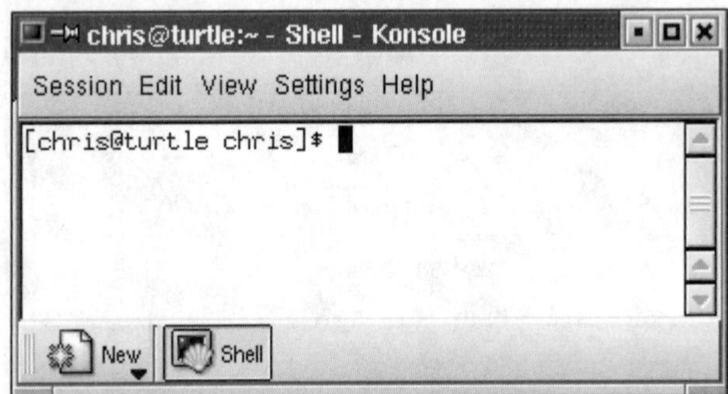

Opened windows are also shown as buttons on the KDE taskbar located on the panel. The taskbar shows the different programs you are running or windows you have open. This is essentially a docking mechanism that lets you change to a window or application just by clicking its button. When you minimize (iconify) a window, it is reduced to its taskbar button. You can then restore the window by clicking its taskbar button.

KDE supports numerous different themes, each displaying window elements in different ways. The default KDE window theme for KDE 3.0 is shown in these examples. In the default KDE 3.0 window, there are two buttons to the left of the title bar at the top of the window. The leftmost button is used to display the window menu and shows an icon representing the type of window open. The button next to it is a Stick Pin button. The Stick Pin button is used to have a window appear on all your virtual desktops, no matter to which one you change. In effect, the window sticks on the screen when you change to another virtual desktop. When active, it appears as a stick pin pressed into the desktop. When inactive, it shows a stick pin on its side.

To the right of the title bar are three small buttons for iconifying, maximizing, or closing the window. The button with a square maximizes the window, letting the window take up the entire screen. Clicking the Maximize button with the middle or right mouse button maximizes vertically or horizontally. The rightmost button showing an *x* is used to close the window.

The button with the Dot icon is used to iconify the icon. When you click it, the window is no longer displayed on the desktop, but its button entry remains in the taskbar on the panel.

Application windows may also display a Help Notes button, shown next to the iconify button and displaying a question mark. Clicking this button changes your cursor to a question mark. You can then move the cursor to an item such as an icon on a toolbar, then click it to display a small help note explaining what the item does. Clicking a Forward button in the file manager taskbar will show a note explaining that this button performs a browser forward operation.

When a window is not active, its contrast is reduced to make it easier for you to notice the active window.

As a multitasking operating system, Linux enables you to run several applications at the same time. This means you can have several applications open and running on your desktop, each with its own window. You can switch between them by moving from one window to another. When an application is open, a button for it is placed in the taskbar at the top of the desktop. You can switch to that application at any time by clicking its taskbar button. From the keyboard, you can use the ALT-TAB key combination to display a list of current applications. Holding down the ALT key and sequentially pressing TAB moves you through the list. You can hide an application at any time by clicking its window's Minimize button. The taskbar button entry for it remains. Click this to restore the application. Table 8-2 shows the KDE keyboard shortcuts.

Keys	Effect
ALT-ESC or CTRL-ESC	Current session manager with Logout button
ALT-TAB and ALT-SHIFT-TAB	Traverse the windows of the current desktop
CTRL-TAB and CTRL-SHIFT-TAB	Traverse the virtual desktops
ALT-F2	Open small command line window
ALT-F3	Window operation menu
ALT-F4	Close window
CTRL-F[1...8]	Switch to a particular virtual desktop
CTRL-ALT-ESC	Force shutdown of X Window System

Table 8-2. *KDE Keyboard Shortcuts*

Virtual Desktops: The KDE Desktop Pager

KDE, like most Linux window managers, supports virtual desktops. In effect, this extends the desktop area on which you can work. You could have Netscape running on one desktop and be using a text editor in another. KDE can support up to 16 virtual desktops, though the default is four. Your virtual desktops can be displayed and accessed using the KDE Desktop Pager located on the panel. The KDE Desktop Pager represents your virtual desktops as miniature screens showing small squares for each desktop. By default there are four squares, numbered 1, 2, 3, and 4.

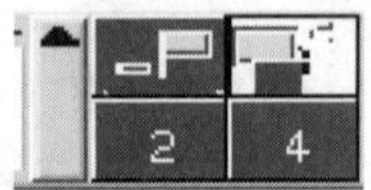

You can have up to 16. To move from one desktop to another, click the square for the destination desktop. Clicking 3 displays the third desktop, and clicking 1 moves you back to the first desktop.

Normally, when you open an application on a particular desktop, it appears only in that desktop. When you move to another desktop, the application disappears from your screen. Moving back again shows the application. For example, if you open KMail on the third desktop, and then move to the second desktop, KMail disappears from your screen. Moving back to the third desktop causes KMail to appear again. Selecting the taskbar button for an application also switches you to the desktop on which the application is open. In the example, clicking the KMail taskbar button switches to the third desktop. You can also use the Window list menu in the panel to display a listing of all open windows in each desktop. Selecting a window entry moves to that desktop. If you want an application to appear on all desktops, no matter which one you move to, click its window's Stick Pin button.

If you want to move a window to a different desktop, first open the window's menu by right-clicking the window's title bar. Then select the To Desktop entry, which lists the available desktops. Choose the one you want. You can also right-click the window's title bar to display the window's menu.

You can also configure KDE so that if you move the mouse over the edge of a desktop screen, it automatically moves to the adjoining desktop. You need to imagine the desktops arranged in a four-square configuration, with two top desktops next to each other and two desktops below them. You enable this feature by selecting the Active Desktop Borders entry in the Desktop panel in the KDE Control Center.

To change the number of virtual desktops, you use the KPanel configuration window. From the K Menu, select Panel and then Configure. On the KPanel configuration window, select the Desktop panel. You then see entries for the current desktops. The visible bar controls the number of desktops. Slide this to the right to add more and to the left to reduce the number. The width bar controls the width of the desktop buttons on the panel. You can change any of the desktop names by clicking a name and entering a new one.

You can also configure desktop features, such as color background, for each virtual desktop. In the K Menu, select Settings and then Desktop. From this menu, you can choose various features to change. Selecting Background displays a Display Settings window. A list of virtual desktops is then shown. Select the one whose background you want to change, and then you can choose from colors and wallpaper. You can select wallpaper from a preselected list or choose your own.

KDE Panel: Kicker

The KDE panel (Kicker), located at the bottom of the screen, provides access to most KDE functions.

The panel includes icons for menus, directory windows, specific programs, and virtual desktops. At the left end of the panel is an icon with a large *K* on a cog wheel, known as the K button. This is the button for the KDE Application Starter that opens the K Menu. Click this button to display the menu of applications you run (you can also open the K Menu by pressing ALT-F1). From the KDE menu, you can access numerous submenus for different kinds of applications. The menu also includes certain key items such as Logout, to log out out of KDE; Lock Screen, to lock your desktop; Configure Panel, to access your Kicker panel configuration options; Run, to run programs from a command line; Quick Browser, to quickly browse your home, KDE, or root directories; and Recent Documents, which lists your recently opened documents.

To add an application to the panel, select the Add entry in the Configure Panel submenu located in the K Menu. You can also right-click anywhere on the panel and select Add from the pop-up menu. The Add menu displays the kind of objects you can add, such as buttons, applets, extensions, and windows. For KDE applications, select the buttons entry. This lists all installed KDE applications. To add a button for an application to the panel, click the application entry. You can also drag applications from a file manager window or from the K menu to the panel directly and have them automatically placed in the panel. The panel only displays desktop files. When you drag and drop a file to the panel, a desktop file for it is automatically generated. Kicker also supports numerous applets and several extensions. Applets are designed to run as icons in the panel. These include a clock, pager, and system monitor. Extensions add components to your desktop. For example, the Kasbar extension sets up its own panel and list icons for each window you open. You can easily move from one window to another by clicking their corresponding icon in the Kasbar extension panel.

To configure the panel position and behavior, right-click the panel and select the Preferences entry. This displays a Panel Configuration dialog box with several tabbed panels: Position, Hiding, Look and Feel, Menus, Buttons, and Applets. The Position panel enables you to specify the edges of the screen where you want your panel and taskbar displayed. You can also enlarge or reduce it in size. On the Look and Feel panel, you can set a background theme. The Menus panel lets you control the size of your menus as well as whether to display recently opened documents as menu items. On the Buttons panel, you can have panel buttons display their background tiles, making each button more distinctive. The Applets panel lets you load only trusted applets or all available applets. Below each panel are buttons that you can use to restore the panel to its original settings (Default) or to its previous settings (Reset). You activate your settings either immediately with the Apply button or when you close the configuration window (OK).

You can add or remove menu items in your K Menu using the Edit Menus program. Right-click its *K* icon and select Configure. This launches the Edit Menus window, displaying two panes. The right pane shows the menu entries, and the left shows information about a selected entry. The right pane has two tabbed panels: General and Advanced. The General pane fields are where the features such as application program, the menu item name, and the icon used are specified. You can edit any of these entries. You can also specify if you want the program opened in a terminal window. On the Advanced panel you can select a keyboard shortcut for the program. To create a new menu entry, you select New in the File menu. You can also move, copy, and delete menu entries.

KDE Themes

For your desktop, you can select a variety of different themes. A *theme* changes the look and feel of your desktop, affecting the appearance of GUI elements, such as scroll bars, buttons, and icons. For example, you use the Mac OS theme to make your K Desktop look like a Macintosh. Themes for the K Desktop can be downloaded from the **kde.themes.org** Web site. Information and links for themes for different window managers can be found at **www.themes.org**. You can use the KthemeMgr program to install and change your themes.

The KDE Help System

The KDE Help viewer provides a browser-like interface for accessing and displaying both KDE Help files and Linux Man and info files. You can start the Help system either by selecting its entry in the K Menu, clicking on the Help icon in the Panel (life-preserver), or by right-clicking the desktop and selecting the Help entry. The Help window is divided into two frames. The left frame of the Help screen holds two tabbed panels, one listing contents and the other providing a search engine. The left frame displays currently selected documents. A help tree on the content's panel lets you choose the kind of Help documents you want to access. Here you can choose manuals, Man pages, or info documents. The Help Center includes a detailed user manual, a FAQ, and KDE Web site access.

You can also use a URL format to access Man and info pages, **`info:`** and **`man:`**. For example, **`man:cp`** displays the Man page for the **`cp`** command. A navigation toolbar enables you to move through previously viewed documents. KDE Help documents use an HTML format with links you can click to access other documents. The Back and Forward commands move you through the list of previously viewed documents. The KDE Help system provides an effective search tool for searching for patterns in Help documents, including Man and info pages. Select the Search entry to display a page where you can enter your pattern. You can also click the small icon in the toolbar of a page with a spyglass.

Applications

You can start an application in KDE in several ways. If an entry for it is in the K Menu, you can select that entry to start the application. Some applications also have buttons on the KDE panel you can click to start them. The panel already holds several of the commonly used programs, such as the Kate text editor and KMail. You can also use the file manager to locate a file using that application or the application program itself. Clicking its icon starts the application. Or you can open a shell window and enter the name of the application at the shell prompt and press ENTER to start an application. You can also press ALT-F2 to open a small window consisting of a box to enter a single command. You can use the UP ARROW and DOWN ARROW keys to display previous commands, and the RIGHT ARROW and LEFT ARROW keys or the BACKSPACE key to edit any of them. Press ENTER to execute a command.

Note *You can create a desktop file on your desktop for any application already on your KDE menu by simply clicking and dragging its menu entry to the desktop. Select Copy and a desktop file for that application is created for you on your desktop, showing its icon.*

You can also access applications directly from your desktop. To access an application from the desktop, either create a desktop file or a standard link file that can link to the original application program. With a desktop file, you can choose your own icon and specify a ToolTip comment. You can also use a desktop file to start a shell-based application running in its own terminal window. A standard link, on the other hand, is a simple reference to the original program file. Using a link starts the program up directly with no arguments. To create a standard link file, locate the application on your file system, usually in the **/bin**, **/usr/bin**, or **/usr/sbin** directories. Then click and drag the application icon to your desktop. In the pop-up menu, select Link. The link has the same icon as the original application. Whenever you then click that icon, you can select Start from the pop-up menu to start the application. You can also use this method to run an application program you have created yourself, locating it in your own directory and creating a link for it on your desktop.

To create a new desktop file for an application, right-click anywhere on the empty desktop, select Create New from the pop-up menu, and then choose Link To Application. Enter the name for the program and a desktop file for it appears on the desktop with that name. A Properties dialog box then opens with four panels: General, Permissions, Execute, and Application. The General panel displays the name of the link. To specify the application the desktop file runs, go to the Execute panel and either enter the application's program name in the Execute box or click Browse to select it. If this is a shell program, you can elect to run it from within a terminal window. To select an icon image for the desktop file, click the Cog icon. The Select Icon window is displayed, listing icons from which you can choose. To run a shell-based program such as Pine or Vi, click the Run In Terminal check box and specify any terminal options. Certain KDE programs can minimize to a small icon, which can be displayed in the panel while they are running. This is referred to as *swallowing on the panel.* Enter the name of the program in the Execute box.

On the Permissions panel, be sure to set execute permissions so that the program can be run. You can set permissions for yourself, for your group, or for any user on the system. In the Application panel, you can specify the type of documents to be associated with this application. The bottom of the panel shows two lists. The left list is for MIME types you want associated with this program, and the right list is the listing of available MIME types from which to choose. To add a MIME type, select an entry in the right list and click the left arrow button. Use the right arrow button to remove a MIME type. On the panel, you also specify the comment, the file manager program name, and the name in your language. The comment is the Help note that appears when you pass your mouse over the icon. For the file manager program name, enter the name followed by a semicolon. This is the name used for the link, if you use the file manager to display it. Desktop files needn't reside on the desktop. You can place them in any directory and access them through the file manager. You can later make changes to a desktop file by right-clicking its icon and selecting Properties from the pop-up menu. This again displays the dialog box for this file. You can change its icon and even the application it runs. You can download other icons from **icons.themes.org**.

You can have KDE automatically display selected directories or start certain applications whenever it starts up. To do so, place links for these windows and applications in the **AutoStart** directory, located in your **.kde** directory. To place a link for a directory in the AutoStart folder, first locate the Directory icon using the file manager. Then click and drag the icon to the AutoStart folder. From the pop-up menu that appears, select Link (do not select Copy or Move). Whenever you start KDE, that directory is displayed in a file manager window. You can do the same for applications and files. Locate the application with the file manager and click and drag it to the AutoStart folder, selecting Link. For a file, do the same. Whenever KDE starts, those applications automatically start. For files, the application associated with a file starts using that file. For example, to start KMail automatically, click and drag its icon to the AutoStart folder, selecting Link.

Mounting CD-ROMs and Floppy Disks from the Desktop

Desktop icons are created for your CD-ROMs and floppies when your distribution installed KDE. Floppy and CD-ROM icons are displayed on the left side of your KDE desktop. To access a CD-ROM disk, place the CD-ROM disk in your CD-ROM drive and click the CD-ROM icon. The file manager window then opens, displaying the contents of the CD-ROM's top-level directory. You can also right-click the icon to display a pop-up menu with an entry to mount or unmount the disk. When the CD-ROM holds a mounted CD disk, the CD-ROM icon displays a small red rectangle on its image. Unlike on Windows systems, the CD-ROM disk remains locked in the CD-ROM drive until you unlock it. To unmount the CD, right-click the CD-ROM's icon and select Unmount from the pop-up menu. You can then open the CD-ROM drive and remove the CD.

To access a floppy disk, you can perform a similar operation using the Floppy Disk icon. Place the floppy disk in the disk drive and click the Floppy Disk icon. This displays a file manager window with the contents of the floppy disk. Alternatively, you can right-click the icon to display a pop-up menu with an entry to mount the disk. Once it is mounted, you can access it, copying files to and from the disk. Be careful not to remove the disk unless you first unmount it. To unmount the disk, right-click its icon and select Unmount from the icon's pop-up menu. You can perform one added operation with floppy disks. If you put in a blank disk, you can format it. You can choose from several file system formats, including MS-DOS. To format a standard Linux file system, select the ext3 entry.

A desktop file you use for your CD-ROM is a special kind of desktop file designed for file system devices. If you add a new CD-ROM or floppy drive, you can create a new desktop file for it to enable you to access the drive from your desktop. To create one, first right-click anywhere on the desktop, select New, and then select either CD-ROM Device for a CD-ROM drive or Floppy Device for a floppy drive. This opens a Properties window with tabs for General, Permissions, and Device. In the General tab you can set the name for the device icon that will appear on the desktop as well as choose the icon you want to show for a mounted CD-ROM or floppy disk (a default is already provided). On the Device panel, you select the actual device, its mount point on your file system, and the type of file system it will mount, as well as the icon used to indicate when it is unmounted. On the Permissions panel, you can also indicate the permissions that have been set to allow access to the device. See the chapter on file administration, Chapter 29, for a discussion on devices and file systems. The desktop file does not perform the necessary system administration operations that enable access to the CD-ROM by ordinary users. Normally, only the systems administrator (root user) can mount or unmount CD-ROMs and floppy disks. You also must make sure an entry is in the **/etc/fstab** file for the CD-ROM or floppy drive. If not, you have to add one. Check Chapter 4 and Chapter 29 for the procedures to use.

KDE File Manager and Internet Client: Konqueror

The KDE file manager is a multifunctional utility with which you can manage files, start programs, browse the Web, and download files from remote sites (see Figure 8-3). Traditionally, the term "file manager" was used to refer to managing files on a local hard disk. The KDE file manager extends its functionality well beyond this traditional function because it is Internet capable, seamlessly displaying remote file systems as if they were your own, as well as viewing Web pages with browser capabilities. It is capable of displaying a multitude of different kinds of files, including image, postscript, and text files. KOffice applications can be run within the Konqueror window.

Note *With KDE 2.2, the original KDE file manager, kfm, was replaced by a new file manager called Konqueror.*

A KDE file manager window consists of a menu bar, a navigation toolbar, a location field, a status bar, and a sidebar that provides different views of user resources such as a tree view of file and directory icons for your home directory. When you first display the file manager window, it displays the file and subdirectory icons for your home directory. Files and directories are automatically refreshed. So if you add or remove

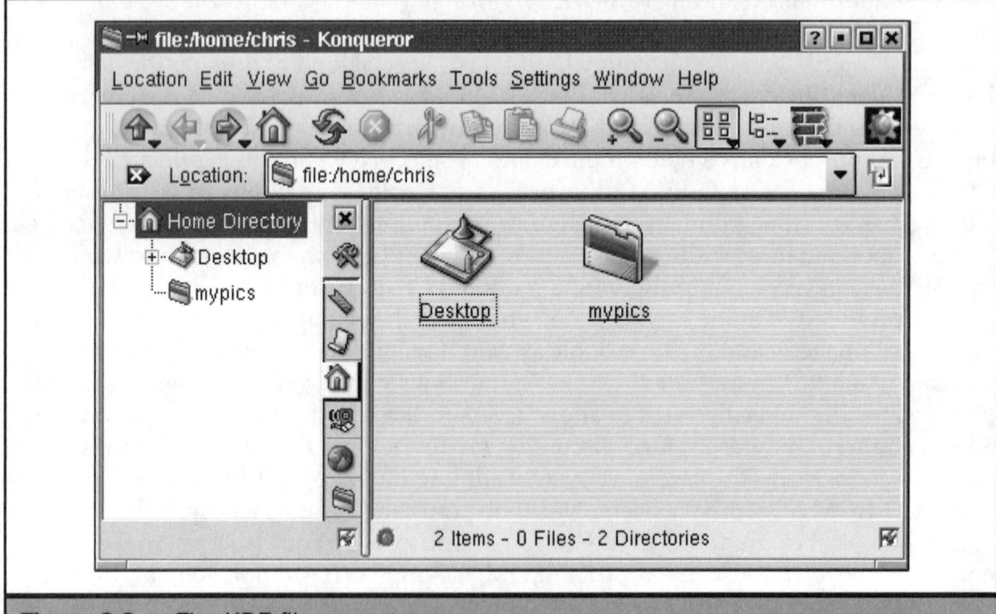

Figure 8-3. *The KDE file manager*

directories, you do not have to manually refresh the file manager window. It automatically updates for you, showing added files or eliminating deleted ones. The files listed in a directory can be viewed in several different ways. You can view files and directories as icons, small icons, or in a detailed listing. The detailed listing provides permissions, owner, group, and size information. Permissions are the permissions controlling access to this file (see Chapter 11). Configuration files are not usually displayed. These are files beginning with a period and are often referred to as *dot files*. To have the file manager display these files, select Show Dot Files from the View menu. Konqueror includes KSSL which provides full SSL support for secure connections. KDE Version 3.1 will feature a secure connection status display.

The sidebar lists different resources that a user can access with Konqueror. The sidebar has both a classic and extended version. You can select which one to use from the Window menu. In the classic version, resources such as file manager history, bookmarks, and your home directory are listed in an expandable tree. Click on an entry to expand it. Double-click on it to access it with Konqueror. For example, to move to a subdirectory, expand your home directory entry and then double-click on the subdirectory you want. Konqueror will now display that subdirectory. To go to a previously bookmarked directory or Web page, find its entry in the Bookmarks listing and select it.

Note *With 3.0, Konqueror also provides a sidebar media player for running selected media files within your file manager window.*

The extended sidebar features a vertical button bar for displaying items such as your file manager history, home directory, bookmarks, and network resources. The history button lists the network resources and directories you have accessed, including Web pages. The network button lists network resources you have access to, such as FTP and Web sites. The folder button displays your system's root directory. If multiple views is enabled, you can display several of these at once, just by clicking the ones you want. If multiple views is not enabled, the previous listing is replaced by the selected one. Turn off a display by clicking its button again. The last button is a classic sidebar button which will display all of the resources in an expandable tree, like the classic sidebar does.

To configure the extended sidebar, click on its configure button in the sidebar button bar. Select the Multiple Views entry to allow the display of several resource listings at once, each in their separate sub-sidebar. You can also add a new resource listing, choosing from a bookmark, history, or directory type. A button will appear for the new listing. You can right-click on the button to select a new icon for it or select a URL, either a directory pathname or a network address. To remove a button and its listing, right-click on it and select the Remove entry.

To search for files, select the Find entry in the Tools menu or click on the Looking Glass icon. This opens a pane within the file manager window in which you can search for filenames using wildcard matching symbols, such as `*`. Click the Find button to run the search and on the Stop button to stop it. The search results are displayed in a pane in the lower half of the file manager window. You can click a file and have it open with its appropriate application. Text files are displayed by the Kate text editor. Images are displayed by KView, and postscript files by KGhostview. Applications are run. The search program also enables you to save your search results for later reference. You can even select files from the search and add them to an archive.

You can open a file either by clicking it, or by selecting it and then choosing the Open entry in the File menu. A single-click, not a double-click, opens the file. If you want to select the file or directory, you need to hold down the CTRL key while you click it. A selection is performed with a CTRL-click. If the file is a program, that program starts up. If it is a data file, such as a text file, the associated application is run using that data file. For example, if you click a text file, the Kate application starts displaying that file. If Konqueror cannot determine the application to use, it opens a dialog box prompting you to enter the application name. You can click the Browse button on this box to use a directory tree to locate the application program you want.

The file manager can also extract tar archives and install RPM packages. An *archive* is a file ending in **.tar.gz**, **.tar**, or **.tgz**. Clicking the archive lists the files in it. You can extract a particular file simply by dragging it out the window. Clicking a text file in the archive displays it with Kate, while clicking an image file displays it with KView. Selecting an RPM package opens it with the kpackage utility, which you can then use to install the package.

Moving Through the File System

A single-click on a directory icon moves to that directory and displays its file and subdirectory icons. Unlike other interfaces, KDE does not use double-clicking to open a directory. To move back up to the parent directory, you click the up arrow button located on the left end of the navigation toolbar. A single-click on a directory icon moves you down the directory tree, one directory at a time. By clicking the up arrow button, you move up the tree. To move directly to a specific directory, you can enter its pathname in the Location box located just above the pane that displays the file and directory icons. Figure 8-3 shows the KDE file manager window displaying the current directory. You can also use several keyboard shortcuts to perform such operations, as listed in Table 8-3.

Like a Web browser, the file manager remembers the previous directories it has displayed. You can use the back and forward arrow buttons to move through this list of prior directories. For example, a user could use the Location field to move to the **~/birthday** directory and use it again to move to the **~/reports** directory. Clicking the back arrow button displays the **~/birthday** directory (the ~ represents the user's home directory). Clicking the forward arrow button moves it back to the **~/reports** directory. You can move directly to your home directory by clicking the Home button. This has the same effect as the `cd` command in the shell.

If you know you want to access particular directories again, you can bookmark them, much as you do a Web page. Just open the directory and select the Add Bookmarks

Keys	Description
ALT-LEFT ARROW	Back in History
ALT-RIGHT ARROW	Forward in History
ALT-UP ARROW	One directory up
ENTER	Open a file/directory
ESC	Open a pop-up menu for the current file
LEFT/RIGHT/UP/DOWN ARROWS	Move among the icons
SPACEBAR	Select/unselect file
PAGE UP	Scroll up fast
PAGE DOWN	Scroll down fast
RIGHT ARROW	Scroll right (on Web pages)
LEFT ARROW	Scroll left (on Web pages)
UP ARROW	Scroll up (on Web pages)
DOWN ARROW	Scroll down (on Web pages)
CTRL-C	Copy selected file to clipboard
CTRL-V	Paste files from clipboard to current directory
CTRL-S	Select files by pattern
CTRL-T	Open a terminal in the current directory
CTRL-L	Open new location
CTRL-F	Find files
CTRL-W	Close window

Table 8-3. *KDE File Manager Keyboard Shortcuts*

entry in the Bookmarks menu. An entry for that directory is then placed in the file manager's Bookmark menu. To move to the directory again, select its entry in the Bookmark menu. This is helpful for directories you might use frequently or for directories you must access with lengthy or complex pathnames. Bookmarks also apply to individual files and applications. You can even bookmark desktop icons. To bookmark a file, first select a file and then choose the Add Bookmarks entry in the

Bookmark menu. Later, selecting that bookmark opens that file. You can do the same thing with applications, where selecting the application's bookmark starts the application. Each bookmark is a file placed in your **.kde2/share/apps/konqueror/bookmarks** directory (kfm instead of Konqueror if you are upgrading from KDE 1.0). You can go to this directory and change the names of any of the files, and they then appear as changed on your Bookmark menu. To change their names, right-click the file and select Properties from the pop-up menu. In the dialog box displayed, you see the filename is the full pathname on the General tab. You can replace the pathname with one of your own choosing. This bookmark would then appear as **myreport**. The pathname used to access the file is actually on the URL panel.

To help you navigate from one directory to another, you can use the Location field or the directory tree. In the Location field, you can enter the pathname of a directory, if you know it, and press ENTER. The file manager then displays that directory. The directory tree provides a tree listing all directories on your system and in your home directory. You can activate the directory tree by selecting the Show Tree entry in the View menu. The directory tree has three main entries: Root, My Home, and Desktop. The Root entry displays the directories starting from the system root directory, the My Home entry displays directories starting from your home directory, and the Desktop entry displays the files and links on your desktop. Click a side triangle to expand a directory entry, and click a down triangle of an expanded directory entry to hide it.

Internet Access

The KDE file manager doubles as a Web browser and an FTP client. It includes a box for entering either a pathname for a local file or a URL for a Web page on the Internet or your intranet. A navigation toolbar can be used to display previous Web pages or previous directories. The Home button will always return you to your home directory. When accessing a Web page, the page is displayed as on any Web browser. With the navigation toolbar, you can move back and forth through the list of previously displayed pages in that session. This feature is particularly convenient for displaying local Web pages, such as documentation in HTML format. Most Linux distributions provide extensive documentation in the form of Web pages you can easily access and display using a KDE file manager window.

The KDE file manager also operates as an FTP client. When you access an FTP site, you navigate the remote directories as you would your own. The operations to download a file are the same as copying a file on your local system. Just select the file's icon or entry in the file manager window and drag it to a window showing the local directory to which you want it downloaded. Then, select the Copy entry from the pop-up menu that appears.

By default, KDE attempts an anonymous login. If you want to perform a non-anonymous login as a particular user, add the username with an @ symbol before the FTP address. You are then prompted for the user password. For example, the following entry logs in to the **ftp.mygames.com** server as the user **chris**:

```
ftp://chris@ftp.mygames.com
```

Copy, Move, Delete, and Archive Operations

To perform an operation on a file or directory, you first have to select it. In KDE, to select a file or directory, you hold the CTRL key down while clicking the file's icon or listing. To select more than one file, continue to hold the CTRL key down while you click the files you want. You can also use the keyboard arrow keys to move from one file icon to another and then use the SPACEBAR to select the file you want.

To copy and move files, you can use the standard drag-and-drop method with your mouse. To copy a file, you locate it by using the file manager. Open another file manager window to the directory to which you want the file copied. Then click and drag the File icon to that window. A pop-up menu appears with selections for Move, Copy, or Link. Choose Copy. To move a file to another directory, follow the same procedure, but select Move from the pop-up menu. To copy or move a directory, use the same procedure as for files. All the directory's files and subdirectories are also copied or moved.

You can also move or copy files using the Copy and Paste commands. First, use CTRL-click to select a file or directory (hold the CTRL key down while clicking the File icon). Either select the Copy entry from the Edit menu or click the Copy button in the navigation bar. Change to the directory to which you want to copy the selected file. Then either select Paste from the Edit menu or click the Paste button. Follow the same procedure for moving files, using the Move entry from the Edit menu or the Move button in the navigation toolbar. Most of the basic file manager operations can be selected from a pop-up menu displayed whenever you right-click a file or directory. Here, you can find entries for copying, moving, and deleting the file, as well as navigating to a different directory.

Distinguishing between a copy of a file or directory and a link is important. A *copy* creates a duplicate, whereas a *link* is just another name for the same item. Links are used extensively as ways of providing different access points to the same document. If you want to access a file using an icon on your desktop, creating a link on the desktop (rather than a copy) is best. With a copy, you have two different documents, whereas with a link you are accessing and changing the same document. To create a link on your desktop, click and drag the File icon from the directory window to the desktop and select Link from the pop-up menu. Clicking the link brings up the original document. Deleting the link only removes the link, not the original document. You can create links for directories or applications using the same procedure. You can also place links in a directory: click and drag the files you want to link to in that directory and select Link from the pop-up menu.

You delete a file by removing it immediately or placing it in a Trash folder to delete later. To delete a file, select it and then choose the Delete entry in the Edit menu. You can also right-click the icon and select Delete. To place a file in the Trash folder, click and drag it to the Trash icon on your desktop or select Move To Trash from the Edit menu. You can later open the Trash folder and delete the files. To delete all the files in the Trash folder, right-click the Trash icon and select Empty Trash Bin from the pop-up menu. To restore any files in the Trash bin, open the Trash bin and drag them out of the Trash folder.

Each file or directory has properties associated with it that include permissions, the filename, and its directory. To display the Properties window for a given file, right-click the file's icon and select the Properties entry. On the General panel, you see the name of the file displayed. To change the file's name, replace the name there with a new one. Permissions are set on the Permissions panel. Here, you can set read, write, and execute permissions for user, group, or other access to the file. See Chapter 11 for a discussion of permissions. The Group entry enables you to change the group for a file.

.directory

KDE automatically searches for and reads an existing **.directory** file located in a directory. A **.directory** file holds KDE configuration information used to determine how the directory is displayed. You can create such a file in a directory and place a setting in it to set display features, such as the icon to use to display the directory folder.

KDE Configuration: KDE Control Center

With the KDE Control Center, you can configure your desktop and system, changing the way it is displayed and the features it supports (see Figure 8-4). You can open the Control Center directly to a selected component by selecting its entry in the K Menu Preferences menu. The Preferences menu displays a submenu listing the configuration categories. Select a category, and then select the component you want. For example, to configure your screen saver, select the Screensaver entry in the Look & Feel menu located in the Settings menu. The Control Center can be directly started by either clicking the Control Center icon in the panel or selecting Control Center from the K Menu.

The Control Center window is divided into two panes. The left pane shows a tree view of all the components you can configure and the right pane displays the dialog windows for a selected component. On the left pane, components are arranged into categories whose titles you can expand or shrink. The Web Browsing heading holds entries for configuring the KDE file manager's Web browser features. Under Look & Feel, you can set different features for displaying and controlling your desktop. For example, the Background entry enables you to select a different background color or image for each one of your virtual desktops. Other entries enable you to configure components such as the screen saver, the language used, and the window style. Some entries enable you to configure your mouse, key mappings, network connections, sound events, and window components. You can change key bindings for any of the window operations or standard operations, such as cut and paste. You can also change any of the specialize key mappings, such as ALT-TAB, which moves through your open

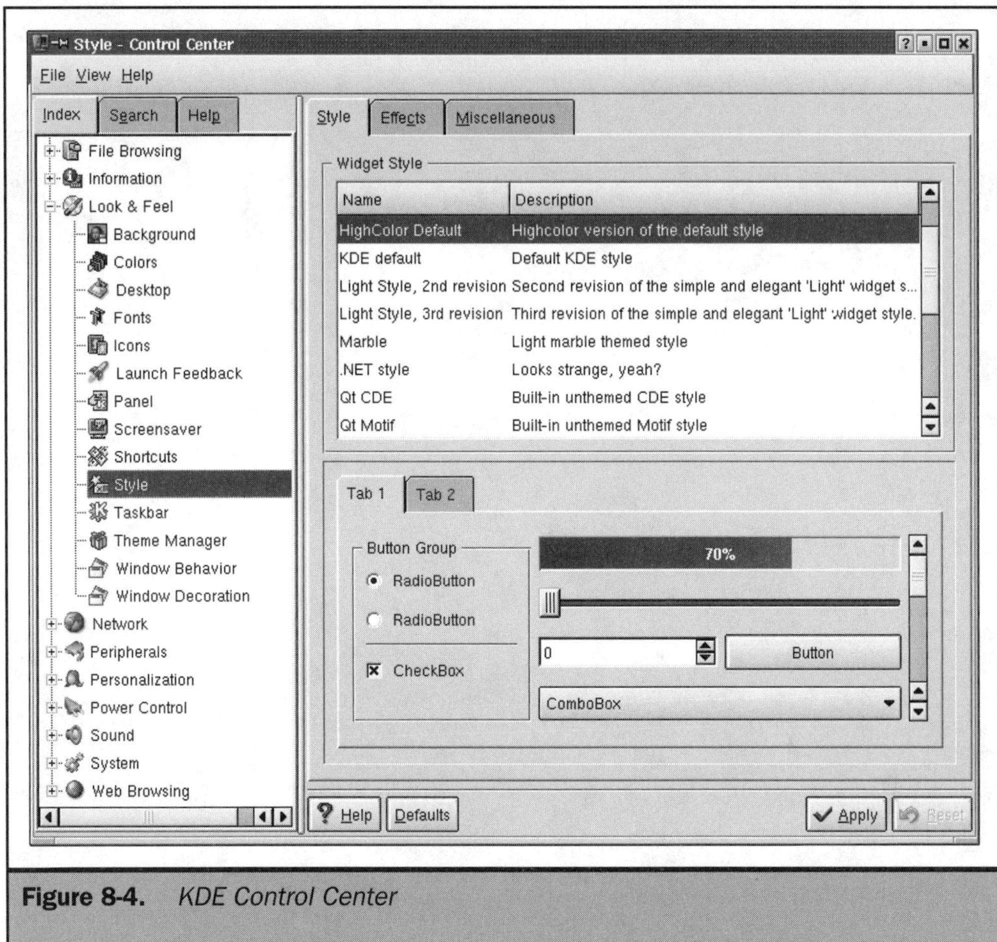

Figure 8-4. *KDE Control Center*

applications; CTRL-TAB, which moves through your virtual desktops; or ALT-f2, which displays a dialog box for executing commands. Configuration components are actually modules. In future releases, more modules will be included as more applications and tools are added to the K Desktop. See the Help viewer for a current listing of K Desktop configuration modules.

Chapter 9

Gnome

The GNU Network Object Model Environment, also known as *Gnome,* is a powerful and easy-to-use environment consisting primarily of a panel, a desktop, and a set of GUI tools with which program interfaces can be constructed. Gnome is designed to provide a flexible platform for the development of powerful applications. Currently, Gnome is strongly supported by several distributions and is the primary interface for Red Hat and Mandrake. Gnome is completely free under the GNU Public License. You can obtain the source directly, as well as documentation and other Gnome software, from the Gnome Web site at **www.gnome.org**. Several companies have joined together to form the Gnome Foundation, an organization dedicated to coordinating the development of Gnome and Gnome software applications. These include such companies as Sun, IBM, and Hewlett-Packard as well as Linux distributors such as Mandrake, Red Hat, Caldera, and TurboLinux, along with Gnome developers such as Ximian. Modeled on the Apache Foundation, which developed the Apache Web server, the Gnome Foundation will provide direction to Gnome development as well as organization, financial, and legal support. Recently, Sun announced that it was adopting Gnome as the desktop interface for its Solaris operating system, replacing the Motif-based Common Desktop Environment (CDE).

The core components of the Gnome desktop consist of a panel for starting programs and desktop functionality. Other components normally found in a desktop, such as a file manager, Web browser, and window manager, are provided by Gnome-compliant applications. Gnome provides libraries of Gnome GUI tools that developers can use to create Gnome applications. Programs that use buttons, menus, and windows that adhere to a Gnome standard can be said to be Gnome-compliant. For a file manager, the Gnome desktop uses Nautilus, originally developed by Eazel. The Gnome desktop does not have its own window manager as KDE does. Instead, it uses any Gnome-compliant window manager. The Sawfish window manager is the one bundled with the Gnome distributions.

Support for component model interfaces is integrated into Gnome, allowing software components to interconnect regardless of the computer language in which they are implemented or the kind of machine on which they are running. The standard used in Gnome for such interfaces is the Common Object Request Broker Architecture (CORBA), developed by the Object Model Group for use on Unix systems. Gnome uses the ORBit implementation of CORBA. With such a framework, Gnome applications and clients can directly communicate with each other, enabling you to use components of one application in another. With Gnome 2.0, Gnome officially adopted GConf and its libraries as the underlying method for configuring Gnome and its applications. GConf can configure independently coordinating programs such as those that make up the Nautilus file manager.

You can find out more about Gnome at its Web site at **www.gnome.org**. This site not only provides a detailed software map of current Gnome projects with links to their development sites, it also maintains extensive mailing lists for Gnome projects to which you can subscribe. The Web site provides online documentation, such as the Gnome User's Guide and FAQs. If you want to develop Gnome programs, check the Gnome developer's Web site at **developer.gnome.org.** The site provides tutorials, programming guides, and development tools. Here you can find the complete API reference manual online, as well as extensive support tools such as tutorials and Interactive Development Environments (IDE). The site also includes detailed online documentation for the GTK+ library, Gnome widgets, and the Gnome desktop.

With Gnome 1.4, the Nautilus file manager officially replaced the Gnome version of GNU Midnight Commander used on previous Gnome releases. Nautilus is designed to operate as a desktop shell that can support numerous components, letting you operate a Web browser within it or decompress files. Originally developed by Eazel, Nautilus development is now being carried on independently. You can download the Nautilus source from the Gnome CVS depository or from **www.ximian.com**. You can find out more about Nautilus from the Nautilus user's manual that is part of the Gnome User's Guide at **www.gnome.org**.

With Gnome 2.0, Gnome has been rewritten to work on the new GTK+ 2.0 graphics library. Gnome 2.0 now supports anti-aliasing fonts as well as more efficient GUI execution. Gnome 2.0 also includes Pango for International language support, and the Accessibility Toolkit (ATK) that provides easier interaction by those with disabilities.

Note *An enhanced version of Gnome known as Ximian Gnome can be downloaded from Ximian at* ***www.ximian.com****. There are versions for most distributions.*

GTK+

GTK+ is the widget set used for Gnome applications. Its look and feel was originally derived from Motif. The widget set is designed from the ground up for power and flexibility. For example, buttons can have labels, images, or any combination thereof. Objects can be dynamically queried and modified at runtime. It also includes a theme engine that enables users to change the look and feel of applications using these widgets. At the same time, the GTK+ widget set remains small and efficient.

The GTK+ widget set is entirely free under the Library General Public License (LGPL). The LGPL enables developers to use the widget set with proprietary software, as well as free software (GPL would restrict it to just free software). The widget set also features an extensive set of programming language bindings, including C++, Perl, Python, Pascal, Objective C, Guile, and Ada. Internalization is fully supported, permitting GTK+-based applications to be used with other character sets, such as those in Asian languages. The drag-and-drop functionality supports both Xdnd and Motif protocols, allowing drag-and-drop operations with other widget sets that support these protocols, such as Qt and Motif.

The Gnome Interface

The Gnome interface consists of the panel and a desktop, as shown in Figure 9-1. The panel appears as a long bar across the bottom of the screen. It holds menus, programs,

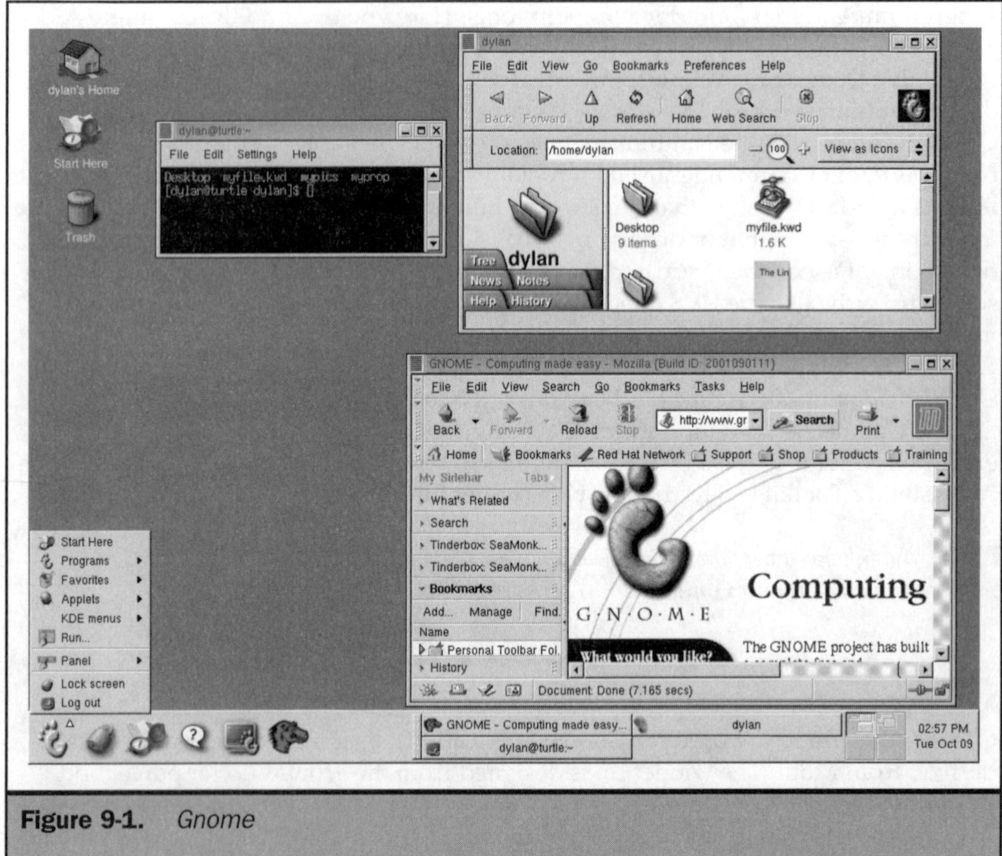

Figure 9-1. *Gnome*

and applets. An *applet* is a small program designed to be run within the panel. On the panel is a button with a large footprint on it. This is the Gnome applications menu, the main menu. The menu operates like the Start menu in Windows, listing entries for applications you can run on your desktop. You can display panels horizontally or vertically, and have them automatically hide to show you a full screen.

The remainder of the screen is the desktop. Here, you can place directories, files, or programs. You can create them on the desktop directly or drag them from a file manager window. A click-and-drag operation with the middle mouse button (two buttons at once on a two-button mouse) enables you to create links on the desktop to installed programs. Initially, the desktop only holds an icon for your home directory. Clicking it opens a file manager window to that directory. A right-click anywhere on the desktop displays a desktop menu (see Table 9-1) with which you can open new windows, create new folders, and mount floppy disks and CD-ROMs.

From a user's point of view, you can think of the Gnome interface as having four components: the desktop, the panel, the main menu, and the file manager. In its standard default configuration, the Gnome desktop displays a Folder icon for your home directory in the upper-left corner. Some distributions may include other icons, such as links to the Gnome Web site or to the Linux documentation site. Initially, a file manager window opens on the desktop, displaying your home directory. The panel has several default icons: The main menu (footprint), a screen lock feature (padlock), the terminal program (monitor), the Gnome Help System (question mark), the Start Here window (pocket compass), the Gnome pager (squares), and a clock. Many distributions will also include Mozilla.

To start a program, you can select its entry in the main menu, click its application launcher button in the panel (if there is one), double-click its icon in either the desktop or the file manager window, drag a data file to its icon, or select the Run Program entry in the main menu. This opens a small window where you can type in the program name.

When you first start Gnome, the Start Here window is displayed. From here you can access your favorite Web sites and files (Favorites), select and run applications (Programs), customize your Gnome desktop (Preferences), and perform administrative tasks for both your system and your servers (Server Configuration and System Settings). Double-clicking an icon opens a window listing icons for subwindows or tools. In effect, the Start Here window is mimicking the main menu. You can select and run applications from the Start Here's Program window, just as you can from the main menu's Program menu. The Preferences window lists Gnome configuration tools (capplets) for setting up your Gnome preferences. In effect, it replaces the Gnome Control Center window used in previous versions. See the Gnome Configuration section for more details. If you need to configure administrative tasks such as setting up network connections or managing servers, you can choose the Server configuration or System settings windows. Most of those tools are accessible only by the root user.

To quit Gnome, you select the Logout entry in the main menu or click the terminal icon displaying the moon (on Ximian Gnome, you choose the Logout entry in the menu panel's System menu). You can also add a Logout button to the panel, which you could use instead. To add the Logout button, right-click the panel and select the Add Logout Button entry. A Logout button then appears in the panel. When you log out, the Logout dialog box is displayed. You have three options. The first option, Logout, quits Gnome, returning you to the login window (or command line shell still logged in to your Linux account, if you started Gnome with **startx**). The second option, Halt, not only quits Gnome, but also shuts down your entire system. The third option, the Reboot entry, shuts down and reboots your system. The Logout entry is selected by default. Halt and Reboot are only available to the root user. If normal users execute them, they are prompted to enter the root user password to shut down. You can also elect to retain your desktop by clicking the Save Current Setup check box. This reopens any programs or directories left open when you logged out. Gnome-compliant window managers also quit when you log out of Gnome. You then must separately quit a window manager that is not Gnome-compliant after logging out of Gnome.

The Gnome Help system provides a browser-like interface for displaying the Gnome user's manual, Man pages, and info documents. It features a toolbar that enables you to move through the list of previously viewed documents. You can even bookmark specific items. A Web page interface enables you to use links to connect to different documents. You can easily move the manual or the list of Man pages and info documents. You can place entries in the location box to access specific documents directly. Special URL-like protocols are supported for the different types of documents: **ghelp**, for Gnome help; **man**, for man pages; and **info**, for the info documents.

The Gnome Desktop

The Gnome desktop provides you with all the capabilities of GUI-based operating systems (see Figure 9-1). You can drag files, applications, and directories to the desktop, and then back to Gnome-compliant applications. If the desktop stops functioning, you can restart it by starting the Gnome file manager (Nautilus). The desktop is actually a backend process in the Gnome file manager. But you needn't have the file manager open to use the desktop. The Gnome 1.4 desktop with Nautilus is described in this section.

Although the Gnome desktop supports drag-and-drop operations, these work only for applications that are Gnome-compliant. You can drag any items from a Gnome-compliant application to your desktop, and vice versa. Any icon for an item that you drag from a file manager window to the desktop also appears on the desktop. However, the default drag-and-drop operation is a **move** operation. If you select a file in your file manager window and drag it to the desktop, you are actually moving the file from its current directory to the Gnome desktop directory, which is located in your home directory and holds all items on the desktop (notice this is a dot file). For Gnome, the desktop directory is **.gnome-desktop**. In the case of dragging directory folders to the desktop, the entire directory and its subdirectories would be copied to the Gnome desktop directory.

In most cases, you only want to create on the desktop another way to access a file without moving it from its original directory. You can do this by creating a link or a program launcher, instead of moving the file. To create a link, click and drag the file while holding down the SHIFT key. A copy of the icon then appears with a small arrow in the right corner indicating it is a link. You can click this link to start the program, open the file, or open the directory, depending on what kind of file you linked to.

You can use that icon to access the item directly. This is often used for starting common programs. For example, you can SHIFT-click and drag the Netscape icon to the desktop to create a Link icon for Netscape. Double-clicking the icon starts Netscape. You can do the same with files. In this case, their respective program is started. If the item is a directory, the file manager starts up opened to that directory. If you want to have an application placed on your desktop that is not Gnome-compliant, you can manually place a link in your home directory's Gnome desktop directory.

You can also copy a file to your desktop by clicking and dragging it from a file manager window to your desktop, and then pressing the CTRL key before you release the left mouse button. You will see the small arrow in the upper-right corner of the copied icon change to a + symbol, indicating that you are creating a copy instead of a link.

As an alternative to the desktop, you can drag any program, file, or directory to the panel; a launcher applet is then automatically created for it on the panel. The item is not moved or copied. You can also right-click anywhere on the empty desktop to display a menu. You will notice entries for a New Folder. Remember, this entry creates a new directory on your desktop, specifically in your Gnome desktop directory. The entries for this menu are listed in Table 9-1.

The desktop also displays icons for any drives you have mounted, such as a CD-ROM or floppy drives, provided they are user-mountable. Nautilus automatically mounts CD-ROMs when you insert them into your CD-ROM drive, displaying the CD-ROM icon and opening a Nautilus window displaying the CD-ROM's contents.

You can manually mount a CD-ROM or floppy disk by right-clicking anywhere on the desktop to display the desktop menu and then selecting the CD-ROM or Floppy entry in the Disks menu. An icon for that device will appear with the name of the CD-ROM or floppy disk. You can then access the disk in the CD-ROM drive either by double-clicking it or right-clicking and selecting the Open entry. A file manager window opens to display the contents of the CD-ROM disk. To unmount a CD-ROM, right-click the CD-ROM icon and select the Unmount entry. The CD-ROM disk is automatically ejected. The same procedure works for floppy disks, using the Floppy Disk icon. Be sure you don't remove a mounted floppy disk until you have first unmounted it, selecting the Unmount entry in the pop-up menu.

Usually, a window manager extends a desktop into several areas that appear as different screens. Gnome's drag-and-drop operation works on desktop areas provided by a Gnome-compliant window manager. Gnome does not directly manage desktop areas, though you can use the Gnome pager to move to them. You use the window manager configuration tool to configure them—in this case Sawfish, which is the default window manager for Gnome. In addition, most window managers, including Sawfish, also support virtual desktops. Instead of being extensions of the same desktop area, virtual desktops are separate entities. The Gnome pager on the Panel supports virtual desktops, creating icons for each in the panel, along with task buttons for any applications open on them. You can use the Gnome pager to move to different virtual desktops and their areas.

Menu Item	Description
New Window	Starts a new Nautilus file manager window on your desktop, showing your home directory.
New Terminal	Launches a new Gnome terminal window that navigates to the desktop directory.
New Folder	Creates a new directory on your desktop.
Clean Up by Name	Arranges your desktop icons.
Disks	Displays a submenu that lists floppy and CD-ROM devices that you can select to mount. Mounted disks will appear as CD-ROM or floppy icons on your desktop, which you can use to access them or unmount later.
Change Desktop Background	Opens Gnome Control Center with the Background capplet selected to let you select a new background for your desktop.

Table 9-1. *The Gnome 1.4 Desktop Menu (Nautilus)*

Window Managers

Gnome works with any window manager. However, desktop functionality, such as drag-and-drop capabilities and the Gnome pager, only work with window managers that are Gnome-compliant. The current release of Gnome uses the Sawfish window manager. It is completely Gnome-compliant and is designed to integrate with the Gnome desktop without any duplication of functionality. However, other window managers such as Enlightenment, FVWM, IceWin, and Window Maker can also be used. Check a window manager's documentation to see if it is Gnome-compliant.

Sawfish employs much the same window operations as used on other window managers. You can resize a window by clicking any of its sides or corners and dragging. You can move the window with a click-and-drag operation on its title bar. You can also right-click and drag any border to move the window, as well as ALT-click anywhere on the window. The upper-right corner shows the Maximize, Minimize, and Close buttons. If the Gnome pager is running in your panel, Minimize creates a button for the window in the panel that you can click to restore it. If the Gnome pager is not present, the window will iconify, minimizing to an icon on the desktop. You can right-click on the title bar of a window to display a window menu with entries for window operations. These include a desktop entry to move the window to another desktop area and the Stick option, which displays the window no matter to what desktop area you move.

You can also access the Sawfish desktop menu. To display the menu, middle-click anywhere on the desktop (hold both mouse buttons down at the same time for a two-button mouse). A pop-up menu appears with submenus for Gnome, user, and other applications, as well as the Desktop, Themes, and Sawfish configurations. You can use this menu to start any application, if you want. With the desktop menus, you move to different desktop areas and virtual desktops. The Themes menu enables you to choose different Sawfish themes (these are separate from KDE themes). Sawfish also has extensive configuration options, discussed in a later section in this chapter.

If you have several window managers installed on your system, you can change from one to the other using the Window Manager capplet. *Capplet* is the term used for a *control applet,* a module used to configure your desktop. Select the Window Manager entry in the main menu to start the Settings menu, or select its icon in the desktop windows opened from Preferences in the Start Here window. A panel is displayed listing your window managers. To add others to the list, click the Add button on the right side of the panel. This opens a window that prompts you to enter an identifying name for the window manager, the command that starts the window manager, and any configuration tool it may use. If the window manager is Gnome-compliant, you can click the button Window Manager Is Session Managed. Once you finish making your entries and click OK, the new window manager appears in the list on the Window Manager panel. Select it and click Try to run that window manager. If you want to run the window manager's configuration tool, click the Run Configuration Tool button.

The Gnome File Manager: Nautilus

With Gnome 1.4, the file manager for Gnome was changed from Gnome Midnight Commander (GMC) to Nautilus. Nautilus supports the standard features for copying, removing, and deleting items as well as setting permissions and displaying items just as GMC does. Nautilus also provides enhancements such as zooming capabilities, user levels, and theme support. You can enlarge or reduce the size of your file icons, select from novice, intermediate, or expert levels of use, and customize the look and feel of Nautilus with different themes. Nautilus also lets you set up customized views of file listings, enabling you to display images for directory icons and run component applications within the file manager window. For example, a directory of MP3 files could have an album cover for its directory icon and run a component MP3 player within the file manager window to play a file.

Nautilus was designed as a desktop shell in which different components can be employed to add functionality. For example, within Nautilus, a Web browser can be executed to provide Web browser capabilities in a Nautilus file manager window. Nautilus is not only a file manager, but also a desktop shell based on a component architecture. Different components, such as a Web browser, compression commands, or an image viewer, can be used to add capabilities to this desktop shell.

The standard Nautilus window displays a menu bar and toolbar of file manager commands along with a Location box at the top (see Figure 9-2). The rest of the window

Figure 9-2. *Nautilus file manager*

is divided into two panes. The left pane is a sidebar used to display information about the current working directory. The right pane is the main panel that displays the list of files and subdirectories in the current working directory. A status bar at the bottom of the window displays information about a selected file or directory.

With the Preferences menu, you can set your level of expertise: advanced, intermediate, or beginner. The different levels allow for simpler methods of managing files. If you only need the basic file management capabilities, you can choose beginner, leaving advanced and intermediate for the more complex tasks. Next to the Location box is an element for zooming in and out the view of the files. Click the + button to zoom in and the – button to zoom out. Next to the zoom element is a drop-down menu for selecting the different views for your files, such as icons, small icons, or details.

The sidebar has five different tabbed views for displaying additional information about files and directories: Tree, History, News, Help, and Notes. The Tree view will display a tree-based hierarchical view of the directories and files on your system, highlighting the one you have currently selected. You can use this tree to move to other directories and files. The tree maps all the directories on your system, starting from the root directory. You can expand or shrink any directory by clicking the + or – symbol before its name. Select a directory by clicking the directory name. The contents of that directory are then displayed in the main panel. The History tab shows previous files or directories you have accessed, handy for moving back and forth between directories or files. The Help tab provides access to documentation such as Gnome manuals, info pages, and Man documentation. On the Notes tab, you can enter notes about your current working directory. The News tab will display breaking news from sites you have selected. Click the Select Site button to display a list of news sites such as CNN, Gnome News, or Linux Today. URLs for different stories will appear in the sidebar when the News panel is selected.

You can view a directory's contents as icons, as a detailed list, as music, or as a custom (other) view. You select the different options from the pop-up menu located on the right side of the Location bar. The List view provides the name, permissions, size, date, owner, and group. For a custom view, you can select the informational fields you want displayed for your files. In the List view, buttons are displayed for each field across the top of the main panel. You can use these buttons to sort the lists according to that field. For example, to sort the files by date, click the Date button; to sort by size, click the Size button.

In the Icon view, you can sort icons, change their sizes, and even preview their contents without opening them. To sort items in the Icon view, select the Lay Out Items entry in the View menu, and then select a layout option. To change an icon's size, select Stretch Icon. Handles will appear on the icon image. Click and drag the handles to change its size. To restore the icon, select Restore Icon's Original Size in the Edit menu. Certain types of files have their icons display previews of their contents—for example, the icons for image files will display a small version of the image. A music file such as an MP3 file will start playing when the mouse pointer moves over its icon. A text file will display in its icon the first few words of its text.

The Music view lets you treat directories of MP3 files as if they were your own digital music albums. When you select the Music view, only MP3 files are displayed. Clicking on a file starts the music player, which will automatically play from track to track. You can even select a cover image for your music directory icon.

You can click anywhere on the main panel to display a pop-up menu with entries for managing and arranging your file manager icon (see Table 9-2). To create a new folder, select New Folder, and to open a new file manager window, select New Window. The Lay Out Items entry displays a submenu with entries for sorting your icons by name, size, type, date, or even emblem. The Manually entry lets you move icons wherever you want on the main panel. The Clean Up By Name entry displays your icons alphabetically. The Zoom In entry enlarges your view of the window, making icons bigger, and Zoom Out reduces your view, making them smaller. Normal Size restores them to the standard size. Reset Background lets you change the background used on the File Manager window, useful for music folders where you display your favorite album cover. You can also cut, copy, and paste files to more easily move or copy them between folders.

Menu Item	Description
New Window	Opens a file or directory in a separate window
New Folder	Creates a new subdirectory in the directory
Lay Out Items	Displays a submenu to arrange files by name, size, type, date, or emblems
Clean Up By Name	Alphabetically orders files
Cut, Copy, Paste	Cuts, copies, or pastes files, letting you move or copy files between folders
Zoom In	Close-up view of icons, making them appear larger
Zoom Out	Distant view of icons, making them appear smaller
Normal Size	Restores view of icons to standard size
Reset Background	Sets the background image for the file manager main panel

Table 9-2. *Nautilus File Manager Menu*

Note *The Lay Out Item submenu is not provided in the Nautilus pop-up menu when the main panel displays files in the list mode.*

The Nautilus file manager operates similarly to a Web browser. It maintains a list of previously viewed directories, and you can move back and forth through that list using the toolbar buttons. The left arrow button moves you to the previously displayed directory, and the right arrow button moves you to the next displayed directory. The up arrow button moves you to the parent directory, and the Home button moves you to your home directory. To use a pathname to go directly to a given directory, you can type the pathname in the Location box and press ENTER.

To search for files or directories, click on the Find icon on the toolbar if there is one (see Note). Depending on the expertise level you set, Nautilus can perform simple or complex searches (simple for beginner level and complex for advanced and intermediate). The Location box is replaced by the Find box, where you can enter the pattern you want to search for. Then click on the Find Them button to the right. Complex searches let you specify different attributes such as type, owner, or even file contents. For complex searches, two pop-up menus are added with which you can further refine your search. These menus specify criteria such as searches by name, content, file type, size, date modified, and owner. Nautilus searches make use of a search daemon called **Medusa** that creates an index of all your files, enabling very fast searches. **Medusa** even indexes by the contents of your file, supporting text searches of file contents. (For **Medusa** to work, the **crond** daemon must be running).

Version 1.0.4 for Nautilus does not include support for Find operations. A Find icon is not displayed. If you are using Ximian Gnome, you can use a Find utility located on the System menu in the Menu panel. It has many of the same features as the Nautilus Find operation.

To open a subdirectory, you can double-click its icon or single-click the icon and select Open from the File menu. If you want to open a separate Nautilus window for that directory, right-click the directory's icon and select Open In A New Window.

As a Gnome-compliant file manager, Nautilus supports GUI drag-and-drop operations for copying and moving files. To move a file or directory, click and drag from one directory to another as you would on Windows or Mac interfaces. The **`move`** operation is the default drag-and-drop operation in Gnome. To copy a file, click and drag with the right mouse button (not the left) and select Copy Here from the pop-up menu. You can also click and drag normally and then press the CTRL key before you lift up on the left mouse button.

Note

If you move a file to a directory on another partition (file system), it will be copied instead of moved.

You can also perform remove, duplicate, and link creation operations on a file by right-clicking its icon and selecting the action you want from the pop-up menu that appears (see Table 9-3). For example, to remove an item, right-click it and select the Move To Trash entry from the pop-up menu. This places it in the Trash directory where you can later delete it by selecting Empty Trash from the Nautilus File menu. To create a copy of a file, you can select Duplicate from the pop-up menu to create a duplicate version in the same directory. The name of the copy will begin with the term "Duplicate." To create a link, right-click the file and select Create Link from the pop-up menu. This creates a new link file that begins with the term "Link."

To rename a file, you can either right-click on the file's icon and select the Rename entry from the pop-up menu or click on the name of the file shown below its icon. The name of the icon will be highlighted in a black background, encased in a small text box. You can then click on the name and delete the old name, typing a new one. You can also rename a file by entering a new name in its Properties dialog box. Use a right-click and select Show Properties from the pop-up menu to display the Properties dialog box. On the General tab, you can change the name of the file.

File operations can be performed on a selected group of files and directories. You can select a group of items in several ways. You can click the first item and then hold down the SHIFT key while clicking the last item. You can also click and drag the mouse across items you want to select. To select separated items, hold the CTRL key down as you click the individual icons. If you want to select all the items in the directory, choose

Menu Item	Description
Open	Opens the file with its associated application. Directories are opened in the file manager.
Open In A New Window	Opens a file or directory in a separate window.
Open With	Selects an application with which to open this file. A submenu of possible applications is displayed.
Show Properties	Displays the Properties dialog box for this file. There are three panels: Statistics, Options, and Permissions.
Move To Trash	Moves a file to the Trash directory, where you can later delete it.
Duplicate	Creates a duplicate copy of the file in the same directory.
Make Link	Creates a link to that file in the same directory.
Rename	Renames the file.
Stretch Icon	Changes the size of a selected icon.
Remove Custom Image	Removes a custom image you selected for the icon.
Restore Icon's Original Size	A selected icon you enlarged earlier is restored to its standard size.

Table 9-3. *The Nautilus File Pop-Up Menu*

the Select All entry in the Edit menu. You can also select files based on pattern matches on the filenames. Choose the Select Files entry in the Edit menu. You can then enter a pattern using Linux file-matching wildcard symbols such as `*` (see Chapter 11). For example, the pattern `*.c` would select all C source code files (those ending with the extension `.c`). You can then click and drag a set of items at once. This enables you to copy, move, or even delete several files at once. To move files between directories, open two file manager windows to the respective directories. Then click and drag the items from one window to the other.

You can start any application in the file manager by double-clicking either the application itself or a data file used for that application. If a file does not have an associated application, you can right-click the file and select the Open With entry. A submenu displays a list of possible applications. If your application is not listed, you can select Other Application to open a dialog box where you can choose the application with which you want to open this file. You can also use a text viewer to display the bare contents of a file within the file manager window. Drag-and-drop operations are also supported for applications. You can drag a data file to its associated application icon (say, one on the desktop); the application then starts up using that data file.

With the Properties dialog box, you can view detailed information on a file and set options and permissions (see Figure 9-3). A Properties box has three panels: Basic, Emblems, and Permissions. The *Basic panel* shows detailed information such as type, size, location, and date modified. The type is a MIME type, indicating the type of application associated with it. The file's icon is displayed at the top with a text box showing the file's name. You can edit the filename in this text box, changing that name. A button at the bottom labeled Select Custom Icon will open a dialog box showing available icons you can use. You can select the one you want from that window. The Remove Custom Icon button will restore the default icon image. The *Emblems panel* enables you to set the emblem you want displayed for this file, displaying all the emblems available. The *Permissions panel* shows the read, write, and execute permissions for user, group, and other, as set for this file. You can change any of the permissions here, provided the file belongs to you. The panel will also show the file's owner and its group. The group name expands to a pop-up menu listing different groups, allowing you to select one to change the file's group.

You can set preferences for your Nautilus file manager in the Preferences dialog box. Access this dialog box by selecting the Edit Preferences item in the Preferences menu. The Preferences dialog box shows a main panel with a sidebar with several

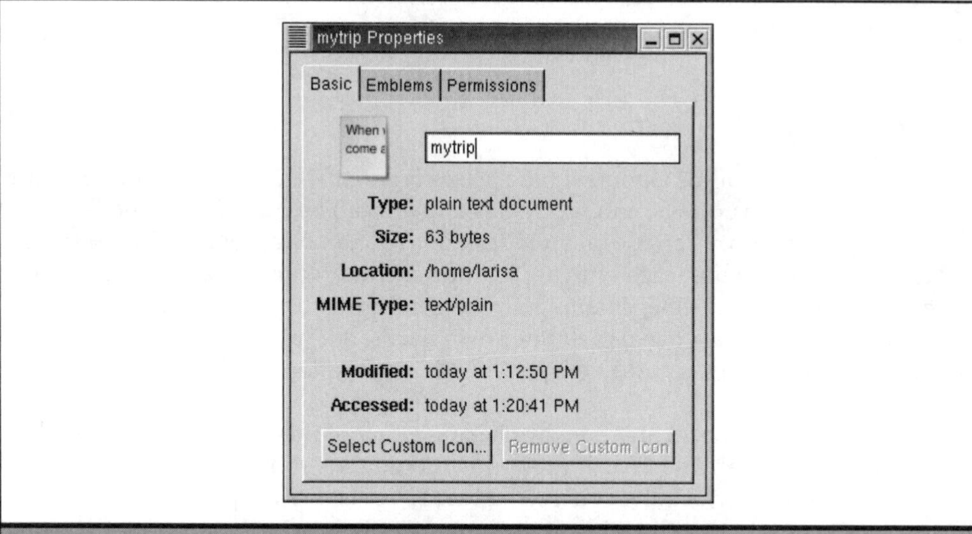

Figure 9-3. *File properties on Nautilus*

configuration entries, including Appearance, Windows & Desktop, Icon & List Views, Sidebar Panel, Search, Navigation, and Speed Tradeoffs. You use these dialog boxes to set the default display properties for your Nautilus file manager. For example, Windows & Desktop allows you to select which bars to display by default, such as the sidebar or the toolbar. Appearance lets you select the style you want to use. For the Sidebar Panel, you can select which tab to display, such as history or tree. On the Search menu, you can specify the default Web search site to use.

Nautilus as a Web Browser

Nautilus is also an operational Web browser. You can use the Location box to access any Web or FTP site. Just enter the URL for the Web site in the Location box and press ENTER (you do not need to specify **www** or **http://**). However, Nautilus is not a fully functional Web browser. When you access a page, it will display buttons in the sidebar to open the page using one of several Web browsers installed on your system, such as Netscape, Mozilla, or Lynx. The Go menu and History tab in the sidebar maintain a history list of Web sites you have previously accessed. You can also right-click on the Back and Forward buttons to display this history list. To clear the history list, select Forget History in the Go menu. Nautilus also supports bookmarks, which can be displayed and edited using the Bookmarks menu. Clicking on the Web Search icon will open the page of your specified favorite Web search engine, such as Yahoo or Google.

Nautilus is also Internet-aware. You can use the Location box to access an FTP site and display the directories on that remote site, and then drag and drop files to another file manager window to download them to your system. Be sure to include the FTP protocol specification, ***ftp://***.

The Gnome Panel

The *panel* is the center of the Gnome interface (see Figure 9-4). Through it you can start your applications, run applets, and access desktop areas. You can think of the Gnome panel as a type of tool you can use on your desktop. You can have several Gnome panels displayed on your desktop, each with applets and menus you have placed in them. In this respect, Gnome is flexible, enabling you to configure your panels any way you want. You can customize a panel to fit your own needs, holding applets and menus of your own selection. You may add new panels, add applications to the panel, and add various applets.

You can hide the panel at any time by clicking either of the Hide buttons located on each end of the panel. The Hide buttons are thin buttons showing a small arrow. This is the direction in which the panel will hide. To redisplay the panel, move your mouse off the screen in that direction at the bottom of the screen. If you want the panel to automatically hide when you are not using it, select the Auto-Hide option in the panel configuration window. Moving the mouse to the bottom of the screen redisplays the panel. You can also move the panel to another edge of the screen by clicking and

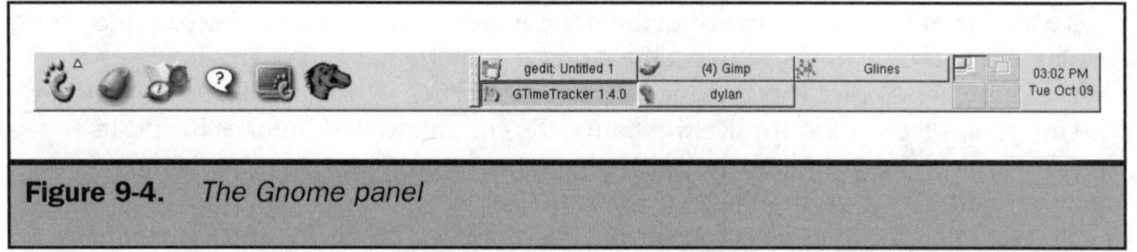

Figure 9-4. *The Gnome panel*

dragging on either end of the panel with your middle mouse button (both buttons simultaneously for two-button mice).

To add a new panel, select the Create Panel entry in the Panel menu. You can then select the panel type, choosing from a menu, edge, floating, sliding, or aligned panel. The default is an edge panel. An *edge panel* is displayed across one of the edges of the screen. Your original panel is an edge panel. A *menu panel* is a panel implemented as a menu bar across the top of the desktop with menus for Programs, Favorites, Settings, and Desktop. It can hold any objects that a standard panel can hold. A *floating panel* is one that you can position anywhere on the desktop. A *sliding panel* is sized to the number of items in the panel and can be placed anywhere on the edge of the desktop. An *aligned panel* is a smaller panel also sized to the number of items on it and is positioned in the center of the edge of a desktop. You can change a panel's type at any time by right-clicking the panel and selecting an alternate configuration.

A panel can contain several different types of objects. These include menus, launchers, applets, drawers, and special objects. The main menu is an example of a panel menu. You can create your own, or even drag submenus down to the panel from the main menu. Launchers are buttons used to start an application or execute a command. The Netscape icon is an example of a launcher button. You can drag any application entry in the main menu to the panel and create a launcher for it on the panel. An applet is a small application designed to run within the panel. The Gnome Desk Guide showing the different desktops is an example of a Gnome applet. A drawer is an extension of the panel that can be open or closed. You can think of a drawer as a shrinkable part of the panel. You can add anything to it that you can to a regular panel, including applets, menus, and even other drawers. Special objects are used for special tasks not supported by other panel objects. For example, the Logout and Lock buttons are special objects.

Adding Applications and Applets

Adding applications to a panel is easy. For an application already in the main menu, you only need to go to its entry and right-click it. Then select the Add This Launcher To Panel entry. An application launcher for that application is then automatically added to the panel. Suppose you use gEdit frequently and want to add its icon to the panel, instead of having to go through the main menu all the time. Right-click the gEdit menu entry and select the Add This Launcher To Panel option. The gEdit icon now appears in your panel.

To add an application icon not in the main menu, first right-click the panel to display the pop-up menu and select the Add New Launcher entry. This opens the Create Launcher Applet window for entering properties for the applications launcher. You are prompted for the application name, the command that invokes it, and its type. To select an icon for your launcher, click the Icon button. This opens the Icon Picker window, listing icons from which you can choose.

You can also group applications under a Drawer icon. Clicking the Drawer icon displays a list of the different application icons you can then select. To add a drawer to your panel, right-click the panel and select the Add Drawer entry. If you want to add a whole menu of applications on the main menu to your panel, right-click the menu title displayed at the top of the menu and select the Add This As Drawer To Panel entry. The entire menu appears as a drawer on your panel, holding icons instead of menu entries. For example, suppose you want to place the Internet applications menu on your panel. Right-click the Internet item and select Add This As Drawer To Panel. A drawer appears on your panel labeled Internet, and clicking it displays a pop-up list of icons for all the Internet applications.

A menu differs from a drawer in that a *drawer* holds application icons instead of menu entries. You can add menus to your panel, much as you add drawers. To add a submenu in the main menu to your panel, right-click the menu title and select the Add This As Menu To Panel entry. The menu title appears in the panel; you can click it to display the menu entries.

You can also add directory folders to a panel. Click and drag the Folder icon from the file manager window to your panel. Whenever you click this Folder button, a file manager window opens, displaying that directory. You already have a Folder button for your home directory. You can add directory folders to any drawer on your panel.

Moving and Removing Panel Objects

To move any object on the panel, even the Menu icon, just drag it with the middle mouse button. You can also right-click on it and choose Move Applet to let you move the applet. You can move it either to a different place on the same panel or to a different panel. When moving objects, you can have them either push over, switch with, or jump over other objects that they run into on the panel. To push over an object, you hold the SHIFT key down while moving the object. To switch with an object, you hold down the CTRL key, and to jump over an object, you hold down the ALT key.

To remove an object from the panel, right-click on it to display a pop-up menu for it, and then choose the Remove From Panel entry.

Main Menu

You open the main menu by clicking its button on the panel. The Main Menu button is a stylized picture of a bare foot. It is initially located on the left side of your panel, the lower-left corner of your screen. You only need to single-click the Main Menu button. You needn't keep holding your mouse button down. The menu pops up much like the Start menu in Windows.

You can configure menus using the Menu Properties dialog box. To change the properties for a menu on the panel, including the main menu, right-click its icon in the panel and select the Properties entry. This displays the Menu Properties dialog box, which has two sections: Menu Type and Main Menu. In the Main Menu section, you can set properties for that main menu. Several possible submenus can be displayed on the main menu, either directly or in other submenus. You can choose from the System, Applets, Favorites, KDE, and Distribution menus. You can place these menus on the main menu or make them submenus. Distribution menus are those used for a specific distribution like Mandrake or Red Hat that are not specifically Gnome applications. KDE is used for KDE applications, if the KDE desktop is also installed on your system.

You can customize the main menu, adding your own entries, with the Menu Editor. To start the Menu Editor, select the Menu Editor entry in the Setting submenu located in the main menu. The Menu Editor is divided into two panes, the left being a tree view of the main menu. You can expand or shrink any of the submenus. The right pane holds configuration information for a selected entry. There are two panels: basic and advanced. The basic panel displays the name, command, and application type, as well as the icon. You can click the icon to change it. You can also change the Name, Command, or Type field.

To add a new application, click the New Item button on the toolbar. The new item is placed in the currently selected menu. Enter the name, command, and type information, and then select an icon. Then click the Save button to add the entry to the menu. You can move the menu item in the menu by clicking the up or down arrow button in the toolbar, or by dragging it with the mouse. If you are a user, remember you can only add entries to the User menu, not to the Systems menu.

An easier way to add an application is to use the drag-and-drop method. Locate the application you want to add with the file manager, and then drag and drop its icon to the appropriate menu in the Menu Editor. The entry is made automatically, using configuration information provided for that application by the file manager.

Panel Configuration

You use the Global Panel Configuration dialog box to configure properties for all Gnome panels. Either right-click the panel and select Global Properties or select Global Properties in the Panel submenu in the main menu to display this dialog window. The Global Panel Configuration dialog box has six tabbed panels: Animation, Launcher Icon, Drawer Icon, Menu Icon, Logout Icon, and Miscellaneous. With the Animation panel, you can enable panel animations, setting various options for them. The various icon panels enable you to select the images you want to use to denote active or inactive elements, among other features, such as border and depth. On the Miscellaneous panel, you set certain options such as allowing pop-up menus on the desktop, prompting before logout, or keeping panels below windows.

To configure individual panels, you use the Panel Properties dialog box. To display this dialog box, you right-click the particular panel and select the This Panel Properties entry in the pop-up menu, or select This Panel Properties in the main menu's Panel menu. For individual panels, you can set features for edge panel configuration and the background. The Panel Properties dialog box includes a tabbed panel for each. On the edge panel, you can choose options for positioning an edge panel and for minimizing it, including the Auto-Hide feature. The Hide Buttons feature enables you to hide the panel yourself.

On the Background panel, you can change the background image used for the panel. You can select an image, have it scaled to fit the panel, and select a background color. For an image, you can also drag and drop an image file from the file manager to the panel, and that image then becomes the background image for the panel.

Special Panel Objects

Special panel objects perform operations not supported by other panel objects. Currently, these include the Lock, Logout, and Run buttons, as well as swallowed applications and the status dock. The Lock button shows a padlock and will lock your desktop, running the screen saver in its place. To access your desktop, click on it and then enter your user password at the password prompt. The Logout button shows a monitor with a half-moon. Clicking it will display the Logout dialog box and you can then log out. It is the same as selecting Logout from the main menu. The Run button shows a hand on a terminal window. It opens the Run dialog box, which allows you to enter or select an application to run.

Any application can be run as applets on the panel. This process is referred to as *swallowing* the application. In effect, instead of being run in a Gnome window, the application is run as an applet on the panel. To swallow an application, you first start the application and take note of its window title. Then, in the Create Swallowed Application dialog box, enter the title of the application to swallow. You can further specify the applet's dimensions. If you want to start the application directly as an applet, you can specify its program name in the Command window.

The status dock is designed to hold status docklets. A status docklet provides current status information on an application. KDE applications that support status docklets can use the Gnome status dock, when run under Gnome.

Gnome Applets

As previously stated, applets are small programs that perform tasks within the panel. To add an applet, right-click the panel and select Add To Panel, and then Applets from the pop-up menu. This, in turn, displays other pop-up menus listing categories of applets with further listings of available applets. Select the one you want. For example, to add the clock to your panel, select Clock from the Utility menu. To remove an applet, right-click it and select the Remove From Panel entry. You can also select the Applets menu in the main menu and select an applet to add to your panel.

Gnome features a number of helpful applets, such as a CPU monitor and a mail checker. Some applets monitor your system, such as the Battery Monitor, which checks the battery in laptops, and CPU/MEM Usage, which shows a graph indicating your current CPU and memory use. There are also separate applets for CPU and memory load: CPULoad and MemLoad. The Mixer applet displays a small scroll bar for adjusting sound levels. The CD player displays a small CD interface for playing music CDs.

For network tasks, there are MailCheck, Modem Lights, and Web Control applets. MailCheck checks for received mail. To configure MailCheck, right-click it and select the Properties entry. You can set the frequency of checks, as well as specify a more sophisticated mail checker to run, such as **`fetchmail`**. The Modem Lights feature monitors your modem connection. You can configure it to monitor a PPP connection to an ISP over a modem. Web Control enables you to start your Web browser with a specified URL.

Several helpful utility applets provide added functionality to your desktop. The Clock applet can display time in a 12- or 24-hour format. Right-click the Clock applet and select the Properties entry to change its setup. You use the Printer applet to print your files. To print a file, drag its icon to the Printer applet. To configure the Printer applet, right-click it and select Properties. Here, you can specify the printer name and the printer command to use—helpful if you have more than one printer. The Drive Mount applet enables you to mount a drive using a single click. You can create a Drive Mount applet for each device you have, such as a floppy drive and a CD-ROM. To mount a file system, all you have to do is click the appropriate Drive Mount icon in the panel. To specify the file systems to mount, use the applet's Drive Mount Settings dialog box.

Gnome Desk Guide

The *Gnome Desk Guide*, shown in Figure 9-5, appears in the panel and shows a view of your virtual desktops along with their desktop areas. Virtual desktops and their desktop areas are defined in the window manager. Desk Guide lets you easily move from one to another with the click of a mouse. The Gnome Desk Guide is a panel applet that works only in the panel.

Note *If the Desk Guide is not already active, you can activate the Gnome Desk Guide by right-clicking the panel and selecting Add New Applet from the pop-up menu. This, in turn, displays other pop-up menus listing categories of applets and their listings of available applets. Select the Utility category and, in that menu, select Desk Guide.*

The Desk Guide shows your entire virtual desktop as separate rectangles within a box. Each rectangle in turn is cut into small adjoining squares to show the desktop areas for each virtual desktop. Open windows show up as small colored rectangles in these squares. You can move any window from one virtual desktop or area to another by clicking and dragging its image in the Desk Guide with your middle mouse button. If you click the small arrow to the right of the Desktop view, the Tasklist window opens, listing all the tasks (windows) currently open and running (if the arrow is not displayed,

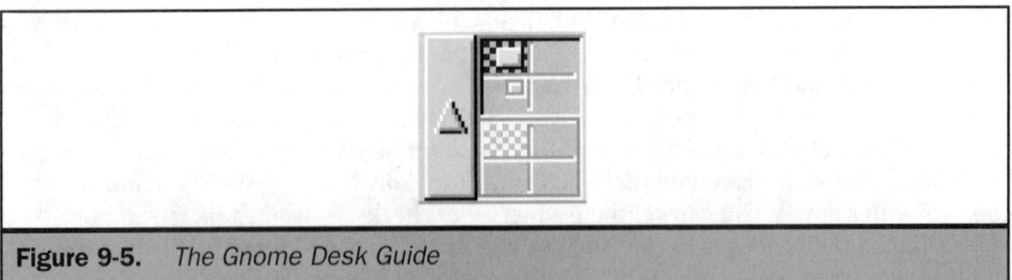

Figure 9-5. *The Gnome Desk Guide*

open the Desk Guide properties and select Show Tasklist Arrow). You can select a task to move to its window and the desktop it is currently positioned in. Figure 9-5 shows a simple Desk View applet displaying two virtual desktops, each with four desktop areas. Figure 9-6 shows a more complex desktop view with four virtual desktops, each with four desktop areas.

Various window managers use different terms to describe virtual desktops and their desktop areas. Enlightenment uses the terms "desktops" and "screens," whereas Sawfish uses "workspaces" that are then divided into "columns" and "rows." Desk Guide officially calls them "desktops" and "viewports."

To configure the Desk Guide, right-click it and select Properties to display the Properties dialog box. Here, you can choose from panels to configure the display, tasks, geometry, and advanced features such as window manager options. You can set the size of the Desk Guide to extend beyond the height of the panel, elect to display any virtual desktop names, or even show hidden tasks. Remember, the window manager you are using may also have a pager you can use that may operate much like the Desk Guide. Check your window manager documentation on how to activate it.

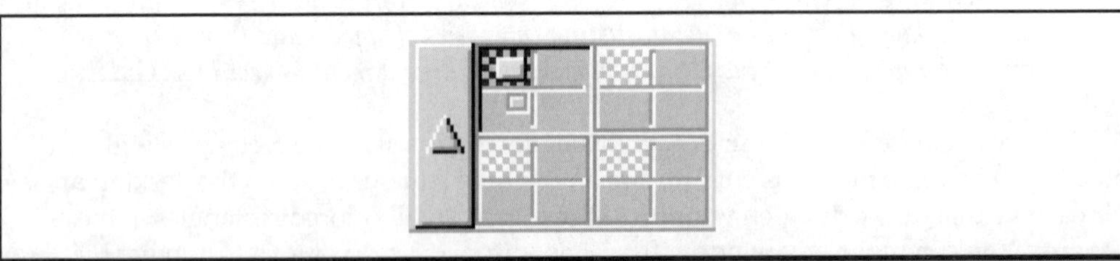

Figure 9-6. *Desk Guide for four virtual desktops with four desktop areas each*

Gnome Tasklist

The *Tasklist* shows currently opened applications. The Tasklist arranges tasks currently running in a series of buttons, one for each window. A task can be any open application, usually denoted by a window displayed on the screen. These can include applications such as a Web browser or a file manager window displaying a directory. You can move from one task to another by clicking on its button, in effect moving from one window to another. When you minimize a window, you can later restore it by clicking on its entry in the Tasklist. Figure 9-7 shows a Tasklist displaying buttons for several different kinds of windowed applications.

Right-clicking on a window's Tasklist entry opens a menu that lets you iconify or restore, shade, stick, or close the window. The iconify operation will reduce the window to its Tasklist entry. Right-clicking on the entry will display the menu with a Restore option instead of an iconify one, which you can then use to redisplay the window. The Shade entry will reduce the window to its title bar, and the Stick entry will display the window in any desktop you move to. The Kill entry will close the window, ending its application.

To configure the Tasklist, right-click on it and select the Properties entry. Here, you can set features such as the size of the Tasklist, the number of rows, whether to display mini-icons, and the tasks to show.

Quicklaunch

You can use the Quicklaunch applet in the panel to start programs. The *Quicklaunch applet* holds a collection of small icons for application launchers. Click them to launch your application. The Quicklaunch applet can use only launchers that are already set up either on the main menu or on your desktop. To add a launcher to Quicklaunch, drag and drop the launcher to the Quicklaunch applet in the panel. A small icon is then created for it in the Quicklaunch applet. For main menu items, click an item and drag it to the Quicklaunch applet. Right-click a particular application's icon and select Properties to configure that launcher.

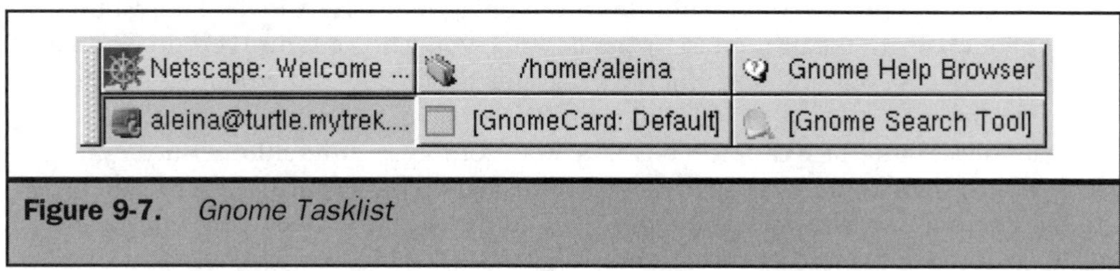

Figure 9-7. *Gnome Tasklist*

Gnome Configuration

You can configure different parts of your Gnome interface using tools called *capplets.* Think of capplets as modules or plug-ins that can be added to enable you to configure various applications. Capplets exist for the core set of Gnome applications, as well as for other applications for which developers may have written capplets. You can access capplets from the Settings menu in the Gnome Programs menu. This menu will display entries for each category of capplets supported by the control center. Selecting one will open a window displaying icons for individual capplets. Double-clicking on a particular icon will open its capplet window. You can have several open at once. You can also select a capplet from the Settings menu on the Gnome main menu.

You can also access capplets using the Control Center, which displays icons for all the capplet categories. Mandrake displays the Control Center as a window of iconified categories. Red Hat does not let you select the Control Center directly. Instead you have to select Preferences in the Red Hat Start Here window.

Tip *On Red Hat, it is possible to also open the Control Center window listing all capplets using an expandable tree. To do so, you need to enter the* **gnomecc** *command in a terminal window.*

Your Gnome system provides several desktop capplets you can use to configure your desktop, such as Background, Screensaver, Theme Selector, and Window Manager. You use the Background capplet to select a background color or image, the Screensaver capplet to select the screen saver images and wait time, the Theme Selector capplet to choose a theme, and the Window Manager capplet to choose the window manager you want to use.

On the Gnome Default Editor entry, you choose an editor as your default editor for Gnome, the editor the Gnome file manager uses to open text files. The Gnome File Types capplet enables you to specify Multipurpose Internet Mail Extensions (MIME) type entries for your system, associating given MIME types with certain applications. Notice that basic MIME type entries are already present. You can edit an entry and change its associated application. Also listed are Multimedia and Peripheral capplets. For the sound configuration, you can select sound files to play for events in different Gnome applications. For your keyboard, you can set the repeat sensitivity and click sound. You can configure mouse buttons for your right or left hand, and adjust the mouse motion. With the Session Manager capplet, you can configure certain Gnome session features, specifying non-Gnome programs to start up and whether you want a logout prompt.

Several User Interface capplets enable you to configure different interface components, such as menus, toolbars, and status bars. There are capplets for setting these features for applications, dialog boxes, and the Multiple Document Interface (MDI). You can specify whether toolbars and menus can be detached, whether they have relief borders, and whether they include icons. For dialog boxes, you can set features such as the arrangement of buttons or the position of the dialog box on the screen when it appears. The default MDI used for Gnome is modal. You can choose two other interfaces: toplevel and notebook.

Gnome sets up several configuration files and directories in your home directory. The **.gnome** directory holds configuration files for different desktop components, such as **gmc** for the file manager, **panel** for the panels, and **gmenu** for the main menu. **.gtkrc** holds configuration directives for the GTK+ widgets. The **.gnome-desktop** directory holds all the items you placed on your desktop.

Gnome Directories and Files

Most distributions install Gnome binaries in the **/usr/bin** directory on your system. Gnome libraries are located in the **/usr/lib** directory. Gnome also has its own **include** directories with header files for use in compiling and developing Gnome applications, **/usr/include/libgnome** and **/usr/include/libgnomeui**. The directories located in **/usr/share/gnome** contain files used to configure your Gnome environment.

Gnome sets up several hidden directories for each user in their home directory that begin with **.gnome** and include a preceding period in the name. **.gnome** holds files used to configure a user's Gnome desktop and applications. Configuration files for the panel, Control Center, GnomeRPM, MIME types, and sessions, among others, are located here. The files **Gnome**, **GnomeHelp**, **Background**, and **Terminal** all hold Gnome configuration commands for how to display and use these components. For example, **Gnome** holds general display features for the desktop, while **GnomeHelp** specifies the history and bookmark files for the help system. Configuration files for particular Gnome applications are kept in the subdirectory **apps**. **gnome-desktop** which holds any files, folders, or links the user has dragged to the desktop. **.gnome-help-browser** holds the bookmark and history files for the Gnome Help system. These are the bookmarks and the list of previous documents the user consulted with the Gnome Help browser. **.gtckrc** is the user configuration file for the GTK+ libraries, which contains current desktop configuration directives for resources such as key bindings, colors, and window styles.

With Gnome 2.0, Gnome will officially implement GConf to provide underlying configuration support. GConf corresponds to the registry use on Windows system. GConf consists of a series of libraries used to implement a configuration database for a Gnome desktop. This standardized configuration database allows for a consistent interactions between Gnome applications. Gnome applications that are built from a variety of other programs, as Nautilus is, can use GConf to configure all those programs according to a single standard, maintaining configurations in a single database. Currently the GConf database is implemented as XML files in the user's **.gconf** directory. Database interaction and access is carried out by the GConf daemon, **gconfd**.

The Complete Reference

Chapter 10

The Shell

The *shell* is a command interpreter that provides a line-oriented interactive and noninteractive interface between the user and the operating system. You enter commands on a command line, they are interpreted by the shell, and then sent as instructions to the operating system. You can also place commands in a script file to be consecutively executed much like a program. This interpretive capability of the shell provides for many sophisticated features. For example, the shell has a set of file expansion characters that can generate filenames. The shell can redirect input and output, as well as run operations in the background, freeing you to perform other tasks.

Several different types of shells have been developed for Linux: the Bourne Again shell (BASH), the Public Domain Korn shell (PDKSH), the TCSH shell, and the Z shell. All shells are available for your use, although the BASH shell is the default. You only need one type of shell to do your work. All the major Linux distributions include all the major shells, although it installs and uses the BASH shell as the default. If you use Linux command line shell, you will be using the BASH shell unless you specify another. This chapter discusses the BASH shell that shares many of the same features as other shells.

Note *You can find out more about the BASH shell at **www.gnu.org/software/bash**. A detailed online manual is available on your Linux system using the* **`man`** *command with the* **`bash`** *keyword.*

The Command Line

The Linux command line interface consists of a single line into which you enter commands with any of their options and arguments. Most Linux distributions, including Red Hat, SUSE, and Caldera, install with the BASH shell. From Gnome or KDE you can access the command line interface by opening a terminal window. Should you start Linux with the command line interface, you will be presented with a BASH shell command line when you log in.

By default, the BASH shell has a dollar sign (**$**) prompt, but Linux has several other types of shells, each with its own prompt. A shell *prompt*, such as the one shown here, marks the beginning of the command line:

```
$
```

The prompt designates the beginning of the command line. You are now ready to enter a command and its arguments at the prompt. In the next example, the user enters the **`date`** command, which displays the date. The user types the command on the first line, and then presses ENTER to execute the command.

```
$ date
Sun July 7 10:30:21 PST 2002
```

The *command line interface* is the primary interface for the shell, which interprets the commands you enter and sends them to the system. The shell follows a special syntax for interpreting the command line. The first word entered on a command line must be the name of a command. The next words are options and arguments for the command. Each word on the command line must be separated from the others by one or more spaces or tabs.

```
$ Command      Options      Arguments
```

An *option* is a one-letter code preceded by a hyphen that modifies the type of action the command takes. One example of a command that has options is the **ls** command. The **ls** command, with no options, displays a list of all the files in your current directory. It merely lists the name of each file with no other information.

With a **-l** option, the **ls** command modifies its task by displaying a line of information about each file, listing such data as its size and the date and time it was last modified. In the next example, the user enters the **ls** command followed by a **-l** option. The hyphen before the **-l** option is required. Linux uses it to distinguish an option from an argument.

```
$ ls -l
```

Another option, **-a**, lists all the files in your directory, including what are known as hidden files. *Hidden files* are often configuration files and they always have names beginning with a period. For this reason, hidden files are often referred to as *dot files*. In most cases, you can also combine options. You do so by preceding the options with an initial hyphen and then listing the options you want. The options **-al**, for example, list information about all the files in your directory, including any hidden files.

```
$ ls -al
```

*Another option for the **ls** command is **-F**. With this option, the **ls** command displays directory names with a preceding slash, so you can easily identify them.*

Most commands are designed to take arguments. An *argument* is a word you type on the command line after any options. Many file management commands take filenames as their arguments. For example, if you only wanted the information displayed for a particular file, you could add that file's name after the **-l** option:

```
$ ls -l mydata
```

The shell you will start working in is the BASH shell, your default shell. This shell has special command line editing capabilities that you may find helpful as you learn Linux. You can easily modify commands you have entered before executing them, moving anywhere on the command line and inserting or deleting characters. This is particularly helpful for complex commands. You can use the CTRL-F or RIGHT ARROW keys to move forward a character, or the CTRL-B or LEFT ARROW keys to move back a character. CTRL-D or DEL deletes the character the cursor is on, and CTRL-H or BACKSPACE deletes the character before the cursor. To add text, you use the arrow keys to move the cursor to where you want to insert text and type the new characters. At any time, you can press ENTER to execute the command. For example, if you make a spelling mistake when entering a command, rather than reentering the entire command, you can use the editing operations to correct the mistake.

*The editing capabilities of the BASH shell command line are provided by Readline. Readline supports numerous editing operations. You can even bind a key to a selected editing operation. You can find out more about Readline in the BASH shell reference manual at **www.gnu.org/manual/bash**.*

You can also use the UP ARROW key to redisplay your previously executed command. You can then reexecute that command or edit it and execute the modified command. You'll find this capability helpful when you have to repeat certain operations over and over, such as editing the same file.

The capability to redisplay a previous command is helpful when you've already executed a command you had entered incorrectly. In this case, you would be presented with an error message and a new, empty command line. By pressing the UP ARROW key, you can redisplay your previous command, make corrections to it, and then execute it again. This way, you would not have to enter the whole command again.

The BASH shell keeps a list, called a *history list*, of your previously entered commands. You can display each command, in turn, on your command line by pressing the UP ARROW key. The DOWN ARROW key moves you down the list. You can modify and execute any of these previous commands when you display them on your command line. This history feature is discussed in more detail in Chapter 12.

Some commands can be complex and take some time to execute. When you mistakenly execute the wrong command, you can interrupt and stop such commands with the interrupt keys—CTRL-C or DEL.

You can enter a command on several lines by typing a backslash just before you press ENTER. The backslash "escapes" the ENTER key, effectively continuing the same command line to the next line. In the next example, the **cp** command is entered on three lines. The first two lines end in a backslash, effectively making all three lines one command line.

```
$ cp -i \
mydata \
newdata
```

Filename Expansion: *, ?, [ ]

Filenames are the most common arguments used in a command. Often you may know only part of the filename, or you may want to reference several filenames that have the same extension or begin with the same characters. The shell provides a set of special characters that search out, match, and generate a list of filenames. These are the asterisk, the question mark, and brackets (`*, ?, []`). Given a partial filename, the shell uses these matching operators to search for files and expand to a list of filenames found. The shell replaces the partial filename argument with the expanded list of matched filenames. This list of filenames can then become the arguments for commands such as **`ls`**, which can operate on many files. Table 10-1 lists the shell's file expansion characters.

Common Shell Symbols	Execution
ENTER	Execute a command line.
;	Separate commands on the same command line.
`'`*command*`'`	Execute a command.
`$(`*command*`)`	Execute a command.
`[]`	Match on a class of possible characters in filenames.
\	Quote the following character. Used to quote special characters.
|	Pipe the standard output of one command as input for another command.
`&`	Execute a command in the background.
`!`	History command.

Table 10-1. *Shell Symbols*

File Expansion Symbols	Execution
*	Match on any set of characters in filenames.
?	Match on any single character in filenames.
[]	Match on a class of characters in filenames.
Redirection Symbols	**Execution**
>	Redirect the standard output to a file or device, creating the file if it does not exist and overwriting the file if it does exist.
>!	The exclamation point forces the overwriting of a file if it already exists. This overrides the **noclobber** option.
<	Redirect the standard input from a file or device to a program.
>>	Redirect the standard output to a file or device, appending the output to the end of the file.
Standard Error Redirection Symbols	**Execution**
2>	Redirect the standard error to a file or device.
2>>	Redirect and append the standard error to a file or device.
2>&1	Redirect the standard error to the standard output.
>&	Redirect the standard error to a file or device.
|&	Pipe the standard error as input to another command.

Table 10-1. *Shell Symbols* (continued)

The asterisk, *****, references files beginning or ending with a specific set of characters. You place the asterisk before or after a set of characters that form a pattern to be searched for in filenames. If the asterisk is placed before the pattern, filenames that end in that pattern are searched for. If the asterisk is placed after the pattern, filenames that begin with that pattern are searched for. Any matching filename is copied into a list of filenames generated by this operation. In the next example, all filenames beginning with the pattern "doc" are searched for and a list generated. Then all filenames ending with the pattern "day" are searched for and a list is generated. The last example shows how the * can be used in any combination of characters.

```
$ ls
doc1 doc2 document docs mydoc monday tuesday
$ ls doc*
doc1 doc2 document docs
$ ls *day
monday tuesday
$ ls m*d*
monday
$
```

Filenames often include an extension specified with a period and followed by a string denoting the file type, such as **.c** for C files, **.cpp** for C++ files, or even **.jpg** for JPEG image files. The extension has no special status and is only part of the characters making up the filename. Using the asterisk makes it easy to select files with a given extension. In the next example, the asterisk is used to list only those files with a **.c** extension. The asterisk placed before the **.c** constitutes the argument for **ls**.

```
$ ls *.c
calc.c main.c
```

You can use * with the **rm** command to erase several files at once. The asterisk first selects a list of files with a given extension, or beginning or ending with a given set of characters, and then it presents this list of files to the **rm** command to be erased. In the next example, the **rm** command erases all files beginning with the pattern "doc":

```
$ rm doc*
```

The asterisk by itself matches all files. If you use a single asterisk as the argument for an **rm** command, all your files will be erased. In the next example, the **ls *** command lists all files, and the **rm *** command erases all files:

```
$ ls *
doc1 doc2 document docs mydoc myletter yourletter
$ rm *
$ ls
$
```

Use the * file expansion character carefully and sparingly with the **rm** command. The combination can be dangerous. A misplaced * in an **rm** command without the

-i option could easily erase all your files. The first command in the next example erases only those files with a **.c** extension. The second command, however, erases all files. Notice the space between the asterisk and the period in the second command. A space in a command line functions as a *delimiter*, separating arguments. The asterisk is considered one argument, and the **.c** another argument. The asterisk by itself matches all files and, when used as an argument with the **rm** command, instructs **rm** to erase all your files.

```
$ rm *.c
$ rm * .c
```

The question mark, **?**, matches only a single incomplete character in filenames. Suppose you want to match the files **doc1** and **docA**, but not **document**. Whereas the asterisk will match filenames of any length, the question mark limits the match to just one extra character. The next example matches files that begin with the word "doc" followed by a single differing letter:

```
$ ls
doc1 docA document
$ ls doc?
doc1 docA
```

Whereas the ***** and **?** file expansion characters specify incomplete portions of a filename, the brackets, **[]**, enable you to specify a set of valid characters to search for. Any character placed within the brackets will be matched in the filename. Suppose you want to list files beginning with "doc", but only ending in *1* or *A*. You are not interested in filenames ending in *2* or *B*, or any other character. Here is how it's done:

```
$ ls
doc1 doc2 doc3 docA docB docD document
$ ls doc[1A]
doc1 docA
```

You can also specify a set of characters as a range, rather than listing them one by one. A hyphen placed between the upper and lower bounds of a set of characters selects all characters within that range. The range is usually determined by the character set in use. In an ASCII character set, the range "a-g" will select all lowercase alphabetic characters from *a* through *g*, inclusive. In the next example, files beginning with the pattern "doc" and ending in characters *1* through *3* are selected. Then, those ending in characters *B* through *E* are matched.

```
$ ls doc[1-3]
doc1 doc2 doc3
$ ls doc[B-E]
docB docD
```

You can combine the brackets with other file expansion characters to form flexible matching operators. Suppose you only want to list filenames ending in either a **.c** or **.o** extension, but no other extension. You can use a combination of the asterisk and brackets: `* [co]`. The asterisk matches all filenames, and the brackets match only filenames with extension **.c** or **.o**.

```
$ ls *.[co]
main.c  main.o  calc.c
```

At times, a file expansion character is actually part of a filename. In these cases, you need to quote the character by preceding it with a backslash to reference the file. In the next example, the user needs to reference a file that ends with the **?** character, **answers?**. The **?** is, however, a file expansion character and would match any filename beginning with "answers" that has one or more characters. In this case, the user quotes the **?** with a preceding backslash to reference the filename.

```
$ ls answers\?
answers?
```

Though not a file expansion operation, `{}` is often useful for generating names that you can use to create or modify files and directories. The braces operation only generates a list of names. It does not match on existing filenames. Patterns are placed within the braces and separated with commas. Any pattern placed within the braces will be used to generate a version of the pattern, using either the preceding or following pattern, or both. Suppose you want to generate a list of names beginning with "doc", but only ending in the patterns "ument", "final", and "draft". Here is how it's done:

```
$ echo doc{ument,final,draft}
document docfinal docdraft
```

Since the names generated do not have to exist, you could use the `{}` operation in a command to create directories, as shown here.

```
$ mkdir {fall,winter,spring}report
$ ls
fallreport winterreport springreport
```

Standard Input/Output and Redirection

When Unix was designed, a decision was made to distinguish between the physical implementation and the logical organization of a file. Physically, Unix files are accessed in randomly arranged blocks. Logically, all files are organized as a continuous stream of bytes. Linux, as a version of Unix, has this same organization. Aside from special system calls, the user never references the physical structure of a file. To the user, all files have the same organization—a byte stream. Any file can be easily copied or appended to another because all files are organized in the same way. In this sense, only one standard type of file exists in Linux, the *byte-stream file*. Linux makes no implementational distinction between a character file and a record file, or a text file and a binary file.

This logical file organization extends to input and output operations. The data in input and output operations is organized like a file. Data input at the keyboard is placed in a data stream arranged as a continuous set of bytes. Data output from a command or program is also placed in a data stream and arranged as a continuous set of bytes. This input data stream is referred to in Linux as the *standard input*, while the output data stream is called the *standard output*. There is also a separate output data stream reserved solely for error messages, called the *standard error* (see the section on the standard error later in this chapter).

Because the standard input and standard output have the same organization as that of a file, they can easily interact with files. Linux has a redirection capability that lets you easily move data in and out of files. You can redirect the standard output so that, instead of displaying the output on a screen, you can save it in a file. You can also redirect the standard input away from the keyboard to a file, so that input is read from a file instead of from your keyboard.

When a Linux command is executed that produces output, this output is placed in the standard output data stream. The default destination for the standard output data stream is a device—in this case, the screen. *Devices*, such as the keyboard and screen, are treated as files. They receive and send out streams of bytes with the same organization as that of a byte-stream file. The screen is a device that displays a continuous stream of bytes. By default, the standard output will send its data to the screen device, which will then display the data.

For example, the `ls` command generates a list of all filenames and outputs this list to the standard output. Next, this stream of bytes in the standard output is directed to the screen device. The list of filenames is then printed on the screen. The `cat` command also sends output to the standard output. The contents of a file are copied to the standard output whose default destination is the screen. The contents of the file are then displayed on the screen.

Redirecting the Standard Output: > and >>

Suppose that instead of displaying a list of files on the screen, you would like to save this list in a file. In other words, you would like to direct the standard output to a file rather than the screen. To do this, you place the output redirection operator,

> (greater-than sign), and the name of a file on the command line after the Linux command. Table 10-2 lists the different ways you can use the redirection operators. In the next example, the output of the **cat** command is redirected from the screen device to a file:

```
$ cat myletter > newletter
```

Command	Execution
ENTER	Execute a command line.
;	Separate commands on the same command line.
command\ *opts args*	Enter backslash before carriage return to continue entering a command on the next line.
`*command*`	Execute a command.
$(*command*)	Execute a command.
BACKSPACE CTRL-H	Erase the previous character.
CTRL-U	Erase the command line and start over.
CTRL-C	Interrupt and stop a command execution.
Special Characters for Filename Expansion	**Execution**
*	Match on any set of characters.
?	Match on any single characters.
[]	Match on a class of possible characters.
\	Quote the following character. Used to quote special characters.
Redirection	**Execution**
command > *filename*	Redirect the standard output to a file or device, creating the file if it does not exist and overwriting the file if it does exist.

Table 10-2. *The Shell Operations*

Redirection	Execution
command < *filename*	Redirect the standard input from a file or device to a program.
command >> *filename*	Redirect the standard output to a file or device, appending the output to the end of the file.
command >! *filename*	In the C shell and the Korn shell, the exclamation point forces the overwriting of a file if it already exists. This overrides the **`noclobber`** option.
command 2> *filename*	Redirect the standard error to a file or device in the Bourne shell.
command 2>> *filename*	Redirect and append the standard error to a file or device in the Bourne shell.
command `2>&1`	Redirect the standard error to the standard output in the Bourne shell.
command >& *filename*	Redirect the standard error to a file or device in the C shell.
Pipes	**Execution**
command | *command*	Pipe the standard output of one command as input for another command.
command |& *command*	Pipe the standard error as input to another command in the C shell.
Background Jobs	**Execution**
&	Execute a command in the background.
`fg` %*jobnum*	Bring a command in the background to the foreground or resume an interrupted program.
`bg`	Place a command in the foreground into the background.
CTRL-Z	Interrupt and stop the currently running program. The program remains stopped and waiting in the background for you to resume it.
`notify` %*jobnum*	Notify you when a job ends.

Table 10-2. *The Shell Operations* (continued)

Background Jobs	Execution
`kill` %*jobnum* `kill` *processnum*	Cancel and end a job running in the background.
`jobs`	List all background jobs. The **jobs** command is not available in the Bourne shell, unless it is using the jsh shell.
`ps`	List all currently running processes, including background jobs.
`at` *time date*	Execute commands at a specified time and date. The time can be entered with hours and minutes and qualified as A.M. or P.M.

Table 10-2. *The Shell Operations* (continued)

The redirection operation creates the new destination file. If the file already exists, it will be overwritten with the data in the standard output. You can set the **noclobber** feature to prevent overwriting an existing file with the redirection operation. In this case, the redirection operation on an existing file will fail. You can overcome the **noclobber** feature by placing an exclamation point after the redirection operator. You can place the **noclobber** command in a shell configuration file to make it an automatic default operation (see Chapter 12). The next example sets the **noclobber** feature for the BASH shell and then forces the overwriting of the **oldletter** file if it already exists:

```
$ set -o noclobber
$ cat myletter >! oldletter
```

Although the redirection operator and the filename are placed after the command, the redirection operation is not executed after the command. In fact, it is executed before the command. The redirection operation creates the file and sets up the redirection before it receives any data from the standard output. If the file already exists, it will be destroyed and replaced by a file of the same name. In effect, the command generating the output is executed only after the redirected file has been created.

In the next example, the output of the **ls** command is redirected from the screen device to a file. First the **ls** command lists files and, in the next command, **ls** redirects its file list to the **listf** file. Then the **cat** command displays the list of files saved in **listf**. Notice the list of files in **listf** includes the **listf** filename. The list of filenames generated by the **ls** command includes the name of the file created by the redirection operation—

in this case, **listf**. The **listf** file is first created by the redirection operation, and then the `ls` command lists it along with other files. This file list output by `ls` is then redirected to the **listf** file, instead of being printed on the screen.

```
$ ls
mydata intro preface
$ ls > listf
$ cat listf
mydata intro listf preface
```

Errors occur when you try to use the same filename for both an input file for the command and the redirected destination file. In this case, because the redirection operation is executed first, the input file, because it exists, is destroyed and replaced by a file of the same name. When the command is executed, it finds an input file that is empty.

In the `cat` command shown next, the file **myletter** is the name for both the destination file for redirected output and the input file for the `cat` operation. As shown in the next example, the redirection operation is executed first, destroying the **myletter** file and replacing it with a new and empty **myletter** file. Then the `cat` operation is executed and attempts to read all the data in the **myletter** file. However, nothing new is now in the **myletter** file.

```
$ cat myletter > myletter
```

You can also append the standard output to an existing file using the **>>** redirection operator. Instead of overwriting the file, the data in the standard output is added at the end of the file. In the next example, the **myletter** and **oldletter** files are appended to the **alletters** file. The **alletters** file will then contain the contents of both **myletter** and **oldletter**.

```
$ cat myletter >> alletters
$ cat oldletter >> alletters
```

The Standard Input

Many Linux commands can receive data from the standard input. The standard input itself receives data from a device or a file. The default device for the standard input is the keyboard. Characters typed on the keyboard are placed in the standard input, which is then directed to the Linux command. The `cat` command without a filename argument reads data from standard input. When you type data on the keyboard, each character will be placed in the standard input and directed to the `cat` command. The `cat` command then sends the character to the standard output—the screen device—which displays the character on the screen.

If you combine the **cat** command with redirection, you have an easy way of saving what you have typed to a file. As shown in the next example, the output of the **cat** operation is redirected to the **mydat** file. The **mydat** file will now contain all the data typed in at the keyboard. The **cat** command, in this case, still has no file arguments. It will receive its data from the standard input, the keyboard device. The redirection operator redirects the output of the **cat** command to the file **mydat**. The **cat** command has no direct contact with any files; it is simply receiving input from the standard input and sending output to the standard output.

```
$ cat > mydat
This is a new line
for the cat
command
^D
$
```

Just as with the standard output, you can also redirect the standard input. The standard input may be received from a file rather than the keyboard. The operator for redirecting the standard input is the less-than sign, **<**. In the next example, the standard input is redirected to receive input from the **myletter** file, rather than the keyboard device. The contents of **myletter** are read into the standard input by the redirection operation. Then the **cat** command reads the standard input and displays the contents of **myletter**.

```
$ cat < myletter
hello Christopher
How are you today
$
```

You can combine the redirection operations for both standard input and standard output. In the next example, the **cat** command has no filename arguments. Without filename arguments, the **cat** command receives input from the standard input and sends output to the standard output. However, the standard input has been redirected to receive its data from a file, while the standard output has been redirected to place its data in a file.

```
$ cat < myletter > newletter
```

Pipes: |

You may find yourself in situations in which you need to send data from one command to another. In other words, you may want to send the standard output of a command to another command, not to a destination file. Suppose you want to send a list of your filenames to the printer to be printed. You need two commands to do this: the **ls** command to generate a list of filenames and the **lpr** command to send the list to the printer. In effect, you need to take the output of the **ls** command and use it as input for the **lpr** command. You can think of the data as flowing from one command to another. To form such a connection in Linux, you use what is called a *pipe*. The *pipe operator*, |, (vertical bar character) placed between two commands forms a connection between them. The standard output of one command becomes the standard input for the other. The pipe operation receives output from the command placed before the pipe and sends this data as input to the command placed after the pipe. As shown in the next example, you can connect the **ls** command and the **lpr** command with a pipe. The list of filenames output by the **ls** command is piped into the **lpr** command.

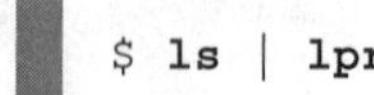

```
$ ls | lpr
```

You can combine the **pipe** operation with other shell features, such as file expansion characters, to perform specialized operations. The next example prints only files with a **.c** extension. The **ls** command is used with the asterisk and ".c" to generate a list of filenames with the **.c** extension. Then this list is piped to the **lpr** command.

```
$ ls *.c | lpr
```

In the previous example, a list of filenames was used as input, but what is important to note is pipes operate on the standard output of a command, whatever that might be. The contents of whole files or even several files can be piped from one command to another. In the next example, the **cat** command reads and outputs the contents of the **mydata** file, which are then piped to the **lpr** command:

```
$ cat mydata | lpr
```

Linux has many commands that generate modified output. For example, the **sort** command takes the contents of a file and generates a version with each line sorted in alphabetic order. The **sort** command works best with files that are lists of items. Commands such as **sort** that output a modified version of its input are referred to as *filters*. Filters are often used with pipes. In the next example, a sorted version of **mylist** is generated and piped into the **more** command for display on the screen. Note that the original file, **mylist**, has not been changed and is not itself sorted. Only the output of **sort** in the standard output is sorted.

```
$ sort mylist | more
```

You can, of course, combine several commands, connecting each pair with a pipe. The output of one command can be piped into another command, which, in turn, can pipe its output into still another command. Suppose you have a file with a list of items you want to print both numbered and in alphabetical order. To print the numbered and sorted list, you can first generate a sorted version with the **sort** command and then pipe that output to the **cat** command. The **cat** command with the **-n** option then takes as its input the sorted list and generates as its output a numbered, sorted list. The numbered, sorted list can then be piped to the **lpr** command for printing. The next example shows the command:

```
$ sort mylist | cat -n | lpr
```

The standard input piped into a command can be more carefully controlled with the standard input argument, **-**. When you use the hyphen as an argument for a command, it represents the standard input. Suppose you want to print a file with the name of its directory at the top. The **pwd** command outputs a directory name, and the **cat** command outputs the contents of a file. In this case, the **cat** command needs to take as its input both the file and the standard input piped in from the **pwd** command. The **cat** command will have two arguments: the standard input as represented by the hyphen and the filename of the file to be printed.

In the next example, the **pwd** command generates the directory name and pipes it into the **cat** command. For the **cat** command, this piped-in standard input now contains the directory name. As represented by the hyphen, the standard input is the first argument to the **cat** command. The **cat** command copies the directory name and the contents of the **mylist** file to the standard output, which is then piped to the **lpr** command for printing. If you want to print the directory name at the end of the file instead, simply make the hyphen the last argument and the filename the first argument, as in **cat mylist -**.

```
$ pwd | cat - mylist | lpr
```

Redirecting and Piping the Standard Error: >&, 2>

When you execute commands, an error could possibly occur. You may give the wrong number of arguments, or some kind of system error could take place. When an error occurs, the system issues an error message. Usually such error messages are displayed on the screen, along with the standard output. Linux distinguishes between standard output and error messages, however. Error messages are placed in yet another standard byte stream called the *standard error*. In the next example, the **cat** command is given as its argument the name of a file that does not exist, **myintro**. In this case, the **cat** command simply issues an error:

```
$ cat myintro
cat : myintro not found
$
```

Because error messages are in a separate data stream from the standard output, error messages still appear on the screen for you to see even if you have redirected the standard output to a file. In the next example, the standard output of the **cat** command is redirected to the file **mydata**. However, the standard error, containing the error messages, is still directed to the screen.

```
$ cat myintro > mydata
cat : myintro not found
$
```

You can redirect the standard error as you can the standard output. This means you can save your error messages in a file for future reference. This is helpful if you need a record of the error messages. Like the standard output, the standard error has the screen device for its default destination. However, you can redirect the standard error to any file or device you choose using special redirection operators. In this case, the error messages will not be displayed on the screen.

Redirection of the standard error relies on a special feature of shell redirection. You can reference all the standard byte streams in redirection operations with numbers. The numbers 0, 1, and 2 reference the standard input, standard output, and standard error, respectively. By default, an output redirection, **>**, operates on the standard output, 1. You can modify the output redirection to operate on the standard error, however, by preceding the output redirection operator with the number 2. In the next example, the **cat** command again will generate an error. The error message is redirected to the standard byte stream represented by the number 2, the standard error.

```
$ cat nodata 2> myerrors
$ cat myerrors
cat : nodata not found
$
```

You can also append the standard error to a file by using the number 2 and the redirection append operator, **>>**. In the next example, the user appends the standard error to the **myerrors** file, which then functions as a log of errors:

```
$ cat nodata 2>> myerrors
```

Shell Variables

You define variables within a shell, and such variables are known—logically enough—as *shell variables*. Many different shells exist. Some utilities, such as the Mail utility, have their own shells with their own shell variables. You can also create your own shell using what are called *shell scripts*. You have a user shell that becomes active as soon as you log in. This is often referred to as the *login shell*. Special system variables are defined within this login shell. Shell variables can also be used to define a shell's environment, as described in Chapter 12.

Note *Shell variables exist as long as your shell is active—that is, until you exit the shell. For example, logging out will exit the login shell. When you log in again, any variables you may need in your login shell must be defined again.*

Definition and Evaluation of Variables: =, $, set, unset

You define a variable in a shell when you first use the variable's name. A variable's name may be any set of alphabetic characters, including the underscore. The name may also include a number, but the number cannot be the first character in the name. A name may not have any other type of character, such as an exclamation point, an ampersand, or even a space. Such symbols are reserved by the shell for its own use. Also, a name may not include more than one word. The shell uses spaces on the command line to distinguish different components of a command such as options, arguments, and the name of the command.

You assign a value to a variable with the assignment operator, `=`. You type the variable name, the assignment operator, and then the value assigned. Do not place any spaces around the assignment operator. The assignment operation **poet = Virgil**, for example, will fail. (The C shell has a slightly different type of assignment operation that is described in the section on C shell variables later in this chapter.) You can assign any set of characters to a variable. In the next example, the variable **poet** is assigned the string **Virgil**:

```
$ poet=Virgil
```

Once you have assigned a value to a variable, you can then use the variable name to reference the value. Often you use the values of variables as arguments for a command. You can reference the value of a variable using the variable name preceded by the **$** operator. The dollar sign is a special operator that uses the variable name to reference a variable's value, in effect evaluating the variable. Evaluation retrieves a variable's value, usually a set of characters. This set of characters then replaces the variable name on the command line. Wherever a **$** is placed before the variable name, the variable name is replaced with the value of the variable. In the next example, the shell variable **poet** is evaluated and its contents, **Virgil**, are then used as the argument for an **echo** command. The **echo** command simply echoes or prints a set of characters to the screen.

```
$ echo $poet
Virgil
```

You must be careful to distinguish between the evaluation of a variable and its name alone. If you leave out the **$** operator before the variable name, all you have is the variable name itself. In the next example, the **$** operator is absent from the variable name. In this case, the **echo** command has as its argument the word "poet", and so prints out "poet":

```
$ echo poet
poet
```

The contents of a variable are often used as command arguments. A common command argument is a directory pathname. It can be tedious to retype a directory path that is being used over and over again. If you assign the directory pathname to a variable, you can simply use the evaluated variable in its place. The directory path you assign to the variable is retrieved when the variable is evaluated with the **$** operator. The next example assigns a directory pathname to a variable and then uses the evaluated variable in a copy command. The evaluation of **ldir** (which is **$ldir**) results in the path name **/home/chris/letters**. The copy command evaluates to **cp myletter /home/chris/letters**.

```
$ ldir=/home/chris/letters
$ cp myletter $ldir
```

You can obtain a list of all the defined variables with the **set** command. The next example uses the **set** command to display a list of all defined variables and their values:

```
$ set
poet   Virgil
ldir   /home/chris/letters
$
```

If you decide you do not want a certain variable, you can remove it with the **unset** command. The **unset** command undefines a variable. The next example undefines the variable **poet**. Then the user executes the **set** command to list all defined variables. Notice that **poet** is missing.

```
$ unset poet
$ set
ldir  /home/chris/letters
$
```

Shell Scripts: User-Defined Commands

You can place shell commands within a file and then have the shell read and execute the commands in the file. In this sense, the file functions as a shell program, executing shell commands as if they were statements in a program. A file that contains shell commands is called a *shell script*.

You enter shell commands into a script file using a standard text editor such as the Vi editor. The **sh** or **.** command used with the script's filename will read the script file and execute the commands. In the next example, the text file called **lsc** contains an **ls** command that displays only files with the extension **.c**:

lsc

```
ls *.c
```

A run of the script follows.

```
$ sh lsc
main.c calc.c
$ . lsc
main.c calc.c
```

You can dispense with the **sh** and **.** commands by setting the executable permission of a script file. When the script file is first created by your text editor, it is only given read and write permission. The **chmod** command with the **+x** option will give the script file executable permission. (Permissions are discussed in Chapter 12.) Once it is executable, entering the name of the script file at the shell prompt and pressing ENTER will execute the script file and the shell commands in it. In effect, the script's filename becomes a new shell command. In this way, you can use shell scripts to design and create your own Linux commands. You only need to set the permission once. In the next example, the **lsc** file's executable permission for the owner is set to on. Then the **lsc** shell script is directly executed like any Linux command.

```
$ chmod u+x lsc
$ lsc
main.c calc.c
```

You may have to specify that the script you are using is in your current working directory. You do this by prefixing the script name with a period and slash combination, **./**, as in **./lsc**. The period is a special character representing the name of your current working directory. The slash is a directory path name separator, as explained more fully in Chapter 12. The following example would show how you would execute the **hello** script:

```
$ ./lsc
main.c calc.c
```

Just as any Linux command can take arguments, so also can a shell script. Arguments on the command line are referenced sequentially starting with 1. An argument is referenced using the **$** operator and the number of its position. The first argument is referenced with **$1**, the second, with **$2**, and so on. In the next example, the **lsext** script prints out files with a specified extension. The first argument is the extension. The script is then executed with the argument **c** (of course, the executable permission must have been set).

lsext

```
ls *.$1
```

A run of the script follows.

```
$ lsext c
main.c calc.c
```

In the next example, the commands to print out a file with line numbers have been placed in an executable file called **lpnum**, which takes a filename as its argument. The **cat** command with the **-n** option first outputs the contents of the file with line numbers. Then this output is piped into the **lp** command, which prints it. The command to print out the line numbers is executed in the background.

lpnum

```
cat -n $1 | lp &
```

You may need to reference more than one argument at a time. The number of arguments used may vary. In **lpnum,** you may want to print out three files at one time and five files at some other time. The **$** operator with the asterisk, **$***, references all the arguments on the command line. Using **$*** enables you to create scripts that take a varying number of arguments. In the next example, **lpnum** is rewritten using **$*** so it can take a different number of arguments each time you use it:

lpnum

```
cat -n $* | lp &
```

Jobs: Background, Kills, and Interruptions

In Linux, you not only have control over a command's input and output, but also over its execution. You can run a job in the background while you execute other commands. You can also cancel commands before they have finished executing. You can even interrupt a command, starting it again later from where you left off. Background operations are particularly useful for long jobs. Instead of waiting at the terminal until a command has finished execution, you can place it in the background. You can then continue executing other Linux commands. You can, for example, edit a file while other files are printing.

Canceling a background command can often save you a lot of unnecessary expense. If, say, you execute a command to print all your files and then realize you have some large files you do not want to print, you can reference that execution of the print command and cancel it. Interrupting commands is rarely used, and sometimes it is unintentionally executed. You can, if you want, interrupt an editing session to send mail and then return to your editing session, continuing from where you left off. The background commands, as well as commands to cancel and interrupt jobs, are listed in Table 10-2.

In Linux, a command is considered a *process*—a task to be performed. A Linux system can execute several processes at the same time, just as Linux can handle several users at the same time. Commands to examine and control processes exist, though they are often reserved for system administration operations. Processes actually include not only the commands a user executes, but also all the tasks the system must perform to keep Linux running.

The commands that users execute are often called *jobs* to distinguish them from system processes. When the user executes a command, it becomes a job to be performed by the system. The shell provides a set of job control operations that enable the user to control the execution of these jobs. You can place a job in the background, cancel a job, or interrupt one.

You execute a command in the background by placing an ampersand on the command line at the end of the command. When you do so, a user job number and a system process number are displayed. The user job number, placed in brackets, is the number by which the user references the job. The system process number is the number by which the system identifies the job. In the next example, the command to print the file **mydata** is placed in the background:

```
$ lpr mydata &
[1]  534
$
```

You can place more than one command in the background. Each is classified as a job and given a name and a job number. The command **jobs** lists the jobs being run in the background. Each entry in the list consists of the job number in brackets, whether it is stopped or running, and the name of the job. The **+** sign indicates the job currently being processed, and the **-** sign indicates the next job to be executed. In the next example, two commands have been placed in the background. The **jobs** command then lists those jobs, showing which one is currently being executed.

```
$ lpr intro &
[1]  547
$ cat *.c > myprogs &
```

```
[2]  548
$ jobs
[1]  +  Running  lpr intro
[2]  -  Running  cat *.c > myprogs
$
```

If you wish, you can place several commands at once in the background by entering the commands on the command line, separated by an ampersand, **&**. In this case, the **&** both separates commands on the command line and executes them in the background. In the next example, the first command, to sort and redirect all files with a **.l** extension, is placed in the background. On the same command line, the second command, to print all files with a **.c** extension, is also placed in the background. Notice the two commands each end with **&**. The **jobs** command then lists the **sort** and **lpr** commands as separate operations.

```
$ sort *.l > ldocs &; lpr *.c &
[1]  534
[2]  567
$ jobs
[1]  +  Running  sort *.l > ldocs
[2]  -  Running  lpr
$
```

After you execute any command in Linux, the system tells you what background jobs, if you have any running, have been completed so far. The system does not interrupt any operation, such as editing, to notify you about a completed job. If you want to be notified immediately when a certain job ends, no matter what you are doing on the system, you can use the **notify** command to instruct the system to tell you. The **notify** command takes a job number as its argument. When that job is finished, the system interrupts what you are doing to notify you the job has ended. The next example tells the system to notify the user when job 2 has finished:

```
$ notify %2
```

You can bring a job out of the background with the foreground command, **fg**. If only one job is in the background, the **fg** command alone will bring it to the foreground. If more than one job is in the background, you must use the job's number with the command. You place the job number after the **fg** command, preceded with a percent sign. A **bg** command also places a job in the background. This command is usually used for interrupted jobs. In the next example, the second job is brought back into the foreground. You may not immediately receive a prompt again because the second command is now in the foreground and executing. When the command is finished executing, the prompt appears and you can execute another command.

```
$ fg %2
cat *.c > myprogs
$
```

If you want to stop a job running in the background, you can force it to end with the **kill** command. The **kill** command takes as its argument either the user job number or the system process number. The user job number must be preceded by a percent sign, **%**. You can find out the job number from the **jobs** command. In the next example, the **jobs** command lists the background jobs; then job 2 is canceled:

```
$ jobs
[1]  +  Running  lpr intro
[2]  -  Running  cat *.c > myprogs
$ kill %2
$
```

You can also cancel a job using the system process number, which you can obtain with the **ps** command. The **ps** command displays a great deal more information than the **jobs** command does. The next example lists the processes a user is running. The PID is the system process number, also known as the process ID. TTY is the terminal identifier. The time is how long the process has taken so far. COMMAND is the name of the process.

```
$ ps
PID     TTY       TIME      COMMAND
523     tty24     0:05      sh
567     tty24     0:01      lpr
570     tty24     0:00      ps
```

You can then reference the system process number in a **kill** command. Use the process number without any preceding percent sign. The next example kills process 567:

```
$ kill 567
```

You can suspend a job and stop it with the CTRL-Z keys. This places the job to the side until it is restarted. The job is not ended; it merely remains suspended until you want to continue. When you're ready, you can continue with the job in either the foreground or the background using the **fg** or **bg** command. The **fg** command restarts a suspended job in the foreground. The **bg** command places the suspended job in the background.

At times, you may need to place a currently running job in the foreground into the background. However, you cannot move a currently running job directly into the background. You first need to suspend it with CTRL-Z, and then place it in the background with the **bg** command. In the next example, the current command to list and redirect **.c** files is first suspended with CTRL-Z. Then that job is placed in the background.

```
$ cat *.c > myprogs
^Z
$ bg
```

The Complete Reference

Chapter 11

The Linux File Structure

In Linux, all files are organized into directories that, in turn, are hierarchically connected to each other in one overall file structure. A file is referenced not just according to its name, but also according to its place in this file structure. You can create as many new directories as you want, adding more directories to the file structure. The Linux file commands can perform sophisticated operations, such as moving or copying whole directories along with their subdirectories. Desktop file managers, such as Konqueror, Nautilus, and Midnight Commander used on the KDE and Gnome desktops, provide a graphical user interface to perform the same operations using icons, windows, and menus (see Chapters 8 and 9).

Linux Files and Directories

You can name a file using any letters, underscores, and numbers. You can also include periods and commas. Except in certain special cases, you should never begin a filename with a period. Other characters, such as slashes, question marks, or asterisks, are reserved for use as special characters by the system and should not be part of a filename. Filenames can be as long as 256 characters.

Linux organizes files into a hierarchically connected set of directories. Each directory may contain either files or other directories. In this respect, directories perform two important functions. A *directory* holds files, much like files held in a file drawer, and a directory connects to other directories, much like a branch in a tree is connected to other branches. With respect to files, directories appear to operate like file drawers, with each drawer holding several files. To access files, you open a file drawer. Unlike file drawers, however, directories can contain not only files, but other directories as well. In this way, a directory can connect to another directory.

Because of the similarities to a tree, such a structure is often referred to as a *tree structure*. This structure could more accurately be thought of as an upside-down bush rather than a tree, however, because no trunk exists. The tree is represented upside down, with the root at the top. Extending down from the root are the branches. Each branch grows out of only one branch, but it can have many lower branches. In this respect, it can be said to have a *parent/child structure*. In the same way, each directory is itself a subdirectory of one other directory. Each directory may contain many subdirectories, but is itself the child of only one parent directory.

The Linux file structure branches into several directories beginning with a root directory, /. Within the root directory system, directories contain files and programs that are features of the Linux system. The root directory also contains a directory called **home** that contains the home directories of all the users in the system. Each user's home directory, in turn, contains the directories the user has made for their own use. Each of these could also contain directories. Such nested directories would branch out from the user's home directory.

You may also need to look at the contents of a file. The **cat** and **more** commands display the contents of a file on the screen. **cat** stands for *concatenate*.

```
$ cat mydata
computers
```

The **cat** command outputs the entire text of a file to the screen at once. This presents a problem when the file is large because its text quickly speeds past on the screen. The **more** command is designed to overcome this limitation by displaying one screen of text at a time. You can then move forward or backward in the text at your leisure. You invoke the **more** command by entering the command name followed by the name of the file you want to view.

```
$ more mydata
```

When **more** invokes a file, the first screen of text is displayed. To continue to the next screen, you press the F key or the SPACEBAR. To move back in the text, you press the B key. You can quit at any time by pressing the Q key.

With the printer commands such as **lpr** and **lprm,** you can perform printing operations such as printing files or canceling print jobs. When you need to print files, use the **lpr** command to send files to the printer connected to your system. In the next example, the user prints the **mydata** file:

```
$ lpr mydata
```

Printing jobs are placed in a queue and printed one at a time in the background. You can continue with other work as your files print. You can see the position of a particular printing job at any given time with the **lpq** command. **lpq** gives the owner of the printing job (the login name of the user who sent the job), the print job ID, the size in bytes, and the temporary file in which it is currently held. In this example, the owner is **chris** and the print ID is **00015**:

```
$ lpq
Owner ID Chars Filename
chris 00015 360 /usr/lpd/cfa00015
```

If you need to cancel an unwanted printing job, you can do so with the **lprm** command. **lprm** takes as its argument either the ID number of the printing job or the owner's name. **lprm** then removes the print job from the print queue. For this task, **lpq** is helpful, for it provides you with the ID number and owner of the printing job you need to use with **lprm**. In the next example, the print job 15 is canceled:

```
$ lprm 00015
```

You can create and remove your own directories, as well as change your working directory, with the **mkdir**, **rmdir**, and **cd** commands. Each of these commands can take as its argument the pathname for a directory. The **pwd** command displays the absolute pathname of your working directory. In addition to these commands, the special characters represented by a single dot, a double dot, and a tilde can be used to reference the working directory, the parent of the working directory, and the home directory, respectively. Taken together, these commands enable you to manage your directories. You can create nested directories, move from one directory to another, and use pathnames to reference any of your directories.

As you create more and more files, you may want to back them up, change their names, erase some of them, or even give them added names. Linux provides you with several file commands that enable you to search for files, copy files, rename files, or remove files. If you have a large number of files, you can also search them to locate a specific one. The commands are shortened forms of full words, consisting of only two characters. The **cp** command stands for "copy" and copies a file, **mv** stands for "move" and renames or moves a file, **rm** stands for "remove" and erases a file, and **ln** stands for "link" and adds another name for a file. One exception to the two-character rule is the **find** command, which performs searches of your filenames to find a file.

Once you have a large number of files in many different directories, you may need to search them to locate a specific file, or files, of a certain type. The **find** command enables you to perform such a search. The **find** command takes as its arguments directory names followed by several possible options that specify the type of search and the criteria for the search. **find** then searches within the directories listed and their subdirectories for files that meet these criteria. The **find** command can search for a file based on its name, type, owner, and even the time of the last update.

```
$ find directory-list -option criteria
```

The **-name** option has as its criteria a pattern and instructs **find** to search for the filename that matches that pattern. To search for a file by name, you use the **find** command with the directory name followed by the **-name** option and the name of the file.

```
$ find directory-list -name filename
```

To make a copy of a file, you simply give **cp** two filenames as its arguments. The first filename is the name of the file to be copied—the one that already exists. This is often referred to as the *source file*. The second filename is the name you want for the copy. This will be a new file containing a copy of all the data in the source file. This second argument is often referred to as the *destination file*. The syntax for the **cp** command follows:

```
$ cp source-file destination-file
```

As you use Linux, you will find the number of files you use increases rapidly. Generating files in Linux is easy. Applications such as editors, and commands such as **cp**, easily create files. Eventually, many of these files may become outdated and useless. You can then remove them with the **rm** command. In the next example, the user erases the file **oldprop**:

```
$ rm oldprop
```

The **rm** command can take any number of arguments, enabling you to list several filenames and erase them all at the same time. You just list them on the command line after you type **rm**.

You can give a file more than one name using the **ln** command. You might want to reference a file using different filenames to access it from different directories. The added names are often referred to as *links*. Linux supports two different types of links, hard and symbolic. Symbolic links are much more flexible and can work over many different file systems, whereas hard links are limited to your local file system. Links are usually implemented as symbolic links.

To set up a symbolic link, you use the **ln** command with the **-s** option and two arguments: the name of the original file and the new, added filename. The **ls** operation lists both filenames, but only one physical file will exist.

```
$ ln -s original-file-name added-file-name
```

In the next example, the **today** file is given the additional name **weather**. It is just another name for the **today** file.

```
$ ls
today
$ ln -s today weather
$ ls
today weather
```

File and Directory Permissions

Each file and directory in Linux contains a set of permissions that determine who can access them and how. You set these permissions to limit access in one of three ways: You can restrict access to yourself alone, you can allow users in a predesignated group to have access, or you can permit anyone on your system to have access. You can also control how a given file or directory is accessed. A file and directory may have read, write, and execute permissions. When a file is created, it is automatically given read and write permissions for the owner, enabling you to display and modify the file. You may change these permissions to any combination you want. A file could have read-only permission, preventing any modifications. A file could also have execute permission, allowing it to be executed as a program.

Three different categories of users can have access to a file or directory: the owner, the group, or others. The owner is the user who created the file. Any file you create, you own. You can also permit your group to have access to a file. Often, users are collected into groups. For example, all the users for a given class or project could be formed into a group by the system administrator. A user can give access to a file to other members of the group. Finally, you can also open up access to a file to all other users on the system. In this case, every user on your system could have access to one of your files or directories. In this sense, every other user on the system makes up the "others" category.

Each category has its own set of read, write, and execute permissions. The first set controls the user's own access to his or her files—the owner access. The second set controls the access of the group to a user's files. The third set controls the access of all other users to the user's files. The three sets of read, write, and execute permissions for the three categories—owner, group, and other—make a total of nine types of permissions.

As you saw in the previous section, the **ls** command with the **-l** option displays detailed information about the file, including the permissions. In the next example, the first set of characters on the left is a list of the permissions set for the **mydata** file:

```
$ ls -l mydata
-rw-r--r-- 1 chris weather 207 Feb 20 11:55 mydata
```

An empty permission is represented by a dash, -. The read permission is represented by **r**, write by **w**, and execute by **x**. Notice there are ten positions. The first character indicates the file type. In a general sense, a directory can be considered a type of file. If the first character is a dash, a file is being listed. If it is **d**, information about a directory is being displayed.

The next nine characters are arranged according to the different user categories. The first set of three characters is the owner's set of permissions for the file. The second set of three characters is the group's set of permissions for the file. The last set of three characters is the other users' set of permissions for the file.

You use the **chmod** command to change different permission configurations. **chmod** takes two lists as its arguments: permission changes and filenames. You can specify the list of permissions in two different ways. One way uses permission symbols and is referred to as the *symbolic method*. The other uses what is known as a "binary mask" and is referred to as either the *absolute* or the *relative method*. Of the two, the symbolic method is the more intuitive and will be presented first.

The symbolic method of setting permissions uses the characters **r**, **w**, and **x** for read, write, and execute, respectively. Any of these permissions can be added or removed. The symbol to add a permission is the plus sign, **+**. The symbol to remove a permission is the minus sign, -. In the next example, the **chmod** command adds the execute permission and removes the write permission for the **mydata** file. The read permission is not changed.

```
$ chmod +x-w mydata
```

Instead of permission symbols, many users find it more convenient to use the absolute method. The *absolute method* changes all the permissions at once, instead of specifying one or the other. It uses a binary mask that references all the permissions in each category. The three categories, each with three permissions, conform to an octal binary format. Octal numbers have a base 8 structure. When translated into a binary number, each octal digit becomes three binary digits. A binary number is a set of 1 and 0 digits. Three octal digits in a number translate into three sets of three binary digits, which is nine altogether—and the exact number of permissions for a file.

If you want others to be able to execute and read the file, but not change it, you can set the read and execute permissions and turn off the write permission with the digit 5 (101). In this case, you would use the octal digits 755, having the binary equivalent of 111 101 101.

```
$ chmod 755 myprog
```

A simple way to calculate the octal number makes use of the fact that any number used for permissions will be a combination derived from adding in decimal terms the numbers 4, 2, and 1. Use 4 for read permission, 2 for write, and 1 for execute. The read, write, execute permission is simply the addition of 4 + 2 + 1 to get 7. The read and execute permission adds 4 and 1, to get 5. You can use this method to calculate the octal number for each category. To get 755, you would add 4 + 2 + 1 for the user read, write, and execute permission, 4 + 1 for the group read and execute permission, and 4 + 1 again for the other read and execute permission.

The mtools Utilities: msdos

Your Linux system provides a set of utilities, known as *mtools,* that enable you to access a floppy and hard disks formatted for MS-DOS easily.The **mcopy** command enables you to copy files to and from an MS-DOS floppy disk in your floppy drive or a Windows partition on your hard drive. No special operations, such as mounting, are required. With mtools, you needn't mount an MS-DOS partition to access it. For an MS-DOS floppy disk, place the disk in your floppy drive, and you can then use mtool commands to access those files. For example, to copy a file from an MS-DOS floppy disk to your Linux system, use the **mcopy** command. You specify the MS-DOS disk with **a:** for the A drive. Unlike normal DOS pathnames, pathnames used with mtool commands use forward slashes instead of backslashes. The directory **docs** on the A drive would be referenced by the pathname **a:/docs**, not **a:\docs**. Unlike MS-DOS, which defaults the second argument to the current directory, you always need to supply the second argument for **mcopy**. The next example copies the file **mydata** to the MS-DOS disk, and then copies the **preface** file from the disk to the current Linux directory.

```
$ mcopy mydata a:
$ mcopy a:/preface  .
```

Note *Currently, mtools cannot access Windows XP, NT, and 2000 NTFS partitions.*

Archive Files and Compression: tar, gzip, and bzip2

The tar utility creates archives for files and directories. With tar, you can archive specific files, update them in the archive, and add new files as you want to that archive. You can even archive entire directories with all their files and subdirectories, all of which can be restored from the archive. The tar utility was originally designed to create archives on tapes. The term "tar" stands for tape archive. You can create archives on any device, such as a floppy disk, or you can create an archive file to hold the archive. The tar utility is ideal for making backups of your files or combining several files into a single file for transmission across a network. As an alternative to tar you can use pax. pax is designed to work with different kinds of Unix archive formats such as cpio, bcpio, and tar. You can extract, list, and create archives. pax is helpful if you are handling archives created on Unix systems that are using different archive formats.

On Linux, tar is often used to create archives on devices or files. You can direct tar to archive files to a specific device or a file by using the **f** option with the name of the device or file. The syntax for the **tar** command using the **f** option is shown in the next example. The device or filename is often referred to as the archive name. When creating a file for a tar archive, the filename is usually given the extension **.tar**. This is a convention only and is not required. You can list as many filenames as you want. If a directory name is specified, all its subdirectories are included in the archive.

```
$ tar optionsf archive-name.tar directory-and-file-names
```

To create an archive, use the **c** option. Combined with the **f** option, **c** creates an archive on a file or device. You enter this option before and right next to the **f** option. Notice no preceding dash is before a tar option. In the next example, the directory **mydir** and all its subdirectories are saved in the file **myarch.tar**.

```
$ tar cvf myarch.tar mydir
```

The user can later extract the directories from the tape using the **x** option. The **xf** option extracts files from an archive file or device. The tar extraction operation generates all subdirectories. In the next example, the **xf** option directs **tar** to extract all the files and subdirectories from the tar file **myarch.tar**:

```
$ tar xvf myarch.tar
```

Several reasons exist for reducing the size of a file. The two most common are to save space or, if you are transferring the file across a network, to save transmission time. You can effectively reduce a file size by creating a compressed copy of it. Anytime you need the file again, you decompress it. Compression is used in combination with archiving to enable you to compress whole directories and their files at once. Decompression generates a copy of the archive file, which can then be extracted, generating a copy of those files and directories.

Several compression utilities are available for use on Linux and Unix systems. Most software for Linux systems use the GNU gzip and gunzip utilities. The gzip utility compresses files and gunzip decompresses them. To compress a file, enter the command **gzip** and the filename. This replaces the file with a compressed version of it, with the extension **.gz**.


```
$ gzip mydata
$ ls
mydata.gz
```

To decompress a gzip file, use either **gzip** with the **-d** option or the command **gunzip**. These commands decompress a compressed file with the **.gz** extension and replace it with a decompressed version with the same root name, but without the **.gz** extension. When you use gunzip, you needn't even type in the **.gz** extension. **gunzip** and **gzip -d** assume it.

```
$ gunzip mydata.gz
```

Another popular compression utility is bzip2. It compresses files using the Burrows-Wheeler block-sorting text compression algorithm and Huffman coding. The command line options are similar to gzip by design, but they are not exactly the same. See the bzip2 Man page for a complete listing. You compress files using the **bzip2** command and decompress with **bunzip2**. The **bzip2** command creates files with the extension **.bz2**. You can use **bzcat** to output compressed data to the standard output. The **bzip2** command compresses files in block and enables you to specify their size (larger blocks give you greater compression). Like gzip, you can use bzip2 to compress tar archive files. The following example compresses the **mydata** file into a bzip compressed file with the extension **.bz2**:

```
$ bzip2 mydata
$ ls
mydata.bz2
```

To decompress, use the **bunzip2** command on a bzip file.

```
$ bunzip2 mydata.bz2
```

The Complete Reference

Chapter 12

Shell Configuration

Four different major shells are commonly used on Linux systems: the Bourne Again shell (BASH), the Public Domain Korn shell (PDKSH), the TCSH shell, and the Z shell. The BASH shell is an advanced version of the Bourne shell, which includes most of the advanced features developed for the Korn shell and the C shell. TCSH is an enhanced version of the C shell, originally developed for BSD versions of Unix. PDKSH is a subset of the Unix Korn shell, whereas the Z shell is an enhanced version of the Korn shell. Although their Unix counterparts differ greatly, the Linux shells share many of the same features. In Unix, the Bourne shell lacks many capabilities found in the other Unix shells. In Linux, however, the BASH shell incorporates all the advanced features of the Korn shell and C shell, as well as the TCSH shell. All four shells are available for your use, though the BASH shell is the default.

So far, all examples in this book have used the BASH shell. You log into your default shell, but you can change to another shell by entering its name. **tcsh** invokes the TCSH shell, **bash** the BASH shell, **ksh** the PDKSH shell, and **zsh** the Z shell. You can leave a shell with the CTRL-D or **exit** command. You only need one type of shell to do your work. This chapter describes common features of the BASH shell, such as history and aliases, as well as how to configure the shell to your own needs using shell variables and initialization files. The other shells share many of the same features, and use similar variables and initialization files.

Command and Filename Completion

The BASH command line has a built-in feature that performs command and filename completion. If you enter an incomplete pattern as a command or filename argument, you can then press the TAB key to activate the command and filename completion feature, which completes the pattern. If more than one command or file has the same prefix, the shell simply beeps and waits for you to add enough characters to select a unique command or filename. In the next example, the user issues a **cat** command with an incomplete filename. Upon pressing the TAB key, the system searches for a match and, when it finds one, fills in the filename. The user can then press ENTER to execute the command.

```
$ cat pre tab
$ cat preface
```

The shell can also perform filename completion to list the partially matching files in your current directory. If you press ESC followed by a question mark, ESC-?, or press the TAB key again, the shell lists all filenames matching the incomplete pattern. In the next example, the ESC-? after the incomplete filename generates a list of possible filenames. The shell then redraws the command line, and you can type in the complete name of the file you want, or type in distinguishing characters and press the TAB key to have the filename completed.

```
$ ls
document docudrama
$ cat doc escape ?
document
docudrama
$ cat docudrama
```

Command Line Editing

The BASH shell has built-in command line editing capabilities that enable you to easily modify commands you have entered before executing them. If you make a spelling mistake when entering a command, rather than reentering the entire command, you can use the editing operations to correct the mistake before executing the command. This is most helpful for commands that use arguments with lengthy pathnames. The command line editing operations are implemented by Readline, which uses a subset of the Emacs editing commands (see Table 12-1). You can use CTRL-F or the RIGHT ARROW key to move forward a character, and the CTRL-B or the LEFT ARROW key to move back a character. CTRL-D or DEL deletes the character the cursor is on. To add text, you move the cursor to where you want to insert text and type in the new characters. At any time, you can press ENTER to execute the command.

Command Line Editing	Description
CTRL-B or LEFT ARROW	Moves left one character (backward to the previous character)
CTRL-F or RIGHT ARROW	Moves right one character (forward to the next character)
CTRL-A	Moves to the beginning of a line
CTRL-E	Moves to the end of a line
ESC-F	Moves forward one word
ESC-B	Moves backward one word
DEL	Deletes the character the cursor is on
BACKSPACE or CTRL-H	Deletes the character before the cursor
CTRL-D	Deletes the character the cursor is on.
CTRL-K	Removes (kills) the remainder of a line

Table 12-1. *Command Line Editing, History Commands, and History Event References*

History Commands	
CTRL-N or DOWN ARROW	Moves down to the next event in the history list
CTRL-P or UP ARROW	Moves up to the previous event in the history list
ESC-<	Moves to the beginning of the history event list
ESC->	Moves to the end of the history event list
ESC-TAB	History of event matching and completion
`fc` *event-reference*	Edits an event with the standard editor and then executes it
Options	
`-l`	Lists recent history events; same as **`history`** command
`-e` *editor event-reference*	Invokes a specified editor to edit a specific event
History Event References	
`!`*event num*	References an event with an event number
`!`*characters*	References an event with beginning characters
`!?`*pattern*`?`	References an event with a pattern in the event
`!-`*event num*	References an event with an offset from the first event
`!`*num*`-`*num*	References a range of events

Table 12-1. *Command Line Editing, History Commands, and History Event References* (continued)

Note *As described in the next section, you can also use the command line editing operations to modify history events—previous commands you have entered.*

History

In the BASH shell, the *history utility* keeps a record of the most recent commands you have executed. The commands are numbered starting at 1, and a limit exists to the number of commands remembered—the default is 500. The history utility is a kind of short-term memory, keeping track of the most recent commands you have executed. To see the set of your most recent commands, type **history** on the command line and press ENTER. A list of your most recent commands is then displayed, preceded by a number.

```
$ history
1 cp mydata today
2 vi mydata
3 mv mydata reports
4 cd reports
5 ls
```

Each of these commands is technically referred to as an event. An *event* describes an action that has been taken—a command that has been executed. The events are numbered according to their sequence of execution. The most recent event has the highest number. Each of these events can be identified by its number or beginning characters in the command.

The history utility enables you to reference a former event, placing it on your command line and enabling you to execute it. The easiest way to do this is to use the UP ARROW and DOWN ARROW keys to place history events on your command line, one at a time. You needn't display the list first with **history**. Pressing the UP ARROW key once places the last history event on your command line. Pressing it again places the next history event on your command. Pressing the DOWN ARROW key places the previous event on the command line.

The BASH shell also has a history event completion operation invoked by the ESC-TAB command. Much like standard command line completion, you enter part of the history event you want. Then you press ESC, followed by TAB. The event that matches the text you have entered is then located and used to complete your command line entry.

Tip *If more than one history event matches what you have entered, you will hear a beep, and you can then enter more characters to help uniquely identify the event you want.*

You can edit the event displayed on your command line using the command line editing operations. The LEFT ARROW and RIGHT ARROW keys move you along the command line. You can insert text wherever you stop your cursor. With BACKSPACE and DEL, you can delete characters. Once the event is displayed on your command line, you can press ENTER to execute it.

You can also reference and execute history events using the **!** history command. The **!** is followed by a reference that identifies the command. The reference can be either the number of the event or a beginning set of characters in the event. In the next example, the third command in the history list is referenced first by number and then by the beginning characters:

```
$ !3
mv mydata reports
```

```
$ !mv
mv mydata reports
```

You can also reference an event using an offset from the end of the list. A negative number will offset from the end of the list to that event, thereby referencing it. In the next example, the fourth command, **cd mydata**, is referenced using a negative offset, and then executed. Remember that you are offsetting from the end of the list—in this case, event 5—up toward the beginning of the list, event 1. An offset of 4 beginning from event 5 places you at event 2.

```
$ !-4
vi mydata
```

If no event reference is used, then the last event is assumed. In the next example, the command **!** by itself executes the last command the user executed—in this case, **ls**:

```
$ !
ls
mydata today reports
```

History Event Editing

You can also edit any event in the history list before you execute it. In the BASH shell, you can do this two ways. You can use the command line editor capability to reference and edit any event in the history list. You can also use a history **fc** command option to reference an event and edit it with the full Vi editor. Each approach involves two different editing capabilities. The first is limited to the commands in the command line editor, which edits only a single line with a subset of Emacs commands. At the same time, however, it enables you to reference events easily in the history list. The second approach invokes the standard Vi editor with all its features, but only for a specified history event.

With the command line editor, not only can you edit the current command, you can also move to a previous event in the history list to edit and execute it. The CTRL-P command then moves you up to the prior event in the list. The CTRL-N command moves you down the list. The ESC-< command moves you to the top of the list, and the ESC-> command moves you to the bottom. You can even use a pattern to search for a given event. The slash followed by a pattern searches backward in the list, and the question mark followed by a pattern searches forward in the list. The **n** command repeats the search.

Once you locate the event you want to edit, you use the Emacs command line editing commands to edit the line. CTRL-D deletes a character. CTRL-F or the RIGHT ARROW moves you forward a character, and CTRL-B or the LEFT ARROW moves you back a character. To add text, you position your cursor and type in the characters you want. Table 12-1 lists the different commands for referencing the history list.

If you want to edit an event using a standard editor instead, you need to reference the event using the **fc** command and a specific event reference, such as an event number. The editor used is the one specified by the shell in the **EDITOR** variable. This serves as the default editor for the **fc** command. You can assign to the **EDITOR** variable a different editor if you wish, such as Emacs instead of Vi. The next example will edit the fourth event, **cd reports**, with the standard editor and then execute the edited event:

```
$ fc 4
```

You can select more than one command at a time to be edited and executed by referencing a range of commands. You select a range of commands by indicating an identifier for the first command followed by an identifier for the last command in the range. An identifier can be the command number or the beginning characters in the command. In the next example, the range of commands 2–4 is edited and executed, first using event numbers and then using beginning characters in those events:

```
$ fc 2 4
$ fc vi c
```

fc uses the default editor specified in the **FCEDIT** special variable. Usually, this is the Vi editor. If you want to use the Emacs editor instead, you use the **-e** option and the term **emacs** when you invoke **fc**. The next example will edit the fourth event, **cd reports**, with the Emacs editor and then execute the edited event:

```
$ fc -e emacs 4
```

Configuring History: HISTFILE and HISTSAVE

The number of events saved by your system is kept in a special system variable called **HISTSIZE**. By default, this is usually set to 500. You can change this to another number by simply assigning a new value to **HISTSIZE**. In the next example, the user changes the number of history events saved to 10 by resetting the **HISTSIZE** variable:

```
$ HISTSIZE=10
```

The actual history events are saved in a file whose name is held in a special variable called **HISTFILE**. By default, this file is the **.bash_history** file. You can change the file in which history events are saved, however, by assigning its name to the **HISTFILE** variable. In the next example, the value of **HISTFILE** is displayed. Then a new filename is assigned to it, **newhist**. History events are then saved in the **newhist** file.

```
$ echo $HISTFILE
.bash_history
$ HISTFILE="newhist"
$ echo $HISTFILE
newhist
```

Aliases

You use the **alias** command to create another name for a command. The **alias** command operates like a macro that expands to the command it represents. The alias does not literally replace the name of the command; it simply gives another name to that command. An **alias** command begins with the keyword **alias** and the new name for the command, followed by an equal sign and the command the alias will reference.

Note *No spaces can be around the equal sign used in the* **alias** *command.*

In the next example, **list** becomes another name for the **ls** command:

```
$ alias list=ls
$ ls
mydata today
$ list
mydata today
$
```

Tip *SuSE Linux runs an /etc/profile.dos script which aliases Linux commands with DOS commands. For example,* **cp** *is aliased as* **copy**, *and* **mv** *as* **move**.

You can also use an alias to substitute for a command and its option, but you need to enclose both the command and the option within single quotes. Any command you alias that contains spaces must be enclosed in single quotes. In the next example, the alias **lss** references the **ls** command with its **-s** option, and the alias **lsa** references the **ls** command with the **-F** option. **ls** with the **-s** option lists files and their sizes in blocks, and the **ls** with the **-F** option places a slash after directory names. Notice single quotes enclose the command and its option.

```
$ alias lss='ls -s'
$ lss
```

```
mydata 14   today  6   reports  1
$ alias lsa='ls -F'
$ lsa
mydata today reports/
$
```

You may often use an alias to include a command name with an argument. If you execute a command that has an argument with a complex combination of special characters on a regular basis, you may want to alias it. For example, suppose you often list just your source code and object code files—those files ending in either a **.c** or **.o**. You would need to use as an argument for **ls** a combination of special characters such as ***.[co]**. Instead, you could alias **ls** with the **.[co]** argument, giving it a simple name. In the next example, the user creates an alias called **lsc** for the command **ls.[co]**:

```
$ alias lsc='ls *.[co]'
$ lsc
main.c main.o lib.c lib.o
```

You can also use the name of a command as an alias. This can be helpful in cases where you should only use a command with a specific option. In the case of the **rm**, **cp**, and **mv** commands, the **-i** option should always be used to ensure an existing file is not overwritten. Instead of constantly being careful to use the **-i** option each time you use one of these commands, the command name can be aliased to include the option. In the next example, the **rm**, **cp**, and **mv** commands have been aliased to include the **-i** option:

```
$ alias rm='rm -i'
$ alias mv='mv -i'
$ alias cp='cp -i'
```

The **alias** command by itself provides a list of all aliases that have been defined, showing the commands they represent. You can remove an alias by using the **unalias** command. In the next example, the user lists the current aliases and then removes the **lsa** alias:

```
$ alias
lsa=ls -F
list=ls
rm=rm -i
$ unalias lsa
```

Controlling Shell Operations

The BASH shell has several features that enable you to control the way different shell operations work. For example, setting the **noclobber** feature prevents redirection from overwriting files. You can turn these features on and off like a toggle, using the **set** command. The **set** command takes two arguments: an option specifying on or off and the name of the feature. To set a feature on, you use the **-o** option, and to set it off, you use the **+o** option. Here is the basic form:

```
$ set -o feature        turn the feature on
$ set +o feature        turn the feature off
```

Three of the most common features are described here: **ignoreeof**, **noclobber**, and **noglob**. Table 12-2 lists these different features, as well as the **set** command.

BASH Shell Special Variables	Description
HOME	Pathname for user's home directory
LOGNAME	Login name
USER	Login name
SHELL	Pathname of program for type of shell you are using
BASH_ENV	Holds name of BASH initialization script executed whenever a BASH shell script is run or BASH shell entered; usually **$HOME/.bashrc**
PATH	List of pathnames for directories searched for executable commands
PS1	Primary shell prompt
PS2	Secondary shell prompt
IFS	Interfield delimiter symbol
MAIL	Name of mail file checked by Mail utility for received messages
MAILCHECK	Interval for checking for received mail
MAILPATH	List of mail files to be checked by Mail for received messages

Table 12-2. *BASH Shell Special Variables and Features*

BASH Shell Special Variables	Description
`TERM`	Terminal name
`CDPATH`	Pathnames for directories searched by **`cd`** command for subdirectories
`EXINIT`	Initialization commands for Ex/Vi editor
BASH Shell Features	
`$ set -+o` *feature*	Bash shell features are turned on and off with the **`set`** command; **`-o`** sets a feature on and **`+o`** turns it off: `$ set -o noclobber` *set noclobber on* `$ set +o noclobber` *set noclobber off*
`ignoreeof`	Disables CTRL-D logout
`noclobber`	Does not overwrite files through redirection
`noglob`	Disables special characters used for filename expansion: **`*`**, **`?`**, **`~`**, and **`[]`**

Table 12-2. *BASH Shell Special Variables and Features* (continued)

Setting **`ignoreeof`** enables a feature that prevents you from logging out of the user shell with CTRL-D. CTRL-D is not only used to log out of the user shell, but also to end user input entered directly into the standard input. CTRL-D is used often for the Mail program or for utilities such as **`cat`**. You could easily enter an extra CTRL-D in such circumstances and accidentally log yourself out. The **`ignoreeof`** feature prevents such accidental logouts. In the next example, the **`ignoreeof`** feature is turned on using the **`set`** command with the **`-o`** option. The user can now only log out by entering the **`logout`** command.

```
$ set -o ignoreeof
$ ctrl-d
Use exit to logout
$
```

Setting **`noclobber`** enables a feature that safeguards existing files from redirected output. With the **`noclobber`** feature, if you redirect output to a file that already exists, the file will not be overwritten with the standard output. The original file is preserved. Situations may occur in which you use, as the name for a file to hold the redirected output, a name you have already given to an existing file. The **noclobber** feature prevents you from accidentally overwriting your original file. In the next example, the user sets the **noclobber** feature on and then tries to overwrite an existing file, **myfile**, using redirection. The system returns an error message.

```
$ set -o noclobber
$ cat preface > myfile
myfile: file exists
$
```

At times, you may want to overwrite a file with redirected output. In this case, you can place an exclamation point after the redirection operator. This will override the **noclobber** feature, replacing the contents of the file with the standard output.

```
$ cat preface >! myfile
```

Setting **noglob** enables a feature that disables special characters in the user shell. The characters *, **?**, **[]**, and **~** will no longer expand to matched filenames. This feature is helpful if you have special characters as part of the name of a file. In the next example, the user needs to reference a file that ends with the **?** character, **answers?**. First, the user turns off special characters using the **noglob** feature. Now the question mark on the command line is taken as part of the filename, not as a special character, and the user can reference the **answers?** file.

```
$ set -o noglob
$ ls answers?
answers?
```

Environment Variables and Subshells: export

When you log in to your account, Linux generates your user shell. Within this shell, you can issue commands and declare variables. You can also create and execute shell scripts. When you execute a shell script, however, the system generates a subshell. You then have two shells, the one you logged into and the one generated for the script. Within the script shell, you could execute another shell script, which would have its own shell. When a script has finished execution, its shell terminates and you return to the shell from which it was executed. In this sense, you can have many shells, each nested within the other. Variables you define within a shell are local to it. If you define a variable in a shell script, then, when the script is run, the variable is defined with that script's shell and is local to it. No other shell can reference that variable. In a sense, the variable is hidden within its shell.

You can define environment variables in all types of shells including the BASH, the Z shell, and the TCSH shell. The strategy used to implement environment variables in the BASH shell, however, is different from that of the TCSH shell. In the BASH shell, environment variables are exported. That is to say, a copy of an environment variable is made in each subshell. For example, if the **EDITOR** variable is exported, a copy is automatically defined in each subshell for you. In the TCSH shell, on the other hand, an environment variable is defined only once and can be directly referenced by any subshell.

In the BASH shell, an environment variable can be thought of as a regular variable with added capabilities. To make an environment variable, you apply the **export** command to a variable you have already defined. The **export** command instructs the system to define a copy of that variable for each new shell generated. Each new shell will have its own copy of the environment variable. This process is called *exporting variables.* Thinking of exported environment variables as global variables is a mistake. A new shell can never reference a variable outside of itself. Instead, a copy of the variable with its value is generated for the new shell.

Note *You can think of exported variables as exporting their values to a shell, not to themselves. For those familiar with programming structures, exported variables can be thought of as a form of "call by value."*

Configuring Your Shell with Special Shell Variables

When you log in to your account, the system generates a shell for you. This shell is referred to as either your login shell or your user shell. When you execute scripts, you are generating subshells of your user shell. You can define variables within your user shell, and you can also define environment variables that can be referenced by any subshells you generate. Linux sets up special shell variables you can use to configure your user shell. Many of these special shell variables are defined by the system when you log in, but you define others yourself. See Table 12-2 for a list of the commonly used ones.

A reserved set of keywords is used for the names of these special variables. You should not use these keywords as the names of any of your own variable names. The special shell variables are all specified in uppercase letters, making them easy to identify. Shell feature variables are in lowercase letters. For example, the keyword **HOME** is used by the system to define the **HOME** variable. **HOME** is a special environment variable that holds the pathname of the user's home directory. On the other hand, the keyword **noclobber**, covered earlier in the chapter, is used to set the **noclobber** feature on or off.

Common Special Variables

Many of the special variables automatically defined and assigned initial values by the system when you log in can be changed, if you wish. Some special variables exist whose values should not be changed, however. For example, the **HOME** variable holds the pathname for your home directory. Commands, such as **cd,** reference the pathname in the **HOME** special variable to locate your home directory. Some of the more common of these special variables are described in this section. Other special variables are defined by the system and given an initial value that you are free to change. To do this, you redefine them and assign a new value. For example, the **PATH** variable is defined by the system and given an initial value; it contains the pathnames of directories where commands are located. Whenever you execute a command, the shell searches for it in these directories. You can add a new directory to be searched by redefining the **PATH** variable yourself, so it will include the new directory's pathname. Still other special variables exist that the system does not define. These are usually optional features, such as the **EXINIT** variable that enables you to set options for the Vi editor. Each time you log in, you must define and assign a value to such variables.

Note *You can obtain a listing of the currently defined special variables using the* **env** *command. The* **env** *command operates like the* **set** *command, but it only lists special variables.*

You can automatically define special variables using special shell scripts called initialization files. An *initialization file* is a specially named shell script executed whenever you enter a certain shell. You can edit the initialization file and place in it definitions and assignments for special variables. When you enter the shell, the initialization file will execute these definitions and assignments, effectively initializing special variables with your own values. For example, the BASH shell's **.bash_profile** file is an initialization file executed every time you log in. It contains definitions and assignments of special variables. However, the **.bash_profile** file is basically only a shell script, which you can edit with any text editor such as the Vi editor; changing, if you wish, the values assigned to special variables.

In the BASH shell, all the special variables are designed to be environment variables. When you define or redefine a special variable, you also need to export it to make it an environment variable. This means any change you make to a special variable must be accompanied by an **export** command. You will see that at the end of the login initialization file, **.bash_profile**, there is usually an **export** command for all the special variables defined in it.

The **HOME** variable contains the pathname of your home directory. Your home directory is determined by the system administrator when your account is created. The pathname for your home directory is automatically read into your **HOME** variable when you log in. In the next example, the **echo** command displays the contents of the **HOME** variable:

```
$ echo $HOME
/home/chris
```

The **HOME** variable is often used when you need to specify the absolute pathname of your home directory. In the next example, the absolute pathname of **reports** is specified using **HOME** for the home directory's path:

```
$ ls $HOME/reports
```

Some of the more common special variables are **SHELL**, **PATH**, **PS1**, **PS2**, and **MAIL**. The **SHELL** variable holds the pathname of the program for the type of shell you log in to. The **PATH** variable lists the different directories to be searched for a Linux command. The **PS1** and **PS2** variables hold the prompt symbols. The **MAIL** variable holds the pathname of your mailbox file. You can modify the values for any of them to customize your shell.

The **PATH** variable contains a series of directory paths separated by colons. Each time a command is executed, the paths listed in the **PATH** variable are searched one by one for that command. For example, the **cp** command resides on the system in the directory **/usr/bin**. This directory path is one of the directories listed in the **PATH** variable. Each time you execute the **cp** command, this path is searched and the **cp** command located. The system defines and assigns **PATH** an initial set of pathnames. In Linux, the initial pathnames are **/usr/bin** and **usr/sbin**.

The shell can execute any executable file, including programs and scripts you have created. For this reason, the **PATH** variable can also reference your working directory; so if you want to execute one of your own scripts or programs in your working directory, the shell can locate it. No spaces are allowed between the pathnames in the string. A colon with no pathname specified references your working directory. Usually, a single colon is placed at the end of the pathnames as an empty entry specifying your working directory. For example, the pathname **/usr/bin:/usr/sbin:** references three directories: **/usr/bin**, **/usr/sbin**, and your current working directory.

```
$ echo $PATH
/usr/bin:/usr/sbin:
```

You can add any new directory path you want to the **PATH** variable. This can be useful if you have created several of your own Linux commands using shell scripts. You could place these new shell script commands in a directory you created and then add that directory to the **PATH** list. Then, no matter what directory you are in, you can execute one of your shell scripts. The **PATH** variable will contain the directory for that script, so that directory will be searched each time you issue a command.

You add a directory to the **PATH** variable with a variable assignment. You can execute this assignment directly in your shell. In the next example, the user **chris** adds a new directory, called **mybin,** to the **PATH**. Although you could carefully type in the

ENVIRONMENTS

complete pathnames listed in **PATH** for the assignment, you can also use an evaluation of **PATH**, **$PATH**, in their place. In this example, an evaluation of **HOME** is also used to designate the user's **home** directory in the new directory's pathname. Notice the empty entry between two colons, which specifies the working directory.

```
$ PATH=$PATH:$HOME/mybin:
$ export PATH
$ echo $PATH
/usr/bin:/usr/sbin::/home/chris/mybin
```

If you add a directory to **PATH** yourself while you are logged in, the directory would be added only for the duration of your login session. When you log back in, the login initialization file, **.bash_profile**, would again initialize your **PATH** with its original set of directories. The **.bash_profile** file is described in detail a bit later in this chapter. To add a new directory to your **PATH** permanently, you need to edit your **.bash_profile** file and find the assignment for the **PATH** variable. Then, you simply insert the directory, preceded by a colon, into the set of pathnames assigned to **PATH**.

The **BASH_ENV** variable holds the name of the BASH shell initialization file to be executed whenever a BASH shell is generated. For example, when a BASH shell script is executed, the **BASH_ENV** variable is checked and the name of the script that it holds is executed before the shell script. The **BASH_ENV** variable usually holds **$HOME/.bashrc**. This is the **.bashrc** file in the user's home directory. The **.bashrc** file is discussed later in this chapter. You could specify a different file if you wish, using that instead of the **.bashrc** file for BASH shell scripts.

The **PS1** and **PS2** variables contain the primary and secondary prompt symbols, respectively. The primary prompt symbol for the BASH shell is a dollar sign, **$**. You can change the prompt symbol by assigning a new set of characters to the **PS1** variable. In the next example, the shell prompt is changed to the **->** symbol:

```
$ PS1= >>-> >>
-> export PS1
->
```

You can change the prompt to be any set of characters, including a string, as shown in the next example:

```
$ PS1="Please enter a command: "
Please enter a command: export PS1
Please enter a command: ls
mydata /reports
Please enter a command:
```

The **PS2** variable holds the secondary prompt symbol, which is used for commands that take several lines to complete. The default secondary prompt is **>**. The added command lines begin with the secondary prompt instead of the primary prompt. You can change the secondary prompt just as easily as the primary prompt, as shown here:

```
$ PS2="@"
```

Like the TCSH shell, the BASH shell provides you with a predefined set of codes you can use to configure your prompt. With them you can make the time, your username, or your directory pathname a part of your prompt. You can even have your prompt display the history event number of the current command you are about to enter. Each code is preceded by a \ symbol. **\w** represents the current working directory, **\t** the time, and **\u** your username. **\!** will display the next history event number. In the next example, the user adds the current working directory to the prompt:

```
$ PS1="\w $"
/home/dylan $
```

The codes must be included within a quoted string. If no quotes exist, the code characters are not evaluated and are themselves used as the prompt. **PS1=\w** sets the prompt to the characters **\w**, not the working directory. The next example incorporates both the time and the history event number with a new prompt:

```
$ PS1="\t \! ->"
```

The following table lists the codes for configuring your prompt:

Prompt Codes	Description
\!	Current history number
\$	Use **$** as prompt for all users except the root user, which has the **#** as its prompt
\d	Current date
\s	Shell currently active
\t	Time of day
\u	Username
\w	Current working directory

If **CDPATH** is undefined, then when the **cd** command is given a directory name as its argument, it searches only the current working directory for that name. If **CDPATH** is defined, however, **cd** also searches the directories listed in **CDPATH** for that directory name. If the directory name is found, **cd** changes to that directory. This is helpful if you are working on a project in which you constantly must change to directories in another part of the file system. To change to a directory that has a pathname very different from the one you are in, you would need to know the full pathname of that directory. Instead, you could simply place the pathname of that directory's parent in **CDPATH**. Then **cd** automatically searches the parent directory, finding the name of the directory you want.

Note *Notice that you assign to **CDPATH** the pathname of the parent of the directory you want to change to, not the pathname of the directory itself.*

Using the **HOME** variable to specify the user's home directory part of the path in any new pathname added to **CDPATH** is advisable. This is because the pathname for your home directory could possibly be changed by the system administrator during a reorganization of the file system. **HOME** will always hold the current pathname of the user's home directory. In the next example, the pathname **/home/chris/letters** is specified with **$HOME/letters**:

```
$ CDPATH=$CDPATH:$HOME/letters
$ export CDPATH
$ echo $CDPATH
:/home/chris/letters
```

Several shell special variables are used to set values used by network applications, such as Web browsers or newsreaders. **NNTPSERVER** is used to set the value of a remote news server accessible on your network. If you are using an ISP, the ISP usually provides a news server you can access with your newsreader applications. However, you first have to provide your newsreaders with the Internet address of the news server. This is the role of the **NNTPSERVER**. News servers on the Internet usually use the NNTP protocol. **NNTPSERVER** should hold the address of such a news server. For many ISPs, the news server address is a domain name that begins with **nntp**. The following example assigns the news server address **nntp.myservice.com** to the **NNTPSERVER** special variables. Newsreader applications automatically obtain the news server address from **NNTPSERVER**. Usually, this assignment is placed in the shell initialization file, **.bash_profile**, so it is automatically set each time a user logs in.

```
NNTPSERVER=nntp.myservice.com
export NNTPSERVER
```

Other special variables are used for specific applications. The **KDEDIR** variable holds the pathname for the KDE Desktop program files. This is usually **/opt/kde** but, at the time of installation, you can choose to install KDE in a different directory and then change the value of **KDEDIR** accordingly.

```
export KDEDIR=/opt/kde
```

Configuring Your Login Shell: .bash_profile

The **.bash_profile** file is the BASH shell's login initialization file, which can also be named **.profile** (as in SuSE Linux). It is a script file that is automatically executed whenever a user logs in. The file contains shell commands that define special environment variables used to manage your shell. They may be either redefinitions of system-defined special variables or definitions of user-defined special variables. For example, when you log in, your user shell needs to know what directories hold Linux commands. It will reference the **PATH** variable to find the pathnames for these directories. However, first, the **PATH** variable must be assigned those pathnames. In the **.bash_profile** file, an assignment operation does just this. Because it is in the **.bash_profile** file, the assignment is executed automatically when the user logs in.

Special variables also need to be exported, using the **export** command, to make them accessible to any subshells you may enter. You can export several variables in one **export** command by listing them as arguments. Usually, at the end of the **.bash_profile** file is an **export** command with a list of all the variables defined in the file. If a variable is missing from this list, you may be unable to access it. Notice the **export** command at the end of the **.profile** file in the example described next. You can also combine the assignment and **export** command into one operation as shown here for **NNTPSERVER**:

```
export NNTPSERVER=nntp.myservice.com
```

A copy of the standard **.bash_profile** file provided for you when your account is created is listed in the next example. Notice how **PATH** is assigned, as is the value of **$HOME**. Both **PATH** and **HOME** are system special variables the system has already defined. **PATH** holds the pathnames of directories searched for any command you enter, and **HOME** holds the pathname of your home directory. The assignment **PATH=$PATH:$HOME/bin** has the effect of redefining **PATH** to include your **bin** directory within your home directory. So your **bin** directory will also be searched for any commands, including ones you create yourself, such as scripts or programs. Notice **PATH** is then exported, so it can be accessed by any subshells. Should you want to have your home directory searched also, you can use any text editor to modify this line in your **.bash_profile** file to **PATH=$PATH:$HOME/bin:$HOME**, adding **:$HOME** at the end. In fact, you can change this entry to add as many directories as you want searched.

.bash_profile

```
#.bash_profile
```

```
# Get the aliases and functions
if [ -f ~/.bashrc ]; then
   . ~/.bashrc
fi

# User specific environment and startup programs

PATH=$PATH:$HOME/bin
BASH_ENV=$HOME/.bashrc
USERNAME=''''

export USERNAME BASH_ENV PATH
```

Your Linux system also has its own profile file that it executes whenever any user logs in. This system initialization file is simply called **profile** and is found in the **/etc** directory, **/etc/profile**. This file contains special variable definitions the system needs to provide for each user. A copy of the system's **.profile** file follows. Notice how **PATH** is redefined to include the **/usr/X11R6/bin** directory. This is the directory that holds the X Window commands you execute when using the desktop. **HISTFILE** is also redefined to include a larger number of history events. An entry has been added here for the **NNTPSERVER** variable. Normally, a news server address is a value that needs to be set for all users. Such assignments should be made in the system's **/etc/profile** file by the system administrator, rather than in each individual user's own **.bash_profile** file. The **/etc/profile** file also executes any scripts in the directory **/etc/profile.d**. This design allows for a more modular structure. Rather than make entries by editing the **/etc/profile** file, you can just add a script to **profile.d** directory. The scripts for the BASH shell have the extension **.sh**. For example, the **kde.sh** script in the **profile.d** directory checks for a definition of the **KDEDIR** variable and makes one if none is in effect.

/etc/profile

```
# /etc/profile


# System wide environment and startup programs
# Functions and aliases go in /etc/bashrc

if ! echo $PATH | /bin/grep -q "/usr/X11R6/bin" ; then
   PATH="$PATH:/usr/X11R6/bin"
if [ `id -u` = 0 ] && ! echo $PATH | /bin/grep -q "/sbin" ; then
   PATH=/sbin:$PATH
fi
if [ `id -u` = 0 ] && ! echo $PATH | /bin/grep -q "/usr/local/sbin" ; then
   PATH=/usr/local/sbin:$PATH
fi
fi
PS1="[\u@\h \W]\\$ "

USER=`id -un`
LOGNAME=$USER
```

```
MAIL="/var/spool/mail/$USER"

HOSTNAME=`/bin/hostname`
HISTSIZE=1000
  NNTPSERVER=nntp.myservice.com

if [ -z "$INPUTRC" -a ! -f "$HOME/.inputrc" ]; then
        INPUTRC=/etc/inputrc
fi

export PATH PS1 HOSTNAME HISTSIZE MAIL NNTPSERVER

for i in /etc/profile.d/*.sh ; do
   if [ -x $i ]; then
      . $i
   fi
done

unset i
```


Your **.bash_profile** initialization file is a text file that can be edited by a text editor, like any other text file. You can easily add new directories to your **PATH** by editing **.bash_profile** and using editing commands to insert a new directory pathname in the list of directory pathnames assigned to the **PATH** variable. You can even add new variable definitions. If you do so, however, be sure to include the new variable's name in the **export** command's argument list. For example, if your **.bash_profile** file does not have any definition of the **EXINIT** variable, you can edit the file and add a new line that assigns a value to **EXINIT**. The definition **EXINIT='set nu ai'** will configure the Vi editor with line numbering and indentation. You then need to add **EXINIT** to the **export** command's argument list. When the **.bash_profile** file executes again, the **EXINIT** variable will be set to the command **set nu ai**. When the Vi editor is invoked, the command in the **EXINIT** variable will be executed, setting the line number and auto-indent options automatically.

In the following example, the user's **.bash_profile** has been modified to include definitions of **EXINIT** and redefinitions of **PATH**, **CDPATH**, **PS1**, and **HISTSIZE**. The **PATH** variable has **$HOME**: added to its value. **$HOME** is a variable that evaluates to the user's home directory and the ending colon specifies the current working directory, enabling you to execute commands that may be located in either the home directory or the working directory. The redefinition of **HISTSIZE** reduces the number of history events saved, from 1,000 defined in the system's **.profile** file, to 30. The redefinition of the **PS1** special variable changes the prompt to include the pathname of the current working directory. Any changes you make to special variables within your **.bash_profile** file override those made earlier by the system's **.profile** file. All these special variables are then exported with the **export** command.

.bash_profile

```
# .bash_profile
# Get the aliases and functions
if [ -f ~/.bashrc ];
```

```
 then
  . ~/.bashrc
fi
# User-specific environment and startup programs
PATH=/usr/local/sbin:/usr/sbin:/sbin:$PATH:$HOME/bin:$HOME:
BASH_ENV=$HOME/.bashrc
USERNAME=''''
CDPATH=$CDPATH:$HOME/bin:$HOME
HISTSIZE=30
NNTPSERVER=nntp.myserver.com
EXINIT='set nu ai'
PS1="\w \$"
export USERNAME BASH_ENV PATH CDPATH HISTSIZE EXINIT PS1
```

Although **.bash_profile** is executed each time you log in, it is not automatically reexecuted after you make changes to it. The **.bash_profile** file is an initialization file that is *only* executed whenever you log in. If you want to take advantage of any changes you make to it without having to log out and log in again, you can reexecute **.bash_profile** with the dot (**.**) command. The **.bash_profile** file is a shell script and, like any shell script, can be executed with the **.** command.

```
$ . .bash_profile
```

Alternatively, you can use the **source** command to execute the **.bash_profile** initialization file, or any initialization file such as **.login** used in the TCSH shell, or **.bashrc**.

```
$ source .bash_profile
```

Configuring the BASH Shell: .bashrc

The **.bashrc** file is a configuration file executed each time you enter the BASH shell or generate any subshells. If the BASH shell is your login shell, **.bashrc** is executed along with your **.bash_login** file when you log in. If you enter the BASH shell from another shell, the **.bashrc** file is automatically executed, and the variable and alias definitions it contains will be defined. If you enter a different type of shell, the configuration file for that shell will be executed instead. For example, if you were to enter the TCSH shell with the **tcsh** command, the **.tcshrc** configuration file is executed instead of **.bashrc**.

The **.bashrc** shell configuration file is actually executed each time you generate a BASH shell, such as when you run a shell script. In other words, each time a subshell is created, the **.bashrc** file is executed. This has the effect of exporting any local variables or aliases you have defined in the **.bashrc** shell initialization file. The **.bashrc** file usually contains the definition of aliases and any feature variables used to turn on shell features. Aliases and feature variables are locally defined within the shell. But the **.bashrc** file defines them in every shell. For this reason, the **.bashrc** file usually holds such aliases as those defined for the **rm**, **cp**, and **mv** commands. The next example is a **.bashrc** file with many of the standard definitions:

.bashrc

```
# Source global definitions
if [ -f /etc/bashrc ];
 then
   .  /etc/bashrc
fi
set  -o ignoreeof
set  -o noclobber
alias rm 'rm -i'
alias mv 'mv -i'
alias cp 'cp -i'
```

Linux systems usually contain a system **.bashrc** file executed for all users. This may contain certain global aliases and features needed by all users whenever they enter a BASH shell. This is located in the **/etc** directory, **/etc/.bashrc**. A user's own **.bashrc** file, located in the **home** directory, contains commands to execute this system **.bashrc** file. The **./etc/bashrc** command in the previous example of **.bashrc** does just that. You can add any commands or definitions of your own to your **.bashrc** file. If you have made changes to **.bashrc** and you want them to take effect during your current login session, you need to reexecute the file with either the **.** or the **source** command.

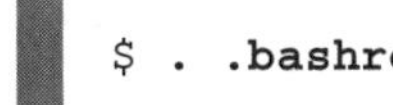

```
$ . .bashrc
```


The BASH Shell Logout File: .bash_logout

The **.bash_logout** file is also a configuration file, which is executed when the user logs out. It is designed to perform any operations you want done whenever you log out. Instead of variable definitions, the **.bash_logout** file usually contains shell commands that form a kind of shutdown procedure—actions you always want taken before you log out. One common logout command is to clear the screen and then issue a farewell message.

As with **.bash_profile**, you can add your own shell commands to **.bash_logout**. In fact, the **.bash_logout** file is not automatically set up for you when your account is first created. You need to create it yourself, using the Vi or Emacs editor. You could then add a farewell message or other operations. In the next example, the user has a **clear** and an **echo** command in the **.bash_logout** file. When the user logs out, the **clear** command clears the screen, and then the **echo** command displays the message "Good-bye for now."

.bash_logout

```
 # ~/.bash_logout
clear
echo "Good-bye for now"
```

Other Initialization and Configuration Files

Each type of shell has its own set of initialization and configuration files. The TCSH shell uses **.login**, **.tcshrc**, **.logout** files in place of **.bash_profile**, **.bashrc**, and **.bash_logout**.

The Z shell has several initialization files: **.zshenv**, **.zlogin**, **.zprofile**, **.zschrc**, and **.zlogout**. See Table 12-3 for a listing. Check the Man pages for each shell to see how they are usually configured. When you install a shell, default versions of these files are automatically placed in the users' home directories. Except for the TCSH shell, all shells use much the same syntax for variable definitions and assigning values (TCSH uses a slightly different syntax, described in its Man pages).

BASH Shell	**Function**
.bash_profile	Login initialization file
.bashrc	BASH shell configuration file
.bash_logout	Logout name
.bash_history	History file
TCSH Shell	
.login	Login initialization file
.tcshrc	TCSH shell configuration file
.logout	Logout file
Z Shell	
.zshenv	Shell login file (first read)
.zprofile	Login initialization file
.zlogin	Shell login file
.zshrc	Z shell configuration file
.zlogout	Logout file
PDKSH Shell	
.profile	Login initialization file
.kshrc	PDKSH shell configuration file

Table 12-3. *Shell Configuration Files*

Configuration Directories and Files

Applications often install configuration files in a user's home directory that contain specific configuration information, which tailors the application to the needs of that particular user. This may take the form of a single configuration file that begins with a period, or a directory that contains several configuration files. The directory name will also begin with a period. For example, Netscape installs a directory called **.netscape** in the user's home directory that contains configuration files. On the other hand, the Mail application uses a single file called **.mailrc** to hold alias and feature settings set up by the user. Most single configuration files end in the letters **rc**. **FTP** uses a file called **.netrc**. Most newsreaders use a file called **.newsrc**. Entries in configuration files are usually set by the application, though you can usually make entries directly by editing the file. Applications have their own set of special variables to which you can define and assign values. Of particular interest is the **.wm_style** file that holds the name of the window manager the user wants to use. You can edit and change the name to another window manager to start up a new one. You can list the configuration files in your home directory with the `ls -a` command.

The Complete Reference

Part IV

Clients and Applications

Chapter 13

Mail and News Clients

Your Linux system supports a wide range of both electronic mail and news clients. Mail clients enable you to send messages to other users on your system or accessible on your network, such as those on the Internet. News clients let you read articles and messages posted in a newsgroups, which are open to access by all users. This chapter reviews mail and news clients installed with most Linux distributions.

Mail Clients

You can send and receive messages in a variety of ways, depending on the type of mail client you use. Although all electronic mail utilities perform the same basic tasks of receiving and sending messages, they tend to have different interfaces. Some mail clients operate on a desktop, such as KDE or Gnome. Others run on any X Window System managers. Several popular mail clients were designed to use a screen-based interface and can be started from only the command line. Other traditional mail clients were developed for just the command line interface, which requires you to type your commands on a single command line. Most mail clients described here are included in standard Linux distributions and come in a standard RPM package for easy installation. For Web-based Internet mail services, such as Hotmail, Lycos, and Yahoo, you use a Web browser instead of a mail client to access mail accounts provided by those services. Table 13-1 lists several popular Linux mail clients.

Mail is transported to and from destinations using mail transport agents. Sendmail and Smail send and receive mail from destinations on the Internet or at other sites on a network (see Chapter 23). To send mail over the Internet, they use the Simple Mail Transport Protocol (SMTP). Most Linux distributions, including Red Hat, automatically install and configure Sendmail for you. On starting up your system, you can send and receive messages over the Internet.

Mail Client	Description
KMail	The K Desktop mail client
Evolution	Ximian Gnome mail client
Balsa, Gmail, Mahagony, etc.	Gnome mail clients (see Table 13-2)
Mozilla Mail	Web browser–based mail client
Netscape	Web browser–based mail client
exmh	X Mail Hander mail client

Table 13-1. *Linux Mail Clients*

Mail Client	Description
GNUEmacs and XEmacs	Emacs mail clients
Pine	Mail client and newsreader
Mutt	Screen-based mail client
Elm	Screen-based mail client
Mail	Original Unix-based command line mail client
nmh	New Mail Handler command line mail client

Table 13-1. *Linux Mail Clients* (continued)

Local and Internet Addresses

Each user on a Linux system has a mail address, and whenever you send mail, you are required to provide the address of the user to whom you are sending the message. For users on your local Linux system, addresses can consist of only the user's login name. When sending messages to users on other systems, however, you need to know not only the login name, but also the address of the system they are on. Internet addresses require the system address to be uniquely identified.

Most systems have Internet addresses you can use to send mail. Internet addresses use a form of addressing called *domain addressing*. A system is assigned a domain name which, when combined with the system name, gives the system a unique address. This domain name is separated from the system name by a period and may be further qualified by additional domain names. Here is the syntax for domain addresses:

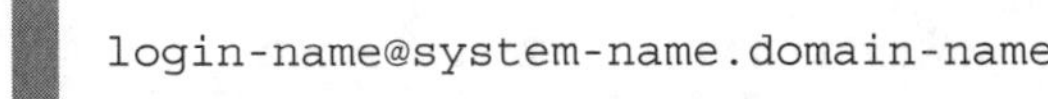

```
login-name@system-name.domain-name
```

Systems that are part of a local network are often given the same domain name. The domain name for both the **garnet** and **violet** systems at U.C. Berkeley is **berkeley.edu**. To send a message to **chris** on the **garnet** system, you simply include the domain name:

```
chris@garnet.berkeley.edu
```

In the next example, a message is sent to **chris,** located on the **garnet** system, using domain addressing:

```
$ mail chris@garnet.berkeley.edu < mydata
```

Early domain names reflect that the Internet was first developed in the United States. They qualify Internet addresses by category, such as commercial, military, or educational systems. The domain name **.com** indicates a commercial organization, whereas **.edu** is used for educational institutions. As the Internet developed into a global network, a set of international domain names was established. These domain names indicate the country in which a system is located—for example, **.fr** represents France, **.jp** represents Japan, and **.us** represents the United States.

You can end your e-mail message with the same standard signature information, such as your name, Internet address or addresses, or farewell phrase. Having your signature information automatically added to your messages is helpful. To do so, you need to create a signature file in your home directory and enter your signature information in it. A *signature file* is a standard text file you can edit using any text editor. Mail clients such as KMail enable you to specify a file to function as your signature file. Others, such as Mail, expect the signature file to be named **.signature**.

MIME

MIME (the term stands for Multipurpose Internet Mail Extensions) is used to enable mail clients to send and receive multimedia files and files using different characters sets such as those for different languages. Multimedia files can be images, sound, or even video. Mail clients that support MIME can send binary files automatically as attachments to messages. MIME-capable mail clients maintain a file called **mailcap** that maps different types of MIME messages to applications on your system that can view or display them. For example, an image file will be mapped to an application that can display images. Your mail clients can then run that program to display the image message. A sound file will be mapped to an application that can play sound files on your speakers. Most mail clients have MIME capabilities built in and use their own version of the **mailcap** file. Others, like Elm, use a program called metamail that adds MIME support. MIME is not only used in mail clients. As noted in Chapters 8 and 9, both the KDE and Gnome file managers use MIME to map a file to a particular application so that you can launch the application directly from the file.

Applications are associated with binary files by means of the **mailcap** and **mime.types** files. The **mime.types** file defines different MIME types, associating a MIME type with a certain application. The **mailcap** file then associates each MIME type with a specified application. Your system maintains its own MIME types file, usually **/etc/mime.types**.

Entries in the MIME types file associate a MIME type and possible subtype of an application with a set of possible file extensions used for files that run on a given kind of application. The MIME type is usually further qualified by a subtype, separated from the major type by a slash. For example, a MIME type image can have several subtypes such as jpeg, gif, or tiff. A sample MIME type entry defining a MIME type for JPEG files is shown here. The MIME type is image/jpeg, and the list of possible file extensions is "jpeg jpg jpe":

```
image/jpeg jpep jpg jpe
```

The applications specified will depend on those available on your particular system. The MIME type is separated from the application with a semicolon. In many cases, X Window System–based programs are specified. Comments are indicated with a **#**. A ***** used in a MIME subtype references all subtypes. The entry **image/*** would be used for an application that can run all types of image files. A formatting code, **%s**, is used to reference the attachment file that will be run on this application. Sample **mailcap** entries are shown here. The first associates all **image** files with the xv image viewer. The next two associate video and video MPEG files with the xanim application.

```
image/*; xv %s
video/*; xanim %s
video/mpeg; xanim %s
```

You can also create and edit MIME types on the Gnome and KDE desktops. For Gnome, use the Gnome Control Center's MIME types capplet. This capplet will list the MIME types defined for your system along with their associated filename extensions. Edit an entry to change the application and icon associated with that MIME type, that type of file. On KDE, use the KDE Control Center's File Association entry under File Browsing. This will list MIME types and their associated filename extensions. Select an entry to edit it and change the applications associated with it. KDE saves its MIME type information in a separate file called **mimelnk** in the KDE configuration directory.

Though you can create your own MIME types, a standard set already is in use. The types text, image, audio, video, application, multipart, and message, along with their subtypes, have already been defined for your system. You will find that commonly used file extensions such as **.tif** and **.jpg** for TIFF and JPEG image files are already associated with a MIME type and an application. Though you can easily change the associated application, it is best to keep the MIME types already installed. The current official MIME types are listed at the IANA Web site (**www.iana.org**) under the name Media Types, provided as part of their Assignment Services. You can access the media types file directly on their FTP site at:


```
ftp.iana.org/in-notes/iana/assignments/media-types/
```

The K Desktop Mail Client: KMail

The K Desktop mail client, KMail, provides a full-featured GUI interface for composing, sending, and receiving mail messages. The KMail window displays three panes for folders, headers, and messages, as shown in Figure 13-1. The upper-left pane displays your mail folders. You have an inbox folder for received mail, an outbox folder for mail you have composed but have not sent yet, and a sent-mail folder for messages you have previously sent. You can create your own mail folders and save selected messages in

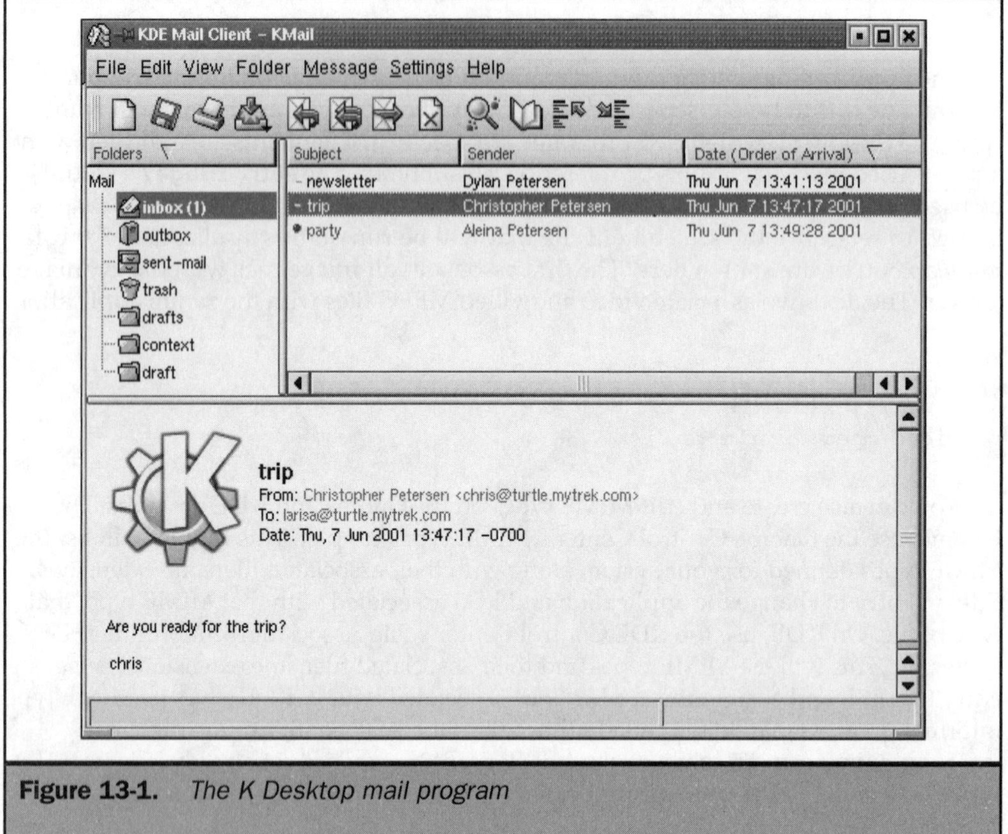

Figure 13-1. *The K Desktop mail program*

them, if you wish. The top-right pane displays mail headers for the currently selected mail folder. You can use the scroll bar to the right to move through the list of headers. The headers are segmented according to fields, beginning with sender and subject. A color code is used to indicate read and unread messages. New messages are listed in red. Read messages are in green. A bullet symbol also appears at the beginning of unread message headers. To display a message, click its header. The message is then displayed in the large pane below the header list. You can also send and receive attachments, including binary files. Pictures and movies that are received are displayed using the appropriate K Desktop utility. If you right-click the message, a pop-up menu displays options for actions you may want to perform on it. You can move or copy it to another folder, or simply delete it. You can also compose a reply or forward the message.

The menus in the menu bar at the top of the window contain the commands and options you can use for managing your mail. An icon bar for commonly used mail commands is displayed below the menu bar. To get new mail, click the icon showing a page with a question mark (?). To print a message, click the Printer icon. To save a message, click the Disk icon. To check your mail, click the Check Mail icon. If you hold the mouse over an icon, a short description of its function is displayed. The icon of an open book opens the KMail address book. Here you can enter a list of e-mail addresses. Also, right-clicking a displayed message gives you the option of automatically adding its e-mail address to your address book. You can use the Help button or the Help menu to obtain more detailed descriptions of the different KMail features. The Help button opens the KMail Handbook, which provides easy reference to different operations.

You click the Blank Page icon to compose and send a new message. If you want to compose a reply, select the header of the message you want to reply to, and then click the icon showing a page with a single curved arrow. A message window opens with the To entry already filled with the sender's address, the From entry with your address, and the Subject line with the sender's subject with a preceding RE:. To forward a message, select the message's header and click the icon showing a page with two curved arrows.

To set up KMail for use with your mail accounts, you must enter account information. Select the Configure entry in the Settings menu. Several panels are available on the Settings window, which you can display by clicking their icons in the left column. For accounts, you select the Network panel. Two sections are on this panel: one for sending mail and one for receiving mail. In the sending-mail section, enter the SMTP server you use. If you have an ISP or you are on a LAN, enter the server name for your network. The default is the Sendmail utility on your own Linux system. In the receiving mail section, you can add any mail accounts you may have. You may have more than one mail account on mail servers maintained by your ISP or LAN. A configure window is displayed where you can enter login, password, and host information. The *host* is the name of the POP or IMAP server this particular account uses. For secure access, KMail now supports SSL, provided OpenSSL is installed. Messages can now be encrypted and decoded by users. It also supports IMAP in addition to POP and SMTP protocols.

Gnome Mail Clients: Balsa, Evolution, Gmail, Mahogany, and Others

Several Gnome-based mail clients are under development, many of which you can currently use (see Table 13-2). These include Balsa, Mahogany, Gmail, Althea, MMC, SMAN, Pygmy, Spruce, and N-tool (Balsa, Evolution, and Mahogany are discussed further). Check the Gnome Web site for more mail clients as they come out. Many are based on the Gnome mail client libraries (camel) currently under development, which provides support for standard mail operations. Balsa is a Gnome mail client with extensive features, though it can operate under any window manager, including KDE, as long as Gnome is installed on your system. Evolution is an integrated mail client, calendar, and contact manager from Ximian. The Mahogany mail client is a Gnome mail client that also has versions for other platforms. Gmail is meant to be a light and fast e-mail client, supporting basic mail operations, such as forwarding, replies, and mailboxes. Althea is a stable IMAP mail client. SMAN simple mail client is used to access POP3 servers. Pygmy is a simple GNOME mail client written in the Python

Application	Description
Balsa	E-mail client for GNOME that supports POP3, IMAP, local folders, and multithreading
Evolution	Ximian integrated mail client, calendar, and contact manager
Eucalyptus	Advanced MIME-compliant e-mail application
Althea	Stable IMAP mail client
SQmaiL	Folder-based e-mail system (using mysql)
SMAN	Simple mail user agent that accesses POP3 servers
LinPopUp	X graphical port of WinPopUp, running over Samba
Mahogany	Cross-platform e-mail application
N-tool	GUI mail tool that supports the Japanese language (ISO-2022-JP)
Pygmy	Gnome mail client written in the Python programming language
Spruce	E-mail client with support for multiple accounts
Grin	Mail client with news reading features
MMC	Gnome mail client
Sonicmail	Gnome POP3 mail notifier applet

Table 13-2. *Gnome Mail Clients*

programming language that supports attachments and MIME messages. The N-tool is a Gnome mail client with Japanese language support, providing standard features, including mailboxes and full MIME support. Spruce is a Gnome e-mail client with support for multiple accounts. LinPopUp is a port of WinPopUp that operates on Samba-connected networks and can send messages to users on Windows machines running WinPopUp.

Evolution is an integrated mail client, calendar, and address book, currently being developed by Ximian. The Evolution mailer is a powerful tool with support for numerous protocols (SMTP, POP, and IMAP), multiple mail accounts, and encryption. With Evolution, you can create multiple mail accounts on different servers, including those that use different protocols such as POP or IMAP. You can also decrypt PGP or GPG-encrypted messages.

The Evolution mailer provides a simple GUI interface, with a toolbar for commonly used commands and a sidebar for shortcuts. A menu of Evolution commands allows access to other operations. The main panel is divided into two panes, one for listing the mail headers and the other for displaying the currently selected message. You can click on any header title to sort your headers by that category. Evolution also supports the use of virtual folders. These are folders created by the user to hold mail that meets specified criteria. Incoming mail can be automatically distributed to their particular virtual folder.

To create a message, click on the Compose icon. This opens a window divided into two sections, one for header information and one for inputting the message. For the headers, you can enter your address, subject, and copy information. You can also use the Evolution address book to automatically enter addresses. You can then use standard GUI editing methods to enter your text. For your message, you can include standard text, images, and HTML (Web page) data. Plug-in Bonobo components will allow you to also include complex data such as audio, video, and PDF data. All such data will be displayed within the message window.

Balsa provides a full-featured GUI interface for composing, sending, and receiving mail messages. The Balsa window displays three panes for folders, headers, and messages (see Figure 13-2). The left pane displays your mail folders. You initially have

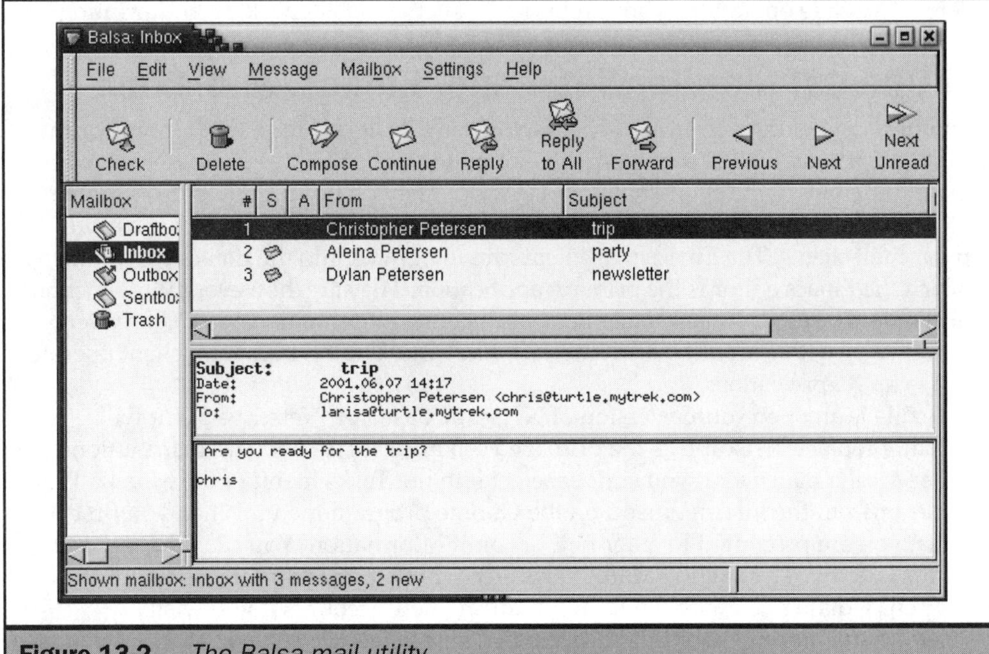

Figure 13-2. *The Balsa mail utility*

three folders: an inbox folder for received mail, an outbox folder for mail you have composed but have not sent yet, and a trash folder for messages you have deleted. You can also create your own mail folders in which you can store particular messages. To place a message in a folder you have created, click and drag the message header for that message to the folder.

The right side of the Balsa window consists of two panes. The top-right pane lists the message headers for the currently selected folder. Message headers are displayed showing the subject, sender, and date. An envelope icon indicates an unread message, and a trashcan icon indicates a message to be deleted. Headers are segmented into fields with buttons for the fields shown at the top of the pane. You can click these buttons to sort headers by different fields, such as subject or sender. To display a message, you click it. It is then displayed in the pane below the message headers. You can click the right and left arrow icons in the icon bar to move through the header list.

The Mahogany mail client window uses a format similar to Balsa. Three panes are there: a left pane for listing folders, and two other panes on the right side for headers and message text. The headers pane has buttons for sorting headers by different fields, such as subject or sender. Mail operations can be performed using the menus or the button bar at the top of the window. To compose a message, you can click the envelope button. This opens a window with entries for From, To, and Subject header fields. Mouse-based editing operations, such as cut and paste, are currently not supported, though you can invoke an external editor. A menu bar and an icon bar at the top of the window list the different message operations you can perform, such as spell-checking and printing.

X Mail Clients: Mozilla, Netscape, Emacs, and exmh

Although many of the newer mail clients are being designed for either Gnome or the K Desktop, several mail clients were developed for use on the X Window System and operate under any window manager or desktop. They do not require either Gnome or the K Desktop. Netscape Messenger, Mozilla mail, and exmh are three of the more popular mail clients. The Emacs mail clients are integrated into the Emacs environment, of which the Emacs editor is the primary application. They are, however, fully functional mail clients. The GNU Emacs mail client can operate either with X Window System capabilities or with a screen-based interface like Pine. The XEmacs mail client operates solely as an X application.

Mozilla is an open source version of Netscape based on Netscape 5.0. It will eventually replace Netscape as the primary Web browser on Red Hat distributions. To use the Mozilla mail client, you simply select it in the Tasks menu of the Mozilla Web browser or from the Internet menu on the Gnome program menu. When you first start Mozilla, you are prompted to enter new account information. You can add and edit accounts later by selecting the Mail/News Account Settings entry in the Edit menu. This opens a dialog box with a button for adding new accounts if you wish.

Netscape Communicator includes a mail client called Messenger. To use the mail client, you have to select the mail window item in Navigator's window menu or select the Messenger icon in the Communicator window. Account information, such as your mail server, username, and password, must be entered in the Mail panel in the Preferences window, accessible from the Edit menu. Received messages are displayed in the Messenger window. The window is divided into two panes, the upper one listing headers of received messages and the lower one for displaying messages. To display a message, click its header. The icon bar displays icons for several common mail operations, such as sending, deleting, or forwarding messages. A sidebar will list your mail and newsgroup accounts, letting you choose among them. To compose a message, click the New Message icon. Messenger supports a wide range of composition features, such HTML addresses, fonts, formatting, and spell-checker. It supports standard GUI editing operations including cut and paste, though you use the ALT key instead of the CTRL key for keyboard equivalents.

The exmh program is an X version of the nmh mail client, described later in this chapter. It displays a window with two panes. The upper pane lists the headers for received mail, and the lower pane displays a selected message. Above each pane is a button bar for various nmh commands (these are the same as the commands for the nmh mail client). To check for new mail, you click the Inc button on the top pane. Headers for unread messages are colored blue, and the selected header is displayed in red. You can add new mailbox folders by clicking the New button.

To read a message, click its header, which is displayed in the lower pane. Buttons for managing a message are listed across the top of that pane. Long messages are displayed screen by screen, and you can see the next screen by clicking the More button. The Next and Previous buttons move you directly to the next or previous message. Comp, Reply, and Forward all open a new message window for composing and sending a message. Comp is for new messages, and Reply and Forward include your address, the sender's, and the current message's subject.

The GNU version of Emacs includes a mail client along with other components, such as a newsreader and editor. GNU Emacs is included on Red Hat distributions. Check the Emacs Web site at **www.emacs.org** for more information. When you start up GNU Emacs, menu buttons are displayed across the top of the screen. If you are running Emacs in an X Window System environment, you have full GUI capabilities and can select menus using your mouse. To access the Emacs mail client, select from the mail entries in the Tools menu. To compose and send messages, just select the Send Mail item in the Tools menu. This opens a screen with prompts for To and Subject header entries. You then type the message below them, using any of the Emacs editing capabilities. On the menu bar, a new menu is added labeled Mail. When you are ready to send the mail, choose the Send Mail entry in this menu. To read mail, select the Read Mail item in the Tools menu, which displays the first mail message received. Use entries in the Move menu to move to the next message or back to a previous one, and use entries in the Delete menu to remove a message. The Mail menu lists entries for message operations, such as sending replies or forwarding the message. GNU Emacs is a working environment within which you can perform a variety of tasks, with each task having its own buffer. When you read mail, a buffer is opened to hold the header list, and when you read a message, another buffer will hold the contents. When you compose a message, yet another buffer holds the text you wrote. The buffers you have opened for mail, news, or editing notes or files are listed in the Buffers menu. You can use this menu to switch among them.

XEmacs is another version of Emacs designed to operate solely with a GUI interface. The Internet applications, which you can easily access from the main XEmacs button bar, include a Web browser, a mail utility, and a newsreader. When composing a message, you have full use of the Emacs editor with all its features, including the spell-checker and search/replace.

Screen-Based Mail Clients

You can invoke several powerful mail clients on the command line that provide a full-screen, cursor-based interface. Menus are displayed on the screen whose entries you can select using your keyboard. Basic cursor movement is supported with arrow keys. Pine and Mutt are mail clients that provide a screen-based interface. Although screen-based, the mail clients are very powerful. Pine, in particular, has an extensive set of features and options.

Pine stands for "Program for Internet News and Email." It features full MIME support, enabling you to send messages, documents, and pictures easily. Pine has an extensive list of options, and it has flexible Internet connection capabilities, letting you receive both mail and Usenet news. Pine also enables you to maintain an address book where you can place frequently used e-mail addresses. You can find more information about Pine, including documentation and recent versions, from the Pine Information Center Web site at **www.washington.edu/pine**. The Pine newsgroup is **comp.mail.pine**, where you can post questions.

Pine runs from the command line using a simple cursor-based interface. Enter the `pine` command to start Pine. Pine supports full-screen cursor controls. It displays a menu whose items you can select by moving the cursor with the arrow keys to the entry of your choice and pressing ENTER. Each item is labeled with a capital letter, which you use to select it. The `O` command brings up a list of other Pine commands you can use.

Mutt incorporates many of the features of both Elm and Pine. It has an easy-to-use screen-based interface similar to Elm. Like Pine, Mutt has an extensive set of features, such as MIME support. You can find more information about Mutt from the Mutt Web page at **www.mutt.org**. Here you can download recent versions of Mutt and access online manuals and help resources. On most distributions, the Mutt manual is located in the `/usr/doc` directory under Mutt. The Mutt newsgroup is **comp.mail.mutt**, where you can post queries and discuss recent Mutt developments.

Command Line Mail Clients

Several mail clients use a simple command line interface. They can be run without any other kind of support, such as the X Window System, desktops, or cursor support. They are simple and easy to use, but include an extensive set of features and options.

Two of the more widely used mail clients of this type are Mail and Mail Handler (nmh). Mail is the mailx mail client that was developed for the Unix system. It is considered a kind of default mail client that can be found on all Unix and Linux systems.

You can also use the Emacs mail client from the command line, as described in the previous section.

Mail

What is known now as the mail utility was originally created for BSD Unix and called, simply, mail. Later versions of Unix System V adopted the BSD mail utility and renamed it mailx. Now, it is simply referred to as Mail. Mail functions as a de facto default mail client on Unix and Linux systems. All systems have the mail client called Mail, whereas they may not have other mail clients.

To send a message with Mail, type **mail** along with the address of the person to whom you are sending the message. Press ENTER and you are prompted for a subject. Enter the subject of the message and press ENTER again. At this point, you are placed in input mode. Anything typed in is taken as the contents of the message. Pressing ENTER adds a new line to the text. When you finish typing your message, press CTRL-D on a line of its own to end the message. You will then be prompted to enter a user to whom to send a carbon copy of the message (Cc). If you do not want to sent a carbon copy, just press ENTER. You will then see *EOT* (*end-of-transmission*) displayed after you press CTRL-D. In the next example, the user sends a message to another user whose address is **robert**. The subject of the message is Birthday. After typing in the text of the message, the user presses CTRL-D, and then presses ENTER to skip the carbon copy prompt.

```
$ mail robert
Subject: Birthday
 Your present is in the mail
 really.

^D
Cc: ENTER

EOT
$
```

The Mail utility receives input from the standard input. By default, the standard input is taken from what the user enters on the keyboard. With redirection, however, you can use the contents of a file as the message for the Mail program. In the next example, the file **mydata** is redirected as input for the Mail utility and sent to **robert**.

```
$ mail robert < mydata
```

You can send a message to several users at the same time by listing those users' addresses as arguments on the command line following the **mail** command. In the next example, the user sends the same message to both **chris** and **aleina**.

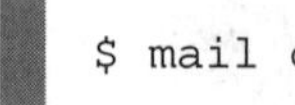

```
$ mail chris aleina
```

You may also want to save a copy of the message you are sending for yourself. You can copy a mail message to a file in your account by specifying a filename on the command line after the addresses. The filename must be a relative or full pathname, containing a slash. A pathname identifies an argument as a filename to which Mail saves a copy of the message being sent. In the next example, the user saves a copy of the message to a file called **birthnote**. A relative pathname is used, with the period denoting the current working directory: **./birthnote**.

```
$ mail robert ./birthnote
```

To receive mail, you enter only the **mail** command and press ENTER. This invokes a Mail shell with its own prompt and mail commands. A list of message headers is displayed. Header information is arranged into fields beginning with the status of the message and the message number. The status of a message is indicated by a single uppercase letter, usually **N** for *new* or **U** for *unread*. A message number, used for easy reference to your messages, follows the status field. The next field is the address of the sender, followed by the date and time the message was received, and then the number of lines and characters in the message. The last field contains the subject the sender gave for the message. After the headers, the Mail shell displays its prompt, an ampersand, **&**. At the Mail prompt, you enter commands that operate on the messages. The commonly used Mail commands are listed in Table 13-3. An example of a Mail header and prompt follows:

```
$ mail
Mail version 8.1 6/6/93. Type ? for help.
"/var/spool/mail/larisa": 3 messages 2 unread
 1 chris@turtle.mytrek. Thu Jun 7 14:17 22/554 "trip"
>U 2 aleina@turtle.mytrek Thu Jun 7 14:18 22/525 "party"
 U 3 dylan@turtle.mytrek. Thu Jun 7 14:18 22/528 "newsletter"
& q
```

Mail references messages either through a message list or through the current message marker (>). The greater-than sign (>) is placed before a message considered the current message. The current message is referenced by default when no message number is included with a Mail command. You can also reference messages using a message list consisting of several message numbers. Given the messages in the previous example, you can reference all three messages with **1-3**. The ^ references the first message; for example, **^-3** specifies the range of messages from the first message to the third message. The **$** references the last message. The period, **.**, references the current message. And the asterisk, *****, references all messages. Simply entering the number of the message by itself will display that message. The message is then output screen by screen. Press the SPACEBAR or the ENTER key to continue to the next screen.

You use the **R** and **r** commands to reply to a message you have received. The **R** command entered with a message number generates a header for sending a message and then places you into the input mode to type in the message. The **q** command quits Mail. When you quit, messages you have already read are placed in a file called **mbox** in your home directory. Instead of saving messages in the **mbox** file, you can use the **s** command to save a message explicitly to a file of your choice. The **s** command, however, saves a message with its header, in effect creating another mailbox file. You can then later access a mailbox file either by invoking the Mail utility with the **-f** option and the mailbox filename or, if you are already using Mail, by executing the **folder** command that switches to a specified mailbox file. For example, the command **mail -f family_msgs** accesses the mailbox file **family_msgs**. Each message in the **family_msgs** mailbox file is then displayed in a message list.

Mail has its own initialization file, called **.mailrc**, that is executed each time Mail is invoked, for either sending or receiving messages. Within it, you can define Mail options and create Mail aliases. You can set options that add different features to mail, such as changing the prompt or saving copies of messages you send. To define an alias, you enter the keyword **alias**, followed by the alias you have chosen and then the list of addresses it represents. In the next example, the alias **myclass** is defined in the **.mailrc** file.

.mailrc

```
alias myclass chris dylan aleina justin larisa
```

In the next example, the contents of the file **homework** are sent to all the users whose addresses are aliased by **myclass**.

```
$ mail myclass < homework
```


Status Codes	Description
N	Newly received messages
U	Previously unread messages
R	Reads messages in the current session

Table 13-3. *Mail Commands*

Status Codes	Description
`P`	Preserved messages, read in the previous session and kept in incoming mailbox
`D`	Deleted messages; messages marked for deletion
`O`	Old messages
`*`	Messages you saved to another mailbox file
Display Messages	**Description**
`h`	Redisplay the message headers
`z+ z-`	If header list takes up more than one screen, scrolls header list forward and backward
`t` *message-list*	Displays a message referenced by the message list; if no message list is used, the current message is displayed
`p` *message-list*	Displays a message referenced by the message list; if no message list is used, the current message is displayed
`n` or +	Displays next message
-	Displays previous message
`top` *message-list*	Displays the top few lines of a message referenced by the message list; if no message list is used, the current message is displayed
Message Lists	**Description**
message-number	References message with message number
num1-num2	References a range of messages beginning with *num1* and ending with *num2*
`.`	Current message
`^`	First message
`$`	Last message
`*`	All the messages waiting in the mailbox
/pattern	All messages with *pattern* in the subject field
Address	All messages sent from the user with *address*

Table 13-3. *Mail Commands* (continued)

Status Codes	Description
:*c*	All messages of the type indicated by *c;* message types are as follows: **n** Newly received messages **o** Old messages previously received **r** Read messages **u** Unread messages **d** Deleted messages
Deleting and Restoring Messages	**Description**
d *message-list*	Deletes a message referenced by the indicated message list from your mailbox
u *message-list*	Undeletes a message referenced by the indicated message list that has been previously deleted
q	Quits the Mail utility and saves any read messages in the **mbox** file
x	Quits the Mail utility and does *not* erase any messages you deleted; this is equivalent to executing a **u** command on all deleted messages before quitting
pre *message-list*	Preserves messages in your waiting mailbox even if you have already read them
Sending and Editing Messages	**Description**
r	Sends a reply to all persons who received a message
R	Sends a reply to the person who sent you a message
m *address*	Sends a message to someone while in the Mail utility
v *message-list*	Edits a message with the Vi editor
Saving Messages	**Description**
s *message-list filename*	Saves a message referenced by the message list in a file, including the header of the message
S *message-list*	Saves a message referenced by the message list in a file named for the sender of the message

Table 13-3. *Mail Commands* (continued)

Status Codes	**Description**
Saving Messages	**Description**
w *message-list filename*	Saves a message referenced by the message list in a file without the header; only the text of the message is saved
`folder` *mailbox-filename*	Switches to another mailbox file
`%`	Represents the name of incoming mailbox file: `folder %` switches to incoming mailbox file
`#`	Represents name of previously accessed mailbox file: `folder #` switches to previous mailbox file
`&`	Represents name of mailbox file used to save your read messages automatically; usually called **mbox**: `folder &` switches to **mbox** file
General Commands	**Description**
`?`	Displays a list of all the Mail commands
`!` *command*	Executes a user shell command from within the Mail shell

Table 13-3. *Mail Commands* (continued)

The New Mail Handler Utility: nmh

The Mail Handler mail client, commonly known as nmh, takes a different approach to managing mail than most other mail clients. nmh consists of a set of commands you execute within your user shell, just as you would execute any other Unix command. No special mail shell exists, as there is for Mail. One nmh command sends a message, another displays your incoming messages, and still another saves a message. The nmh commands and their options are listed in Table 13-4. A set of environment variables provides a context for the nmh commands you execute, such as keeping track of the current messages or mail folders.

Note *Instead of working from a command line interface, you can use xmh or exmh, which provides an X interface for accessing nmh messages.*

To send a message using nmh, you first need to compose the message using the **comp** command, and then send the message with the **send** command. To compose a message, type the word **comp** on the command line by itself and press ENTER. With nmh, you are placed in an input mode for the default editor used for nmh (usually the Vi editor). Fields at the top of the screen show prompts for the address, carbon copy, and subject. Below the dotted line, you enter your message. You can use your arrow keys to move from one field to another. Once you type the contents of the message, save and quit the editor as you normally would (ESC-SHIFT-ZZ for Vi). At the **What now?** prompt, you can send the message, edit it, save it to a file, display it again, or quit without sending the message. The **send** command sends the message. Pressing ENTER at the **What now?** prompt displays a list of commands you can enter. In the next example, the user composes a message for another user whose address is **robert**.

```
$ comp
To: robert
cc:
Subject: Birthday
--------------------
Your present is in the mail
really.

What now? send
$
```

To read your mail with nmh, you first need to store newly received mail into a designated nmh mailbox file with the **inc** command. The **inc** command displays a list of headers for each mail message in your incoming mailbox. An nmh message header consists only of the message number, the month and year, the address of the sender, and the beginning of the message text.

```
$ inc
1+ 06/07 Christopher Peter trip<<Are you ready for the trip? chris >>
2 06/07 Aleina Petersen party<<its on for tomorrow night. Aleina >>
3 06/07 Dylan Petersen newsletter<<Did you write your article yet? Dyla
$
```

If you want to redisplay the headers, you need to use another nmh command called **scan**.

```
$ scan
1+ 06/07 Christopher Peter trip<<Are you ready chris >>
2 06/07 Aleina Petersen party<<its on for Aleina >>
3 06/07 Dylan Petersen newsletter<<Did you Dylan >>
$
```

You use the **show**, **next**, and **prev** commands to display a message. The **show** command displays the current message, the **next** command displays the message after the current one, and the **prev** command displays the message before the current one. Initially, the current message is the first of the newly received messages. If you want to display a particular message, you can use the **show** command with the number of the message. The command **show 2** displays message 2. You can also reference several messages at once by listing their message numbers. The command **show 1 3** displays messages 1 and 3. You can also designate a range of messages by specifying the first message number in the range and the last number, separated by a minus sign. The command **show 1-3** displays messages 1, 2, and 3.

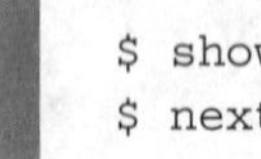

```
$ show
$ next
```

To print a message, you first output it with **show**, and then pipe the output to a printer. You save a message to a text file in much the same way. First you output the message using the **show** command, and then you redirect that output to a file.

```
$ show | lpr
$ show > myfile
```

Commands	Descriptions
inc	Places received mail in your incoming mailbox and displays message headers
show *num*	Displays current message or specified messages
prev	Displays the previous message
next	Displays the next message
scan	Redisplays message headers
Mhl	Displays formatted listing of messages
folders	Lists all mail folders
forw	Forwards a message
repl	Replies to a message

Table 13-4. *nmh Commands*

Commands	Descriptions
`send`	Resends a message or sends a file as a message
`pick`	Selects messages by specified criteria and assigns them a sequence
`folder`	Changes to another mailbox file (folder)

Table 13-4. *nmh Commands* (continued)

Notifications of Received Mail

As your mail messages are received, they are automatically placed in your mailbox file, but you are not automatically notified when you receive a message. To find out if you have any messages waiting, you can use a mail client to retrieve messages or you can use a mail monitor tool to tell you if you have any mail waiting. There are also a number of mail monitors available for use on Gnome. Several operate as applets on the Gnome panel. On the Red Hat Gnome desktop, there are two mail monitors you can choose from: the Mail Check and Clock and Mail Notify monitors. Both are applets that run inside a Gnome panel. The Mail Check applet will display a mail envelope when mail arrives, and the Clock and Mail Notify applet displays a small envelope and the number of messages received below the time. Other applets like Sonicmail will notify you of any POP3 mail arrivals. PyBiff performs much the same kind of mail monitoring as Korn. gbox_applet will monitor mailboxes, assigning priorities to each. GMailWatch is a mail monitor applet that will display a summary of incoming mail.

The KDE Desktop has a mail monitor utility called Korn that works in much the same way. Korn shows an empty inbox tray when there is no mail and a tray with slanted letters in it when mail arrives. If old mail is still in your mailbox, letters are displayed in a neat square. You can set these icons as any image you want. You can also specify the mail client to use and the polling interval for checking for new mail. If you have several mail accounts, you can set up a Korn profile for each one. Different icons can appear for each account telling you when mail arrives in one of them.

If you are just using a window manager, such as fvwm2 or Enlightenment, you can use the xbiff utility to perform the same function. xbiff displays an icon of a mailbox, which has a flag on it, on your desktop. When mail arrives, the flag goes up. xbiff can also beep or produce some other sound, if you prefer.

For command line interfaces you can use the biff utility. The biff utility notifies you immediately when a message is received. This is helpful when you are expecting a message and want to know as soon as it arrives. biff automatically displays the header and beginning lines of messages as they are received. To turn on biff, you enter **`biff y`** on the command line. To turn it off, you enter **biff n**. To find out if biff is turned on, enter **biff** alone.

You can temporarily block biff by using the **mesg n** command to prevent any message displays on your screen. **mesg n** not only stops any Write and Talk messages, it also stops biff and Notify messages. Later, you can unblock biff with a **mesg y** command. A **mesg n** command comes in handy if you don't want to be disturbed while working on some project.

Accessing Mail on Remote POP Mail Servers

Most newer mail clients are equipped to access mail accounts on remote servers. For such mail clients, you can specify a separate mail account with its own mailbox. For example, if you are using an ISP, most likely you will use that ISP's mail server to receive mail. You will have set up a mail account with a username and password for accessing your mail. Your e-mail address is usually your username and the ISP's domain name. For example, a username of **larisa** for an ISP domain named **mynet.com** would have the address **larisa@mynet.com**. The username would be **larisa**. The address of the actual mail server could be something like **mail.mynet.com**. The user **larisa** would log into the **mail.mynet.com** server using the username **larisa** and password to access mail sent to the address **larisa@mynet.com**. Newer mail clients, such as KMail, Balsa, and Netscape, enable you to set up a mailbox for such an account and access your ISP's mail server to check for and download received mail. You must specify what protocol a mail server uses. This is usually the Post Office Protocol (POP). This procedure is used for any remote mail server. Using a mail server address, you can access your account with your username and password.

Instead of creating separate mailboxes in different mail clients, you can arrange to have mail from remote accounts sent directly to the inbox maintained by your Linux system for your Linux account. All your mail, whether from other users on your Linux system or from ISP mail servers, will appear in your local inbox. Such a feature is helpful if you are using a mail client, such as Elm or Mail, that does not have the capability to access mail on your ISP's mail server. You can implement such a feature with Fetchmail. Fetchmail checks for mail on remote mail servers and downloads it to your local inbox, where it appears as newly received mail (you will have to be connected to the Internet or the remote mail server's network).

To use Fetchmail, you have to know a remote mail server's Internet address and mail protocol. Most remote mail servers use the POP3 protocol, but others may use the IMAP, ETRM, or POP2 protocols. Enter **fetchmail** on the command line with the mail server address and any needed options. The mail protocol is indicated with the **-p** option and the mail server type, usually POP3. If your e-mail username is different from your Linux login name, you use the **-u** option and the e-mail name. Once you execute the **fetchmail** command, you are prompted for a password. The syntax for the **fetchmail** command for a POP3 mail server follows:

```
fetchmail -p POP3 -u username mail-server
```

To use Fetchmail, connect to your ISP and then enter the **fetchmail** commands with the options and the POP server name on the command line. You will see messages telling you if mail is there and, if so, how many messages are being downloaded. You can then use a mail client to read the messages from your inbox. You can run Fetchmail in daemon mode to have it automatically check for mail. You have to include an option specifying the interval in seconds for checking mail.

```
fetchmail -d 1200
```

You can specify options such as the server type, username, and password in a **.fetchmailrc** file in your home directory. You can also have entries for other mail servers and accounts you may have. Instead of entering options directly into the **.fetchmailrc** file, you can use the fetchmailconf program. fetchmailconf provides a GUI interface for selecting Fetchmail options and entering mail account information. fetchmailconf runs only under X and requires that python and Tk be installed. It displays windows for adding news servers, configuring a mail server, and configuring a user account on a particular mail server. The expert version displays the same kind of windows, but with many more options. Initially, fetchmailconf displays a window with buttons for choosing a novice or expert version (see Figure 13-3). Choosing the novice version displays a window with an entry labeled "New Server." Type the address of your mail server in the adjoining box and press ENTER. The server address then appears in a list below. To configure that server, click the server name and then the Edit button at the bottom of the window. A new window opens with entries such as user accounts and server protocols. You can add as many user accounts as you may have on that server. You can then further configure an individual account by selecting the username and clicking the Edit button. This opens another window for user account options. You can specify a password and specify any corresponding local users for which you want mail for this account downloaded.

Once it is configured, you can enter **fetchmail** with no arguments; it will read entries from your **.fetchmailrc** file. Accounts you have specified are checked and any new mail is placed in your inbox. If you want Fetchmail to automatically check for new mail periodically, you can activate its daemon mode. To do so, place a daemon entry in the **.fetchmailrc** file. The following entry activates the Fetchmail daemon mode, checking for mail every 1,200 seconds:

```
Set daemon 1200
```

You can also make entries directly in the **.fetchmailrc** file. An entry in the **.fetchmailrc** file for a particular mail account consists of several fields and their values: poll, protocol, username, and password. *Poll* is used to specify the mail server name,

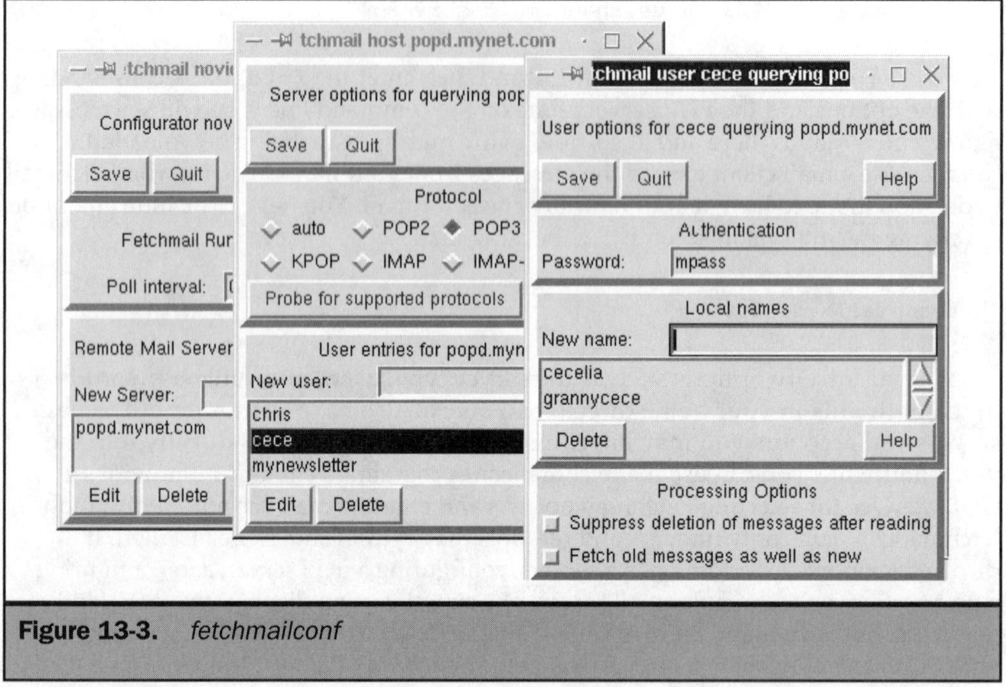

Figure 13-3. *fetchmailconf*

and *protocol*, the type of protocol used. Notice you can also specify your password, instead of having to enter it each time Fetchmail accesses the mail server. The syntax for an entry follows:

```
poll SERVERNAME protocol PROTOCOL username NAME password PASSWORD
```

You can use abbreviations for certain field names if you want: *proto* for protocol, *user* for username, and *pass* for password. An example follows for a POP3 server and an account with the username **chris** and the password **mypass**:

```
poll popd.mynet.com proto pop3 user chris password mypass
```

You can specify a default entry for any of these fields and not have to repeat them for each account entry. The default must be placed before the mail server entries. The following example sets the default protocol to POP3 and the username to **chris**:

```
defaults protocol pop3 user chris
```

This next example would reference the **chris** account with the password **newpass** on the **popd.train.com** mail server using the POP3 protocol. The missing fields are filled in by default.

```
poll popd.train.com password newpass
```

Fetchmail enables you to download messages to a specific user on your local system. In fact, you can access several accounts on the remote system and have them downloaded to specific users on the your local system. This is useful when running Fetchmail in daemon mode. Essentially, Fetchmail is transferring mail from one set of remote accounts to corresponding ones on your local system. You could even have Fetchmail download from one remote account to several local ones, sending copies of the same mail to each. This is helpful if you are using several accounts on your Linux system, or if a group of users is using an account on the remote server for group mail. Local users are specified with the keyword **is** or **to** followed by the usernames, terminating with the keyword **here**. The following examples show different ways of specifying local users. The last entry will send all mail retrieved from the **mynewsletter** account to the users **larisa**, **aleina**, and **dylan**.

```
poll popd.mynet.com proto pop3 user chris password mypass is chris here
poll popd.othernet.com proto pop3 user neil password mypass is chris here
poll popd.mynet.com proto pop3 user cece password mypass  \
  to cecelia grannycece here
poll popd.mynet.com proto pop3 user mynewsletter password mypass \
  to larisa aleina dylan here
```

Note *Fetchmail also supports a multidrop mailbox feature. You can have several users' mail sent to one mailbox on the mail server, and then download it from there to the inboxes for their Linux accounts.*

Usenet News

Usenet is an open mail system on which users post news and opinions. It operates like a systemwide mailbox that any user on your Linux system can read or send messages to. Users' messages are incorporated into Usenet files, which are distributed to any system signed up to receive them. Each system that receives Usenet files is referred to as a *site.* Certain sites perform organizational and distribution operations for Usenet, receiving messages from other sites and organizing them into Usenet files, which are then broadcast to many other sites. Such sites are called *backbone sites*, and they operate like publishers, receiving articles and organizing them into different groups.

To access Usenet news, you need access to a news server. A news server receives the daily Usenet newsfeeds and makes them accessible to other systems. Your network may have a system that operates as a news server. If you are using an Internet service provider (ISP), a news server is probably maintained for your use. To read Usenet articles, you use a *newsreader*—a client program that connects to a news server and accesses the articles. On the Internet and in TCP/IP networks, news servers communicate with newsreaders using the Network News Transfer Protocol (NNTP) and are often referred to as NNTP news servers. Or you could also create your own news server on your Linux system to run a local Usenet news service or to download and maintain the full set of Usenet articles. Several Linux programs, called *news transport agents,* can be used to create such a server. This chapter focuses on the variety of news readers available for the Linux platform. The configuration administration and architecture of the NNTP server are covered in Chapter 24.

Usenet files were originally designed to function like journals. Messages contained in the files are referred to as *articles.* A user could write an article, post it in Usenet, and have it immediately distributed to other systems around the world. Someone could then read the article on Usenet, instead of waiting for a journal publication. Usenet files themselves were organized as journal publications. Because journals are designed to address specific groups, Usenet files were organized according to groups called *newsgroups.* When a user posts an article, it is assigned to a specific newsgroup. If another user wants to read that article, he or she looks at the articles in that newsgroup. You can think of each newsgroup as a constantly updated magazine. For example, to read articles on computer science, you would access the Usenet newsgroup on computer science. Usenet files are also used as bulletin boards on which people carry on debates. Again, such files are classified into newsgroups, though their articles read more like conversations than journal articles. You can also create articles of your own, which you can then add to a newsgroup for others to read. Adding an article to a newsgroup is called *posting* the article.

Each newsgroup has its own name, which is often segmented to classify newsgroups. Usually, the names are divided into three segments: a general topic, a subtopic, and a specific topic. The segments are delimited by periods. For example, you may have several newsgroups dealing with the general topic *rec,* which stands for recreation. Of those, some newsgroups may deal with only the subtopic food. Again, of those, a group may only discuss a specific topic, such as recipes. In this case, the newsgroup name would be **rec.food.recipes**.

Many of the bulletin board groups are designed for discussion only, lacking any journal-like articles. A good number of these begin with either *alt* or *talk* as their general topic. For example, **talk.food.chocolate** may contain conversations about how wonderful or awful chocolate is perceived, while **alt.food.chocolate** may contain informal speculations about the importance of chocolate to the basic structure of civilization as we know it. Here are some examples of Usenet newsgroup names:

```
comp.ai.neural-nets
comp.lang.pascal
```

```
sci.physics.fusion
rec.food.recipes
talk.politics.theory
```

Note *The Google Web site also maintains online access to Usenet newsgroups. It has the added capability of letting you search extensive newsgroup archives. You can easily locate articles on similar topics that may reside in different newsgroups. Other sites like Yahoo maintain their own groups that operate much like Usenet newsgroups, but with more supervision.*

Linux has newsgroups on various topics. Some are for discussion, and others are sources of information about recent developments. On some, you can ask for help for specific problems. A selection of some of the popular Linux newsgroups is provided here:

Newsgroup	Topic
comp.os.linux.announce	Announcements of Linux developments
comp.os.linux.admin	System administration questions
comp.os.linux.misc	Special questions and issues
comp.os.linux.setup	Installation problems
comp.os.linux.help	Questions and answers for particular problems
linux.help	Obtain help for Linux problems

You read Usenet articles with a newsreader, such as KNode, Pan, Pine, Mozilla, Netscape, trn, or tin, which enables you to first select a specific newsgroup and then read the articles in it. A newsreader operates like a user interface, enabling you to browse through and select available articles for reading, saving, or printing. Most newsreaders employ a sophisticated retrieval feature called *threads* that pulls together articles on the same discussion or topic. Newsreaders are designed to operate using certain kinds of interfaces. For example, KNode is a KDE newsreader that has a KDE interface and is designed for the KDE desktop. Pan has a Gnome interface and is designed to operate on the Gnome desktop. Pine is a cursor-based newsreader, meaning that it provides a full-screen interface that you can work with using a simple screen-based cursor that you can move with arrow keys. It does not support a mouse or any other GUI feature. trn uses a simple command line interface with limited cursor support. Most commands you type in and press ENTER to execute. Several popular newsreaders are listed in Table 13-5.

Newsreader	Description
Pan	Gnome Desktop newsreader
KNode	KDE Desktop newsreader
Mozilla	Web utility with newsreader capabilities (X based)
Netscape	Web utility with newsreader capabilities (X based)
Pine	Mail client with newsreader capabilities (cursor based)
Slrn	Newsreader (cursor based)
Emacs	Emacs editor, mail client, and newsreader (cursor based)
trn	Newsreader (command line interface)
tin	Newsreader (command line interface)

Table 13-5. *Linux Newsreaders*

Note *Numerous newsreaders currently are under development for both Gnome and KDE. You can check for KDE newsreaders on the software list on the K Desktop Web site at **apps.kde.com**. For Gnome newsreaders, check Internet tools on the software map on the Gnome Web site at **www.gnome.org**. The Mozilla newsreader is integrated into the Mozilla Web browser and is available from **www.mozilla.org**.*

Most newsreaders can read Usenet news provided on remote news servers that use the NNTP. Many such remote news servers are available through the Internet. Desktop newsreaders, such as KNode and Pan, have you specify the Internet address for the remote news server in their own configuration settings. Several shell-based newsreaders, however, such as trn, tin, and Pine, obtain the news server's Internet address from the **NNTPSERVER** shell variable. Before you can connect to a remote news server with such newsreaders, you first have to assign the Internet address of the news server to the **NNTPSERVER** shell variable, and then export that variable. You can place the assignment and export of **NNTPSERVER** in a login initialization file, such as **.bash_profile,** so it is performed automatically whenever you log in. Administrators could place this entry in the **/etc/profile** file for a news server available to all users on the system.

```
$ NNTPSERVER=news.domain.com
$ export NNTPSERVER
```

The Complete Reference

Chapter 14

Web, FTP, and Java Clients

Most Linux distributions will provide powerful Web and FTP clients for accessing the Internet. Many are installed automatically and are ready to use when you first start up your Linux system. Linux also includes full Java development support, letting you run and construct Java applets. This chapter will cover some of the more popular clients available on Linux.

Web and FTP clients connect to sites which are servers that use Web pages and FTP files to provide services to users. Sites are accessed using their Internet addresses. Local networks use the same addressing format. Though discussed in more detail in Chapter 36, a quick review is provided here. The Internet uses a set of network protocols called TCP/IP, which stands for Transmission Control Protocol/Internet Protocol. In a TCP/IP network, messages are broken into small components called *datagrams,* which are then transmitted through various interlocking routes and delivered to their destination computers. Once received, the datagrams are reassembled into the original message. Datagrams are also referred to as *packets.* Sending messages as small components has proved far more reliable and faster than sending them as one large bulky transmission. With small components, if one is lost or damaged, only that component has to be resent, whereas if any part of a large transmission is corrupted or lost, the entire message must be resent.

On a TCP/IP network such as the Internet, each computer is given a unique address called an *IP address.* The IP address is used to identify and locate a particular host—a computer connected to the network. It consists of a number, usually four sets of three numbers separated by periods. An example of an IP address is **192.168.187.4.** IP addressing is described in detail in Chapter 36. Non-Internet machines use a gateway to connect to the Internet (see Chapters 7 and 37).

All hosts on the Internet are identified by their IP addresses. When you send a message to a host on the Internet, you must provide its IP address. Using a sequence of four numbers of an IP address, however, can be difficult. They are hard to remember, and it's easy to make mistakes when typing them. To make identifying a computer on the Internet easier, the Domain Name Service (DNS) was implemented. The DNS establishes a domain name address for each IP address. The domain name address is a series of names separated by periods. Whenever you use a domain name address, it is automatically converted to an IP address, which is then used to identify that Internet host. The domain name address is far easier to use than its corresponding IP address.

A domain name address needs to be registered with an Internet domain name registry such as the American Registry for Internet Numbers (ARIN) so that each computer on the Internet can have a unique name (see **www.iana.org** for more information). Creating a name follows specified naming conventions. The domain name address consists of the hostname, the name you gave to your computer; a domain name, the name that identifies your network, and an extension that identifies the type of network you are on. Here is the syntax for domain addresses:

```
host-name.domain-name.extension
```

In the following example, the domain address references a computer called **metalab** on a network referred to as **unc**. It is part of an educational institution, as indicated by the extension **edu**.

```
metalab.unc.edu
```

With the **whois** command, you can obtain information for domain name servers about different networks and hosts connected to the Internet. Enter **whois** and the domain name address of the host or network, and **whois** displays information about the host, such as the street address and phone number, as well as contact persons.

```
$ whois domain-address
```

Web Clients

The World Wide Web (WWW, or the Web) is a hypertext database of different types of information, distributed across many different sites on the Internet. A *hypertext database* consists of items linked to other items, which, in turn, may be linked to yet other items, and so on. Upon retrieving an item, you can use that item to retrieve any related items. For example, you could retrieve an article on the Amazon rain forest and then use it to retrieve a map or a picture of the rain forest. In this respect, a hypertext database is like a web of interconnected data you can trace from one data item to another. Information is displayed in pages known as *Web pages.* On a Web page, certain keywords or graphics are highlighted that form links to other Web pages or to items, such as pictures, articles, or files.

To quickly review, the Web links data across different sites on the Internet throughout the world. The Web originated in Europe at CERN research laboratories. An Internet site that operates as a Web server is known as a *Web site.* Such Web sites are often dedicated to specialized topics or institutions—for example, the Smithsonian Web site or the NASA Web site. These Web sites usually have an Internet address that begins with "www", as in **www.redhat.com**, the Web site for Red Hat, Inc. Once connected to a Web site, you can use hypertext links to move from one Web page to another.

To access the Web, you use a client program called a *browser.* You can choose from many different Web browsers. Browsers are available for use on Unix, Windows, Macintosh, and Linux. Certain browsers, such as Netscape and Mozilla, have versions that operate on all such systems. On your Linux system, you can choose from several Web browsers, including Netscape Navigator. Navigator is available as part of all Linux distributions. Netscape and Mozilla are X Window System–based browsers that provide full picture, sound, and video display capabilities. Most distributions also include the Lynx browser, a line-mode browser that displays only lines of text. The K Desktop incorporates Web browser capabilities into its file manager, letting a directory window operate as a Web browser. Gnome-based browsers, such as Express and Mnemonic, are also designed to be easily enhanced.

Web browsers and FTP clients are commonly used to conduct secure transactions such as logging into remote sites, ordering items, or transferring files. Such operations are currently secured by encryption methods provided by the Secure Socket Layer (SSL). See Chapters 21 and 37 for more information about SSL and its counterpart, SSH, the Secure Shell. If you use a browser for secure transactions, it should be SSL enabled. Most browsers such as Netscape, Mozilla, and Links include SSL support. For FTP operations, you can use the SSH version of ftp, sftp, or the Kerberos 5 version (see Chapter 37). Linux distributions install SSL as part of a standard installation.

URL Addresses

An Internet resource is accessed using a Universal Resource Locator (URL). A URL is composed of three elements: the transfer protocol, the hostname, and the pathname. The transfer protocol and the hostname are separated by a colon and two slashes, **://**. The *pathname* always begins with a single slash:

```
transfer-protocol://host-name/path-name
```

The *transfer protocol* is usually HTTP (Hypertext Transfer Protocol), indicating a Web page. Other possible values for transfer protocols are **gopher**, **ftp**, and **file**. As their names suggest, **gopher** and **ftp** initiate Gopher and FTP sessions, whereas **file** displays a local file on your own system, such as a text or an HTML file. Table 14-1 lists the various transfer protocols.

Protocol	Description
http	Uses Hypertext Transfer Protocol for Web site access
gopher	Accesses Gopher site
ftp	Uses File Transfer Protocol for anonymous FTP connections
telnet	Makes a Telnet connection
news	Reads Usenet news; uses Net News Transfer Protocol (NNTP)

Table 14-1. *Web Protocols*

The *hostname* is the computer on which a particular Web site is located. You can think of this as the address of the Web site. By convention, most hostnames begin with **www**. In the next example, the URL locates a Web page called **guides.html** on the **www.kernel.org** Web site in the LDP directory:

```
http://www.kernel.org/LDP/guides.html
```

If you do not want to access a particular Web page, you can leave the file reference out, and then you automatically access the Web site's home page. To access a Web site directly, use its hostname. If no home page is specified for a Web site, the file **index.html** in the top directory is often used as the home page. In the next example, the user brings up the Red Hat home page:

```
http://www.redhat.com/
```

The pathname specifies the directory where the resource can be found on the host system, as well as the name of the resource's file. For example, **/pub/Linux/newdat.html** references an HTML document called **newdat** located in the **/pub/Linux** directory. As you move to other Web pages on a site, you may move more deeply into the directory tree. In the following example, the user accesses the **FAQ.html** document in the directory **support/docs/faqs/rhl_general_faq/FAQ.html/**:

```
http://www.redhat.com/support/docs/faqs/rhl_general_faq/FAQ.html
```

If you specify a directory pathname without a particular Web page file, the Web site looks for a specified default file. Often this is called **index.html** and is located in that directory. In the next example, the **index.html** Web page in the /**apps/support** directory is displayed:

```
http://www.redhat.com/apps/support/index.html
```

You can use this technique to access local Web pages on your system. For example, once installed, the demo Web pages for Java are located in **/usr/local/java/**. Because this is on your local system, you needn't include a hostname. An **index.html** page in the **/usr/local/java/** directory is automatically displayed when you specify the directory path. You can do the same for your system documentation, which, on most distributions, is in Web page format located in the **/usr/doc/HTML/ldp** directory.

```
file:/usr/local/java
file:/usr/doc/HTML/ldp
```

If you reference a directory that has no **index.html** file, the Web server, if so configured, can create one for you that your browser can display (see Chapter 21). This index simply lists the different files and directories in that directory. You can click an entry to display a file or to move to another directory. The first entry is a special entry for the parent directory.

The resource file's extension indicates the type of action to be taken on it. A picture has a **.gif** or **.jpeg** extension and is converted for display. A sound file has a **.au** or **.wav** extension and is played. The following URL references a **.gif** file. Instead of displaying a Web page, your browser invokes a graphics viewer to display the picture. Table 14-2 provides a list of the different file extensions.

```
http://www.train.com/engine/engine1.gif
```

Web Browsers

Most Web browsers are designed to access several different kinds of information. Web browsers can access a Web page on a remote Web site or a file on your own system.

File Type	Description
.html	Web page document formatted using HTML, the Hypertext Markup Language
Graphics Files	
.gif	Graphics, using GIF compression
.jpeg	Graphics, using JPEG compression
Sound Files	
.au	Sun (Unix) sound file
.wav	Microsoft Windows sound file
.aiff	Macintosh sound file
Video Files	
.QT	QuickTime video file, multiplatform
.mpeg	Video file
.avi	Microsoft Windows video file

Table 14-2. *Web File Types*

Some browsers can also access a remote news server or an FTP site. The type of information for a site is specified by the keyword **http** for Web sites, **nntp** for news servers, **ftp** for FTP sites, and **file** for files on your own system.

To access a Web site, you enter `http://` followed by the Internet address of the Web site. If you know a particular Web page you want to access on that Web site, you can add the pathname for that page, attaching it to the Internet address. Then simply press ENTER. The browser connects you to that Web site and displays its home page or the page you specified.

You can just as easily use a Web browser to display Web pages on your own system by entering the term `file` followed by a colon, `file:`, with the pathname of the Web page you want to display. You do not specify an Internet site. Remember, all Web pages usually have the extension **.html**. Links within a Web page on your own system can connect you to other Web pages on your system or to Web pages on remote systems. When you first start a Web browser, your browser displays a local Web page on your own system. The default page on Red Hat is a local page with links to the Red Hat Web site where you can obtain online support. If you want, you can create your own Web pages, with their own links, and make one of them your default Web page.

Web pages on a Web site often contain links to other Web pages, some on the same site and others at other Web sites. Through these links, you can move from one page to another. As you move from Web page to Web page using the links or buttons, your browser displays the URL for the current page. Your browser keeps a list of the different Web pages you have accessed in a given session. Most browsers have buttons that enable you to move back and forth through this list. You can move to the Web page you displayed before the current one and then move back further to the previous one. You can move forward again to the next page, and so on.

To get to a particular page, you may have moved through a series of pages, using links in each to finally reach the Web page you want. To access any Web page, all you need is its URL address. If you want to access a particular page again, you can enter its URL address and move directly to it, without moving through the intervening pages as you did the first time. Instead of writing down the URL addresses and entering them yourself, most Web browsers can keep bookmarks—a list of favorite Web pages you want to access directly. When you are displaying a Web page you want to access later, instruct your browser to place it on the Bookmarks list. The Web page is usually listed in the Bookmarks list by its title, not its URL. To access that Web page later, select the entry in the Bookmark list.

Most Web browsers can also access FTP and Gopher sites. You may find using a Web browser to access an FTP site with anonymous access is easier than using an FTP client. Directories and files are automatically listed, and selecting a file or directory is only a matter of clicking its name. First enter `ftp://` and then the Internet address of the FTP site. The contents of a directory are then displayed, listing files and subdirectories. To move to another directory, just click it. To download a file, click its name. You see an entry listed as double periods (..), representing the parent directory. You can move down the file structure from one subdirectory to another and move back up one directory at a time by selecting the parent directory to return to the previous directory.

Most browsers can connect to your news server to access specified newsgroups or articles. This is a local operation, accessing the news server to which you are already connected. You enter `nntp` followed by a colon and the newsgroup or news article. Some browsers, such as Netscape, have an added newsreader browser that allows them to access any remote news servers.

As noted previously, several popular browsers are available for Linux. Three distinctive ones are described here: Netscape Navigator, Konqueror, and Lynx. Netscape is an X Window System–based Web browser capable of displaying graphics, video, and sound, as well as operating as a newsreader and mailer. Konqueror is the K Desktop file manager. KDE has integrated full Web-browsing capability into the Konqueror file manager, letting you seamlessly access the Web and your file system with the same application. Lynx and Links are command line–based browsers with no graphics capabilities, but in every other respect are fully functional Web browsers.

Netscape Navigator and Mozilla

Hypertext databases are designed to access any kind of data, whether it is text, graphics, sound, or even video. Whether you can actually access such data depends to a large extent on the type of browser you use. Mozilla is a browser based on the Netscape core source code known as mozilla. In 1998, Netscape made this source code freely available under the Netscape Public License (NPL). The Mozilla Project, based at **www.mozilla.org**, has developed a commercial-level browser based on mozilla source code. Mozilla is developed on an open source model much like Linux, KDE, and Gnome. Developers can submit modifications and additions over the Internet to the Mozilla Web site. Mozilla releases are referred to as Milestones. Mozilla is currently released under both the NPL license for modifications of mozilla code and the MPL license (Mozilla Public License) for new additions. In future releases, Red Hat will use Mozilla as its primary browser, in place of Netscape.

Mozilla is an X Window System application you operate from your desktop. Red Hat has a Mozilla entry for in the desktop's Internet menu. Mozilla displays an area at the top of the screen for entering a URL address and a series of buttons for various Web page operations. Drop-down menus provide access to Mozilla features. To access a Web site, you enter its address in the URL area and press ENTER. The icon bar across the top of the browser holds buttons for moving from one page to another and performing other operations (see Figure 14-1).

Mozilla refers to the URLs of Web pages you want to keep in a hotlist as *bookmarks*, marking pages you want to access directly. The Bookmarks menu enables you to add your favorite Web pages to a hotlist. You can then view your bookmarks and select one to view. You can also edit your list of bookmarks, adding new ones or removing old ones. History is a list of previous URLs you have accessed. If you want to return to a Web page you did not save as a bookmark, you can find it in the History list. Additionally, you can use Mozilla to receive and send mail, as well as to access Usenet newsgroups.

The Options menu in Mozilla enables you to set several different kinds of preferences for your browser. You can set preferences for mail and news, the network,

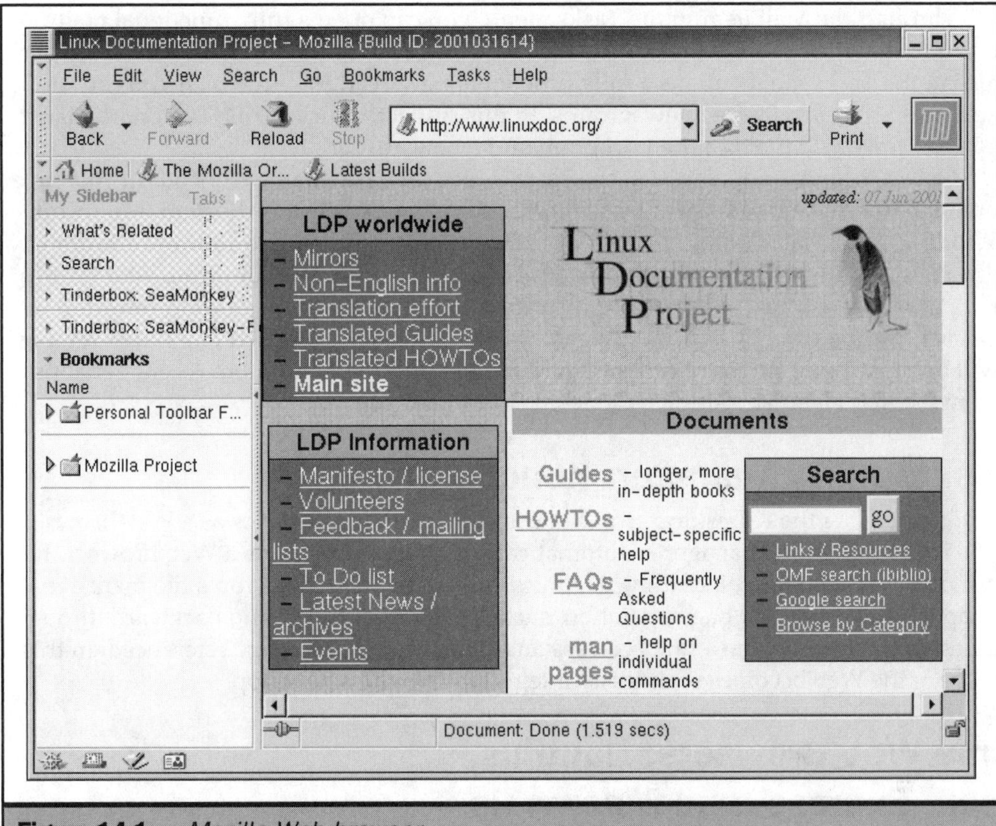

Figure 14-1. *Mozilla Web browser*

and security, as well as general preferences. In general preferences, you can determine your home page and how you want the toolbar displayed. In the Mail/News Account Settings, you can enter the mail and news servers you use on the Internet. Mozilla can be set to access any number of news servers you subscribe to and that use the NNTP transfer protocols. You can switch from one news server to another if you want.

If you are on a network that connects to the Internet through a firewall, you must use the Proxies screen to enter the address of your network's firewall gateway computer. A *firewall* is a computer that operates as a controlled gateway to the Internet for your network. Several types of firewalls exist. One of the most restrictive uses programs called *proxies,* which receive Internet requests from users and then make those requests on their behalf. There is no direct connection to the Internet. From the Options menu, select Network and then choose the Proxies screen. Here, enter the IP address of your network's firewall gateway computer.

Through the Mail item in the Tasks menu, you can open a fully functional mail client with which you can send and receive messages over the Internet. The News item, also in the Tasks menu, opens a fully functional newsreader with which you can read and post articles in Usenet newsgroups. In this respect, your Mozilla is more than just a Web browser. It is also a mail program and a newsreader.

One of the more popular Web browsers is Netscape Navigator. Versions of Netscape operate on different graphical user interfaces such as X Window System, Microsoft Windows, and Macintosh. Using X Window System, the Netscape browser can display graphics, sound, video, and Java-based programs (you learn about Java a little later in the chapter). You can obtain more information about Netscape on its Web site: **www.netscape.com**. Netscape Navigator is now included with Red Hat Linux 7.1, but will be replaced in future releases with Mozilla. You can obtain more recent versions from the Red Hat distribution FTP site at **ftp.redhat.com**.

K Desktop File Manager: Konqueror

If you are using the K Desktop, you can use a file manager window as a Web browser. The K Desktop's file manager is automatically configured to act as a Web browser. It can display Web pages, including graphics and links. The K Desktop's file manager supports standard Web page operation, such as moving forward and backward through accessed pages. Clicking a link accesses and displays the Web page referenced. In this respect, the Web becomes seamlessly integrated into the K Desktop.

Gnome Web Browsers: Nautilus, Galeon, Express, and Mnemonic

The new Gnome file manager, Nautilus, used in Gnome 1.4, is a functional Web browser, just like Konqueror. In the Nautilus location box, you can enter a Web address and Nautilus will access and display that Web page. The file manager Forward and Backward buttons, as well as bookmarks, help you navigate through previously viewed pages. However, it is not a fully functional Web browser. Nautilus will display icons in its sidebar for dedicated Web browsers installed on your system. Click on one to start using that Web browser instead of Nautilus.

Midnight Commander, the Gnome 1.2 file manager used in Red Hat 7.1, does not have Web browser capability.

Several other Gnome-based Web browsers are also available. Galeon, Express, and Mnemonic support standard Web operations. Galeon is a Gnome Web browser designed to be fast with a very light interface. It supports drag-and-drop operations, multiple selections, and bookmark imports. It is based on Gecko (the mozilla rendering engine). You can find out more about Galeon at **galeon.sourceforge.net**. Express is designed to rely on plug-ins for Web features. This way, the browser can be made as complex or simple as you want. All major operations, such as viewers and protocols, are handled as plug-ins. This design allows new features to be easily added in this way. Mnemonic is an extensible and modular Web browser.

Lynx and Links: Line-Mode Browser

Lynx is a line-mode browser you can use without X Window System. A Web page is displayed as text only. A text page can contain links to other Internet resources, but does not display any graphics, video, or sound. Except for the display limitations, Lynx is a fully functional Web browser. You can use Lynx to download files or to make Telnet connections. All information on the Web is still accessible to you. Because it does not require much of the overhead that graphics-based browsers need, Lynx can operate much faster, quickly displaying Web page text. To start the Lynx browser, you enter **`lynx`** on the command line and press ENTER.

Another useful text-based browser shipped with most distributions is Links. Links is a powerful screen-based browser that includes features such as frame, form, and table support. It also supports SSL secure encryption.

Web Search Utilities

To search for files on FTP sites, you can use search engines provided by Web sites, such as Yahoo!, Excite, Google, AltaVista, or Lycos. These usually search for both Web pages and FTP files. To find a particular Web page you want on the Internet, you can use the search engines mentioned above, or perform searches from any number of Web portals, such as Netscape or Linux online. Web searches have become a standard service of most Web sites. Searches carried out on documents within a Web site may use local search indexes set up and maintained by indexing programs like ht:/Dig. Sites using ht:/Dig use a standard Web page search interface.

Creating Your Own Web Site

To create your own Web site, you need access to a Web server. Red Hat automatically installs the Apache Web server on its Linux systems. You can also rent Web page space on a remote server—a service many ISPs provide, some free. On Red Hat systems, the directory set up by your Apache Web server for your Web site pages is **/var/httpd/html**. Other servers provide you with a directory for your home page. Place the Web pages you create in that directory. You place your home page here. You can make other subdirectories with their own Web pages to which these can link. Web pages are not difficult to create. Links from one page to another move users through your Web site. You can even create links to Web pages or resources on other sites. Many excellent texts are available on Web page creation and management.

Web pages are created using either HTML, the Hypertext Markup Language, or the newer extended version, XML, the Extended Markup Language. They are a subset of Standard Generalized Markup Language (SGML). Creating an HTML or XML document is a matter of inserting HTML or XML tags in a text file. In this respect, creating a Web page is as simple as using a tag-based word processor. You use the HTML tags to format text for display as a Web page. XML tags can include more detailed information about a particular connection such as object data or transaction characteristics. The Web page itself is a text file you can create using any text editor, such as Vi. If you are familiar with tag-based word processing on Unix systems, you will find it conceptually similar to nroff. Some HTML tags indicate headings, lists, and paragraphs, as well as links to reference Web resources.

Instead of manually entering HTML or XML code, you can use Web page composers. A Web page composer provides a graphical interface for constructing Web pages. The Linux version of WordPerfect can automatically generate a Web page from a WordPerfect document. You can create Web pages using all the word processing features of WordPerfect and Star Office. Special Web page creation programs, such as Netscape Composer, also can easily help you create complex Web pages without ever having to type any HTML tags explicitly. Remember, though, no matter what tool you use to create your Web page, the Web page itself will be an HTML document.

Note *Many of the standard editors for the K Desktop and Gnome include Web page construction features. Many enable you to insert links or format headings. For example, the KEdit program supports basic text-based Web page components. You can add headings, links, or lines, but not graphics.*

Java for Linux: Blackdown

To develop Java applications, use Java tools, and run many Java products, you must install the Java 2 Software Development Kit (SDK) and the Java 2 Runtime Environment (JRE) on your system. Together they make up the Java 2 Platform, Standard Edition (J2SE). Sun currently supports and distributes Linux versions of these products. You can download them from Sun at **java.sun.com/j2se** and install them on your system. You can even select an RPM package version for easy installation on Red Hat. The current version of the J2SE is known as Java version 1.3. An earlier version, 1.2, will not work on Red Hat 7.0, though 1.3 will work on 7.1.

Though Sun supports Linux versions of Java, more thorough and effective Linux ports of Java can be obtained from the Blackdown project at **www.blackdown.org**. The Blackdown project has ported the J2SE, including versions 1.3 of the SDK and JRE. They have also ported previous versions of Java, including 1.1 and 1.2. More information and documentation is also available at this Blackdown Web site. The SDK and JRE 1.3 are usually available in the form of compressed archives, **.tar.bz2**. You use the `bunzip2` command to decompress the file and the tar `xvf` command to extract it. Extraction should be done in the **/usr/local** file. Follow the instructions in the **INSTALL** file to install the software.

Numerous additional Java-based products and tools are currently adaptable for Linux. Tools include Java 3D, Java Media Framework (JMF), and Java Advanced Imaging (JAI), all Blackdown projects (see Table 14-3). Many of the products run directly as provided by Sun. These include the HotJava Web browser and the Java Web server. You can download several directly from the Sun Java Web site at **java.sun.com**.

Application	Description
Java 2 Software Development Kit (SDK) 1.3	A Java development environment with a compiler, interpreters, debugger, and more. Part of the Java 2 Platform. Download the Linux port from **www.blackdown.org**.
Java 2 Runtime Environment 1.3 (J2RE)	A Java Runtime Environment used to run Java applets. Part of the Java 2 Platform. Download the Linux port from **www.blackdown.org**.
Java 2 Platform SE (J2SE) for Linux	Java 2 Platform, Standard Edition, which includes Java 2 SDK and RE. Download the Linux port from **www.blackdown.org**.
Java 3D for Linux	Sun's 3D Application Program Interface for 3D Java programs. Download the Linux port from **www.blackdown.org**.
Java Media Framework (JMF) for Linux	Enable audio and video to be added to Java. Download the Linux port from **www.blackdown.org**.
Java Advanced Imaging (JAI) for Linux	Java Advanced Imaging API. Download the Linux port from **www.blackdown.org**.
Java 1.1 Development Kit (JDK) and Java 1.1 Runtime Environment (JRE)	The older Java 1.1 development environment with a compiler, interpreters, debugger, and more. Download the Linux port for your distribution's update through **www.blackdown.org**.
HotJava browser	Sun's HTML 3.2– and JDK 1.1–compliant Web browser. Download the Linux version from **java.sun.com**.
Java Web Server	A Web server implemented with Java. Available at Java Web site at **java.sun.com**.

Table 14-3. *Blackdown Java Packages and Java Web Applications*

*See **java.sun.com/products** for an extensive listing of Java applications.*

The Java 2 Software Development Kit: SDK

The Java Software Development Kit (SDK) provides tools for creating and debugging your own Java applets and provides support for Java applications, such as the HotJava browser. The kit includes demonstration applets with source code. You can obtain detailed documentation about the SDK from the Sun Web site at **java.sun.com**. Two major releases of the SDK are currently available—1.2, 1.3.*x*—with corresponding versions for the Java 2 Runtime Environment (J2RE) for 1.2 and 1.3. Java SDK adds capabilities for security, Swing, and running Java enhancements, such as Java3D and Java Sound.

SDK includes standard features found in the JDK features for internationalization, signed applets, JAR file format, AWT (window toolkit) enhancements, JavaBeans component model, networking enhancements, a math package for large numbers, database connectivity (JDBC), object serialization, and inner classes. Java applications include a Java compiler (javac), a Java debugger (jdb), and an applet viewer (appletviewer). In addition, the SDK offers the Java Naming and Directory Interface (JNDI), integrated Swing, Java 2d, network and security enhancements, and CORBA. With SDK, you can run the Blackdown port of Java 3D, Java Advanced Imaging, Java Media Framework, and Java Sound. Detailed descriptions of these features can be found in the SDK documentation.

Java Applets

You create a Java applet much as you would create a program using a standard programming language. You first use a text editor to create the source code, which is saved in a file with a **.java** extension. Then you can use the java compiler to compile the source code file, generating a Java applet. This applet file has the extension **.class**. For example, the JDK demo directory includes the Java source code for a Blink applet called **Blink.java.** You can go to that directory and then compile the **Blink.java** file, generating a **Blink.class** file. The **example1.html** file in that directory runs the **Blink.class** applet. Start your browser and access this file to run the Blink applet.

```
# javac Blink.java
```

An applet is called within a Web page using the <applet> HTML tag. This tag can contain several attributes, one of which is required: code. You assign to code the name of the compiled applet. You can use several optional attributes to set features, such as the region used to display the applet and its alignment. You can even access applets on a remote Web site. In the following example, the applet called **Blink.class** is displayed in a box on the Web browser that has a height of 140 pixels and a width of 100 pixels, and is aligned in the center.

```
<applet code="Blink.class" width=100 height=140 align=center></applet>
```

To invoke the debugger, use the **appletviewer** command with the **-debug** option and the name of the HTML file that runs the applet.

```
appletviewer -debug mypage.html
```

Numerous Interface Development Environments (IDE) applications are available for composing Java applets and applications. Although most are commercial, some provide free shareware versions. An IDE provides a GUI interface for constructing Java applets. You can link to and download several IDE applications through the Blackdown Web page.

FTP Clients

The Internet is a network of computers around the world you can access with an Internet address and a set of Internet tools. Many computers on the Internet are configured to operate as servers, providing information to anyone who requests it. The information is contained in files you can access and copy. Each server, often referred to as a *site,* has its own Internet address by which it can be located. Linux provides a set of Internet tools you can use to access sites on the Internet, and then locate and download information from them. These tools are known as *clients.* A client application, such as an FTP or a Web client, can communicate with a corresponding server application running on a remote system. An FTP client can communicate with an FTP server program on another system. The server lets the client access certain specified resources on its system and lets an FTP client transfer certain files. Several popular FTP clients are shown in Table 14-4.

FTP Clients	Description
Konquerer	K Desktop file manager
Nautilus and GNU Midnight Commander	Gnome file managers
gFTP	Gnome FTP client
NcFTP	Screen-based FTP client
ftp	Command line FTP client

Table 14-4. *Linux FTP Clients*

To access Internet sites, your computer must be connected to the Internet. You may be part of a network already connected to the Internet. If you have a standalone computer, such as a personal computer, you can obtain an Internet connection from an Internet service provider (ISP). Once you have an Internet address of your own, you can configure your Linux system to connect to the Internet and use various Internet tools to access different sites. Chapter 36 describes how to configure your Linux system to make such a connection.

The primary tools for accessing Internet sites are FTP clients and Web browsers. With FTP clients, you can connect to a corresponding FTP site and download files from it. FTP clients are commonly used to download software from FTP sites that operate as software repositories. Most Linux software applications can be downloaded to your Linux system from such sites. A distribution site like **ftp.redhat.com** is an example of one such FTP site, holding an extensive set of packaged Linux applications you can download using an FTP client and then easily install on your system. In the last few years, Web browsers have become the primary tool for accessing information on the Internet. Most of the tasks you perform on the Internet can be done easily with a Web browser. You only need to use an FTP client to download or upload files from or to a specific FTP site.

Other Internet tools are also available for your use, such as Telnet and IRC clients. The *Telnet* protocol enables you to log into an account directly on another system. *IRC clients* set up chat rooms through which you can communicate with other users over the Internet. Web clients are discussed in the next chapter, and Telnet and IRC clients are discussed in Chapter 15.

Network File Transfer: FTP

You can use File Transfer Protocol (FTP) clients to transfer extremely large files directly from one site to another. FTP can handle both text and binary files. This is one of the TCP/IP protocols, and it operates on systems connected to networks that use the TCP/IP protocols, such as the Internet. FTP performs a remote login to another account on another system connected to you on a network. Once logged into that other system, you can transfer files to and from it. To log in, you need to know the login name and password for the account on the remote system. For example, if you have accounts at two different sites on the Internet, you can use FTP to transfer files from one to the other. Many sites on the Internet allow public access using FTP, however. Such sites serve as depositories for large files anyone can access and download. These sites are often referred to as *FTP sites,* and in many cases, their Internet address begins with the word *ftp,* such as **ftp.gnome.org** or **ftp.redhat.com**. Others begin with other names, such as **metalab.unc.edu**. These public sites allow anonymous FTP login from any user. For the login name, you use the word "anonymous," and for the password you use your Internet address. You can then transfer files from that site to your own system.

You can perform FTP operations using any one of a number of FTP client programs. For Linux systems, you can choose from several FTP clients. Many now operate using GUI interfaces such as Gnome. Some, such as Netscape, have limited capabilities, whereas others, such as NcFTP, include an extensive set of enhancements. The original FTP client is just as effective, though not as easy to use. It operates using a simple command line interface and requires no GUI or cursor support, as do other clients.

The Internet has a great many sites open to public access. They contain files anyone can obtain using file transfer programs, such as NcFTP. Unless you already know where a file is located, however, finding it can be difficult. To search for files on FTP sites, you can use search engines provided by Web sites, such as Yahoo!, Excite, AltaVista, Google, or Lycos. For Linux software, you can check sites such as **freshmeat.net, sourceforge.net**, **rpmfind.net**, **apps.kde.com**, and **www.linuxapps.com**. These sites usually search for both Web pages and FTP files.

Note *Linux tools like Ganesha and Karchie will search FTP sites for requested software.*

Web Browser–Based FTP: Netscape

You access an FTP site and download files from it with any Web browser. A Web browser is effective for checking out an FTP site to see what files are listed there. When you access an FTP site with a Web browser, the entire list of files in a directory is listed as a Web page. You can move to a subdirectory by clicking its entry. With Mozilla or Netscape Navigator, you can easily browse through an FTP site to download files. To download a file with Mozilla, hold down the SHIFT key and then double-click the file (for Netscape, hold the SHIFT key down and single-click). This will start the transfer operation. This opens a box for selecting your local directory and the name for the file. The default name is the same as on the remote system. Mozilla and Netscape Navigator have some important limitations. You cannot upload a file, and you cannot download more than one file at a time. They are useful for locating individual files, though not for downloading a large set of files, as is usually required for a system update.

The K Desktop File Manager: Konqueror

On the K Desktop, the desktop file manager (Konqueror) has a built-in FTP capability. The FTP operation has been seamlessly integrated into standard desktop file operations. Downloading files from an FTP site is as simple as copying files by dragging them from one directory window to another, but one of the directories happens to be located on a remote FTP site. On the K Desktop, you can use a file manager window to access a remote FTP site. Files in the remote directory are listed just as your local files are. To download files from an FTP site, you open a window to access that site, entering the URL for the FTP site in the window's location box. Open the directory you want, and then open another window for the local directory to which you want the remote files copied. In the window showing the FTP files, select the ones you want to download. Then simply click and drag those files to the window for the local directory. A pop-up menu appears with choices for Copy, Link, or Move. Select Copy. The selected files are then downloaded. Another window then opens, showing the download progress and displaying the name of each file in turn, and a bar indicating the percentage downloaded so far.

Gnome FTP: Nautilus, GNU Midnight Commander, gFTP

The easiest way to download files is to use the built-in FTP capabilities of the Gnome file manager, Midnight Commander. You can also use several Gnome-based FTP clients that offer more features, including gFTP. Check the Gnome Web site at **www.gnome.org** for more. gFTP is included with the current Gnome release.

On Gnome, the desktop file managers—GNU Midnight Commander and Nautilus—have a built-in FTP capability much like the KDE file manager. The FTP operation has been seamlessly integrated into standard desktop file operations. Downloading files from an FTP site is as simple as dragging files from one directory window to another, where one of the directories happens to be located on a remote FTP site. Use the Gnome file manager to access a remote FTP site, listing files in the remote directory, just as local files are. Just enter the FTP URL following the prefix **ftp://** and press ENTER. The top directory of the remote FTP site will be displayed. Simply use the file manager to progress through the remote FTP site's directory tree until you find the file you want. Then open another window for the local directory to which you want the remote files copied. In the window showing the FTP files, select those you want to download. Then CTRL-click and drag those files to the window for the local directory. CTRL-click performs a copy operation, not a move. As files are downloaded, a dialog window appears showing the progress.

Note *Nautilus replaces Midnight Commander in Gnome 1.4 and later versions.*

gFTP

The gFTP program is a simpler Gnome FTP client designed to let you make standard FTP file transfers. It has an interface similar to WS_FTP used on Windows. The gFTP window consists of several panes. The top-left pane lists files in your local directory, and the top-right pane lists your remote directory. Subdirectories have folder icons preceding their names. The parent directory can be referenced by the double period entry (..) with an up arrow at the top of each list. Double-click a directory entry to access it. The pathnames for all directories are displayed in boxes above each pane. You can enter a new pathname for a different directory to change to it, if you want.

Two buttons between the panes are used for transferring files. The left arrow button, <-, downloads selected files in the remote directory, and the right arrow button, ->, uploads files from the local directory. To download a file, click it in the right-side pane and then click the left arrow button, <-. When the file is downloaded, its name appears in the left pane, your local directory. Menus across the top of the window can be used to manage your transfers. A connection manager enables you to enter login information about a specific site. You can specify whether to perform an anonymous login or to provide a username and password. Click the Connect button to connect to that site. A drop-down menu for sites enables you to choose the site you want.

NcFTP

The NcFTP program has a screen-based interface that can be run from any shell command line. It does not use a desktop interface. FTP operations are executed using commands you enter at a prompt. Options and bookmarks can be selected using cursor-based menus. To start up NcFTP, you enter the **ncftp** command on the command line. If you are working in a window manager, such as KDE, Gnome, or FVWM, open a shell terminal window and enter the command at its prompt. The main NcFTP screen consists of an input line at the bottom of the screen with a status line above it. The remainder of the screen is used to display commands and responses from remote systems. For example, when you download files, a message specifying the files to be downloaded is displayed in the status line. NcFTP lets you set preferences for different features, such as anonymous login, progress meters, or a download directory. Enter the **pref** command to open the preferences screen. From there, you can select and modify the listed preferences.

To connect to an FTP site, you enter the **open** command on the input line, followed by the site's address. The address can be either an IP address or a domain name, such as **ftp.gnome.org**. If you don't supply an address, a list of your bookmarked sites is displayed, and you can choose one from there. By default, NcFTP attempts an anonymous login, using the term "anonymous" as your username and your e-mail address as the password. When you successfully connect, the status bar displays the remote site's name on the left and the remote directory name on the right.

```
open ftp.gnome.org
```

If you want to log into a specific account on a remote site, have yourself prompted for the username and password by using the **-u** option with the **open** command. The **open** command remembers the last kind of login you performed for a specific site and repeats it. If you want to change back to an anonymous login from a user login, you use the **-a** option with the **open** command. For busy sites, you may be unable to connect on the first try and you must repeat the open process. NcFTP has a redial capability you turn on with the **-r** option. The **-d** option sets the delay for the next attempt, and the **-g** option sets the maximum number of connection attempts. With the **lookup** command, you can obtain the IP and domain name addresses for an FTP site. The **lookup** command takes as an argument either the IP or domain name address and then displays both. This is useful for finding a site's IP address. With the **-v** option, more information, such as aliases, is retrieved. The NcFTP open options are shown in Table 14-5.

Once connected, you enter commands on the input line to perform FTP operations such as displaying file lists, changing directories, or downloading files. With the **ls** command, you can list the contents of the current remote directory. Use the **cd** command to change to another remote directory. The **dir** command displays a detailed listing of files. With the **page** command, you view the contents of a remote file, a screen at a time. To download files, you use the **get** command, and to upload files, you use the **put** command. During a download, a progress meter above the status bar displays

Option	Description
`-a`	Connect anonymously
`-u`	Connect with username and password prompts
`-p` *num*	Use specified port number when connecting
`-r`	Redial until connected
`-d` *num*	Set delay (*num*) in number of seconds for redial option
`-g` *num*	Specify the maximum number of redials

Table 14-5. *NcFTP Open Options*

how much of the file has been downloaded so far. The **get** command has several features described in more detail in the following section. When you finish, you can disconnect from the site with the **close** command. You can then use **open** to connect to another site, or quit the NcFTP program with the **quit** command. The **help** command lists all NcFTP commands. You can use the **help** command followed by the name of a command to display specific information on it.

The NcFTP program supports several commands that operate on your local system. These are usually standard FTP command names preceded by an *l*. **lcd** changes your local working directory, **lls** lists the contents of your local directory, **lpage** displays the contents of a local file a screen at a time, and **lpwd** displays the local directory's full pathname. For any other local commands or scripts you need to execute, use the shell escape command, **!**. Simply precede the shell command or script with a **!**.

The NcFTP program also provides commands for managing files and directories on your remote site, provided you have the permission to do so. You can use **mkdir** to create a remote directory, and **rmdir** to remove one. Use the **rm** command to erase remote files. With the **rename** command, you can change their names. The NcFTP commands are listed in Table 14-6.

The NcFTP program also has a colon mode of operation that enables you to issue a single **ncftp** command to download a file. Enter the **ncftp** command, followed by a URL, for the file you want. You can enter the command on the shell command line or place it within a script. For example, the following command downloads the **readme** file on the Red Hat FTP site:

```
$ ncftp ftp.redhat.com/pub/README
```

Command	Description
help [*command*]	Lists names of NcFTP commands
cd [*directory*]	Changes the working directory on the remote host
create [*filename*]	Creates an empty file on the remote host, enabling you to use the filename as a message
debug	Turns debugging on or off
version	Displays version information
dir	Displays a detailed directory listing
echo	Displays a string, useful for macros
get	Downloads files from a remote host to your working directory
lcd [*directory*]	Changes the local working directory
lls	Lists files in your local working directory
lookup *host*	Looks up entries for remote hosts
lpage *filename*	Displays contents of local file, a page at time
lpwd	Displays the local current working directory
mkdir *directory name*	Creates a directory on the remote host
mode *mode*	Specifies transfer mode (*b* for block mode, *s* for stream mode)
open [*option*] *hostname*	Connects to a remote host. If no hostname is specified, the bookmark editor displays a host list from which you can choose one: **-a** forces anonymous login **-u** forces user login **-r** redials automatically **-d** specifies time delay before redial; used with **-r** **-g** specifies the maximum number of redials; used with **-r**
page *filename*	Displays the contents of a remote file

Table 14-6. *NcFTP Commands*

Command	Description
pdir	Same as **dir**, but outputs to your pager, enabling you to display a remote file list a page at a time. Used for command line interface.
pls	Same as **ls**, but outputs to your pager. Used for command line interface.
redir	Redisplays the last directory listing
predir	Redisplays the last directory listing and outputs to pager if working in command line interface
put *filename*	Uploads a file to a remote host
pwd	Displays the remote current working directory
rename *orig-name new-name*	Changes the name of a remote file
quit	Quits NcFTP
quote	Sends an FTP protocol command to the remote server
rhelp [*command*]	Sends a help request to the remote host
rm *filenames*	Erases remote files
rmdir *directories*	Removes remote directories
site *command*	Executes site-specific commands
type *type*	Changes transfer type (ASCII, binary, image)
! *command*	Escapes to the shell and executes the following shell command or script

Table 14-6. *NcFTP Commands* (continued)

In the colon mode, the **-c** option sends the file to the standard output and the **-m** option pipes it to your pager:

```
$ ncftp -c ftp.redhat.com/pub/README > ~/redhatinfo/readme
$ ncftp -m ftp.redhat.com/pub/README
```

NcFTP Download Features

The NcFTP **get** command differs significantly from the original FTP client's **get** command. Whereas the original FTP client uses two commands, **get** and **mget**, to perform download operations, NcFTP uses only the **get** command. However, the NcFTP **get** command combines the capabilities of both **mget** and **get** into the **get** command, as well as adding several new features. Table 14-7 lists the various **get** command options. By default, the NcFTP **get** command performs wildcard matching for filenames. If you enter only part of a filename, the **get** command tries to download all files beginning with that name. You can turn off wildcard matching with the **-G** option, in which case you must enter the full names of the files you want. The following example downloads all files with names beginning with "Xfree86" and is similar to using **mget Xfree86*** in the original FTP:

```
get Xfree86
```

The **get** command checks to see if you already have a file you are trying to download. If so, it skips the download. The **get** command also checks if the file you already have is a newer version, in which case it also skips the download. This is a helpful feature for easily maintaining upgrade files. You can simply access the update directory on the remote site, and then use the **get** command with the * to download to the directory you are using to keep your upgrade file. Only newer versions or newly added upgrade files

Command	Description
-G	Turns wildcard matching for filenames on or off
-R *directory*	Downloads a directory and all its subdirectories (recursive)
-f *filenames*	Forces the download of all specified files, even if older or the same as local ones
-C	Forces resumption of a download from where it was interrupted
-z *remote-file local-file*	Renames a remote file on your local system
-n *num*	Downloads files no older than the specified number of days

Table 14-7. *NcFTP get Options*

are downloaded, instead of the entire set. If you want to download a file, even though you have it already, you can force the download with the **-f** option. For example, to download upgrades for Red Hat manually, you can connect to the Red Hat upgrade directory in the Red Hat FTP site and then issue the following **get** command:

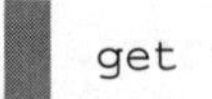

```
get *
```

Tip *If you were interrupted during a download, you can restart the download from where you left off. This feature is built into NcFTP. (On other FTP programs, it can be invoked with the* **reget** *command.) NcFTP checks to see if you have already started to download a file and then continues from where you left off.*

Certain features require you to enter an option on the command line after the **get** command. For example, adding the **-R** command specifies a recursive capability, enabling you to download and create subdirectories and their files. This command is particularly helpful in downloading upgrade directories, such as Red Hat's, which contain several subdirectories. The following example downloads the **i386** directory and all its subdirectories:

```
get -R i386
```

If you want to give a file a different name on your local system, use the **-z** option. Enter the local filename you want after the remote filename. The following example downloads the **readme** file and renames it **calinfo**. If you did not use the **-z** option, both names would be taken as files to be downloaded, instead of only the first.

```
get -z readme calinfo
```

To obtain recent files only, you can use the **-n** option, which takes as its argument a number of days. Files older than the specified number of days are not retrieved. The following example downloads files posted within the last 30 days:

```
get -n 30 *
```

Bookmarks and Macros

When you disconnect (close) from a site, NcFTP automatically saves information about it. This includes the site address, the directory you were in, and the login information. This information is placed in a file called **bookmarks** in your **.ncftp** directory. The site information is given a bookmark name you can use to access the site easily again. The bookmark name is usually the key name in the site's address. You can use this name to connect to the site. For example, **ftp.redhat.com** could be named **redhat**. You could then connect to it with the following command:

```
open redhat
```

You can edit your bookmark entries using the bookmark editor. Enter the command **bookmarks** to bring up the editor. Remote systems you have accessed are listed on the right side of the screen. Bookmark commands are listed on the left. You can change the bookmark name or edit login information, such as the username or password, the remote directory, or the transfer mode.

The NcFTP program supports macros for simple operations. You create macros by entering macro definitions in the macros file located in your **.ncftp** directory. Initially, no such file will exist, so you have to create one using any text editor. The **macros** file is a simple text file you can edit with any text editor. The syntax for a macro definition follows:

```
macro macro-name
 ftp-commands
end
```

A macro executes NcFTP commands. Remember, however, the **!** is an NcFTP command that enables you to execute any Linux command or script. With a preceding **!** you can define an NcFTP macro that executes any shell command or any script you have written. A simple example of a macro is as follows:

```
macro ascii
 type ascii
end
```

Macros support parameters similar to those used by shell programs. Arguments entered after a macro name can be referenced in the macro using a **$** sign and the number of the argument in the argument list. **$1** references the first argument, **$2** the second, and so on. **$*** is a special parameter that references all arguments, and **$@** references all arguments, encasing each in double quotes.

```
macro cdls
 cd $1
 ls
end
```

The NcFTP program also supports a limited numbers of event macros. These are macros executed when a certain event is detected, such as when the program starts or shuts down. For example, a macro defined with the name **.start.ncftp** has its commands executed every time you start NcFTP; **.quit.ncftp** executes its commands when you quit. Site-specific macros also execute whenever it is necessary to access or disconnect from certain sites. These macros begin with either the open or close event, followed by the site's bookmark. For example, a macro defined with the name **.open.redhat** would execute its commands whenever you connected to the Red Hat site. A macro named **.open.any** has its commands executed whenever you connect to any site, and one named **.close.any** executes whenever you disconnect from a site.

ftp

The name ftp designates the original FTP client used on Unix and Linux systems. ftp uses a command line interface, and it has an extensive set of commands and options you can use to manage your FTP transfers. You start the ftp client by entering the command **`ftp`** at a shell prompt. If you have a specific site you want to connect to, you can include the name of that site on the command line after the ftp keyword. Otherwise, you need to connect to the remote system with the ftp command **`open`**. You are then prompted for the name of the remote system with the prompt "(to)". Upon entering the remote system name, ftp connects you to the system and then prompts you for a login name. The prompt for the login name consists of the word "Name" and, in parentheses, the system name and your local login name. Sometimes the login name on the remote system is the same as the login name on your own system. If the names are the same, press ENTER at the prompt. If they are different, enter the remote system's login name. After entering the login name, you are prompted for the password. In the next example, the user connects to the remote system **garnet** and logs into the **robert** account:

```
$ ftp
ftp> open
(to) garnet
Connected to garnet.berkeley.edu.
220 garnet.berkeley.edu FTP server ready.
Name (garnet.berkeley.edu:root): robert
password required
Password:
user robert logged in
ftp>
```

Once logged in, you can execute Linux commands on either the remote system or your local system. You execute a command on your local system in ftp by preceding the command with an exclamation point. Any Linux commands without an exclamation point are executed on the remote system. One exception exists to this rule. Whereas you can change directories on the remote system with the **`cd`** command, to change directories on your local system, you need to use a special ftp command called **`lcd`**.

The Complete Reference

Chapter 15

Network Tools

You can use a variety of network tools to perform tasks such as obtaining information about other systems on your network, accessing other systems, and communicating directly with other users. Network information can be obtained using utilities such as **ping**, **finger**, and **host**. Talk, ICQ, and IRC clients enable you to communicate directly with other users on your network. Telnet performs a remote login to an account you may have on another system connected on your network. Each has a corresponding K Desktop or Gnome version. These provide a GUI interface, so you no longer have to use the shell command line to run these tools. In addition, your network may make use of older remote access commands. These are useful for smaller networks and enable you to access remote systems directly to copy files or execute commands.

Network Information: ping, finger, and host

You can use the **ping**, **finger**, **traceroute**, and **host** commands to find out status information about systems and users on your network. **ping** is used to check if a remote system is up and running. You use **finger** to find out information about other users on your network, seeing if they are logged in or if they have received mail. **host** displays address information about a system on your network, giving you a system's IP and domain name addresses. **traceroute** can be used to track the sequence of computer networks and systems your message passed through on its way to you. Table 15-1 lists various network information tools.

On the Gnome desktop, the Gnetutil utility provides a Gnome interface for entering the **ping**, **finger**, and **host** commands. On the K Desktop, you can use the KDE network utilities (knu) to issue **ping** , **finger**, **traceroute**, and **host** commands. Select the appropriate tabbed panel. For the Ping panel, enter the address of the remote system at the box labeled Host and click Go.

ping

The **ping** command detects whether a system is up and running. **ping** takes as its argument the name of the system you want to check. If the system you want to check is down, **ping** issues a timeout message indicating a connection could not be made. The next example checks to see if **www.redhat.com** is up and connected to the network:

```
$ ping www.redhat.com
PING www.portal.redhat.com (206.132.41.231): 56 data bytes
64 bytes from 206.132.41.231: icmp_seq=0 ttl=248 time=24.0 ms
64 bytes from 206.132.41.231: icmp_seq=1 ttl=248 time=124.5 ms
64 bytes from 206.132.41.231: icmp_seq=2 ttl=248 time=77.9 ms
64 bytes from 206.132.41.231: icmp_seq=3 ttl=248 time=220.1 ms
64 bytes from 206.132.41.231: icmp_seq=4 ttl=248 time=14.9 ms
```

```
--- www.portal.redhat.com ping statistics ---
6 packets transmitted, 5 packets received, 16% packet loss
round-trip min/avg/max = 14.9/92.2/220.1 ms
```

You can also use **ping** with an IP address instead of a domain name. With an IP address, **ping** can try to detect the remote system directly without having to go through a domain name server to translate the domain name to an IP address. This can be helpful for situations where your network's domain name server may be temporarily down and you want to check if a particular remote host on your network is connected. In the next example, the user checks the Red Hat site using its IP address:

```
$ ping 206.132.41.231
PING 206.132.41.231 (206.132.41.231): 56 data bytes
64 bytes from 206.132.41.231: icmp_seq=0 ttl=248 time=16.6 ms
64 bytes from 206.132.41.231: icmp_seq=1 ttl=248 time=65.1 ms
64 bytes from 206.132.41.231: icmp_seq=2 ttl=248 time=70.1 ms
64 bytes from 206.132.41.231: icmp_seq=3 ttl=248 time=336.6 ms
64 bytes from 206.132.41.231: icmp_seq=4 ttl=248 time=53.6 ms
64 bytes from 206.132.41.231: icmp_seq=5 ttl=248 time=42.1 ms

--- 206.132.41.231 ping statistics ---
6 packets transmitted, 6 packets received, 0% packet loss
round-trip min/avg/max = 16.6/97.3/336.6 ms
```

Note *__ping__ operation could also fail if __ping__ access is denied by a network's firewall. See Chapter 37 for more details.*

finger and who

You can use the **finger** command to obtain information about other users on your network and the **who** command to see what users are currently online on your system. The **who** command lists all users currently connected along with when, how long, and where they logged in. It has several options for specifying the level of detail. **who** is meant to operate on a local system or network. **finger** can operate on large networks, including the Internet, though most systems block it for security reasons. It may be of more use within a secure local network. **finger** checks to see when a user last logged in, the type of shell that he or she is using, the pathname of the home directory, and whether any mail has been received. **finger** then checks for a **.plan** file in a user's home directory that may contain information about the user. The **.plan** file is a file you create yourself on your own home directory. You can place information you want made publicly available into the **.plan** file. You can enter the command **finger** on the command line with the login name of the user you want to check.

On the Gnome desktop you can use the gfinger utility to issue finger commands, and in the K Desktop you can use the KDE network utilities (knu). Click the Finger panel and enter the address of the host you want to check. On the K Desktop, the KFinger tool also provides a GUI for easily sending **finger** queries. It features entries for users and remote servers. You can search for users on specific remote systems.

host

With the **host** command, you can find network address information about a remote system connected to your network. This information usually consists of a system's IP address, domain name address, domain name nicknames, and mail server. This information is obtained from your network's domain name server. For the Internet, this includes all systems you can connect to over the Internet.

The **host** command is an effective way to determine a remote site's IP address or URL. If you have only the IP address of a site, you can use **host** to find out its domain name. For network administration, an IP address can be helpful for making your own domain name entries in your **/etc/host** file. That way, you needn't rely on a remote domain name server (DNS) for locating a site. On the K Desktop, you can use the KDE network utilities for running **host** commands. Click the Host resolution panel and enter the address of the host you want to check. On Gnome, you can use the gHostLookup utility.

```
$ host www.gnome.org
www.gnome.org is a nickname for gnome.labs.redhat.com
gnome.labs.redhat.com has address 199.183.24.235
gnome.labs.redhat.com mail is handled (pri=10) by mail.redhat.com

$ host 199.183.24.235
235.24.183.199.IN-ADDR.ARPA domain name pointer
gnome.labs.redhat.com
```

The Gwhois program is a Gnome-based client that displays information about hosts obtained from NIC network services. Gwhois provides an X Window System interface with a list of NIC servers from which to choose. gHostLookup is a simple Gnome application that returns a machine's IP address when you give it the hostname.

Network Information Tools	Description
ping	Detects whether a system is connected to the network

Table 15-1. *Network Tools*

Network Information Tools	Description
finger	Obtains information about users on the network
who	Checks what users are currently online
host	Obtains network address information about a remote host
traceroute	Tracks the sequence of computer networks and hosts your message passes through
knu	The KDE Network utilities featuring **finger**, **ping**, **traceroute**, and **host** commands
Gnetutil	The Gnome Network utilities featuring **finger**, **ping**, **traceroute**, and **host** commands
gfinger	Gnome finger client
KFinger	KDE **finger** utility
gHostLookup	Gnome utility to find IP addresses for hostnames
Gwhois	Obtains information about networks, hosts, and users

Table 15-1. *Network Tools* (continued)

Network Talk and Messenger Clients

You may, at times, want to communicate directly with other users on your network. You can do so with talk, ICQ, instant messenger, and IRC utilities, provided the other user is also logged into a connected system at the same time (see Table 15-2). The Talk utility operates like a telephone, enabling you to have a direct two-way conversation with another user. Talk is designed for users on the same system or connected on a local network. ICQ (I Seek You) is an Internet tool that notifies you when other users are online and enables you to communicate with them. ICQ works much like an instant messenger. With an Internet Relay Chat utility (IRC), you can connect to a remote server where other users are also connected and talk with them. Instant messenger (IM) clients operate much the same way, allowing users on the same IM system to communicate anywhere across the Internet. Currently the major IM systems are AOL, Microsoft Network (MSN), Yahoo, ICQ, and Jabber. Unlike the others, Jabber is an open source instant messenger service (**www.jabber.org**).

Clients	Description
Kicq, KXicq2	KDE ICQ clients
GnomeICU	Gnome ICQ client
X-Chat	Internet Relay Chat (IRC) client
Kit	KDE AOL Instant Messenger (AIM) client
Kaim	KDE AIM client
Gabber	Jabber client
Gaim	Gnome AIM client
GNU Talk	Talk client and server

Table 15-2. *Talk and Messenger Clients*

ICQ Clients

The ICQ protocol enables you to communicate directly with other users online, but like an instant messenger utility. Using an ICQ client, you can send users messages, chat with them, or send files. You can set up a contact list of users who you may want to contact when they are online. You are then notified in real time when they connect, and you can communicate with them if you wish. Several modes of communication are supported. These include chat, message, e-mail, file transfer, or games. To use ICQ, you register with an ICQ server that provides you with an ICQ number, also known as a Universal Internet Number (UIN). You can find out more about the ICQ protocol at **www.icq.com**.

Several Gnome-based ICQ clients are available for your use. Check the Gnome software map at **www.gnome.org** for new versions and recent updates. GnomeICU is an ICQ client that can communicate with other ICQ users on any platform, whether Linux, Windows, or Macintosh. GnomeICU features include message history for individual users, chat, messages, and sound events. Kicq and Kxicq2 are K Desktop ICQ clients currently under development. They will support instant messaging, client lists, and other ICQ features.

Internet Relay Chat

Internet Relay Chat (IRC) operates like a chat room, where you can enter channels and talk to other users already there. First, you select an IRC server to connect to. Various servers are available for different locales and topics. Once connected to a server, you can choose from a list of channels to enter. The interface works much like a chat room. When you connect to the server, you can choose a nickname by which you will be referred. Several Internet Relay Chat clients are available for use on Linux systems. Most operate on either X Window System, KDE, or Gnome platforms. Irssi and X-Chat are Gnome IRC clients, though there are versions for other platforms. Both have support for multiple concurrent server connections, multiple windows, Direct Client Communication (DCC) to bypass intermediate servers, and Perl scripts. X-Chat has a plug-in interface for adding new features (see **xchat.linuxpower.org** for more details). Irssi has an easy-to-use interface with support for the Gnome panel. Kvirc is a K Destop IRC client. Kvirc features an alias and events editor, DCC, and scripting. X-Chat is the only one currently installed with Red Hat, and works equally well on Gnome and KDE.

AOL Instant Messenger Client: Kit

AOL Instant Messenger (AIM) is a free service provided by AOL for anyone who registers for it, as well as those who are already members of AOL. With AIM, you can send messages to members instantly, play games with them, and receive stock alerts. You can even share images, sounds, and photographs. AOL already provides clients for Windows and Macintosh. A new version called AIM Express is designed to run on any Web browser and will run on systems with JDK 1.1 or greater. You can find out more about AIM at **www.aol.com/aim**.

Kit is the KDE desktop AOL Instant Messenger (AIM) client, providing support for panel docking and session management. Kit is included as a standard part of KDE 2.x. When you first start Kit you are asked to create an initial profile, providing a screen name and password. Once selected, the main window will list your buddy list, organizing them by group. From the Settings menu you can open a configuration window where you can enter your buddy list as well as set permissions and edit your user information. If a buddy is also logged in, you can click on his or her entry and open an instant messenger window to send and receive messages. You can find out more about Kit at **kitclient.sourceforge.net**. Other AIM clients also available are Kaim and Gaim.

Several Gnome instant messaging clients are designed to work with all instant messaging systems, including AIM, Yahoo, MSN, and ICQ. Gaim has plug-ins that let you connect to ICQ, Yahoo, MSN, IRC, Jabber, and Zephyr. Gabber is a Jabber client which is an open source instant messaging system that allows communication with all other systems, including AIM, Yahoo, MSN, and ICQ. Everybuddy is designed to be a universal instant messenger service for all the major services.

Talk

Talk is the original Unix talk utility designed to set up an interactive two-way communication between you and another user using a command line interface. It works much like instant messenger. Both you and the other user can type in messages simultaneously—where two people are constantly talking back and forth to each other. You initiate the communication by entering the **talk** command followed by the other user's address, usually the login name. This displays a message on the other user's screen asking if she or he wants to talk and giving your address. The user then responds with a **talk** command of her or his own, using your address. Both your screen and the other user's screen then split into two segments. The top segment displays what you type and the bottom segment displays what the other user types. Either user can end the session with an interrupt character, usually CTRL-C.

A K Desktop version of Talk called KTalk displays user screens as panes in a K Desktop window. KTalk includes an address book and supports word-wrap and file transfer features. KTalkd is a KDE-aware Talk daemon with answering machine features and forwarding capabilities. GNU Talk is a Gnome version of Talk that supports multiple clients, file transfers, encryption, shared applications, auto-answer, and call forwarding. GNU Talk includes both clients and a daemon. The client can operate using different front ends such as Emacs, screen-based cursors (curses), X Window System, Motif, and Gnome. Among applications included with GNU Talk is one that enables you to draw pictures with another user.

Telnet

You use the **telnet** command to log in remotely to another system on your network. The system can be on your local area network or available through an Internet connection. Telnet operates as if you were logging into another system from a remote terminal. You will be asked for a login name and, in some cases, a password. In effect, you are logging into another account on another system. In fact, if you have an account on another system, you could use telnet to log into it. You invoke the Telnet utility with the keyword **telnet**. If you know the name of the site you want to connect with, you can enter **telnet** and the name of the site on the Linux command line. As an alternative, you can use the K Desktop KTelnet utility. This provides a GUI interface to connecting and logging into remote systems.

```
$ telnet garnet.berkeley.edu
Connected to garnet
login:
```

The Telnet program also has a command mode with a series of commands you can use to configure your connection. You can enter the Telnet command mode either by invoking Telnet with the keyword **telnet** or by pressing CTRL-] during a session. The Telnet **help** command lists all the Telnet commands you can use. A comprehensive list is available on the Man pages (**man telnet**). In the next example, the user first invokes the Telnet utility. A prompt is displayed next, indicating the command mode, **telnet>**. The Telnet command **open** then connects to another system.

```
$ telnet
telnet> open garnet.berkeley.edu
Connected to garnet.berkeley.edu
login:
```

Once connected, you follow the login procedure for that system. If you are logging into a regular system, you must provide a login name and password. Once logged in, you are provided with the operating system prompt that, in the case of Linux or Unix, will either be **$** or **%**. You are then directly connected to an account on that system and can issue any commands you want. When you finish your work, you log out. This breaks the connection and returns you to the Telnet prompt on your own system. You can then quit Telnet with the **quit** command.

```
telnet> quit
```

When using Telnet to connect to a site that provides public access, you needn't provide a login name or password. Access is usually controlled by a series of menus that restrict what you can do on that system.

If you are logging into a specific account on another system, you can use the **-l** option to specify the login name of that account. This enables you to skip the login prompt. You can use the **-l** option either with the **telnet** invocation on the command line or with the **open** command, as shown in the next examples. Here, the user is logging into a specific account called **dylan** on the **rose.berkeley.edu** system:

```
$ telnet rose.berkeley.edu -l dylan
telnet> open rose.berkeley.edu -l dylan
```

Note *You can also use Telnet to connect to different Internet-based services like FTP.*

Remote Access Commands: rwho, rlogin, rcp, and rsh

The remote access commands were designed for smaller networks, such as intranets. They enable you to log in remotely to another account on another system and to copy files from one system to another. You can also obtain information about another system, such as who is logged on currently (see Table 15-3). Many of the remote commands have comparable network communication utilities used for the Internet. For example, **rlogin**, which remotely logs into a system, is similar to **telnet**. The **rcp** command, which remotely copies files, performs much the same function as **ftp**.

There are security risks with the use of remote operations like **telnet**, **rlogin**, and **rsh**. Such commands allow easy unencrypted remote access to a Linux system. These commands should only be used within a local secure network. For Internet operations like these, you should use the secure versions of these commands provided by the Secure SHell (SSH) such as **ssh**, **slogin**, **scp**. (see Chapter 37). SSH commands are encrypted, provided a much higher level of security.

*For added security, you can also use Kerberos versions for **telnet**, **rlogin**, **rcp**, **rsh**, and **ftp**, which provide authentication and encryption. The Kerberos versions operate using the same commands and options as the originals, making their use transparent to the user.*

You can use several commands to obtain information about different systems on your network. You can find out who is logged in, get information about a user on another system, or find out if a system is up and running. For example, the **rwho** command functions in the same way as the **who** command. It displays all the users currently logged into each system in your network.

```
$ rwho
violet robert:tty1 Sept 10 10:34
garnet chris:tty2 Sept 10 09:22
```

The **ruptime** command displays information about each system on your network. The information shows how each system has been performing. **ruptime** shows whether a system is up or down, how long it has been up or down, the number of users on the system, and the average load on the system for the last five, ten, and fifteen minutes.

```
$ ruptime
violet up 11+04:10, 8 users, load 1.20 1.10 1.00
garnet up 11+04:10, 20 users, load 1.50 1.40 1.30
```

Remote Access Permission: .rhosts

You use a **.rhosts** file to control access to your account by users using TCP/IP commands. Users create the **.rhosts** file on their own accounts using a standard editor such as Vi. It must be located in the user's home directory. In the next example, the user displays the contents of a **.rhosts** file:

```
$ cat .rhosts
garnet chris
violet robert
```

The **.rhosts** file is a simple way to allow other people access to your account without giving out your password. To deny access to a user, simply delete the system's name and the user's login name from your **.rhosts** file. If a user's login name and system are in a **.rhosts** file, then that user can directly access that account without knowing the password (in place of using **.rhosts**, you could use a password instead). The **.rhosts** file is required for other remote commands, such as remotely copying files or remotely executing Linux commands. If you want to execute such commands on an account in a remote system, that account must have your login name and system name in its **.rhosts** file.

The type of access **.rhosts** provides enables you to use TCP/IP commands to access other accounts directly that you might have on other systems. You do not have to log into them first. In effect, you can treat your accounts on other systems as extensions of the one you are currently logged into. Using the **rcp** command, you can copy any files from one directory to another no matter what account they are on. With the **rsh** command, you can execute any Linux command you want on any of your other accounts.

rlogin, rcp, and rsh

You may have accounts on different systems in your network, or you may be permitted to access someone else's account on another system. You could access an account on another system by first logging into your own and then remotely logging in across your network to the account on the other system. You can perform such a remote login using the **rlogin** command, which takes as its argument a system name. The command connects you to the other system and begins login procedures. Bear in mind that if you are using an SSH-enabled network connection, you would use **slogin** instead of **rlogin**. **slogin** will provide secure encrypted login access.

Login procedures using **rlogin** differ from regular login procedures in that the user is not prompted for a login name. **rlogin** assumes the login name on your local system is the same as the login name on the remote system. Upon executing the **rlogin** command, you are immediately prompted for a password. After entering the password, you are logged into the account on the remote system. Once logged into a remote system, you can execute any command you want. You can end the connection with **exit**, CTRL-D, **~.**, or **logout** (TCSH or C shell). **rlogin** assumes the login name on the remote system is the same as the one on the local system because most people use **rlogin** to access accounts they have on other systems with their own login name. When the login name on the remote system is different from the one on the local system, however, the **-l** option enables you to enter it. The syntax is shown here:

```
$ rlogin system-name -l login-name
```

You can use the **rcp** command to copy files to and from remote and local systems. (For SSH-enabled network connections, you would use **scp** instead of **rcp**.) **rcp** is a file transfer utility that operates like the **cp** command, but across a network connection to a remote system. The **rcp** command requires the remote system to have your local system and login name in its **.rhosts** file. The **rcp** command begins with the keyword **rcp** and has as its arguments the source file and copy filenames. To specify the file on the remote system, you need to place the remote system name before the filename, separated by a colon. When you are copying a file on the remote system to your own, the source file is a remote file and requires the remote system's name. The copy file is a file on your own system and does not require a system name:

```
$ rcp remote-system-name:source-file copy-file
```

In the next example, the user copies the file **wednesday** from the remote system **violet** to her own system and renames the file **today**:

```
$ rcp violet:wednesday today
```

You can also use **rcp** to copy whole directories to or from a remote system. The **rcp** command with the **-r** option copies a directory and all its subdirectories from one system to another. Like the **cp** command, **rcp** requires source and copy directories. The directory on the remote system requires the system name and colon be placed before the directory name. When you copy a directory from your own system to a remote system, the copy directory is on the remote system and requires the remote system's name. In the next example, the user copies the directory **letters** to the directory **oldnotes** on the remote system **violet**:

```
$ rcp -r letters violet:oldnotes
```

At times, you may need to execute a single command on a remote system. The **rsh** command executes a Linux command on another system and displays the results on your own. Your system name and login name must, of course, be in the remote system's **.rhosts** file. For SSH-enabled network connections, you would use **ssh** instead of **rsh**. The **rsh** command takes two general arguments: a system name and a Linux command. The syntax is as follows:

```
$ rsh remote-system-name Linux-command
```

In the next example, the **rsh** command executes an **ls** command on the remote system **violet** to list the files in the **/home/robert** directory on **violet**:

```
$ rsh violet ls /home/robert
```

Special characters are evaluated by the local system unless quoted. This is particularly true of special characters that control the standard output, such as redirection operators or pipes. The next example lists the files on the remote system and sends them to the standard output on the local system. The redirection operator is evaluated by the local system and redirects the output to **myfiles**, which is a file on the local system.

```
$ rsh violet ls /home/robert > myfiles
```

If you quote a special character, it becomes part of the Linux command evaluated on the remote system. Quoting redirection operators enables you to perform redirection operations on the remote system. In the next example, the redirection operator is quoted. It becomes part of the Linux command, including its argument, the filename **myfiles**. The `ls` command then generates a list of filenames that is redirected on the remote system to a file called **myfiles**, also located on the remote system.

```
$ rsh violet ls /home/robert '>' myfiles
```

The same is true for pipes. The first command (shown next) prints the list of files on the local system's printer. The standard output is piped to your own line printer. In the second command, the list of files is printed on the remote system's printer. The pipe is quoted and evaluated by the remote system, piping the standard output to the printer on the remote system.

```
$ rsh violet ls /home/robert | lpr
$ rsh violet ls /home/robert '|' lpr
```

Remote Commands	Effect
`rwho`	Displays all users logged into systems in your network.
`ruptime`	Displays information about each system on your network.
`rlogin` *system-name*	Allows you to log in remotely to an account on another system.

Table 15-3. *Remote Access Commands*

Remote Commands	Effect
`-l`	Allows you to specify the login name of the account.
`slogin` *system-name*	Secure login to an account on another system.
`rcp` *sys-name:file1 sys-name:file2*	Allows you to copy a file from an account on one system to an account on another system. If no system name is given, the current system is assumed.
`-r`	With the `-r` option, allows you to copy directories instead of just files.
`-p`	Preserves the modification times and modes of source files.
`scp` *sys-name:file1 sys-name:file2*	Secure copy of a file from an account on one system to an account on another system.
`rsh` *sys-name Linux-command*	Allows you to remotely execute a command on another system.
`-l`	Allows you to specify the login name.
`-n`	Redirects input from the null special device, **/dev/null**.
`ssh` *sys-name Linux-command*	Secure remote execution of a command on another system.

Table 15-3. *Remote Access Commands* (continued)

Chapter 16

Office Applications

A variety of office suites are now available for Linux. These include professional-level word processors, presentation managers, drawing tools, and spreadsheets. The freely available versions are described in this chapter. Currently, you can download personal (noncommercial) versions for both WordPerfect and StarOffice from the Internet for free. KOffice is an entirely free office suite designed for use with KDE. The Gnome Office integrates Gnome applications into a productivity suite that is freely available. Ximian is developing a professional-level office suite for Gnome. In addition, Sun has initiated the development of an open source office suite using StarOffice code. The applications are known as OpenOffice and will provide office applications integrated with Gnome. Different distributions may emphasize certain office suites. For example, Caldera, which uses only KDE, supports KOffice. Red Hat, which supports both KDE and Gnome, includes both KOffice and Gnome Office. Mandrake incorporates Sun's StarOffice, as well as both KOffice and Gnome Office. You can, of course, manually install any office suite on any Linux distribution.

You can also purchase commercial office suites such as Applixware from Red Hat and Corel Office from Corel. Applixware includes a word processor, a spreadsheet, a presentation graphics tool, a drawing tool, an e-mail client, and an object-oriented application builder. Table 16-1 lists freely available Linux Office projects. Most distributions also include AbiWord, a professional-level word processor.

Accessibility to Microsoft Office

One of the primary concerns for new Linux users is what kind of access they will have to their Microsoft Office files, particularly Word files. The Linux operating system and many applications for it are designed to provide seamless access to MS Office files. The

Web Site	Description
www.koffice.org	KOffice Suite, for KDE
www.gnome.org/gnome-office	Gnome Office, for Gnome
www.sun.com/staroffice	Star Office Suite
www.openoffice.org	OpenOffice open source office suite based on Star Office
www.ximian.com	Ximian Gnome desktop and office applications
linux.corel.com	WordPerfect word processor

Table 16-1. *Linux Office Projects*

Intel version of Linux can directly mount and access any Windows partition and its files. The major Linux Office suites, including WordPerfect, KOffice, and particularly Star Office, all read and manage any Microsoft Office files. In addition, these office suites are fast approaching the same level of support for office tasks as found in Microsoft Office.

Note *If you want to use any Windows application on Linux, one important alternative is the VMware virtual platform technology, a commercial package. With VMware, you can run any Windows application directly on your Linux system. For more information, check the VMware Web site at* ***www.vmware.com****. The Wine project has also developed a Windows 3.1 and Win32 interface that works on X running on Unix and Linux systems. Check* ***www.winehq.com*** *for more details.*

KOffice

KOffice is an integrated office suite for the KDE (K Desktop Environment) consisting of several office applications, including a word processor, a spreadsheet, and graphic applications. All applications are written for the KOM component model, which allows components from any one application to be used in another. This means you can embed a spreadsheet from KSpread or a drawing from Kontour in a KWord document. You can obtain more information about KOffice from the KOffice Web site at **www.koffice.org**.

Currently, KOffice includes KSpread, KPresenter, Kontour, Karbon, KWord, KFormula, KChart, Kugar, Krita, Kivio, and KPlato (see Table 16-2). KSpread is a spreadsheet, KPresenter is a presentation application, Kontour is a vector drawing program, Karbon is a vector graphics program, KWord is a Publisher-like word processor, KFormula is a formula editor, and KChart generates charts and diagrams. Kugar is a report generator, Krita is a bitmap image editor, Kivio creates flow charts, and KPlato handles project management.

Embedded components support real-time updates. For example, if you use KChart to generate a chart in a KWord document using data in a KSpread spreadsheet and then change the selected data in the spreadsheet, KChart automatically updates the chart in the KWord document. In effect, you are creating a compound document—one made up of several applications. This capability is implemented by the KDE component model known as KParts. KParts replaces K Object Model/OpenParts (KOM/OP) component model used in KDE version 1.0, which was based directly on CORBA. Like KOM/OP, KParts provides communication between distributed objects. In this respect, you can think of an application working also as a server, providing other applications with the services it specializes in. A word processor, specializing in services like paragraph formatting or spell-checking, could provide these services to all KOffice applications. In that way, other applications do not need to have their own text formatting functions written into them.

KParts is implemented with DCOP, the Desktop Communications Protocol. This is a very simple, small, and fast IPC/RPC mechanism for InterProcess Communication

Application	Description
KSpread	Spreadsheet
KPresenter	Presentation program
Kontour	Vector drawing program
Karbon	Vector graphics program
KWord	Word processor (desktop publisher)
KFormula	Mathematical formula editor
KChart	Tool for drawing charts and diagrams
Kugar	Report generator
Krita	Image manipulation program
Kivio	Flow chart generator and editor (similar to Vivio)
KPlato	Project management

Table 16-2. *KOffice Applications*

(IPC) and is based on the X Window System's ICE (Inter-client Exchange) protocol. KDE applications now use DCOP libraries to manage their communications with each other. DCOP makes development of KOffice applications much easier and more stable.

With KOffice, you create one kind of document rather than separate ones for different applications. The different applications become views of this document, adding their components to it. KWord sets up the publishing and word processing components, Kontour adds drawing components, while KSpread adds spreadsheet components. You use the appropriate application to view the different components in the single document. This means you can have separate windows open at the same time for different components of the document.

KSpread is the spreadsheet application, which incorporates the basic operations found in most spreadsheets, with formulas similar to those used in Excel. You can extend KSpread capabilities with Python scripts. It supports features such as embedded buttons for customized functions, automatic completion for cell contents, and formatting options such as backgrounds, borders, and font styles. To generate a diagram using selected cells, select the Insert Diagram entry from the KSpread menu. This starts up KChart, which you then use to create the diagram—which is then embedded in the spreadsheet. You can also embed pictures or formulas using Krita, Kontour, or KFormula.

With KChart, you can create different kinds of charts, such as bar graphs, pie charts, and line graphs, as well as create diagrams. To generate a chart, you can use data in

KSpread to enter your data. With KPresenter, you can create presentations consisting of text and graphics modeled using different fonts, orientations, and attributes such as colors. You can add such elements as speech bubbles, arrows, and clip art, as well as embed any KOffice component. KPresenter supports standard editing operations such as shading, rotating, and coloring objects, as well as cut-and-paste and undo/redo capabilities. You can generate templates from a KPresenter document, in effect enabling you to use a document's configuration to create other documents. With KPresenter, you can also create special effects such as simple animation.

Kontour is a vector-based graphics program, much like Adobe Illustrator and Corel Draw. It supports the standard graphic operations such as rotating, scaling, and aligning objects. Kontour also includes text formatting capabilities such as alignment to irregular boundaries. You can create complex illustrations using layers, using a layer manager to control the layers. Kontour also supports a number of import and export filters for image files of different types like **.jpeg**, **.gif**, and **.eps**.

KWord can best be described as a desktop publisher, with many of the features found in publishing applications like Microsoft Publisher and FrameMaker (see Figure 16-1). Although it is also a fully functional word processor, KWord is not page-based like Word or WordPerfect. Instead, text is set up in frames that are placed on the page like objects. Frames, like objects in a drawing program, can be moved, resized, and even reoriented. You can organize frames into a frame set, having text flow from one to the other. Formatting can be applied to a frame set, changing features in all the frames

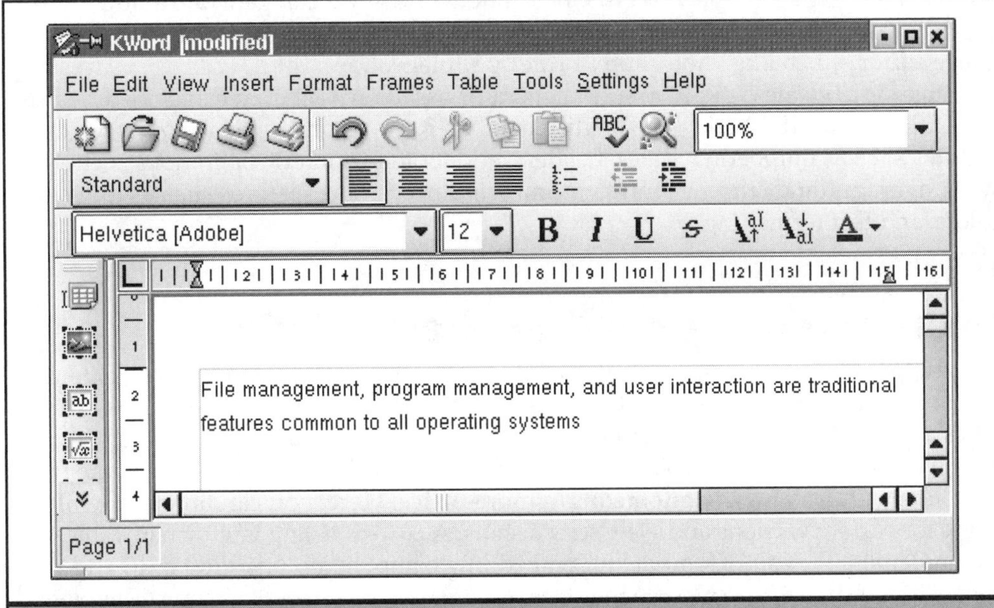

Figure 16-1. *KWord, KOffice word processor and publisher*

belonging to it at once. The default frame set up for you when you first create a document is the same size as the page. This gives you the effect of a page-based word processor, enabling you to work as if you were using a standard word processor. You can, of course, change the size of your frame and add new ones, if you want.

You can also insert images, illustrations, tables, and other KOffice components such as diagrams and spreadsheets. You can set up a frame to contain an image and place it on top of a text frame, configuring the text frame to flow its text around it.

KWord uses templates to set up a document. You have two different sets of templates from which to choose: one for desktop publishing (DTP) and the other for standard word processing (word processing). The desktop publishing templates enable you to move frames freely, whereas in the word processing templates the frames are fixed to the size of the page.

KWord supports the standard word processing features for formatting paragraphs, text, and document elements, such as headers and footers, as well as lists and multiple columns. You can also define your own paragraph layouts, specifying features such as indentation, fonts, borders, and alignment. Layouts are the same as styles used in other word processors. Tables are implemented as frames, where each cell is its own frame.

KFormula is a formula editor used to generate mathematical formulas. Although KFormula does not have the power of TeX, you can use it to create fairly complex formulas. It supports standard components like roots, integral, and fractions, as well as fonts for Greek symbols.

Kivio is a flow chart application similar to Vivio. Kivio has the ability to generate flow charts using scriptable objects. Given a network, Kivio can generate a flow chart for it. With Java header files it can generate a flow chart of Java objects. Krita is an image editor, much like Photoshop (formerly KImageShop).

Kugar is a business-quality report generator based on XML that can embed reports in KOffice applications and even be displayed on Konqueror. Kugar supports page features such as numbering, dates, headers, and footers; numeric operations such as sums, averages, and currency formats; and word processing features such as fonts, colors, and text formatting.

Gnome Office, OpenOffice, and Ximian

Office applications for Gnome have been developed independently, such as the Gnumeric spreadsheet. Currently, Gnome Office is an attempt to integrate the various office applications into a productivity suite. Although most are still under development, some have working stable versions you can download and install. You can find out more from the Gnome Office at **www.gnome.org/gnome-office**. Here, you can link to download pages for current versions and view screen shots. A current listing is shown in Table 16-3. All implement the CORBA model for embedding components, ensuring drag-and-drop capability throughout the Gnome interface. All are based on a set of Gnome technologies, including Bonobo, Gnome-Print, and XML. Bonobo is the Gnome architecture for supporting compound documents and reusable software components. Gnome-Print is the Gnome printing architecture designed to support graphics applications as

Application	Description
Achtung	Presentation manager
AbiWord	Cross-platform word processor
Balsa	E-mail client
Gfax	Send and receive faxes
Galeon	Web browser
Gnumeric	Spreadsheet
GnuCash	Personal finance manager
Dia	Diagram and flow chart editor
Evolution	E-mail and calendar
Eye of Gnome	Image viewer
GIMP	GNU image manipulation program
Gnome-DB	Database connectivity
Gnumeric	Spreadsheet
Gnome Personal Information Manager	Calendar/organizer and address book
Guppi	Plotting and graphing program
Sketch	Vector drawing package
Toutdoux	Project manager

Table 16-3. *Gnome Office*

well as work easily with any printing resource. XML is usesd as the native file format to support the easy exchange of data between Gnome applications.

Currently, Gnome Office includes AbiWord, Gnumeric, GIMP, Dia, Eye of Gnome, Gnome-PIM, and Gnome-DB. AbiWord is a word processor, Gnumeric is a spreadsheet, GIMP is the Gnome image editing application, Dia is a diagram composer, Eye of Gnome is an image viewer, the Gnome Personal Information Manager (Gnome-PIM) is a personal information manager, and Gnome-DB provides database connectivity (see Table 16-3).

Gnumeric is the Gnome spreadsheet, a professional-level program meant to replace commercial spreadsheets. Like Gnome, Gnumeric is freely available under the GNU

Public License. Gnumeric is included with the Gnome release, and you will find it installed with Gnome on any distribution that supports Gnome. Its development is currently managed by Ximian. You can download current versions from **www.ximian.com** or **www.gnome.org/projects/gnumeric**. Gnumeric supports standard GUI spreadsheet features, including autofilling and cell formatting, and it provides an extensive number of formats. It supports drag-and-drop operations, enabling you to select and then move or copy cells to another location. Gnumeric also supports plug-ins, making it possible to extend and customize its capabilities easily.

AbiWord is an open source word processor that supports such features as unlimited undo operations and Word97 imports. It is part of a set of desktop productivity applications being developed by the AbiSource project (**www.abisource.com**).

GIMP is the GNU image manipulation program, which supports operations such as photo retouching, image composition, and image authoring (see the section on graphics in Chapter 17). You can obtain more information from **www.gimp.org**.

Dia is a drawing program designed to create diagrams. You can select different kinds of diagrams to create, such as database, circuit object, flow chart, and network diagrams. You can easily create elements along with lines and arcs with different types of endpoints such as arrows or diamonds. Data can be saved in XML format, making it easily transportable to other applications.

Eye of Gnome (EOG) is an image viewer that can also function as an image cataloging program. It is designed to be fast and provide high-quality image displays.

Gnome Personal Information Manager (Gnome-PIM) is a personal information manager that currently includes both a calendar and an address book. Gnome-PIM is included with the current distribution of Gnome. You can obtain updates from **www.gnome.org/gnome-office**.

Gnome-DB is a suite of libraries and applications that allow easy access to different database systems. It provides an API to which databases can plug in. These backend connections are based on CORBA. Through this API, Gnome applications can then access a database. You can find out more about Gnome-DB at **www.gnome.org/gnome-db**.

Ximian is a Gnome project designed to provide a professional-level desktop for Gnome that will include a full range of office applications. You can find out more about Ximian at **www.ximian.com**. Ximian currently provides an enhanced version of the Gnome desktop called Ximian Gnome. It also supports development of the Gnumeric spreadsheet. Its first office application is a contact, calendar, and mail client application called Evolution (see Chapter 13). You can download Evolution from the Ximian Web site, but it currently requires the Ximian Gnome desktop to run. Their next project is a word processor.

The OpenOffice Suite of applications currently covers several core applications used in StarOffice. StarOffice code has been released as an open source project called OpenOffice.org, at **www.openoffice.org**. The open source versions of StarOffice applications, known as OpenOffice, are being integrated with Gnome. This, in effect, creates a Gnome OpenOffice. The applications recently released are listed in Table 16-4.

Application	Description
OpenCalc	OpenOffice spreadsheet
OpenDraw	OpenOffice drawing application
OpenWriter	OpenOffice word processor
Impress	OpenOffice presentation manager

Table 16-4. *Gnome OpenOffice*

Like StarOffice, OpenOffice is an integrated suite of applications. Initially the suite opens with the OpenWriter window. You can select New from the file menu and then select a different application. The application will open in a separate window. OpenOffice is still very much in development, but holds the promise of providing professional-level office applications integrated into the Gnome desktop.

WordPerfect

The personal version of Corel's WordPerfect word processor is now available for Linux and is free. The personal version is a fully functional word processor. You can download WordPerfect from the Corel Web site at **linux.corel.com**. WordPerfect is more than just a word processor. You can use it to create drawings, spreadsheets, and charts, as well as to edit and publish Web pages.

When you first start WordPerfect, a small window is displayed with the WordPerfect logo and four menus: Program, Preferences, Window, and Help. From the Program menu, you can select WordPerfect. In the Preferences menu, you can open a window with icons for configuring your printer, selecting fonts, choosing colors, and selecting conversion filters. The Window menu moves you to different open windows.

WordPerfect provides many of the standard word processing features, including cut-and-paste operations, font and paragraph styles, and document formatting. The extensive features for WordPerfect are indicated by its set of toolbars. WordPerfect includes such editing features as Grammar-As-You-Go, which checks and highlights suspicious phrases and offers suggestions. With Spell-As-You-Go, words that might be misspelled are identified as you type them. Corel Versions keeps track of document revisions for workgroup collaboration.

WordPerfect includes a chart and drawing tool for creating figures. You can perform drawing operations such as sizing and rotating images, as well as contouring text over image shapes. The drawing tool supports features such as gradients, patterns, and groupings. You can create a variety of different charts, including 3-D, area, and line charts. WordPerfect supports a number of spreadsheet functions with which you can create tables with spreadsheet cells. You can use such data to generate charts.

You can also use WordPerfect as a Web page editor and publisher, adding or changing HTML components. Use WordPerfect to create your HTML document with hyperlinks and bookmarks, and then place them on your Web site. Any text beginning with an Internet protocol, such as **www**, **ftp**, and **http**, is automatically set up as a hyperlink. You can also save Web pages as WordPerfect documents for easy editing.

WordPerfect supports an extensive number of file formats, including Microsoft Word files. With WordPerfect, you can effectively edit your Word files.

WordPerfect also has its own file manager. You can use the file manager to locate and open files, but it also performs other operations. You can create directories and modify file permissions, as well as move and copy files.

StarOffice

StarOffice is a fully integrated and Microsoft Office–compatible suite of office applications developed and supported by Sun Microsystems. It includes Web-enabled word processing, spreadsheet, presentation, e-mail, news, chart, and graphic applications (see Table 16-5). Versions of StarOffice exist for Linux, Windows, and Solaris. With StarOffice, you can access Microsoft Office (including NT) files and data to create spreadsheets, presentations, and word processing documents. You can save StarOffice documents in Microsoft formats or as HTML files that you can post on Web sites.

StarOffice is free for all noncommercial, private users, as well as students. You can download a free copy of StarOffice from the Sun Web site at **www.sun.com/staroffice**. The Web site also contains information such as online manuals and FAQs. Sun has plans to make StarOffice version 6.0 a commercial product, though the current 5.2 version is still free.

Note

*Development for StarOffice is being carried out as an open source project called openoffice.org. The core code for StarOffice is now open source and anyone can download and use it. See the OpenOffice.org Web site at **www.openoffice.org** for more information. The code developed in the openoffice.org project will then be incorporated into future releases of StarOffice. Currently the word processor, presentation manager, drawing tool, and chart tool, and spreadsheet are under open source development at OpenOffice.org.*

StarOffice describes itself as implementing a task-oriented approach to office projects. It provides an integrated solution letting you perform a variety of tasks using the same interface. In addition, StarOffice applications are fully Internet-aware, enabling you to connect directly to Web sites and access information from your word processor, spreadsheet, or presenter.

Application	Description
StarDesktop	Main desktop window for StarOffice applications
StarWriter	Word processor
StarImpress	Presentation manager
StarDraw	Drawing tool
StarChart	Chart and graph creator
StarMail	E-mail client
StarDiscussion	Newsgroup client
StarMath	Mathematical formulas
StarImage	Image editor
StarCalc	Spreadsheet
StarSchedule	Schedule manager
StarBase	Relational database

Table 16-5. *StarOffice Applications*

Note *StarOffice is now included with Mandrake Linux.*

When you start up StarOffice, you are presented with the StarOffice desktop window. From here, you can create documents and access other StarOffice applications. The left pane in this window is the Explorer. This is a tree menu that lists the different resources you can use, such as an address book, a gallery of clip art, and FTP server URLs. The main window of the StarOffice desktop shows icons for applications you can use, your StarOffice documents, and other tools.

You use StarOffice by creating projects. In a particular project, you can place resources such as images, Internet links, e-mail messages, or office documents, such as spreadsheets and word processing documents. To create a new document, click the New button in the bottom status bar and select the application you want to use from the pop-up menu. You can create spreadsheets, word processing documents, presentation files, mail messages, charts, images, mathematical formulas, and even Web pages (see Table 16-5). You can also create frame sets for use in Web page frames. Initially, windows are attached (docked) to the desktop window. You can detach them to their own floating windows by double-clicking the gray area between them.

StarOffice has its own mail and news clients. With StarMail, you can define mail accounts and access your e-mail, as well as compose and send messages. With StarDiscussion, you can access newsgroups, saving articles and posting your own. You can set up icons and entries for mail accounts and newsgroups on your desktop and Explorer window.

The StarWriter word processor supports standard word processing features, such as cut and paste, spell-checker, and text formatting, as well as paragraph styles. You can also insert objects in your text, such as images, diagrams, or text frames. Text can be configured to flow around them. A text frame can be further edited to create banner-like text, coloring, blending, and shaping text. The Navigator enables you to move through the document by page or by object, such as from one image to another.

You can open and save documents in the MS Office, WordPerfect, Lotus 1-2-3, and AmiPro formats. This means you can effectively edit MS Word documents with StarOffice. StarWriter also functions as a Web browser—capable of displaying HTML pages—and supports Java, JavaScript, Navigator, and Explorer plug-ins. At the same time, you can edit a Web page, turning StarWriter into a Web page editor.

You can embed objects within documents, such as using StarChart to create a bar chart using data in the spreadsheet. With StarMath, you can create formulas that you can then embed in a text document.

With the presentation manager (StarImpress), you can create images for presentations, such as circles, rectangles, and connecting elements like arrows, as well as vector-based illustrations. StarImpress supports advanced features such as morphing objects, grouping objects, and defining gradients. You can also create animation effects and use layers to generate complex images. Any components from other StarOffice applications can be embedded in a presentation document. You can also import Microsoft PowerPoint files and save presentation files as HTML files. An AutoPilot Wizard for StarImpress walks you through the steps for creating a presentation.

StarDraw is a sophisticated drawing tool that includes 3-D modeling tools. You can create simple or complex images, including animation text aligned on curves. You can use it to create buttons and icons for your Web page.

StarSchedule provides scheduling and task management that can be used to coordinate efforts by a group of users. You can use it to track events and to-do lists, connecting automatically to the address book. StarSchedule includes a reminder system to display pop-up alerts and to send e-mail reminders. The StarSchedule server operates independently from StarOffice to provide scheduling services to any client on your network. StarBase is a relational database, somewhat like MS Access, which supports drag-and-drop operations for importing data to your StarOffice applications.

Chapter 17

Database Management Systems, Graphic Tools, and Multimedia

A variety of database management systems are now available for Linux. These include high-powered, commercial-level database management systems, such as Oracle, IBM, and Sybase. Most of the database management systems available for Linux are designed to support large relational databases. For small personal databases, you can use the desktop database management systems being developed for KDE and Gnome. In addition, some software is available for databases accessed with the Xbase database programming language. These are smaller databases using formats originally developed for dBase on the PC. Various database management systems available to run under Linux are listed in Table 17-1.

You can also use a wide range of graphic tools, ranging from simple image viewers like KImage to sophisticated image manipulation programs like GIMP. You also have newer graphic tools for Gnome and KDE desktops, as well as the older X Window System, from which to choose. Graphics tools available for use under Linux are listed in Table 17-2. There is also strong support for multimedia tasks from video and DVD

System	Site
Oracle	Oracle database **www.oracle.com**
Sybase	Sybase database **www.sybase.com**
DB2	IBM database **www.software.ibm.com/data/db2/linux**
Informix	Informix database **www.informix.com/linux**
Adabas D	Adabas D database **www.softwareag.com/adabas**
MySQL	MySQL database **www.mysql.com**
GNU SQL	The GNU SQL database **www.ispras.ru/~kml/gss**
PostgreSQL	The PostgreSQL database **www.postgresql.org**
Flagship	Interface for Xbase database files **www.fship.com/free.html**
Katabase	KDE desktop database **www.koffice.org**
Gaby	Gnome desktop personal database **gaby.sourceforge.net**.

Table 17-1. *Database Management Systems for Linux*

KDE	Description
KView	Simple image viewer for GIF and JPEG image files
KSnapshot	Screen grabber
KFourier	Image processing tool that uses the Fourier transform
KuickShow	Image browser and viewer
imageview	Simple image viewer
KPaint	Paint program
KRayon	Image editor
Gnome	
GQview	Image viewer
ImageShaker	Digital image processing
GIMP	GNU Image Manipulation Program
Electric Eyes	Image viewer
gPhoto2	Digital camera application
X Window System	
xv	Screen grabber and image converter
Xpaint	Paint program
Xfig	Drawing program
Xmorph	Tool that morphs images
Xfractals	Fractal image generator

Table 17-2. *Graphic Tools for Linux*

to sound and music editing (see Table 17-3). Thousands of multimedia and graphic projects, as well as standard projects, are under development or currently available from **www.sourceforge.net**. Be sure to check the SourceForge site for any kind of application you may need.

Application	Description
GTV	Gnome MPEG video player
Xine	Multimedia player for video, DVD, and audio
Gnome-tv	TV tuner
aKtion	KDE video player
Kscd	Music CD player
Knapster2	Napster-like MP3 download utility
XMMS	MP3 and CD Player
Xplaycd	Music CD player
Noatun	KDE multimedia player
Xanim	Animation and video player
mpg123	Command line MP3 player
RealPlayer	RealMedia and RealAudio streaming media (**www.real.com**)
KReateCD	KDE CD writing interface for cdrecord, mkisofs, and cdda2wav
CD-Rchive	KDE CD burner and ripper
Gnome Toaster	Gnome CD burner

Table 17-3. *Multimedia Applications*

Database Management Systems

Database software can be generally organized into three categories: SQL, Xbase, and desktop databases. *SQL-based databases* are professional-level relational databases whose files are managed by a central database server program. Applications that use the database do not access the files directly. Instead, they send requests to the database server, which then performs the actual access. *SQL* is the query language used on these industrial-strength databases.

The *Xbase language* is an enhanced version of the dBase programming language used to access database files whose formats were originally developed for dBase on the PC. With Xbase, database management systems can directly access the database files. Xbase is used mainly for smaller personal databases, with database files often located on a user's own system.

Desktop databases are being developed for both Gnome and KDE. Currently, these are personal databases designed for individual users. Katabase is meant to be used with a user's KOffice applications, and Gaby for a user's personal records. Both, however, are designed with a plug-in structure that can easily extend their capabilities.

SQL Databases (RDMS)

SQL databases are relational database management systems (RDMSs) designed for extensive database management tasks. Many of the major SQL databases now have Linux versions, including Oracle, Informix, Sybase, and IBM (but not, of course, Microsoft). These are commercial and professional database management systems of the highest order. Linux has proved itself capable of supporting complex and demanding database management tasks. In addition, many free SQL databases are available for Linux that offer much the same functionality. Most commercial databases also provide free personal versions, as do Oracle, Adabas D, and MySQL.

PostgreSQL

PostgreSQL is based on the POSTGRES database management system, though it uses SQL as its query language. POSTGRES is a next-generation research prototype developed at the University of California, Berkeley. Linux versions of PostgreSQL are included in most distributions, including Red Hat, Debian, and Mandrake distributions. You can download current versions from the PostgreSQL Web site at **www.postgresql.org**. Development is being managed by a team of developers over the Internet.

PostgreSQL is often used to provide database support for Internet servers with heavy demand such as Web servers. With a few simple commands you can create relational database tables. Use the `createuser` command to create a PostgreSQL user that you can then log into the server with. You can then create a database with the `createdb` command and construct relational tables using the create table directive. With an `insert` command you can add records and then view them with the `select` command. Access to the server by remote users is controlled by entries in the **pg_hba.conf** file located in PostgreSQL directory, usually **/var/lib/pgsql**.

Oracle

Oracle offers a fully functional version of its Oracle8*i* (soon to be superseded by Oracle9*i*) database management system for Linux, as well as the Oracle Application Server. You can download trial versions from the Oracle Web site at **www.oracle.com**. Oracle8*i* is a professional database for large databases specifically designed for Internet e-business tasks. Expect to use a gigabyte of memory just to install it. The Oracle Application Server provides support for real-time and commerce applications on the Web. As Linux is a fully functional version of Unix, Oracle is particularly effective on it. Oracle was originally designed to operate on Unix, and Linux is a far better platform for it than other PC operating systems.

Oracle offers extensive documentation for its Linux version that you can download from its Documentation page, to which you can link from the Support pages on its Web site. The documentation available includes an installation guide, an administrator's reference, and release notes, as well as the generic documentation. You can find specific information on installing and configuring Oracle for Linux in the Oracle Database HOW-TO.

Informix

Informix (now controlled by IBM) offers an integrated platform of Internet-based applications called Informix Internet Foundation.2000 on Linux. These include the Informix Dynamic Server, their database server. Informix Dynamic Server features Dynamic Scalable Architecture, making it capable of effectively using any hardware setup. Informix only provides commercial products. No free versions exist, though the company currently provides special promotions for Linux products. You can find out more about Informix at **www-4.ibm.com/software/data/informix**.

Informix strongly supports Linux development of its Informix line. It provides developer support through its Informix Developer Network (**www7b.boulder.ibm.com/dmdd/zones/informix**).

Sybase

For Linux, Sybase offers the Sybase Adaptive Server Enterprise server (see **www.sybase.com**). You can currently download the Adaptive Server Enterprise server from the Web site. The Sybase Enterprise database features data integration that coordinates all information resources on a network. SQL Anywhere is a database system designed for smaller databases, though with the same level of complexity found in larger databases.

DB2

IBM provides a Linux version of its DB2 Universal Database software. You can download it free from the IBM DB2 Web page for Linux, **www.software.ibm.com/data/db2/linux/**. DB2 Universal Database for Linux includes Internet functionality along with support for Java and Perl. With the Web Control Center, administrators can maintain databases from a Web browser. DB2 features scalability to expand the database easily, support for Binary Large Objects, and cost-based optimization for fast access. DB2 is still very much a mainframe database, though IBM is currently working on refining its Unix/Linux version.

Adabas D

Adabas D is an intermediate relational database, not quite as powerful or as large as Oracle, which is meant for use on smaller networks of personal databases. It still provides the flexibility and power found in all relational databases. Adabas D provides a personal version for Linux free. For commercial uses, you have to purchase a copy. You can also check the Adabas D Web site at **www.softwareag.com/adabas**.

MySQL

MySQL is a true multiuser, multithreaded SQL database server, supported by MySQL AB. MySQL is an open source product available free under the GPL license. You can download a copy from its Web site at **www.mysql.com**. The site also includes detailed documentation, including manuals and FAQs.

MySQL is structured on a client/server model with a server daemon (mysqld) filling requests from client programs. MySQL is designed for speed, reliability, and ease of use. It is meant to be a fast database management system for large databases and, at the same time, reliable with intensive use.

GNU SQL

GNU SQL is the GNU relational database developed by a group at the Institute for System Programming of the Russian Academy of Sciences and supported by the GNU organization. It is a portable multiuser database management system with a client/server structure that supports SQL. The server processes requests and performs basic administrative operations, such as unloading parts of the database used infrequently. The clients can reside on any computer of a local network. GNU SQL uses a dialect of SQL based on the SQL-89 standard and is designed for use on a Unix-like environment. You can download the database software from the GNU FTP site at **ftp.gnu.org**. For more information, contact the GNU SQL Web site at **www.ispras.ru/~kml/gss**.

Xbase Databases

Databases accessed with Xbase are smaller in scale, designed for small networks or for personal use. Many are originally PC database programs, such as dBaseIII, Clipper, FoxPro, and Quicksilver. Currently, only Flagship provides an interface for accessing Xbase database files.

Flagship is a compiler with which you can create interfaces for querying Xbase database files. The interfaces support menus and dialog boxes, and they have function calls that execute certain database queries. Flagship can compile dBaseIII+ code and up. It is compatible with dBase and Clipper and can access most Xbase file formats, such as **.dbf**, **.dbt**, **.fmt**, and **.frm**. One of Flagship's key features is that its interfaces can be attached to a Web page, enabling users to update databases. Flagship is commercial software, though you can download a free personal version from its Web site at **www.fship.com/free.html**.

Desktop Database

Both Gnome and KDE also have database management applications that take advantage of their respective desktops. KDE's Katabase is part of KOffice and is fully integrated with its other applications. Gnome's Gaby takes advantage of the interface to display and search user databases.

Katabase

Katabase is a database management system under development for the KDE desktop. It is a desktop database, somewhat like Microsoft Access and Paradox; however, it makes full use of its integration with other KOffice programs by means of KOM/OpenParts. As part of KOffice, any part of Katabase can be embedded into another KOffice application, and KOffice components can be embedded into Katabase. You can find out more about Katabase at **www.koffice.org**.

Gaby

Gaby is a small personal database manager using GTK+ and Gnome. It provides access to user databases, such as those for addresses, books, and even photos. Gaby's plug-in design makes it easily extensible. You can find out more about Gaby at **gaby.sourceforge.net**. Its interface has the same browser-like tools found in most Gnome applications. You can download the current version of Gaby from the Gnome software map at **www.gnome.org**.

Graphic Tools

Gnome, KDE, and the X Window System support an impressive number of graphic tools, including image viewers, window grabbers, image editors, and paint tools. On the KDE and Gnome desktops, these tools can be found under either a Graphics submenu or the Utilities menu.

KDE Graphic Tools

The KView program is a simple image viewer for GIF and JPEG image files. The KSnapshot program is a simple screen grabber for KDE, which currently supports only a few image formats. The KFourier program is an image-processing tool that uses the Fourier transform to apply several filters to an image at once. The imageview program is a simple image viewer. The KuickShow program is an easy-to-use, comfortable image browser and viewer, based on imlib. The KPaint program is a simple paint program with brushes, shapes, and color effects. Krayon is a professional image paint and editing application that is part of KOffice 2.1 (formerly KImageShop).

Gnome Graphic Tools

ImageShaker is a digital image-processing tool that includes an extensive set of graphic filters, such as alpha blending and median. It uses a stream-like approach that allows batch processing.

Electric Eyes is a simple image viewer. Right-click its window to display a pop-up menu with options. You can load images and also move back and forth through previously viewed ones. You can even make an image your background.

GQview is a simple image viewer supporting features such as click file viewing, thumbnail preview, zoom, drag and drop, and external editor support, as well as slideshow and full-screen options. Multiple files can be selected for moving, copying, deleting, renaming, or dragging. See **gqview.sourceforge.net** for more information.

GIMP is the GNU Image Manipulation Program, a sophisticated image application much like Adobe Photoshop. You can use GIMP for such tasks as photo retouching, image composition, and image authoring. It supports features such as layers, channels, blends, and gradients. GIMP makes particular use of the GTK+ widget set. You can find out more about GIMP and download the newest versions from its Web site at **www.gimp.org**. GIMP is freely distributed under the GNU Public License.

The gPhoto2 program is a digital camera tool that can load, select, and edit photos from a digital camera connected to your system. With gPhoto2, you can generate thumbnail images to let you select and organize your photos. You can also process photos, changing their orientation.

X Window System Graphic Programs

The xv program is a screen capture and image-editing program. After displaying the main screen, right-click it to display its control screen. Use the Grab button to scan a window or a section you select with a drag operation using your middle mouse button (both right and left at once on a two button mouse). Once you have scanned a window or screen section, you can crop it with a drag operation with your left mouse key and then use crop to reduce it to that selected section. With xv, you can also convert an image file from one format to another. Just load the image and then save it as another file using a different image format.

The Xpaint program is a painting program, much like MacPaint. You can load paint pictures or photographs, and then create shapes, add text, and add colors. You can use brush tools with various sizes and colors. The Xfig program is a drawing program, and Xmorph enables you to morph images, changing their shapes.

Multimedia

Many applications are available for both video and sound, including sound editors, MP3 players, and video players (see Table 17-3). Linux sound applications include mixers, digital audio tools, CD audio writers, MP3 players, and network audio support. There are literally thousands of projects currently under development at **www.sourceforge.net**. If you are looking for a specific kind of application, odds are you will find it there. Currently projects include a full-featured video player, a digital video recorder, and a digital audio mixer. Many applications designed specifically for the Gnome or KDE user interface can be found at their respective software sites (**www.gnome.org** and **apps.kde.com**).

Many sound applications are currently under development for Gnome, including sound editors, MP3 players, and audio players. Check the software map at **www.gnome.org** for current releases. A variety of applications are available for KDE, including a media player (Kaimain), a mixer (KMix), an MP3 player (KJukeBoxMgr), a CD player (Kscd), and even a Napster-like MP3 download utility (KNapster2). Check **apps.kde.com** for recent additions. Several X Window System–based multimedia applications are installed with most distributions. These include XMMS, an MP3 and CD player, Xplaycd, a CD music player, and Xanim, an animation and video player. The Open Sound System (OSS) site provides an extensive listing of available multimedia software at **www.opensound.com/ossapps.html**. Here you can find digital audio players, mixers, MP3 and MPEG players, and even speech tools. You can also download a copy of RealPlayer, the Internet streaming media player, from **www.real.com**. Be sure to choose RealPlayer for Unix, and select as your OS, Linux 2.x (libc i386) RPM.The Linux Midi and Sound pages currently at **www.xdt.com/ar/linux-snd** also hold links to Web and FTP sites for many of these applications.

Note *Several CD Write programs that can be used for CD Music and MP3 writing (burners and rippers) are available from* ***apps.kde.com****. These include KreateCD, CD-Rchive, and KOnCD. For Gnome you can use cd-rec and Gnome Toaster. All use mkisofs, cdrecord, and cdda2wav CD writing programs, which are installed by most distributions. You can download, compile, and install them. Make sure that any CD-R, CD-RW, and CD-ROM drives that are IDE drives are installed as SCSI drives (see Chapter 4).*

Several projects are under way to provide TV, video, DVD, and DTV support for Linux (see Table 17-4). The site **linuxtv.org** provides detailed links to DVD, digital video broadcasting (DVB), and multicasting. The site also provides downloads of many Linux video applications. For DVD, the Linux Video and DVD Project (LiViD) at **www.linuxvideo.org** supports the development of MPEG 2 (DVD) software. The development of an open source DVD player has been hampered by the concerns and restrictions of the MPAA and their control over the DVD decoding software. Information about efforts to develop Linux DVD software can be had at **www.opendvd.org.** Xine is a multipurpose video player for Linux/Unix systems that can play video, DVD, and audio disks. See **xine.sourceforge.net** for more information. At **dvr.sourceforge.net** you can download DVR software for use on KDE.

Projects	Description
Linux MIDI and Sound Pages	Information and links to Linux sound projects and site: **www.xdt.com/ar/linux-snd**
Advanced Linux Sound Architecture (ALSA)	Advanced Linux Sound Architecture project (ALSA) is developed on Linux under the GPL: **www.alsa-project.org**
Open Sound System	Open Sound System; extensive software links **www.opensound.com**
linuxtv.org	Links to video, TV, and DVD sites
LiViD	Linux Video and DVD Project **www.linuxvideo.org**
GATOS	General ATI TV and Overlay Software **www.linuxvideo.org/gatos**
Xine	Xine video player **xine.sourgeforge.net**

Table 17-4. *Linux Multimedia Projects*

For KDE, several video applications are available or currently under development, including video players (aKtion, and Noatun). Check **apps.kde.com** for downloads. Currently available or under development for Gnome are TV tuners (Gnomevision and Gnome-tv), a video player (Gnome-Video), and a video editor (trinity). Check **www.gnome.org**.

Chapter 18

Editors

Linux distributions normally include several text editors that range from simple text editors for simple notes to editors with more complex features such as spell-checkers, buffers, or pattern matching. All generate character text files and can be used to edit any Linux text files. Text editors are often used in system administration tasks to change or add entries in Linux configuration files found in the **/etc** directory or a user's initialization or application dot files located in a user's home directory. You can use any text editor to work on source code files for any of the programming languages or shell program scripts.

Note *Many distributions, including Red Hat, now include a very easy to use GUI-based text editor called Nedit. You can access it on both Gnome and KDE desktops.*

Traditionally, most Linux distributions, including Red Hat, install the cursor-based editors Vim and Emacs. *Vim* is an enhanced version of the Vi text editor used on the Unix system. These editors use simple, cursor-based operations to give you a full-screen format. You can start these editors from the shell command line without any kind of X Window System support. In this mode, their cursor-based operations do not have the ease of use normally found in window-based editors. There are no menus, scroll bars, or mouse-click features. However, the K Desktop and Gnome do support powerful GUI text editors with all these features. These editors operate much more like those found on Mac and Windows systems. They have full mouse support, scroll bars, and menus. You may find them much easier to use than the Vi and Emacs editors. These editors operate from their respective desktops, requiring you first have either KDE or Gnome installed, though the editors can run on either desktop. Vi and Emacs have powerful editing features that have been refined over the years. Emacs, in particular, is extensible to a full-development environment for programming new applications. Newer versions of Emacs, such as GNU Emacs and XEmacs, provide X Window System support with mouse, menu, and window operations. They can run on any window manager or desktop. In addition, the gvim version of the Vim editor also provides basic window operations. Table 18-1 lists several GUI-based editors for Linux.

Note *Most popular Linux distributions include two full functional word processors, KWord and Abiword. You can find out more on Abiword at* ***www.abiword.com****.*

Gnome Editor: gedit

gedit is a basic text editor for the Gnome desktop. It provides full mouse support, implementing standard GUI operations, such as cut-and-paste to move text, and click-and-drag to select text. It supports standard text editing operations such as Find and Replace. You can use gedit to create and modify any of your text files, including as configuration files. gedit also provides more advanced features such as print preview and configurable levels of undo/redo operations, and can read data from pipes.

The K Desktop	Description
KEdit	Text editor
Kate	Text and program editor
KJots	Notebook editor
KWord	Desktop publisher, part of KOffice
Gnome	
gedit	Text editor
Abiword	Word processor
Nedit	GUI-based text editor
X Window System	
GNU Emacs	Emacs editor with X Window System support
XEmacs	X Window System version of Emacs editor
gvim	Vim version with X Window System support
WordPerfect	Word processor that can edit text files

Table 18-1. *Desktop Editors*

It features a plug-in menu that provides added functionality, and it includes plug-ins for spell-checking, encryption, e-mail, and text-based Web page display.

K Desktop Editors: Kate, KEdit, and KJots

All the K Desktop editors provide full mouse support, implementing standard GUI operations, such as cut-and-paste to move text, and click-and-drag to select text. Kate is an advanced editor, with such features as a spell-checking, font selection, and highlighting. Most commands can be selected using menus. A toolbar of icons for common operations is displayed across the top of the Kate window. A sidebar displays panels for a file selector and file list. With the file selector you can navigate through the file system selecting files to work on. Kate also supports multiple views of a document, letting you display segments in their own windows, vertically or horizontally. You can also open several documents at the same time, moving between them with the file list.

Kate is designed to be a program editor for editing software programming/ development-related source code files. Although Kate does not have all the features of Emacs or Vi, it can handle most major tasks. Kate can format the syntax for different programming languages, such as C, Perl, Java, and XML. In addition, Kate also has the capability to access and edit files on an FTP or Web site.

KEdit is an older simple text editor meant for editing simple text files such as configuration files. A toolbar of buttons at the top of the KEdit window enables you to execute common editing commands easily using just a mouse click. With KEdit, you can also mail files you are editing over a network. The entry for KEdit in the K menu is listed simply as Text Editor. You can start up KEdit by entering the **`kedit`** command in a terminal window. The KOffice Office Suite also includes a word processor called KWord, which is a high-powered word processor you can also use as a simple editor.

The editor KJots is designed to enable you to jot down notes in a notebook. It organizes notes you write into notebooks, called simply *books*. You can select the one you want to view or add to from the Books menu. To start KJots, select its entry in the Utilities menu or enter the **`kjots`** command in a terminal window.

The Emacs Editor

Emacs can best be described as a working environment featuring an editor, a mailer, a newsreader, and a Lisp interpreter. The editor is tailored for program development, enabling you to format source code according to the programming language you use. Many versions of Emacs are currently available for use on Unix and Linux systems. The versions usually included with Linux distributions are either GNU Emacs or XEmacs. The current version for GNU Emacs is 20.*x*; it is X Window System–capable, enabling GUI features such as menus, scroll bars, and mouse-based editing operations. (See Chapter 13 for a discussion of the GNU Emacs mailer and its newsreader.) Check the update FTP sites for your distribution for new versions as they come out, and also check the GNU Web site at **www.gnu.org**, and the Emacs Web site at **www.emacs.org**. You can find out more information about XEmacs at its Web site, **www.xemacs.org**.

Emacs derives much of its power and flexibility from its capability to manipulate buffers. Emacs can be described as a buffer-oriented editor. Whenever you edit a file in any editor, the file is copied into a work buffer, and editing operations are made on the work buffer. Emacs can manage many work buffers at once, enabling you to edit several files at the same time. You can edit buffers that hold deleted or copied text. You can even create buffers of your own, fill them with text, and later save them to a file. Emacs extends the concept of buffers to cover any task. When you compose mail, you open a mail buffer; when you read news, you open a news buffer. Switching from one task to another is simply a matter of switching to another buffer.

The Emacs editor operates much like a standard word processor. The keys on your keyboard represent input characters. Commands are implemented with special keys, such as control (CTRL) keys and alternate (ALT) keys. There is no special input mode, as in Vi or Ed. You type in your text, and if you need to execute an editing command, such as moving the cursor or saving text, you use a CTRL key. Such an organization makes the Emacs editor easy to use. However, Emacs is anything but simple—it is a sophisticated and flexible editor with several hundred commands. Emacs also has special features, such as multiple windows. You can display two windows for text at the same time. You can also open and work on more than one file at a time, and display each on the screen in its own window. You invoke the Emacs editor with the command **emacs**. You can enter the name of the file you want to edit, and if the file does not exist, it is created. In the next example, the user prepares to edit the file **mydata** with Emacs:

```
$ emacs mydata
```

Emacs is a full-screen editor that supports menus even when used on the command line. In the case of a newly created file, the screen is empty except for the bottom two lines. The cursor is positioned in the upper-left corner. The bottom line is called the *Echo area*, and it functions as a kind of Emacs command line. The Echo area is also used to display Emacs messages. The line above it is called the *Mode line*; it is used to display status information about the text being edited. The Mode line is highlighted in reverse video. The GNU version of Emacs also displays a list of menus at the top of the screen. If you are working from the shell, you can access the menu entries by pressing the F10 key. If you are working on a desktop, you can use your mouse.

To enter text, simply start typing—you are always in the input mode. Editing commands, such as movement commands, are implemented with CTRL keys. For example, to move the cursor right, use CTRL-F, and to move the cursor left, use CTRL-B. To move up one line, use CTRL-P, and to move down one line, use CTRL-N. You can save your text at any time with the CTRL-X-CTRL-S command sequence. Many Emacs commands are made up of CTRL key combinations. The command sequence to quit the editor is CTRL-X-CTRL-C. When you finish editing the file, first save the file with CTRL-X-CTRL-S before quitting the editor with CTRL-X-CTRL-C.

Emacs provides several help utilities, such as an online manual and a tutorial. You access the help utilities through a CTRL-H sequence. CTRL-H followed by another CTRL-H lists the many possible options. An option of special note is the tutorial. CTRL-H-T places you into an online tutorial that provides you with special lessons on Emacs.

You can run GNU Emacs either from an X Window System window manager or from the shell command line. Many window managers or desktops may already have an entry in their main menu. If not, you can open a terminal window and enter the command **emacs**. When run from a terminal window, Emacs operates with X Window System support, enabling mouse-based editing and menu selection. You can also run Emacs from a standard shell command line, without X. In this case, mouse-based operations are not enabled. However, the Emacs menu headings are still displayed at the top of the screen. You can access a menu by pressing F10. The screen will split, with the lower section listing menus and keys you press to access them. Once you select a menu, the items for that menu are listed with keys to press to select one. For example, to open a file, you press F10, then **f** to list the file menu items, and then **o** to select the open item.

The GNU Emacs editor now supports an X Window System graphical user interface. To enable X support, start Emacs within an X Window System environment, such as a KDE, Gnome, or FVWM desktop. The basic GUI editing operations are supported: selection of text with click-and-drag mouse operations; cut, copy, and paste; and a scroll bar for moving through text. The Mode line and Echo areas are displayed at the bottom of the window, where you can enter keyboard commands. The scroll bar is located on the left side. To move the scroll bar down, click it with the left mouse button. To move the scroll bar up, click it with the right mouse button.

Note *XEmacs is the complete Emacs editor with a graphical user interface and Internet applications. The Internet applications, which you can easily access from the main XEmacs button bar, include a Web browser, a mail utility, and a newsreader.*

The Vi Editor: vim and gvim

The Vim editor included with most Linux distributions is an enhanced version of the Vi editor. It includes all the commands and features of the Vi editor. Vi, which stands for *visual*, remains one of the most widely used editors in Linux. Keyboard-based editors like Vim and Emacs use a keyboard for two different operations: to specify editing commands and to receive character input. Used for editing commands, certain keys perform deletions, some execute changes, and others perform cursor movement. Used for character input, keys represent characters that can be entered into the file being edited. Usually, these two different functions are divided among different keys on the keyboard. Alphabetic keys are reserved for character input, while function keys and control keys specify editing commands, such as deleting text or moving the cursor. Such editors can rely on the existence of an extended keyboard that includes function and control keys. Editors in Unix, however, were designed to assume a minimal keyboard with alphanumeric characters and some control characters, as well as the ESC and ENTER keys. Instead of dividing the command and input functions among different keys, the Vi editor has three separate modes of operation for the keyboard: command and input modes, and a line editing mode. In *command* mode, all the keys on the keyboard become editing commands; in the *input* mode, the keys on the keyboard become input characters. Some of the editing commands, such as `a` or `i`, enter the input mode. On pressing the `i` key, you leave the command mode and enter the input mode. Each key now represents a character to be input to the text. Pressing ESC automatically returns you to the command mode, and the keys once again become editor commands. As you edit text, you are constantly moving from the command mode to the input mode and back again. With Vim, you can use the CTRL-O command to jump quickly to the command mode and enter a command, and then automatically return to the input mode. Table 18-2 lists this basic set of Vi commands you need to get started in Vi.

Although the Vi command mode handles most editing operations, it cannot perform some, such as file saving and global substitutions. For such operations, you need to execute line editing commands. You enter the line editing mode using the Vi colon command, `:`. The colon is a special command that enables you to perform a one-line

Key	Cursor Movement
`h`	Moves the cursor left one character
`l`	Moves the cursor right one character
`k`	Moves the cursor up one line
`j`	Moves the cursor down one line
`w`	Moves the cursor forward one word
`b`	Moves the cursor back one word
`0`	Moves the cursor to the beginning of the line
`$`	Moves the cursor to the end of the line
ENTER	Moves the cursor to beginning of next line
`(`	Moves the cursor to beginning of sentence
`)`	Moves the cursor to the end of sentence; successive command moves to beginning of next sentence
`{`	Moves the cursor to beginning of paragraph
`}`	Moves the cursor to end of paragraph
CTRL-F	Moves forward by a screen of text; the next screen of text is displayed
CTRL-B	Moves backward by a screen of text; the previous screen of text is displayed
`G`	Moves the cursor to last line in the text
num`G`	Moves the cursor to specific line number: **45G** places the cursor on line 45
Input	*(All input commands place the user in input; the user leaves input with* ESC.*)*
`a`	Enters input after the cursor
`A`	Enters input at the end of a line
`i`	Enters input before the cursor
`I`	Enters input at the beginning of a line
`o`	Enters input below the line the cursor is on; inserts a new empty line below the one the cursor is currently on
`O`	Enters input above the line the cursor is on; inserts a new empty line above the one the cursor is currently on

Table 18-2. *Vi Editor Commands*

Text Selection (vim)	Cursor Movement
`v`	Visual mode; move the cursor to expand selected text by character. Once selected, press key to execute action: **c** change, **d** delete, **y** copy, **:** line editing command, **J** join lines, **U** uppercase, **u** lowercase.
`V`	Visual mode; move cursor to expand selected text by line
`o`	Expand selected text backward
Delete	**Effect**
`x`	Deletes the character the cursor is on
`dw`	Deletes the word the cursor is on
`dd`	Deletes the line the cursor is on
`D`	Deletes the rest of the line the cursor is on
`J`	Joins the line below the cursor to the end of the current line; in effect, deleting the newline character of the line the cursor is on
Change	*(Except for the replace command, **r**, all change commands place the user into input after deleting text.)*
`s`	Deletes the character the cursor is on and places the user into the input mode
`C`	Deletes the rest of the line the cursor is on and places the user into input mode
`cw`	Deletes the word the cursor is on and places the user into the input mode
`r`	Replaces the character the cursor is on; after pressing **r**, the user enters the replacement character; the change is made without entering input; the user remains in the Vi command mode
`R`	First places into the input mode, and then overwrites character by character; appears as an overwrite mode on the screen, but actually is in input mode
Move	Moves text by first deleting it, moving the cursor to desired place of insertion, and then pressing the **p** command. (When text is deleted, it is automatically held in a special buffer.)
`p`	Inserts deleted or copied text after the character or line the cursor is on
`P`	Inserts deleted or copied text before the character or line the cursor is on
`dw p`	Deletes a word, and then moves it to the place you indicate with the cursor (press **p** to insert the word *after* the word the cursor is on)
`yy` or `Y`	Copies the line the cursor is on

Table 18-2. *Vi Editor Commands* (continued)

Component References	Description
`w`	Word the cursor is on
`b`	To beginning of a word
`W`	Space-delimited word
`B`	Beginning of a space-delimited word
`)`	Sentence
`}`	Paragraph
`G`	Rest of the file
Search	The two search commands open up a line at the bottom of the screen and enable the user to enter a pattern to be searched for; press ENTER after typing in the pattern
/*pattern*	Searches forward in the text for a pattern
?*pattern*	Searches backward in the text for a pattern
`n`	Repeats the previous search, whether it was forward or backward
`/`	Repeats the previous search in forward direction
`?`	Repeats the previous search in backward direction
Help (vim)	**Effect**
`:help` *command*	Starts help utility; you can specify a command
`F1`	Same as `:help`
Line Editing Commands	**Effect**
`w`	Saves file
`r` *filename*	Inserts file text
`q`	Quits editor, `q!` quits without saving
`d`	Deletes a line or set of lines

Table 18-2. *Vi Editor Commands* (continued)

editing operation. When you type the colon, a line opens up at the bottom of the screen with the cursor placed at the beginning of the line. You are now in the line editing mode. In this mode, you enter an editing command on a line, press ENTER, and the command is executed. Entry into this mode is usually only temporary. Upon pressing ENTER, you are automatically returned to the Vi command mode, and the cursor returns to its previous position on the screen.

Although you can create, save, close, and quit files with the Vi editor, the commands for each are not all that similar. Saving and quitting a file involves the use of special line editing commands, whereas closing a file is a Vi editing command. Creation of a file is usually specified on the same shell command line that invokes the Vi editor. To edit a file, type **vi** or **vim** and the name of a file on the shell command line. If a file by that name does not exist, the system creates it. In effect, giving the name of a file that does not yet exist instructs the Vi editor to create that file. The following command invokes the Vi editor, working on the file **booklist**. If **booklist** does not yet exist, the Vi editor creates it.

```
$ vim booklist
```

After executing the **vim** command, you enter Vi's command mode. Each key becomes a Vi editing command, and the screen becomes a window onto the text file. Text is displayed screen by screen. The first screen of text is displayed, and the cursor is positioned in the upper-left corner. With a newly created file, there is no text to display. This fact is indicated by a column of tildes at the left side of the screen. The tildes represent the part of a screen that is not part of the file.

Remember, when you first enter the Vi editor, you are in the command mode. To enter text, you need to enter the input mode. In the command mode, the **a** key is the editor command for appending text. Pressing this key places you in the input mode. Now the keyboard operates like a typewriter and you can input text to the file. If you press ENTER, you merely start a new line of text. With Vim, you can use the arrow keys to move from one part of the entered text to another and work on different parts of the text. After entering text, you can leave the input mode and return to the command mode by pressing ESC. Once finished with the editing session, you exit Vi by typing two capital Z's, **ZZ**. Hold down the SHIFT key and press **Z** twice. This sequence first saves the file and then exits the Vi editor, returning you to the Linux shell. To save a file while editing, you use the line editing command **w**, which writes a file to the disk. **w** is equivalent to the Save command found in other word processors. You first type a colon to access the line editing mode, and then type **w** and press ENTER.

You can use the **:q** command to quit an editing session. Unlike the **ZZ** command, the **:q** command does not perform any save operation before it quits. In this respect, it has one major constraint. If any modifications have been made to your file since the last save operation, the **:q** command will fail and you will not leave the editor. However, you can override this restriction by placing a **!** qualifier after the **:q** command. The command **:q!** will quit the Vi editor without saving any modifications made to the file in that session since the last save.

To obtain online help, enter the **:help** command. This is a line editing command. Type a colon, enter the word **help** on the line that opens at the bottom of the screen, and then press ENTER. You can add the name of a specific command after the word **help**. The F1 key also brings up online help.

As an alternative to using Vim in a command-line interface, you can use gvim, which provides X Window System–based menus for basic file, editing, and window operations. To use gvim, enter the **gvim** command at an X Window System terminal prompt or select it from a window manager menu. The standard Vi interface is displayed, but with several menu buttons displayed across the top. All the standard Vi commands work just as they are described previously. However, you can use your mouse to select items on these menus. You can open and close a file, or open several files using split windows or different windows. The editing menu enables you to cut, copy, and paste text as well as undo or redo operations. In the editing mode, you can select text with your mouse with a click-and-drag operation, or use the Editing menu to cut or copy and then paste the selected text. Text entry, however, is still performed using the **a**, **i**, or **o** commands to enter the input mode.

Part V

Servers

The Complete Reference

Chapter 19

Server Management

Reflecting the close relationship between Unix and the development of the Internet, Linux is particularly good at providing Internet services, such as the Web, FTP, and e-mail. In the case of the Web, instead of only accessing other sites, you can set up your own Linux system as a Web site. Other people can then access your system using Web pages you created or download files you provide for them. A system that operates this way is called a *server* and is known by the service it provides. You can set up your system to be a Web server or an FTP server, connecting it to the Internet and turning it into a site others can access. A single Linux system can provide several different services. Your Linux system can be a Web server and an FTP server, as well as a mail and news server, all at the same time. One user could download files using your FTP services, while another reads your Web pages. All you have to do is install and run the appropriate server software for each service. Each one operates as a continually running daemon looking for requests for its particular services from remote users. A *daemon* is any program that continually runs, checking for certain requests and performing appropriate actions.

When you install Linux, you have the option of installing several Internet servers, including Web and FTP servers. Linux was designed with Internet servers in mind. For many Linux distributions, a standard install installs these servers automatically and configures them for you (check to make sure the servers are included). Every time you start your system, you also start the Web and FTP server daemons. Then, to turn your Linux system into a Web server, all you have to do is create Web pages. For an FTP server, you only have to place the files you want to make available in the FTP directories.

You can operate your Linux system as a server on the Internet or an intranet (local area network), or you can set it up to service only the users on your own system. To operate servers as Internet servers, you must obtain a connection to the Internet and provide access to your system for remote users. Access is usually a matter of enabling anonymous logins to directories reserved for server resources. Linux systems are usually already configured to enable such access for Web and FTP users. Connections to the Internet that can accommodate server activity can be difficult to find. You may need a dedicated connection, or you may need to use a connection set up by an Internet service provider (ISP). You are no longer connecting only yourself to the Internet, but you are allowing many other users to make what could be a great many connections to you through the Internet. This will involve security risks to your system, and precautions should be taken to protect it (see Chapter 37). If you only want to provide the services to a local area network (LAN), you don't need a special connection. Also, you can provide these services to users by allowing them to connect over a modem and to log in directly. Users could dial into your system and use your Web pages or use FTP to download files. Furthermore, users with accounts on your own machine can also make use of the servers. In whatever situation you want to use these services, you need the appropriate server software installed and running. This chapter examines how servers are started and stopped on your system, as well as different ways of accessing the servers.

Starting Servers: Standalone and xinetd

A *server* is a daemon that runs concurrently with your other programs, continuously looking for a request for its services, either from other users on your system or from remote users connecting to your system through a network. When it receives a request from a user, a server starts up a session to provide its services. For example, if users want to download a file from your system, they can use their own FTP client to request that your FTP server start a session for them. In the session, they can access and download files from your system. Your server needs to be running for a user to access its services. For example, if you set up a Web site on your system with HTML files, you must have the httpd Web server program running before users can access your Web site and display those files. See Chapters 20 and 21 on how to install FTP and Web servers.

You can start a server in several ways. One way is to do it manually from the command line by entering the name of the server program and its arguments. When you press ENTER, the server starts, although your command line prompt reappears. The server runs concurrently as you perform other tasks. To see if your server is running, you can enter the following command to list all currently running processes. You should see a process for the server program you started. To refine the list, you can add a **grep** operation with a pattern for the server name you want. The second command lists the process for the Web server.

```
# ps -aux
# ps -aux | grep 'httpd'
```

On Mandrake, SuSE, Caldera, and Red Hat Linux systems, you use special startup scripts to start and stop your server manually. These scripts are located in the **/etc/rc.d/init.d** directory (**/etc/rc.d** on SuSE) and have the same name as the server programs. For example, the **/etc/rc.d/init.d/httpd** script with the **start** option starts the Web server (**/etc/rc.d/httpd** on SuSE). Using this script with the **stop** option stops it. On Red Hat and Mandrake, instead of using the complete pathname for the script, you can use the **service** command and the script name. The following commands are equivalent.

```
/etc/rc.d/init.d/httpd stop
service httpd stop
```

Instead of manually executing all the server programs each time you boot your system, you can have your system automatically start the servers for you. You can do this in two ways, depending on how you want to use a server. You can have a server running continuously from the time you start your system until you shut it down, or you can have the server start only when it receives a request from a user for its services. If a server is being used frequently, you may want to have it running all the time. If it is used rarely, you may only want the server to start when it receives a request. For example, if you are running a Web site, your Web server is receiving requests all the time from remote hosts on the Internet. For an FTP site, however, you may receive requests infrequently, in which case you may want to have the FTP server start only when it receives a request. Of course, certain FTP sites receive frequent requests, which would warrant a continuously running FTP server.

A server that starts automatically and runs continuously is referred to as a *standalone* server. Mandrake, Caldera, SuSE, and Red Hat use the System V Init procedure to start servers automatically whenever your system boots. This procedure uses special startup scripts for the servers located in the **/etc/rc.d/init.d** directory (**/etc/rc.d** on SuSE). Most Linux systems configure the Web server to start automatically and to run continuously by default. A script for this is called **httpd** and is in the **/etc/rc.d/init.d** directory.

To start the server only when a request for its services is received, you configure it using either the **xinetd** or **inetd** daemons. The **xinetd** daemon is a newer version of **inetd** and is used on Mandrake and Red Hat. If you add, change, or delete server entries in the **/etc/xinetd** files, you will have to restart the **xinetd** daemon for these changes to take effect. You can restart the **xinetd** daemon using the **/etc/rc.d/init.d/xinetd** script with the **restart** argument, as shown here:

```
# service xinetd restart
```

You can also use the **xinetd** script to start and stop the **xinetd** daemon. Stopping effectively shuts down all the servers that the **xinetd** daemon manages (those listed in the **/etc/xinetd.conf** file or **xinetd.d** directory).

```
# service xinetd stop
# service xinetd start
```

You can also directly restart the **xinetd** by sending its process a SIGHUP signal, forcing it to restart. To do this, you use the **kill** command with the **-HUP** option and the process ID of the **xinetd** daemon. You can find the process ID using the **ps -aux** command to list all process and then use **grep** to locate the **xinetd** entry as shown here. The process ID will also be held in the **/var/run/xinetd.pid** file.

```
# ps -aux | grep sinetd
# kill -HUP xinetd-process-id
```

*Earlier versions of Linux systems used the **inetd** daemon (the term stands for the Internet Services Daemon) instead of **xinetd**. **xinetd** is meant to be the enhanced replacement for **inetd**. If you are upgrading from **inetd**, you can use the **inetdconvert** command to convert **inetd** entries into **xinetd** configurations.*

Service Management Tools: chkconfig and System V Init

On most distributions, the KDE System V Init Editor and the **chkconfig** command provide simple interfaces you can use to choose what servers you want started up and how you want them to run. In addition, most distributions provide their own tools such as serviceconf on Red Hat, the Services panel on the Mandrake Control Center, or SuSE's YaST Control Center. You can also use Linuxconf and Webmin to make these changes. You use these tools to control any daemon you want started up, including system services such as cron, the print server, and remote file servers for Samba and NFS, authentication servers for Kerberos, and, of course, Internet servers for FTP or HTTP. Such daemons are referred to as services, and you should think of these tools as managing these services. Any of these services can be set up to start or start at different runlevels.

These tools manage services that are started up by scripts in the **/etc/rc.d/init.d** directory. If you add a new service, both **chkconfig** and System V Init Editor can manage it. As described in the following section, services are started up at specific runlevels using startup links in various runlevel directories. These links are connected to the startup scripts in the **init.d** directory. Runlevel directories are numbered from 0 to 6 in the **/etc/rc.d** directory, such as **/etc/rc.d/rc3.d** for runlevel 3 and **/etc/rc.d/rc5.d** for runlevel 5. Removing a service from a runlevel only removes its link in the corresponding runlevel **rc.d** directory. It does not touch the startup script in the **init.d** directory. Having a server start at a specified runlevel puts the link back in that runlevel directory. For example, if you specify that httpd is no longer to start at runlevel 3, then the **S85httpd** startup link in the **rc3.d** directory is deleted. Having httpd start at runlevel 5 recreates the **S85htppd** link in the **rc5.d** directory. See the following section on SysV Init scripts for more details, and Chapter 25 for more information on runlevels.

chkconfig

With the **chkconfig** command you can specify the service you want to start and the level you want to start it at. Unlike other service management tools, **chkconfig** works equally well on standalone and on **xinetd** services. Though standalone services can be run at any runlevel, you can also turn **xinetd** services on or off for the runlevels that **xinetd** runs in. Table 19-1 lists the different **chkconfig** options.

You use the **on** option to have a service started at certain runlevels, and the **off** option to not have it started. You can specify the runlevel to effect with the **--level** option. If no level is specified, **chkconfig** will use any **chkconfig** default information in a service's **init.d** startup script. Mandrake and Red Hat install their services with **chkconfig** default information already entered (should this be missing, **chkconfig** will use runlevels 3, 4, and 5). The following example will have the Web server (httpd) started at runlevel 5.

```
chkconfig --level 5 httpd on
```

Option	Description
--level *runlevel*	Specifies a runlevel to turn on, off, or reset a service.
--list *service*	Lists startup information for services at different runlevels. **xinetd** services are just on or off. With no argument, all services are listed, including **xinetd** services.
--add *service*	Adds a service, creating links in default specified runlevels (or all if none specified).
--del *service*	Deletes all links for the service (startup and shutdown) in all runlevel directories.
service **on**	Turns a service on, creating a startup link in the specified or default runlevel directories.
service **off**	Turns a service off, creating shutdown links in specified or default directories.
service **reset**	Resets service startup information, creating default links as specified in the **chkconfig** entry in the service's **init.d** startup script.

Table 19-1. *chkconfig Options*

The **off** option will actually configure a service to shut down if it enters a specified runlevel. The next example will shut down the Web server if runlevel 3 is entered. If it is not running, it remains shut down.

```
chkconfig --level 3 httpd off
```

The **reset** option will restore a service to its **chkconfig** default options as specified in the service's **init.d** startup script.

```
chkconfig wu-ftpd reset
```

To see just the startup information for a service, you use just the service name with the **--list** option.

```
chkconfig --list httpd
httpd   0:off  1:off  2:off    3:on     4:off     5:on   6:off
```

Unlike the System V Init Editor, **chkconfig** also has the ability to have **xinetd** services enabled or disabled. Simply enter the **xinetd** service with either an **on** or **off** option. The service will be started up or shut down and its **xinetd** configuration script in the **/etc/xinetd.d** directory will have its disable line edited accordingly. For example, to start swat, the Samba configuration server, which runs on **xinetd**, you simply enter:

```
chkconfig swat on
chkconfig --list swat
     swat          on
```

The swat configuration file for **xinetd**, **/etc/xinetd.d/swat**, will have its disable line edited to **no**, as shown here.

```
disable=no
```

If you want to shut down the swat server, you can use the **off** option. This will change the disable line in **/etc/xinetd.d/swat** to read **disable=yes**.

```
chkconfig swat off
```

The same procedure works for other **xinetd** services such as wu-ftpd, the FTP server, and finger.

If you want a service removed entirely from the entire startup and shutdown process in all runlevels, you can use the **--del** option. This removes all startup and shutdown links in all the runlevel directories.

```
chkconfig --del httpd
```

You can also have services added to management by **chkconfig** with the **--add** option. **chkconfig** will create startup links for it in the appropriate startup directories, **/etc/rc.d/rc*n*.d**. If you have previously removed all links for a service, you can restore them with the **add** option.

```
chkconfig --add httpd
```

To see a list of services managed by https, you use the **--list** option. A sampling of services managed by **chkconfig** are shown here. The on and off status of the service is shown at each runlevel. xinted services and their status are also shown.

```
chkconfig -list
dhcpd   0:off  1:off  2:off  3:off   4:off  5:off  6:off
httpd   0:off  1:off  2:off  3:off   4:off  5:off  6:off
```

```
named    0:off  1:off  2:off  3:off  4:off  5:off  6:off
tux      0:off  1:off  2:off  3:off  4:off  5:off  6:off
kudzu    0:off  1:off  2:off  3:on   4:on   5:on   6:off
innd     0:off  1:off  2:off  3:off  4:off  5:off  6:off
lpd      0:off  1:off  2:on   3:on   4:on   5:on   6:off
nfs      0:off  1:off  2:off  3:off  4:off  5:off  6:off
smb      0:off  1:off  2:off  3:off  4:off  5:off  6:off
crond    0:off  1:off  2:on   3:on   4:on   5:on   6:off
xinetd   0:off  1:off  2:off  3:on   4:on   5:on   6:off
xinetd based services:
     time:        off
     finger:      off
     pop3s:       off
     swat:        on
     wu-ftpd:     off
```

chkconfig works by creating startup and shutdown links in the appropriate runlevel directories in the **/etc/rc.d** directory. For example, when **chkconfig** added the httpd service at runlevel 5, it created a link in the **/etc/rc.d/rc5.d** directory to the startup script **httpd** in the **/etc/rc.d/init.d** directory. When it turned off the Web service from runlevel 3, it created a shutdown link in the **/etc/rc.d/rc3.d** directory to use the script **httpd** in the **/etc/rc.d/initd** directory to make sure the Web service is not started. In the following example, the user turns on the Web service (httpd) on runlevel 3, creating the startup link in **rc5.d, S85httpd**, and then turns off the Web service on runlevel 3, creating a shutdown link in **rc3.d, K15httpd**.

```
chkconfig --level 5 httpd on
ls /etc/rc.d/rc3.d/*httpd
   /etc/rc.d/rc3.d/K15httpd
chkconfig -level 3 httpd off
ls /etc/rc.d/rc3.d/*httpd
   /etc/rc.d/rc3.d/K15httpd
```

Default runlevel information should be placed in the startup scripts that are to be managed by **chkconfig**. Mandrake and Red Hat have already placed this information in the startup scripts for the services that are installed with its distribution. You can edit these scripts to change the default information if you wish. This information is entered as a line beginning with a # sign and followed by the **chkconfig** keyword and a colon. Then you list the default runlevels that the service should start up on, along with the start and stop priorities. The following entry lists runlevels 3 and 5 with a start priority of 85 and a stop of 15.

```
# chkconfig: 35 85 15
```

So when a user turns on the httpd service with no level option specified, **chkconfig** will start up httpd at runlevels 3, 4, and 5.

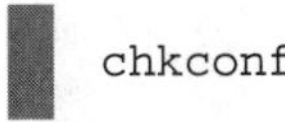

```
chkconfig httpd on
```

A description line should also be added that **chkconfig** can use to describe the service. With the description you enter a short description of the service, using the \ symbol before a newline to use more than one line.

```
# description: Apache is a World Wide Web server. It is used to serve \
# HTML files and CGI.
```

System V Init Editor

The KDE System V Init Editor features a GUI interface to enable you to manage any daemons on your system easily—Internet servers as well as system daemons, such as print servers. The Init Editor window is divided into three major panes. To the left is a scroll window labeled "available" that lists all the daemons available for use on your system. These include the daemons for Internet servers, such as **httpd**. To the right, taking up most of the window, are an upper pane and a lower pane. The upper pane has scroll windows, one for each runlevel. These list the daemons currently configured to run in their respective runlevels. The lower pane also holds scroll windows, one for each runlevel. These are daemons that will be shut down if you switch to that respective runlevel. System administrators can switch from one level to another. All the servers that start up under normal processing are listed in the start runlevel 5 (graphical login) and runlevel 3 (command line) scroll windows. Figure 19-1 shows the System V Init Editor.

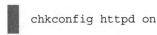

Note *An older program called System V Runlevel Editor is still used on some distributions. It operates much the same as the System V Init Editor, with few differences.*

You can easily configure a server to start automatically when you boot at a certain runlevel. Your system operates at certain runlevels, each specified by a given number, such as the standard multiuser level (runlevel 3), a graphical login level (runlevel 5), and an administrative level (runlevel 1). See Chapter 25 for a discussion of runlevels. To have a server start at a given runlevel, click and drag its entry in the available scroll window to the scroll window for the runlevel you want it to start at. For example, if you use a graphical login, your runlevel when you start up is 5. To have the Web server, httpd, start up automatically whenever you boot your system, check to see if it is in the runlevel 5 startup scroll window. If not, then click and drag the httpd entry in the available window to the runlevel 5 startup window. Select a position in that window where there appear to be available numbers, such as between 15 or 17, or at the end of the scroll window. An httpd entry will then appear in the scroll window. If you do not want to

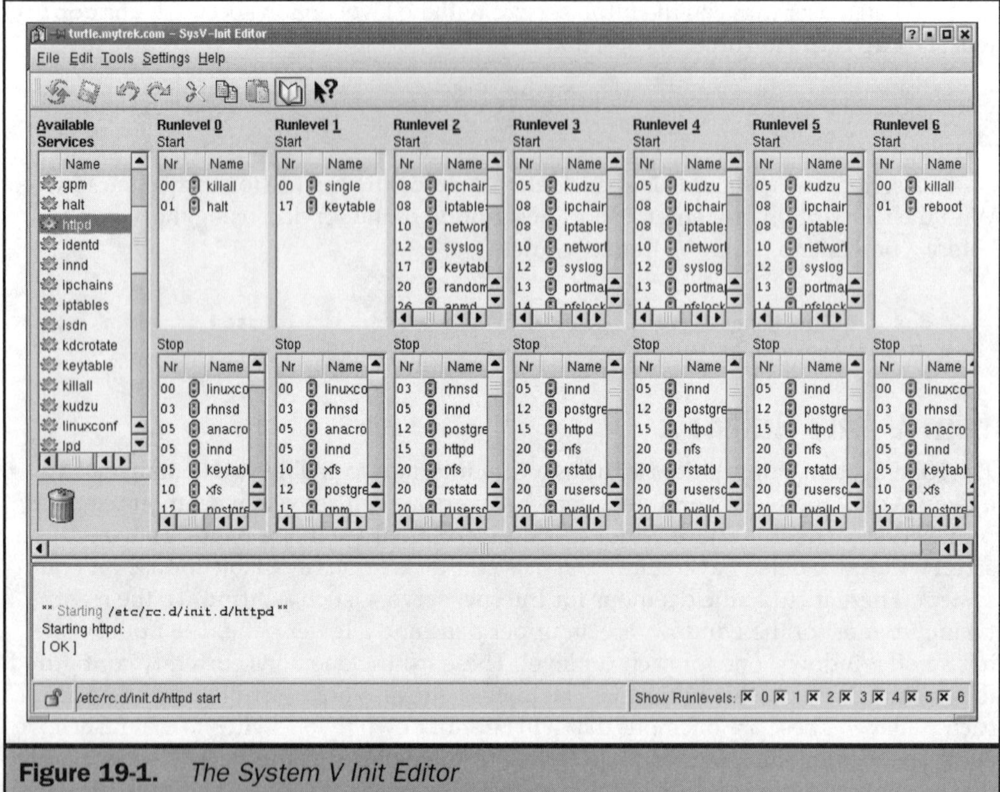

Figure 19-1. *The System V Init Editor*

have the service started up automatically, you can remove it from its startup scroll window by clicking on it and selecting Cut from the pop-up menu. So, to remove httpd from the runlevel 5 startup window, click on its entry in that window and select Cut.

To start or stop a server manually, click its entry in the available scroll window. A Properties window appears where you can select whether you want to start, stop, or restart the server. Do the same procedure to start the server, clicking the Start button. An Edit button will open the server's startup script in an editor and let you modify it directly. Figure 19-2 shows the System V Init Editor httpd Properties window.

Servers that operate under **xinetd** are not listed by the System V Init Editor. The FTP wu-ftpd server is usually installed to run under **xinetd**, so you won't find entries for them here. The System V Editor reads its list of servers from the server scripts in the **/etc/rc.d/init.d** directory. If you add a new script, you can have the System V Editor rescan that directory and then see it appear in the available list. Removing a server

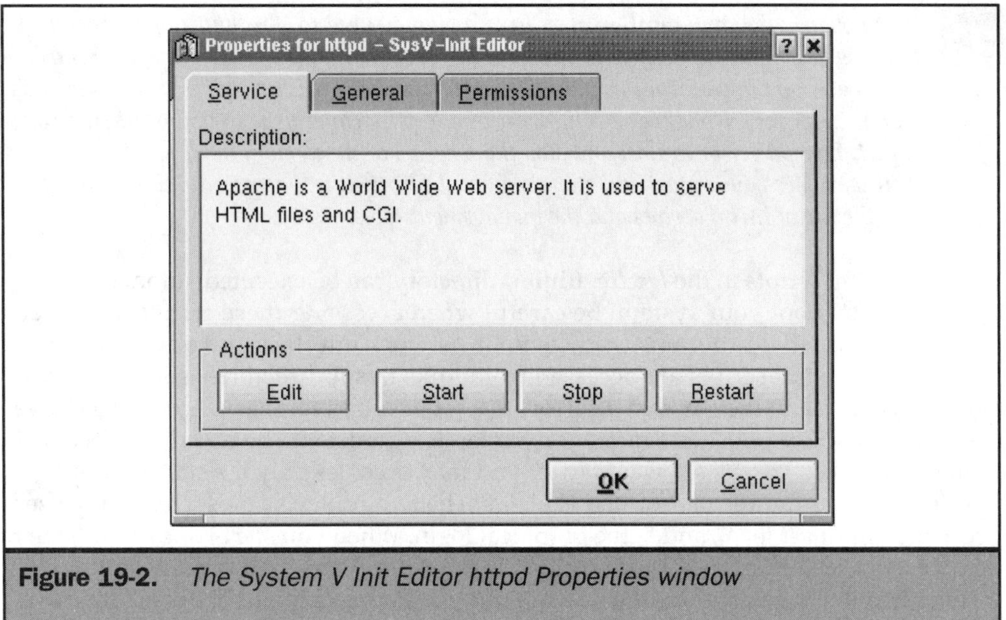

Figure 19-2. *The System V Init Editor httpd Properties window*

from a runlevel window only removes its link in the corresponding runlevel **rc.d** directory. It does not touch the startup script in the **init.d** directory. Adding in the server to the start runlevel window puts the link back in that runlevel directory. Adding a server to a stop window adds a *K* link in the corresponding **rc.d** directory, which stops a server when the system switches to that runlevel. For example, if you remove httpd from the runlevel 3 start window, the **S85httpd** link in the **rc3.d** directory is deleted. Adding httpd back to the runlevel 3 start window recreates the **S85htppd** link in the **rc3.d** directory. Adding httpd to the runlevel 2 stop directory would create a **K85httpd** link in the **rc2.d** directory, shutting down the server when switching to runlevel 2.

SysV Init: init.d Scripts

The startup and shutdown of server daemons is managed using special startup scripts located in the **/etc/rc.d/init.d** directory. These scripts often have the same name as the server's program. For example, for the **/usr/sbin/httpd** Web server program, a corresponding script is called **/etc/rc.d/init.d/httpd**. This script actually starts and stops the Web server. This method of using **init.d** startup scripts to start servers is called *SysV Init,* after the method used in Unix System V.

Note *If you change the configuration of a server, you may need to start and stop it several times as you refine the configuration. Several servers provide special management tools that enable you to perform this task easily. The apachectl utility enables you to start and stop the Apache Web server easily. It is functionally equivalent to using the **/tec/rc.d/init.d/httpd** script to start and stop the server. For the domain name server, the ndc utility enables you to start and stop the named server. It is, however, advisable not to mix the use of **init.d** scripts and the management tools.*

The startup scripts in the **/etc/rc.d/init.d** directory can be executed automatically whenever you boot your system. Be careful when accessing these scripts, however. These start essential programs, such as your network interface and your printer daemon. These init scripts are accessed from links in subdirectories set up for each possible runlevel. In the **/etc/rc.d** directory is a set of subdirectories whose names have the format **rc*N.d***, where *N* is a number referring to a runlevel. The **rc** script detects the runlevel in which the system was started, and then executes only the startup scripts specified in the subdirectory for that runlevel. The two runlevels most commonly used are 3, the multiuser level, and 5, the graphical login. When you start your system, the **rc** script executes the startup scripts specified in the **rc3.d** directory if you are performing a command line login, and **rc5.d** if you are using a graphical login. The **rc3.d** and **rc5.d** directories hold symbolic links to certain startup scripts in the **/etc/rc.d/init.d** directory. So the **httpd** script in the **/etc/rc.d/init.d** directory is actually called through a symbolic link in the **rc3.d** or the **rc5.d** directory. The symbolic link for the **/etc/rc.d/httpd** script in the **rc3.d** directory is **S85httpd**. The *S* prefixing the link stands for "startup" and calls the corresponding **init.d** script with the **start** option. The number indicates the order in which startup scripts are run, lower ones first. **S85httpd** invokes **/etc/rc.d/init.d/httpd** with the option **start**. The numbers in these links are simply there for ordering purposes. If you change the name of the link to start with a *K*, the script is invoked with the **stop** option, stopping it. Such links are used in the runlevels 0 and 6 directories, **rc6.d** and **rc0.d**. Runlevel 0 halts the system and runlevel 6 reboots it. You can use the **runlevel** command to find out what runlevel you are currently operating at (see Chapter 25 for more details on runlevels). A listing of runlevels is shown here:

Runlevel	rc.d Directory	Description
0	rc0.d	Halt (shut down) the system
1	rc1.d	Single-user mode (no networking, limited capabilities)
2	rc2.d	Multiuser mode with no NFS support (limited capabilities)
3	rc3.d	Multiuser mode (full operational mode)

Runlevel	rc.d Directory	Description
5	rc5.d	Multiuser mode with graphical login (full operation mode with graphical login added)
6	rc6.d	Reboot system

Most server software using RPM packages will automatically install the startup scripts and create the needed links in the appropriate **rc*N*.d** directories. Startup scripts, though, can be used for any program you may want to run when your system starts up. To have such a program start automatically, you first create a startup script for it in the **/etc/rc.d/init.d** directory, and then create symbolic links to that script in the **/etc/rc.d/rc3.d** and **/etc/rc.d/rc5.d** directories. A shutdown link (*K*) should also be placed in the **rc6.d** directory used for runlevel 6 (reboot).

A simplified version of the startup script **httpd** is shown here. You can see the different options listed under the case statement: **start**, **stop**, **status**, **restart**, and **reload**. If no option is provided (*), then the script use syntax is displayed. The **httpd** script first executes a script to define functions used in these startup scripts. The **daemon** function with httpd actually executes the **/usr/sbin/httpd** server program.

```
echo -n "Starting httpd: "
 daemon httpd
 echo
 touch /var/lock/subsys/httpd
```

The **killproc** function shuts down the daemon. The lock file and the process ID file (**httpd.pid**) are then deleted.

```
killproc httpd
echo
rm -f /var/lock/subsys/httpd
rm -f /var/run/httpd.pid
```

The **daemon**, **killproc**, and **status** scripts are shell scripts defined in the **functions** script also located in the **inet.d** directory. The **functions** script is executed at the beginning of each startup script to activate these functions. A list of these functions is provided in Table 19-2.

```
. /etc/rc.d/init.d/functions
```

The beginning of the startup script holds tags used to configure the server. These tags, which begin with an initial **#**, are used to provide runtime information about the service to your system. The tags are listed in Table 19-2 along with the startup functions.

Init Script Functions	Description
`daemon [+/-`*nicelevel*`]` *program* `[`*arguments*`] [&]`	Starts a daemon, if it is not already running.
`killproc` *program* `[`*signal*`]`	Sends a signal to the program; by default it sends a SIGTERM, and if the process doesn't stop, it sends a SIGKILL. It will also remove any PID files, if it can.
`pidofproc` *program*	Used by another function, it determines the PID of a program.
`status` *program*	Displays status information.
Init Script Tags	**Description**
`# chkconfig:` *startlevellist startpriority endpriority*	Required. Specifies the default start levels for this service as well as start and end priorities.
`# description [`*ln*`]:` *description of service*	Required. The description of the service, continued with `'\'` characters. Use an initial **#** for any added lines. With the *ln* option, you can specify the language the description is written in.
`# autoreload: true`	Optional. If this line exists, the daemon checks its configuration files and reloads them automatically when they change.
`# processname:` *program*	Optional, multiple entries allowed. Name of the program or daemon started in the script.
`# config:` *configuration-file*	Optional, multiple entries allowed. Specify a configuration file used by the server.
`# pidfile:` *pid-file*	Optional, multiple entries allowed. Specifies the PID file.
`# probe: true`	Optional, used *in place* of **autoreload**, **processname**, **config**, and **pidfile** entries to automatically probe and start the service.

Table 19-2. *System V Init Script Functions and Tags*

You enter a tag with a preceding **#** symbol, the tag name with a colon, and then the tag arguments. For example, the **processname** tag will specify the name of the program being executed, in this example httpd.

```
# processname: httpd
```

If your script starts more than one daemon, you should have a **processname** entry for each. For example, the Samba service starts up both the **smdb** and **nmdb** daemons.

```
# processname: smdb
# processname: nmdb
```

The end of the tag section is indicated by an empty line. After this line, any lines beginning with a **#** are treated as comments. The chkconfig line will list the default runlevels that the service should start up on, along with the start and stop priorities. The following entry lists runlevels 3, 4, and 5 with a start priority of 85 and a stop of 15.

```
# chkconfig: 345 85 15
```

With the description you enter a short description of the service, using the \ symbol before a newline to use more than one line. **pidfile** indicates the file where the server process ID is held. With config tags, you specify the configuration files the server may use. In the case of the Apache Web server, there may be three configuration files:

```
# config: /etc/httpd/conf/access.conf
# config: /etc/httpd/conf/httpd.conf
# config: /etc/httpd/conf/srm.conf
```

As an example, a simplified version of the Web server startup script is shown here. Most scripts are much more complicated, particularly when determining any arguments or variables a server may need to specify when it starts up. It has the same name as the Web server daemon, **httpd**.

/etc/rc.d/init.d/httpd

```
#!/bin/sh
#
# Startup script for the Apache Web Server
#
# chkconfig: 35 85 15
# description: Apache is a World Wide Web server. It is used to serve \
# HTML files and CGI.
# processname: httpd
# pidfile: /var/run/httpd.pid
# config: /etc/httpd/conf/access.conf
# config: /etc/httpd/conf/httpd.conf
# config: /etc/httpd/conf/srm.conf


# Source function library.
. /etc/rc.d/init.d/functions
```

```
# See how we were called.
case "$1" in
     start)
            echo -n "Starting httpd: "
             daemon httpd
             echo
             touch /var/lock/subsys/httpd
              ;;
    stop)
             killproc httpd
             echo
             rm -f /var/lock/subsys/httpd
             rm -f /var/run/httpd.pid
             ;;
    status)
             status httpd
             ;;
    restart)
             $0 stop
             $0 start
             ;;
    reload)
             echo -n "Reloading httpd: "
             killproc httpd -HUP
             echo
             ;;
    *)
             echo "Usage: $0 {start|stop|restart|reload|status}"
             exit 1
   esac

exit 0
```

The RPM packaged versions for an Internet server include the startup script for that server. Installing the RPM package installs the script in the **/etc/rc.d/init.d** directory and creates its appropriate links in the runlevel directories, such as **/etc/rc.h/rc3.d**. If you decide, instead, to create the server using its source code files, you can then manually install the startup script. If no startup script exists, you first make a copy of the **httpd** script—renaming it—and then edit the copy to replace all references to **httpd** with the name of the server daemon program. Then place the copy of the script in the **/etc/rc.d/init.d** directory and make a symbolic link to it in the **/etc/rc.d/rc3.d** directory. Or you could use the System V Init Editor to create the link in the **/etc/rc.d/rc3.d** directory. Have the editor scan the **init.d** directory by selecting Re-scan from the File menu, click the entry in the Available listing, click the Add button, and then select the Runlevel and Start options in the Add window. When you start your system now, the new server is automatically started up, running concurrently and waiting for requests.

Extended Internet Services Daemon (xinetd)

If your system averages only a few requests for a specific service, you don't need the server for that service running all the time. You only need it when a remote user is accessing its service. The Extended Internet Services Daemon (**xinetd**) manages Internet servers, invoking them only when your system receives a request for their services. **xinetd** checks continuously for any requests by remote users for a particular Internet service; when it receives a request, it then starts the appropriate server daemon.

The **xinetd** program is designed to be a replacement for **inetd**, providing security enhancements, logging support, and even user notifications. For example, with **xinetd** you can send banner notices to users when they are not able to access a service, telling them why. **xinetd** security capabilities can be used to prevent denial-of-service attacks, limiting remote hosts' simultaneous connections or restricting the rate of incoming connections. **xinetd** also incorporates TCP, providing TCP security without the need to invoke the **tcpd** daemon. Furthermore, you do not have to have a service listed in the **/etc/services** file. **xinetd** can be set up to start any kind of special-purpose server. Current Red Hat and Mandrake Linux versions 7 use **xinetd**. Many older Linux systems may still be using **inetd**.

You can start, stop, and restart **xinetd** using its startup script in the **/etc/rc.d/init.d** directory, as shown here:

```
# /etc/rc.d/init.d/xinetd stop
# /etc/rc.d/init.d/xinetd start
# /etc/rc.d/init.d/xinetd restart
```

On Red Hat and Mandrake you can use the service command.

```
# service xinetd restart
```

You can also turn on and off particular **xinetd** services with **`chkconfig`**, as described earlier. Use the **`on`** and **`off`** options to enable or disable a service. **`chkconfig`** will edit the disable option for the service, changing its value to **`yes`** for off and **`no`** for on. For example, to enable the swat server you could enter:

```
chkconfig swat on
```

The **xinetd.conf** file is the configuration file for **xinetd**. Entries in it define different servers to be activated when requested along with any options and security precautions. An entry consists of a block of attributes defined for different features, such as the name of the server program, the protocol used, and security restrictions. Each block for an Internet service such as a server is preceded by the keyword **service** and the name by which you want to identify the service. A pair of braces encloses the block of attributes. Each attribute entry begins with the attribute name followed by an assignment operator such as = and then the value or values assigned. A special block specified by the keyword **default** contains default attributes for services. The syntax is shown here:

```
service <service_name>
{
<attribute> <assign_op> <value> <value> ...
  ...
}
```

Most attributes take a single value for which you use the standard assignment operator, =. Some attributes can take a list of values. You can assign values with the = operator, but you can also add or remove items from these lists with the += and -= operators. Use the += to add values and -= to remove values. You often use the += and -= operators to add values to attributes that may have an initial value assigned in the default block.

Attributes are listed in Table 19-3. Certain attributes are required for a service. These include **socket_type** and **wait**. **socket_type** can be **stream** for stream-based service, **dgram** for datagram-based service, **raw** for service that requires direct access,

Attributes	Description
id	Identifies a service. By default, the service ID is the same as the service name.
type	Type of service: **RPC**, **INTERNAL** (provided by **xinetd**), **UNLISTED** (not listed in a standard system file).
flags	Possible flags include **REUSE**, **INTERCEPT**, **NORETRY**, **IDONLY**, **NAMEINARGS** (allows use of **tcpd**), **NODELAY**, **DISABLE** (disable the service). See the **xinetd.conf** Man page for more details.
disable	Specifies **yes** to disable the service.
socket_type	Specifies **stream** for a stream-based service, **dgram** for a datagram-based service, **raw** for a service that requires direct access to IP, and the **seqpacket** service for reliable sequential datagram transmission.

Table 19-3. *xinetd Attributes*

Attributes	Description
`protocol`	Specifies a protocol for the service. The protocol must exist in **/etc/protocols**. If this attribute is not defined, the default protocol employed by the service will be used.
`wait`	Specifies whether the service is single-threaded or multithreaded (**`yes`** or **`no`**). If **`yes`**, the service is single-threaded, which means that **xinetd** will start the server and then stop handling requests for the service until the server stops. If **`no`**, the service is multithreaded and **xinetd** will continue to handle new requests for it.
`user`	Specifies the user ID (UID) for the server process. The username must exist in **/etc/passwd**.
`group`	Specifies the GID for the server process. The group name must exist in **/etc/group**.
`instances`	Specifies the number of server processes that can be simultaneously active for a service.
`nice`	Specifies the server priority.
`server`	Specifies the program to execute for this service.
`server_args`	Lists the arguments passed to the server. This does not include the server name.
`only_from`	Controls the remote hosts to which the particular service is available. Its value is a list of IP addresses. With no value, service is denied to all.
`no_access`	Controls the remote hosts to which the particular service is unavailable.
`access_times`	Specifies the time intervals when the service is available. An interval has the form *hour:min-hour:min*.
`log_type`	Specifies where the output of the service log is sent, either syslog facility (**`SYSLOG`**) or a file (**`FILE`**).
`log_on_ success`	Specifies the information that is logged when a server starts and stops. Information you can specify includes **`PID`** (server process ID), **`HOST`** (the remote host address), **`USERID`** (the remote user), **`EXIT`** (exit status and termination signal), and **`DURATION`** (duration of a service session).

Table 19-3. *xinetd Attributes* (continued)

Attributes	Description
`log_on_failure`	Specifies the information that is logged when a server cannot be started. Information you can specify includes **`HOST`** (the remote host address), **`USERID`** (user ID of the remote user), **`ATTEMPT`** (logs a failed attempt), **`RECORD`** (records information from the remote host to allow monitoring of attempts to access the server).
`rpc_version`	Specifies the RPC version for a RPC service.
`rpc_number`	Specifies the number for an UNLISTED RPC service.
`env`	Defines environment variables for a service.
`passenv`	Lists the environment variables from **xinetd**'s environment that will be passed to the server.
`port`	Specifies the service port.
`redirect`	Allows a TCP service to be redirected to another host.
`bind`	Allows a service to be bound to a specific interface on the machine.
`interface`	Synonym for **`bind`**.
`banner`	The name of a file to be displayed for a remote host when a connection to that service is established.
`banner_success`	The name of a file to be displayed at the remote host when a connection to that service is granted.
`banner_fail`	Takes the name of a file to be displayed at the remote host when a connection to that service is denied.
`groups`	Allows access to groups the service has access to (**`yes`** or **`no`**).
`enabled`	Specifies the list of service names to enable.
`include`	Inserts the contents of a specified file as part of the configuration file.
`includedir`	Takes a directory name in the form of "includedir /etc/xinetd.d". Every file inside that directory will be read sequentially as an **xinetd** configuration file, combining to form the **xinetd** configuration.

Table 19-3. *xinetd Attributes* (continued)

and **seqpacket** service for sequential datagram transmission. The **wait** attribute can have a yes or no value to specify if the server is single-threaded (**yes**) or multithreaded (**no**). If **yes**, **xinetd** will wait, calling the server initially and letting that server handle further requests until the server stops. If the value is **no** (multithreaded), **xinetd** will continue to handle new requests for the server, generating new server processes to handle them. For a standard Internet service, you would also need to provide the user (user ID for the service), the server (name of the server program), and the protocol (protocol used by the server). With **server_arguments**, you can also list any arguments you want passed to the server program (this does not include the server name as with **tcpd**). If protocol is not defined, the default protocol for the service is used.

```
service ftp
   {
    socket_type = stream
    wait = no
    user = root
    protocol = ftp
    server = /usr/sbin/in.ftpd
    server_args = -l -a
    disable = yes
   }
```

Services can be turned on and off with the **disable** attribute. In the previous example, the **disable** attribute has turned off the FTP service, keeping the FTP server shut down. To enable a service, you would set the **disable** attribute to **no**, as shown here:

```
disable = no
```

You then have to restart **xinetd** to start the service.

```
# /etc/rc.d/init.d/xinetd restart
```

Note *Your distribution may disable all the services it initially set up when it installed* ***xinetd****. To enable a particular service, you have to set its* ***disable*** *attribute to* ***no****.*

To enable management by **chkconfig**, a commented default and description entry need to be placed before each service segment. Where separate files are used, these are placed at the head of each file. Red Hat already provides these for the services it installs with its distribution such as wu-fptd and swat. A default entry can be either on or off. For example, the **chkconfig** default and description entries for the FTP service are shown here.

```
# default: on
# description: The wu-ftpd FTP server serves FTP connections. It \
```

```
#    uses normal, unencrypted usernames and passwords for \
#    authentication.
```

If you want to turn on a service that is off by default, you will have to set its **disable** attribute to **no**, and restart **xinetd**. The Red Hat entry for the wu-ftpd FTP server is shown here. An initial comment tells us that it is on by default, but then the **disable** attribute turns it off.

```
# default: on
# description: The wu-ftpd FTP server serves FTP connections. It \
#    uses normal, unencrypted usernames and passwords for \
#    authentication.
service ftp
{
        socket_type     = stream
        wait            = no
        user            = root
        server          = /usr/sbin/in.ftpd
        server_args     = -l -a
        log_on_success  += DURATION USERID
        log_on_failure  += USERID
        nice            = 10
        disable         = yes
}
```

You can further add a variety of other attributes such as logging information about connections and server priority (**nice**). In the following example, the **log_on_success** attribute will log the duration (**DURATION**) and the user ID (**USERID**) for connections to a service, **log_on_failure** will log the users that failed to connect, and **nice** will set the priority of the service to 10.

```
log_on_success += DURATION USERID
log_on_failure += USERID
nice = 10
```

The default attributes defined in the defaults block often set global attributes such as default logging activity and security restrictions. **log_type** specifies where logging information is to be sent, such as to a specific file (**FILE**) or to the system logger (**SYSLOG**). **log_on_success** will specify information to be logged when connections are made, and **log_on_failure** will specify information to be logged when they fail.

```
log_type = SYSLOG authpriv
log_on_success = HOST PID
log_on_failure = HOST RECORD
```

For security restrictions, you can use **only_from** to restrict access by certain remote hosts. **no_access** denies access by the listed hosts, but no others. These controls take as their values IP addresses. You can list individual IP addresses, a range of IP addresses, or a network using the network address. The **instances** attribute will limit the number of server processes that can be active at once for a particular service. The following examples restrict access to a local network 192.168.1.0 and the localhost, deny access from 192.168.1.15, and use the **instances** attribute to limit the number of server processes at one time to 60.

```
only_from = 192.168.1.0
only_from = localhost
no_access = 192.168.1.15
instances = 60
```

A sample default block is shown here:

```
defaults
{
 instances = 60
 log_type = FILE /var/log/servicelog
 log_on_success = HOST PID
 log_on_failure = HOST RECORD
 only_from = 192.168.1.0
 only_from = localhost
 no_access = 192.168.1.15
}
```

The **xinetd** program also provides several internal services including time, services, servers, and xadmin. The services service provides a list of currently active services, and servers provide information about servers. xadmin provides **xinetd** administrative support.

Instead of having one large **xinetd.conf** file, you can split it into several configuration files, one for each service. You do this by creating an **xinetd.conf** file with an **includedir** attribute that specifies a directory to hold the different service configuration files. In the following example, the **xinetd.d** directory will hold **xinetd** configuration files for services like wu-ftpd. Mandrake and Red Hat use just such an implementation. This approach has the advantage of letting you add services by just creating a new configuration file for it. Modifying a service only involves editing its configuration file, not an entire **xinetd.conf** file.

```
includedir /etc/xinetd.d
```

The following example shows the **xinetd.conf** file used for Red Hat Linux.

xinetd.conf

```
#
# Simple configuration file for xinetd
#
# Some defaults, and include /etc/xinetd.d/

defaults
{
    instances          = 60
    log_type           = SYSLOG authpriv
    log_on_success     = HOST PID
    log_on_failure     = HOST
}

includedir /etc/xinetd.d
```

A few of the files in the **xinetd.d** directory are shown here. Notice that some are disabled by default, whereas others are not.

swat

```
# default: off
# description: SWAT is the Samba Web Admin Tool. Use swat \
#    to configure your Samba server. To use SWAT, \
#    connect to port 901 with your favorite web browser.
service swat
{
    port               = 901
    socket_type        = stream
    wait               = no
    only_from          = localhost
    user               = root
    server             = /usr/sbin/swat
    log_on_failure     += USERID
    disable            = yes
}
```

telnet

```
# default: on
# description: The telnet server serves telnet sessions; it uses \
# unencrypted username/password pairs for authentication.
service telnet
{
    flags                  = REUSE
```

```
    socket_type         = stream
    wait                = no
    user                = root
    server              = /usr/sbin/in.telnetd
    log_on_failure      += USERID
    disable             = yes
}
```

inetd Server Management

Like **xinetd**, **inetd** is used when your system averages only a few requests for a specific service, so you don't need the server for that service running all the time. You only need it when a remote user is accessing its service. **inetd** is the precursor to **xinetd**, and is still used on some distribution and older Linux systems.

The **inetd** daemon manages Internet servers, invoking them only when your system receives a request for their services. **inetd** checks continuously for any requests by remote users for a particular Internet service; when it receives a request, it then starts the appropriate server daemon. For example, the Washington University FTP daemon, **wu-ftpd**, is usually installed to run using **inetd**, rather than as a standalone daemon. When **inetd** receives a request from a user to access FTP, it starts **in.ftpd**, the FTP daemon. **in.ftpd** then handles the request, enabling the remote user to download files.

For **inetd** to call the appropriate server daemon, it must be configured for that service. You place entries for that server in the **/etc/services** and **/etc/inetd.conf** files. The **/etc/services** file lists services available on your system. An entry in **/etc/services** consists of the name of the service followed by its port and protocol, separated by a slash. Entries for FTP as they appear in your **/etc/service** file are shown here. Other distributions may require only one entry for FTP.

```
ftp-data      20/tcp
ftp           21/tcp
```

The **/etc/inetd.conf** file is the **inetd** configuration file. For its entries, you specify the service, its protocol, and the server program to invoke. An entry for FTP is shown here. Server paths and arguments may vary according to different Linux distributions. Some programs have a special script, link, or alternate program to use for **inet.d** activation, instead of directly using the program file. Such scripts or links begin with the prefix **in** followed by a period, followed by the program name. For example, the ProFTP server is called **proftpd**, but uses the **in.proftpd** as the program name in an **inetd.conf** entry. Other programs, such as the Apache Web server, use the same program name—in this case, **httpd**.

```
#<service> <sock_type> <proto> <flags> <user> <server_path>     <args>
ftp        stream      tcp     nowait  root   /usr/sbin/in.ftpd in.ftpd
```

For some services, the configuration lines may exist, but they may be commented out with a preceding **#** symbol. Remove the **#**. If no configuration entries exist, you need to add them. The standard entries in **inetd.conf** for Internet services are shown here:

```
# These are standard services.
#
ftp      stream   tcp   nowait   root   /usr/sbin/in.ftpd   in.ftpd
-l -a
telnet   stream   tcp   nowait   root   /usr/sbin/in.telnetd
in.telnetd
gopher   stream   tcp   nowait   root   /usr/sbin/in.gn   gn
```

TCP Wrappers

TCP wrappers add another level of security to **xinetd**-managed servers. In effect, the server is wrapped with an intervening level of security, monitoring connections and controlling access. A server connection made through **xinetd** is monitored verifying remote user identities and checking to make sure they are making valid requests. Connections are logged with the **syslogd** daemon (see Chapter 25) and may be found in **syslogd** files such as **/var/log/secure**. With TCP wrappers, you can also restrict access to your system by remote hosts. Lists of hosts are kept in the **hosts.allow** and **hosts.deny** files. Entries in these files have the format **service:hostname:domain**. The domain is optional. For the service, you can specify a particular service, such as FTP, or you can enter **ALL** for all services. For the hostname, you can specify a particular host or use a wildcard to match several hosts. For example, **ALL** will match on all hosts. Table 19-4 lists the available wildcards you can use. In the following example, the first

Wildcard	Description
ALL	Matches all hosts.
LOCAL	Matches any host specified with just a hostname without a domain name. Used to match on hosts in the local domain.
UNKNOWN	Matches any user or host whose name or address is unknown.
KNOWN	Matches any user or host whose name or address is known.

Table 19-4. *TCP Wrapper Wildcards*

Wildcard	Description
`PARANOID`	Matches any host whose hostname does not match its IP address.
`EXCEPT`	An operator that lets you provide exceptions to matches. It takes the form of *list1* **`EXCEPT`** *list2* where those hosts matched in *list1* that are also matched in *list2* are excluded.

Table 19-4. *TCP Wrapper Wildcards* (continued)

entry allows access by all hosts to the Web service, **http**. The second entry allows access to all services by the **pango1.train.com** host. The third and fourth entries allow **rabbit.trek.com** and **sparrow.com** FTP access.

```
http:ALL
ALL:pango1.train.com
ftp:rabbit.trek.com
ftp:sparrow.com
```

The **hosts.allow** file holds hosts to which you allow access. If you want to allow access to all but a few specific hosts, you can specify **`ALL`** for a service in the **hosts.allow** file, but list the ones you are denying access to in the **hosts.deny** file. Using IP addresses instead of hostnames is more secure because hostnames can be compromised through the DNS records by spoofing attacks where an attacker pretends to be another host.

When **xinetd** receives a request for an FTP service, a TCP wrapper monitors the connection and starts up the **in.ftpd** server program. By default, all requests are allowed. To allow all requests specifically for the FTP service, you would enter the following in your **/etc/hosts.allow** file. The entry **`ALL:ALL`** opens your system to all hosts for all services.

```
ftp:ALL
```

Originally, TCP wrappers were managed by the **tcpd** daemon. However, **xinetd** has since integrated support for TCP wrappers into its own program. You can explicitly invoke the **tcpd** daemon to handle services if you wish. The **tcpd** Man pages (**man tcpd**) provide more detailed information about **tcpd**.

If you are using **inetd** instead of **xinetd**, you will need to make **tcpd** entries in the **inted.conf** file. To have **tcpd** monitor a server, you have to place the pathname for **tcpd** in the pathname field of a server's entry for the **inetd.conf** file. This is what has already been done for the **ftpd** server entry in the Red Hat **inetd.conf** file. Instead of the pathname for the **ftpd** program, **/usr/sbin/in.ftpd**, there is the pathname for the **tcpd** daemon, **/usr/sbin/tcpd**. The argument field that follows then lists the **in.ftpd** server program.

```
# <service> <sock_type> <proto> <flags> <user>  <server_path>   <args>
ftp         stream      tcp     nowait  root    /usr/sbin/tcpd  in.ftpd
```

When **inetd** receives a request for an FTP service, it calls the **tcpd** daemon, which then takes over and monitors the connection. Then it starts up the **in.ftpd** server program. By default, **tcpd** allows all requests. To allow all requests specifically for the FTP service, you would enter the following in your **/etc/hosts.allow** file. The entry **`ALL:ALL`** opens your system to all hosts for all services.

```
ftp:ALL
```

The standard Internet services listed in the **/etc/initd.conf** file all use the **tcpd** daemon, as shown here.

```
# These are standard services.
#
ftp     stream   tcp   nowait   root   /usr/sbin/tcpd   in.ftpd -l -a
telnet  stream   tcp   nowait   root   /usr/sbin/tcpd   in.telnetd
```

Chapter 20

FTP Servers

The File Transfer Protocol (FTP) is designed to transfer large files across a network from one system to another. Like most Internet operations, FTP works on a client/server model. FTP client programs can enable users to transfer files to and from a remote system running an FTP server program. Chapter 14 discusses FTP clients. Any Linux system can operate as an FTP server. It only has to run the server software—an FTP daemon with the appropriate configuration. Transfers are made between user accounts on client and server systems. A user on the remote system has to log in to an account on a server and can then transfer files to and from that account's directories only. A special kind of user account, named *ftp,* allows any user to log in to it with the username "anonymous." This account has its own set of directories and files that are considered public, available to anyone on the network who wants to download them. The numerous FTP sites on the Internet are FTP servers supporting FTP user accounts with anonymous login. Any Linux system can be configured to support anonymous FTP access, turning them into network FTP sites. Such sites can work on an intranet or on the Internet.

Note *On Mandrake and Red Hat, the configuration files for anonymous FTP are in packages beginning with the term* ***anonftp****. Installing this package sets up your FTP directories and configures the FTP account.*

FTP Daemons

FTP server software consists of an FTP daemon and configuration files. The *daemon* is a program that continuously checks for FTP requests from remote users. When a request is received, it manages a login, sets up the connection to the requested user account, and executes any FTP commands the remote user sends. For anonymous FTP access, the FTP daemon allows the remote user to log in to the FTP account using anonymous or ftp as the username. The user then has access to the directories and files set up for the FTP account. As a further security measure, however, the daemon changes the root directory for that session to be the FTP home directory. This hides the rest of the system from the remote user. Normally, any user on a system can move around to any directories open to him or her. A user logging in with anonymous FTP can only see the FTP home directory and its subdirectories. The remainder of the system is hidden from that user. This effect is achieved by the `chroot` operation (discussed later) that literally changes the system root directory for that user to that of the FTP directory. By default, the FTP server also requires a user be using a valid shell. It checks for a list of valid shells in the **/etc/shells** file. Most daemons have options for turning off this feature.

Several FTP server daemons are available for use on Linux systems. Most Linux distributions come with the Washington University FTP server called *wu-ftpd.* You can download RPM package updates for particular distributions from their FTP sites, such as **ftp.redhat.com**. The software package usually begins with the term **wu-ftpd**. You can obtain the original compressed archive from the Washington University archive at **http://wuarchive.wustl.edu/packages/wuarchive-ftpd**.

ProFTPD is a newer and popular FTP daemon based on an Apache Web server design. It features simplified configuration and support for virtual FTP hosts. Although not currently included with most distributions, you can download RPM packages from distribution sites, as well as the ProFTPD site. The package begins with the term **proftpd**. The compressed archive of the most up-to-date version, along with documentation, is available at the ProFTPD Web site at **www.proftpd.net**. Another FTP daemon, ncftpd, is a commercial product produced by the same programmers who did the ncftp FTP client. ncftpd is free for academic use and features a reduced fee for small networks. Check **www.ncftpd.org** for more information.

Note *Several security-based FTP servers are also available, including SSLftp and SSH sftpd. SSLftp uses SSL (Secure Sockets Layer) to encrypt and authenticate transmissions, as well as MD5 digests to check the integrity of transmitted files. SSH sftpd is an FTP server now part of the Open SSH package, using SSH encryption and authentication to establish secure FTP connections.*

Most distributions, including Red Hat, Mandrake, and Caldera, currently install the wu-ftpd server and the **anon** anonymous FTP package during installation. At that time, an **ftp** directory along with several subdirectories are created where you can place files for FTP access. The directories have already been configured to control access by remote users, restricting use to only the **ftp** directories and any subdirectories. The **ftp** directory is placed in different directories by different distributions.

Note *On Mandrake and Red Hat, the* ***ftp*** *directory is placed in the* ***/var*** *directory,* ***/var/ftp****. Place the files you want to allow access to in the* ***ftp/pub*** *directory. For example, on Mandrake and Red Hat this would be at* ***/var/ftp/pub****.*

You can also create subdirectories and place files there. Once connected to a network, a remote user can connect to your system and download files you placed in **ftp/pub** or any of its subdirectories. The **anon** FTP package implements a default configuration for those directories and their files. You can change these if you want. If you are installing an FTP server yourself, you need to know the procedures detailed in the following sections to install an FTP server and create its data directories.

The **anon** FTP package does not create a directory where users can upload files to the FTP site. Such a directory is usually named the incoming directory, located at **ftp/pub/incoming**. If you want such a directory, you will have to create it, make it part of the **ftp** group, and then set its permissions to allow user's write access.

```
chgrp ftp /var/ftp/pub/incoming
chmod g+w /var/ftp/pub/incoming
```

Normal users with accounts on an FTP server can gain full FTP access simply by logging into their accounts. Such users can access and transfer files directly from their own accounts or any directories they may have access to. You can also create users, known as guest users, that have restricted access to the FTP publicly accessible directories. This involves setting standard user restrictions, with the FTP public directory as their home directory.

Anonymous FTP: anon

An anonymous FTP site is essentially a special kind of user on your system with publicly accessible directories and files in its home directory. Anyone can log in to this account and access its files. Because anyone can log in to an anonymous FTP account, you must be careful to restrict a remote FTP user to only the files on that anonymous FTP directory. Normally, a user's files are interconnected to the entire file structure of your system. Normal users have write access that lets them create or delete files and directories. The anonymous FTP files and directories can be configured in such a way that the rest of the file system is hidden from them and remote users are given only read access. In ProFTPD, this is achieved through configuration directives placed in its configuration file. An older approach used by wu-ftpd and implemented by the **anon** package involves having copies of certain system configuration, command, and library files placed within subdirectories of the FTP home directory. Restrictions placed on those subdirectories then control access by other users. Within the FTP home directory, you then have a publicly accessible directory that holds the files you want to make available to remote users. This directory usually has the name **pub**, for public.

An FTP site is made up of an FTP user account, an FTP home directory, and certain copies of system directories containing selected configuration and support files. Newer FTP daemons, such as ProFTPD, do not need the system directories and support files. Most distributions, including Red Hat, have already set up an FTP user account when you installed your system.

*On distributions that support RPM packages like Red Hat, you can use the **anon** RPM package to set up the home directory and the copies of the system directories. If you do not have access to the **anon** package, you may have to create these system directories yourself.*

The FTP User Account: anonymous

To allow anonymous FTP access by other users to your system, you must have a user account named *FTP*. Most distributions already create this account for you. If your system does not have such an account, you will have to create one. You can then place restrictions on the FTP account to keep any remote FTP users from accessing any other part of your system. You must also modify the entry for this account in your **/etc/passwd** file to prevent normal user access to it. The following is the entry you find in your **/etc/passwd** file on Mandrake and Red Hat systems that sets up an FTP login as an anonymous user:

```
ftp:*:14:50:FTP User:/var/ftp:
```

The asterisk in the password field blocks the account, which prevents any other users from gaining access to it, thereby gaining control over its files or access to other parts of your system. The user ID, 14, is a unique ID. The comment field is FTP User. The login directory is **/var/ftp**. When FTP users log in to your system, this is the directory in which they are placed. If a home directory has not been set up, create one and then change its ownership to the FTP user with the **chown** command.

The group ID is the ID of the **ftp** group, which is set up only for anonymous FTP users. You can set up restrictions on the **ftp** group, thereby restricting any anonymous FTP users. Here is the entry for the **ftp** group you find in the **/etc/group** file. If your system does not have one, you should add it.

```
ftp::50:
```

Anonymous FTP Server Directories

As previously noted, on Red Hat, the FTP home directory is named **ftp** and is placed in the **/var** directory. When users log in anonymously, they are placed in this directory. An important part of protecting your system is preventing remote users from using any commands or programs not in the restricted directories. For example, you would not let a user use your **ls** command to list filenames because **ls** is located in your **/bin** directory. At the same time, you want to let the FTP user list filenames using an **ls** command. Newer FTP daemons like ProFTPD solve this problem by creating secure access to needed system commands and files, while restricting remote users to only the FTP site's directories. Another more traditional solution, used by wu-ftpd, is to create copies of certain system directories and files needed by remote users and to place them in the **ftp** directory where users can access them. A **bin** directory is placed in the **ftp** directory and remote users are restricted to it, instead of the system's **bin** directory. Whenever they use the **ls** command, remote users are using the one in **ftp/bin**, not the one you use in **/bin**.

On Red Hat, the **anon** RPM package will set up these copies of system directories and files. Otherwise, you may have to create these directories and support files yourself. On Red Hat, the **anon** package installs **etc**, **bin**, and **lib** directories in the **/var/ftp** directory. These contain localized versions of system files needed to let an FTP client execute certain **FTP** commands, such as listing files or changing directories. The **ftp/etc** directory contains versions of the password and group configuration files, the **ftp/bin** directory contains copies of shell and compression commands, and the **ftp/lib** directory holds copies of system libraries. The directories set up by the **anon** package are shown here:

```
ftp
ftp/bin
ftp/etc
ftp/lib
ftp/pub
```

The **ftp/etc** directory holds a version of your **passwd** and **group** files specially configured for FTP access. Again, the idea is to prevent any access to the original files in the **/etc** directory by FTP users. The **ftp/etc/passwd** file should not include any entries for regular users on your system. All entries should have their passwords set to * to block access. The **group** file should not include any user groups and all passwords should be set to *.

```
ftp/etc/passwd
root:*:0:0:::
bin:*:1:1:::
operator:*:11:0:::
ftp:*:14:50:::
nobody:*:99:99:::

ftp/etc/group
root::0:
bin::1:
daemon::2:
sys::3:
adm::4:
ftp::50:
```

If, for some reason, you do not have access to the **anon** package, you can set up the anonymous FTP directories yourself. Again, remember, if you are using ProFTPD, you do not need any of these files, except for an FTP home directory. You must use the **chmod** command to change the access permissions for the directories so remote users cannot access the rest of your system. Create an **ftp** directory and use the **chmod** command with the permission 555 to turn off write access: **chmod 555 ftp**. Next, make a new **bin** directory in the **ftp** directory, and then make a copy of the **ls** command and place it in **ftp/bin**. Do this for any commands you want to make available to FTP users. Then create an **ftp/etc** directory to hold a copy of your **passwd** and **group** files. Again, the idea is to prevent any access to the original files in the **/etc** directory by FTP users.

The **ftp/etc/passwd** file should be edited to remove any entries for regular users on your system. All other entries should have their passwords set to * to block access. For the **group** file, remove all user groups and set all passwords to *. Create an **ftp/lib** directory, and then make copies of the libraries you need to run the commands you placed in the **bin** directory.

Anonymous FTP Files

A directory named **pub**, located in the FTP home directory, usually holds the files you are making available for downloading by remote FTP users. When FTP users log in, they are placed in the FTP home directory (**/var/ftp** on Red Hat) and they can then change to the **pub** directory to start accessing those files (**/var/ftp/pub** on Red Hat). Within the **pub** directory, you can add as many files and directories as you want. You can even designate some directories as upload directories, enabling FTP users to transfer files to your system.

In each subdirectory set up under the ***pub*** *directory to hold FTP files, you should create a* ***Readme*** *file and an* ***index*** *file as a courtesy to FTP users. The* ***Readme*** *file contains a brief description of the kind of files held in this directory. The* ***index*** *file contains a listing of the files and a description of what each one holds.*

Permissions

Technically, any remote FTP user gaining access to your system is considered a user and, unless restricted, could access other parts of your file system, create directories and files, or delete the ones already there. Permissions can be used to restrict remote users to simple read access, and the rest of your file system can be hidden from the FTP directories. The **anon** package and the ProFTPD daemon already implement these restrictions. If you are manually creating your anonymous FTP files, you must be sure to set the permission correctly to restrict access.

Normally, a Linux file structure interconnects all the directories and files on its system. Except where prevented by permissions set on a directory or file, any user can access any directory or file on your system. Technically, any remote FTP user gaining anonymous access is an anonymous user and, as a user, could theoretically access an unrestricted directory or file on your system. To restrict FTP users to the FTP home directory, such as **ftp**, and its subdirectories, the rest of the file structure must be hidden from them. In effect, the FTP home directory should appear to be the root directory as far as FTP users are concerned. The FTP home directory **ftp** would appear to the remote FTP user as the root directory. The real root directory, **/**, and the rest of the directory structure remain hidden. The FTP daemon attains this effect by using the `chroot` command to make the FTP home directory appear as a root directory, with the FTP user as the argument. When a remote FTP user issues a `cd /` command to change to the root, they always change to the FTP home directory, not the system's root directory. For example, the `cd /` command would change to **ftp**.

As a further restriction, all the directories that hold commands in the FTP home directory, as well as the commands themselves, should be owned by the root, not by the FTP user. In other words, no FTP user should have any control over these directories. The root has to own the FTP home directory's **bin** and **etc** subdirectories and all the files they contain (**/var/ftp/bin** and **/var/ftp/etc** on Red Hat). The **anon** package already has set the ownership of these directories to the root. If you need to set them manually, you can use the **chown** command. The following example changes the ownership of the **/var/ftp/bin** directory to the root:

```
# chown root  /var/ftp/bin
```

Permissions for the FTP directories should be set to allow access for FTP users. You recall that three sets of permissions exist—read, write, and execute for the owner, the group, and others. To allow access by FTP users, the group and other permissions for directories should be set to both read and execute. The execute permission allows FTP users to access that directory, and the read permission allows listing the contents of the directory. Directories should not allow write permission by FTP users. You don't want them to be able to delete your directories or make new ones. For example, the FTP **bin** directory needs both read and execute permissions because FTP users have to access and execute its commands. This is particularly true for directories, such as **pub**, that hold the files for downloading. They must have both read and execute permissions set.

You, as the owner of the directories, may need write permission to add new files or subdirectories. Of course, you only need this when you are making changes. To add further security, you could set these directories at just read and execute, even for the owner when you are not making changes. You can set all permissions to read and execute with the **chmod** command and the number 555 followed by the directory name. This sets the owner, group, and other permissions to read and execute. The permissions currently in place for the FTP directories set up by the **anon** package are designated by the number 755, giving the owner write permission.

```
# chmod 555 /var/ftp/bin
```

Permissions for files within the FTP **bin** directory and other special FTP directories can be more restrictive. Some files only need to be read, while others must be execute. Files in the FTP **bin** or **lib** directories only have to be execute. These could have their permissions set to 555. Files in the FTP **etc** directory such as **passwd** and **group** should have their permissions set to 111. They only have to be read. You always use the **chmod** command to set permissions for files, as shown in the following example. The **anon** package sets these permissions at read and execute, 555.

```
# chmod 111 /var/ftp/etc/passwd
```

FTP Server Tools

Both the wu-ftpd and ProFTPD daemons provide a set of FTP tools you can use to manage your FTP server. With the **ftpshut** command, you can smoothly shut down a running server, warning users of the shutdown well before it happens. **ftpwho** can tell you who is currently connected and what they are doing. **ftpcount** can give you the number of connections currently in effect. Although each daemon has its own set of tools, they perform the same action with much the same set of options. Tools provided by both ProFTPD and wu-ftpd have the same name and options, though ProFTPD provides more information on virtual hosts and has some added options.

ftpshut

With the **ftpshut** command, you can have the FTP server shut down at a given time, rather than suddenly shutting it down by killing its process. This gives you the chance to warn users the server is shutting down and not to start any long downloads. **ftpshut** takes several options for specifying the time and including a warning message. **ftpshut** takes as its arguments the time until the shutdown, followed by the warning message you want sent to users. The time can be a word such as "now" that effects an immediate shutdown, a **+** sign with the number of minutes remaining, or a specific time of day indicated by an HHMM format, where HH is the hour in a 24-hour cycle and MM is the minute. The following example shuts down the FTP server in ten minutes, issuing a warning to users:

```
ftpshut +10  "Shutdown in ten minutes"
```

Shutdown disables new FTP access ten minutes before a scheduled shutdown, though this can be changed using the **-l** option with the number of minutes you want. Five minutes before a scheduled shutdown, all current connections are disconnected. You can adjust the time with the **-d** option. The warning message is formatted at 75 characters and you can use special formatting symbols for in-place substitutions of certain values in the warning message, such as the shutdown time. These symbols are called *magic cookies*. For example, **%s** is the shutdown time, **%r** is the time when new connections are refused, **%d** is the time when current connections are cut, **%M** is the maximum number of users, and **%L** is the local hostname.

ftpwho and ftpcount

With the **ftpwho** command, you can find out who is currently connected to your FTP server. **ftpwho** shows the current process information for each user. The output displays five fields: the process ID, the tty connection, the status of the connection, the amount of CPU time used so far for the process, and the connection details. The status of the connection is *R* for running, *S* for sleeping, and *Z* for crashed. The connection details include the Internet address from where the connection is made, the user making the connection, and the task currently being performed, such as downloading a file. The field begins with the name of the FTP daemon, usually **ftpd**, followed by the different segments separated by colons.

`ftpcount` displays the number of users connected to your FTP server, broken down according to the classes specified in your **.ftpaccess** file. Along with the number of users, it shows the maximum number allowed to connect.

The Washington University FTP daemon: wu-ftpd

The Washington University FTP daemon is currently the most widely used FTP server on Linux systems. It is the FTP server installed by most Linux distributions. The name of the Washington University FTP daemon is wu-ftpd. The wu-ftpd options are shown in Table 20-1. wu-ftpd must be running to allow FTP access by remote users. As with other servers, you can start the FTP server at boot time, through **xinetd** when a request is received, or directly from the command line. By default, the wu-ftpd server is installed to run using **xinetd**. The use of **xinetd** for the servers is described in detail in the previous chapter. The command name for the FTP server invoked by **xinetd** is **in.ftpd.** This is

Option	Effect
`-d`	Writes debugging information to the **syslog**
`-l`	Logs each FTP session in the **syslog**
`-t`*seconds*	Sets the inactivity timeout period to specified seconds (default is 15 minutes)
`-T`*seconds*	The maximum timeout period allowed when timeout is set by user (default is two hours)
`-a`	Enables use of the **ftpaccess** configuration file
`-A`	Disables use of the **ftpaccess** configuration file
`-L`	Logs commands sent to the **ftpd** server to the **syslog**
`-I`	Logs files received by **ftpd** to **xferlog**
`-o`	Logs files transmitted by **ftpd** to the **syslog**

Table 20-1. *wu-ftpd Options*

a link to the **wu-ftpd** command. **xinetd** will run a file called **wu-ftpd** located in the **/etc/xinetd.d** directory. A copy of the script is shown here.

wu-ftpd

```
# default: on
# description: The wu-ftpd FTP server serves FTP connections. It uses \
# normal, unencrypted usernames and passwords for authentication.
service ftp
{
    socket_type                 = stream
    wait                        = no
    user                        = root
    server                      = /usr/sbin/in.ftpd
    server_args                 = -l -a
    log_on_success             += DURATION USERID
    log_on_failure             += USERID
    nice                        = 10
    disable                     = yes
}
```

Initially, the server will be turned off. You can turn it on with the **chkconfig** command and the **on** argument, as shown here. Use the **off** argument to disable the server.

```
chkconfig wu-ftpd on
```

Restart **xinetd** with the **service** command to restart the wu-ftpd server, should you make configuration changes.

```
service xinetd restart
```

If you want to run your server continually (like a Web server), you have to configure it to start up initially with your system. On Red Hat and Caldera, this means creating an **init** script for it in the **/etc/rc.d/init.d** directory, so it starts when you boot your system. You can also start the FTP server directly from the command line by entering the **wu-ftpd** command with any options or arguments. The wu-ftpd server can be called with several options. Usually, it is called with the **-l** option that allows logins. The **-t** and **-T** options set timeouts for users, cutting off those that have no activity after a certain period of time. The **-d** option displays debugging information, and **-u** sets the umask value for uploaded files.

Configuring the wu-ftpd Server with kwuftpd

Distributions that install KDE, such as Red Hat, Caldera, and SUSE, include a GUI wu-ftpd configuration tool for the KDE desktop called kwuftpd. Though still under development, current versions can be used to configure your **ftpaccess** file easily. You can access kwuftpd from the KDE desktop. Kwuftpd presents a set of tabbed panels for tasks such as controlling users and uploads, specifying server directories, and setting up virtual hosts. In the Security panel you can specify files that can't be accessed, control access to basic commands by real, guest, and anonymous users, and specify the allowable number of failed logins.

With kwuftpd, you can also set up virtual hosts. On the Virtual Hosts panel, you can specify the virtual host information such as the hostname, root directory, and log file. Click the Add button to create a Virtual Host entry, then enter its information. You can also control access by real users.

You can also use Linuxconf and Webmin to configure the wu-ftpd server. Linuxconf requires that you load its wu-ftpd module.

wu-ftpd Server Configuration Files

You can use numerous configuration options to tailor your FTP server to your site's particular needs. wu-ftpd makes use of several configuration files located in the system's **/etc** directory. All begin with the pattern **ftp**. The primary configuration file is named **ftpaccess**. Here, you provide basic server information and access for specified directories. The **ftphosts**, **ftpusers**, and **ftpgroups** files control access by systems, particular users, and groups. **ftpconversions** specifies how archive and compression operations are to be performed on files before or after they are transferred. **xferlog** is the log file that stores a running log of all transactions performed by the server.

ftpaccess

The **ftpaccess** file determines capabilities users have after they gain access to your FTP site. Access, information, permissions, logging, and several miscellaneous capabilities can be designated. You can have entries that create aliases for certain directories, display a message when FTP users log in, or prevent anonymous users from deleting files. A **loginfails** entry determines the number of login tries a user can make before being cut off, and the **email** entry specifies the e-mail address of the FTP administrator. The Man page for **ftpaccess** lists the possible entries. The **ftpaccess** file with the configuration used on Red Hat systems is shown in this section. For commonly used **ftpaccess** entries, see Table 20-2. For more detailed information, check the **ftpaccess** Man page and wu-ftpd documentation.

In the **ftpaccess** file, you set capabilities for different types of users, called *classes*. Three different types of users exist: anonymous, guest, and real. *Anonymous users* are any users using the anonymous login name. *Guest users* are those given special guest access with `guestgroup` or `guestuser` options. A *real user* is one who has an account on the system and is using an FTP connection to access it. You can define your own class using the `class` option. In the **ftpaccess** file shown here, a class called **all** is created that consists of all users of the anonymous, guest, and real types.

Access Capabilities	Description
autogroup *group classglob* [*classglob*...]	Allows access to a group's read-only files and directories by particular classes of anonymous users. *group* is a valid group from **/etc/group**.
class *class typelist addrglob* [*addrglob*...]	Defines *class* of users, with source addresses of the form *addrglob*. *typelist* is a comma-separated list of the user types: anonymous, guest, and real.
deny *host-addrglob message_file*	Always denies access to host(s) matching *host-addrglob*. *message_file* is displayed.
guestgroup *groupname* [*groupname*...]	Allows guest access by a real user, where the user is a member of the specified group. A password entry for the guest user specifies a home directory within the FTP site directories.
guestuser *usrname* [*userpname*...]	Allows guest access by a real user.
limit *class n times message_file*	Limits class to *n* users at times—*times*, displaying *message_file* if access is denied.
noretrieve *file-list*	Denies retrieval ability of these files.
loginfails *number*	After *number* login failures, terminates the FTP connection. Default value is 5.
Private *yes*|*no*	The user becomes a member of the group specified in the group access file **ftpgroups**.
Informational Capabilities	
banner *file*	The banner is displayed before login. File requires full pathname.
email *email-address*	Defines the e-mail address of the FTP manager.
message *file* { *when* { *class* ...}}	FTP displays the contents of the *file* at login time or upon changing directories. The **when** parameter may be LOGIN or CWD=*dir*; *dir* specifies the directory that displays the message when entered. Magic cookies can be in the message file that causes the FTP server to replace the cookie with a specified text string, such as the date or the username.
readme *file* { *when* { *class*}}	The user is notified at login time or upon using a change working directory command (**cd**) that *file* exists and was modified on such and such date.

Table 20-2. */etc/ftpaccess wu-ftpd Configuration File*

Logging Capabilities	Description
log commands *typelist*	Enables logging of individual commands by users.
log transfers *typelist directions*	Enables logging of file transfers. *directions* is a comma-separated list of the terms "inbound" and "outbound," and logs transfers for files sent to the server and sent from the server.
Miscellaneous Capabilities	
alias *string dir*	Defines an alias, *string*, for a directory.
cdpath *dir*	Defines an entry in **cdpath**. This defines a search path used when changing directories.
compress yes|no *classglob* [*classglob* **tar** yes|no *classglob* [*classglob...*] ...]	Enables **compress** or **tar** capabilities for any class matching of *classglob*. The actual conversions are defined in the external file **ftconversion**.
shutdown *path*	If the file pointed to by *path* exists, the server checks the file regularly to see if the server is going to be shut down.
virtual *address* root| banner|logfile *path*	Enables the virtual FTP server capabilities. Specify the root, banner, and logfile files.
virtual *address* hostname|email *string*	Specifies the hostname and e-mail for the virtual host.
virtual *address* allow *user-list*	Lists users allowed access to the virtual host.
virtual *address* deny *user-list*	Lists users denied access to the virtual host.
virtual *address* private	Denies access by anonymous users.
virtual *address* password *path*	Uses a different password file for the virtual host.
virtual *address* shadow *path*	Uses a different shadow password file for the virtual host.
Permission Capabilities	Allows or disallows the ability to perform the specified function. By default, all users are allowed.
chmod yes | no *typelist*	Allows or disallows changing file permissions.
delete yes | no *typelist*	Allows or disallows deleting files, **rm**.
overwrite yes | no *typelist*	Allows or disallows modifying files.

Table 20-2. */etc/ftpaccess wu-ftpd Configuration File* (continued)

Permission Capabilities	Description
rename yes | no *typelist*	Allows or disallows renaming files, **mv**.
umask yes | no *typelist*	Allows or disallows file creation permissions.
passwd-check *none* | *trivial* | *rfc822* (*enforce* | *warn*)	Defines the level and enforcement of password checking done by the server for anonymous FTP. *rfc822* requires an e-mail address in a valid e-mail address format.
path-filter *typelist* *mesg allowed_charset* { *disallowed regexp...*}	For users in *typelist*, **path-filter** defines regular expressions that control what a filename can or cannot be. Multiple disallowed *regexps* may occur.
upload *root-dir dirglob* yes|no *owner group mode* ["dirs"|"nodirs"]	Defines a directory with *dirglob*, which permits or denies uploads.

Table 20-2. */etc/ftpaccess wu-ftpd Configuration File* (continued)

The message entry specifies a file with the message to be displayed and when that message is to appear. You can have one message appear when users log in and other messages displayed when users enter certain directories. For example, the following entry will display the message in the **/welcome.msg** file when a user logs in:

```
message /welcome.msg              login
```

To set permissions, you use the command followed by a yes or a no and then a list of the user types or classes. An example of the **ftpaccess** file on Red Hat systems is shown here. In this example, all users can perform **tar** and **compress** operations, but anonymous and guest users are prohibited from using **chmod**, **delete**, **overwrite**, and **rename** operations. They also cannot erase files, modify them, or change their names or permissions.

/etc/ftpaccess

```
# define the class of users
class   all   real,guest,anonymous *
# Email address of FTP managerm
email root@localhost
# Allow only 5 login failures per connection
loginfails 5
# Login and change directory README files
readme  README*    login
readme  README*    cwd=*
# Login and change directory message files
message /welcome.msg     login
```

```
message .message                    cwd=*

# Set permissions
# Allow access to compress and tar operations.
compress     yes      all
tar          yes      all
# Deny access by guests and anonymous users to commands
chmod        no       guest,anonymous
delete       no       guest,anonymous
overwrite    no       guest,anonymous
rename       no       guest,anonymous

# Log file transfers, shutdown notice, password email address
log transfers anonymous,real inbound,outbound
shutdown /etc/shutmsg
passwd-check rfc822 warn
```

You can further modify your **ftpaccess** file to control access to particular users or groups of users by defining a class for them and placing restrictions on that class. For example, you could define a class for connections from a particular host as shown here:

```
class  manycons   192.168.1.55  *
```

Then apply controls such as limiting the number of connections from that host to five. This would be helpful for cases where you know many users from a particular host are trying to use your FTP site.

```
limit manycons  5  Any
```

If you want to allow users to upload files to a specific directory, you will need to specify that directory with an **upload** entry. For the **upload** entry, you need to specify the root directory of the FTP site (root directory for the **ftp** user), the directory to which files can be uploaded, whether uploads are permitted (**yes** | **no**), and the owner, group, and the file permissions for the files in that directory. The **dirs** and **nodirs** options will allow and disallow the user from creating subdirectories in that upload directory. In the next example, the **/var/ftp/pub/incoming** directory is the directory to which users can upload copies (**/var/ftp** is the FTP root directory). Any files in that directory will be owned by the **ftp** user, which is part of the **ftp** group, and will have the permissions 0666 (read/write access). Users are also not allowed to create subdirectories.

```
upload  /var/ftp   /pub/incoming   yes  ftp  ftp   066   nodirs
```

The wu-ftpd server also supports virtual hosts. These are FTP sites that have different addresses but use the same server. To enable wu-ftpd to service a virtual host, you need to specify information about it, such as its root directory, its hostname, and user access. You specify this information with the **virtual** command using different options. The first argument is usually the IP address of the virtual FTP server. Then different options let you specify certain information. With the **root** option you can specify the server's root directory. The **banner**, **password**, and **logfile** options specify the banner, password, and log files. With the **hostname** and **email** options, you give the virtual host's hostname and the e-mail address for its administrator. The **deny** and **allow** options let you list real and guest users that can or cannot have access to the virtual server. The **private** option denies access to anonymous users.

In the following example, a virtual FTP server called **ftp.mypics.com** is created whose IP address is at 10.0.0.1. This virtual server has a root directory at **/var/ftp/mypics** and uses the log file at **/var/log/syslog**. The administrator's e-mail address is aleina@turtle.mytrek.com.

```
virtual 10.0.0.1 hostname ftp.mypics.com
virtual 10.0.0.1 root   /var/ftp/mypics
virtual 10.0.0.1 logfile  /var/ftp/syslog
virtual 10.0.0.1 email  aleina@turtle.mytrek.com
```

ftphosts

You use the **ftphosts** file to allow or deny access by other host computers to your FTP site. When the remote system accesses your system, it does so by logging in as a registered user. Access is made through a user account already set up on your system. You allow the remote host to log in as a certain specific user or deny access as a certain user. You could use this kind of control to allow or deny anonymous access to the FTP user by a remote host.

The file **ftphosts** has two kinds of entries: one for allowing access and the other for denying access. Entries to allow access begin with the keyword **allow**, then the user account on your system to which the host is allowed access, followed by the address of the remote host. The address can be a pattern that can be used to match several hosts. You can use any of the filename generation symbols (see Chapter 10). Entries to deny access begin with the keyword **deny**, then the user account on your system to which the host is denied access, followed by the address of the remote host. The terms **deny** and **allow** can be misleading. **allow** is a much more restrictive control, whereas **deny** is a much more open control. **allow** only allows access from the remote host to the specified account. No other access is permitted. You could use **allow** to permit a remote host anonymous access only. **deny**, on the other hand, only denies access to the specified account. You could use **deny** to deny anonymous access by a certain system, but not any direct FTP access from one user to another.

ftpusers and ftpgroups

The **ftpusers** files list users that cannot access the FTP service. For example, the root user should not be accessible through an FTP connection, even if you knew the password. This file will initially hold a listing of all your system users such as **root**, **mail**, and **bin**.

ftpgroups is a group access file that allows FTP users to become members of specified groups on your system. This file lists special group passwords. For these to work, the **Private** entry must be set to **yes** in the **ftpaccess** file.

ftpconversions

The **ftpconversions** file holds possible FTP conversions for compression and archive operations. It operates as an FTP conversions database, listing all possible conversions. A default **ftpconversions** file is included with the installation package that already has entries for the most common conversion operations. Each line in the file is a record of eight fields, with the fields separated by colons. The fields are Strip Prefix and Postfix, Addon Prefix and Postfix, External Command, Types, Options, and Description. The Prefix and Postfix fields refer to changes made to the filename after the specified action is performed. The Strip Postfix removes a specified suffix from a filename, and the Add Postfix adds a suffix. For example, a gzipped compressed file has a suffix of **.gz**. If the command is to compress a file with gzip, then the Add Postfix entry should have the **.gz** placed in it. When the file is compressed, **.gz** is added to the end. If you were decompressing a file with gunzip, then you would want to remove the **.gz** suffix. For this, you would place **.gz** in the Strip Postfix field. The Strip and Add Prefix fields perform the same kind of action for prefixes.

The **external** command is the command you would use to convert the file. You can list command options after the command. The filename you are operating on is specified with **%s**, usually placed after any options. For example, you would use the **tar** command to extract a **.tar** archived file and **gunzip** to decompress a **.gz** file. The Type field lists the type of files that can be operated on by the command. These can be regular files, character files, or directories, as indicated by the entries **T_REG**, **T_ASCII**, and **T_DIR**. You can specify more than one entry by placing a | between them. The Options field specifies the type of operation the command performs. Currently, options exist for compression, decompression, and use of the **tar** command: **O_COMPRESS**, **O_UNCOMPRESS**, and **O_TAR**. You can list more than one by separating them with a | symbol. The description provides some documentation as to what the conversion operation does. Here is the **ftpconversion** file used on Red Hat systems:

```
:.Z:  :  :/bin/compress -d -c %s:T_REG|T_ASCII:O_UNCOMPRESS:UNCOMPRESS
:   : :.Z:/bin/compress -c %s:T_REG:O_COMPRESS:COMPRESS
:.gz: :  :/bin/gzip -cd %s:T_REG|T_ASCII:O_UNCOMPRESS:GUNZIP
:    : :.gz:/bin/gzip -9 -c %s:T_REG:O_COMPRESS:GZIP
:    : :.tar:/bin/tar -c -f - %s:T_REG|T_DIR:O_TAR:TAR
:    : :.tar.Z:/bin/tar -c -Z -f -
                             %s:T_REG|T_DIR:O_COMPRESS|O_TAR:TAR+COMPRESS
:    : :.tar.gz:/bin/tar -c -z -f -
                             %s:T_REG|T_DIR:O_COMPRESS|O_TAR:TAR+GZIP
```

FTP log file: xferlog

This file contains log information about connections and tasks performed by your FTP server. On Red Hat systems, this file is found in the **/var/log** directory. On other systems, this file may be on the **/usr/adm** directory. The file is made up of server entries, one on each line. The entry is divided into several fields separated by spaces. The fields are current-time, transfer-time, remote-host, file-size, filename, transfer-type, special-action-flag, direction, access-mode, username, service-name, authentication-method, and authenticated-user-id. The *transfer-time* is the time in seconds for the transfer. The *remote-host* is the address of the remote system making the connection, and *username* is the name of the user on that system. The *transfer-type* is either an *a* for ASCII or *b* for binary. The *access-mode* is the method by which the user logged in: *a* for anonymous, *g* for guest, and *r* for a real login (to another account on your system). The direction is either *o* for outgoing or *i* for incoming. The following example shows the file **mydoc** transferred by user **larisa**. The entry first shows the time, the FTP server host, and the size of the file along with the filename. The file transfer was binary, outgoing, and made by an anonymous user (**b o a**). The user's name and the service used, ftp, are also shown.

```
Sun Oct 29 11:15:40 2000 1 turtle.mytrek.com 55945
/var/ftp/pub/mydoc b o a larisa@turtle.mytrek.com ftp 0 * c
```

Professional FTP Daemon: ProFTPD

ProFTPD is based on the same design as the Apache Web server, implementing a similar simplified configuration structure and supporting such flexible features as virtual hosting. ProFTPD is an open source project made available under a GPL license. You can download the current version from its Web sites at **www.proftpd.net** and **www.proftpd.org.** There you will also find detailed documentation including FAQs, user manuals, and sample configurations. Check the site for new releases and updates.

RPM packages are available for many distributions, including Red Hat, and from **www.proftpd.net**. Unlike other FTP daemons, you do not need to set up special subdirectories of system files in the FTP home directory. No special **bin** or **etc** files are needed. You can also set up ProFTPD to alternate automatically between xinetd startups or as a standalone server constantly running, depending on the system load.

ProFTPD's tools operate in the same way as the wu-ftpd tools. **ftpshut** shuts down the system at specified times with warnings. With ProFTPD, you can shut down a virtual host while the main server continues to run. **ftpwho** displays a list of all remote users currently connected, broken down according to virtual hosts and servers. **ftpcount** shows the number of current connections by server and virtual hosts. See the previous section on FTP tools for more information.

install and startup

If you install ProFTPD using distribution RPM packages such as the one for Red Hat, the required configuration entries are made in your **proftpd.conf** files. If you installed from compiled source code, you may have to modify the entries in the default **proftpd.conf** file provided. Make sure the FTP user and group specified in the **proftpd.conf** file actually exist.

You can download ProFTPD from the ProFTPD Web site at **www.proftpd.net**. The RPM package version will contain three packages: a core application, a standalone version, and an inetd version that will run on xinetd. Download and install the core package first. Then, depending on whether you want to run ProFTPD as a standalone or inetd process, install either the inetd or the standalone package.

```
proftpd-core-1.2.0pre10-1.i686.rpm
proftpd-inetd-1.2.0pre10-1.i686.rpm
proftpd-standalone-1.2.0pre10-1.i686.rpm
```

You can run ProFTPD either as a standalone process or from xinetd. Make sure the appropriate entry is made in the ServerType directive in your **proftpd.conf** file. The standalone RPM package will install **proftpd** to run as a standalone server, setting the ServerType to standalone. **proftpd** options are listed in Table 20-3. On Red Hat systems, a startup script named **proftpd** is placed in the **/etc/rc.d/inet.d** directory that starts up the daemon when you boot your system. A standalone process is continually running. You can start, stop, and restart the server using the **`service`** command, as shown here:

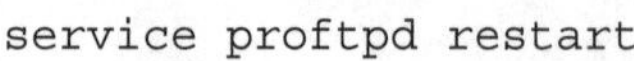

```
service proftpd restart
```

Option	Description
-h,--help	Uses description, including options.
-n,--nodaemon	Runs the **proftpd** process in standalone mode (must also specify standalone as ServerType in the configuration file).
-v,--version	Displays ProFTPD version number.
-d,--debug *debuglevel*	Sets ProFTPD's internal debug level (1–5).
-c,--config *config-file*	Specifies alternate configuration file.
-p,--persistent 0|1	Disables (0) or enables (1) the default persistent password support, which is determined at configure time for each platform.
-l,--list	Lists all modules compiled into **proftpd**.

Table 20-3. *ProFTPD Daemon Startup Options*

To set the runlevels at which it will start automatically, you can use **chkconfig**, Sys V Runlevel Editor, or Sys V Init Editor tools. The following command sets **proftpd** to run automatically from runlevels 3 and 5:

```
chkconfig--level 35 proftpd on
```

The following command would disable **proftpd**:

```
chkconfig--del proftpd
```

If you want to run **proftpd** as an **xinetd** process, you first must change the ServerType to inetd and disable the **proftpd** startup script in the **/etc/rc.d/inet.d** directory. To run ProFTPD from **xinetd**, make sure to create an appropriate file for it in the **/etc/xinetd.d directory**. Currently, the **proftpd** inetd RPM package implements an **in.proftpd** link to the **proftpd** daemon. Use this link to invoke ProFTPD in the ProFTPD **xinetd** file. A simple ProFTPD **xinetd** file, named **proftpd**, would look like this:

```
service proftp
{
        socket_type          = stream
        wait                 = no
        user                 = root
        server               = /usr/sbin/in.proftpd
        disable              = no
}
```

Use the **chkconfig** command with the **off** and **on** arguments to disable or enable **proftpd** running under **xinetd**.

```
chkconfig proftpd on
```

proftpd.config and .ftpaccess

ProFTPD uses only one configuration file, named **proftpd.conf**, located in the **/etc** directory. Configuration entries take the form of directives. This format is purposely modeled on Apache configuration directives. With the directives, you can enter basic configuration information, such as your server name, or perform more complex operations, such as implementing virtual FTP hosts. The design is flexible enough to enable you to define configuration features for particular directories, users, or groups.

To configure a particular directory, you can use an **.ftpaccess** file with configuration options placed within that directory. These **.ftpaccess** options take precedence over those in the **proftpd.conf** directory. **.fptaccess** files are designed to operate like **.htaccess** files in the Apache Web server that configures particular Web site directories.

You can find a complete listing of ProFTPD configuration parameters at the ProFTPD Web site (**www.proftpd.net**) and in the ProFTPD documentation installed in **/usr/doc** as part of the ProFTPD software package. Several of the more commonly used parameters are listed in Table 20-4. When creating a new configuration, you should make a copy of the **proftpd.conf** configuration file and modify it. Then you can test its syntax using the **proftpd** command with the **-c** option and the name of the file.

```
proftpd -c newfile.conf
```

Directive	Description
AccessGrantMsg *message*	Response message sent to an FTP client indicating the user has logged in or anonymous access has been granted. The magic cookie **'%u'** is replaced with the username specified by the client. Default: Dependent on login type Context: server config, <VirtualHost>, <Anonymous>, <Global>
Allow ["from"] "all"|"none"|*host*|*network* [,*host*|*network*[,...]]	Used inside a <Limit> context to specify explicitly which hosts and/or networks have access to the commands or operations being limited. Used with Order and Deny to create access control rules. Default: Allow from all Context: <Limit>
AllowAll	Allows access to a <Directory>, <Anonymous> or <Limit> block Default: Default is to implicitly AllowAll, but not explicitly Context: <Directory>, <Anonymous>, <Limit>, .ftpaccess
AllowFilter *regular-expression*	Allows the configuration of a regular expression that must be matched for all commands sent to ProFTPD. Default: None Context: server config, <VirtualHost>, <Anonymous>, <Global>
AllowForeignAddress on|off	Allows clients to transmit foreign data connection addresses that do not match the client's address. Default: AllowForeignAddress off Context: server config, <VirtualHost>, <Anonymous>, <Global>

Table 20-4. *ProFTPD Configuration Directives, proftpd.conf*

Directive	Description
`AllowGroup` *`group-expression`*	List of groups allowed in a Limit block. Default: None Context: <Limit>
`AllowUser` *`user-expression`*	Users allowed access. Default: None Context: <Limit>
`AnonRequirePassword` *`on`*|*`off`*	Requires anonymous logins to enter a valid password that must match the password of the user that the anonymous daemon runs as. This is used to create guest accounts that function like anonymous logins but require a valid password. Default: AnonRequirePassword off Context: <Anonymous>
`<Anonymous` *`root-directory`*`>`	Creates an anonymous FTP login, terminated by a matching </Anonymous> directive. The root directory parameter is the directory **`proftpd`** first moves to and then **`chroot`** to, hiding the rest of the file system. Default: None Context: server config,<VirtualHost>
`AuthGroupFile` *`path`*	Alternates group's file with the same format as the system **/etc/group** file. Default: None Context: server config, <VirtualHost>, <Global>
`AuthUserFile` *`path`*	Alternates **passwd** file with the same format as the system **/etc/passwd** file. Default: None Context: server config,<VirtualHost>, <Global>
`Bind` *`address`*	Allows additional IP addresses to be bound to a main or VirtualHost configuration. Multiple Bind directives can be used to bind multiple addresses. Default: None Context: server config, <VirtualHost>
`DefaultRoot` *`directory`* `[group-expression]`	Default root directory assigned to user on login. The **`group-expression`** argument restricts the DefaultRoot directive to a group or set of groups. Default: DefaultRoot / Context: server config, <VirtualHost>, <Global>

Table 20-4. *ProFTPD Configuration Directives, proftpd.conf* (continued)

Directive	Description
`Deny ["from"] "all"|"none"|host|network [,host|network[,...]]`	List of hosts and networks explicitly denied access to a given <Limit> context block. **all** indicates all hosts are denied access, and **none** indicates no hosts are explicitly denied. Default: None Context: <Limit>
`DenyAll`	Denies access to a directory, anonymous FTP, or Limit block. Default: None Context: <Directory>, <Anonymous>, <Limit>, .ftpaccess
`DenyFilter` *regular-expression*	Specifies a regular expression, which must *not* match any command. Default: None Context: server config, <VirtualHost>, <Anonymous>, <Global>
`DenyUser` *user-expression*	Users denied access within a Limit block. Default: None Context: <Limit>
`<Directory` *pathname*`>`	Directory-specific configuration. Used to create a block of directives that apply to the specified directory and its subdirectories. Default: None Context: server config, <VirtualHost>, <Anonymous>, <Global>
`DisplayFirstChdir` *filename*	Specifies the text file displayed to a user the first time he or she changes into a given directory during an FTP session. Default: None Context: server config, <VirtualHost>, <Anonymous>, <Directory>, <Global>
`DisplayLogin` *filename*	Specifies the text file displayed to a user who logs in. Default: None Context: server config, <VirtualHost>, <Anonymous>, <Global>
`<Global>`	Global configuration block used to create a set of configuration directives applied universally to both the main server configuration and all VirtualHost configurations. Default: None Context: server config, <VirtualHost>

Table 20-4. *ProFTPD Configuration Directives, proftpd.conf* (continued)

Directive	Description
`<Limit` *command* | *command-group* `[command2 ..]>`	Access restrictions on FTP commands, within a given context. The **`command-group`** refers to groupings of commands as defined in the ProFTPD documentation. Default: None Context: server config, <VirtualHost>, <Directory>, <Anonymous>, <Global>, ftpaccess
`LsDefaultOptions` "*options* string"	Default options for directory listings (as in the **`ls`** command). Default: None Context: server config, <VirtualHost>, <Global>
`MaxClients` *number* | *none message*	Maximum number of connected clients allowed. The message specified is displayed when a client is refused connection. Default: MaxClients none Context: server config, <Anonymous>, <VirtualHost>, <Global>
`MaxLoginAttempts` *number*	Maximum number of times a client may attempt to log in to the server during a given connection. Default: MaxLoginAttempts 3 Context: server config, <VirtualHost>, <Global>
`Order` *allow,deny* | *deny,allow*	Configures the order that Allow and Deny directives are checked inside a <Limit> block. Default: Order allow,deny Context: <Limit>
`PersistentPasswd on` | `off`	When on, **proftpd**, during login, opens the system-wide **/etc/passwd**, **/etc/group** files, accessing them even during a **`chroot`** operation that changes the root directory. Default: Platform dependent Context: server config
`RequireValidShell` *on* | *off*	Allows or denies logins not listed in **/etc/shells**. By default, **proftpd** disallows logins if the user's default shell is not listed in **/etc/shells**. Default: RequireValidShell on Context: server config, <VirtualHost>, <Anonymous>, <Global>
`ScoreboardPath` *path*	Directory that holds **proftpd** runtime **Scoreboard** files. Default: ScoreboardPath /var/run Context: server config

Table 20-4. *ProFTPD Configuration Directives, proftpd.conf* (continued)

Directive	Description
`ServerAdmin` *`"admin-email-address"`*	E-mail address of the server or virtual host administrator. Default: ServerAdmin root@[ServerName] Context: server config, <VirtualHost>
`ServerType` *`type-identifier`*	The server daemon's operating mode, either inetd or standalone. Default: ServerType standalone Context: server config
`TimeoutIdle` *`seconds`*	Maximum number of seconds proftpd allows clients to stay connected without any activity. Default: TimeoutIdle 600 Context: server config
`Umask` *`octal-mask`*	Permissions applied to newly created file and directory within a given context. Default: None Context: server config, <Anonymous>, <VirtualHost>, <Directory>, <Global>, .ftpaccess
`User` *`userid`*	The user the **proftpd** daemon runs as. Default: None Context: server config, <VirtualHost>, <Anonymous>, <Global>
`UserAlias` *`login-user`* `userid`	Maps a login name used by a client to a user ID on the server. A client logging in as *login-user* is actually logged in as *user ID*. Often used inside an <Anonymous> block to allow specified *login-names* to perform an anonymous login. Default: None Context: server config, <VirtualHost>, <Anonymous>, <Global>
`<VirtualHost` *`address`*`>`	Configuration directives that apply to a particular hostname or IP address. Often used with virtual servers that run on the same physical machine. The block is terminated with a </VirtualHost> directive. By using the Port directive inside a VirtualHost block, it is possible to create a virtual server that uses the same address as the master server, but that listens on a separate TCP port. Default: None Context: server config

Table 20-4. *ProFTPD Configuration Directives, proftpd.conf* (continued)

Different kinds of directives exist. Many set values, such as MaxClients, which set the maximum number of clients, or NameServer, which sets the name of the FTP server. Others create blocks that can hold directives that apply to specific FTP server components. Block directives are entered in pairs: a beginning directive and a terminating directive. The terminating directive defines the end of the block and consists of the same name, beginning with a slash. Block directives take an argument that specifies the particular object to which the directives will apply. For the Directory block directive, you must specify a directory name to which it will apply. The <Directory *mydir*> block directive creates a block whose directives within it apply to the *mydir* directory. The block is terminated by a </Directory> directive. <Anonymous *ftp-dir*> configures the anonymous service for your FTP server. You need to specify the directory on your system used for your anonymous FTP service, such as **/var/ftp**. The block is terminated with the </Anonymous> directive. The <VirtualHost *hostaddress*> block directive is used to configure a specific virtual FTP server and must include the IP or the domain name address used for that server. </VirtualHost> is its terminating directive. Any Directives you place within this block are applied to that virtual FTP server. The <Limit *permission*> directive specifies the kind of access you want to limit. It takes as its argument one of several keywords indicating the kind of permission to be controlled: **WRITE** for write access, **READ** for read access, **STOR** for transfer access (uploading), and **LOGIN** to control user login.

A sample of the standard **proftpd.conf** file installed as part of the ProFTPD software package is shown here. Notice the default ServerType is standalone. If you want to use xinetd to run your server, you must change this entry to inetd. Detailed examples of **proftpd.conf** files, showing various anonymous FTP and virtual host configurations, can be found with the ProFTPD documentation, located in **/usr/doc**, and on the ProFPTD Web site at **www.proftpd.net**.

```
# This is a basic ProFTPD configuration file (rename it to
# 'proftpd.conf' for actual use).  It establishes a single server
# and a single anonymous login.  It assumes that you have a user/group
# "nobody" and "ftp" for normal operation and anon.

ServerName          "ProFTPD Default Installation"
ServerType          standalone
DefaultServer          on

# Port 21 is the standard FTP port.
Port            21
Umask         022
MaxInstances         30

# Set the user and group that the server normally runs at.
User            nobody
Group         nobody
```

```
# Normally, we want files to be overwriteable.
<Directory /*>
     AllowOverwrite      on
</Directory>

# A basic anonymous configuration, with one incoming directory.
<Anonymous ~ftp>
     User              ftp
  Group              ftp
  RequireValidShell       off
  MaxClients          10
  # We want clients to be able to login with "anonymous" as well as "ftp"
  UserAlias           anonymous ftp
  # We want 'welcome.msg' displayed at login, and '.message' displayed
  # in each newly chdired directory.
  DisplayLogin          welcome.msg
  DisplayFirstChdir       .message

  # Limit WRITE everywhere in the anonymous chroot except incoming
  <Directory *>
     <Limit WRITE>
        DenyAll
     </Limit>
  </Directory>

  <Directory incoming>
     <Limit WRITE>
           AllowAll
     </Limit>
     <Limit READ>
           DenyAll
     </Limit>
  </Directory>

</Anonymous>
```

Anonymous Access

You use the Anonymous configuration directive to create an anonymous configuration block in which you can place directives that configure your anonymous FTP service. The directive includes the directory on your system used for the anonymous FTP service. The ProFTPD daemon executes a **`chroot`** operation on this directory, making it the root directory for the remote user accessing the service. By default, anonymous logins are supported, expecting users to enter their e-mail address as a password. You can modify an anonymous configuration to construct more controlled anonymous services, such as guest logins and required passwords.

For ProFTPD, your anonymous FTP directory does not require any system files. Before ProFTPD executes a **chroot** *operation, hiding the rest of the system from the directory, it accesses and keeps open any needed system files outside the directory.*

The following example shows a standard anonymous FTP configuration. The initial Anonymous directive specifies **/var/ftp** as the anonymous FTP home directory. The User directive specifies the user that the Anonymous FTP daemon will run as, and Group indicates its group. In both cases, FTP, the standard username, is used on most systems for anonymous FTP. A Directory directive with the * file matching character then defines a Directory block that applies to all directories and files in **/var/ftp**. The * symbol matches on all filenames and directories. Within the Directory directive is a Limit directive that you use to place controls on a directory. The directive takes several arguments including **READ** for read access and **WRITE** for write access. In this example, the Limit directive places restrictions on the write capabilities of users. Within the Limit directive, the DenyAll directive denies write permission, preventing users from creating or deleting files and effectively giving them only read access. A second Directory directive creates an exception to this rule for the incoming directory. An incoming directory is usually set up on FTP sites to let users upload files. For this directory, the first Limit directive prevents both **READ** and **WRITE** access by users with its DenyAll directive, effectively preventing users from deleting or reading files here. The second Limit directive lets users upload files, however, permitting transfers only (**STOR**) with the AllowAll directive.

One important directive for anonymous FTP configurations is the RequireValidShell. By default, the FTP daemon first checks to see if the remote user is attempting to log in using a valid shell, such as the BASH shell or the C shell. The FTP daemon obtains the list of valid shells from the **/etc/shells** file. If the remote user does not have a valid shell, a connection is denied. You can turn off the check using the RequireValidShell directive and the **off** option. The remote user can then log in using any kind of shell.

```
<Anonymous /var/ftp>
    User ftp
    Group ftp
    UserAlias anonymous ftp
    RequireValidShell off
 <Directory *>
       <Limit WRITE>
               DenyAll
       </Limit>
    </Directory>
     # The only command allowed in incoming is STOR
     # (transfer file from client to server)
    <Directory incoming>
```

SERVERS

```
            <Limit READ WRITE>
                DenyAll
            </Limit>
            <Limit STOR>
                AllowAll
            </Limit>
        </Directory>
    </Anonymous>
```

Recall that FTP was originally designed to let a remote user connect to an account of his or her own on the system. Users can log in to different accounts on your system using the FTP service. Anonymous users are restricted to the anonymous user account. However, you can create other users and their home directories that also function as anonymous FTP accounts with the same restrictions. Such accounts are known as *guest accounts.* Remote users are required to know the username and, usually, the password. Once connected, they only have read access to that account's files; the rest of the file system is hidden from them. In effect, you are creating a separate anonymous FTP site at the same location with more restricted access.

To create a guest account, first create a user and the home directory for it. You then create an Anonymous block in the **proftpd.conf** file for that account. The Anonymous directive includes the home directory of the guest user you create. You can specify this directory with a ~ for the path and the directory name, usually the same as the username. Within the Anonymous block, you use the User and Group directives to specify the user and group name for the user account. Set the AnonRequirePassword directive to **on** if you want remote users to provide a password. A UserAlias directive defines aliases for the username. A remote user can use either the alias or the original username to log in. You then enter the remaining directives for controlling access to the files and directories in the account's home directory. An example showing the initial directives is listed here. The User directive specifies the user as **myproject**. The home directory is **~myproject**, which usually evaluates to **/var/myproject**. The UserAlias lets remote users log in either with the name **myproject** or **mydesert**.

```
<Anonymous ~myproject>
    User myproject
    Group other
    UserAlias mydesert myproject
    AnonRequirePassword on
    <Directory *>
```

You could just as easily create an account that requires no password, letting users enter in their e-mail addresses instead. The following example configures an anonymous user named **mypics**. A password isn't required and neither is a valid shell. The remote user still needs to know the username, in this case **mypics**.

```
<Anonymous /var/mypics>
    AnonRequirePassword off
    User mypics
    Group nobody
    RequireValidShell off
    <Directory *>
```

The following example provides a more generic kind of guest login. The username is **guest** with the home directory located at **~guest**. Remote users are required to know the password for the guest account. The first Limit directive lets all users log in. The second Limit directive allows write access from users on a specific network, as indicated by the network IP address, and denies write access by any others.

```
<Anonymous ~guest>
  User                guest
  Group                nobody
  AnonRequirePassword      on

  <Limit LOGIN>
        AllowAll
  </Limit>

  # Deny write access from all except trusted hosts.
  <Limit WRITE>
        Order          allow,deny
        Allow          from 10.0.0.
        Deny          from all
  </Limit>

</Anonymous>
```

Virtual FTP Servers

The ProFTPD daemon can manage more than one FTP site at once. Using a VirtualHost directive in the **proftpd.conf** file, you can create an independent set of directives that configure a separate FTP server. The VirtualHost directive is usually used to configure virtual servers as FTP sites. You can configure your system to support more than one IP address. The extra IP addresses can be used for virtual servers, not independent machines. You can use such an extra IP address to set up a virtual FTP server, giving you another FTP site on the same system. This added server would use the extra IP address as its own. Remote users could access it using that IP address, instead of the system's main IP address. Because such an FTP server is not running independently on a separate machine but is, instead, on the same machine, it is known as a *virtual FTP server* or *virtual host*. This feature lets you run what appear to others as several different FTP servers on one machine. When a remote user uses the virtual FTP server's IP address to access it, the ProFTPD daemon detects that request and operates as the FTP service for that site. ProFTPD can handle a great many virtual FTP sites at the same time on a single machine.

Note *Given its configuration capabilities, you can also tailor any of the virtual FTP sites to specific roles, such as a guest site, an anonymous site for a particular group, or an anonymous site for a particular user.*

You configure a virtual FTP server by entering a <VirtualHost> directive for it in your **proftpd.conf** file. Such an entry begins with the VirtualHost directive and the IP address, and ends with a terminating VirtualHost directive, </VirtualHost>. Any directives placed within these are applied to the virtual host. For anonymous or guest sites, add Anonymous and Guest directives. You can even add Directory directives for specific directories. With the Port directive on a standalone configuration, you can create a virtual host that operates on the same system but connects on a different port.

```
<VirtualHost 10.0.0.1>
      ServerName "My virtual FTP server"
</VirtualHost>
```

Xinetd and standalone configurations handle virtual hosts differently. Xinetd detects a request for a virtual host, and then hands it off to an FTP daemon. The FTP daemon then examines the address and port specified in the request and processes the request for the appropriate virtual host. In the standalone configuration, the FTP daemon continually listens for requests on all specified ports and generates child processes to handle ones for different virtual hosts as they come in. In the standalone configuration, ProFTPD can support a great many virtual hosts at the same time.

The following example shows a sample configuration of a virtual FTP host. The VirtualHost directives use domain name addresses for its arguments. When a domain name address is used, it must be associated with an IP address in the network's domain name server. The IP address, in turn, has to reference the machine on which the ProFTPD daemon is running. On the **ftp.mypics.com** virtual FTP server, an anonymous guest account named **robpics** is configured that requires a password to log in. An anonymous FTP account is also configured that uses the home directory **/var/ftp/virtual/pics**.

```
<VirtualHost ftp.mypics.com>

  ServerName          "Mypics FTP Server"
  MaxClients          10
  MaxLoginAttempts       1
  DeferWelcome          on
  <Anonymous ~robpics>
    User          robpics
    Group          robpics
    AnonRequirePassword       on

  <Anonymous /var/ftp/virtual/pics>
    User          ftp
    Group          ftp
    UserAlias          anonymous ftp
  </Anonymous>
</VirtualHost>
```

Chapter 21

Web Servers: Apache

Linux distributions provide several Web servers for use on your system. The primary Web server is normally Apache, which has almost become the standard Web server for Linux. It is a very powerful, stable, and fairly easy to configure system. Other Web servers are also available, such as Tux. Tux is smaller, but very fast, and can handle Web data that does not change with great efficiency. Most Linux distributions provide default configurations for the Web servers, making them usable as soon as they are installed.

Other Web servers available for Linux include the Red Hat Secure Server (**www.redhat.com**), Apache-SSL (**www.apache-ssl.org**), Stronghold (**www.c2.net**), and Netscape Enterprise Server (**home.netscape.com**). Apache-SSL is an encrypting Web server based on Apache and OpenSSL (**www.openssl.org**). Stronghold is a commercial version of the Apache Web server featuring improved security and administration tools. You can also use the original NCSA Web server, though it is no longer supported (**hoohoo.ncsa.uiuc.edu**). AOLserver is America Online's Web server that is now available under the GPL license (**www.aolserver.com**).

There are also private cryptographic products available only with licensing fees. Instead of obtaining the licensing directly, you can simply buy a commercial version of Apache that includes such licensing as Stronghold and Raven (**www.covalent.net**). Formerly this kind of restriction only applied to the use of RSA technology in the United States, where it was once patented. The RSA patent has since expired and is now available for use in freely distributed products like OpenSSL.

Tux

Tux is a static content Web server designed to be run very fast from within the Linux kernel. In effect, it runs in kernel space, making response times much faster than standard user-space Web servers like Apache. As a kernel-space server, Tux can handle static content such as images very efficiently. At the same time it can coordinate with a user-space Web server, like Apache, to provide the dynamic content, like CGI programs. Tux can even make use of a cache to hold previously generated dynamic content, using it as if it were static. The ability to coordinate with a user-space Web server lets you use Tux as your primary Web server. Anything that Tux cannot handle, it will pass off to the user-space Web server.

Note *Tux is freely distributed under the GNU Public License and is included with many distributions.*

The Tux configuration file is located in **/proc/sys/net/tux**. Here you enter parameters such as **`serverport`**, **`max_doc_size`**, and **`logfile`** (check the Tux reference manual at **www.redhat.com/support/manuals** for a detailed listing). Defaults are already entered. **`serverport`**, **`clientport`**, and **`documentroot`** are required parameters that must be set. **`serverport`** is the port Tux will use—80 if it is the primary Web server. **`clientport`** is the port used by the user-space Web server Tux coordinates with, like Apache. `documentroot` specifies the root directory for your Web documents (**/var/www/html** on Mandrake and Red Hat).

Ideally, Tux is run as the primary Web server and Apache as the secondary Web server. To configure Apache to run with Tux, the port entry in the Apache **httpd.conf** file needs to be changed from 80 to 8080:

```
Port 8080
```

You can start, stop, and restart the server with the **/etc/rd.d/init.d/tux** command. Several parameters like `DOCROOT` can be specified as arguments to this Tux command. You can enter them in the **/etc/sysconfig/tux** file.

*You can also run Tux as an FTP server. In the **/proc/sys/net/tux** directory, you change the contents of the file **serverport** to 21, **application_protocol** to 1, and **nonagle** to 0, and then restart Tux. Use the `generatetuxlist` command in the document root directory to generate FTP directory listings.*

Apache Web Server

The Apache Web server is a full-featured free HTTP (Web) server developed and maintained by the Apache Server Project. The aim of the project is to provide a reliable, efficient, and easily extensible Web server, with free open source code. The server software includes the server daemon, configuration files, management tools, and documentation. The Apache Server Project is maintained by a core group of volunteer programmers and supported by a great many contributors worldwide. The Apache Server Project is one of several projects currently supported by the Apache Software Foundation (formerly known as the Apache Group). This nonprofit organization provides financial, legal, and organizational support for various Apache open source software projects, including the Apache HTTPD Server, Java Apache, Jakarta, and XML-Apache. The Web site for the Apache Software Foundation is at **www.apache.org**. Table 21-1 lists various Apache-related Web sites.

Apache was originally based on the NCSA Web server developed at the National Center for Supercomputing Applications, University of Illinois, Urbana-Champaign. Apache has since emerged as a server in its own right and has become one of the most popular Web servers in use. Although originally developed for Linux and Unix systems, Apache has become a cross-platform application with Windows and OS/2 versions. Apache provides online support and documentation for its Web server at **httpd.apache.org**. An HTML-based manual is also provided with the server installation. You can use the Apache Configuration Tool to help configure your Apache server easily. It operates on any X Window System window manager, including Gnome and KDE. In addition, you

Web Site	Description
www.apache.org	Apache Software Foundation
httpd.apache.org	Apache HTTP Server Project
java.apache.org	Java Apache Project
jakarta.apache.org	Jakarta Apache Project
gui.apache.org	Apache GUI Project
www.comanche.org	Comanche (Configuration Manager for Apache)
www.apache-ssl.org	Apache-SSL server
www.openssl.org	OpenSSL project (Secure Socket Layer)
www.modssl.org	The SSL module (mod_ssl) project to add SSL encryption to an Apache Web server
www.php.net	PHP Hypertext PreProcessor, embedded Web page programming language

Table 21-1. *Apache-Related Web Sites*

can use the Comanche configuration tool. Webmin and Linuxconf also provide Apache configuration support.

Java: Jakarta and Apache-Java

The Java Apache Project develops open source Java software and has its Web site located at **java.apache.org**. Currently, the Java Apache Project supports numerous projects, including JServ, JSSI, JMeter, and mod_java, among others. The Apache JServ Project has developed a Java servlet engine compliant with the JavaSoft Java Servlet API's 2.0 specification. The Apache JSSI project has developed a Java servlet for dynamic servlet output from HTML files through the `<SERVLET>` tag as designated by the JavaSoft Java Web Server. JMeter is a Java desktop application to test performance of server resources, such as servlets and CGI scripts. The mod_java project has developed a mod_java extension module for Apache Web servers that allows Apache modules to be written in Java instead of in C. It functions much like mod_perl (which allows modules to be written in Perl).

Jakarta is an Apache project to develop server-side Java capabilities on Linux. Jakarta's main product, called Tomcat, is an open source implementation of the Java Servlet 2.2 and JavaServer Pages 1.1 specifications. Tomcat is designed for use in Apache servers. The Jakarta Web site is at **jakarta.apache.org**.

Linux Distribution Apache Installations

Your Linux distribution will normally provide you with the option of installing the Apache Web server during your initial installation of your Linux system. All the necessary directories and configuration files are automatically generated for you. Then, whenever you run Linux, your system is already a fully functional Web site. Every time you start your system, the Web server will also start up, running continuously. On most distributions, the directory reserved for your Web site data files is **/var/www/html**. Place your Web pages in this directory or in any subdirectories. Your system is already configured to operate as a Web server. All you need to do is perform any needed network server configurations, and then designate the files and directories open to remote users. You needn't do anything else. Once your Web site is connected to a network, remote users can access it.

The Web server normally sets up your Web site in the **/var/www** directory. It also sets up several directories for managing the site. The **/var/www/cgi-bin** directory holds the CGI scripts, and **/var/www/html/manual** holds the Apache manual in HTML format. You can use your browser to examine it. Your Web pages are to be placed in the **/var/www/html** directory. Place your Web site home page there. Your configuration files are located in a different directory, **/etc/httpd/conf**. Table 21-2 lists the various Apache Web server directories and configuration files.

To upgrade your Apache server, either use your distribution's upgrade tool (such as those included with Red Hat, SuSE, or Mandrake) or look for recent Apache update files at your Linux distribution's FTP sites. For binary versions for an RPM supported distribution like Mandrake, Caldera, and Red Hat, you can download RPM packages containing the latest version of the Apache Web server, specially configured for your Linux distribution. Then use the **`rpm`** command with the **`-Uvh`** options to install the upgrade (the **`-U`** option specifies an upgrade option).

```
rpm -Uvh apache-1.3.12-20.i386.rpm
rpm -Uvh apache-docs-1.3.12-20.i386.rpm
```

Alternatively, you can download the source code version for the latest Apache Web server directly from Apache and compile it on your system. You must decompress the file and extract the archive. Many of the same directories are created, with added ones for the source code. The server package includes installation instructions for creating your server directories and compiling your software. Make sure the configuration files are set up and installed.

Web Site Directories	Description
/var/www	Directory for Apache Web site files on Mandrake, SuSE, and Red Hat systems.
/var/www/html	Web site Web files.
/var/www/cgi-bin	CGI program files.
/var/www/html/manual	Apache Web server manual.
Configuration Files	
.htaccess	Directory-based configuration files; an **.htaccess** file holds directives to control access to files within the directory in which it is located.
/etc/httpd/conf	Directory for Apache Web server configuration files.
/etc/httpd/conf/httpd.conf	Apache Web server configuration file.
Startup Scripts	
/etc/rc.d/init.d/httpd (/etc/rc.d/htppd on SuSE)	Startup script for Web server daemon.
/etc/rc.d/rc3.d/S85httpd	Link in runlevel 3 directory (**/etc/rc3.d**) to the **httpd** startup script in the **/etc/rc.d/init.d** directory.
Application Files	
/usr/sbin	Location of the Apache Web server program file and utilities.
/usr/share/doc/	Apache Web server documentation.
/var/log/http	Location of Apache log files.

Table 21-2. *Apache Web Server Files and Directories (RPM Installation)*

Note *If you are installing Apache from the source code, notice that versions of the configuration files ending with the extension **.conf-dist** are provided. You have to make copies of these configuration files with the same prefix, but only with the extension **.conf** to set up a default configuration. The Web server reads configuration information only from files with a **.conf** extension.*

Apache Web Server 2.0

Many distributions (including Red Hat 7.3) still use Apache version 1.3, which is described here. Apache recently released 2.0, which is designed to be less dependent on Linux/Unix systems. Most directives and features for Apache 1.3 still work on Apache 2.0. However, Apache 2.0 has introduced a new architecture that uses Multi-Processing Modules (MPM), which are designed to customize Apache to different operating systems. A Linux system would use the threaded MPM, whereas Windows would use the mpm_winnt MPM. To maintain compatibility with Apache 1.3 configurations, you would use the prefork MPM.

Apache 2.0 has adopted a much more modular architecture than 1.3. Many directives that once resided in the Apache core are now placed in respective modules and MPMs. With this modular design, several directives have been dropped, such as ServerType. Such directives deprecated in Apache 2.0 are noted in Table 21-3.

A selected MPM is usually integrated into Apache when it is compiled. Future Linux distributions of Apache should use the Linux/Unix default MPM, which is named "threaded."

Module	Description
mod_access	Access control based on client hostname or IP address
mod_actions	Executes CGI scripts based on media type or request method
mod_alias	Maps different parts of the host file system in the document tree; performs URL redirection
mod_asis	Sends files that contain their own HTTP headers
mod_auth	User authentication using text files
mod_auth_anon	Anonymous user access to authenticated areas
mod_auth_db	User authentication using Berkeley DB files
mod_auth_dbm	User authentication using DBM files
mod_auth_digest	MD5 authentication
mod_autoindex	Automatic directory listings

Table 21-3. *Apache Modules (Apache 2.0)*

Module	Description
mod_cern_meta	Support for HTTP header metafiles
mod_cgi	Invokes CGI scripts
mod_cgid	Invokes CGI scripts using an external daemon
mod_charset_lite	Configures character set translation
mod_dav	Distributed Authoring and Versioning, WebDAV HTTP extensions
mod_dir	Basic directory handling
mod_env	Passes environments to CGI scripts
mod_example	Demonstrates Apache API
mod_expires	Applies Expires: headers to resources
mod_ext_filter	Filters output with external programs
mod_file_cache	Caches files in memory for faster serving
mod_headers	Adds arbitrary HTTP headers to resources
mod_imap	Image-map file handler
mod_include	Server-parsed documents
mod_info	Server configuration information
mod_isapi	Windows ISAPI Extension support
mod_log_config	User-configurable logging replacement for mod_log_common
mod_mime	Determines document types using file extensions
mod_mime_magic	Determines document types using "magic numbers"
mod_negotiation	Content negotiation
mod_proxy	Caches proxy abilities
mod_rewrite	Powerful URI-to-filename mapping using regular expressions
mod_setenvif	Sets environment variables based on client information
mod_so	Support for loading modules at runtime

Table 21-3. *Apache Modules (Apache 2.0)* (continued)

Module	Description
mod_spelling	Automatically corrects minor typos in URLs
mod_status	Server status display
mod_userdir	User home directories
mod_unique_id	Generates unique request identifier for every request
mod_usertrack	User tracking using cookies (replacement for mod_cookies.c)
mod_vhost_alias	Support for dynamically configured mass virtual hosting

Table 21-3. *Apache Modules (Apache 2.0)* (continued)

Starting and Stopping the Web Server

On most systems, Apache is installed as a standalone server, continually running. As noted in Chapter 19, in the discussion of init scripts, your system automatically starts up the Web server daemon, invoking it whenever you start your system. On Mandrake, Red Hat, and Caldera systems, a startup script for the Web server called **httpd** is in the **/etc/rc.d/init.d** directory (**/etc/rc.d** on SuSE). Symbolic links through which this script is run are located in corresponding runlevel directories. You will usually find the **S85httpd** link to **/etc/rc.d/init.d/httpd** in the runlevel 3 and 5 directories, **/etc/rc.d/rc3.d** and **/etc/rc.d/rc5.d**. You can use the **chkconfig** command or the System V Init Editor to set the runlevels at which the httpd server will start, creating links in appropriate runlevel directories. The following command will set up the Web server (httpd) to start up at runlevels 3 and 5 (see Chapter 19 for more details on runlevels).

```
chkconfig—level 35 httpd on
```

On Mandrake and Red Hat, you can also use **service** command to start and stop the httpd server manually. This may be helpful when you are testing or modifying your server. The **httpd** script with the **start** option starts the server, the **stop** option stops it, and **restart** will restart it. Simply killing the Web process directly is not advisable.

```
service httpd restart
```

Apache also provides a control tool called **apachectl** (Apache control) for managing your Web server. With **apachectl**, you can start, stop, and restart the server from the command line. **apachectl** takes several arguments: **start** to start the server, **stop** to stop it, **restart** to shut down and restart the server, and **graceful** to shut down and restart gracefully. In addition, you can use **apachectl** to check the syntax of your configuration files with the **config** argument. You can also use **apachectl** as a system startup file for your server in the **/etc/rc.d** directory.

Remember, **httpd** is a script that calls the actual **httpd** daemon. You could call the daemon directly using its full pathname. This daemon has several options. The **-d** option enables you to specify a directory for the httpd program if it is different from the default directory. With the **-f** option, you can specify a configuration file different from **httpd.conf**. The **-v** option displays the version.

```
/usr/sbin/httpd -v
```

To check your Web server, start your Web browser and enter the Internet domain name address of your system. For the system **turtle.mytrek.com,** the user enters **http://turtle.mytrek.com**. This should display the home page you placed in your Web root directory. A simple way to do this is to use Lynx, the command line Web browser. Start Lynx, and type **g** to open a line where you can enter a URL for your own system. Lynx displays your Web site's home page. Be sure to place an **index.html** file in the **/var/www/html** directory first.

Once you have your server running, you can check its performance with the **ab** benchmarking tool, also provided by Apache. **ab** shows you how many requests at a time your server can handle. Options include **-v,** which enables you to control the level of detail displayed, **-n,** which specifies the number of requests to handle (default is 1), and **-t,** which specifies a time limit.

Currently there is no support for running Apache under xinetd. In Apache 2.0, such support is determined by choosing an MPM module designed to run on xinetd. Currently there are none.

Apache Configuration and Directives

Configuration directives are placed in the **httpd.conf** configuration file. A documented version of the **httpd.conf** configuration file is installed automatically in **/etc/httpd**. It is strongly recommended that you consult this file on your system. It contains detailed documentation and default entries for Apache directives.

Any of the directives in the main configuration files can be overridden on a per-directory basis using an **.htaccess** file located within a directory. Although originally designed only for access directives, the **.htaccess** file can also hold any resource directives, enabling you to tailor how Web pages are displayed in a particular directory. You can configure access to .**htaccess** files in the **httpd.conf** file.

Note *With Apache version 1.3.4, all configuration directives are placed in one file, the* ***httpd.conf*** *file. Older versions used two other files, the* ***srm.conf*** *and* ***access.conf*** *files. The* ***srm.conf*** *file handled document specifications, configuring file types and locations. The* ***access.conf*** *file was designed to hold directives that control access to Web site directories and files. Though you will still find these files on current Apache versions, they will be empty.*

Apache configuration operations take the form of directives entered into the Apache configuration files. With these directives, you can enter basic configuration information, such as your server name, or perform more complex operations, such as implementing virtual hosts. The design is flexible enough to enable you to define configuration features for particular directories and different virtual hosts. Apache has a variety of different directives performing operations as diverse as controlling directory access, assigning file icon formats, and creating log files. Most directives set values such as **DirectoryRoot**, which holds the root directory for the server's Web pages, or **Port**, which holds the port on the system that the server listens on for requests. Table 21-3 provides a listing of the more commonly used Apache directives. The syntax for a simple directive is shown here:

```
directive option option ...
```

Certain directives create blocks able to hold directives that apply to specific server components (also referred to as sectional directives). For example, the **Directory** directive is used to define a block within which you place directives that apply only to a particular directory. Block directives are entered in pairs: a beginning directive and a terminating directive. The terminating directive defines the end of the block and consists of the same name beginning with a slash. Block directives take an argument that specifies the particular object to which the directives apply. For the **Directory** block directive, you must specify a directory name to which it will apply. The **<Directory *mydir*>** block directive creates a block whose directives within it apply to the *mydir* directory. The block is terminated by a **</Directory>** directive. The **<VirtualHost *hostaddress*>** block directive is used to configure a specific virtual Web server and must include the IP or domain name address used for that server. **</VirtualHost>** is its terminating directive. Any directives you place within this block are applied to that virtual Web server. The **<Limit *method*>** directive specifies the kind of access method you want to limit, such as GET or POST. The access control directives located within the block list the controls you are placing on those methods. The syntax for a block directive is as follows:

```
<block-directive option ... >
 directive option ...
 directive option ...
</block-directive>
```

SERVERS

Usually, directives are placed in one of the main configuration files. **Directory** directives in those files can be used to configure a particular directory. However, Apache also makes use of directory-based configuration files. Any directory may have its own **.htaccess** file that holds directives to configure only that directory. If your site has many directories, or if any directories have special configuration needs, you can place their configuration directives in their **.htaccess** files, instead of filling the main configuration file with specific **Directory** directives for each one. You can control what directives in an **.htaccess** file take precedence over those in the main configuration files. If your site allows user- or client-controlled directories, you may want to carefully monitor or disable the use of **.htaccess** files in them. (It is possible for directives in an **.htaccess** file to override those in the standard configuration files unless disabled with **AllowOverride** directives.)

Much of the power and flexibility of the Apache Web server comes from its use of modules to extend its capabilities. Apache is implemented with a core set of directives. Modules can be created that hold definitions of other directives. They can be loaded into Apache, enabling you to use those directives for your server. A standard set of modules is included with the Apache distribution, though you can download others and even create your own. For example, the mod_autoindex module holds the directives for automatically indexing directories (as described in the following section). The mod_mime module holds the MIME type and handler directives. Modules are loaded with the **LoadModule** directive. You can find **LoadModule** directives in the **httpd.conf** configuration file for most of the standard modules.

```
LoadModule mime_module modules/mod_mime.so
```

The apxs application provided with the Apache package can be used to build Apache extension modules. With the apxs application, you can compile Apache module source code in C and create dynamically shared objects that can be loaded with the **LoadModule** directive. The apxs application requires that the mod_so module be part of your Apache application. It includes extensive options such as `-n` to specify the module name, `-a` to add an entry for it in the **httpd.conf** file, and `-i` to install the module on your Web server.

You can find a complete listing of Apache Web configuration directives at the Apache Web site, **httpd.apache.org**, and in the Apache manual located in your site's Web site root directory. On many systems, this is located in the manual subdirectory in the Web site default directory set up by the distribution (on Mandrake and Red Hat, this is **/var/www/manual**). Many of the more commonly used directives are listed in Table 21-4.

Server Configuration

Certain directives are used to configure your server's overall operations. These directives are placed in the **httpd.conf** configuration file. Some require pathnames, whereas others only need to be turned on or off with the keywords **on** and **off**. Apache provides a default **httpd.conf** configuration file. The **httpd.conf** file already contains these directives. Some are commented out with a preceding **#** symbol. You can activate a directive by removing its **#** sign. Many of the entries are preceded by comments explaining their purpose. The following is an example of the **ServerAdmin** directive used to set the address where users can send mail for administrative issues. You replace the **you@your.address** entry with the address you want to use to receive system administration mail. By default, this is set to **root@localhost**.

```
# ServerAdmin: Your address, where problems should be e-mailed.
ServerAdmin you@your.address
```

Some directives require specific information about your system. For example, **ServerName** holds the hostname for your Web server. Specifying a hostname is important to avoid unnecessary DNS lookup failures that can hang your server. Notice the entry is commented with a preceding **#**. Simply remove the **#** and type your Web server's hostname in place of **new.host.name**.

```
# ServerName allows you to set a hostname which is sent
# back to clients for your server if it's different than the
# one the program would get (i.e. use
# "www" instead of the host's real name).

#ServerName new.host.name
```

On Mandrake, SuSE, and Red Hat systems, entries have already been made for the standard Web server installation using **/var/www** as your Web site directory. You can tailor your Web site to your own needs by changing the appropriate directives. The **DocumentRoot** directive determines the home directory for your Web pages. The **ServerRoot** directive specifies where your Web server configuration, error, and log files are kept.

```
DocumentRoot /var/www/html
ServerRoot /etc/httpd
```

The **MaxClients** directive sets the maximum number of clients that can connect to your server at the same time.

```
MaxClients 150
```

Directory-Level Configuration: .htaccess and <Directory>

One of the most flexible aspects of Apache is its ability to configure individual directories. With the **Directory** directive, you can define a block of directives that apply only to a particular directory. Such a directive can be placed in the **httpd.conf** or **access.conf** configuration file. You can also use an .htaccess file within a particular directory to hold configuration directives. Those directives are then applied only to that directory. The name ".htaccess" is actually set with the **AccessFileName** directive. You can change this if you want.

```
AccessFileName .htaccess
```

A **Directory** block begins with a **<Directory** ***pathname*****>** directive, where *pathname* is the directory to be configured. The ending directive uses the same **<>** symbols, but with a slash preceding the word "Directory": **</Directory>**. Directives placed within this block apply only to the specified directory. The following example denies access to only the **mypics** directory by requests from **www.myvids.com**.

```
<Directory /var/www/html/mypics>
 Order Deny,Allow
 Deny from www.myvids.com
</Directory>
```

With the Options directive, you can enable certain features in a directory, such as the use of symbolic links, automatic indexing, execution of CGI scripts, and content negotiation. The default is the **All** option, which turns on all features except content negotiation (multiviews). The following example enables automatic indexing (**Indexes**), symbolic links (**FollowSymLinks**), and content negotiation (**Multiviews**).

```
Options Indexes FollowSymLinks Multiviews
```

Configurations made by directives in main configuration files or in upper-level directories are inherited by lower-level directories. Directives for a particular directory held in **.htaccess** files and **Directory** blocks can be allowed to override those configurations. This capability can be controlled by the **AllowOverride** directive. With the **`all`** argument, **.htaccess** files can override any previous configurations. The **`none`** argument disallows overrides, effectively disabling the **.htaccess** file. You can further control the override of specific groups of directives. **AuthConfig** enables use of authorization directives, **FileInfo** is for type directives, **Indexes** is for indexing directives, **Limit** is for access control directives, and **Options** is for the **options** directive.

```
AllowOverride all
```

Access Control

With access control directives, such as **allow** and **deny**, you can control access to your Web site by remote users and hosts. The **allow** directive followed by a list of hostnames restricts access to only those hosts. The **deny** directive with a list of hostnames denies access by those systems. The argument `all` applies the directive to all hosts. The **order** directive specifies in what order the access control directives are to be applied. Other access control directives, such as **require**, can establish authentication controls, requiring users to log in. The access control directives can be used globally to control access to the entire site or placed within **Directory** directives to control access to individual directives. In the following example, all users are allowed access:

```
order allow,deny
allow from all
```

You can further qualify access control directives by limiting them to certain HTML access methods. HTML access methods are ways a browser interacts with your Web site. For example, a browser could get information from a page (GET) or send information through it (POST). You can control such access methods using the **<Limit>** directive. **Limit** takes as its argument a list of access methods to be controlled. The directive then pairs with a **</Limit>** directive to define a **Limit** block within which you can place access control directives. These directives only apply to the specified access methods. You can place such **Limit** blocks with a **Directory** block to set up controls of access methods for a specific directory. The following **Directory** block in the **/etc/config/httpd.conf** file controls access methods for your Web site's home directory, **/var/www/html**.

```
# This should be changed to whatever you set DocumentRoot to.
<Directory /var/www/html>
Options Indexes FollowSymLinks
AllowOverride All
<Limit GET>
order allow,deny
allow from all
</Limit>
</Directory>
```

Controls are inherited from upper-level directories to lower-level ones. If you want to control access strictly on a per-directory basis to your entire Web site, you can use the following entry to deny access to all users. Then, in individual directories, you can allow access to certain users, groups, or hosts.

```
<Directory /var/www/html>
 Order Deny,Allow
 Deny from All
 </Directory>
```

URL Pathnames

Certain directives can modify or complete pathname segments of a URL used to access your site. The pathname segment of the URL specifies a particular directory or Web page on your site. Directives enable you to alias or redirect pathnames, as well as to select a default Web page. With the **Alias** directive, you can let users access resources located in other parts of your system, on other file systems, or on other Web sites. An alias can use a URL for sites on the Internet, instead of a pathname for a directory on your system. With the **Redirect** directive, you can redirect a user to another site.

```
Alias /mytrain /home/dylan/trainproj
Redirect /mycars http://www.myautos.com/mycars
```

If Apache is given only a directory to access, rather than a specific Web page, it looks for an index Web page located in that directory and displays it. The possible names for a default Web page are listed by the **DirectoryIndex** directive. The name usually used is **index.html**, but you can add others. The standard names are shown here. When Apache is given only a Web directory to access, it looks for and displays the **index.html** Web page located in it.

```
DirectoryIndex index.html index.shtml index.cgi
```

Apache also lets a user maintain Web pages located in a special subdirectory in the user's home directory, rather than in the main Web site directory. Using a ~ followed by the username accesses this directory. The name of this directory is specified with the **UserDir** directive. The default name is **public_html**, as shown here. The site **turtle.mytrek.com/~dylan** accesses the directory **turtle.mytrek.com/home/dylan/public_html** on the host **turtle.mytrek.com**.

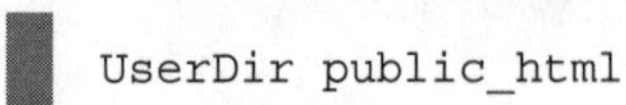

```
UserDir public_html
```

MIME Types

When a browser accesses Web pages on a Web site, it is often accessing many different kinds of objects, including HTML files, picture or sound files, and script files. To display these objects correctly, the browser must have some indication of what kind of objects they are. A JPEG picture file is handled differently from a simple text file. The server provides this type information in the form of MIME types (see Chapter 13). MIME types are the same types used for sending attached files through Internet mailers, such as Pine. Each kind of object is associated with a given MIME type. Provided with the MIME type, the browser can correctly handle and display the object.

The MIME protocol associates a certain type with files of a given extension. For example, files with a **.jpg** extension would have the MIME type image/jpeg. The **TypesConfig** directive holds the location of the **mime.types** file, which lists all the MIME types and their associated file extensions. **DefaultType** is the default MIME type for any file whose type cannot be determined. **AddType** enables you to modify the **mime.type** types list without editing the MIME file.

```
TypesConfig /etc/mime.types
DefaultType text/plain
```

Other type directives are used to specify actions to be taken on certain documents. **AddEncoding** lets browsers decompress compressed files on the fly. **AddHandler** maps file extensions to actions, and **AddLanguage** enables you to specify the language for a document. The following example marks filenames with the **.gz** extension as gzip-encoded files and files with the **.fr** extension as French language files:

```
AddEncoding x-gzip gz
AddLanguage fr .fr
```

A Web server can display and execute many different types of files and programs. Not all Web browsers are able to display all those files, though. Older browsers are the most limited. Some browsers, such as Lynx, are not designed to display even simple graphics. To allow a Web browser to display a page, the server negotiates with it to determine the type of files it can handle. To enable such negotiation, you need to enable the multiviews option.

```
Option multiviews
```

CGI Files

Common Gateway Interface (CGI) files are programs that can be executed by Web browsers accessing your site. CGI files are usually initiated by Web pages that execute the program as part of the content they display. Traditionally, CGI programs were placed in a directory called **cgi-bin** and could only be executed if they resided in such a special directory. Usually, only one **cgi-bin** directory exists per Web site. Distributions will normally set up a **cgi-bin** directory in the default Web server directory (**/var/www/cgi-bin** on Mandrake and Red Hat). Here, you place any CGI programs that can be executed on your Web site. The **ScriptAlias** directive specifies an alias for your **cgi-bin** directory. Any Web pages or browsers can use the alias to reference this directory.

```
ScriptAlias /cgi-bin/ /var/www/cgi-bin/
```

If you want to execute CGI programs that reside anywhere on your Web site, you can specify that files with a **.cgi** extension are treated as executable CGI programs. You do this with the **AddHandler** directive. This directive applies certain handlers to files of a given type. The handler directive to do this is included in the default **httpd.conf** file, provided with the Apache source code files, though commented out. You can remove the comment symbol (#) to enable it.

```
AddHandler cgi-script cgi
```

Automatic Directory Indexing

When given a URL for a directory instead of an HTML file, and when no default Web page is in the directory, Apache creates a page on the fly and displays it. This is usually only a listing of the different files in the directory. In effect, Apache indexes the items in the directory for you. You can set several options for generating and displaying such an index. If **FancyIndexing** is turned on, Web page items are displayed with icons and column headers that can be used to sort the listing.

```
FancyIndexing on
```

Icon directives tell Apache what icon to display for a certain type of file. The **AddIconByType** and **AddIconByEncoding** directives use MIME-type information to determine the file's type and then associate the specified image with it. **AddIcon** uses the file's extension to determine its type. In the next example, the **text.gif** image is displayed for text files with the extension **.txt**. You can also use **AddIcon** to associate an image with a particular file. The **DefaultIcon** directive specifies the image used for files of undetermined type.

```
AddIcon /icons/text.gif .txt
DefaultIcon /icons/unknown.gif
AddIconByType (VID,/icons/movie.gif) video/*
```

With the **AddDescription** directive, you can add a short descriptive phrase to the filename entry. The description can be applied to an individual file or to filenames of a certain pattern.

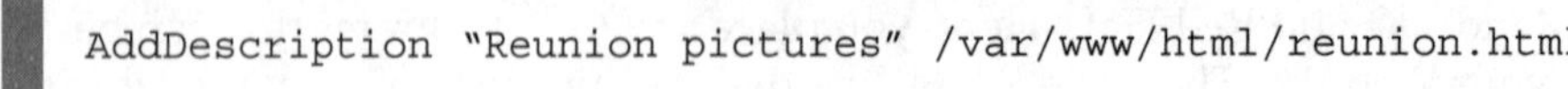

```
AddDescription "Reunion pictures" /var/www/html/reunion.html
```

Within a directory, you can place special files that can be used to display certain text both before and after the generated listing. The **HeaderName** directive is used to set the name of the file whose text is inserted before the listing. The **ReadmeName** directive sets the name of the file whose text is placed at the end of the listing. You can use these directives in an **.htaccess** file or a **<Directory>** block to select particular files within a directory. The **ReadmeName** directive is usually set to readme, and **HeaderName** to HEADER. In that case, Apache searches for files named **HEADER** and **README** in the directory.

```
HeaderName HEADER
ReadmeName README
```

With the **IndexOptions** directive, you can set different options for displaying a generated index. Options exist for setting the height and width of icons and filenames. The **IconsAreLinks** option makes icons part of filename anchors. The **ScanHTMLTitles** option reads the titles in HTML documents and uses those to display entries in the index listing instead of filenames. Various options exist for suppressing different index display features such as sorting, descriptions, and header/readme inserts. You can set options for individual directories using a **Directory** block or an **.htaccess** file. Normally, options set in higher-level directories are inherited by lower-level ones. If you use an **IndexOption** directive to set any new option, however, all previously inherited options are cleared. If you want to keep the inherited options, you can set options using the plus (**+**) or minus (**-**) symbols. These add or remove options. If you were also to set an option without the **+** or **-** symbols, though, all inherited options would be cleared.

```
IndexOptions IconsAreLinks FancyIndexing
IndexOptions +ScanHTMLTitles
```

Authentication

Your Web server can also control access on a per-user or per-group basis to particular directories on your Web site. You can require various levels for authentication. Access can be limited to particular users and require passwords, or expanded to allow members of a group access. You can dispense with passwords altogether or set up an anonymous type of access, as used with FTP.

To apply authentication directives to a certain directory, you place those directives within either a **Directory** block or the directory's **.htaccess** file. You use the **require** directive to determine what users can access the directory. You can list particular users or groups. The **AuthName** directive provides the authentication realm to the user, the name used to identify the particular set of resources accessed by this authentication process. The **AuthType** directive specifies the type of authentication, such as basic or digest. A **require** directive requires also **AuthType**, **AuthName**, and directives specifying the locations of group and user authentication files. In the following example, only the users george, robert, and mark are allowed access to the **newpics** directory:

```
<Directory /var/www/html/newpics
AuthType Basic
```

```
AuthName Newpics
AuthUserFile /web/users
AuthGroupFile /web/groups
<Limit GET POST>
 require users george robert mark
</Limit>
</Directory>
```

The next example allows group access by administrators to the CGI directory:

```
<Directory /var/www/html/cgi-bin
AuthType Basic
AuthName CGI
AuthGroupFile /web/groups
<Limit GET POST>
 require groups admin
</Limit>
</Directory>
```

To set up anonymous access for a directory, place the **Anonymous** directive with the user anonymous as its argument in the directory's Directory block or **.htaccess** file. You can also use the **Anonymous** directive to provide access to particular users without requiring passwords from them.

Apache maintains its own user and group authentication files specifying what users and groups are allowed to which directories. These files are normally simple flat files, such as your system's password and group files. They can become large, however, possibly slowing down authentication lookups. As an alternative, many sites have used database management files in place of these flat files. Database methods are then used to access the files, providing a faster response time. Apache has directives for specifying the authentication files, depending on the type of file you are using. The **AuthUserFile** and **AuthGroupFile** directives are used to specify the location of authentication files that have a standard flat file format. The **AuthDBUserFile** and **AuthDBGroupFile** directives are used for DB database files, and the **AuthDBMGUserFile** and **AuthDBMGGroupFile** are used for DBMG database files.

The programs htdigest, htpasswd, and dbmmanage are tools provided with the Apache software package for creating and maintaining *user authentication files,* which are user password files listing users who have access to specific directories or resources on your Web site. htdigest and htpasswd manage a simple flat file of user authentication records, whereas dbmmanage uses a more complex database management format. If your user list is extensive, you may want to use a database file for fast lookups. htdigest takes as its arguments the authentication file, the realm, and the username, creating or updating the user entry. htpasswd can also employ encryption on the password.

dbmmanage has an extensive set of options to add, delete, and update user entries. A variety of different database formats are used to set up such files. Three common ones are Berkeley DB2, NDBM, and GNU GBDM. dbmmanage looks for the system libraries for these formats in that order. Be careful to be consistent in using the same format for your authentication files.

Log Files

Apache maintains logs of all requests by users to your Web site. By default, these logs include records using the Common Log Format (CLF). The record for each request takes up a line composed of several fields: host, identity check, authenticated user (for logins), the date, the request line submitted by the client, the status sent to the client, and the size of the object sent in bytes. Using the **LogFormat** and **CustomLog** directives, you can customize your log record to add more fields with varying levels of detail. These directives use a format string consisting of field specifiers to determine the fields to record in a log record. You add whatever fields you want and in any order. A field specifier consists of a percent (`%`) symbol followed by an identifying character. For example, **`%h`** is the field specifier for a remote host, **`%b`** for the size in bytes, and **`%s`** for the status. See the documentation for the mod_log_config module for a complete listing. Table 21-4 lists several of the commonly used ones. You should quote fields whose contents may take up more than one word. The quotes themselves must be quoted with a backslash to be included in the format string. The following example is the Common Log Format implemented as a **FormatLog** directive:

```
FormatLog "%h %l %u %t \"%r\" %s %b"
```

Instead of maintaining one large log file, you can create several log files using the **CustomLog** or **TransferLog** directive. This is helpful for virtual hosts where you may want to maintain a separate log file for each host. You use the **FormatLog** directive to define a default format for log records. The **TransferLog** then uses this default as its format when creating a new log file. **CustomLog** combines both operations, enabling you to create a new file and to define a format for it.

```
FormatLog "%h %l %u %t \"%r\" %s %b"
# Create a new log file called myprojlog using the FormatLog format
TransferLog myprojlog
# Create a new log file called mypicslog using its own format
CustomLog mypicslog "%h %l %u %t \"%r\" %s %b"
```

Certain field specifiers in the log format can be qualified to record specific information. The **`%i`** specifier records header lines in requests the server receives. The reference for the specific header line to record is placed within braces between the `%` and the field specifier. For example, **`User-agent`** is the header line that indicates the browser software

Field Specifier	Description
`%a`	Remote IP address
`%A`	Local IP address
`%b`	Bytes sent, excluding HTTP headers
`%{`*variable*`}e:`	The contents of the environment *variable*
`%f`	Filename
`%h`	Remote host
`%l`	Remote logname (from **identd**, if supplied)
`%m`	The request method
`%P`	The process ID of the child that serviced the request
`%r`	First line of request
`%s`	Status
`%t`	Time, in Common Log Format time format (standard English format)
`%u`	Remote user (from auth; may be bogus if return status (`%s`) is 401)
`%U`	The URL path requested
`%v`	The canonical ServerName of the server serving the request

Table 21-4. *Apache Log Field Specifiers*

used in the request. To record User-agent header information, use the conversion specifier **%{User-agent}i**.

To maintain compatibility with NCSA servers, Apache originally implemented **AgentLog** and **RefererLog** directives to record User-agent and Referer headers. These have since been replaced by qualified **%i** field specifiers used for the **LogFormat** and **CustomLog** directives. A Referer header records link information from clients, detecting who may have links to your site. The following is an NCSA-compliant log format:

```
"%h %l %u %t \"%r\" %s %b\"%{Referer}i\" \"%{User-agent}i\"".
```

Apache provides two utilities for processing and managing log files. logresolve resolves IP addresses in your log file to hostnames. rotatelogs rotates log files without having to kill the server. You can specify the rotation time.

Virtual Hosting on Apache

Virtual hosting allows the Apache Web server to host multiple Web sites as part of its own. In effect, the server can act as several servers, each hosted Web site appearing separate to outside users. Apache supports both IP address and name-based virtual hosting. IP address virtual hosts use valid registered IP addresses, whereas name-based virtual hosts use fully qualified domain addresses. These domain addresses are provided by the host header from the requesting browser. The server can then determine the correct virtual host to use on the basis of the domain name alone. Note that SSL servers require IP virtual hosting. See **httpd.apache.org** for more information.

IP Address Virtual Hosts

In the IP address virtual hosting method, your server must have a different IP address for each virtual host. The IP address you use is already set up to reference your system. Network system administration operations can set up your machine to support several IP addresses. Your machine could have separate physical network connections for each one, or a particular connection could be configured to listen for several IP addresses at once. In effect, any of the IP addresses can access your system.

You can configure Apache to run a separate daemon for each virtual host, separately listening for each IP address, or you can have a single daemon running that listens for requests for all the virtual hosts. To set up a single daemon to manage all virtual hosts, use **VirtualHost** directives. To set up a separate daemon for each host, also use the **Listen** directive.

A **VirtualHost** directive block must be set up for each virtual host. Within each **VirtualHost** block, you place the appropriate directives for accessing a host. You should have **ServerAdmin**, **ServerName**, **DocumentRoot**, and **TransferLog** directives specifying the particular values for that host. You can use any directive within a **VirtualHost** block, except for **ServerType (1.3)**, **StartServers**, **MaxSpareServers**, **MinSpareServers**, **MaxRequestsPerChild**, **Listen**, **PidFile**, **TypesConfig**, **ServerRoot**, and **NameVirtualHost**.

Although you can use domain names for the address in the **VirtualHost** directive, using the actual IP address is preferable. This way, you are not dependent on your domain name service to make the correct domain name associations. Be sure to leave an IP address for your main server. If you use all the available IP addresses for your machine for virtual hosts, you can no longer access your main server. You could, of course, reconfigure your main server as a virtual host. The following example shows two IP-based virtual hosts blocks: one using an IP address, and the other a domain name that associates with an IP address:

```
<VirtualHost 192.168.1.23>
 ServerAdmin webmaster@mail.mypics.com
 DocumentRoot /groups/mypics/html
 ServerName www.mypics.com
 ErrorLog /groups/mypics/logs/error_log
 .....
```

```
</VirtualHost>

<VirtualHost www.myproj.org>
 ServerAdmin webmaster@mail.myproj.org
 DocumentRoot /groups/myproj/html
 ServerName www.myproj.org
 ErrorLog /groups/myproj/logs/error_log
 ....
</VirtualHost>
```

Name-Based Virtual Hosts

With IP-based virtual hosting, you are limited to the number of IP addresses your system supports. With name-based virtual hosting, you can support any number of virtual hosts using no additional IP addresses. With only a single IP address for your machine, you can still support an unlimited number of virtual hosts. Such a capability is made possible by the HTTP/1.1 protocol, which lets a server identify the name by which it is being accessed. This method requires the client, the remote user, to use a browser that supports the HTTP/1.1 protocol, as current browsers do (though older ones may not). A browser using such a protocol can send a host header specifying the particular host to use on a machine.

To implement name-based virtual hosting, use a **VirtualHost** directive for each host and a **NameVirtualHost** directive to specify the IP address you want to use for the virtual hosts. If your system has only one IP address, you need to use that address. Within the **VirtualHost** directives, you use the **ServerName** directive to specify the domain name you want to use for that host. Using **ServerName** to specify the domain name is important to avoid a DNS lookup. A DNS lookup failure disables the virtual host. The **VirtualHost** directives each take the same IP address specified in the **NameVirtualHost** directive as their argument. You use Apache directives within the **VirtualHost** blocks to configure each host separately. Name-based virtual hosting uses the domain name address specified in a host header to determine the virtual host to use. If no such information exists, the first host is used as the default. The following example implements two name-based virtual hosts. Here, **www.mypics.com** and **www.myproj.org** are implemented as name-based virtual hosts instead of IP-based hosts:

```
ServerName turtle.mytrek.com

NameVirtualHost 192.168.1.5

<VirtualHost 192.168.1.5>
 ServerName www.mypics.com
```

```
  ServerAdmin webmaster@mail.mypics.com
  DocumentRoot /var/www/mypics/html
  ErrorLog /var/www/mypics/logs/error_log
  ...
</VirtualHost>

<VirtualHost 192.168.1.5>
  ServerName www.myproj.org
  ServerAdmin webmaster@mail.myproj.org
  DocumentRoot /var/www/myproj/html
  ErrorLog /var/www/myproj/logs/error_log
  ….
</VirtualHost>
```

If your system has only one IP address, implementing virtual hosts prevents access to your main server with that address. You could no longer use your main server as a Web server directly; you could only use it indirectly to manage your virtual host. You could configure a virtual host to manage your main server's Web pages. You would then use your main server to support a set of virtual hosts that would function as Web sites, rather than the main server operating as one site directly. If your machine has two or more IP addresses, you can use one for the main server and the other for your virtual hosts. You can even mix IP-based virtual hosts and name-based virtual hosts on your server. You can also use separate IP addresses to support different sets of virtual hosts. You can further have several domain addresses access the same virtual host. To do so, place a **ServerAlias** directive listing the domain names within the selected VirtualHost block.

```
ServerAlias www.mypics.com www.greatpics.com
```

Requests sent to the IP address used for your virtual hosts have to match one of the configured virtual domain names. To catch requests that do not match one of these virtual hosts, you can set up a default virtual host using *_default_*:*. Unmatched requests are then handled by this virtual host.

```
<VirtualHost _default_:*>
```

Dynamic Virtual Hosting

If you have implemented many virtual hosts on your server that have basically the same configuration, you can use a technique called *dynamic virtual hosting* to have these virtual hosts generated dynamically. The code for implementing your virtual hosts becomes much smaller, and as a result, your server accesses them faster. Adding yet more virtual hosts becomes a simple matter of creating appropriate directories and adding entries for them in the DNS server.

To make dynamic virtual hosting work, the server uses commands in the mod_vhost_alias module (supported in Apache version 1.3.6 and up) to rewrite both the server name and the document root to those of the appropriate virtual server (for older Apache versions before 1.3.6, you use the mod_rewrite module). Dynamic virtual hosting can be either name-based or IP-based. In either case, you have to set the **UseCanonicalName** directive in such a way as to allow the server to use the virtual hostname instead of the server's own name. For name-based hosting, you simply turn off **UseCanonicalName**. This allows your server to obtain the hostname from the host header of the user request. For IP-based hosting, you set the **UseCanonicalName** directive to DNS. This allows the server to look up the host in the DNS server.

```
UseCanonicalName Off
UseCanonicalName DNS
```

You then have to enable the server to locate the different document root directories and CGI bin directories for your various virtual hosts. You use the **VirtualDocumentRoot** directive to specify the template for virtual hosts' directories. For example, if you place the different host directories in the **/var/www/hosts** directory, then you could set the **VirtualDocumentRoot** directive accordingly.

```
VirtualDocumentRoot /var/www/hosts/%0/html
```

The %0 will be replaced with the virtual host's name when that virtual host is accessed. It is important that you create the dynamic virtual host's directory using that host's name. For example, for a dynamic virtual host called **www.mygolf.org**, you would create a directory named **/var/www/hosts/www.mygolf.org**. Then create subdirectories for the document root and CGI programs as in **/var/www/hosts/www.mygolf.org/html**. For the CGI directory, use the **VirtualScriptAlias** directive to specify the CGI subdirectory you use.

```
VirtualScriptAlias /var/www/hosts/%0/cgi-bin
```

A simple example of name-based dynamic virtual hosting directives follows:

```
UseCanonicalName Off
VirtualDocumentRoot /var/www/hosts/%0/html
VirtualScriptAlias /var/www/hosts/%0/cgi-bin
```

If a request was made for **www.mygolf.com/html/mypage**, that would evaluate to:

```
/var/www/hosts/www.mygolf.com/html/mypage
```

The mod_vhosts_alias module supports various interpolated strings, each beginning with a `%` symbol and followed by a number. As you have seen, `%0` references the entire Web address. `%1` references only the first segment, `%2` references the second, `%-1` references the last part, and `%2+` references from the second part on. For example, if you only want to use the second part of a Web address for the directory name, you would use the following directives:

```
VirtualDocumentRoot /var/www/hosts/%2/html
VirtualScriptAlias /var/www/hosts/%2/cgi-bin
```

In this case, a request made for **www.mygolf.com/html/mypage** would use only the second part of the Web address. This would be "mygolf" in **www.mygolf.com**, and would evaluate to:

```
/var/www/hosts/mygolf/html/mypage
```

If you used `%2+` instead, as in **/var/www/hosts/%2/html**, the request for **www.mygolf.com/html/mypage** would evaluate to

```
/var/www/hosts/mygolf.com/html/mypage
```

The same method works for IP addresses, where `%1` references the first IP address segment, `%2` references the second, and so on.

A simple example of dynamic virtual hosting is shown here:

```
UseCanonicalName Off

NameVirtualHost 192.168.1.5

<VirtualHost 192.168.1.5>
 ServerName www.mygolf.com
 ServerAdmin webmaster@mail.mygolf.com
 VirtualDocumentRoot /var/www/hosts/%0/html
 VirtualScriptAlias /var/www/hosts/%0/cgi-bin
 ...
</VirtualHost>
```

To implement IP-based dynamic virtual hosting instead, set the **UseCanonicalName** to DNS instead of Off.

```
UseCanonicalName DNS
VirtualDocumentRoot /var/www/hosts/%0/html
VirtualScriptAlias /var/www/hosts/%0/cgi-bin
```

One drawback of dynamic virtual hosting is that you can only set up one log for all your hosts. However, you can create your own shell program to simply cut out the entries for the different hosts in that log.

```
LogFormat "%V %h %l %u %t \"%r\" %s %b" vcommon
CustomLog logs/access_log vcommon
```

Implementing IP-based dynamic virtual hosting in the standard way as shown previously will slow down the process, as your server will have to perform a DNS lookup to discover the name of your server using its IP address. You can avoid this step by simply using the IP address for your virtual host's directory. So, for IP virtual host 192.198.1.6, you would create a directory **/var/www/hosts/192.198.1.6**, with an **html** subdirectory for that host's document root. You would use the **VirtualDocumentRootIP** and **VirtualScriptAliasIP** directives to use IP addresses as directory names. Now the IP address can be mapped directly to the document root directory name, no longer requiring a DNS lookup. Also be sure to include the IP address in your log, **%A**.

```
UseCanonicalName DNS
LogFormat "%A %h %l %u %t \"%r\" %s %b" vcommon
CustomLog logs/access_log vcommon

VirtualDocumentRootIP /var/www/hosts/%0/html
VirtualScriptAliasIP /var/www/hosts/%0/cgi-bin
```

You can mix these commands in with other virtual host entries as you need them. For example, to specify the document root directory for a nondynamic name-based virtual host, you could simply use the **VirtualDocumentRoot** directive. In other words, you can simply use the same directories for both dynamic and nondynamic virtual hosts. You could still specify other directories for different nondynamic virtual hosts as you wish. In the following example, the **www.mypics.com** name-based virtual host uses the dynamic virtual host directive **VirtualDocumentRoot** to set its document root directory. It now uses **/var/www/www.mypics.com/html** as its document root directory. The CGI directory, however, is set as a nondynamic directory, **/var/www/mypics/cgi-bin**.

```
UseCanonicalName Off

NameVirtualHost 192.168.1.5

<VirtualHost 192.168.1.5>
 ServerName www.mypics.com
 ServerAdmin webmaster@mail.mypics.com
 VirtualDocumentRoot /var/www/%0/html
 ScriptAlias /var/www/mypics/cgi-bin
 ...
</VirtualHost>
```

Server-Side Includes

Server-side includes (SSIs) are designed to provide a much more refined control of your Web site content, namely the Web pages themselves. Server-side includes are Apache directives placed within particular Web pages as part of the page's HTML code. You can configure your Apache Web server to look for SSI directives in particular Web pages and execute them. First, you have to use the **Options** directive with the **include** option to allow SSI directives.

```
Options Includes
```

You need to instruct the server to parse particular Web pages. The easiest way to enable parsing is to instruct Apache to parse HTML files with specified extensions. Usually, the extension **.shtml** is used for Web pages that have SSI directories. In fact, in the default Apache configuration files, you can find the following entry to enable parsing for SSI directives in HTML files. The **AddType** directive here adds the **.shtml** type as an HTML type of file, and the **AddHandler** directive specifies that **.shtml** files are to be parsed (server-parsed).

```
# To use server-parsed HTML files
AddType text/html .shtml
AddHandler server-parsed .shtml
```

Instead of creating a separate type of file, you can use the **XBitHack** directive to have Apache parse any executable file for SSI directives. In other words, any file with execute permission (see Chapter 10) will be parsed for SSI directives.

SSI directives operate much like statements in a programming language. You can define variables, create loops, and use tests to select alternate directives. An SSI directive consists of an element followed by attributes that can be assigned values. The syntax for an SSI directive is shown here:

```
<!--#element attribute=value ... -->
```

You can think of an element as operating much like a command in a programming language and attributes as its arguments. For example, to assign a value to a variable, you use the **set** element with the variable assignment as its attribute. The **if** directive displays any following text on the given Web page. The **if** directive takes as its attribute **expr**, which is assigned the expression to test. The test is able to compare two strings using standard comparison operators such as **<=**, **!=**, or **=**. Variables used in the test are evaluated with the **$** operator.

```
<!--#set myvar="Goodbye" -->
<!--#if expr="$myvar = Hello" -->
```

Other helpful SSI elements are **exec**, which executes CGI programs, or shell commands, which read the contents of a file into the Web page and also execute CGI files. The **echo** element displays values such as the date, the document's name, and the page's URL. With the **config** element, you can configure certain values, such as the date or file size.

PHP

PHP (PHP Hypertext PreProcessor) is a scripting language designed for use in Web pages. PHP enabled pages allow you to create dynamic Web pages that can perform tasks instead of just displaying data. PHP is an official project of the Apache Software Foundation. You can find out more about PHP at **www.php.net**.

Unlike CGI programs, which are executed separately from a Web page, PHP commands are embedded as tags within the page itself, much like SSI commands are. PHP support to interpret and execute these commands is provided directly by the Web server. This embedded support is enabled in Apache with the mod_php module. Instead of having to separately construct programs to be invoked and run outside the Web server, with PHP, such commands are embedded within a Web page and run by the Web server. The Web server maintains complete control at all times whenever tasks are being performed. It is possible, however, to implement PHP in a CGI mode, where PHP pages are constructed as separate programs, invoked by a Web page much like a Perl-based CGP program is.

PHP has flexible and powerful programming capabilities on the same level as C and Perl. As in those languages, you can create control structures such as if statements and loops. In addition, PHP has capabilities specifically suited to Web page tasks. PHP can interact directly with databases such as Oracle, MySQL, and IBM DB2. It can easily interact with all the standard protocols such as IMAP, LDAP, HTTP, and POP3. It even has text processing abilities such as interpreting regular expressions and displaying XML documents. There are also extensions for searches, compression tools like gzip, and language translations. PHP supports a massive collection of possible operations. Check its Web site for a complete listing, as well as online manuals and tutorials.

Apache GUI Configuration Tools

Red Hat provides a GUI configuration tool called the Apache Configuration Tool, accessible from the Gnome and KDE desktops. Also available is Comanche, a popular Apache Configuration Tool that you download from the Internet. The Apache GUI Project (**gui.apache.org**) provides a set of GUI tools for configuring and managing your Apache Web server. Its currently active projects are Comanche and TkApache. In the Linuxconf utility, you can also configure your Apache Web server. Webmin provides a very complete Apache Web server module.

Apache Configuration Tool

The Apache Configuration Tool opens with a window displaying panels for Main, Virtual Hosts, Server, and Performance Tuning. In each of these you will see buttons to open dialog boxes where you can enter default settings. You will also be able to enter settings for particular items such as virtual hosts and particular directories. For example, in the Virtual Hosts panel you can enter default settings for all virtual hosts, as well as add and edit particular virtual hosts. Click the Help button to display a Web page–based reference manual that details how to use each panel. On the Main panel, you enter your Web server address, the Web master's e-mail address, and the ports the Web server will be listening on.

On the Virtual Hosts panel, be sure to click the Edit Default Settings button to set the default settings for pages searches, error codes, log files, and directories. To add a virtual host, click the Add button to open a window where you can enter host information such as the virtual hostname and IP address. On the sidebar, you can select different configuration panels for the virtual host, such as log files and directory controls.

On the server panel, you set administrative settings such as the Apache server's user ID and the process ID file. The Performance Tuning panel lets you set different usage limits such as the maximum number of requests and the number of requests per connection.

When the Apache Configuration Tool saves its settings, it will overwrite the Apache configuration file, **/etc/httpd/conf/httpd.conf**. It is advisable that you first make a backup copy of your **httpd.conf** file in case you want to restore the original settings created by your distribution for Apache. If you have already manually edited this file, you will receive a warning, and the Apache Configuration Tool will make a backup copy in **/etc/httpd/conf/httpd.conf.bak.**

Comanche

Comanche (Configuration Manager for Apache) is an easy-to-use, full-featured Apache configuration utility that runs on any X Window System window manager. You can download the current version and documentation from the Comanche Web site at **www.comanche.org**. Comanche uses a simple, directory tree–like structure to enable you to access and configure your main Web server, and any virtual server you have set up. Comanche can configure the server on your local machine as well as on remote servers.

When you first start the program, a window is displayed where you select the kind of Apache installation you have. The main Comanche window has a sidebar that shows a tree of Apache servers, and the main panel shows the items in the selected entry in the tree. The main tree entry will display the Apache Web server and under it, the Apache server. Here you will find entries for Server Management and the Default Web server, the primary Web server. To perform actions on any of these entries, select the entry and then select the list of actions on the main panel. The Server Management entry displays a list of items to start, stop, restart, and query the server status, as well as to save your configuration. Any changes you make with Comanche are not made in your Apache configuration files until you explicitly save the configuration. Be sure to save before you quit. When you save your configuration, this version overwrites your **httpd.conf** file.

To configure your Default Web server, click on it and then select the default configuration entry on the mail panel. This opens a dialog box. If you double-click the Default Web server icon, the tree expands to list server locations. These are the root directory, your Web server home directory, the CGI program directory, and the documentation directory. To create new directories, right-click the Web server entry and select the New item in the menu that pops up.

Initially, only one server is listed, labeled Default Web Server. If you add virtual hosts, they are listed at the same level. To create a virtual host, right-click the Apache Server entry and then select New on the pop-up menu. This activates a drop-down menu with a Virtual Host entry. Select the Virtual Host entry to create your virtual host.

To configure a directory, right-click its entry and select the Properties item from the pop-up menu displayed. This opens a new window for configuring your selection. The window is divided into sidebar and main panel: the sidebar shows a tree of configuration items, and the main panel displays the configuration dialog windows for these items. For example, by selecting the Basic configuration entry, you can display text boxes for entering items such as the document root directory and the name of your server. Other entries let you set server options, proxy settings, and indexing formats.

Web Server Security: SSL

Web server security deals with two different tasks: protecting your Web server from unauthorized access, and providing security for transactions carried out between a Web browser client and your Web server. To protect your server from unauthorized access, you use a proxy server such as Squid. Squid is a GNU proxy server often used with Apache on Linux systems. (See Chapter 24 for a detailed explanation of the Squid server.) Apache itself has several modules that provide security capabilities. These include mod_access for mandatory controls; mod_auth, mod_auth_db, mod_auth_digest, and mod_auth_dbm, which provide authentication support; and mod_auth_anon for anonymous FTP-like logging (see previous sections on access control and authentication).

To secure transmissions, you need to perform three tasks. You have to verify identities, check the integrity of the data, and ensure the privacy of the transmission. To verify the identities of the hosts participating in the transmission, you perform authentication procedures. To check the integrity of the data, you add digital signatures containing a digest value for the data. The digest value is a value that uniquely represents the data. Finally, to secure the privacy of the transmission, you encrypt it. Transactions between a browser and your server can then be encrypted, with the browser and your server alone able to decrypt the transmissions. The protocol most often used to implement secure transmissions with Linux Apache Web servers is the Secure Sockets Layer (SSL) protocol, which was originally developed by Netscape for secure transactions on the Web.

Like the Secure Shell (SSH) described in Chapter 37 and GPG discussed in Chapter 6, SSL uses a form of public- and private-key encryption for authentication. Data is encrypted with the public key, but can only be decrypted with the private key. Once authenticated, an agreed-upon cipher is used to encrypt the data. Digital signatures encrypt an MD5 digest value for data to ensure integrity. Authentication is carried out with the use of certificates of authority. Certificates identify the different parties in a secure transmission, verifying that they are who they say they are. A Web server will have a certificate verifying its identity, verifying that it is the server it claims to be. The browser contacting the server will also have a certificate identifying who it is. These certificates are, in turn, both signed by a certificate authority, verifying that they are valid certificates. A certificate authority is an independent entity that both parties trust.

A certificate contains the public key of the particular server or browser it is given to, along with the digital signature of the certificate authority and identity information such as the name of the user or company running the server or browser. The effectiveness of a certificate depends directly on the reliability of the certificate authority issuing it. To run a secure Web server on the Internet, you should obtain a certificate from a noted certificate authority such as Verisign. A commercial vendor such as Stronghold can do this for you. Many established companies already maintain their own certificate authority, securing transmissions within their company networks. An SSL session is set up using a handshake sequence in which the server and browser are authenticated by exchanging certificates, a cipher is agreed upon to encrypt the transmissions, and the kind of digest integrity check is chosen. There is also a choice in the kind of public key encryption used for authentication, either RSA or DSA. For each session, a unique session key is set up that the browser and server use.

A free version of SSL called OpenSSL is available for use with Apache (see **www.openssl.org**). It is based on SSLeay from Eric A. Young and Tim J. Hudson. However, U.S. government restrictions prevent the Apache Web server from being freely distributed with SSL capabilities built in. You have to separately obtain SSL and update your Apache server to incorporate this capability.

The U.S. government maintains export restrictions on encryption technology over 40 bits. SSL, however, supports a number of ciphers using 168-, 128-, and 40-bit keys (128 is considered secure, and so by comparison, the exportable 40-bit versions are useless). This means that if Apache included SSL, it could not be distributed outside the United States. Outside the United States, however, there are projects that do distribute SSL for Apache using OpenSSL. These are free for noncommercial use in the United States, though export restrictions apply. The Apache-SSL project freely distributes Apache with SSL built-in, apache+ssl. You can download this from their Web site at **www.apache-ssl.org** (though there are restrictions on exporting encryption technology, there is none on importing it). In addition, the mod_ssl project provides an SSL module with patches you can use to update your Apache Web server to incorporate SSL (**www.modssl.org**). mod_ssl is free for both commercial and noncommercial use under an Apache style license.

Red Hat includes the mod_ssl module with its distribution in the mod_ssl package.

```
rpm -i mod_ssl-2.8.1-5.i386.rpm
```

The mod_ssl implementation of SSL provides an alternate access to your Web server using a different port (443) and a different protocol, https. In effect, you have both an SSL server and a non-secure version. To access the secure SSL version, you use the protocol https instead of http for the Web server's URL address. For example, to access the SSL version for the web server running at **www.mytrek.com** you would use the protocol https in its URL, as shown here:

```
https://www.mytrek.com
```

You can configure mod_ssl using a number of configuration directives in the Apache configuration file, **smb.conf**. On Red Hat, the default configuration file installed with Apache contains a section for the SSL directives along with detailed comments. Check the online documentation for mod_ssl at **www.modssl.org** for a detailed reference listing all the directives. There are global, server-based, and directory-based directives available.

In the Red Hat **smb.conf** file, the inclusion of SSL directives are controlled by IfDefine blocks enabled by the HAVE_SSL flag. For example, the following code will load the SSL module:

```
<IfDefine HAVE_SSL>
LoadModule ssl_module          modules/libssl.so
</IfDefine>
```

The SSL version for your Apache Web server is set up in the **smb.conf** file as a virtual host. The SSL directives are enabled by an ifDefine block using the HAVE_SSL flag.

Several default directives are implemented such as the location of SSL key directories and the port that the SSL version of the server will listen on (443). Others are commented out. You can enable them by removing the preceding # symbol, setting your own options. Several of the directives are shown here:

```
<IfDefine HAVE_SSL>
## SSL Virtual Host Context

#  Apache will only listen on port 80 by default.
#  Defining the virtual server
#  (below) won't make it automatically listen on the virtual server's port.
Listen 443

<VirtualHost _default_:443>

#  General setup for the virtual host
DocumentRoot "/var/www/html"

#   SSL Engine Switch:
#   Enable/Disable SSL for this virtual host.
SSLEngine on
#SSLCipherSuite
ALL:!ADH:RC4+RSA:+HIGH:+MEDIUM:+LOW:+SSLv2:+EXP:+eNULL

#   Server Certificate:
SSLCertificateFile /etc/httpd/conf/ssl.crt/server.crt
#SSLCertificateFile /etc/httpd/conf/ssl.crt/server-dsa.crt

#   Server Private Key:
SSLCertificateKeyFile /etc/httpd/conf/ssl.key/server.key

#   Certificate Authority (CA):
#SSLCACertificatePath /etc/httpd/conf/ssl.crt
#SSLCACertificateFile /etc/httpd/conf/ssl.crt/ca-bundle.crt
```

In the /etc/httpd/conf directory, mod_ssl will set up several SSL directories that will contain SSL authentication and encryption keys and data. The **ssl.crt** directory will hold certificates for the server. The **ssl.key** directory holds the public and private keys used in authentication encryption. Revocation lists for revoking expired certificates are kept in **ssl.crl**. The **ssl.csr** directory holds the certificate signing request used to request an official certificate from a certificate authority. **ssl.prm** holds parameter files used by the DSA key encryption method. Check the README files in each directory for details on the SSL files they contain.

The mod_ssl installation will provide you with a demonstration certificate called snakeoil that you can use to test your SSL configuration. When you have an official certificate, you can install it with the **`make certificate`** command within the **ssl.crt** directory. This will overwrite the **server.crt** server certificate file.

*Check the Apache documentation at **httpd.apache.org** for a complete listing of Apache directives.*

The Complete Reference

Chapter 22

Domain Name Service

The Domain Name Service (DNS) is an Internet service that converts domain names into their corresponding IP addresses. As you may recall, all computers connected to the Internet are addressed using an Internet Protocol (IP) address. The IP address may be implemented in either the newer IPv6 (Internet Protocol Version 6) format or on the older and more common IPv4 (Internet Protocol Version 4) format. Since most systems still use the IPv4 addressing, that format will be used in these examples. In the older IPv4 format, the IP address consists of a number composed of four segments separated by periods. Depending on the type of network, several of the first segments are used for the network address and several of the last segments are used for the host address. In a standard class C network used in smaller networks, the first three segments are the computer's network address and the last segment is the computer's host ID (as used in these examples). For example, in the address 192.168.0.2, 192.168.0 is the network address and 2 is the computer's host ID within that network. Together, they make up an IP address by which the computer can be addressed from anywhere on the Internet. IP addresses, though, are difficult to remember and easy to get wrong.

As a normal user on a network might have to access many different hosts, keeping track of the IP addresses needed quickly became a problem. It was much easier to label hosts with names and use the names to access them. Names were associated with IP addresses. When a user used a name to access a host, the corresponding IP address was looked up first and then used to provide access.

IP addresses were associated with corresponding names, called fully qualified domain names. A *fully qualified domain name* is composed of three or more segments. The first segment is the name that identifies the host, and the remaining segments are for the network in which the host is located. The network segments of a fully qualified domain name are usually referred to simply as the domain name, while the host part is referred to as the hostname (though this is also used to refer to the complete fully qualified domain name). In effect, subnets are referred to as domains. The fully qualified domain name **www.linux.org** has an IP address 198.182.196.56, where 198.182.196 is the network address and 56 is the host ID. Computers can be accessed only with an IP address, so a fully qualified domain name must first be translated into its corresponding IP address to be of any use. The parts of the IP address that make up the domain name and the hosts can vary. See Chapter 36 for a detailed discussion of IP addresses, including network classes and Classless Interdomain Routing (CIDR).

Any computer on the Internet can maintain a file that manually associates IP addresses with domain names. On Linux and Unix systems, this file is called the **/etc/hosts** file. Here, you can enter the IP addresses and domain names of computers you commonly access. Using this method, however, each computer needs a complete listing of all other computers on the Internet, and that listing must be updated constantly. Early on, this became clearly impractical for the Internet, though it is still feasible for small isolated networks. The Domain Name Service has been implemented to deal with the task of translating the domain name of any computer on the Internet to its IP address. The task is carried out by interconnecting servers that manage the Domain Name Service (also referred to as DNS servers or name servers). These DNS servers keep lists of fully qualified domain names and their IP addresses, matching one up with the other. This service that they provide to a network is referred to as the Domain Name Service. The Internet is composed of many connected subnets called *domains*, each with its own Domain Name Service (DNS) servers that keep track of all the fully qualified domain names and IP addresses for all the computers on its network. DNS servers are hierarchically linked to root servers, which, in turn, connect to other root servers and the DNS servers on their subnets throughout the Internet. The section of a network for which a given DNS server is responsible is called a *zone*. Although a zone may correspond to a domain, many zones may, in fact, be within a domain, each with its own name server. This is true for large domains where too many systems exist for one name server to manage.

When a user enters a fully qualified domain name to access a remote host, a resolver program queries the local network's DNS server requesting the corresponding IP address for that remote host. With the IP address the user can then access the remote host. In Figure 22-1, the user at **rabbit.mytrek.com** wants to connect to the remote host **lizard.mytrek.com**. **rabbit.mytrek.com** first sends a request to the network's DNS server—in this case, **turtle.mytrek.com**—to look up the name **lizard.mytrek.com** and find its IP address. It then returns the IP address for **lizard.mytrek.com**, 192.168.0.3, to the requesting host, **rabbit.mytrek.com**. With the IP address, the user at **rabbit.mytrek.com** can then connect to **lizard.mytrek.com**.

The names of the DNS servers that service a host's network are kept in the host's **/etc/resolv.conf** file. When setting up an Internet connection, the name servers provided

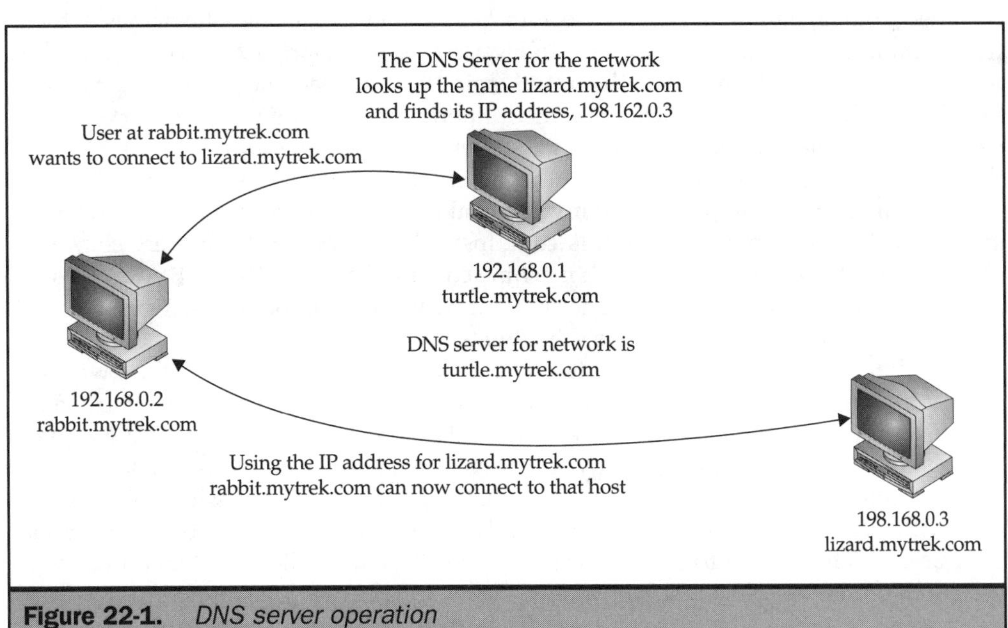

Figure 22-1. *DNS server operation*

by your Internet service provider (ISP) were placed in this file. These name servers resolve any fully qualified domain names that you use when you access different Internet sites. For example, when you enter a Web site name in your browser, the name is looked up by the name servers and the name's associated IP address is then used to access the site.

Local Area Network Addressing

If you are setting up a DNS server for a local area network (LAN) that is not connected to the Internet, you should use a special set of IP numbers reserved for such non-Internet networks (also known as *private networks* or *intranets*). This is especially true if you are implementing IP masquerading, where only a gateway machine has an Internet address, and the others make use of that one address to connect to the Internet. For a class C network (254 hosts or less), these are numbers that have the special network number 192.168, as used in these examples. If you are setting up a LAN, such as a small business or home network, you are free to use these numbers for your local machines. You can set up a private network, such as an intranet, using network cards such as Ethernet cards and Ethernet hubs, and then configure your machines with IP addresses starting from 192.168.0.1. The host segment can range from 1 to 254, where 255 is used for the broadcast address. If you have three machines on your home network, you can give them the addresses 192.168.0.1, 192.168.0.2, and 192.168.0.3. You can then set up domain name services for your network by running a DNS server on one of the machines. This machine becomes your network's DNS server. You can then give your machines fully qualified domain names and configure your DNS server to translate the names to their corresponding IP addresses. As shown in Figure 22-2, for example, you could give the machine 192.168.0.1 the name **turtle.mytrek.com**, and the machine 192.168.0.2 the name **rabbit.mytrek.com**. You can also implement Internet services on your network such as FTP, Web, and mail services by setting up servers for them on your machines. You can then configure your DNS server to let users access those services using fully qualified domain names. For example, for the **mytrek.com** network, the Web server could be accessed using the name **www.mytrek.com**. Instead of a Domain Name Service, you could have the **/etc/hosts** files in each machine contain the entire list of IP addresses and domain names for all the machines in your network. But, for any changes, you would have to update each machine's **/etc/hosts** file.

Numbers are also reserved for class A and class B non-Internet local networks. Table 22-1 lists these addresses. The possible addresses available span from 0 to 255 in the host segment of the address. For example, class B network addresses range from 172.16.0.0 to 172.16.255.255, giving you a total of 65,534 possible hosts. The class C network ranges from 192.168.0.0 to 192.168.255.255, giving you 254 possible subnetworks, each with 254 possible hosts. The number 127.0.0.0 is reserved for a system's loopback interface, which allows it to communicate with itself, as it enables users on the same system to send messages to each other.

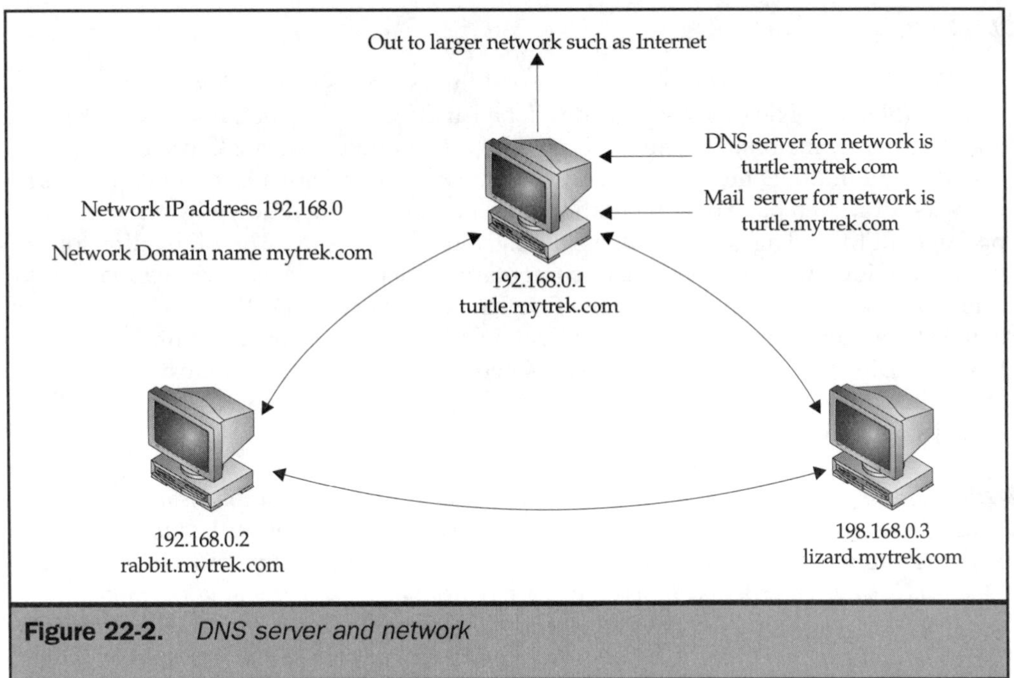

Figure 22-2. *DNS server and network*

These numbers were originally designed for class-based addressing. However, they can just as easily be used for Classless Interdomain Routing (CIDR) addressing, where you can create subnetworks with a smaller number of hosts. For example, the 254 hosts addressed in a class C network could be split into two subnetworks, each with 125 hosts. See Chapter 36 for more details.

Address	Networks
10.0.0.0	Class A network
172.16.0.0 to 172.31.255.255	Class B network
192.168.0.0	Class C network
127.0.0.0	Loopback network (for system self-communication)

Table 22-1. *Non-Internet Private Network IP Addresses*

BIND

The DNS server software currently in use on Linux systems is Berkeley Internet Name Domain (BIND). BIND was originally developed at the University of California, Berkeley, and is currently maintained and supported by the Internet Software Consortium (ISC). You can obtain BIND information and current software releases from its Web site at **www.isc.org**. Web page documentation and manuals are included with the software package. RPM packages are available at distribution FTP sites. The BIND directory in **/usr/share/doc** contains extensive documentation, including Web page manuals and examples. The Linux HOW-TO for the Domain Name Service, DNS-HOWTO, provides detailed examples. Documentation, news, and DNS tools can be obtained from the DNS Resource Directory (DNSRD) at **www.dns.net/dnsrd**. The site includes extensive links and online documentation, including the *BIND Operations Guide* (*BOG*). See Table 22-2 for a list of DNS resources.

Note *Several alternative DNS servers are now available. These include djbdns, noted for its security features, CustomDNS, a dynamic server implemented in Java (**customdns.sourceforge.net**), and Yaku-NS, an embedded server. djbdns (**dgbdns.org**), written by D. J. Bernstein, is designed specifically with security in mind, providing a set of small server daemons, each performing specialized tasks. In particular, djbdns separates the name server, caching server, and zone transfer tasks into separate programs. tinydns implements the authoritative name server for a network, whereas dnscache implements a caching server that will resolve requests from DNS clients like Web browsers. In effect, dnscache operates as the name server that your applications will use to resolve addresses. dnscache will then query tinydns to resolve addresses on your local network. Zone transfers are handled separately by axfrdns and asfget.*

Currently ISC has contracted with two companies, Nominum and Mind, to provide BIND support. Nominum is an ISC support partner and has taken an active role in BIND development. At its Web site at **www.nominum.com** you can find BIND documentation,

Web Site	Resource
www.isc.org	Internet Software Consortium
www.dns.net/dnsrd	DNS Resource Directory
www.nominum.com	Nominum, BIND support and consulting
mind.be	Mind, BIND support and consulting for Europe

Table 22-2. *BIND Resources*

including the BIND 9 Administrator's Reference. Nominum, like many commercial companies that support open source software, provides professional consultant and support services, while freely contributing to open source development. Mind provides consulting services for the European market.

The BIND DNS server software consists of a name server daemon, several sample configuration files, and resolver libraries. As of 1998, a new version of BIND, beginning with the series number 8.*x*, implemented a new configuration file using a new syntax. Version 9.0 adds new security features. Older versions, which begin with the number 4.*x*, use a different configuration file with an older syntax. Most distributions currently install the newer 9.*x* version of BIND.

The name of the BIND name server daemon is **named**. To operate your machine as a name server, simply run the **named** daemon with the appropriate configuration. The **named** daemon listens for resolution requests and provides the correct IP address for the requested hostname. You can use the Remote Name Daemon Controller utility, `rndc`, provided with BIND to start, stop, restart, and check the status of the server as you test its configuration. `rndc` with the `stop` command stops **named** and, with the `start` command, starts it again, reading your **named.conf** file. `rndc` with the `help` command provides a list of all `rndc` commands. Once your name server is running, you can test it using the dig or nslookup utility, which queries a name server, providing information about hosts and domains. If you start dig with no arguments, it enters an interactive mode where you can issue different dig commands to refine your queries. Numerous other DNS tools are also available, such as nslint and host. Check the DNS Resource Directory at **www.dns.net/dnsrd** for a listing. Table 22-3 lists several DNS administrative tools.

On Mandrake, Red Hat, and Caldera systems, the **named** daemon is started using a startup script in the **/etc/rc.d/init.d** directory called **named** (On SuSE it is in the **/etc/rc.d** directory). You can use this script to start, stop, and restart the daemon using the `stop`,

Tool	Description
dig *domain*	Domain Information Groper, tool to obtain information on a DNS server. Preferred over nslookup.
host *hostname*	Simple lookup of hosts.
nslookup *domain*	Tool to query DNS servers for information about domains and hosts.
rndc *command*	Remote Name Daemon Controller is an administrative tool for managing a DNS server (version 9.*x*).
ndc	Name Daemon Controller (version 8.*x*).

Table 22-3. *BIND Diagnostic and Administration Tools*

start, and **restart** arguments. You can invoke the script with the **service** command as shown here:

```
service named restart
```

On most distributions, **named** runs as a standalone daemon, starting up when the system boots and constantly runs. If you don't want **named** to start up automatically, you can use the System V Runlevel Editor or Setup to change its status.

Domain Name Service Configuration

You configure a DNS server using a configuration file, several zone files, and a cache file. The part of a network for which the name server is responsible is called a zone. A *zone* is not the same as a domain, because in a large domain you could have several zones, each with its own name server. You could also have one name server service several zones. In this case, each zone has its own zone file. The zone files hold resource records that provide hostname and IP address associations for computers on the network for which the DNS server is responsible. Zone files exist for the server's network and the local machine. Zone entries are defined in the **named.conf** file. Here, you place zone entries for your master, slave, and forward DNS servers. The most commonly used zone types are described here:

- **Master zone** This is the primary zone file for a network. It holds the mappings from domain names to IP addresses for all the hosts on the network.
- **Slave zone** These are references to other DNS servers for your network. Your network can have a master DNS server and several slave DNS servers to help carry the workload. A slave DNS server automatically copies its configuration files, including all zone files, from the master DNS server. Any changes to the master configuration files trigger an automatic download of these files to the slave servers. In effect, you only have to manage the configuration files for the master DNS server, as they are automatically copied to the slave servers.
- **Forward zone** The forward zone lists name servers outside your network that should be searched if your network's name server fails to resolve an address.
- **IN-ADDR.ARPA zone** DNS can also provide reverse resolutions, where an IP address is used to determine the associated domain name address. Such lookups are provided by **IN-ADDR.ARPA** zone files. Each master zone file usually has a corresponding **IN-ADDR.ARPA** zone file to provide reverse resolution for that zone. For each master zone entry, a corresponding reverse mapping zone entry named **IN-ADDR.ARPA** also exists, as well as one for the localhost. This entry performs reverse mapping from an IP address to its domain name. The name of the zone entry uses the domain IP address, which is the IP address with segments listed starting from the host, instead of the network. So, for the

IP address 192.168.0.4 where 4 is the host address, the corresponding domain IP address is 4.1.168.192, listing the segments in reverse order. The reverse mapping for the localhost is 0.0.127.

- **Hint zone** A hint zone specifies the root name servers and is denoted by a period (.). A DNS server is normally connected to a larger network, such as the Internet, which has its own DNS servers. DNS servers are connected this way hierarchically, with each server having its root servers to which it can send resolution queries. The root servers are designated in the hint zone.

On Red Hat you can use bindconf, the BIND Configuration Tool, to configure a DNS server for a simple local network. bindconf provides a Gnome interface for setting up the master, slave, forward, and IN-ADDR.ARPA zones you would need for a server. Be aware, though, that it will overwrite your ***/etc/named.conf*** *file. bindconf can be accessed from the Gnome System menu.*

DNS Servers

There are several kinds of DNS servers, each designed to perform a different type of task under the Domain Name Service. The basic kind of DNS server is the *master* server. Each network must have at least one master server that is responsible for resolving names on the network. Large networks may need several DNS servers. Some of these can be slave servers that can be updated directly from a master server. Others may be *alternative master* servers that hosts in a network can use. Both are commonly referred to as *secondary* servers. For DNS requests a DNS server cannot resolve, the request can be forwarded to specific DNS servers outside the network, such as on the Internet. DNS servers in a network can be set up to perform this task and are referred to as *forwarder* servers. To help bear the workload, local DNS servers can be set up within a network that operate as caching servers. Such a server merely collects DNS lookups from previous requests it sent to the main DNS server. Any repeated requests can then be answered by the caching server.

A server that can answer DNS queries for a given zone with authority is known as an *authoritative* server. An authoritative server holds the DNS configuration records for hosts in a zone that will associate each host's DNS name with an IP address. For example, a master server is an authoritative server. So are slave and stealth servers (see the list that follows). A caching server is not authoritative. It only holds whatever associations it picked up from other servers and cannot guarantee that the associations are valid.

- **Master server** This is the primary DNS server for a zone.
- **Slave server** A DNS server that receives zone information from the master server.
- **Forwarder server** A server that forwards unresolved DNS requests to outside DNS servers. Can be used to keep other servers on a local network hidden from the Internet.

- **Caching only server** Caches DNS information it receives from DNS servers and uses it to resolve local requests.
- **Stealth server** A DNS server for a zone not listed as a name server by the master DNS server.

Note *As an alternative to making entries in the configuration files manually, you can configure DNS with Linuxconf or Webmin.*

named.conf

The configuration file for the **named** daemon is **named.conf**, located in the **/etc** directory. It uses a flexible syntax similar to C programs. The format enables easy configuration of selected zones, enabling features such as access control lists and categorized logging. The **named.conf** file consists of BIND configuration commands with attached blocks within which specific options are listed. A **`configuration`** command is followed by arguments and a block that is delimited with braces. Within the block are lines of option and feature entries. Each entry is terminated with a semicolon. Comments can use the C, C++, or Shell/Perl syntax: enclosing **`/* */`**, preceding **`//`**, or preceding **#**. The following example shows a **`zone`** statement followed by the zone name and a block of options that begin with an opening brace, **{**. Each option entry ends with a semicolon. The entire block ends with a closing brace, also followed by a semicolon. The format for a **named.conf** entry is show here, along with the different kinds of comments allowed. Table 22-6 later in this chapter lists several commonly used options.

```
// comments
/* comments */
# comments

statements {
 options and features; //comments
};
```

The following example shows a simple caching server entry.

```
// a caching only nameserver config
//
zone "." {
       type hint;
       file "named.ca";
       };
```

Note *The **named.conf** file is a new feature implemented with BIND version 8.x. and 9.x. The older BIND 4.x versions use a file called **named.boot**. This file is no longer used by version 8.x. The syntaxes used in these configuration files differ radically. If you upgrade to 8.x, you can use the **named-bootconf.pl** Perl script provided with the BIND software to convert your **named.boot** file to a **named.conf** file.*

The **zone** statement is used to specify the domains the name server will service. You enter the keyword **zone,** followed by the name of the domain placed within double quotes. Do not place a period at the end of the domain name. In the following example, a period is within the domain name, but not at the end, **"mytrek.com"**; this differs from the zone file, which requires a period at the end of a complete domain name.

After the zone name, you can specify the class **in**, which stands for Internet. You can also leave it out, in which case **in** is assumed (there are only a few other esoteric classes that are rarely used). Within the zone block, you can place several options (see Table 22-6). Two essential options are **type** and **file**. The **type** option is used to specify the zone's type. The **file** option is used to specify the name of the zone file to be used for this zone. You can choose from several types of zones: master, slave, stub, forward, and hint. *Master* specifies that the zone holds master information and is authorized to act on it. A master server was called a primary server in the older 4.*x* BIND configuration. *Slave* indicates that the zone needs to update its data periodically from a specified master name server. You use this entry if your name server is operating as a secondary server for another primary (master) DNS server. A *stub zone* only copies other name server entries, instead of the entire zone. A *forward zone* directs all queries to name servers specified in a **forwarders** statement. A *hint zone* specifies the set of root name servers used by all Internet DNS servers. You can also specify several options that can override any global options set with the **options** statement. Table 22-4 lists the BIND zone types. The following example shows a simple **zone** statement for the

Type	Description
master	Primary DNS zone
slave	Slave DNS server; controlled by a master DNS server
hint	Set of root DNS Internet servers
forward	Forwards any queries in it to other servers
stub	Like a slave zone, but only holds names of DNS servers

Table 22-4. *DNS BIND Zone Types*

mytrek.com domain. Its class is Internet (in) and its type is master. The name of its zone file is usually the same as the zone name, in this case, **"mytrek.com"**.

```
zone "mytrek.com" in {
        type master;
        file "mytrek.com";
        };
```

Other statements, such as **`acl`**, **`server`**, **`options`**, and **`logging`**, enable you to configure different features for your name server (see Table 22-5). The **`server`** statement defines the characteristics to be associated with a remote name server, such as the transfer

Statements	Description
/* *comment* */	BIND comment in C syntax
// *comment*	BIND comment in C++ syntax
# *comment*	BIND comment in Unix shell and Perl syntax
`acl`	Defines a named IP address matching list
`include`	Includes a file, interpreting it as part of the **named.conf** file
`key`	Specifies key information for use in authentication and authorization
`logging`	Specifies what the server logs and where the log messages are sent
options	Global server configuration options and defaults for other statements
`controls`	Declares control channels to be used by the ndc utility
`server`	Sets certain configuration options for the specified server basis
`sortlists`	Gives preference to specified networks based on a queries source
`trusted-keys`	Defines DNSSEC keys preconfigured into the server and implicitly trusted
`zone`	Defines a zone
`view`	Defines a view

Table 22-5. *BIND Configuration Statements*

method and key ID for transaction security. The **control** statement defines special control channels. The **key** statement defines a key ID to be used in a **server** statement that associates an authentication method with a particular name server (see DNSSEC). The **logging** statement is used to configure logging options for the name server, such as the maximum size of the log file and a severity level for messages. Table 22-5 lists the BIND statements.

The **options** statement defines global options and can be used only once in the configuration file. An extensive number of options cover such components as forwarding, name checking, directory path names, access control, and zone transfers, among others (see Table 22-7). A complete listing can be found in the BIND documentation. A critically important option found in most configuration files is the **directory** option, which holds the location of the name server's zone and cache files on your system. The following example is taken from the Red Hat **/etc/named.conf** file. This example specifies the zone files are located in the **/var/named** directory. In this directory, you can find your zone files, including those used for your local system.

```
options {
        directory "/var/named";
        forwarders { 192.168.0.34;
                    192.168.0.47;
                   };
       };
```

Another commonly used global option is the **forwarders** option. With the **forwarders** option, you can list several DNS servers to which queries can be forwarded if they cannot be resolved by the local DNS server. This is helpful for local networks that may need to use a DNS server connected to the Internet. The **forwarders** option can also be placed in forward zone entries.

With the **notify** option turned on, the master zone DNS servers send messages to any slave DNS servers whenever their configuration has changed. The slave servers can then perform zone transfers in which they download the changed configuration files. Slave servers always use the DNS configuration files copied from their master DNS servers. **notify** takes one argument, **yes** or **no**, where **yes** is the default. With the **no** argument, you can have the master server not send out any messages to the slave servers, in effect preventing any zone transfers.

The **sortlists** statement lets you specify preferences to be used when a query returns multiple responses. For example, you could give preference to your localhost network or to a private local network such a 192.168.0.0.

The following example is a simple **named.conf** file based on the example provided in the BIND documentation. This example shows samples of several of the configuration statements. The file begins with comments using C++ syntax, **//**. The **options** statement has a directory entry that sets the directory for the zone and cache files to **/var/named**. Here, you find your zone files, such as **named.local** and reverse mapping files, along with the cache file, **named.ca**. The first **zone** statement (**.**) defines a hint zone specifying the root name servers. The cache file listing these servers is **named.ca**.

Ophtions	Description
`type`	Specifies a zone type
`file`	Specifies the zone file for the zone
`directory`	Specifies a directory for zone files
`forwarders`	Lists hosts for DNS servers where requests are to be forwarded
`masters`	Lists hosts for DNS master servers for a slave server
`notify`	Allows master servers to notify their slave servers when the master zone data changes and updates are needed
`allow-transfer`	Specifies which hosts are allowed to receive zone transfers
`allow-query`	Specifies hosts that are allowed make queries
`allow-recursion`	Specifies hosts that are allowed to perform recursive queries on the server

Table 22-6. *Zone Options*

Options	Description
`sortlist`	Gives preference to specified networks based on a queries source
`directory`	Specifies a directory for zone files
`forwarders`	Lists hosts for DNS servers where requests are to be forwarded
`allow-transfer`	Specifies which hosts are allowed to receive zone transfers
`allow-query`	Specifies hosts that are allowed make queries
`allow-recursion`	Specifies hosts that are allowed to perform recursive queries on the server
`notify`	Allows master servers to notify their slave servers when the master zone data changes and updates are needed
`blackhole`	Option to eliminate denial response by `allow-query`

Table 22-7. *options Options*

The second **zone** statement defines a zone for the **mytrek.com** domain. Its type is master, and its zone file is named **"mytrek.com"**. The next zone is used for reverse IP mapping of the previous zone. Its name is made up of a reverse listing of the **mytrek.com** domain's IP address with the term **IN-ADDR.ARPA** appended. The domain address for **mytrek.com** is 192.168.0, so the reverse is 1.168.192. The **IN-ADDR.ARPA** domain is a special domain that supports gateway location and Internet address to host mapping. The last **zone** statement defines a reverse mapping zone for the loopback interface, the method used by the system to address itself and enable communication between local users on the system. The zone file used for this local zone is **named.local**.

named.conf

```
//
// A simple BIND 9 configuration
//

logging {
        category cname { null; };
       };

options {
        directory "/var/named";
        };

zone "." {
         type hint;
         file "named.ca";
         };

zone "mytrek.com" {
              type master;
              file "mytrek.com";
              };
zone "1.168.192.IN-ADDR.ARPA" {
               type master;
               file "192.168.0";
               };

zone "0.0.127.IN-ADDR.ARPA" {
               type master;
               file "named.local";
               };
```

When BIND is initially installed, it creates a default configuration for what is known as a caching only server. A *caching only server* copies queries made by users and saves them in a cache, for use later if the queries are repeated. This can save DNS lookup response times. The cache is held in memory and only lasts as long as **named** runs. The following example is the **named.conf** file initially installed for a caching only server. Only the local and cache zones are defined.

named.conf (caching only server)

```
// generated by named-bootconf.pl
```

SERVERS

```
options {
        directory "/var/named";
        };

//
// a caching only nameserver config
//
zone "." {
        type hint;
        file "named.ca";
        };

zone "0.0.127.IN-ADDR.ARPA" {
                type master;
                file "named.local";
                };
```

Resource Records

Your name server holds domain name information about the hosts on your network in resource records placed in zone and reverse mapping files. Resource records are used to associate IP addresses with fully qualified domain names. You need a record for every computer in the zone that the name server services. A record takes up one line, though you can use parentheses to use several lines for a record, as is usually the case with SOA records. A resource record uses the Standard Resource Record Format as shown here:

```
name [<ttl>] [<class>] <type> <rdata> [<comment>]
```

Here, **name** is the name for this record. It can be a domain name for a fully qualified domain name. If you only specify the hostname, the default domain is appended. If no name entry exists, the last specific name is used. If the **@** symbol is used, the name server's domain name is used. **ttl** (time to live) is an optional entry that specifies how long the record is to be cached. ***class*** is the class of the record. The class used in most resource record entries is IN, for Internet. By default, it is the same as that specified for the domain in the **named.conf** file. *type* is the type of the record. *rdata* is the resource record data. The following is an example of a resource record entry. The name is **rabbit.mytrek.com**, the class is Internet (IN), the type is a host address record (A), and the data is the IP address 192.168.0.2.

```
rabbit.mytrek.com. IN A 192.168.0.2
```

Different types of resource records exist for different kinds of hosts and name server operations (see Table 22-8 for a listing of resource record types). A, NS, MX, PTR, and CNAME are the types commonly used. A is used for host address records that match

Type	Description
A	Host address, maps hostname to IP address
A6	An IPv6 host address
NS	Authoritative name server for this zone
CNAME	Canonical name, used to define an alias for a hostname
SOA	Start of Authority, starts DNS entries in zone file, specifies name server for domain, and other features such as server contact and serial number
WKS	Well-known service description
PTR	Pointer record, for performing reverse domain name lookups, maps IP address to hostname
RP	Text string that contains contact information about a host
HINFO	Host information
MINFO	Mailbox or mail list information
MX	Mail exchanger, informs remote site of your zone's mail server
TXT	Text strings, usually information about a host
KEY	Domain private key
SIG	Resource record signature
NXT	Next resource record

Table 22-8. *Domain Name Service Resource Record Types*

domain names with IP addresses. NS is used to reference a name server. MX specifies the host address of the mail server that services this zone. The name server has mail messages sent to that host. The PTR type is used for records that point to other resource records and is used for reverse mapping. CNAME is used to identify an alias for a host on your system.

Start of Authority: SOA

A zone and reverse mapping files always begin with a special resource record called the Start of Authority (SOA) record. This record specifies that all the following records are authoritative for this domain. It also holds information about the name server's domain, which is to be given to other name servers. An SOA record has the same format as other resource records, though its data segment is arranged differently. The format for an SOA record follows:

```
name {ttl} class SOA Origin Person-in-charge (
                                      Serial number
                                      Refresh
                                      Retry
                                      Expire
                                      Minimum )
```

Each zone has its own SOA record. The SOA begins with the zone name specified in the **named.conf** zone entry. This is usually a domain name. An @ symbol is usually used for the name and acts like a macro expanding to the domain name. The *class* is usually the Internet class, IN. *SOA* is the type. *Origin* is the machine that is the origin of the records, usually the machine running your name server daemon. The *person-in-charge* is the e-mail address for the person managing the name server (use dots, not @, for the e-mail address, as this symbol is used for the domain name). Several configuration entries are placed in a block delimited with braces. The first is the *serial number.* You change the serial number when you add or change records, so that it is updated by other servers. The serial number can be any number, as long as it is incremented each time a change is made to any record in the zone. A common practice is to use the year-month-day- number for the serial number, where number is the number of changes in that day. For example, 1999120403 would be the year 1999, December 4, for the third change. Be sure to update it when making changes.

Refresh specifies the time interval for refreshing SOA information. *Retry* is the frequency for trying to contact an authoritative server. *Expire* is the length of time a secondary name server keeps information about a zone without updating it. *Minimum* is the length of time records in a zone live. The times are specified in the number of seconds.

The following example shows an SOA record. The machine running the name server is **turtle.mytrek.com,** and the e-mail address of the person responsible for the server is **hostmaster.turtle.mytrek.com**. Notice the periods at the end of these names. For names with no periods, the domain name is appended. **turtle** would be the same as **turtle.mytrek.com**. When entering full hostnames, be sure to add the period so that the domain is not appended.

```
@ IN SOA turtle.mytrek.com. hostmaster.turtle.mytrek.com. (
                                        1997022700 ; Serial
                                        28800 ; Refresh
                                        14400 ; Retry
                                        3600000 ; Expire
                                        86400 ) ; Minimum
```

Name Server: NS

The name server record specifies the name of the name server for this zone. These have a resource record type of NS. If you have more than one name server, list them in NS records. These records usually follow the SOA record. As they usually apply to the same domain as the SOA record, their name field is often left blank to inherit the server's domain name specified by the @ symbol in the previous SOA record.

```
IN   NS      turtle.mytrek.com.
```

You can, if you wish, enter the domain name explicitly as shown here:

```
mytrek.com.   IN   NS      turtle.mytrek.com.
```

Address Record: A and A6

Resource records of type A are address records that associate a fully qualified domain name with an IP address. Often, only their hostname is specified. Any domain names without a terminating period automatically have the domain appended to them. Given the domain **mytrek.com**, the **turtle** name in the following example is expanded to **turtle.mytrek.com**:

```
rabbit.mytrek.com. IN    A      192.168.0.2
turtle             IN    A      192.168.0.1
```

BIND versions 8.2.2 and 9.1 support IPv6 addresses. IPv6 IP addresses have a very different format from that of the IPv4 addresses commonly used (see Chapter 36). Instead of the numerals arranged in four segments, IPv6 uses hexadecimal numbers arranged in seven segments. Though BIND checks for both IPv4 and IPv6 addresses, currently you should always use a system's IPv4 address if it has one. In the following example, **divit.mygolf.com** is associated with its IPv6 address:

```
divit.mygolf.com.    IN    A6    3ffe:8050:201:1860:1::3
```

BIND also supports IPv6 resolution features such as A6 chains, which allow you to specify part of the address as a network domain name. This would be the name of a network through which the host connects to the Internet. The network domain name is then used to complete the address.

```
divit.mygolf.com.    IN    A6    0:0:0:0:1::3mytrek.com.
```

Mail Exchanger: MX

The Mail Exchanger record, MX, specifies the mail server that is used for this zone or for a particular host. The mail exchanger is the server to which mail for the host is sent. In the following example, the mail server is specified as **turtle.mytrek.com**. Any mail sent to the address for any machines in that zone will be sent to the mail server, which in turn will send it to the specific machines. For example, mail sent to a user on **rabbit.mytrek.com** will first be sent to **turtle.mytrek.com**, which will then send it on to **rabbit.mytrek.com**. In the following example, the host 192.168.0.1 (**turtle.mytrek.com**) is defined as the mail server for the **mytrek.com** domain:

```
mytrek.com.  IN     MX   10   turtle.mytrek.com.
```

You could also inherit the domain name from the SOA record, leaving the domain name entry blank.

```
IN     MX   turtle.mytrek.com.
```

You could use the IP address instead, but in larger networks, the domain name may be needed to search for and resolve the IP address of a particular machine, which could change.

```
mytrek.com.  IN     MX   10   192.168.0.1
```

An MX record recognizes an additional field that specifies the ranking for a mail exchanger. If your zone has several mail servers, you can assign them different rankings in their MX records. The smaller number has a higher ranking. This way, if mail cannot reach the first mail server, it can be routed to an alternate server to reach the host. In the following example, mail for hosts on the **mytrek.com** domain is first routed to the mail server at 192.168.0.1 (**turtle.mytrek.com**), and if that fails, it is routed to the mail server at 192.168.0.2 (**rabbit.mytrek.com**).

```
mytrek.com. IN MX 10 turtle.mytrek.com.
            IN MX 20 rabbit.mytrek.com.
```

You can also specify a mail server for a particular host. In the following example, the mail server for **lizard.mytrek.com** is specified as **rabbit.mytrek.com**:

```
lizard.mytrek.com. IN     A        192.168.0.3
                   IN     MX  10   rabbit.mytrek.com.
```

Aliases: CNAME

Resource records of type CNAME are used to specify alias names for a host in the zone. Aliases are often used for machines running several different types of servers, such as both Web and FTP servers. They are also used to locate a host when it changes its name. The old name becomes an alias for the new name. In the following example, **ftp.mytrek.com** is an alias for a machine actually called **turtle.mytrek.com**:

```
ftp.mytrek.com. IN CNAME turtle.mytrek.com.
```

The term CNAME stands for canonical name. The canonical name is the actual name of the host. In the example above the canonical name is **turtle.mytrek.com**. The alias, also known as the CNAME, is **ftp.mytrek.com**. In a CNAME entry, the alias points to the canonical name. Aliases cannot be used for NS (name server) or MX (mail server) entries. For those records you need to use the original domain name or IP address.

A more stable way to implement aliases is simply to create another address record for it. You can have as many hostnames for the same IP address as you want, provided they are certified. For example, to make **www.mytrek.com** an alias for **turtle.mytrek.com**, you only have to add another address record for it, giving it the same IP address as **turtle.mytrek.com**.

```
turtle.mytrek.com.    IN    A    192.168.0.1
www.mytrek.com.       IN    A    192.168.0.1
```

Pointer Record: PTR

A PTR record is used to perform reverse mapping from an IP address to a host. PTR records are used in the reverse mapping files. The name entry holds a reversed IP address and the data entry holds the name of the host. The following example maps the IP address 192.168.0.1 to **turtle.mytrek.com**:

```
1.1.168.192    IN    PTR    turtle.mytrek.com.
```

In a PTR record you can specify just that last number segment of the address (the host address), and let DNS fill in the domain part of the address. In the next example, 1 has the domain address, 1.168.192, automatically added to give 1.1.168.192:

```
1 IN PTR turtle.mytrek.com.
```

Host Information: HINFO, RP, MINFO, and TXT

The HINFO, RP, MINFO, and TXT records are used to provide information about the host. The RP record enables you to specify the person responsible for a certain host.

The HINFO record provides basic hardware and operating system identification. The TXT record is used to enter any text you want. MINFO provides a host's mail and mailbox information. These are used sparingly as they may give too much information out about the server.

Zone Files

A DNS server uses several zone files covering different components of the DNS. Each zone uses two zone files: the principal zone file and a reverse mapping zone file. The *zone file* contains the resource records for hosts in the zone. A *reverse mapping file* contains records that provide reverse mapping of your domain name entries, enabling you to map from IP addresses to domain names. The name of the file used for the zone file can be any name. The name of the file is specified in the **zone** statement's file entry in the **named.conf** file. If your server supports several zones, you may want to use a name that denotes the specific zone. Most systems use the domain name as the name of the zone file. For example, the zone **mytrek.com** would have a zone file also called **mytrek.com**. These could be placed in a subdirectory called **zones** or **master**. The zone file used in the following example is called **mytrek.com**. The reverse mapping file can also be any name, though it is usually the reverse IP address domain specified in its corresponding zone file. For example, in the case of **mytrek.com** zone file, the reverse mapping file might be called **192.168.0**, the IP address of the **mytrek.com** domain defined in the **mytrek.com** zone file. This file would contain reverse mapping of all the host addresses in the domain, allowing their hostname addresses to be mapped to their corresponding IP addresses. In addition, BIND sets up a cache file and a reverse mapping file for the localhost. The cache file holds the resource records for the root name servers to which your name server connects. The cache file can be any name, although it is usually called **named.ca**. The localhost reverse mapping file holds reverse IP resource records for the local loopback interface, localhost. Although localhost can be any name, it usually has the name **named.local**.

Zone Files for Internet Zones

A zone file holds resource records that follow a certain format. The file begins with general directives to define default domains or to include other resource record files. These are followed by a single SOA, name server, and domain resource records, and then resource records for the different hosts. Comments begin with a semicolon and can be placed throughout the file. The @ symbol operates like a special macro, representing the domain name of the zone to which the records apply. The @ symbol is used in the first field of a resource or SOA record as the zone's domain name. Multiple names can be specified using the * matching character. The first field in a resource record is the name of the domain to which it applies. If the name is left blank, the next previous explicit name entry in another resource record is automatically used. This way, you can list several entries that apply to the same host without having to repeat the hostname. Any host or domain name used throughout this file that is not terminated with a period has the zone's domain appended to it. For example, if the zone's domain is **mytrek.com** and a resource record has only the name **rabbit** with no trailing period, the zone's domain is automatically appended to it, giving you **rabbit.mytrek.com.** Be sure to include the trailing period whenever you enter the complete fully qualified domain name as in **turtle.mytrek.com.**. You can also use several directives to set global attributes. $ORIGIN sets a default domain name to append to address names that do not end in a period. $INCLUDE includes a file. $GENERATE can generate records whose domain or IP addresses differ only by an iterated number.

A zone file begins with an SOA record specifying the machine the name server is running on, among other specifications. The @ symbol is used for the name of the SOA record, denoting the zone's domain name. After the SOA, the name server resource records (NS) are listed. Just below the name server records are resource records for the domain itself. Resource records for host addresses (A), aliases (CNAME), and mail exchangers (MX) follow. The following example shows a sample zone file, which begins with an SOA record and is followed by an NS record, resource records for the domain, and then resource records for individual hosts:

```
; Authoritative data for turle.mytrek.com
;
@ IN SOA turtle.mytrek.com. hostmaster.turtle.mytrek.com.(
                              93071200 ; Serial number
                                 10800 ; Refresh 3 hours
                                  3600 ; Retry 1 hour
                               3600000 ; Expire 1000 hours
                               86400 ) ; Minimum 24 hours

             IN      NS         turtle.mytrek.com.
             IN      A          192.168.0.1
             IN      MX    10   turtle.mytrek.com.
             IN      MX    15   rabbit.mytrek.com.

turtle       IN      A          192.168.0.1
             IN      HINFO      PC-686 LINUX
gopher       IN      CNAME      turtle.mytrek.com.
ftp          IN      CNAME      turtle.mytrek.com.
www          IN      A          192.168.0.1

rabbit       IN      A          192.168.0.2

lizard       IN      A          192.168.0.3
             IN      HINFO      MAC MACOS
localhost    IN      A          127.0.0.1
```

The first two lines are comments about the server for which this zone file is used. Notice that the first two lines begin with a semicolon. The class for each of the resource records in this file is IN, indicating these are Internet records. The SOA record begins with an @ symbol that stands for the zone's domain. In this example, it is **mytrek.com**. Any host or domain name used throughout this file that is not terminated with a period has this domain appended to it. For example, in the following resource record, **turtle** has no period, so it automatically expands to **turtle.mytrek.com**. The same happens for **rabbit** and **lizard**. These are read as **rabbit.mytrek.com** and **lizard.mytrek.com**. Also, in the SOA, notice that the e-mail address for hostmaster uses a period instead of an @ symbol; @ is a special symbol in zone files and cannot be used for any other purpose.

The next resource record specifies the name server for this zone. Here, it is **mytrek.com.** Notice the name for this resource record is blank. If the name is blank, a resource record inherits the name from the previous record. In this case, the NS record inherits the value of @ in the SOA record, its previous record. This is the zone's domain and the NS record specifies **turtle.mytrek.com** is the name server for this zone.

```
IN   NS    turtle.mytrek.com.
```

Here the domain name is inherited. The entry can be read as the following. Notice the trailing period at the end of the domain name.

```
mytrek.com. IN   NS    turtle.mytrek.com.
```

The following address records set up an address for the domain itself. This is often the same as the name server, in this case 192.168.0.1 (the IP address of **turtle.mytrek.com**). This enables users to reference the domain itself, rather than a particular host in it. A mail exchanger record follows that routes mail for the domain to the name server. Users can send mail to the **mytrek.com** domain and it will be routed to **turtle.mytrek.com.**

```
IN    A     192.168.0.1
```

Here the domain name is inherited. The entry can be read as the following:

```
mytrek.com.   IN   A     192.168.0.1
```

The next records are mail exchanger (MX) records listing **turtle.mytrek.com** and **fast.mytrek.com** as holding the mail servers for this zone. You can have more than one mail exchanger record for host. More than one host may exist through which mail can be routed. These can be listed in mail exchanger records for which you can set priority rankings (smaller number ranks higher). In this example, if **turtle.mytrek.com** cannot be reached, its mail is routed through **rabbit.mytrek.com**, which has been set up also to handle mail for the **mytrek.com** domain.

```
            IN      MX      100     turtle.mytrek.com.
            IN      MX      150     rabbit.mytrek.com.
```

Again the domain name is inherited. The entries can be read as the following:

```
mytrek.com.       IN       MX  100   turtle.mytrek.com.
mytrek.com.       IN       MX  150   rabbit.mytrek.com.
```

The following resource record is an address record (A) that associates an IP address with the fully qualified domain name **turtle.mytrek.com**. The resource record name only holds **turtle** with no trailing period, so it is automatically expanded to **turtle.mytrek.com.** This record provides the IP address to which **turtle.mytrek.com** can be mapped.

```
turtle    IN    A     192.168.0.1
```

Several resource records immediately follow that have blank names. These inherit their names from the preceding full record—in this case, **turtle.mytrek.com.** In effect, these records also apply to that host. Using blank names is an easy way to list additional resource records for the same host (notice that an apparent indent occurs). The first record is an information record, providing the hardware and operating system for the machine.

```
          IN    HINFO    PC-686 LINUX
```

If you are using the same machine to run several different servers, such as Web, FTP, and Gopher servers, you may want to assign aliases to these servers to make accessing them easier for users. Instead of using the actual domain name, such as **turtle.mytrek.com,** to access the Web server running on it, users may find using the following is easier: for the Web server, **www.mytrek.com**; for the Gopher server, **gopher.mytrek.com**; and for the FTP server, **ftp.mytrek.com**. In the DNS, you can implement such a feature using alias records. In the example zone file, two CNAME alias records exist for the **turtle.mytrek.com** machine: FTP and Gopher. The next record implements an alias for **www** using another address record for the same machine. None of the name entries ends in a period, so they are appended automatically with the domain name **mytrek.com**. **www.mytrek.com**, **ftp.mytrek.com**, and **gopher.mytrek.com** are all aliases for **turtle.mytrek.com**. Users entering those URLs automatically access the respective servers on the **turtle.mytrek.com** machine.

Address and main exchanger records are then listed for the two other machines in this zone: **rabbit.mytrek.com** and **lizard.mytrek.com**. You could add HINFO, TXT, MINFO, or alias records for these entries. The file ends with an entry for localhost, the special loopback interface that allows your system to address itself.

Reverse Mapping File

Reverse name lookups are enabled using a reverse mapping file. *Reverse mapping files* map fully qualified domain names to IP addresses. This reverse lookup capability is unnecessary, but it is convenient to have. With reverse mapping, when users access remote hosts, their domain name address can be used to identify their own host, instead of only the IP address. The name of the file can be anything you want. On most current distributions, it is the zone's domain address (the network part of a zone's IP address). For example, the reverse mapping file for a zone with the IP address of 192.168.0.1 is 192.168.0. Its full pathname would be something like **/var/named/192.168.0.** On some systems using older implementations of BIND, the reverse mapping filename may consist of the root name of the zone file with the extension **.rev**. For example, if the zone file is called **mytrek.com,** the reverse mapping file would be called something like **mytrek.rev**. The zone entry for a reverse mapping in the **named.conf** file uses a special domain name consisting of the IP address in reverse, with an **IN-ADDR.ARPA** extension. This reverse IP address becomes the zone domain referenced by the @ symbol in the reverse mapping file. For example, the reverse mapping zone name for a domain with the IP address of **192.168.43** would be **43.168.192.IN-ADDR.ARPA**. In the following example, the reverse domain name for the domain address **192.168.0** is **1.168.192.IN-ADDR.ARPA**:

```
zone "1.168.192.IN-ADDR.ARPA" in {
        type master;
        file "192.168.0";
        };
```

A reverse mapping file begins with an SOA record, which is the same as that used in a forward mapping file. Resource records for each machine defined in the forward mapping file then follow. These resource records are PTR records that point to hosts in the zone. These must be actual hosts, not aliases defined with CNAME records. Records for reverse mapping begin with a reversed IP address. Each segment in the IP address is sequentially reversed. Each segment begins with the host ID, followed by reversed network numbers. If you list only the host ID with no trailing period, the zone domain is automatically attached. In the case of a reverse mapping file, the zone domain as specified in the `zone` statement is the domain IP address backward. The 1 expands to 1.1.168.192. In the following example, **turtle** and **lizard** inherit the domain IP address, whereas **rabbit** has its address explicitly entered:

```
; reverse mapping of domain names 1.168.192.IN-ADDR.ARPA
;
@ IN SOA turtle.mytrek.com. hostmaster.turtle.mytrek.com.(
                        92050300 ; Serial (yymmddxx format)
                           10800 ; Refresh 3hHours
                            3600 ; Retry 1 hour
                         3600000 ; Expire 1000 hours
                         86400 ) ; Minimum 24 hours

@            IN    NS      turtle.mytrek.com.
1            IN    PTR     turtle.mytrek.com.
2.1.168.192  IN    PTR     rabbit.mytrek.com.
3            IN    PTR     lizard.mytrek.com.
```

Localhost Reverse Mapping

A localhost reverse mapping file implements reverse mapping for the local loopback interface known as *localhost*, whose network address is 127.0.0.1. This file can be any name. On most systems, localhost is given the name **named.local**. On other systems, localhost may use the network part of the IP address, 127.0.0. This file allows mapping the domain name localhost to the localhost IP address, which is always 127.0.0.1 on every machine. The address 127.0.0.1 is a special address that functions as the local address for your machine. It allows a machine to address itself. In the **zone** statement for this file, the name of the zone is **0.0.127.IN-ADDR.ARPA**. The domain part of the IP address is entered in reverse order, with **IN-ADDR.ARPA** appended to it, **0.0.127.IN-ADDR.ARPA**. The **named.conf** entry is shown here:

```
zone "0.0.127.IN-ADDR.ARPA" {
          type master;
          file "named.local";
          };
```

The name of the file used for the localhost reverse mapping file is usually **named.local**, though it can be any name. The NS record specifies the name server localhost should use. This file has a PTR record that maps the IP address to the localhost. The 1 used as the name expands to append the zone domain—in this case, giving you 1.0.0.127, a reverse IP address. The contents of the **named.local** file are shown here. Notice the trailing periods for localhost.

```
@ IN SOA localhost. root.localhost. (
                        1997022700 ; Serial
                             28800 ; Refresh
```

SERVERS

```
                              14400 ; Retry
                            3600000 ; Expire
                            86400 ) ; Minimum

            IN      NS     turtle.mytrek.com.
  1         IN      PTR    localhost.
```

Subdomains and Slaves

Adding a subdomain to a DNS server is a simple matter of creating an additional master entry in the **named.conf** file, and then placing name server and authority entries for that subdomain in your primary DNS server's zone file. The subdomain, in turn, has its own zone file with its SOA record and entries listing hosts, which are part of its subdomain, including any of its own mail and news servers.

The name for the subdomain could be a different name altogether or a name with the same suffix as the primary domain. In the following example, the subdomain is called **beach.mytrek.com**. It could just as easily be called **mybeach.com**. The name server to that domain is on the host **crab.beach.mytrek.com**, in this example. Its IP address is 192.168.0.33 and its zone file is **beach.mytrek.com**. The **beach.mytrek.com** zone file holds DNS entries for all the hosts being serviced by this name server. The following example shows zone entries for its **named.conf**:

```
zone "beach.mytrek.com" {
          type master;
          file "beach.mytrek.com";
          };

zone "1.168.192.IN-ADDR.ARPA" {
          type master;
          file "192.168.0";
          };
```

On the primary DNS server, in the example **turtle.mytrek.com**, you would place entries in the master zone file to identify the subdomain server's host and designate it as a name server. Such entries are also known as *glue records*. In this example, you would place the following entries in the **mytrek.com** zone file on **turtle.mytrek.com**:

```
beach.mytrek.com.       IN    NS    beach.mytrek.com.
beach.mytrek.com.       IN    A     192.168.0.33.
```

URL references to hosts serviced by **beach.mytrek.com** can now be reached from any host serviced by **mytrek.com**, which does not need to maintain any information about the **beach.mytrek.com** hosts. It simply refers such URL references to the **beach.mytrek.com** name server.

A slave DNS server is tied directly to a master DNS server and periodically receives DNS information from it. You use a master DNS server to configure its slave DNS servers automatically. Any changes you make to the master server are automatically transferred to its slave servers. This transfer of information is called a *zone transfer*. Zone transfers are automatically initiated whenever the slave zone's refresh time is reached or the slave server receives a notify message from the master. The *refresh time* is the second argument in the zone's SOA entry. A notify message is automatically sent by the master whenever changes are made to the master zone's configuration files and the **named** daemon is restarted. In effect, slave zones are automatically configured by the master zone, receiving the master zone's zone files and making them their own.

Using the previous examples, suppose you want to set up a slave server on **rabbit.mytrek.com**. Zone entries, as shown in the following example, are set up in the **named.conf** configuration file for the slave DNS server on **rabbit.mytrek.com**. The slave server is operating in the same domain as the master, and so it has the same zone name, **mytrek.com**. Its SOA file is named **slave.mytrek.com**. The term "slave" in the filename is merely a convention that helps identify it as a slave server configuration file. The **masters** statement lists its master DNS server—in this case, 192.168.0.1. Whenever the slave needs to make a zone transfer, it transfers data from that master DNS server. The entry for the reverse mapping file for this slave server lists its reverse mapping file as **slave.192.168.0**.

```
zone "mytrek.com" {
        type slave;
        file "slave.mytrek.com";
        masters { 192.168.0.1;
        };

zone "1.168.192.IN-ADDR.ARPA" {
         type slave;
         file "slave.192.168.0";
         masters { 192.168.0.1;
         };
```

On the master DNS server, the master SOA zone file has entries in it to identify the host that holds the slave DNS server and to designate it as a DNS server. In this example, you would place the following in the **mytrek.com** zone file:

```
        IN       NS       192.168.0.2
```

SERVERS

You would also place an entry for this name server in the **mytrek.com** reverse mapping file:

```
IN        NS        192.168.0.2
```

The master DNS server can control which slave servers can transfer zone information from it using the **allow-transfer** statement. Place the statement with the list of IP addresses for the slave servers for which you want to allow access. Also, the master DNS server should be sure the **notify** option is not disabled. The **notify** option is disabled by a "notify no" statement in the options or zone **named.conf** entries. Simply erase the "no" argument to enable notify.

With BIND versions 8.2.2 and 9.0, BIND now supports incremental zone transfers (IXFR). Previously, all the zone data would be replaced in an update, rather than simply editing in changes such as the addition of a few resource records. With incremental zone transfers, a database of changes is maintained by the master zone. Then only the changes are transferred to the slave zone, which uses this information to update its own zone files. To implement incremental zone transfers, you have to turn on the **maintain-ixfr-base** option in the options section.

```
maintain-ixfr-base yes;
```

You can then use the **ixfr-base** option in a zone section to specify a particular database file to hold changes.

```
ixfr-base "db.mytrek.com.ixfr";
```

IP Virtual Domains

IP-based virtual hosting allows more than one IP address to be used for a single machine. If a machine has two registered IP addresses, either one can be used to address the machine. If you want to treat the extra IP address as another host in your domain, you need only create an address record for it in your domain's zone file. The domain name for the host would be the same as your domain name. If you want to use a different domain name for the extra IP, however, you have to set up a virtual domain for it. This entails creating a new **zone** statement for it with its own zone file. For example, if the extra IP address is 192.168.0.42 and you want to give it the domain name **sail.com**, you must create a new **zone** statement for it in your **named.conf** file with a new zone file. The **zone** statement would look something like this. The zone file is called **sail.com**.

```
zone "sail.com" in {
        type master;
```

```
            file "sail.com";
            };
```

In the **sail.com** file, the name server name is **turtle.mytrek.com** and the e-mail address is **hostmaster@turtle.mytrek.com**. In the name server (NS) record, the name server is **turtle.mytrek.com.** This is the same machine using the original address that the name server is running as. **turtle.mytrek.com** is also the host that handles mail addressed to **sail.com** (MX). An address record then associates the extra IP address 192.168.0.42 with the **sail.com** domain name. A virtual host on this domain is then defined as **jib.sail.com**. Also, **www** and **ftp** aliases are created for that host, creating **www.sail.com** and **ftp.sail.com** virtual hosts.

```
; Authoritative data for sail.com
;
@ IN SOA turtle.mytrek.com. hostmaster.turtle.mytrek.com. (
                              93071200 ; Serial (yymmddxx)
                                 10800 ; Refresh 3 hours
                                  3600 ; Retry 1 hour
                               3600000 ; Expire 1000 hours
                               86400 ) ; Minimum 24 hours

        IN      NS          turtle.mytrek.com.
        IN      MX    10    turtle.mytrek.com.
        IN      A           192.168.0.42 ;address of the sail.com domain

jib     IN      A          192.168.0.42
www     IN      A          jib.sail.com.
ftp     IN      CNAME      jib.sail.com.
```

In your reverse mapping file (**/var/named/1.168.192**), add PTR records for any virtual domains.

```
42.1.168.192       IN      PTR      sail.com.
42.1.168.192       IN      PTR      jib.sail.com.
```

You also have to configure your network connection to listen for both IP addresses on your machine (see Chapter 7).

Cache File

The *cache file* is used to connect the DNS server to root servers on the Internet. The file can be any name. On many systems, the cache file is called **named.ca**. Other systems may call the cache file **named.cache** or **roots.hints**. The cache file is usually a standard file installed by your BIND software, which lists resource records for designated root servers for the Internet. You can obtain a current version of the **named.ca** file from the **rs.internic.net** FTP site. The following example shows sample entries taken from the **named.ca** file:

```
; formerly NS.INTERNIC.NET
;
. 3600000 IN NS A.ROOT-SERVERS.NET.
A.ROOT-SERVERS.NET. 3600000 A 198.41.0.4
;
; formerly NS1.ISI.EDU
;
. 3600000 NS B.ROOT-SERVERS.NET.
B.ROOT-SERVERS.NET. 3600000 A 128.9.0.107
```

If you are creating an isolated intranet, you need to create your own root DNS server until you connect to the Internet. In effect, you are creating a fake root server. This can be another server on your system pretending to be the root or the same name server.

DNS Security: Access Control Lists and DNSSEC

DNS security currently allows you to control specific access by hosts to the DNS server, as well as providing encrypted communications between servers. With access control lists, you can determine who will have access to your DNS server. The DNS Security Extensions (DNSSEC), included with BIND 9.*x*, provide private/public key encrypted authentication and transmissions.

Access Control Lists

To control access by other hosts, you use access control lists, implemented with the **acl** statement. **allow** and **deny** options with access control host lists enable you to deny or allow access by specified hosts to the name server. With **allow-query** you can restrict queries to specified hosts or networks. Normally this will result in a response saying that access is denied. You can further eliminate this response by using the **blackhole** option in the **options** statement.

You define an acl list with the **acl** statement followed by the label you want to give the list and then the list of addresses. Addresses can be IP addresses, network addresses, or a range of addresses based on CNDR notation. You can also use an acl list defined earlier. The following example defines an acl list called **mynet**:

```
acl mynet { 192.168.0.1; 192.168.0.2; };
```

If you are specifying a range, such as a network, you also add exceptions to the list by preceding such addresses with an **!**. In the following example, the mynetx acl lists all those in the 192.168.0.0 network, except for 192.168.0.3:

```
acl myexceptions {192.168.0.0; !192.168.0.3; };
```

Four default acl lists are already defined for you. You can use them wherever an option uses a list of addresses as an argument. These are **any** for all hosts, **none** for no hosts, **localhost** for all local IP addresses, and **localnet** for all hosts on local networks served by the DNS server.

Once a list is defined, you can then use it with the **allow-query**, **allow-transfer**, **allow-recursion**, and **blackhole** options in a **zone** statement to control access to a zone. **allow-query** specifies hosts that can query the DNS server. **allow-transfer** is used for master/slave zones, designating whether update transfers are allowed. **allow-recursion** specifies those hosts that can perform recursive queries on the server. The **blackhole** option will deny contact from any hosts in its list, without sending a denial response. In the next example, an acl list of mynet is created. Then in the **mytrek.com** zone, only these hosts are allowed to query the server. As the server has no slave DNS serves, zone transfers are disabled entirely. The **blackhole** option denies access from the myrejects list, without sending any rejection notice.

```
acl mynet { 192.168.0.0; };
acl myrejects { 10.0.0.44; 10.0.0.93; };

zone "mytrek.com" {
        type master;
        file "mytrek.com";
        allow-query { mynet; };
        allow-recursion { mynet; };
        allow-transfer { none; };
        blackhole {myrejects};
        };
```

DNSSEC

DNSSEC provides DNS encrypted authentication. With DNSSEC, you can create a signed zone that is securely identified with an encrypted signature. This form of security is used primarily to secure the connections between master and slave DNS servers, so that a master server transfers update records only to authorized slave servers and does so with a secure encrypted communication. Two servers that establish such a secure connection do so using a pair of public and private keys. In effect, you have a parent zone that can securely authenticate child zones, using encrypted transmissions. This involves creating zone keys for each child and having those keys used by the parent zone to authenticate the child zones.

You generate a zone key using the **dnssec-keygen** command. A zone key will require the name ZONE (**-n**) and the name of the zone's domain name. The following example creates a zone key for the **mytrek.com** zone.

```
dnssec-keygen -n ZONE mytrek.com.
```

You can further designate an encryption algorithm (**-a**) and key size (**-b**). Use the **-h** option to obtain a listing of the **dnssec-keygen** options. The following example creates a zone key using a 768-bit key and the DSA encryption algorithm:

```
dnssec-keygen -a DSA -b 768 -n ZONE mytrek.com.
```

dnssec-keygen will create public and private keys, each in corresponding files with the suffixes **.private** and **.key**. The private key is used to generate signatures for the zone, and the public key is used to verify the signatures. You add the public key to the DNS configuration file, **named.conf**, using the **$INCLUDE** statement to include the **.key** file.

In the **named.conf** file, you then use three DNSSEC DNS resource records to implement secure communications for a given zone: KEY, SIG, and NXT. In these records you use the signed keys for the zones you have already generated. The KEY record holds public keys associated with zones, hosts, or users. The SIG record stores digital signatures and expiration dates for a set of resource records. The NXT record is used to determine that a resource record for a domain does not exist. In addition, several utilities let you manage DNS encryption. With the dnskeygen utility, you generated the public and private keys used for encryption. dnssigner signs a zone using the zone's private key, setting up authentication.

To secure a DNS zone with DNSSEC you first use dnskeygen to create public and private keys for the DNS zone. Then use dnssigner to create an authentication key. In the DNS zone file, you enter a KEY resource record in which you include the public key. The public key will appear as a lengthy string of random characters. For the KEY record, you enter in the domain name followed by the KEY and then the public key.

```
mytrek.com. KEY 0x4101 3 3 (
AvqyXgKk/uguxkJF/hbRpYzxZFG3x8EfNX38917GX6w7rlLy
BJ14TqvrDvXr84XsShg+OFcUJafNr84U4ER2dg6NrlRAmZA1
jFfV0UpWDWcHBR2jJnvgV9zJB2ULMGJheDHeyztM1KGd2oGk
Aensm74NlfUqKzy/3KZ9KnQmEpj/EEBr48vAsgAT9kMjN+V3
NgAwfoqgS0dwj5OiRJoIR4+cdRt+s32OUKsclAODFZTdtxRn
vXF3qYV0S8oewMbEwh3trXilc7nDMQC3RmoY8RVGt5U6LMAQ
KITDyHU3VmRJ36vn77QqSzbeUPz8zEnbpik8kHPykJZFkcyj
jZoHT1xkJ1tk )
```

For authentication, you can sign particular resource records for a given domain or host. Enter the domain or host followed by the term **SIG** and then the resource record's signature.

```
mytrek.com. SIG KEY 3 86400 19990321010705 19990218010705 4932 com. (
Am3tWJzEDzfU1xwg7hzkiJ0+8UQaPtlJhUpQx1snKpDUqZxm
igMZEVk= )
```

The NXT record lets you negatively answer queries.

```
mytrek.com. NXT ftp.mytrek.com. A NS SOA MX SIG KEY NXT
```

To set up secure communications between a parent (master) and child (slave) DNS server, the public key then needs to be sent to the parent zone. There, the key can be signed by the parent. As you may have more than one zone key, you create a keyset using the **dnssec-makekeyset** command. This generates a file with the extension **.keyset**, that is then sent to the parent. The parent zone then uses the **dnssec-signkey** command to sign a child's keyset. This generates a file with the prefix **signedkey-**. This is sent back to the child and now contains both the child's keyset and the parent's signatures. Once the child has the **signedkey-** files, the **dnssec-signedzone** command can be used to sign the zone. The **dnssec-signedzone** command will generate a file with the extension **.signed**. This file is then included in the **named.conf** file with the INCLUDE operation. The **trusted-keys** statement needs to list the public key for the parent zone.

Note *TSIG (transmission signatures) also provide secure DNS communications, but they use a shared private key instead of a private/public key pair. They are usually used for communications between two local DNS servers.*

Split DNS: Views

BIND 9.*x* allows you to divide DNS space into internal and external views. This organization into separate views is referred to as *split DNS*. Such a configuration is helpful to manage a local network that is connected to a larger network, such as the Internet. Your internal view would include DNS information on hosts in the local network, whereas an external view would show only the part of the DNS space that is accessible to other networks. DNS views are often used when you have a local network that you want to protect from a larger network such as the Internet. In effect, you protect DNS information for hosts on a local network from a larger external network such as the Internet.

To implement a split DNS space, you need to set up different DNS servers for the internal and external views. The internal DNS servers will hold DNS information about local hosts. The external DNS server maintains connections to the Internet through a gateway as well as manages DNS information about any local hosts that allow external access, such as FTP or Web sites. The gateways and Internet-accessible sites make up the external view of hosts on the network. The internal servers handle all queries to the local hosts or subdomains. Queries to external hosts such as Internet sites are sent to the external servers, which then forward them on to the Internet. Queries sent to those local hosts that operate external servers such as Internet FTP and Web sites are sent to the external DNS servers for processing. Mail sent to local hosts from the Internet are handled first by the external servers, which then forward them on to the internal servers. With a split DNS configuration, local hosts can access other local hosts, Internet sites, and local hosts maintaining Internet servers. Internet users, on the other hand, can only access those hosts open to the Internet (served by external servers) such as those with Internet servers like FTP and HTTP. Internet users can, however, send mail messages to any of the local hosts, internal and external.

You can also use DNS views to manage connections between a private network that may use only one Internet address to connect its hosts to the Internet. In this case, the internal view holds the private addresses (192.168…) and the external view connects a gateway host with an Internet address to the Internet. This adds another level of security, providing a result similar to IP masquerading (see Chapter 37).

DNS views are configured with the allow statements such as **`allow-query`** and **`allow-transfer`**. With these statements you can specify the hosts that a zone can send and receive queries and transfers from. For example, the internal zone could accept queries from other local hosts, but not from local hosts with external access such as Internet servers. The local Internet servers, though, can accept queries from the local hosts. All Internet queries are forwarded to the gateway. In the external configuration, the local Internet servers can accept queries from anywhere. The gateways receive queries from both the local hosts and the local Internet servers.

In the following example, a network of three internal hosts and one external host is set up into a split view. There are two DNS servers: one for the internal network and one for external access, based on the external host. In reality these make up one network, but they are split into two views. The internal view is known as **mygolf.com** and the external as **greatgolf.com**. In each configuration, the internal hosts are designated in an acl list labeled internals, and the external host is designated in an acl list labeled externals. Should you want to designate an entire IP address range as internal, you could simply use the network address, as in 192.168.0.0/24. In the options section, **`allow-query`**, **`allow-recursion`**, and **`allow-transfers`** restrict access within the network.

The following example shows only the configuration entries needed to implement an internal view. In the **mygolf.com** zone, queries and transfers are allowed only among internal hosts. The global **`allow-recursion`** option allows recursion among internals.

Internal DNS server

```
acl internals { 192.168.0.1; 192.168.0.2; 192.168.0.3; };
acl externals {10.0.0.1;};
options {
        forward only;
        forwarders {10.0.0.1;}; // forward to external servers
```

```
        allow-transfer { none; }; // allow-transfer to no one by default
        allow-query { internals; externals; };// restrict query access
         allow-recursion { internals; }; // restrict recursion to internals
         }
zone "mygolf.com" {
       type master;
       file "mygolf";
       forwarders { };
       allow-query { internals; };
       allow-transfer { internals; }
       };
```

In the configuration for the external DNS server, the same acl lists are set up for internals and externals. In the `options` statement, recursion is now allowed for both externals and internals. In the **mygolf.com** zone, queries are allowed from anywhere, and recursion is allowed for externals and internals. Transfers are not allowed at all.

External DNS server

```
acl internals { 192.168.0.1; 192.168.0.2; 192.168.0.3; };
acl externals {10.0.0.1;};
options {
        allow-transfer { none; }; // allow-transfer to no one
        allow-query { internals; externals; };// restrict query access
        allow-recursion { internals; externals }; // restrict recursion
        };

zone "greatgolf.com" {
        type master;
        file "greatgolf";
        allow-query { any; };
        allow-transfer { internals; externals; };
};
```

Chapter 23

Mail Servers: SMTP, POP, and IMAP

Mail servers provide Internet users with electronic mail services. They have their own TCP/IP protocols such as Simple Mail Transfer Protocol (SMTP), the Post Office Protocol (POP), and the Internet Mail Access Protocol (IMAP). Messages are sent across the Internet through mail servers that service local domains. A *domain* can be seen as a subnet of the larger Internet, with its own server to handle mail messages sent from or received for users on that subnet. When a user mails a message, it is first sent from their host system to the mail server. The mail server then sends the message to another mail server on the Internet, the one servicing the subnet on which the recipient user is located. The receiving mail server then sends the message to the recipient's host system.

At each stage, a different type of operation takes place using different agents (programs). A mail user agent (MUA) is a mail client program, such as mail or Elm. With a MUA, a user composes a mail message and sends it. Then a mail transport agent (MTA) transports the messages over the Internet. MTAs are mail servers that use SMTP to send messages across the Internet from one mail server to another, transporting them among subnets. On Linux and Unix systems, the commonly used MTA is Sendmail, a mail server daemon that constantly checks for incoming messages from other mail servers and sends outgoing messages to appropriate servers. Other MTAs becoming more popular are Postfix, exim, and Qmail (see Table 23-1). Incoming messages received by a mail server are distributed to a user with mail delivery agents (MDAs). Most Linux systems use procmail as their MDA, taking messages received by the mail server and delivering them to user accounts (see **www.procmail.org** for more information).

Agent	Description
Sendmail	Sendmail mail transfer agent **www.sendmail.com**
Postfix	Fast, easy to configure, and secure mail transfer agent compatible with Sendmail and designed to replace it **www.postfix.org**
Qmail	Fast, flexible, and secure MTA with its own implementation and competitive with Postfix **www.qmail.org**
Exim	MTA based on smail3 **www.exim.org**
Courier	Courier MTA **www.courier-mta.org**

Table 23-1. *Mail Transfer Agents*

Most Linux distributions automatically install and configure Sendmail for you, though several also include Postfix. On starting your system, you can send and receive messages between local users using Sendmail. You can also set up your Linux system to run a POP server. POP servers hold users' mail until they log in to access their messages, instead of having mail sent to their hosts directly. As Sendmail is the default MTA installed automatically with almost every distribution, it will be discussed in detail in this chapter.

Messages sent within a single standalone system require a loopback interface. Most Linux distributions do this automatically for you during the installation process. A *loopback interface* enables your system to address itself, allowing it to send and receive mail to and from itself. A loopback interface uses the hostname **localhost** and a special IP address reserved for use by local systems, 127.0.0.1. You can examine your **/etc/hosts** file to see if your loopback interface has been configured as the local host. You see **127.0.0.1 localhost** listed as the first entry. If, for some reason, no entry exists for **localhost**, you may have to create a loopback interface yourself using the `ifconfig` and `route` commands as shown here (`lo` is the term for loopback):

```
ifconfig lo 127.0.0.1
route add -net 127.0.0.0
```

Received Mail: MX Records

As noted in Chapter 13, a mail address consists of a username and a host address. The host address takes the form of a fully qualified domain name, listing the hostname and the domain name, separated by periods. Most usage of a hostname, such as FTP connections, translate the hostname into an IP address and use the IP address to locate the host system. Mail messages operate nearly the same way. However, they make use of the Domain Name Service to determine which host to actually send a message to. The host specified in the mail address may not be the host to which delivery should actually be made. Different networks will often specify a mail server to which mail for the hosts in a network should be delivered. For example, mail addressed to the **rabbit.mytrek.com** host may actually be delivered to the **turtle.mytrek.com** host. **turtle.mytrek.com** may be running a POP mail server that users on **rabbit.mytrek.com** can access to read their mail.

Such mail servers are associated with different hosts by mail exchange records, known as MX records, in a network's DNS configuration (see Chapter 22). When mail is received in a network, the network's DNS configuration is first checked for MX records to determine if the mail is to be delivered to a host different from that in the mail message address. For example, the following MX record says that any mail for the **rabbit.mytrek.com** host is to be delivered to the **turtle.mytrek.com host**. **turtle.mytrek.com** is the mail exchanger for **rabbit.mytrek.com**.

```
rabbit.mytrek.com.   IN   MX   0   turtle.mytrek.com.
```

A host could have several mail exchangers, each with a different priority. If one is down, the one with next highest priority will be accessed. Such a design provides for more robust mail delivery, letting a few well-maintained servers handle received mail, instead of each host on its own.

Mail exchange records are also used for mail addresses for which there are no hosts. For example, you could designate virtual hosts or use the domain name as an address. To use a domain name, you would have an MX record with the domain name mapped to a mail server on the network. Mail addressed to the domain name would be sent to the mail server. For example, with the following MX record, mail sent to **mytrek.com** would be delivered to **turtle.mytrek.com**, which would be running a mail server like Sendmail:

```
mytrek.com.    IN    MX      0    turtle.mytrek.com.
```

Mail addressed to **george@mytrek.com** would be sent to **george@turtle.mytrek.com**.

MX records are not only used for mail coming in, but also for mail going out. An MX record can specify a mail server to use for relaying mail from a given host out to a larger network.

MX records come into play with certain Sendmail configurations such as masquerading or centralized mail services. MX records are not required. If you have a standalone system or a small network with only a few hosts, you may want mail received directly by different hosts.

Postfix and Qmail

Postfix is a fast, secure, and flexible MTA designed to replace Sendmail while maintaining as much compatibility as possible. Written by Witese Venema and originally released as the IBM Secure Mailer, it is now available under the GNU license. Postfix uses many of the same Sendmail directories and files and makes use of Sendmail wrappers, letting Sendmail clients interact seamlessly with Postfix servers. Postfix is also easier to configure, using its own configuration file. Several distributions, including Red Hat, now provide Postfix along with Sendmail. Instead of one large program, Postfix is implemented as a collection of smaller programs, each designed to perform a specific mail-related task. Each program operates like a daemon, running only as needed. In addition, Postfix was created with security in mind, treating all incoming mail as potential security risks.

Qmail is also a fast and secure MTA, but has little compatibility with Sendmail. It has its own configuration and maintenance files. Like Postfix, it has a modular design, using a different program for each mail task. It also focuses on security, speed, and easy configuration.

Sendmail

Sendmail operates as a server to both receive and send mail messages. Sendmail listens for any mail messages received from other hosts and addressed to users on the network hosts it serves. At the same time, Sendmail handles messages users are sending out to remote users, determining what hosts to send them to. You can learn more about Sendmail at **www.sendmail.org** and **www.sendmail.net**, including online documentation and current software packages. The Sendmail newsgroup is **comp.mail.sendmail**. You can also obtain a commercial version from **www.sendmail.com**.

The domain name server for your network designates the host that runs the Sendmail server. This is your mail host. Messages are sent to this host, whose Sendmail server then sends the message to the appropriate user and its host. In your domain name server configuration file, the mail host entry is specified with an MX entry. To print the mail queue of messages for future delivery, you can use **`mailq`** (or **`sendmail -v -q`**). This runs Sendmail with instructions to print the mail queue.

The Sendmail software package contains several utilities for managing your Sendmail server (see Table 23-2). These include mailq, which displays the queue of outgoing messages; mailstats, which shows statistics on mail server use; hoststat, which provides the stats of remote hosts that have connected with the mail server; and praliases, which prints out the mail aliases listed in the **/etc/aliases** file. Some, like mailq and hoststat, simply invoke Sendmail with certain options. Others, like mailstats and praliases, are separate programs.

Tool	Description
hoststat	Displays status of hosts recently in contact with the mail server (Sendmail).
mailq	Displays list of outgoing messages (Sendmail).
newaliases	Generates database version of aliases file (Sendmail).
purgestat	Clears status information (Sendmail).
mailstats	Displays mail server statistics.
makemap	Generates database version of table files. With no argument, it regenerates all database files.
praliases	Print the aliases file.
smrsh	A security tool that restricts programs that Sendmail can run to a secure directory.

Table 23-2. *Sendmail Tools*

Sendmail now maintains all configuration and database files in the **/etc/mail** directory. Here you will find the Sendmail macro configuration file, **sendmail.mc**, as well as several database files (see Table 23-3). Many have changed their names with the

File	Description
/etc/mail/sendmail.cf	Sendmail configuration file (on Red Hat, this is at **/etc/sendmail.cf**).
/etc/mail/sendmail.mc	Sendmail M4 macro configuration file.
/etc/aliases	Sendmail aliases file for mailing lists.
/etc/aliases.db	Sendmail aliases database file generated by the **newaliases** command using the aliases file.
/etc/mail/access	Sendmail access text file. Access control for screening or relaying messages from different hosts, networks, or users. Used to generate the **access.db** file.
/etc/mail/access.db	Sendmail access database file. Generated from the access text file.
/etc/mail/local-host-names	Sendmail local hosts file for multiple hosts using the same mail server (formerly **sendmail.cw**).
/etc/mail/trusted-users	Sendmail trusted users file (formerly **sendmail.ct**).
/etc/mail/error-header	Sendmail error header file (formerly **sendmail.oE**).
/etc/mail/helpfile	Sendmail help file (formerly **sendmail.ht**).
/etc/mail/statistics	Sendmail statistics file (formerly **sendmail.st**).
/etc/mail/virtusertable	Sendmail virtual user table text file. Maps user virtual domain addresses, allowing virtual domains to be hosted on one system. Make entries in this file and then use it to generate the **virtusertable.db** file.
/etc/mail/virtusertable.db	Sendmail virtual user table database generated from the **virtusertable** file.
/etc/mail/mailertable	Sendmail mailer table text file, used to override routing for your domains.

Table 23-3. *Sendmail Files and Directories*

File	Description
/etc/mail/mailertable.db	Sendmail mailer table database file, generated from the **mailertable** file.
/etc/mail/userdb	Sendmail user database file.
/etc/mail/domaintable	Sendmail **domaintable** file, maps a domain name to another domain name.
/etc/mail/domaintable.db	Sendmail **domaintable** database file, generated from the **domaintable** file.
/var/spool/mail	Incoming mail.
/var/spool/mqueue	Outgoing mail.
/var/spool/maillog	Mail log file.

Table 23-3. *Sendmail Files and Directories* (continued)

release of Sendmail 8.10. For example, the help file is now **/etc/mail/helpfile** instead of **/etc/sendmail.ht**. Specialized files provide support for certain features such as access, which lets you control access by different hosts and networks to your mail server. **virtusertable** lets you designate virtual hosts. These files have both a text and database version. The database version ends with the extension **.db** and is the file actually used by Sendmail. You would make your entries in the text version and then effect the changes by generating a corresponding database version. Database versions are generated using the **makemap** command with the **hash** option and a redirection operation for the text and database file. For example, to deny access to a particular host, you would place the appropriate entry for it in the **/etc/mail/access** file, editing the file using any text word processor. Then, to generate the **/etc/mail/access.db** version of the access file, you would change to the **/etc/mail directory** and use the following command:

```
cd /etc/mail
makemap hash access < access
```

To regenerate all the database files, just use the **make** command in the **/etc/mail** directory:

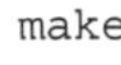

```
make
```

Certain files and directories are used to manage the mail received and sent. Incoming mail is usually kept in the **/var/spool/mail** directory, and outgoing messages are held in the **/var/spool/mqueue** directory, with subdirectories for different users. Monitoring and error messages are logged in the **/var/log/maillog** file.

*Red Hat still places the Sendmail configuration file, **sendmail.cf**, in the **/etc** directory instead of the **/etc/mail** directory.*

*If your mail server services several hosts, you will need to enter them in the **/etc/mail/local-host-names** file.*

Aliases and LDAP

With Sendmail 8.10, Sendmail can now support the Lightweight Directory Access Protocol (LDAP). LDAP enables the use of a separate server to manage Sendmail queries about user mail addresses. Instead of maintaining aliases and **virtusertable** files on different servers, LDAP support allows Sendmail to simply use one centralized LDAP server to locate recipients. Mail addresses are looked up in the LDAP server, instead of having to search several aliases and **virtusertable** files on different servers. LDAP also provides secure authentication of users, allowing controlled access to mail accounts. The following example enables LDAP support on Sendmail in the **sendmail.mc** file:

```
FEATURE('ldap_routing')dnl
LDAPROUTE_DOMAIN('mytrek.com')dnl
```

Alternatively, Sendmail still supports the use of aliases, either for sent or received mail. It checks an aliases database file called **aliases.db** that holds alias names and their associated e-mail addresses. This is often used for administrator mail, where mail may be sent to the system's root user and then redirected to the mail address of the actual system administrator. You can also alias host addresses, enabling you to address hosts on your network using only their aliases. Alias entries are kept in the **/etc/aliases** file. This file consists of one-line alias records associating aliases with user addresses. You can edit this file to add new entries or to change old ones. They are then stored for lookup in the **aliases.db** file using the command **`newaliases`**, which runs Sendmail with instructions to update the **aliases.db** file.

Aliases allow you to give different names for an e-mail address or collection of e-mail addresses. One of its most useful features is to create a mailing list of users. Mail addresses to an alias will be sent to the user or list of users associated with the alias. An alias entry consists of an alias name terminated by a colon and followed by a username or comma-separated list of users. For example, to alias **filmcritic** with the user **george@rabbit.mytrek.com**, you would use the following entry:

```
filmcritic:   george@rabbit.mytrek.com
```

To alias **singers** with the local users **aleina** and **larisa**, you would use

```
singers:     aleina, larisa
```

You can also use aliases as the target addresses, in which case they will expand to their respective user addresses. For example, the **performers** alias will expand through the **filmcritic** and **singers** aliases to the users **george@rabbit.mytrek.com**, **aleina**, and **larisa**.

```
performers:     filmcritic, singers
```

Once you have made your entries in the **/etc/mail/aliases** file, you need to generate a database version using the **newaliases** command:

```
newaliases
```

Sendmail Configuration

The main Sendmail configuration file is **sendmail.cf,** located in the **/etc** directory. This file consists of a sometimes lengthy list of mail definitions that set general options, designate MTAs, and define the address rewrite rules. A series of options set features, such as maximum size of mail messages or the name of host files. The MTAs are those mailers through which Sendmail routes messages. The rewrite rules "rewrite" a mail address to route through the appropriate Internet connections to its destination (these rules can be complex). Check the Sendmail HOW-TO and the online documentation for a detailed explanation.

The **sendmail.cf** definitions can be complex and confusing. To simplify the configuration process, Sendmail supports the use of macros you can use to generate the **sendmail.cf** file using the m4 preprocessor (this requires installation of the sendmail-cf package). Macros are placed in the **/etc/mail/sendmail.mc** file. Here, you can use macros to designate the definitions and features you want for Sendmail, and then the macros are used to generate the appropriate definitions and rewrite rules in the **sendmail.cf** file. As part of the Sendmail package, several specialized versions of the **sendmail.mc** file are made available in the **/usr/share/sendmail-cf** directory. These begin with a system name and have the suffix **.mc**. On many distributions, a specialized version tailored to your distribution is already installed as your **/etc/mail/sendmail.mc** file.

Once you configure your **sendmail.mc** file, you use the following command to generate a **sendmail.cf** file (be sure first to back up your original **sendmail.cf** file). You can rename the **sendmail.mc** file to reflect the specific configuration. You can have as many different **.mc** files as you want and use them to implement different configurations.

```
m4 sendmail.mc > /etc/mail/sendmail.cf
```

You will then need to restart the Sendmail server to make the configuration effective:

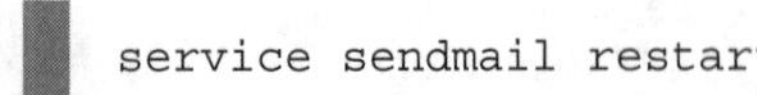

```
service sendmail restart
```

Note *You can also perform basic Sendmail configuration using Linuxconf and Webmin.*

In the **sendmail.mc** file, you configure different aspects of Sendmail using either a **`define`** command to set the value of Sendmail variables or a Sendmail macro that has already been defined to set a particular Sendmail feature. For example, to assign the **`PROCMAIL_PATH`** variable to the directory **/usr/bin/procmail**, you would use the following:

```
define('PROCMAIL_MAILER_PATH','/usr/bin/procmail')
```

Similarly, if there are variables that you do not want defined, you can remove them with the **`undefine`** command:

```
undefine('UUCP_RELAY')
```

To specify the type of operating system that your Sendmail server is running on, you would use the **`OSTYPE`** Sendmail macro. The following example specifies the Linux operating system:

```
OSTYPE('linux')
```

The **`MAILER`** macro specifies the mail delivery agents (MDAs) to be used. You may have more than one. Usually, you will need a mail delivery agent such as procmail for delivering mail to hosts on your network. In addition, Sendmail in effect operates as an MDA to receive messages from hosts in its local network, which it will then send out to the larger network.

```
MAILER(procmail)
MAILER(smtp)
```

Sendmail also supports an extensive number of features that you need to explicitly turn on. You can do this with the Sendmail **`FEATURE`** macro. See Table 23-4 for a list of Sendmail features. The following example turns on the **`redirect`** feature, which is used to inform a sender that a recipient is now at a different address:

```
FEATURE(redirect)
```

Feature	Description
`use_cw_file`	Checks for hosts served by the mail server **/etc/mail/local-host-names** file.
`use_ct_file`	Reads a list of users from the **/etc/trusted-users** file. These are trusted users that can change the sender name for their messages.
`redirect`	Rejects all mail addressed to "address.REDIRECT" , providing a forwarding address is placed in the **/etc/aliases** file.
`nouucp`	Does nothing special with UUCP addresses.
`nocanonify`	Doesn't pass addresses for canonification.
`mailertable`	Uses a mailer table file, **/etc/mail/mailertable**, to override routing for particular domains.
`domaintable`	Uses a domain table file, **/etc/mail/domaintable,** to map one domain to another. Useful if you change your domain name.
`uucpdomain`	Domain feature for UUCP hosts.
`always_add_domain`	Adds the local host domain to local mail on your system (those for which you would only need a username).
`allmasquerade`	Causes recipient addresses to also masquerade as being from the masquerade host.
`masquerade_entire_domain`	Masquerades all hosts within the domain specified in **`MASQUERADE_AS`**.
`masquerade_envelope`	Masquerades envelope sender and recipient along with headers.
`virtusertable`	For virtual hosts, maps virtual addresses to real addresses.
`nullclient`	Turns a Sendmail server into a null client, which simply forwards mail messages to a central mail server for processing.
`local_lmtp`	Uses an LMTP-capable local mailer.

Table 23-4. *Sendmail Features*

Feature	Description
`local_procmail`	Uses procmail as the local mailer.
`smrsh`	Uses the Sendmail Restricted Shell (smrsh) for mailing.
`promiscuous_relay`	Allows you to relay mail, allowing mail to be received from outside your domain and sent on to hosts outside your domain.
`relay_entire_domain`	Allows any host in your domain to relay mail (default limits this to hosts in the access database).
`relay_hosts_only`	Checks for relay permission for particular hosts instead of domains.
`accept_unqualified_ senders`	Allows sender e-mail address to be single usernames instead of just fully qualified names that include domain names.
`accept_unresolvable_ domains`	Allows Sendmail to accept unresolvable domain names. Useful for those users in a local network blocked by a firewall from the full DNS namespace. By default, Sendmail requires domains in addresses to be resolvable with DNS.
`access_db`	Accepts or rejects mail from domains and hosts in the access database.
`blacklist_ recipients`	Blocks mail to certain users, such as those that should never receive mail—like the users **nobody**, **host**, and **yp**.
`rbl`	Rejects hosts in the Realtime Blackhole List. Managed by MAPS (Mail Abuse Prevention System LLC) and designed to limit transport of unwanted mass e-mail. **maps.vix.com/rbl/**.
`ldap_routing`	Enables LDAP use.

Table 23-4. *Sendmail Features* (continued)

In addition, you can set certain configuration options. These are variables beginning with the prefix **conf** that you can set and assign values to using the **define** command. There are an extensive number of configuration options, most of which you will not need to change. Table 23-5 lists several of the commonly used ones. The following example defines the **confAUTO_REBUILD** configuration option, which will automatically rebuild the aliases database if needed.

```
define('confAUTO_REBUILD')
```

Options	Description
confMAILER_NAME	The sender name used for internally generated outgoing messages.
confDOMAIN_NAME	Your domain name. Used only if your system cannot determine your local domain name.
confCF_VERSION	Appended to the configuration version name.
confCW_FILE	File that holds alternate hostnames for server.
confCT_FILE	File that holds trusted users.
confCR_FILE	File that holds relay domains.
confUSERDB_SPEC	Specifies the user database.
confALIAS_WAIT	Time to wait to rebuild aliases database.
confMIN_FREE_BLOCKS	Minimum number of free blocks needed on file system for Sendmail to accept new mail.
confMAX_MESSAGE_SIZE	The maximum size of messages that will be accepted (in bytes).
confDELIVERY_MODE	Default delivery mode.
confAUTO_REBUILD	Automatically rebuilds alias file if needed.
confERROR_MODE	Error message mode.
confERROR_MESSAGE	Error message header/file.
confBIND_OPTS	Default options for DNS resolver.
confLOG_LEVEL	Set the Sendmail log level.
confTO_CONNECT	The timeout waiting for an initial connect to complete.
confME_TOO	Includes sender in group expansions.

Table 23-5. *Sendmail Configuration Options*

Options	Description
confTO_INITIAL	The timeout waiting for a response on the initial connect.
confTO_IDENT	The timeout waiting for a response to an IDENT query.
confTO_QUEUERETURN	The timeout before a message is returned as undeliverable.
confTRY_NULL_MX_LIST	If the server is the best MX for a host and hasn't made other arrangements, try connecting to the host directly.
confDEF_USER_ID	Default user ID.
confDOUBLE_BOUNCE_ADDRESS	If an error occurs when sending an error message, send that "double bounce" error message to this address.
confDONT_PROBE_INTERFACES	If set, Sendmail will *not* insert the names and addresses of any local interfaces into the list of known "equivalent" addresses.
confMAX_RCPTS_PER_MESSAGE	Allow no more than the specified number of recipients in an SMTP envelope.

Table 23-5. *Sendmail Configuration Options* (continued)

Certain macros and types of macros need to be placed in the **sendmail.mc** file in a particular sequence as shown here. Notice that **MAILER** is toward the end and **OSTYPE** at the beginning. Local macro definitions (**define**) and **FEATURE** entries follow the **OSTYPE** and **DOMAIN** entries.

```
VERSIONID
OSTYPE
DOMAIN
define
FEATURE
local macro definitions
MAILER
LOCAL_RULE_*
LOCAL_RULESETS
```

The local macro and configuration option definitions that affect a particular feature need to be entered before the **FEATURE** entry. For example, the **redirect** feature uses the aliases file. Any local definition of the aliases file needs to be entered before the **redirect** feature.

```
define('ALIAS_FILE','/etc/aliases')
FEATURE(redirect)
```

You need to be careful how you enter comments into a **sendmail.mc** file. This file is read as a stream of macros, ignoring all white spaces, including newlines. There are no special comment characters that are looked for. Instead, you have to simulate comment indicators using the **dnl** or **divert** commands. The **dnl** command instructs that all characters following that **dnl** command up to and including the next newline are to be ignored. If you place a **dnl** command at the beginning of a text line in the **sendmain.mc** file, it has the effect of turning that line into a comment, ignoring everything on that line—including its newline. Even empty lines will require a **dnl** entry to ignore the newline character:

```
dnl you will have to /etc/mail/sendmail.cf by running this the m4
dnl macro config through preprocessor:
dnl
```

Alternatively, you can use the **divert** command. The **divert** command will ignore all data until another **divert** command is reached:

```
divert(-1)
 This is the macro config file used to generate
 the /etc/mail/sendmail.cf file. If you modify the file regenerate
you will have to regenerate /etc/mail/sendmail.cf by running the m4
macro
divert(0)
```

For Sendmail to work at all, it only requires that the **OSTYPE** and **MAILERS** macros be defined, along with any needed features and options. A very simple Sendmail file is shown here.

mysendmail.mc

```
dnl My sendmail.mc file
OSTYPE('linux')
define('PROCMAIL_MAILER_PATH','/usr/bin/procmail')
FEATURE(redirect)
```

```
MAILER(procmail)
MAILER(smtp)
```

A **sendmail.mc** file usually contains many more entries, particularly for parameters and features. The default Red Hat **sendmail.mc** file is shown here.

/etc/sendmail.mc

```
divert(-1)
dnl This is the sendmail macro config file. If you make changes to this file,
dnl you need the sendmail-cf rpm installed and then have to generate a
dnl new /etc/sendmail.cf by running the following command:
dnl
dnl        m4 /etc/mail/sendmail.mc > /etc/sendmail.cf
dnl
include('/usr/share/sendmail-cf/m4/cf.m4')
VERSIONID('linux setup for Red Hat Linux')dnl
OSTYPE('linux')
define('confDEF_USER_ID',''8:12'')dnl
undefine('UUCP_RELAY')dnl
undefine('BITNET_RELAY')dnl
define('confAUTO_REBUILD')dnl
define('confTO_CONNECT', '1m')dnl
define('confTRY_NULL_MX_LIST',true)dnl
define('confDONT_PROBE_INTERFACES',true)dnl
define('PROCMAIL_MAILER_PATH','/usr/bin/procmail')dnl
define('ALIAS_FILE', '/etc/aliases')dnl
define('STATUS_FILE', '/var/log/sendmail.st')dnl
define('UUCP_MAILER_MAX', '2000000')dnl
define('confUSERDB_SPEC', '/etc/mail/userdb.db')dnl
define('confPRIVACY_FLAGS', 'authwarnings,novrfy,noexpn,restrictqrun')dnl
define('confAUTH_OPTIONS', 'A')dnl
dnl TRUST_AUTH_MECH('DIGEST-MD5 CRAM-MD5 LOGIN PLAIN')dnl
dnl define('confAUTH_MECHANISMS', 'DIGEST-MD5 CRAM-MD5 LOGIN
PLAIN')dnl
dnl define('confTO_QUEUEWARN', '4h')dnl
dnl define('confTO_QUEUERETURN', '5d')dnl
dnl define('confQUEUE_LA', '12')dnl
dnl define('confREFUSE_LA', '18')dnl
dnl FEATURE(delay_checks)dnl
FEATURE('no_default_msa','dnl')dnl
FEATURE('smrsh','/usr/sbin/smrsh')dnl
FEATURE('mailertable','hash -o /etc/mail/mailertable')dnl
FEATURE('virtusertable','hash -o /etc/mail/virtusertable')dnl
FEATURE(redirect)dnl
FEATURE(always_add_domain)dnl
FEATURE(use_cw_file)dnl
FEATURE(use_ct_file)dnl
FEATURE(local_procmail)dnl
FEATURE('access_db')dnl
FEATURE('blacklist_recipients')dnl
EXPOSED_USER('root')dnl
dnl This changes sendmail to only listen on the loopback device 127.0.0.1
dnl and not on any other network devices. Comment this out if you want
dnl to accept email over the network.
```

```
DAEMON_OPTIONS('Port=smtp,Addr=127.0.0.1, Name=MTA')dnl
dnl We strongly recommend to comment this one out if you want to protect
dnl yourself from spam. However, the laptop and users on computers that do
dnl not have 24x7 DNS do need this.
FEATURE('accept_unresolvable_domains')dnl
MAILER(smtp)dnl
MAILER(procmail)dnl
```

Sendmail Masquerading

For a mail server that is relaying messages from local hosts to the Internet, you may want to masquerade the source of the messages. In large networks that have their own mail servers connected to the Internet, Sendmail masquerading can make messages sent by local hosts appear to be sent by the mail server. Their host address will be replaced by the mail server's address. Returned mail can then be sent to the mail server and held in POP or IMAP server mailboxes that can be later accessed by users on the local hosts. Also, entries in the server's virtual user table could forward mail to corresponding users in local hosts.

Masquerading is often used to masque local hosts with a domain name. Any subdomains can also be masqueraded. This method can be applied to situations where an ISP or your network administrator has assigned your network its own domain name. You can then masque all mail messages as coming from your domain name instead of from particular hosts or from any subdomains you may have. For example, if a network's official domain name is **mytrek.com**, all messages from the hosts in the **mytrek.com** network, such as **rabbit.mytrek.com** and **turtle.mytrek.com**, could be masqueraded to appear as just coming from **mytrek.com**. Should the **mytrek.com** network have a subnetwork whose domain is **mybeach.com**, any messages from **mybeach.com** could also be masqueraded as coming from **mytrek.com**.

You could also use masquerading to allow you to use your own Sendmail server to send mail through an ISP that has not given you your own domain. This is the case for many standalone Internet connections where the ISP connects just one host to the Internet, making it part of its own ISP domain. In this case you would masquerade your local domain as that of the ISP's mail domain. Any mail from hosts in **mytrek.com** would be masqueraded as coming from **myisp.com**. The users sending mail would have to correspond to user mail accounts already set up for you by your ISP. Received mail would still be handled by the ISP mail servers. On the other hand, it is just as easy to use the ISP's mail servers for sending mail (provided they are up and running).

Masquerading is turned on with the **MASQUERADE_AS** command. This takes as its argument the name you want to masquerade your mail as. Normally, the name used is just the domain name, without the mail host. In the following example, the mail is masqueraded as simply **mytrek.com**. Mail sent from a local host like **turtle.mytrek.com** will appear to be sent by just **mytrek.com**:

```
MASQUERADE_AS('mytrek.com')dnl
```

You will also have to specify the hosts and domains on your local network that your Sendmail server should masquerade. If you have decided to masquerade all the hosts in your local network, you just need to set the **masquerade_entire_domain** feature, as in:

```
FEATURE('masquerade_entire_domain')dnl
```

If, instead, you want to masquerade particular hosts or your domain has several subdomains that you want masqueraded, you list them in the **MASQUERADE_DOMAIN** entry. You can list either particular hosts or entire domains. For example, given a local network with the local hosts **turtle.mytrek.com** and **rabbit.mytrek.com** you can list them with the **MASQUERADE_DOMAIN** to have them masqueraded. The domain they are masqueraded as is specified in the **MASQUERADE_AS** entry.

```
MASQUERADE_DOMAIN('turtle.mytrek.com rabbit.mytrek.com')dnl
```

If you want to masquerade all the hosts in your local network, you can simply list your local network's domain name. If your local network also supports several subdomains, you can list those as well to masquerade them. For example, to masquerade all the hosts in the **mybeach.com** domain, you would use the following entry:

```
MASQUERADE_DOMAIN('mytrek.com mybeach.com')dnl
```

If you have a long list of domains or hosts, or you want to be able to easily change those that should be masqueraded, you can place them in a file to be read by Sendmail. Specify the file with the **MASQUERADE_DOMAIN_FILE** command:

```
MASQUERADE_DOMAIN_FILE('mydomains')dnl
```

If you just want to masquerade all the hosts in your local domain, you use the **masquerade_entire_domain** feature:

```
FEATURE(masquerade_entire_domain)dnl
```

A common configuration for a local network would specify the domain name in the **MASQUERADE_AS** entry and in the **MASQUERADE_DOMAIN** entry. Using the example **myisp.com** for the domain, the entries would look like this:

```
MASQUERADE_AS(''mytrek.com')dnl
FEATURE(masquerade_entire_domain)dnl
```

If you wanted to masquerade as an ISP's mail domain, you would use the ISP's domain in the **MASQUERADE_AS** entry as shown here:

```
MASQUERADE_AS('myisp.com')dnl
MASQUERADE_DOMAIN('mytrek.com')dnl
```

You can use the **EXPOSED_USER** feature to override masquerading for certain users. The following example exposes the user **root** in **turtle.mytrek.com**, allowing mail to be addressed using the **turtle** hosts, as in **admin@turtle.mytrek.com**, instead of **admin@mytrek.com**:

```
EXPOSED_USER('root')dnl
```

When mail is received from the outside bearing just the address **mytrek.com**, your network needs to know what host to send it to. This is the host designated as the mail server for the **mytrek.com** network. This information is provided by a mail exchange record (MX) in your DNS configuration that will specify that mail sent to **mytrek.com** will be handled by the mail server—in this case, **turtle.mytrek.com**:

```
mytrek.com.      IN     MX      0      turtle.mytrek.com.
```

You further have to be sure that MX relaying is enabled with the **relay_based_on_MX** feature:

```
FEATURE(relay_based_on_MX)dnl
```

All messages will appear to originate from the mail server's host. For example, if your Sendmail mail server is running on **turtle.mytrek.com**, mail sent from a local host called **rabbit.mytrek.com** will appear to have been sent from **turtle.mytrek.com**.

To further masquerade envelopes as well as headers, you add the **masquerade_envelope** feature:

```
FEATURE(masquerade_envelope)dnl
```

You can also masquerade recipient addresses, so that mail sent to users on your local host will be sent instead to the masqueraded address. Use the **allmasquerade** feature to enable recipient masquerading:

```
FEATURE(allmasquerade)dnl
```

Configuring Mail Servers and Mail Clients

Sendmail can be used as either a mail server, handling mail for various hosts on a network, or as a mail client, managing mail for local users on a particular host. In a simple network configuration, you would have each host running Sendmail in a client configuration, and one host operating as a mail server, relaying mail for the network hosts. For a local network connected to the Internet, your local hosts would run Sendmail in a client configuration, and your gateway would run Sendmail in a server configuration (though the mail server would not have to necessarily run on the gateway). The mail server would relay messages from the local network hosts out to the Internet. The mail server could also be used to block unwanted access from outside hosts, such as those sending spam mail. A basic client or server Sendmail configuration involves just a few features in the **/etc/mail/sendmail.mc** file. The default Red Hat configuration listed in the previous section only allows use on a single host, managing messages between users on that host. To enable client and server use, you will need to make changes to the **/etc/mail/sendmail.mc** file.

Configuring Sendmail for a Simple Network Configuration

Most distributions initially configure Sendmail to work only on the system they are running on, localhost. To use Sendmail to send messages to other hosts on a local network, you need to change and add settings in the **sendmail.mc** and **/etc/mail/access** files. A simple network configuration would have Sendmail running on each host, handling both mail sent between users on that host and mail to and from users on other hosts. For each Sendmail server configuration, you would make the changes described in the following section on simple local network configuration.

Simple Local Network Configuration

For messages sent between hosts on your network, you only need to run the Sendmail server on each, making a few changes to their Sendmail configurations. The Sendmail sever on one of your hosts can be configured to handle the task of relaying messages between hosts. Using the network example described earlier, the hosts turtle, rabbit, and lizard will be running their own Sendmail servers. The Sendmail sever on the turtle host will be configured to relay messages between all the hosts, itself included.

On each host on your network, edit the **/etc/mail/sendmail.mc** file and make the following changes. On Red Hat systems, comment out the **`DAEMON_OPTIONS`** line in the default **sendmail.mc** file by placing a **`dnl`** word in front of it, as shown here. Removing this feature will allow you to receive messages over your local network. This entry is restricting Sendmail to the localhost (127.0.0.1):

```
dnl DAEMON_OPTIONS('Port=smtp,Addr=127.0.0.1, Name=MTA')dnl
```

In the **sendmail.mc** file located on the host that you want to handle the relaying of messages, you need to also add the following line.

```
FEATURE(relay_entire_domain)dnl
```

Run the m4 operation to install the changed configuration and then restart the server with the service operation, as described earlier.

You can now e-mail messages from one user to another across your network. For example, **george@turtle.mytrek.com** can now email a message to **larisa@rabbit.mytrek.com.** The local Sendmail servers will take care of sending and delivering mail to users both within their hosts and those located on other network hosts.

Simple Internet Connections

To send mail to and from the Internet, you should make use of the e-mail services provided by your ISP. This can vary depending upon the kind of service you have. For a small network, like a home network, you may have only one Internet connection. In this case, your ISP normally provides e-mail services for you such as a number of mailboxes for designated users. If you have a larger network, your ISP may have set up a separate official domain for you and is relaying mail to your network. In this case you can set up your own mail server to handle Internet mail.

To make use of the mail services that your ISP provides you can use a mail client like those described in Chapter 13. For a basic Internet connection, ISPs will normally provide you with an e-mail address, along with the choice of several other addresses. You could assign these to different users on your network. Your ISP will be operating a smtp and POP or IMAP mail server to handle mail for their users. You users could then access their mail on these servers directly. Mail clients like Netscape, Mozilla, and Kmail let you specify a remote smtp or POP server. The smtp server is used to send mail out and the POP and IMAP servers are used to receive mail. As also discussed in Chapter 13, you can also arrange to have mail delivered directly to a user account on one of your hosts, using fetchmail.

Using your own Sendmail servers to handle Internet mail is a much more complicated process.

Configuring Sendmail for a Centralized Mail Server

Alternatively, you could set up a central mail server to handle all the mail on your network. Mail clients on various hosts could send their messages to the central mail server, which would then relay them out to the larger network or Internet. Mail could then be received at the central mail server, where clients could later retrieve it. There are several ways to set up a central mail server. One of the simplest is to run a central mail server on your gateway host, and then have null client versions of the Sendmail server running on local hosts. Any mail sent from local hosts would be automatically forwarded to the central mail server. Received mail could only be delivered to the central server, usually to a POP or IMAP server also running on the central server's host. Users could then access the POP server to retrieve their mail.

For a centralized configuration, it would make sense to treat users as having their network domain as their address, rather than separate hosts in their network. So the user **cece** on **rabbit.mytrek.com** would have the mail address **cece@mytrek.com**, not **cece@rabbit.mytrek.com**. Users could have the same name as those on their respective hosts, but corresponding users would be set up on the gateway host to handle received mail managed by the POP or IMAP servers.

An effective simple mail server would involve several components:

- A central mail server running on the gateway host
- Each client running Sendmail as a null client
- Masquerading all mail to use the domain address only, not host addresses
- A POP or IMAP server running on the gateway host to handle received mail

Sendmail nullclient Configuration for Central Server

The **nullclient** version of Sendmail is a stripped-down configuration that simply forwards all mail to the central server. It will not relay mail, nor will it deliver any mail locally. To configure a Sendmail client, you first need to comment out the **DAEMON_OPTIONS** line, if present, in the default **sendmail.mc** file by placing a **dnl** word in front of it, as shown here. Removing this feature will allow you to receive messages over your local network. This entry is restricting Sendmail to the localhost (127.0.0.1):

```
dnl DAEMON_OPTIONS('Port=smtp,Addr=127.0.0.1, Name=MTA')dnl
```

In your network, you will want your Sendmail clients to relay their messages through a central mail server, not to operate as servers themselves. You do this by specifying that they are null clients, as well as listing the mail server operating as the mail hub for their network. To configure Sendmail as a null client, you use the **nullclient** feature. Then define the **MAIL_HUB** feature to list the mail server for the network. In this example, the Sendmail mail server is running on **turtle.mytrek.com**.

```
FEATURE('nullclient')dnl
define('MAIL_HUB', 'turtle.mytrek.com')dnl
```

You could also specify the hub with the **nullclient** feature.

```
FEATURE('nullclient', 'turtle.mytrek.com')dnl
```

Once you have made your changes on a host, restart Sendmail on it:

```
service sendmail restart
```

Sendmail Server Configuration

To configure Sendmail as a server, you need to allow it to accept and relay messages for hosts in your local domain. You do this by adding the feature **relay_entire_domain**:

```
FEATURE(relay_entire_domain)dnl
```

If your local network also specifies mail exchange servers where mail is to be sent and received for certain hosts, you also have to add the **relay_based_on_MX** feature:

```
FEATURE(relay_based_on_MX)dnl
```

This feature is needed if your DNS configuration includes any MX entries specifying mail exchange servers for different hosts or subnetworks.

Be sure to also comment out the **DAEMON_OPTIONS** line as you did for the client configuration:

```
dnl DAEMON_OPTIONS('Port=smtp,Addr=127.0.0.1, Name=MTA')dnl
```

The default configuration enables the **access_db** feature, which restricts access only to those hosts or networks listed in the **/etc/mail/access** file. The **relay_entire_domain** feature will override the list of hosts in the access file and allow all hosts on your local network to access the mail server. However, if you want more refined control, you could use the access database instead of the **relay_entire_domain** feature to limit access to certain hosts or subdomains.

These changes are enough to configure a mail server. However, if you also want to masquerade your mail, you will have to add masquerading options in the server's **sendmail.mc** file. These are similar to those described earlier in the Sendmail masquerading section. To masquerade all outgoing mail, giving it your domain address, you use the **MASQUERADE_AS** entry and the **masquerade_entire_domain** feature:

```
FEATURE(masquerade_entire_domain)dnl
MASQUERADE_AS('mytrek.com')dnl
```

In addition, your mail server host has to be configured to accept mail whose messages have just that domain address (not a host address). In this example, the host running the mail server is **turtle.mytrek.com**. This host needs to also be configured to accept mail meant for **mytrek.com**, not just **turtle.mytrek.com**. You can do this by adding **mytrek.com** to the **/etc/mail/local-host-names** file. This makes **mytrek.com** an alias for **turtle.mytrek.com**. Once you have made all your changes, be sure to restart Sendmail:

```
service sendmail restart
```

Receiving Centralized Mail

In a centralized setup, one of the hosts operates as a mail hub in which all mail is delivered to the mail server on that hub. A POP server could also be running on that hub that users could use to access their mail. MX records in the local network's DNS configuration would direct all mail meant for different hosts to the mail hub.

Masquerading would establish a single domain name for all the users on your network, regardless of their hosts. Mail could be sent to just the mail hub and users would access their mail through a POP server. An MX record would direct mail for the masquerade domain to the mail hub.

For example, as noted previously, all users on the **mytrek.com** network would use an address with the domain name **mytrek.com**, as in **chris@mytrek.com**. The hostname would be left out. Masquerading would masquerade any mail sent from **chris@rabbit.mytrek.com** as **chris@mytrek.com**. Received mail would be addressed to **chris@mytrek.com**, which would be directed to an MX mail server, a mail hub, **turtle.mytrek.com**. The MX record would look like this:

```
mytrek.com.        IN     MX    0       turtle.mytrek.com.
```

A corresponding account for each user on all the hosts through the network would be set up at **turtle.mytrek.com**. A POP server on that mail hub could then be used by users to access their mail. With this kind of configuration, e-mail can become network-based instead of host-based. In effect, mail appears to be sent and received directly by all users on the network, instead of through their respective hosts.

Configuring a Workstation with Direct ISP Connection

If you are running a Linux system that is not part of a network, but does have a direct connection to the Internet through an ISP (Internet service provider), then you could simply use the ISP mail servers for sending and receiving mail. Normally, you would have an SMTP mail server for outgoing mail and a POP server for incoming mail. However, you can also configure Sendmail to interface with your ISP.

Be sure to first comment out the **DAEMON_OPTIONS** option as shown in the previous sections.

Normally, your ISP will provide a mail server that will handle mail for its hosts. To make use of the ISP mail server, you can define it with the **SMART_HOST** option. Mail will be sent through the ISP mail server. **SMART_HOST** has the format *type:hostname*, where *type* is the kind of mail server used, usually SMTP. The default is relay. Define the **SMART_HOST** option to use your ISP to send and receive mail:

```
define ('SMART_HOST', 'smtp:mail.my-isp.com')dnl
```

The **SMART_HOST** option is used to indicate a specific remote mail server that you want to have handle the relaying of your network messages. It can be an ISP mail server, as well as any mail server in a larger network.

For a dial-up connection over a modem, you can use various configuration options to control your connection. The **confMESSAGE_TIMEOUT** option lets you control how long mail can remain on the output queue, letting you keep mail until you are ready to dial in and send it. Setting the **confDELIVERY_MODE** option to **queueonly** lets you send mail when you are ready.

The Mailer Table

You can use the mailer table to have mail addressed to a virtual domain routed to the mail server for your network. To reference an entire domain, prefix the domain name with a period. The host to which the mail is routed is prefixed by the mailer used, usually **smtp** for Sendmail. The following entry will route mail addressed to **.mybeach.com** to the mail server **turtle.mytrek.com**:

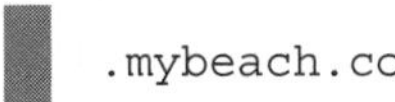

```
.mybeach.com        smtp:turtle.mytrek.com
```

Entries are placed in the **/etc/mail/mailertable** file. Once you have made your entries, generate the **mailertable.db** database file with the **make** command:

```
make mailertable
```

Virtual Hosting: Virtual User Table

As seen in Chapter 22, you can define virtual domains for your network. These virtual domains are mapped to one or more real domains by your DNS server. However, you can receive messages with mail addresses for users on your virtual domains. In this case, you need to map these addresses to users on your real domain so that the mail can be delivered to an existing location. This mapping is carried out by the virtual user table called **/etc/mail/virtusertable**. The virtual user table lets you map mail addresses for virtual domains to users on real domains.

Within a virtual domain, you will have virtual hosts, which will operate off of real hosts on your network. For example, you may have two DNS names for the same host, one real and one virtual. Your host operating as your mail server may also have a virtual hostname by which it can be referenced. Such alternate names should be entered in the local-hostname file. A mail server supporting a virtual domain will have an alternate name consisting of the virtual domain name.

Virtual domains are designated in your DNS configuration, as discussed in Chapter 22. For such a virtual domain, you will need an MX record to specify which real mail server will handle mail for that virtual domain. Make sure there is an MX record connecting your mail server with your virtual host in the DNS zone file for your network. In the following example, the virtual domain **mybeach.com** will have its mail handled by the mail server **turtle.mytrek.com**:

```
mybeach.com.    IN    MX    10    turtle.mytrek.com.
```

Once your mail server for the virtual domain and any alternate names the server may have are specified, you then need to configure your virtual user table. The virtual user table file is specified in the **sendmail.mc** configuration file with the following entry:

```
FEATURE('virtusertable', 'dbm /etc/mail/virtusertable')dnl
```

In the **/etc/mail** directory you will find two versions of the **virtusertable** file, **virtusertable** and **virtusertable.db**. The **virtusertable** file is an editable text version where you enter your virtual host information. The **virtusertable.db** file is a database version of the text file that can be read by Sendmail. You first edit the **virtusertable** file, making your entries. Then you use it to generate the **virtusertable.db** version that can be used by Sendmail:

```
make virtusertable
```

An entry in the **virtusertable** file consists of a virtual address followed by the real address it is mapped to. In the following example, the users **dylan** and **christopher** at the virtual domain **mybeach.com** are mapped to their actual users on real hosts. **dylan@mybeach.com** is mapped to **dylan@turtle.mytrek.com**, and **christopher@mybeach.com** is mapped to **chris@rabbit.mytrek.com**:

```
dylan@mybeach.com             dylan@turtle.mytrek.com
christopher@mybeach.com       chris@rabbit.mytrek.com
```

You can also map all the addresses for a virtual domain to one real user, as shown here. All the mail to users with the virtual address **mytrains.com** will be sent to the user **trainmail@turtle.mytrek.com**:

```
@mytrains.com                 trainmail@turtle.mytrek.com
```

Once you have made your entries, build a **virtusertable.db** database file with the **`make`** command and the **`virtusertable`** option, as shown here:

```
make virtusertable
```

Security

For security, Sendmail lets you screen specific messages as well as provide authentication and encryption for Sendmail transmissions. With version 8.11, Sendmail incorporated support for the Secure Socket Layer (SSL) and the Simple Authentication and Security Layer (SASL). Support for SSL goes by the Sendmail command **STARTTLS**, which stands for "start transport layer security." SSL provides authentication, encryption, and integrity checks for Sendmail operations (see Chapter 37). OpenSSL must first be installed to allow use of SSL encryption and authentication methods.

The SASL is implemented by the **AUTH** command and is referred to as SMTP AUTH. SASL provides authentication for mail users and servers. It can make use of already installed Kerberos services to provide authentication.

Sendmail also provides you with the capability of screening out messages from specific domain, host, IP, and user addresses. Rules to perform such screening are kept in the **/etc/mail/access** file. You can edit this file and add your own rules. A rule consists of an address followed by an action to take. The actions supported are listed in Table 23-6. For example, to remove all messages from the **myannoyingad.com** domain, you would enter:

```
myannoyingad.com DISCARD
```

The next example rejects any message from **larisa@turtle.mycar.com** and sends a notice of the rejection:

```
larisa@turtle.mycar.com REJECT
```

Action	Description
OK	Accepts message even if other rules would reject (exception to the rules)
DISCARD	Discards the message completely
REJECT	Rejects the message, sending a rejection notice to the sender
RELAY	Relays messages for specified domain
SMTP-code message	Code and message to be sent to sender

Table 23-6. *Access Actions*

You can also specify an error message to return, as shown here:

```
cecelia@rabbit.mytrek.com    ERROR:"Retired yesterday"
```

To send an error message to spammers, you could include a message as shown here. The first number is an error code.

```
cyberspammer.com     ERROR:"550 We don't accept mail from spammers"
```

An **/etc/mail/access** file with the previous entries would look like the following:

```
myannoyingad.com                DISCARD
larisa@turtle.mycar.com     REJECT
cecelia@rabbit.mytrek.com ERROR:"Retired yesterday"
cyberspammer.com            ERROR:"550 We don't accept mail from spammers"
```

Sendmail actually reads the access rules from a database file called **access.db**, also located in the **/etc/mail** directory. To implement your rules, you have to regenerate the **access.db** file using the access file. You can do this with the **make** command using **access** as the argument, as shown here:

```
make access
```

Sendmail then has to be restarted to read the new **access.db** file.

The use of the access file is enabled in the **sendmail.mc** file with the **access_db** feature:

```
FEATURE('access_db')dnl
```

The access file will deny mail received from the listed addresses. However, you can also reject any mail sent to them. You can also reject received mail for certain hosts on your network. You do this by enabling the **blacklist_recipients** option in the **sendmail.mc** file. This option governs recipients, whereas **access** normally governs senders. Those addresses listed will not be able to receive any mail. This feature is also used for certain administrative users that should never receive mail, such as **nobody** (the guest user) or **ftp** (the FTP user):

```
FEATURE('blacklist_recipients')dnl
```

The following example will not allow mail to be sent to **cyberspammer.com** (a recipient), nor can mail be received for **justin@lizard.mytrek.com**, **secretproject@rabbit.mytrek.com**, or **mysurfboard.com**:

```
mysurfboard.com                    ERROR:"Domain does not exist"
justin@lizard.mytrek.com           "Moved to Hawaii"
secretproject@rabbit.mytrek.com  REJECT
cyberspammer.com                  REJECT
```

Your distribution version of **smb.conf** may configure Sendmail to use **access_db**. (as is the case with Red Hat). Access is granted only to users on the local host. If your system is being used as a mail server for a network, and you have not enabled the **relay_entire_domain** feature, you will need to allow access by other hosts on your network. In the access file, you can place a **RELAY** rule for your network. The **RELAY** rule will let other hosts use your mail server to send messages out to other hosts. This is normally done for a gateway host that needs to relay messages from a local network out to the Internet. The following example allows access from the **mytrek.com** network:

```
mytrek.com      RELAY
```

For a specific host, place an entry for it in the access file as shown here:

```
rabbit.mytrek.com    RELAY
```

A public list of known spammers is maintained in the Realtime Blackhole List (RBL) by the Mail Abuse Prevention System (MAPS project). Sendmail will automatically check this list for spammers if you use the **rbl** option:

```
FEATURE('rbl')dnl
```

To further secure Sendmail, you should disable the use of **VRFY**. This option allows remote users to try to verify the existence of a user address. This can be used to guess valid users on your system. This option is disabled with the **noverify** feature:

```
FEATURE('noverify')dnl
```

Another potential security breach is the **EXPN** option, which expands mailing lists and aliases to their actual addresses. Use the **noexpn** feature to turn it off:

```
FEATURE('noexpn')dnl
```

By default, Sendmail will refuse mail from any domain that cannot be resolved. You can override this restriction with the **accept_unresolvable_domains** feature. Sendmail will also reject mail whose addresses do not have fully qualified domain names, host and domain. You can override this feature with **accept_unqualified_senders**.

With the sslwrap service, POP3, IMAP, and SMTP service can be encrypted with SSL. sslwrap requires that you have installed OpenSSL or ssleay. See www.rickk.com/sslwrap.

Sendmail Configuration Operators: sendmail.cf

It is not advisable that you modify the **sendmail.cf** file directly. However, it may be helpful to know how it is set up. This section describes the type of entries you will find there. Table 23-7 lists the basic Sendmail configuration operators found in the **sendmail.cf** file. These operators consist of a single uppercase character, some with no spaces separating their arguments. The **D** operator defines macros. These are often used for specific information, such as the name of a host. The macro name usually consists of

Operators	Action
D	Define a macro
C	Define a class
F	Define a class read from a file
H	Define mail header
O	Set an option
P	Set message priority
V	Specify version level of **sendmail.cf** file
K	Specify key file
M	Specify mailer
S	Label and start a ruleset
R	Define a rule
#	Comment

Table 23-7. *Sendmail Configuration Operators*

one character. Uppercase macro names are reserved for use by Sendmail, whereas lowercase macro names are used for user-defined macros. The following example defines a macro called **T** for **turtle.mytrek.com.** You can then reference the macro anywhere in other operations by preceding it with a **$**, as in **$T**. To have a macro name longer than one character, encase the name within braces, as shown here for **rabbit**. To evaluate the **rabbit** macro use **${rabbit}**:

```
DTturtle.mytrek.com
D{rabbit}rabbit.mytrek.com
```

Much of the **sendmail.cf** file consists of options that are specified by the **O** operator followed by the option and its arguments. For example, the following entries determine the location of the alias file and the maximum size of a message:

```
O AliasFile=/etc/aliases
O HelpFile=/usr/lib/sendmail.hf
O MaxMessageSize=1000000
```

The **H** operator is used to define mail headers. The **P** operator is used to define the priority of mail messages based on keywords, such as the term "bulk" in the mail header. The **K** operator specifies the location of key database files, such as the **aliases** databases. The **C** operator is used to define a class, such as a collection of hosts, while the **F** operator is used to define a class from names read from a file:

```
# file containing names of hosts for which we receive email
Fw/etc/sendmail.cw
```

The **M** operator is used to define the mailers used by Sendmail. The **S** and **R** operators are used to define rulesets and rewriting rules. Rulesets and rewriting rules are used to determine how a message is to be routed and, if necessary, to rewrite its address so Sendmail's MTAs can handle it. You can think of rulesets as functions in a program, which are called as needed to work on message addresses—and can themselves call other rulesets. A ruleset consists of a set of rules, much like a function consists of a set of programming statements. Each ruleset is labeled with a number defined by an initial **S** operator. The rules making up the ruleset are then defined by **R** operators. Sendmail uses the rulesets first to format an address into a standard form. Then, for messages being sent, it determines the MTA to use. Special rules called *rewriting rules* can rewrite the address into a form that can be better handled by the MTA. Rewriting rules consist of a left-hand and a right-hand pattern. An address that matches the pattern on the left side is rewritten in the format of the pattern on the right side.

POP Servers

The Post Office Protocol (POP) allows a remote server to hold mail for users who can then fetch their mail from it when they are ready. Unlike Sendmail and procmail, which deliver mail messages directly to a user account on a Linux system, the POP protocol holds mail until a user accesses their account on the POP server. The POP server then transfers any received messages to the user's local mailbox. Servers are often used by ISPs to provide Internet mail services for users. Instead of sending mail directly to a user's machine, the mail resides in the POP server until it's retrieved. Linux distributions normally install the University of Washington POP server. Other popular POP servers used are Qpopper, the Qmail POP server, and the Courier POP server.

You can access the POP server from different hosts; however, when you do, all the messages are transferred to that host. They are not kept on the POP server (though you can set an option to keep them). The POP server simply forwards your messages on the requesting host. When you access your messages from a certain computer, they will be transferred to that computer and erased from the POP server. If you access your POP server again from a different computer, those previous messages will be gone.

The POP protocol provides a set of commands you can use to directly test a POP server. You can access the POP server on port 110 using Telnet and then enter a series of POP commands to check the server's performance. The following example connects to the **turtle.mytrek.com** POP server using Telnet on port 110:

```
telnet turtle.mytrek.com 110
```

You can then log in to an account using the **USER** and **PASSWORD** commands. The **LIST** command will list messages and the **RETR** command will display a message. Use **DELE** to delete a message. Use the **QUIT** command to end the session.

Note *The current version of the POP protocol is known as POP3, whereas POP2 is an earlier one that still may be in use in some places.*

Washington POP Server

Linux distributions include the University of Washington POP server (**ftp.cac.washington.edu/imap**), which is part of the University of Washington's **imap** RPM package. Simply install the package, which is already done as part of the standard install (both POP2 and POP3 servers are installed). The server daemons are called **ipop2d** and **ipop3d**. Your Linux system then runs as a POP2 and POP3 server for your network. These servers are run through xinetd. The POP3 server uses the **ipop3** file in the **/etc/xinetd.d** as shown here.

```
# default: off
# description: The POP3 service allows remote users to access their mail \
#   using a POP3 client such as Netscape Communicator, mutt, \
```

```
#   or fetchmail.
service pop3
{
     disable           = no
     socket_type       = stream
     wait              = no
     user              = root
     server            = /usr/sbin/ipop3d
     log_on_success   += USERID
     log_on_failure   += USERID
}
```

The following command would turn the server on:

```
chkconfig ipop3 on
```

Once you have installed a POP server, you add accounts to it by simply adding standard user accounts on the host it is running on. You do not need to set up a home directory for them, though. Users access their account using a username and password set up on the POP server's host. For example, to set up a POP user account for a POP server running on the host **turtle.mytrek.com**, you log in as **root** on **turtle.mytrek.com** and create a new user as you normally would for that host. To create a POP user account for **larisa**, just create a **larisa** user on the **turtle.mytrek.com** host.

Both the POP and IMAP Washington servers support Open SSL authentication and encryption. The SSL-enabled versions of the POP and IMAP servers have the names **pop3s** and **imaps**. Use **chkconfig** to turn them on or off.

```
chkconfig pop3s on
```

You also have to have appropriate SSL POP and IMAP certificates installed in the **ssl/certs** directory under the names **ipop3d.pem** and **imapd.pem**.

Qpopper

Qpopper is the current version of the Berkeley POP server (popper). Qpopper is supported by Qualcomm, makers of Eudora e-mail software. The Qpopper Web page is **www.eudora.com/free/qpop.html**. You can obtain a current source code version from **ftp.qualcomm.com/eudora/servers/unix**. RPM package versions are located at distribution sites or included in the distribution.

Once you have installed Qpopper and have the POP server running, you can add user accounts. Then users on remote systems can access the POP server using various mail clients or fetchmail. fetchmail, as described in Chapter 13, will fetch mail from a user account and place it in the mailbox on their local host. The following example fetches mail from a POP server running on **turtle.mytrek.com**:

```
fetchmail -p POP3 -u chris   turtle.mytrek.com
```

You can install Qpopper software on your Linux system and have it operate as a POP server for your network. It consists of both the **qpopper** daemon and the popauth program, which manages an authentication database with password encryption for secure user access. popauth creates a database file called **/etc/pop.auth**. To add a user, enter the **popauth** command with the options **-user** and the username. You are then prompted for a password with which the user can access their POP account.

If you download the source code version, you use the **./configure**, **make**, and **make install** sequence to configure, compile, and install the server. For the configure stage, you may need to enter several options to make Qpopper compatible with your system. For example, if your system uses shadow passwords (as most do), you will need to use the **--enable-specialauth** option. The **--enable-apop** option enables the use of the APOP (Authenticated POP) extension to provide encryption that is managed by the **popauth** command:

```
./configure --enable-specialauth --enable-apop
```

Qpopper is usually run through xinetd. You would create a popper file in the **/etc/xinetd.d** directory similar to that shown here:

```
service pop-3
{
    socket_type         = stream
    wait                = no
    user                = root
    server              = /usr/bin/popper
    disable             = no
}
```

You can turn the server on or off with the **chkconfig** command:

```
chkconfig pop-3 on
```

Be sure that the pop-3 service is listed in **/etc/services** along with its port, 110:

```
pop-3 110/tcp
```

IMAP

The Internet Mail Access Protocol (IMAP) allows a remote server to hold mail for users who can then log in to access their mail. Unlike the POP servers, IMAP servers retain user mail messages. Users can even save their mail on the IMAP mail server. This has the advantage of keeping a user's mail in one centralized location accessible anywhere on the network. Users can log in to the mail server from any host on the network and read, send, and save their mail. This interactive connection requires more connect time than the POP protocol and is best suited to an Ethernet LAN where users are always connected, rather than dial-up access through a modem.

Unlike POP, IMAP allows users to set up multiple folders on their mail server in which they can organize their mail. IMAP also supports the use of shared folders to which several users can access mail on a given topic.

The University of Washington IMAP server is normally included with most distributions. Other IMAP servers are also available such as Courier-IMAP server and the Cyrus IMAP server (**asg.web.cmu.edu/cyrus**). Cyrus IMAP servers feature security controls and authentication.

The name of the University of Washington IMAP server daemon is **imapd**. On systems running xinetd, it has a file called **imap** in the **/etc/xinetd.d** directory. You turn it on or off with the **chkconfig** command:

```
# default: off
# description: The IMAP service allows remote\
# users to access their mail using \
#  an IMAP client such as Mutt, Pine, \
#  fetchmail, or Netscape Communicator.
service imap
{
     socket_type          = stream
     wait                 = no
     user                 = root
     server               = /usr/sbin/imapd
     log_on_success      += DURATION USERID
     log_on_failure      += USERID
     disable              = no
}
```

The Washington IMAP server also supports SSL as described earlier for the POP server. In addition, IMAP supports both APOP and CRAM-MD5 authentication methods. These methods use MD checksum values rather than plain text passwords to authenticate users. The server, however, needs to know the plain text version of passwords. These are stored in the **/etc/cram-md5.pwd** file. Entries consist of a username followed by the user's password, separated by a tab. The existence of this file will enable CRAM-MD5 authentication procedures.

Chapter 24

News, Proxy, and Search Servers

News servers provide Internet users with Usenet news services. They have their own TCP/IP protocol, Network News Transfer Protocol (NNTP). In addition, servers exist that provide better access to Internet resources. Proxy servers maintain current copies of commonly accessed Web pages, speeding Web access times by eliminating the need to access the original site constantly. They also perform security functions, protecting servers from unauthorized access. The search and indexing server ht:/Dig enables document searches of Web and FTP sites. With it, you can index documents and carry out complex search requests. Table 24-1 lists different news, proxy, and search servers.

News Servers: INN

The InterNetNews (INN) news server accesses Usenet newsfeeds, providing news clients on your network with the full range of newsgroups and their articles. Newsgroup articles are transferred using NNTP, and servers that support this protocol are known as *NNTP servers*. INN was written by Rich Salz, and is currently maintained and supported by the Internet Software Consortium (ISC). You can download current versions from its Web site at **www.isc.org**. INN is also included with most Linux distributions. The documentation directory for INN in **/usr/share/doc** contains extensive samples. The primary program for INN is the **innd** daemon.

Various INN configuration files can be found in **/etc/news,** including **inn.conf, storage.conf, readers.conf,** and **incoming.conf** (see Table 24-2). **inn.conf** sets options for INN, and the **incoming.conf** file holds the hosts from which you receive newsfeeds. Place entries for remote hosts in the **readers.conf** file to allow them access to your news server. Actual newsfeeds are managed in directories in the **/var/spool/news** directory. Here you will find directories such as **article**, which holds newsgroup articles, **outgoing** for articles being posted by your users to newsgroups, and **overview,** which holds summary information about articles. Correct configuration of INN can be a complex and time-consuming process, so be sure to consult references and online resources,

Web Sites	Description
www.isc.org	InterNetNews news server, INN
www.leafnode.org	Leafnode news server
squid.nlanr.net	Squid proxy server
www.htdig.org	ht://Dig search and indexing server

Table 24-1. *News, Proxy, and Search Servers*

File	Description
inn.conf	General INN configuration file.
incoming.conf	Specifies hosts from which newsfeeds are received.
cycbuff.conf	Configures buffers used in cnfs storage format.
storage.conf	Defines storage classes. These consist of a storage method and the newsgroups that use it. Storage methods are the storage formats: tradspool, timehash, timecaf, and cnfs. An additional method, trash, throws out the articles.
expire.ctl	Sets the expiration policy for articles on the news server.
readers.conf	Designates hosts whose users can access the news server with newsreaders.
ovdb.conf	Configures ovdb storage method for overviews.
newsfeeds	Defines how your news server feeds articles to other news servers.
moderated	Moderated newsgroups.
cleanfeed.conf	Configures cleanfeed spam-blocking utility.
innfeed.conf	Configures newsfeed processes for innfeed.
innreport.conf	Configures innreport utility for generating log-based reports.
buffindexed.conf	Configures overview buffer for buffindexed method.

Table 24-2. *INN Configuration Files*

such as the documents. When you change configurations, be sure to restart the INN server. An **innd** script is in the **/etc/rc.d/init.d** directory, which has similar arguments to the Web **httpd** script. You can use `start`, `restart`, and `stop` arguments with the **innd** script to start, restart, and stop the INN server.

There is a Man page for each configuration file in INN, providing detailed information on how to configure their features.

On many distributions, a basic **inn.conf** file is already set up for you with default settings. Several of the initial parameters you will have to set yourself, such as `domain`, which holds the domain name for your server; `pathhost`, in which you specify the name for your newsreader as you want it to appear in the Path header field for news articles you post; and **server**, in which you specify your newsreader's IP or fully qualified domain name address, as in **mynews.mytrek.com**. Different Path options have already been set up for you defining the location of different INN directories, such as **patharticles** set to **/var/spool/news** articles that holds your newsgroup articles, and **pathetc** set to **/etc/news** for your configuration files.

Storage formats for the vast number of news articles that are often downloaded and accessed are a central concern for a full-scale news server like INN. INN lets you choose among four possible storage formats: tradspool, timehash, timecaf, and cnfs. tradspool is the traditional method where articles are arranged in a simple directory structure according to their newsgroups. This is known to be very time-consuming to access and store. timehash stores articles in directories organized by the time they were received, making it easier to remove outdated articles. timecaf is similar to timehash, but articles received at a given time are placed in the same file, making access much faster. cnfs stores articles into buffer files that have already been set up. When a buffer file becomes full, the older articles are overwritten by new ones as they come in. This is an extremely fast method since no new files are created. There is no need to set maximum article limits, but there is also no control on how long an article is retained. In the **storage.conf** file, storage formats are assigned as storage methods to different newsgroups.

INN also supports overviews. These are summaries of articles that readers can check, instead of having to download the entire article to see what it is. Overviews have their own storage methods: tradindexed, buffindexed, and ovdb. You specify the one you want to use in the ovmethod feature in **inn.conf**. tradindexed is fast for readers, but difficult for the server to generate. buffindexed is fast for news servers, but slow for readers. ovdb uses Berkeley DB database files and is very fast for both, but uses more disk space. If you choose ovdb, you can set configuration parameters for it in **ovdb.conf**.

On many distributions, a **news** user is already created with a newsgroup for use by your INN daemon and sets up the news directories in **/var/spool/news**. INN software also installs **cron** scripts, which are used to update your news server, removing old articles and fetching new ones. These are usually placed in the **/etc/cron.daily** directory, though they may reside anywhere. **inn-cron-expire** removes old articles and **inn-cron-rnews** retrieves new ones. **inn-cron-nntpsend** sends articles posted from your system to other news servers.

INN also includes several support programs to provide maintenance and crash recovery, and perform statistical analysis on server performance and usage. cleanfeed implements spam protection, and innreport generates INN reports based on logs. INN also features a very strong filter system for screening unwanted articles.

Leafnode News Server

Leafnode is an NNTP news server designed for small networks that may have slow connections to the Internet. You can obtain the Leafnode software package along with documentation from its Web site at **www.leafnode.org**. You can also download it from software repositories like **freshmeat.net** or **linuxapps.com**. Along with the Leafnode NNTP server, the software package includes several utilities such as Fetchnews, Texpire, and Newsq. Fetchnews retrieves and sends articles to your upstream news servers. Texpire deletes old news, and Newsq shows articles waiting to be sent out.

Leafnode is tailored to very low usage requirements. Only newsgroups that users on your local network have accessed within the last week are actually downloaded. Newsgroups not accessed in over a week are no longer downloaded. Its usage levels are comparable to a news client, accessing only the news that users on your network want. For a small network, this means having the advantages of a news service with few of the disadvantages. Much less disk space is used, and less time is needed to download newsfeeds.

Note *slrnpull is a simple single-user version of Leafnode that can be used only with the slrn newsreader. With it, you can automatically download articles in specified newsgroups from your network's news server and view them offline (see Chapter 14).*

Configuring Leafnode is a relatively simple process. You need to enter news server information in the Leafnode configuration file and make sure that there is a file for Leafnode in the **xinetd.d** directory so that users on your network can access it. The Leafnode configuration file is **/etc/leafnode/config**. You can edit this file directly or use one of several GUI Leafnode configuration utilities such as Keafnode or leafwa. Keafnode is a KDE program that provides a simple dialog box to configure your Leafnode servers, expire messages in selected newsgroups, and control download operations. leafwa provides a Web-page-based interface letting you configure Leafnode using any Web browser.

You can think of Leafnode as more of a news client that provides news server services to a small local network. It assumes that you already have a connection to a larger network such as the Internet and to an NNTP news server on that network. You then configure Leafnode to download newsgroup articles from that NNTP news server. In the Leafnode configuration file, you need to specify the name of that NNTP news server in the **`server`** entry, as shown here:

```
server = mynewsever.mynet.com
```

If you have access to other news servers, you can list them in the **`supplement`** entry:

```
supplement = myothernewserver.mynet.com
```

If you need a username and password to access the news server, you can list them in **username** and **password** entries following the **server** entry:

```
username = mylogin
password = mypassword
```

In the configuration file, you can also specify a default expiration time for unread newsgroup articles:

```
expire = 20
```

The Leafnode server does not perform the task of downloading articles. For this task, use Fetchnews. Fetchnews will download articles for specified newsgroups from the NNTP news server and send posted articles to it submitted by users on your local network. Similarly, you use the Texpire application to expire articles that have been previously downloaded. You can further automate these operations by scheduling them in a Leafnode **crontab** file, **leafnode.crontab**.

To allows users on your network to access the Leafnode server set up for them, you place a file for it in the **xinetd.d** directory that would call **/user/local/sbin/leafnode**.

Squid Proxy-Caching Server

Squid is a proxy-caching server for Web clients, designed to speed Internet access and provide security controls for Web servers. It implements a proxy-caching service for Web clients that caches Web pages as users make requests. Copies of Web pages accessed by users are kept in the Squid cache and, as requests are made, Squid checks to see if it has a current copy. If Squid does have a current copy, it returns the copy from its cache instead of querying the original site. In this way, Web browsers can then use the local Squid cache as a proxy HTTP server. Squid currently handles Web pages supporting the HTTP, FTP, Gopher, SSL, and WAIS protocols (Squid cannot be used with FTP clients). Replacement algorithms periodically replace old objects in the cache.

As a proxy, Squid does more that just cache Web objects. It operates as an intermediary between the Web browsers (clients) and the servers they access. Instead of connections being made directly to the server, a client connects to the proxy server. The proxy then relays requests to the Web server. This is useful for situations where a Web server is placed behind a firewall server, protecting it from outside access. The proxy is accessible on the firewall, which can then transfer requests and responses back and forth between the client and the Web server. The design is often used to allow Web servers to operate on protected local networks and still be accessible on the Internet. You can also use a Squid proxy to provide Web access to the Internet by local hosts. Instead of using a gateway providing complete access to the Internet, local hosts could use a proxy to allow them just Web access (see Chapter 7). You could also combine the two, allowing gateway access, but using the proxy server to provide more control for Web access. In addition, the caching capabilities of Squid would provide local hosts with faster Web access.

Technically, you could use a proxy server to simply manage traffic between a Web server and the clients that want to communicate with it, without doing caching at all. Squid combines both capabilities as a proxy-caching server.

Squid also provides security capabilities that let you exercise control over hosts accessing your Web server. You can deny access by certain hosts and allow access by others. Squid also supports the use of encrypted protocols such as SSL (see Chapter 37). Encrypted communications are tunneled (passed through without reading) through the Squid server directly to the Web server.

Squid is supported and distributed under a GNU Public License by the National Laboratory for Applied Network Research (NLANR) at the University of California, San Diego. The work is based on the Harvest Project to create a Web indexing system that included a high-performance cache daemon called **cached**. You can obtain current source code versions and online documentation from the Squid home page at **squid.nlanr.net** and the Squid FTP site at **ftp.nlanr.net**. The Squid software package consists of the Squid server, a domain name lookup program called dnsserver, an FTP client called ftpget, and a cache manager script called **cachemgr.cgi**. The dnsserver resolves IP addresses from domain names, and the ftpget program is an FTP client Squid uses to retrieve files from FTP servers. **cachemgr.cgi** lets you view statistics for the Squid server as it runs.

On Mandrake and Red Hat, you can start, stop, and restart the squid server using the squid script, as shown here:

```
service squid restart
```

Configuring Client Browsers

If users on a host want to access the Web through a proxy, the users need to specify their proxy server in their Web browser configuration. For this they will need the IP address of the host running the Squid proxy server as well as the port it is using. Proxies usually make use of port 3128. To configure use of a proxy server running on the local sample network described in Chapter 7, you would enter the following. The proxy server is running on **turtle.mytrek.com** (192.168.0.1) and using port 3128.

```
192.168.0.1 3128
```

On Mozilla and Netscape, the user on the sample local network would first select the Proxy panel located in Preferences under the Edit menu. Then, in the Manual proxy configuration's View panel, enter the previous information. The user will see entries for FTP, Gopher, HTTP, Security, and WAIS proxies. For standard Web access, enter the IP address in the FTP, Gopher, and Web boxes. For their port boxes, enter 3128.

For Konqueror on the KDE Desktop, select the Proxies panel on the Settings window. Here, you can enter the proxy server address and port numbers.

If your local host is using Internet Explorer (such as a Windows system does), you would set the proxy entries in the Local Area Network settings accessible from the Internet Options window.

On Linux or Unix systems, local hosts can set the **http_proxy**, **gopher_proxy**, and **ftp_proxy** shell variables to configure access by Linux-supported Web browsers such as lynx. You can place these definitions in your **.bash_profile** or **/etc/profile** files to have them automatically defined whenever you log in.

```
http_proxy=192.168.0.1:3128
ftp proxy=192.168.0.1:3128
gopher_proxy=192.168.0.1:3128
export http_proxy ftp_proxy gopher_proxy
```

Before a client on a local host could use the proxy server, access permission would have to be given to them in the server's **squid.conf** file, described in the following section on security. Access can easily be provided to an entire network. For the sample network used here, you would have to place the following entries in the **squid.conf** file. These are explained in detail in the following sections.

```
acl mylan src 192.168.0.0/255.255.255.0
http_access allow mylan
```

Web clients that need to access your Squid server will need to know the server's address and the port for Squid's HTTP services, by default 3128.

squid.conf

The Squid configuration file is **squid.conf**, located in the **/etc/squid** directory. In the **/etc/squid/squid.conf** file, you set general options such as ports used, security options controlling access to the server, and cache options for configuring caching operations. You can use a backup version called **/etc/squid/squid.conf.default** to restore your original defaults. The default version of **squid.conf** provided with Squid software includes detailed explanations of all standard entries, along with commented default entries. Entries consist of tags that specify different attributes. For example, **maximum_object_size** and **maximum_object** set limits on objects transferred.

```
maximum_object_size 4096 KB
```

As a proxy, Squid will use certain ports for specific services, such as port 3128 for HTTP services like Web browsers. Default port numbers are already set for Squid.

Should you need to use other ports, you can set them in the **/etc/squid/squid.conf** file. The following entry shows how you would set the Web browser port:

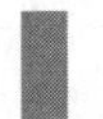

```
http_port 3128
```

Squid uses the Simple Network Management Protocol (SNMP) to provide status information and statistics to SNMP agents managing your network. You can control SNMP with the ***snmp access*** *and* ***port*** *configurations in the* ***squid.conf*** *file.*

Security

Squid can use its role as an intermediary between Web clients and a Web server to implement access controls, determining who can access the Web server and how. Squid does this by checking access control lists (ACLs) of hosts and domains that have had controls placed on them. When it finds a Web client from one of those hosts attempting to connect to the Web server, it executes the control. Squid supports a number of controls with which it can deny or allow access to the Web server by the remote host's Web client (see Table 24-3). In effect, Squid sets up a firewall just for the Web server.

The first step in configuring Squid security is to create ACLs. These are lists of hosts and domains for which you want to set up control. You define ACLs using the **acl** command, in which you create a label for the systems on which you are setting controls. You then use commands, such as **http_access**, to define these controls.

Options	Description
src *ip-address/netmask*	Client's IP address
src *addr1-addr2/netmask*	Range of addresses
dst *ip-address/netmask*	Destination IP address
myip *ip-address/netmask*	Local socket IP address
srcdomain *domain*	Reverse lookup, client IP
dstdomain *domain*	Destination server from URL; for **dstdomain** and **dstdom_regex**, a reverse lookup is tried if an IP-based URL is used
srcdom_regex [-i] *expression*	Regular expression matching client name
dstdom_regex [-i] *expression*	Regular expression matching destination

Table 24-3. *Squid ACL Options*

Options	Description
time *[day-abbrevs] [h1:m1-h2:m2]*	Time as specified by day, hour, and minutes. Day abbreviations: S = Sunday, M = Monday, T = Tuesday, W = Wednesday, H = Thursday, F = Friday, A = Saturday
url_regex [-i] *expression*	Regular expression matching on whole URL
urlpath_regex [-i] *expression*	Regular expression matching on URL path
port *ports*	Specify a port or range of ports
proto *protocol*	Specify a protocol, such as HTTP or FTP
method *method*	Specify methods, such as GET and POST
browser [-i] regexp	Pattern match on user-agent header
ident *username*	String match on **ident** output
src_as *number*	Used for routing of requests to specific caches
dst_as *number*	Used for routing of requests to specific caches
proxy_auth *username*	List of valid usernames
snmp_community *string*	A community string to limit access to your SNMP agent

Table 24-3. *Squid ACL Options* (continued)

You can define a system, or a group of systems, based on several **acl** options, such as the source IP address, the domain name, or even the time and date (refer back to Table 24-2). For example, the **src** option is used to define a system or group of systems with a certain source address. To define a **mylan acl** entry for systems in a local network with the addresses 192.168.0.0 through 192.168.0.255, use the following ACL definition:

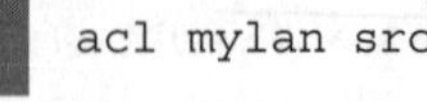

```
acl mylan src 192.168.0.0/255.255.255.0
```

Once defined, you can use an ACL definition in a Squid option to specify a control you want to place on those systems. For example, to allow access by the mylan group of local systems to the Web through the proxy, use an **http_access** option with the **allow** action specifying **mylan** as the **acl** definition to use, as shown here:

```
http_access allow mylan
```

By defining ACLs and using them in Squid options, you can tailor your Web site with the kind of security you want. The following example allows access to the Web through the proxy by only the mylan group of local systems, denying access to all others. Two **acl** entries are set up: one for the local system and one for all others. **http_access** options first allow access to the local system, and then deny access to all others.

```
acl mylan src 192.168.0.0/255.255.255.0
acl all src 0.0.0.0/0.0.0.0
http_access allow mylan
http_access deny all
```

The default entries that you will find in your **squid.conf** file, along with an entry for the mylan sample network, are shown here. You will find these entries in the ACCESS CONTROLS section of the **squid.conf** file.

```
acl all src 0.0.0.0/0.0.0.0
acl manager proto cache_object
acl localhost src 127.0.0.1/255.255.255.255
acl mylan src 192.168.0.0/255.255.255.0
acl SSL_ports port 443 563
```

The order of the **http_access** options is important. Squid starts from the first and works its way down, stopping at the first **http_access** option with an ACL entry that matches. In the previous example, local systems that match the first **http_access** command are allowed, whereas others fall through to the second **http_access** command and are denied.

For systems using the proxy, you can also control what sites they can access. For a destination address, you create an **acl** entry with the **dst** qualifier. The **dst** qualifier takes as its argument the site address. Then you can create an **http_access** option to control access to that address. The following example denies access by anyone using the proxy to the destination site **rabbit.mytrek.com**. If you have a local network accessing the Web through the proxy, you can use such commands to restrict access to certain sites.

```
acl myrabbit dst rabbit.mytrek.com
http_access deny myrabbit
```

The **http_access** entries already defined in the **squid.conf** file, along with an entry for the mylan network, are shown here. Access to outside users is denied, whereas access by hosts on the local network and the localhost (Squid server host) is allowed.

```
http_access allow localhost
http_access allow mylan
http_access deny all
```

You can also qualify addresses by domain. Often, Web sites can be referenced using only the domain. For example, a site called **www.mybeach.com** can be referenced using just the domain **mybeach.com.** To create an **acl** entry to reference a domain, use either the **dstdomain** or **srcdomain** options for destination and source domains, respectively. Remember, such a reference refers to all hosts in that domain. An **acl** entry with the **dstdomain** option for **mybeach.com** restricts access to **www.mybeach.com**, **ftp.mybeach.com**, **surf.mybeach.com**, and so on. The following example restricts access to the **www.mybeach.com** site along with all other **.mybeach.com** sites and any hosts in the **mybeach.com** domain:

```
acl thebeach dstdomain .mybeach.com
http_access deny thebeach
```

You can list several domains or addresses in an **acl** entry to reference them as a group, but you cannot have one domain that is a subdomain of another. For example, if **mybeachblanket.com** is a subdomain of **mybeach.com**, you cannot list both in the same **acl** list. The following example restricts access to both **mybeach.com** and **mysurf.com**:

```
acl beaches dstdomain .mybeach.com .mysurf.com
http_access deny beaches
```

An **acl** entry can also use a pattern to specify certain addresses and domains. In the following example, the access is denied to any URL with the pattern "chocolate", and allows access from all others:

```
acl Choc1 url_regex chocolate
http_access deny Choc1
http_access allow all
```

Squid also supports ident and proxy authentication methods to control user access. The following example only allows the users **dylan** and **chris** to use the Squid cache:

```
ident_lookup on
acl goodusers user chris dylan
http_access allow goodusers
http_access deny all
```

Caches

Squid uses the Internet Cache Protocol (ICP) to communicate with other Web caches. Using the ICP protocols, your Squid cache can connect to other Squid caches or other cache servers, such as Microsoft proxy server, Netscape proxy server, and Novell BorderManager. This way, if your network's Squid cache does not have a copy of a requested Web page, it can contact another cache to see if it is there instead of accessing the original site. You can configure Squid to connect to other Squid caches by connecting it to a cache hierarchy. Squid supports a hierarchy of caches denoted by the terms *child*, *sibling*, and *parent*. Sibling and child caches are accessible on the same level and are automatically queried whenever a request cannot be located in your own Squid's cache. If these queries fail, a parent cache is queried, which then searches its own child and sibling caches—or its own parent cache, if needed—and so on. Use **cache_host** to set up parent and sibling hierarchical connections.

```
cache_host sd.cache.nlanr.net parent 3128 3130
```

You can set up a cache hierarchy to connect to the main NLANR server by registering your cache using the following entries in your **squid.conf** file:

```
cache_announce 24
announce_to sd.cache.nlanr.net:3131
```

Squid keeps several logs. **access.log** holds requests sent to your proxy, **cache.log** holds Squid server messages such as errors and startup messages, and **store.log** holds information about the Squid cache such as objects added or removed. You can use the cache manager (**cachemgr.cgi**) to manage the cache and view statistics on the cache manager as it runs. To run the cache manager, use your browser to execute the **cachemgr.cgi** script (this script should be placed in your Web server's **cgi-bin** directory). You can also monitor Squid using the Multi Router Traffic utility.

Dig Server

Dig, known officially as ht:/Dig, is a Web indexing and search system designed for small networks or intranets. Dig is not considered a replacement for full-scale Internet search systems, such as Lycos, Infoseek, or AltaVista. Unlike Web server–based search engines, Dig can span several Web servers at a site. Dig was developed at San Diego State University and is distributed free under the GNU Public License. You can obtain information and documentation at **www.htdig.org**, and you can download software packages—including RPM packages—from **ftp.htdig.org**.

Dig supports simple and complex searches, including complex Boolean and fuzzy search methods. *Fuzzy searching* supports a number of search algorithms, including exact, soundex, and synonyms. Searches can be carried out on both text and HTML documents. HTML documents can have keywords placed in them for more accurate retrieval, and you can also use HTML templates to control how results are displayed.

Searches can be constrained by authentication requirements, location, and search depth. To protect documents in restricted directories, Dig can be informed to request a specific username and password. You can also restrict a search to retrieve documents in a certain URL, to search subsections of the database, or to retrieve only documents that are a specified number of links away.

All the ht:/Dig programs use the same configuration file, **htdig.conf**, located in the **/etc/htdig** directory. The configuration file consists of attribute entries, each beginning with the attribute line and followed by the value after a colon. Each program takes only the attributes it needs:

```
max_head_length: 10000
```

You can specify attributes such as **allow_virtual_hosts**, which index virtual hosts (see Chapter 21) as separate servers, and **search_algorithm**, which specifies the search algorithms to use for searches.

Dig consist of five programs: htdig, htmerge, htfuzzy, htnotify, and htsearch. htdig, htmerge, and htfuzzy generate the index, while htsearch performs the actual searches. First, htdig gathers information on your database, searching all URL connections in your domain and associating Web pages with terms. The htmerge program uses this information to create a searchable database, merging the information from any previously generated database. htfuzzy creates indexes to allow searches using fuzzy algorithms, such as soundex and synonyms. Once the database is created, users can use Web pages that invoke htsearch to search this index. Results are listed on a Web page. You can use META tags in your HTML documents to enter specific htdig keywords, exclude a document from indexing, or provide notification information such as an e-mail address and an expiration date. htnotify uses the e-mail and expiration date to notify Web page authors when their pages are out of date.

htsearch is a CGI program that expects to be invoked by an HTML form, and it accepts both the GET and POST methods of passing data. The htsearch program can accept a search request from any form containing the required configuration values. Values include search features such as config (configuration file), method (search method), and sort (sort criteria). For the Web page form that invokes htsearch, you can use the default page provided by htdig or create your own. Output is formatted using templates you can modify. Several sample files are included with the htdig software: **rundig** is a sample script for creating a database, **searchform.html** is a sample HTML document that contains a search form for submitting htdig searches, **header.html** is a sample header for search headers, and **footer.html** is for search footers.

Part VI

System Administration

Chapter 25

Basic System Administration

Linux is designed to serve many users at the same time, as well as to provide an interface among the users and the computer with its storage media, such as hard disks and tapes. Users have their own shells through which they interact with the operating system, but you may need to configure the operating system itself in different ways. You may need to add new users, printers, and even file systems. Such operations come under the heading of system administration. The person who performs such actions is referred to as either a *system administrator* or a *superuser*. In this sense, two types of interaction with Linux exist: regular users' interaction and the superuser, who performs system administration tasks. The chapters in the "System Administration" section cover operations such as changing system runlevels, managing users, and configuring printers and compiling the kernel. You rarely perform most of these tasks, such as adding a new printer or mounting a file system. Other tasks, such as adding users, you perform on a regular basis. Basic system administration covers topics such as system access by superusers, selecting the runlevel to start, system configuration files, and performance monitoring. These are discussed in detail in this chapter.

System Management: Superuser

To perform system administration operations, you must first have the correct password that enables you to log in as the root user, making you the superuser. Because a superuser has the power to change almost anything on the system, such a password is usually a carefully guarded secret given only to those whose job is to manage the system. With the correct password, you can log in to the system as a system administrator and configure the system in different ways. You can start up and shut down the system, as well as change to a different operating mode, such as a single-user mode. You can also add or remove users, add or remove whole file systems, back up and restore files, and even designate the system's name. To become a superuser, you log in to the root user account. This is a special account reserved for system management operations with unrestricted access to all components of your Linux operating system. When you log in to the system as the root user, you are placed in a shell from which you can issue administrative Linux commands. The prompt for this shell is a sharp sign, **#**. In the next example, the user logs in to the system as the root user. The password is, of course, not displayed.

```
login: root
password:
#
```

As the root user, you can use the **passwd** command to change the password for the root login, as well as for any other user on the system.

```
# passwd root
New password:
```

```
Re-enter new password:
#
```

While you are logged in to a regular user account, it may be necessary for you to log in to the root and become a superuser. Ordinarily, you would have to log out of your user account first, and then log in to the root. Instead, you can use the **su** command (switch user) to log in directly to the root while remaining logged in to your user account. A CTRL-D or **exit** command returns you to your own login. When logged in as the root, you can use **su** to log in as any user, without providing the password. In the next example, the user is logged in already. The **su** command then logs the user in to the root, making the user a superuser. Some basic superuser commands are shown in Table 25-1.

```
$ pwd
/home/chris
$su
 password:
# cd
# pwd
/root
# exit
$
```

Command	Description
su root	Logs a superuser in to the root from a user login; the superuser returns to the original login with CTRL-D.
passwd *login-name*	Sets a new password for the login name.
crontab *options file-name*	With *file-name* as an argument, installs **crontab** entries in the file to a **crontab** file; these entries are operations executed at specified times: **-e** Edits the **crontab** file. **-l** Lists the contents of the **crontab** file. **-r** Deletes the **crontab** file.

Table 25-1. *Basic System Administration*

Command	Description
`telinit` *runelevl*	Changes the system runlevels (see Table 25-2).
`lilo` *options Config-file*	Reinstalls the Linux Loader (LILO).
`shutdown` *options time*	Shuts down the system; similar to CTRL-ALT-DEL.
`date`	Sets the date and time for the system.
TimeTool	GUI tool to set system time and date.
Kcron	KDE cron management tool.

Table 25-1. *Basic System Administration* (continued)

Note *For security reasons, Linux distributions do not allow the use of* **su** *in a Telnet session to access the root user.*

System Configuration

Although many different specialized components go into making up a system, such as servers, users, and devices, some operations apply to the system in general. These include setting the system date and time, specifying shutdown procedures, and determining the services to start up and run whenever the system boots. In addition, you can use numerous performance analysis tools to control processes and check on resource use.

System Time and Date

You can use several different tools to set the system time and date, depending on the distribution you use. On all distributions, you can set the system time and date using the shell **date** command. Most users prefer to use a configuration tool such as those provided by a distribution's administrative center. Recall that you set the time and date when you first installed your system. You should not need to do so again. If you entered the time incorrectly or moved to a different time zone, though, you could use this utility to change your time.

You can use the **date** command on your root user command line to set the date and time for the system. As an argument to **date**, you list (with no delimiters) the month, day, time, and year. In the next example, the date is set to 2:59 P.M., March 6, 2002 (03 for March, 06 for the day, 1459 for the time, and 02 for the year 2002):

```
# date 0506145902
Mon May 6 02:59:27 PST 2002
```

Note *You can also set the time and date with a variety of different administrative time tools to change the time and date. Many distributions and administrative utilities provide their own time tools. On Red Hat you can use the TimeTool and on Mandrake the Date and Time tool in the Mandrake Control Center. On KDE you can use the Date & Time tool in the KDE Control Center. You can also change the time and date on Webmin or Linuxconf, if you have them installed. On SuSE you can use the time tool on the YaST Control Center's System panel.*

Scheduling Tasks: crontab

Although it is not a system file, a crontab file is helpful in maintaining your system. A *crontab* file lists actions to take at a certain time. The **cron** daemon constantly checks the user's crontab file to see if it is time to take these actions. Any user can set up a crontab file of their own. The root user can set up a crontab file to take system administrative actions, such as backing up files at a certain time each week or month.

A crontab entry has six fields: the first five are used to specify the time for an action, while the last field is the action itself. The first field specifies minutes (0–59), the second field specifies the hour (0–23), the third field specifies the day of the month (1–31), the fourth field specifies the month of the year (1–12), and the fifth field specifies the day of the week (0–6), starting with 0 as Sunday. In each of the time fields, you can specify a range, a set of values, or use the asterisk to indicate all values. For example, 1–5 for the day-of-week field specifies Monday through Friday. In the hour field, 8, 12, 17 would specify 8 A.M., 12 noon, and 5 P.M. An ***** in the month-of-year field indicates every month. The following example backs up the **projects** directory at 2:00 A.M. every weekday:

```
0 2 1-5 * * tar cf /home/chris/backp /home/chris/projects
```

You use the **crontab** command to install your entries into a crontab file. To do this, you first create a text file and type your crontab entries. Save this file with any name you want, such as **mycronfile**. Then, to install these entries, enter **crontab** and the name of the text file. The **crontab** command takes the contents of the text file and creates a crontab file in the **/var/spool/cron** directory, adding the name of the user who issued the command. In the next example, the root user installs the contents of the **mycronfile** as the root's crontab file. This creates a file called **/var/spool/cron/root**. If a user named **justin** installed a crontab file, it would create a file called **/var/spool/cron/justin**. You can control use of the **crontab** command by regular users with the **/etc/cron.allow** file. Only users with their names in this file can create crontab files of their own.

```
# crontab mycronfile
```

Never try to edit your crontab file directly. Instead, use the **crontab** command with the **-e** option. This opens your crontab file in the **/var/spool/cron** directory with the standard text editor, such as Vi. `crontab` uses the default editor as specified by the EDITOR shell environment variable. To use a different editor for `crontab`, change the default editor by assigning the editor's program name to the EDITOR variable and exporting that variable. Running `crontab` with the `-l` option displays the contents of your **crontab** file, and the `-r` option deletes the entire file. Invoking `crontab` with another text file of **crontab** entries overwrites your current **crontab** file, replacing it with the contents of the text file.

To more easily manage and create cron jobs you can use the Kcron utility, accessible on the KDE desktop. When you use Kron as the root user, it will list all the users on your system, and allow you to create and manage jobs for them. These include the system cron jobs as specified in the system **crontab** file. For each user you can specify the jobs to be performed as well as any variables you want to set for those jobs. Each user entry has two folders, one for cron jobs, named Tasks, and the other for the jobs' variables, named Variables. You can add entries to either. The Edit menu will list operations you can perform on jobs such as disabling them, running them immediately, modifying their times, or deleting them altogether. When you create or modify a job, the Edit Task dialog box opens, where you can select the months, days, hours, and minutes when to run a job. You also select the program to run along with its arguments. Once you have made your changes, you select Save from the File menu to save them to your **crontab** file. Individual users can also run Kcron to manage their own cron jobs. In this case, Kcron will only show a single Tasks and Variables folder, where the user can enter their jobs and variables.

Note *You can also schedule tasks with crontab using Webmin. On Webmin, select the Scheduled Cron Jobs icon on the System panel. This opens a page listing the scheduled jobs in your crontab file where you can create and edit cron jobs.*

System Runlevels: telinit and shutdown

Your Linux system can run in different states, depending on the capabilities you want to give it. For example, you can run your system in an administrative state, keeping user access shut down. Normal full operations are activated by simply running your system at a certain state. These states (also known as modes) are referred to as *runlevels*, the level of support that you are running your system at. Your Linux system has several runlevels, numbered from 0 to 6. When you power up your system, you enter the default runlevel. You can then change to other runlevels with the `telinit` command. Runlevels 0, 1, and 6 are special runlevels that perform certain functions. Runlevel 0 is the power-down state and is invoked by the `halt` command. The command `telinit 0` shuts down your system. Runlevel 6 is the reboot state—it shuts down the system and reboots. Runlevel 1 is the single-user state, allowing access only to the superuser, and does not run any network services. This enables you, as administrator, to perform administrative actions without interference from others. Other runlevels reflect how you want the system to be used. Runlevel 2 is a partial multiuser state, allowing access by many users, but without network services such as NFS or xinetd. It is useful for a system that is not part of a network. Both runlevel 3 and runlevel 5 run a fully operational Linux system, with multiuser support and remote file sharing access. They differ in terms of the interface they use. Runlevel 3 starts up your system with the command line interface (also known as the text mode interface). Runlevel 5 starts up your system with an X session, running the X Window System server and invoking a graphical login, using display managers, such as gdm or xdm. If you choose to use graphical logins during installation, this will be your default runlevel. The runlevels are listed in Table 25-2.

Changing runlevels can be helpful if you have problems at a particular runlevel. For example, if your video card is not installed properly, any attempt to start up in Runlevel 5 will likely crash your system, as this level immediately starts your graphical interface. Instead you would want to use the command line interface, Runlevel 3, to first fix your video card installation.

State	Description
`telinit` *runlevel*	Changes the system runlevel; you can use it to power up or power down a system, or allow multiuser or single-user access. The **`telinit`** command takes as its argument a number representing a system state. **`telinit`** is a link to **`init`** which performs the state change operation.
System Runlevels (States)	
0	Halt (do *not* set the default to this); this shuts down the system completely.
1	Administrative single-user mode; denies other users access to the system, but allows root access to the entire multiuser file system. Startup scripts are not run. (Use **`s`** or **`S`** to enter single user mode with startup scripts run.)
2	Multiuser, without network services like NFS, xinetd, and NIS (the same as 3, but you do not have networking).

Table 25-2. *System Runlevels (States)*

State	Description
3	Full multiuser mode with login to command line interface; allows remote file sharing with other systems on your network. Also referred to as the text mode state.
4	Unused level.
5	Full multiuser mode that starts up in an X session, initiating a graphical login. Allows remote file sharing with other systems on your network (same as 3, but with graphical login).
6	Reboots; shuts down and restarts the system (do *not* set the default to this).

Table 25-2. *System Runlevels (States)* (continued)

Note *You can use the single user runlevel (1) as a recovery mode state, allowing you to start up your system without running startup scripts for services like DNS. This is helpful if your system hangs when trying to start such services. Networking will be disabled as well as any multiuser access. Also, you can use* **`linux -s`** *at the LILO prompt to enter runlevel 1. If you want to enter the single-user state (Runlevel 1) and also run the startup scripts, you can use the special* **`s`** *or* **`S`** *runlevels.*

When your system starts up, it uses the default runlevel as specified in the default **init** entry in the **/etc/inittab** file. For example, if your default **init** runlevel is 5 (the graphical login), the default **init** entry in the **/etc/inittab** file would be:

```
init:5:default
```

You can change the default runlevel by editing the **/etc/inittab** file and changing the **`init`** default entry. Editing the **/etc/inittab** file can be dangerous. You should do this with great care. As an example, if the default runlevel is 3 (command line), the entry for your default runlevel in the **/etc/inittab** file should look like the following:

```
id:3:initdefault:
```

You can change the 3 to a 5, to change your default runlevel from the command line interface (3) to the graphical login (5). Change only this number and nothing else.

```
id:5:initdefault:
```

Should your **/etc/inittab** file become corrupted, you can reboot and enter **linux single** at the boot prompt to start up your system, bypassing the **inittab** file. You can then edit the file to fix it.

No matter what runlevel you start in, you can change from one runlevel to another with the **telinit** command. If your default runlevel is 3, you power up in Runlevel 3, but you can change to, say, Runlevel 5 with **telinit 5**. In the next example, the **telinit** command changes to Runlevel 1, the administrative state:

```
# telinit 1
```

telinit is really a link to the **init** command. It is the **init** command that performs the actual startup operations and is automatically invoked when your system starts up. Though you could use **init** to also change runlevels, it is best to use **telinit**. When invoked as **telinit**, **init** functions to merely change runlevels.

Tip *You can use distribution configuration tools like the Mandrake Control Center and SuSE's Yast, as well as independent tools like Linuxconf or Webmin, to change the default startup runlevel between the graphical login runlevel (5) and a command line runlevel (text mode) (3).*

Use the **runlevel** command to see what state you are currently running in. It will list the previous state followed by the current one. If you have not changed states, the previous state will be listed as **N**, indicating no previous state. This is the case for the state you boot up in. In the next example, the system is running in state 3, with no previous state change.

```
# runlevel
N 3
```

Although you can power down the system with the **telinit** command and the 0 state, you can also use the **shutdown** command. The **shutdown** command has a time argument that gives users on the system a warning before you power down. You can specify an exact time to shut down or a period of minutes from the current time. The exact time is specified by *hh:mm* for the hour and minutes. The period of time is indicated by a **+** and the number of minutes. The **shutdown** command takes several options with which you can specify how you want your system shut down. The **-h** option, which stands for halt, simply shuts down the system, whereas the **-r** option shuts down the system and then reboots it. In the next example, the system is shut down after ten minutes. The shutdown options are listed in Table 25-3.

```
# shutdown -h +10
```

Command	Description
shutdown [-rkhncft] *time* [*warning-message*]	Shuts the system down after the specified time period, issuing warnings to users; you can specify a warning message of your own after the *time* argument. If neither **-h** nor **-r** is specified to shut down the system, the system sets to the administrative mode, Runlevel state 1.
Argument	
time	Has two possible formats: it can be an absolute time in the format *hh:mm*, with *hh* as the hour (one or two digits) and *mm* as the minute (in two digits); it can also be in the format *+m*, with *m* as the number of minutes to wait. The word **now** is an alias for **+0**.
Option	
-t *sec*	Tells **init** to wait *sec* seconds between sending processes the warning and the kill signals, before changing to another runlevel.
-k	Doesn't actually shut down; only sends the warning messages to everybody.
-r	Reboots after shutdown, Runlevel state 6.
-h	Halts after shutdown, Runlevel state 0.
-n	Doesn't call **init** to do the shutdown; you do it yourself.
-f	Does a *fast* reboot.
-c	Cancels an already running shutdown; no time argument.

Table 25-3. *System Shutdown Options*

To shut down the system immediately, you can use **+0** or the word **now**. The following example has the same effect as the CTRL-ALT-DEL method of shutting down your system, as described in Chapter 3. It shuts down the system immediately, and then reboots.

```
# shutdown -r now
```

With the **shutdown** command, you can include a warning message to be sent to all users currently logged in, giving them time to finish what they are doing before you shut them down.

```
# shutdown -h +5 "System needs a rest"
```

If you do not specify either the **-h** or the **-r** option, the **shutdown** command shuts down the multiuser mode and shifts you to an administrative single-user mode. In effect, your system state changes from 3 (multiuser state) to 1 (administrative single-user state). Only the root user is active, allowing the root user to perform any necessary system administrative operations with which other users might interfere.

Tip *You can also shut down your system from the Gnome or KDE desktops.*

System Directories and Files

Your Linux system is organized into directories whose files are used for different system functions. Directories with **bin** in the name are used to hold programs. The **/bin** directory holds basic user programs, such as login, shells (**bash**, **tcsh**, and **zsh**), and file commands (**cp**, **mv**, **rm**, **ln**, and so on). The **/sbin** directory holds specialized system programs for such tasks as file system management (**fsck**, **fdisk**, **mkfs**) and system operations like shutdown and startup (**lilo**, **init**). The **/usr/bin** directory holds program files designed for user tasks. The **/usr/sbin** directory holds user-related system operation, such as **useradd** to add new users. The **/lib** directory holds all the libraries your system makes use of, including the main Linux library, **libc**, and subdirectories such as **modules**, which holds all the current kernel modules.

```
# ls /
bin boot dev etc home lib lost+found mnt proc root sbin tmp usr var
```

The **/etc** directory holds your system, network, server, and application configuration files. Here you can find the **fstab** file listing your file systems, the **hosts** file with IP addresses for hosts on your system, and **lilo.conf** for the boot systems provided by LILO. This directory includes various subdirectories, such as **apache** for the Apache Web server configuration files and **X11** for the X Window System and window manager configuration files.

The **/mnt** directory is usually used for mount points for your CD-ROM, floppy, or zip drives. These are file systems you may be changing frequently, unlike partitions on fixed disks. The **/home** directory holds user home directories. When a user account is set up, a home directory for it is set up here, usually with the same name as the user. The **/var** directory holds subdirectories for tasks whose files change frequently, such as lock files, log files, or printer spool files. On many systems, the **/var** directory also holds server data directories, such as **/var/www** for the Apache Web server Web site files or **/var/ftp** for your FTP site files. Mandrake and Red Hat currently place their server data directories in the **/var** directory. The **/tmp** directory is simply a directory to hold any temporary files programs may need to perform a particular task.

The **/usr** directory holds programs for user-related operations. The **/usr/lib** directory holds many of the libraries for particular applications. The **/usr/X11R6** directory holds the X Window System programs and libraries for revision 6 of the X Window System. Many of the files and directories in the **/usr/X11R6/lib/X11** directory such as **XF86Conig** and **xinit** are links to corresponding files and directories in the **/etc/X11** directory, which holds the X Window System configuration files. The **/usr/src** directory holds source files; in particular, **/usr/src/linux** holds the kernel source files you use to update the kernel. Data that is meant to be shared by different applications is kept in the **/usr/share** directory. For example, the **/usr/share/doc** directory holds documentation that is usually installed with different applications. Here, you can also find HOW-TO documents. The **/usr/local** directory is used for programs meant to be used only on this particular system. The **/usr/opt** directory is where optional packages are installed.

```
# ls /usr
X11R6 bin cgi-bin dict doc etc games include info lib libexec local
man sbin share src tmp
```

Standard system directories and configuration files are shown in Tables 25-4 and 25-5. See Chapter 33 for network configuration files.

Directories	Description
/bin	System-related programs.
/sbin	System programs for specialized tasks.
/lib	System libraries.
/etc	Configuration files for system and network services and applications.
/home	The location of user home directories and server data directories, such as Web and FTP site files.

Table 25-4. *System Directories*

Directories	Description
/mnt	The location where CD-ROM and floppy disk files systems are mounted
/var	The location of system directories whose files continually change, such as logs, printer spool files, and lock files
/usr	User-related programs and files. Includes several key subdirectories, such as **/usr/bin**, **/usr/X11**, and **/usr/doc**
/usr/bin	Programs for users
/usr/X11	X Window System configuration files
/usr/share	Shared files
/usr/share/doc	Documentation for applications
/tmp	Directory for system temporary files

Table 25-4. *System Directories* (continued)

File	Description
/etc/inittab	Sets the default state, as well as terminal connections
/etc/passwd	Contains user password and login configurations
/etc/shadow	Contains user-encrypted passwords
/etc/group	Contains a list of groups with configurations for each
/etc/fstab	Automatically mounts file systems when you start your system
/etc/lilo.conf	The LILO configuration file for your system
/etc/conf.modules	Modules on your system to be automatically loaded
/etc/printcap	Contains a list of each printer and its specifications
/etc/termcap	Contains a list of terminal type specifications for terminals that could be connected to the system
/etc/gettydefs	Contains configuration information on terminals connected to the system

Table 25-5. *Configuration Files*

File	Description
/etc/skel	Directory that holds the versions of initialization files, such as **.bash_profile,** which are copied to new users' home directories
/etc/ttys	List of terminal types and the terminal devices to which they correspond
/etc/services	Services run on the system and the ports they use
/etc/profile	Default shell configuration file for users
/etc/shells	Shells installed on the system that users can use
/etc/motd	System administrator's message of the day

Table 25-5. *Configuration Files* (continued)

System Startup Files: /etc/rc.d and /etc/sysconfig

Each time you start your system, it reads a series of startup commands from system initialization files located in your **/etc/rc.d** directory. These initialization files are organized according to different tasks. Some are located in the **/etc/rc.d** directory itself, while others are located in a subdirectory called **init.d** (SuSE uses only **rc.d**) You should not have to change any of these files. The organization of system initialization files varies among Linux distributions. The Mandrake, SuSE, and Red Hat organizations are described here. Some of the files you find in **/etc/rc.d** are listed in Table 25-6.

File	Description
/etc/sysconfig	Directory on Red Hat, Mandrake, and SuSE Linux that holds system configuration files and directories.
/etc/rc.d	Directory that holds system startup and shutdown files.
/etc/rc.d/rc.sysinit	Initialization file for your system.
/etc/rc.d/rc.local	Initialization file for your own commands. You can freely edit this file to add your own startup commands; this is the last startup file executed.

Table 25-6. *System Startup Files*

File	Description
/etc/rc.d/rc.modules	Loads kernel modules (not implemented by default on Red Hat Linux).
/etc/rc.d/init.d	Directory that holds many of the daemons, servers, and scripts such as **httpd** for Web servers and networks to start up network connections.
/etc/rc.d/rc*num*.d	Directories for different runlevels where *num* is the runlevel. The directories hold links to scripts in the **/etc/rc.d/init.d** directory.
/etc/rc.d/init.d/halt	Operations performed each time you shut down the system, such as unmounting file systems. Called **rc.halt** in other distributions.
/etc/rc.d/init.d/lpd	Operations to start up and shut down the **lpd** daemon.
/etc/rc.d/init.d/inet	Operations to start up and shut down the **inetd** daemon.
/etc/rc.d/init.d/network	Operations to start up and shut down your network connections.
/etc/rc.d/init.d/httpd	Operations to start up and shut down your Web server daemon, **httpd**.

Table 25-6. *System Startup Files* (continued)

The **/etc/rc.d/rc.sysinit** file holds the commands for initializing your system, including the mounting of your file systems. Kernel modules for specialized features or devices can be loaded in an **rc.modules** file. The **/etc/rc.d/rc.local** file is the last initialization file executed. You can place commands of your own here. If you look at this file, you see the message displayed for you every time you start the system. You can change that message if you want. When you shut down your system, the **halt** file, which contains the commands to do this, is called. The files in **init.d** are then called to shut down daemons, and the file systems are unmounted. In Mandrake and Red Hat, **halt** is located in the **init.d** directory. For other distributions, such as SuSE, it may be called **rc.halt** and located in the **/etc/rc.d** directory.

The **/etc/rc.d/init.d** directory is designed primarily to hold scripts that both start up and shut down different specialized daemons (on SuSE, scripts are placed in **/etc/rc.d**). Network and printer daemons are started up here. You also find files here to start font servers and Web site daemons. These files perform double duty, starting a daemon when the system starts up and shutting down the daemon when the system shuts down. The files in **init.d** are designed in a way to make it easy to write scripts for starting up and shutting down specialized applications. It uses functions defined in the **functions** file, as do many of the other **init.d** files. Many of these files are set up for you automatically. You needn't change them. If you do change them, be sure you know how these files work first. Chapter 19 describes this process in detail.

When your system starts up, several programs are automatically started and run continuously to provide services such as Web site operations. Depending on what kind of services you want your system to provide, you can add or remove items in a list of services to be automatically started. In the installation process, you could determine what services those would be. For example, the Web server is run automatically when your system starts up. If you are not running a Web site, you would have no need, as yet, for the Web server. You could have the service not started, removing an extra task the system does not need to perform. Several of the servers and daemons perform necessary tasks. The **sendmail** server enables you to send messages across networks, while the **lpd** server performs printing operations.

When your system starts up, it uses links in special runlevel directories in the **/etc/rc.d/** directory to run the startup scripts in the **/etc/rc.d/init.d** directory. A runlevel directory bears the number of its runlevel, as in **/etc/rc.d/rc3.d** for Runlevel 3, and **/etc/rc.d/rc5.d** for Runlevel 5. To have a service not start up, remove its link from that runlevel directory. You can use any of these scripts to start and stop a daemon manually at any time by using the `stop` argument to stop it, the `start` argument to start it again, and the `restart` argument to restart the daemon.

Most administration tools provide interfaces displaying a simple list of services from which you can select the ones you want to start up. The Mandrake Control Center and SuSE's Yast Control Center let you select services to start and stop. On the Red Hat Text setup menu, select System Services and then choose from the list of servers and daemons provided. Toggle an entry on or off with the SPACEBAR. On Linuxconf, the Control Service Activity panel lists different daemons and servers that you can have start by just clicking a check box. On Webmin, select Bootup and Shutdown on the System panel to display a list of available services that you can then configure to start up.

In addition, you can use a KDE System V Init Editor (**ksysv**, see Chapter 19) to determine which servers and daemons are to start and stop at what runlevel. **ksysv** provides an easy-to-use GUI interface for managing the servers and daemons in your **/etc/rc.d/init.d** directory. You can stop, start, and assign servers to different runlevels. **ksysv** is easier to use because it supports drag-and-drop operations. To assign a server to a particular runlevel, drag its entry from the Services box to the appropriate runlevel box. To remove it from a particular runlevel, drag its entry out of that runlevel box to the Trash icon. To start and stop a daemon manually, right-click it and select either the Stop or Start entry from the pop-up menu.

Many distributions still support the older System V Runlevel Editor, which operates similarly to the KDE System V Init Editor.

On Mandrake, SuSE and Red Hat systems, configuration and startup information is also kept in the **/etc/sysconfig** directory. Here you will find files containing definitions of system variables used to configure devices such as your keyboard and mouse. These entries were defined for you when you configured your devices during installation. You will also find network definitions as well as scripts for starting and stopping your network connections. A sample of the keyboard file is shown here.

/etc/sysconfig/keyboard

```
KEYBOARDTYPE="pc"
KEYTABLE="us"
```

Several of these files are generated by distribution configuration tools such as Red Hat's **mouseconfig**. For example, **mouseconfig** will generate configuration variables for the mouse device name, type, and certain features, placing them in the **/etc/sysconfig/mouse** file, shown here:

```
FULLNAME="Generic - 3 Button Mouse (USB)"
MOUSETYPE="imps2"
XEMU3="no"
XMOUSETYPE="IMPS/2"
```

Other files such as **hwconf** will list all your hardware devices, defining configuration variables such as its class (video, CD-ROM, hard drive, and so on) the bus it uses (PCI, IDE, and so on), its device name (such as hdd or st0), the drivers it uses, and a description of the device. A CD-ROM entry is shown here:

```
class: CDROM
bus: IDE
detached: 0
device: hdd
driver: ignore
desc: "TOSHIBA DVD-ROM SD-M1402"
```

Several directories are included. These include **network-scripts**, which lists several startup scripts for network connections, such as **ifup-ppp**, which starts up PPP connections.

System Logs: /var/log and syslogd

Various system logs kept for tasks performed on your system are kept in the **/var/log** directory. Here you can find logs for mail, news, and all other system operations. The **/var/log/messages** file is a log of all system tasks not covered by other logs. This usually includes startup tasks, such as loading drivers and mounting file systems. If a driver for a card failed to install at startup, you find an error message for it here. Logins are also logged in this file, showing you who attempted to log in to what account. The **/var/log/maillog** file logs mail message transmissions and news transfers.

Logs are managed by the **syslogd** daemon. This daemon will manage all the logs on your system as well as coordinating with the logging operations of other systems on your network. Configuration information for **syslogd** is held in the **/etc/syslog.conf** file. This file contains the names and locations for your system log files. Here you find entries for **/var/log/messages** and **/var/log/maillog**, among others. An entry consists of two fields: a selector and an action. The selector is the kind of service to be logged, such as mail or news, and the action is the location where messages are to be placed. The action is usually a log file, but it can also be a remote host or a pipe to another program. The kind of service is referred to as a facility. **syslogd** has several terms it uses to specify certain kinds of service (see Table 25-7). A facility can be further qualified by a priority. A priority specifies the kind of message generated by the facility. **syslogd** uses several designated terms to indicate different priorities. A sector is constructed from both the facility and priority, separated by

Facilities	Description
auth–priv	Security/authorization messages (private)
cron	Clock daemon (cron and at) messages
daemon	Other system daemon messages
kern	Kernel messages
lpr	Line printer subsystem messages
mail	Mail subsystem messages
mark	Internal use only
news	Usenet news subsystem messages
syslog	Syslog internal messages
user	Generic user-level messages
uucp	UUCP subsystem messages
local0 through local7	Reserved for local use
priorities	**Description**
debug	7, Debugging messages, lowest priority
info	6, Informational messages
notice	5, Notifications, normal, but significant, condition

Table 25-7. *Syslogd Facilities, Priorities, and Operators*

Facilities	Description
warning	4, Warnings
err	3, Error messages
crit	2, Critical conditions
alert	1, Alerts, action must be taken immediately
emerg	0, Emergency messages, system is unusable, highest priority
Operators	**Description**
*	Matches all facilities or priorities in a sector
=	Restricts to a specified priority
!	Excludes specified priority and higher ones
/	A file to save messages to
@	A host to send messages to
|	FIFO pipe to send messages to

Table 25-7. *Syslogd Facilities, Priorities, and Operators* (continued)

a period. For example, to save error messages generated by mail systems, you use a sector consisting of the mail facility and the **err** priority, as shown here:

```
mail.err
```

To save these messages to the **/var/log/maillog** file, you specify that file as the action, giving you the following entry:

```
mail.err /var/log/maillog
```

syslogd also supports the use of ***** as a matching character to match either all the facilities or priorities in a sector. **cron.*** would match on all cron messages no matter what the priority, ***.err** would match on error messages from all the facilities, and ***.*** would match on all messages. The following example saves all mail messages to the **/var/log/maillog** file and all critical messages to the **/var/log/mycritical** file:

```
mail.* /var/log/maillog
*.crit /var/log/mycritical
```

When you specify a priority for a facility, that will in fact include all the messages with a higher priority. So the **err** priority also includes the **crit**, **alert**, and **emerg** priorities. If you just want to select the message for a specific priority, you qualify the priority with the = operator. For example, **mail.=err** will select only error messages, not **crit**, **alert**, and **emerg** messages. You can also restrict priorities with the **!** operator. This will eliminate messages with the specified priority and higher. For example, **mail.!crit** will exclude **crit** messages and the higher **alert** and **emerg** messages. To specifically exclude all the messages for an entire facility, you use the **none** priority. **mail.none** excludes all mail messages. This is usually used when you define several sectors in the same entry.

You can list several priorities or facilities in a given sector by separating them with commas. You can also have several sectors in the same entry by separating them with semicolons. The first example saves to the **/var/log/messages** file all messages with **info** priority, excluding all mail, news, and authentication messages (**authpriv**). The second saves all **crit** messages and higher for the **uucp** and **news** facilities to the **/var/log/spooler** file:

```
*.info;mail.none;news.none;authpriv.none /var/log/messages
uucp,news.crit /var/log/spooler
```

For the action field, you can specify files, remote systems, users, or pipes. An action entry for a file must always begin with a / and specify its full pathname, such as **/var/log/messages**. To log messages to a remote host, you simply specify the hostname preceded by an @ sign. The following example saves all kernel messages on **rabbit.trek.com**:

```
kern.* @rabbit.trek.com
```

For users, you just list the login names of the users you want to receive the messages. The following example will send critical news messages to the consoles for the users **chris** and **aleina**:

```
news.=crit chris,aleina
```

You can also output messages to a named pipe (FIFO). The pipe entry for the action field begins with a |. The following example pipes kernel debug messages to the named pipe **|/usr/adm/debug**:

```
kern.=debug |/usr/adm/debug
```

Whenever you make changes to the **syslog.conf** file, you need to restart the **syslogd** daemon using the following command:

```
/etc/rc.d/init.d/syslog restart
```

The default **/etc/syslog.conf** file for Red Hat systems is shown here. Messages are logged to various files in the **/var/log** directory.

/etc/syslog.conf

```
# Log all kernel messages to the console.
# Logging much else clutters up the screen.
#kern.*                                  /dev/console

# Log anything (except mail) of level info or higher.
# Don't log private authentication messages!
*.info;mail.none;news.none;authpriv.none                /var/log/messages

# The authpriv file has restricted access.
authpriv.* /var/log/secure

# Log all the mail messages in one place.
mail.* /var/log/maillog

# Everybody gets emergency messages, plus log them on another
# machine.
*.emerg *

# Save mail and news errors of level err and higher in a
# special file.
uucp,news.crit /var/log/spooler

# Save boot messages also to boot.log
local7.* /var/log/boot.log

#
# INN
#
news.=crit /var/log/news/news.crit
news.=err /var/log/news/news.err
news.notice /var/log/news/news.notice
```

Performance Analysis Tools and Processes

Each task performed on your system is treated by Linux as a process, and is assigned a number and a name. You can examine these processes and even stop them. From the command line, you can use the **ps** command to list processes. With the **-aux** command, you can list all processes. Piping the output to a **grep** command with a pattern enables you to search for a particular process. The following command lists all X Window System processes:

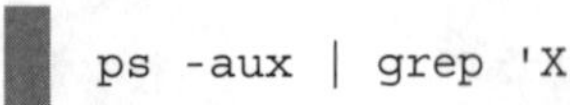

```
ps -aux | grep 'X'
```

A number of utilities on your system provide detailed information on your processes, as well as other system information such as CPU and disk use (see Table 25-8). Although these tools were designed to be used on a shell command line, displaying output in text lines, several now have KDE and Gnome versions that provide a GUI interface for displaying results and managing processes. The **vmstat** command outputs a detailed listing indicating the performance of different system components, including CPU, memory, I/O, and swap operations. A report is issued as a line with fields for the different components. If you provide a time period as an argument, it repeats at the specified interval—usually a few seconds. The **top** command provides a listing of the processes on your system that are the most CPU intensive, showing what processes are using most of your resources. The listing is in real time and updated every few seconds. Commands are provided for changing a process's status, such as its priority.

The **free** command lists the amount of free RAM memory on your system, showing how much is used and how much is free, as well as what is used for buffers and swap memory. **Xload** is an X Window System tool showing the load, CPU, and memory. **iostat** will display your disk usage, and **sar** will show system activity information.

On the Gnome System Manager (GTop), you can also sort the processes according to their fields by clicking the field's button at the top of the process list. If you right-click an

Performance Tool	Description
vmstat	Performance of system components
top	Listing of most CPU intensive processes
free	Listing for free RAM memory
sar	System activity information
iostat	Disk usage
Xload	View of system load
Gtop	Gnome System Manager
Kpm	KDE Process Manager

Table 25-8. *Performance Tools*

entry, a pop-up menu displays with actions you can perform on it. System statistic summary graphs are displayed at the top of the window showing the CPU load, memory use, and disk use. You can add more graphs or change their display features, such as the colors used. The GTop window displays three tabbed panels for detailed reports showing processes, memory use, and file system use. You can add more, showing customized reports such as only the user processes. Process lists can be further refined to show user, system, or all processes. To configure Gtop, you select the Preferences entry in the Settings menu. This displays a menu with tabbed panels for specifying the update frequency for different statistics, determining the summaries you want displayed and what process fields to show. You can find the Gnome System Manager in the Utilities menu.

The K Desktop provides the KDE Process Manager (kpm) for viewing and managing your processes. You can sort the processes according to their fields by clicking the field's button at the top of the process list. If you select a process, you can then choose to perform several different actions on it, such as ending it (killing the process) or suspending it (putting it to sleep). A right-click on a process entry displays a pop-up menu with the different actions you can take. You can further refine your process list by choosing to view only your own processes, system processes, or all processes.

Chapter 26

Boot Management Tools

With Linux, you have the ability to load up different versions of the Linux kernel as well as different operating systems that you have installed on your system. The task of selecting and starting up an operating system or kernel is managed by a boot management utility of which there are currently two in use, the Grand Unified Bootloader (Grub) and the Linux Loader (LILO). These are versatile tools, letting you load operating systems that share the same disk drive, as well as letting you choose from different Linux kernels that may be installed on the same Linux system.

Grand Unified Bootloader (GRUB)

The Grand Unified Bootloader (GRUB) is a multi-boot boot loader that operates like LILO. With many distributions, it is now the default boot loader. GRUB offers extensive compatibility with a variety of operating systems. Users can select operating systems to run from a menu interface displayed when a system boots up. Use arrow keys to move to an entry and press ENTER. Type **e** to edit a command, which lets you change kernel arguments or specify a different kernel. The **c** command places you in a command line interface, similar to LILO. Provided your system bios supports very large drives, GRUB can boot from anywhere on them. Linux and Unix operating systems are known as multi-boot operating systems and take arguments passed to them at boot time. Here, you can specify features like the kernel module to user for an IDE CD-R/RW drive (see Chapter 4). Use **info** grub to list detailed documentation or check the **grub** Man pages.

GRUB configuration is held in the **/etc/grub.conf** file. You only need to make your entries and GRUB will automatically read them when you reboot. There are several options you can set, such as the timeout period and the background image to use. You can specify a system to boot by creating a title entry for it, beginning with the term **title**. You then have to specify where the operating system kernel or program is located, which hard drive and what partition on that hard drive. This information is listed in parentheses following the **root** option. Numbering starts from 0, not 1, and hard drives are indicated with an **hd** prefix, whether they are IDE or SCSI hard drives. So **root (hd0,2)** references the first hard drive (**hda**) and the third partition on that hard drive (**hda3**). For Linux systems, you will also have to use the **kernel** option to indicate the kernel program to run, using the full pathname and any options the kernel may need. The RAM disk is indicated by the **initrd** option.

```
title Red Hat Linux (2.4.7-10)
      root (hd0,2)
      kernel /boot/vmlinuz-2.4.7-10 ro root=/dev/hda3
      initrd /boot/initrd-2.4.7-10.img
```

For another operating system such as Windows, you would use the **rootnoverify** option to specify where Windows is installed. This option instructs GRUB not to try to mount the partition. Use the **imakeactive** and **chainloader+1** options to allow GRUB to access it. The **chainloader** option tells GRUB to use another boot program for that operating system. The number indicates the sector on the partition where the boot program is located—for example, **+1** indicates the first sector.

```
title Windows XP
      rootnoverify (hd0,0)
      imakeactive
      chainloader +1
```

Windows systems will all want to boot from the first partition on the first disk. This becomes a problem if you want to install several versions of Windows on different partitions or install Windows on a partition other than the first one. GRUB lets you work around this by letting you hide other partitions in line, and then un-hiding the one you want, making it appear to be the first partition. In this example, the first partition is hidden, and the second is un-hidden. This assumes there is a Windows system on the second partition on the first hard drive (**hd0,1**). Now that the first partition is hidden, the second one appears as the first partition.

```
hide (hd0,0)
unhide (hd0,1)
rootnoverify (hd0,1)
```

A sample **grub.conf** file follows with entries for both Linux and Windows. Notice that kernel parameters are listed in the **kernel** option as arguments to the kernel.

/etc/grub.conf

```
# grub.conf generated by anaconda
#
#boot=/dev/hda
default=0
timeout=30
splashimage=(hd0,2)/boot/grub/splash.xpm.gz
title Red Hat Linux (2.4.7-10)
      root (hd0,2)
      kernel /boot/vmlinuz-2.4.7-10 ro root=/dev/hda3 hdc=ide-scsi
      initrd /boot/initrd-2.4.7-10.img
title Windows XP
      rootnoverify (hd0,0)
      imakeactive
      chainloader +1
```

LILO

Most Linux distributions also provide the older Linux Loader (LILO) as its boot manager. It performs the same kind of tasks as GRUB. You can modify your LILO configuration either by using an administration tool like Boot Manager (LILO-config) or by editing the **/etc/lilo.conf** configuration file directly. If installed, you can access Boot Manager on the KDE Desktop Control Center, under the System entry. The Boot Manager will display four panels: General Options, Operating Systems, Expert, and About. The General Options panel lets you set basic options such as the drive for the boot record. On the Operating System panel, you create the entries for different operating systems on your computer. For Linux systems, you can specify the root partition and the Linux kernel, as well as a label. On the Expert panel, you can edit the **lilo.conf** file directly, typing in options and adding stanzas.

Note *You can also configure LILO with Webmin and Linuxconf, or with the KDE Klilo2 tool.*

You can directly modify your LILO configuration by editing the **/etc/lilo.conf** configuration file and executing the command **`lilo`**. If you examine your **/etc/lilo.conf** file, you find it organized into different segments called *stanzas*, one for each operating system that LILO is to start up. If your Linux system shares your computer with a Windows system, you should see two stanzas listed in your **/etc/lilo.conf** file: one for Linux and one for Windows. Each stanza indicates the hard disk partition on which the respective operating system is located. It also includes an entry for the label. This is the name you enter at the LILO prompt to start that operating system.

Entries in the **lilo.conf** file consist of options to which you assign values with the = operator (see Table 26-1). At the beginning of the file, you enter global options. The entries you need will already be generated for you if you have already set up LILO during installation. An example of a Linux global entry follows. To set the timeout period when LILO waits for you to make an entry before starting the default, you create a **`timeout`** entry and assign to it the number of seconds you want to wait.

```
timeout = 200
```

Since LILO is invoking your Linux system, you can specify any options you would normally pass to that system in the **lilo.conf** file. You do this with the **append** option. Instead of manually entering the same options at the boot prompt, you can specify them in the **lilo.conf** file with the **append** option. You have already seen how this is done for IDE CD-R and CD-RW devices in Chapter 29. The following example configures the IDE CD-RW drive on the secondary IDE master connection (**hdc**) as a SCSI device by loading the **ide-scsi** module for it.

```
append="hdc=ide-scsi"
```

Another useful global entry is **`default`**, with which you can set the default operating system to start. It takes as its argument the label for the stanza. In the following example, the stanza labeled **win** will be executed by default—in this case, starting Windows:

```
default = win
```

Then you start a Linux stanza with an **`image`** or **`other`** option. You use the **`image`** option for Linux boot images files, and the **`other`** option for other operating systems such as Windows. The next example starts a stanza for Linux loading a Linux 2.4.2-2:

```
image = /boot/vmlinuz-2.4.2-2
```

You can then enter options for a stanza, such as its label and the partition that holds its root device:

```
label = linux
root = /dev/hda4
```

The **`other`** option will start a stanza for a non-Linux system. It is used in the following example to reference a Windows operating system located on the first hard drive partition.

```
other = /dev/hda1
```

One helpful option is **`password`**, where you can restrict access to a particular boot image file or operating system with a specified password. When the user selects that image or operating system, they are prompted for the password.

```
password = mypassword
```

Certain options are designed to be used only in the stanzas, and of those, some are to be used only for Linux image files or for other operating systems. For example, **`table`**, **`label`**, **`password`**, and **`restricted`** are used only for a particular stanza. They are not global options. The **`append`**, **`literal`**, **`read-only`**, and **`read-write`** options are to be used only in stanzas for Linux kernel images. The **`append`** and **`literal`** options are used to pass kernel image arguments to the kernel.

A stanza continues until another image or other option is reached, starting a new stanza. You can, if you want, make changes directly to the **/etc/lilo.conf** file using a text editor. Whenever you make a change, you must execute the **`lilo`** command to have it take effect. Type **`lilo`** and press ENTER.

```
# lilo
```

This command will read the **/etc/lilo.conf** and generate a corresponding boot record it will then write to your system's boot sector.

In the following **lilo.conf** example, the boot device is the hard drive labeled **/dev/hda**. This is the first IDE hard drive on a PC system. The timeout period where LILO waits for a user to enter a system's label is 200 seconds. The message it displays before the prompt is located in the file **/boot/message**. The user will be prompted (**`prompt`**) to enter a label. The default operating system (**`default`**) that will be started if the user does not enter one is labeled **`win`**—in this case, Windows. The VGA mode (**`vga`**) that LILO will use is **`normal`**. The map (**`map`**) is located in the **/boot/map** file, and **/boot/boot.p** is the file used as the new boot sector (**`install`**). The first stanza is a Linux image file (**`image`**) named **/boot/vmlinuz-2.4.2-2**. It is labeled **`linux`**, and the root partition (**`root`**) for this Linux system is at **/dev/hda4**, the fourth partition on the first IDE hard drive. The Linux image will first be mounted as read-only, and then later mounted as read/write. The second stanza denotes that there is another operating system (**`other`**) on the first partition in the first IDE hard drive. It is labeled **`win`**. The partition table (**`table`**) for this operating system is on the first IDE hard drive.

/etc/lilo.conf

```
# general section
boot = /dev/hda
# wait 20 seconds (200 10ths) for user to select the entry to load
timeout = 200
message = /boot/message
prompt
 # default entry
default = win
vga = normal
map=/boot/map
install=/boot/boot.b

    image = /boot/vmlinuz-2.4.2-2
                  label = linux
                  root = /dev/hda4
                  read-only

    other = /dev/hda1
                 label = win
                 table=/dev/hda
```

Unless specified by the default entry, the default operating system LILO boots is the one whose segment is the first listed in the **lilo.conf** file. Because the Linux stanza is the first listed, this is the one LILO boots if you don't enter anything at the LILO prompt. If you want to have your Windows system be the default, you can use **`lilo`** with the **`-D`** option to reset the default or you can edit the **lilo.conf** file to assign a value to **`default`**. You could also use a text editor to place the Windows stanza first, before the Linux stanza. Be sure to execute **`lilo`** to have the change take effect. The next time you start your system, you could press ENTER at the LILO prompt to have Windows loaded, instead of typing **win**.

```
# lilo -D win
```

You can set a number of LILO options using either command line options or making entries in the **lilo.conf** file. These options are listed in Table 26-1.

If you are booting an operating system from a location other than the first hard disk, you need to include a loader line for the **chain.b** file in its stanza.

```
loader=/boot/chain.b
```

Command Line Options	lilo.conf Options	Description
`-u`		Uninstalls LILO by copying the saved boot sector back.
`-V`		Prints version number.
`-t`		Test only. Does not actually write a new boot sector or map file. Use together with **-v** to learn what LILO is about to do.
`-I` *label*		Displays label and pathname of running kernel. Label is held in **BOOT_IMAGE** shell variable.
Global Options	**lilo.conf Options**	**Description**
`-b` *bootdev*	`boot=`*bootdev*	Boot device.
`-c`	`compact`	Enables map compaction. Speeds up booting.
`-d` *dsec*	`delay=`*dsec*	Timeout delay to wait for you to enter the label of an operating system at the LILO prompt when you boot up.

Table 26-1. *LILO Options for the Command Line and lilo.conf Entries*

Global Options	lilo.conf Options	Description
`-D` *label*	`default=`*label*	Uses the kernel with the specified label, instead of the first one in the list, as the default kernel to boot.
`-i` *bootsector*	`install=`*bootsector*	File to be used as the new boot sector.
`-f` *file*	`disktab=`*file*	Disk geometry parameter file.
`-l`	`linear`	Generates linear sector addresses, instead of sector/head/cylinder addresses (for large hard disks). This option can cause a conflict with **`compact`**.
`-m` *mapfile*	`map=`*mapfile*	Uses specified map file instead of the default.
	`message=`*message-file*	Specifies the message to be displayed before the LILO prompt.
	`prompt`	Displays the **`lilo:`** prompt. If timeout is not specified, the automatic reboots are disabled.
	`timeout=`*dsec*	Timeout delay to wait for you to enter the label of an operating system at the LILO prompt when you boot up.
`-p` fix	`fix-table`	Fixes corrupt partition tables.
`-P` ignore	`ignore-table`	Ignores corrupt partition tables.
`-s` *file*	`backup=`*file*	Alternate save file for the boot sector.
`-S` *file*	`force-backup=`*file*	Allows overwriting of existing save file.

Table 26-1. *LILO Options for the Command Line and lilo.conf Entries* (continued)

Global Options	lilo.conf Options	Description
	vga=*mode*	VGA text mode that LILO uses.
Stanza Options	**lilo.conf Options**	**Description**
	image=*Linux-kernel*	Pathname for boot image of a Linux kernel.
	other=*os-boot-image*	Pathname for boot image of a non-Linux operating system.
	alias=*name*	Another name for the kernel image or operating system label.
	table=*device*	Drive that holds the partition table.
	password=*password*	Protects access to an OS or kernel image with a password, as specified.
	restricted	User must enter a password if any command line parameters are passed to the kernel image.
-v	**verbose=***level*	Increases verbosity.
Linux Image Stanza Options	**lilo.conf Options**	**Description**
	root=*path*	Partition for the kernel root.
	append=*string*	Arguments to append to arguments specified for the invocation of the kernel image. Used to add needed hardware specifications for a kernel image.
	literal=*string*	Arguments to replace the arguments specified for the invocation of the kernel image.

Table 26-1. *LILO Options for the Command Line and lilo.conf Entries* (continued)

Linux Image Stanza Options	lilo.conf Options	Description
	`read-only`	Boots Linux kernel as read-only (system startup remounts as read/write).
	`read-write`	Mounts the root system as read/write.

Table 26-1. *LILO Options for the Command Line and lilo.conf Entries* (continued)

Chapter 27

Managing Users

Linux is designed to serve many users at the same time, as well as provide an interface between the users and the computer with its storage media, such as hard disks and tapes. Users have their own shells through which they interact with the operating system. As a system administrator, you can manage user logins on your system. You can add or remove users, as well as add and remove groups. You also have access to system initialization files you can use to configure all user shells. And you have control over the default initialization files copied into an account when it is first created. With them, you can decide how accounts should initially be configured.

*Every file is owned by a user, even those that are used by services like FTP. In such a case, a special user is created for just that service. For example, for FTP there will be a user named **ftp** that will own FTP files.*

You can find out which users are currently logged in with the **who** command. Add the **-u** option to display information about each connected user, such as from where they have logged in and how long they have been inactive. The command displays the login name, the login port, the date and time of login, the length of inactivity (if still active), and the process ID for the login shell. For example:

```
# who -u
root console Oct 12 10:34 . 1219
valerie tty1 Oct 12 22:18 10 1492
```

Any utility to add a user, such as kuser or Red Hat User Manager, makes use of certain default files, called configuration files, and directories to set up the new account. A set of path names is used to locate these default files or to know where to create certain user directories. For example, **/etc/skel** holds initialization files for a new user. **/etc/password** is the file that holds user passwords. A new user's home directory is placed in the **/home** directory. Certain files provide added security, such as **/etc/shadow**, which encrypts password entries. A list of the pathnames follows

Directory	Description
/home	Location of the user's own home directory.
/etc/skel	Holds the default initialization files for the login shell, such as **.bash_profile, .bashrc,** and **.bash_logout**. Includes menu user setup directories and files such as **.kde** for KDE and **Desktop** for Gnome.
/etc/shells	Holds the login shells, such as BASH or TCSH.
/etc/passwd	Holds the password for a user.
/etc/group	Holds the group to which the user belongs.

Directory	Description
/etc/shadow	Encrypted password file.
/etc/gshadow	Encrypted password file for groups.
/etc/login.defs	Default login definitions for users.

The Password Files

When you add a user, an entry for that user is made in the **/etc/passwd** file, commonly known as the *password file.* Each entry takes up one line that has several fields separated by colons. The fields are as follows:

Field	Description
Username	Login name of the user.
Password	Encrypted password for the user's account.
User ID	Unique number assigned by the system.
Group ID	Number used to identify the group to which the user belongs.
Comment	Any user information, such as the user's full name.
Home directory	The user's home directory.
Login shell	Shell to run when the user logs in; this is the default shell, usually **/bin/bash**.

The following is an example of a **/etc/passwd** entry. The entry for **chris** has an `*` in its Password field, indicating a password has not yet been created for this user. For such entries, you must use **`passwd`** to create a password. Notice also, user IDs in this particular system start at 500 and increment by one.

```
dylan:YOTPd3Pyy9hAc:500:500:User:/home/dylan:/bin/bash
chris:*:501:501:User:/home/chris:/bin/bash
```

The **/etc/passwd** file is a text file you can edit using a text editor. You can change fields in entries and even add new entries. The only field you cannot effectively change is Password, which must be encrypted. To change the Password field, you should always use the **`passwd`** command.

Although you can make entries directly to the **/etc/passwd** file, an easier and safer way is to use the userconf, adduser, and useradd utilities. These programs not only make entries in the **/etc/passwd** file, but they also create the home directory for the user and install initialization files in the user's home directory.

The **/etc/passwd** file is a simple text file and is vulnerable to security breaches. If anyone gains access to the **/etc/password** file, they might be able to decipher or brute force crack the passwords. On most Linux distributions, the shadow suite of applications implements a greater level of security. These include versions of useradd, groupadd, and their corresponding update and delete programs. Most other user configuration tools support shadow security measures. With shadow security, passwords are no longer kept in the **/etc/password** file. Instead, passwords are kept in a separate file called **/etc/shadow** and are heavily encrypted. Access is restricted to the root user. A corresponding password file, called **/etc/gshadow,** is also maintained for groups that require passwords. As part of the standard installation for most distributions, shadow passwords were implemented by default. You can manually specify whether you want to use shadow passwords with the authconfig tool in the Text Mode Setup utility.

Note *Most distributions provide tools you can use to enable and configure various authentication tools such as NIS and LDAP servers, as well as enabling shadow passwords, LDAP, and Kerberos authentication.*

Managing User Environments: /etc/skel and /etc/login.defs

Each time a user logs in, two profile scripts are executed. A system profile script is the same for every user, and each user has the **.bash_profile** script in their home directory. The system profile script is located in the **/etc** directory and named **profile** with no preceding period. As a superuser, you can edit the profile script and put in any commands you want executed for each user when he or she logs in. For example, you may want to define a default path for commands, in case the user has not done so. Or you may want to notify the user of recent system news or account charges.

When you first add a user to the system, you must provide the user with a skeleton version of their login, shell, and logout initialization files. For the BASH shell, this would be the **.bash_profile**, **.bashrc**, and **.bash_logout** files. The **useradd** command and other user management tools like kuser and Red Hat User Manager add this file automatically, copying any files in the directory **/etc/skel** to the user's new home directory. The **/etc/skel** directory contains a skeleton initialization file for the **.bash_profile**, **.bashrc**, and **.bash_logout** files or, if you are using the TCSH shell as your login shell, the **.login**, **.tcshrc,** and **.logout** files. The **/etc/skel** directory also contains default files and directories for your desktops. These include a **.screenrc** file for the X Window System, a **.kde** directory for the KDE desktop, and a **Desktop** directory that contains default configuration files for the Gnome desktop.

As a superuser, you can configure the **.bash_profile** or **.bashrc** file in the **/etc/skel** any way you want. Usually, basic system variable assignments are included that define pathnames for commands and command aliases. The **PATH** and **BASH_ENV** variables are defined in **.bash_profile**. Once users have their own **.bash_profile** or **.bashrc** file, they can redefine variables or add new commands as they choose. The **.bashrc** file will also run the **/etc/bashrc** to implement any global definitions such as the **PS1** and **TERM** variables. The **/etc/bashrc** file also executes any specialize initialization file in the **/etc/profile.d** directory such as those used for KDE and Gnome. The **.bash_profile** file runs the **.bashrc** file, and through it, the **/etc/bashrc** file, implementing global definitions.

Systemwide values used by user and group creation utilities such as useradd and usergroup are kept in the **/etc/login.defs** file. Here you will find the range of possible user and group IDs listed. **`UID_MIN`** holds the minimum number, and **`UID_MAX`** the maximum number for user IDs. Various password options control password controls—such as **`PASS_MIN_LEN`**, which determines the minimum number of characters allowable in a password. Options such as **`CREATE_HOME`** can be set to tell useradd to create home directories for new accounts by default.

login.defs

```
# *REQUIRED*
# Directory where mailboxes reside, _or_ name of file, relative to the
# home directory. If you _do_ define both, MAIL_DIR takes precedence.
# QMAIL_DIR is for Qmail
#
#QMAIL_DIR Maildir
MAIL_DIR /var/spool/mail
#MAIL_FILE .mail

# Password aging controls:
# PASS_MAX_DAYS Maximum number of days a password may be used.
# PASS_MIN_DAYS Minimum number of days allowed between password changes.
# PASS_MIN_LEN Minimum acceptable password length.
# PASS_WARN_AGE Number of days warning given before a password expires.
PASS_MAX_DAYS 99999
PASS_MIN_DAYS 0
PASS_MIN_LEN 5
PASS_WARN_AGE 7

# Min/max values for automatic uid selection in useradd
UID_MIN 500
UID_MAX 60000

# Min/max values for automatic gid selection in groupadd
GID_MIN 500
GID_MAX 60000

# If defined, this command is run when removing a user.
#USERDEL_CMD /usr/sbin/userdel_local

# If useradd should create home directories for users by default
# On RH systems, we do.
CREATE_HOME yes
```

Login Access

You can control user login access to your system with the **/etc/login.access** file. The file consists of entries listing users, whether they are allowed access, and from where they can access the system. A record in this file consists of three colon-delimited fields: a plus (+) or minus (-) sign indicating whether users are allowed access, user login names allowed access, and the remote system (host) or terminal (tty device) from which they are trying to log in. The following enables the user **dylan** to access the system from the **rabbit.mytrek.com** remote system:

```
+:chris:rabbit.mytrek.com
```

You can list more than one user or location. You can also use the **ALL** option in place of either users or locations to allow access by all users and locations. The **ALL** option can be qualified with the **EXCEPT** option to allow access by all users except certain specified ones. The following entry allows any user to log in to the system using the console, except for the users **larisa** and **aleina**:

```
+:ALL EXCEPT larisa aleina:console
```

Other access control files are used to control access for specific services, such as the **hosts.deny** and **hosts.allows** files used with the **tcpd** daemon for xinetd-supported servers.

Controlling Access to Directories and Files

Recall from Chapter 12 that you can control access to your files and directories by user, group, or others. This is a capability given to any user for their own files and directories. Access in each of these categories can be controlled according to write, read, and execute permissions. Write access lets users modify a file, read access lets them display it, and execute access (used for programs) lets them run it. For directories, write access lets them delete it, read access lists its contents, and execute access lets users change to that directory. You could allow anyone on the system to read one of your files by assigning a read access to its other permission. Chapter 11 describes how you can use the **chmod** command to set permissions, using **u** for user, **g** for group, and **o** for other, as well as **r** for read, **w** for write, and **x** for execute. The following command provides read and write group permissions for the file **ourdraft1**:

```
chmod g+rx ourdraft1
```

On Gnome, you can set a directory or file permission using its Permissions panel in its Properties window (see Figure 27-1). Right-click on the file or directory entry in the file manager window and select Properties. Then select the Permissions panel. Here you will find a table of boxes with columns for Read, Write, and Execute along with rows for Owner, Group, and Other. Check the appropriate box for the permission you want. Normally, the Read and Write boxes for user permission will already be set. You can

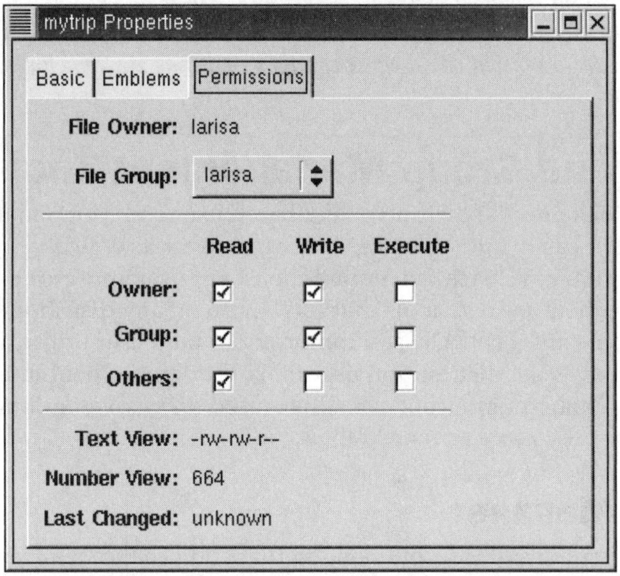

Figure 27-1. *File and directory permissions on Gnome*

specify the group you want access provided to from the Group drop-down menu. This displays the groups a user belongs to.

In addition to the read/write/execute permissions, you can manually set ownership permissions for executable programs. Normally, the user who runs a program owns it while it is running, even though the program file itself may be owned by another user. The set user ID permission allows the original owner of the program to always own it, even while another user is running the program. For example, most software on the system is owned by the root user, but is run by ordinary users. Some such software may have to modify files owned by the root. In this case, the ordinary user would need to run that program with the root retaining ownership so the program could have the permissions to change those root-owned files. The group ID permission works the same way, except for groups. Programs owned by a group retain ownership even when run by users from another group. The program can then change the owner group's files.

To add both the user ID and group ID permissions to a file, you use the **s** option. The following example adds the user ID permission to the **pppd** program, which is owned by the root user. When an ordinary user runs **pppd**, the root user retains ownership, allowing the **pppd** program to change root-owned files.

```
# chmod +s /usr/sbin/pppd
```

Where a program is owned by the root, setting the user ID permission will give the user the ability to execute the program with root permissions. This can be a serious security risk for any program that could effect changes—such as **rm***, which removes files.*

GUI User and Group Management Tools

Several distributions provide their own GUI-based user and group management tools. With these you can easily add, remove, or change users as well as groups. Red Hat, Mandrake, and SuSE have each developed their own user and group administrative tools. In addition, there are user tools that can be run on any distribution such as kuser, Webmin, and Linuxconf. The KDE desktop provides the kuser utility, which has many of the same features as the distribution user tools. Caldera's OpenLinux uses Webmin to manage users. Though Linuxconf can still be used on many distributions, it has been superseded on most by more advanced tools.

Red Hat User Manager

For Red Hat distributions, it is recommended that you use the Red Hat User Manager to manage user accounts. You can access the Red Hat User Manager from the System Settings window in the Start Here window. It will be labeled simply as User Manager. You can also access it from the Gnome System menu.

The User Manager window will display panels for listing both users and groups (see Figure 27-2). You use the User Manager to manage your groups, as well as users. Click on the appropriate tab to display either users or groups. Within the user and group panels, field labels are displayed at the top for usernames, group, the user's full name, login shell, or home directories. A button bar will list various tasks you can perform, including creating new users or groups, editing current ones (Properties), or deleting a selected user or group. The number of users and groups on a system can be extensive. The User Manager provides an easy-to-use search tool. You can enter a search string in the box labeled Filter By. When you click the Apply Filter button, only those matching users or groups are listed.

To create a new user, click the New button. This opens a window with entries for the username, password, login shell, along with options to create a home directory and a new group for that user. Once you have created a user, you can edit its properties to add or change features. Select the user's entry and click the Properties button. This displays a window with tabbed panels for User Data, Account Info, Password Info, and Groups. You can change basic features such as the password and login shell in the User Data panel. Account Info lets you lock an account and set an expiration date for it. Password Info will let you set password expiration limits to force a user to change the password or to render the account inactive after a certain time. On the Groups panel, you can select the groups that the user belongs to, adding or removing group membership (see Figure 27-5).

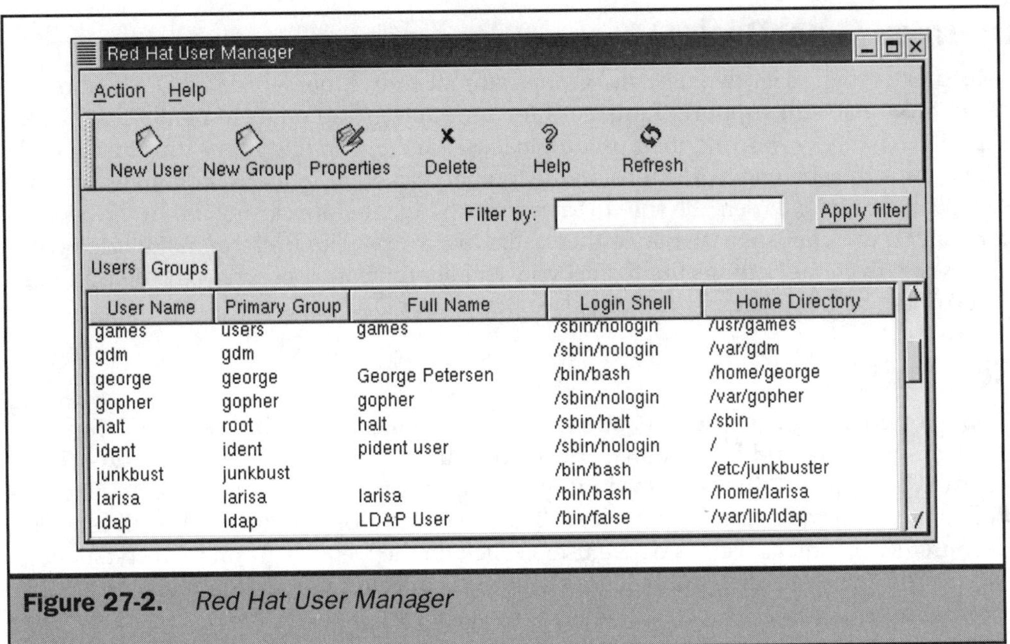

Figure 27-2. *Red Hat User Manager*

Note *You can also manage users with Linuxconf, as was done in older versions of Red Hat.*

You can add, remove, and modify any groups easily with the Red Hat User Manager. First access the Red Hat User Manager by clicking on the User Manager icon in the System Settings window, listed on the Start Here window. Then click on the tabbed panel labeled Groups in the Red Hat User Manager window. This will list all your current groups. There will be two fields for each entry, the group name and the group members.

To add a group, just click the New Group button. This opens a small window where you can enter the group name. When you click the Refresh button, the new group will be listed in the User Manager's Group listing. To add users as members of the group, you select the group's entry and click the Properties button. This opens a window with tabbed panels for both the Group Data and the Group Users. The Groups Users panel will list all current users with check boxes. Select the check boxes for the users you want to be members of this group. If you want to remove a user as member, click its check box to remove its check. Click Apply to effect your changes.

If you want to remove a group, just select its entry in the User Manager's Group panel and then click the Delete button.

Mandrake (userDrake)

Mandrake provides its own user and groups administrative tool called userDrake (though Mandrake also still supports Linuxconf for user and group management). Users are listed in a window showing their user logins, user and group IDs, home directories, and the groups they belong to. Buttons on the toolbar as well as in the Action menu let you add, edit, or remove users. Be sure to save your changes before closing. From the Settings menu you can choose to display either users or groups. The Preferences dialog box, accessible from the Settings menu, lets you set general features such as the default user shell or the home directory. You can also specify an LDAP server.

SuSE (YaST)

SuSE provides its own basic user and group management tools through YaST Control Center's Security and Users panel. Here you can create, edit, or remove users. The Create User tool is a simple wizard for quickly creating a user, requiring only the user's full name, a username, and a password. The Edit User tool lets you modify all aspects of a user's account, as well as delete users. Click on the Details button to open a panel where you can select the kind of login shell to use or select groups that the user will belong to.

Managing Users with Webmin

To manage users with Webmin, select the Users and Groups entry in the System panel. This displays a listing of all your users and groups. To create a new user, click the Create A New User link below the list of users. The Create User page displays segments for User Details, Password Options, and Group Memberships. For User Details, you enter the username (login name), the real name, the shell (login shell), the home directory, and the password (see Figure 27-3). For the shell entry, you can choose the shell you want from a drop-down menu. For the home directory, you can type in the directory name or click the button next to the entry box labeled with three dots. This opens a file manager interface where you can browse to the directory and file you want.

For the password options, you can specify the period when the user needs to change the password and even set an expiration date. For group membership, you can select the primary (default) group (usually **users**) and add any secondary groups.

Once a group is created, an entry for it will appear in the Users and Groups page. The username will appear as a link. To make any changes or to delete the group, simply click on its name. The Edit User page will appear with entries for changing the password, changing secondary groups, or deleting the user.

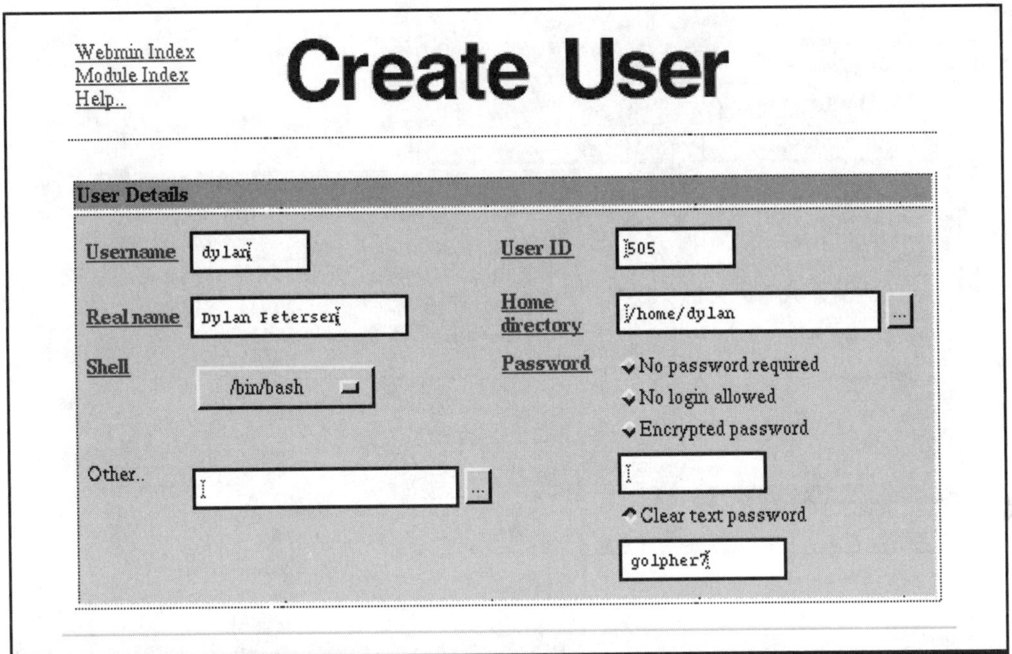

Figure 27-3. *Webmin user details*

Managing Users with kuser

The K Desktop also provides a simple user management utility called kuser that works much like Webmin and Linuxconf (see Figure 27-4). You can use it to manage both users and groups. The window is divided into two panes: one for users and the other for groups. Add, Edit, and Delete icons easily enable you to add new users, change their configuration, or remove them. When you add a new user, a new window opens with entries such as the shell and home directory. To add the password, click Password and enter the password in the window displayed.

Managing Users with Linuxconf

You can access Linuxconf user configuration panels either through the main Linuxconf interface or through a special user-configuration interface invoked with the **`userconf`** command. To add a new user, click the Add button on the User Accounts panel. This

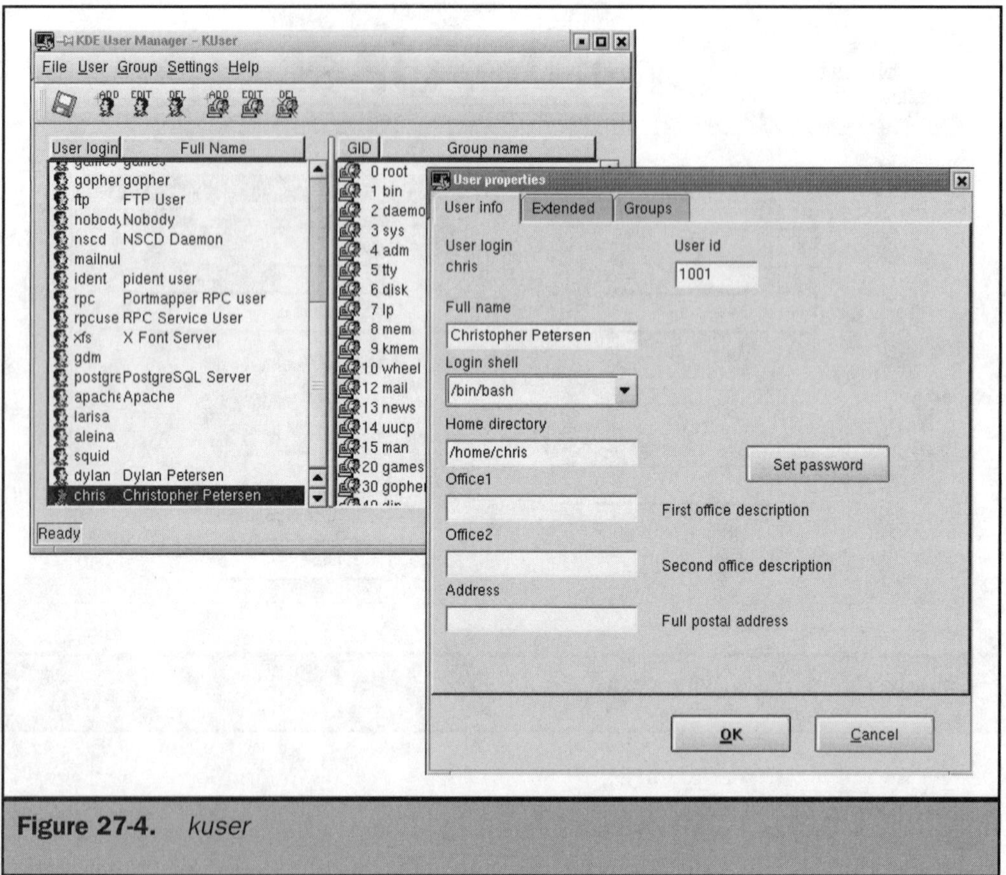

Figure 27-4. *kuser*

displays a User Information panel that contains several tabbed panels, labeled Base Info, Params, and Privileges. To create a user account, all you have to do is enter the login name you want to give the user and the user's full name. Linuxconf will add default entries for the remaining fields, adding a home directory, group, login shell (command interpreter), and user ID. Click the Accept button to create the user. You can select values for these fields yourself, if you wish. The home directory has the default of **/home** and the user's login name, as in **/home/aleina**. Both the group and the shell have drop-down menus listing available groups and shells from which to choose. To give the user an initial password, click the Password button. A Changing Password panel is displayed where you can enter the new password.

There is an entry for both a default group and supplementary groups. The default group (also known as the primary group) is determined by the files and processes the user account needs to have access to. For user accounts, this has traditionally been the group named **users**.

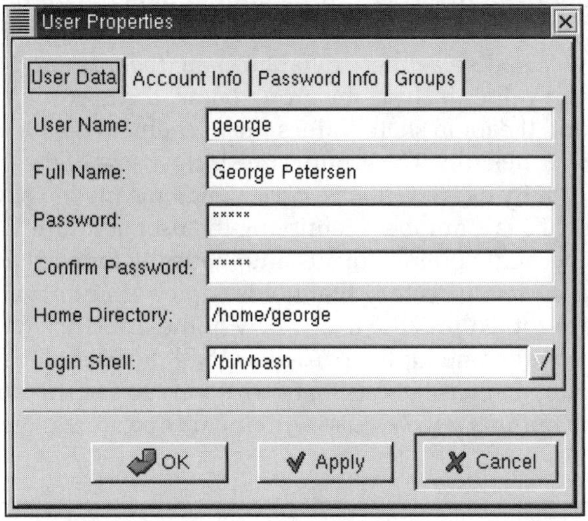

Figure 27-5. *Red Hat User Manager user information*

When you finish, click Accept. You now see the new user displayed in the User Accounts panel. If you need to change or delete a user, double-click its entry in this panel to display its User Information panel. To remove the user, click DELETE. If you want to make some changes, such as adding the user to a different group or giving the user a different home directory, edit the appropriate entries and click Accept. The user information is then updated.

Adding and Removing Users with useradd, usermod, and userdel

Linux also provides the **useradd**, **usermod**, and **userdel** commands to manage user accounts. All these commands take in all their information as options on the command line. If an option is not specified, they use predetermined default values. With the **useradd** command, you enter values as options on the command line, such as the name of a user to create a user account. It then creates a new login and directory of that name using all the default features for a new account.

```
# useradd chris
```

The useradd utility will first check the **/etc/login.defs** file for default values for creating a new account. For those defaults not defined in **/etc/login.defs** file, useradd supplies its own. You can display these defaults using the **useradd** command with the **-D** option. The default values include the group name, the user ID, the home directory, the **skel** directory, and the login shell. Values the user enters on the command line will override corresponding defaults. The group name is the name of the group in which the new account is placed. By default, this is *other*, which means the new account belongs to no group. The user ID is a number identifying the user account. This normally starts at 500 with the first account and increments automatically for each new account. The **skel** directory is the system directory that holds copies of initialization files. These initialization files are copied into the user's new home directory when it is created. The login shell is the pathname for the particular shell the user plans to use.

The **useradd** command has options that correspond to each default value. Table 27-1 holds a list of all the options you can use with the **useradd** command. You can use

Command	Description
useradd *username options*	Adds new users to the system.
usermod *username options*	Modifies a user's features.
userdel -r *username*	Removes a user from the system.
useradd, usermod Options	
-c *str*	Adds a comment to the user's entry in the system password file: **/etc/passwd**.
-d *dir*	Sets the home directory of the new user.
-D	Displays defaults for all settings. Can also be used to reset default settings for the home directory (**-b**), group (**-g**), shell (**-s**), expiration date (**-e**), and password expirations (**-f**).
-e *mm/dd/yy*	Set an expiration date for the account (None, by default). Specify by month/day/year.
-f *days*	Sets the number of days an account remains active after its password expires.
-g *group*	Sets a group.
-G *group*	Sets additional groups.

Table 27-1. *User and Group Management Commands*

Command	Description
-m	Creates user's home directory if it does not exist.
-m -k *skl-dir*	Sets the skeleton directory that holds skeleton files, such as **.profile** files, which are copied to the user's home directory automatically when it is created; the default is **/etc/skel**.
-M	Does not create user's home directory.
-n	Turns off the default procedure whereby a new group is created with the same name as a new account's username. For example, a new user, **dylan**, would have **dylan** as its group name.
-p *password*	Supplies an encrypted password (crypt or MD5). With no argument, the account is immediately disabled.
-r	A Red Hat–specific option that creates a system account (one whose user ID is lower than the minimum set in **logon.defs**). No home directory is created unless specified by **-m**.
-s *shell*	Sets the login shell of the new user. This is the **/bin/bash** by default, the BASH shell.
-u *userid*	Sets the user ID of the new user. The default is the increment of the highest number used so far.
Group Management Commands	
groupadd *groupname options*	Creates a new group.
groupdel *groupname options*	Removes a group.
groupmod *groupname options*	Modifies a group.
useradd, usermod Options	
-g *gid*	Changes a group ID.
-n *groupname*	Changes a group name.
-f	Detects if group already exists.
-r	Creates a system group, one lower than the group minimum specified in **login.defs**.

Table 27-1. *User and Group Management Commands* (continued)

specific values in place of any of these defaults when creating a particular account. The login is inaccessible until you do. In the next example, the group name for the **chris** account is set to **intro1** and the user ID is set to 578:

```
# useradd chris -g intro1 -u 578
```

Once you add a new user login, you need to give the new login a password. Password entries are placed in the **/etc/passwd** and **/etc/shadow** files. Use the **passwd** command to create a new password for the user, as shown here. The password you enter will not appear on your screen. You will be prompted to repeat the password. A message will then be issued indicating that the password was successfully changed.

```
# passwd chris
Changing password for user chris
New UNIX password:
Retype new UNIX password:
passwd: all authentication tokens updated successfully
#
```

The **usermod** command enables you to change the values for any of these features. You can change the home directory or the user ID. You can even change the username for the account.

When you want to remove a user from the system, you can use the **userdel** command to delete the user's login. In the next example, the user **chris** is removed from the system:

```
# userdel -r chris
```

You can also add a new user to the system with the adduser utility. The adduser utility takes as its argument the username for the account you are creating. adduser has options similar to useradd.

Managing Groups

You can manage groups using either shell commands or window utilities like Webmin, Linuxconf, or the Red Hat User Manager. The system file that holds group entries is called **/etc/group**. The file consists of group records, with one record per line and its fields separated by colons. A group record has four fields: a group name, a password, its ID, and the users who are part of this group. The Password field can be left blank. The fields for a group record are as follows:

Group name	Name of the group; must be unique
Password	Usually an asterisk to allow anyone to join the group; a password can be added to control access.
Group ID	Number assigned by the system to identify this group.
Users	List of users that belong to the group.

Here is an example of an entry in an **/etc/group** file. The group is called **engines**, there is no password, the group ID is 100, and the users who are part of this group are **chris**, **robert**, **valerie**, and **aleina**.

```
engines::100:chris,robert,valerie,aleina
```

As in the case of the **/etc/passwd** file, you can edit the **/etc/group** file directly using a text editor, unless you have implemented shadow security. Instead of using **`groupdel`**, you could simply delete the entry for that group in the **/etc/group** file. This can be risky, however, if you make accidental changes. If you have implemented shadow security measures, group entries are kept in an encrypted **/etc/gshadow** file. You cannot edit this file. Changes can only be made through a utility like **`groupmod`**.

As for users, you can also create a home directory for a group. Several administration utilities such as Linuxconf support this feature. To do so manually, you simply create a directory for the group in the **/home** directory and change its group to that of the group, along with allowing access by any member of the group. The following example creates a directory called **engines** and changes its group to that of the **engines** group:

```
mkdir /home/engines
chgrp engines /home/engines
```

Then the read, write, and execute permissions for the group level should be set:

```
chmod g+rwx /home/engines
```

Any member of the **engines** group can now access the **/home/engines** directory and any shared files placed therein. This directory becomes a shared directory for the group. You can, in fact, use the same procedure to make other shared directories at any location on the file system.

Files within the shared directory should also have their permissions set to allow access by other users in the group. When a user places a file in a shared directory, permissions on that file need to be changed to allow other members of the group to access it. A read permission will let others display it, write lets them change it, and execute lets them run it (used for scripts and programs). The following example first changes the group for the **mymodel** file to **engines**. Then it copies the **mymodel** file to the **/home/engines** directory and sets the group read and write permission for the **engines** group.

```
$ chgrp engines mymodel
$ cp mymodel /home/engines
$ chmod g+rw /home/engines/mymodel
```

A new user can be assigned to a special group set up for just that user and given the user's same name. So the new user **dylan** is given a default group also called **dylan**. The group **dylan** will also show up in the listing of groups. This method of assigning default user groups is called the User Private Group (UPG) scheme. UPG is currently used on Red Hat systems. The supplementary groups are additional groups that the user may want to belong to. Traditionally, users were all assigned to one group named **users** that would subject all users to the group permission controls for the **users** group. With UPG, each user has its own group, with its own group permissions.

Managing Groups Using groupadd, groupmod, and groupdel

You can also manage groups with the **`groupadd`**, **`groupmod`**, and **`groupdel`** commands. With the **`groupadd`** command, you can create new groups. When you add a group to the system, the system places the group's name in the **/etc/group** file and gives it a group ID number. If shadow security is in place, then changes are made to the **/etc/gshadow** file. The **`groupadd`** command only creates the group category. Users are individually added to the group. In the next example, the **`groupadd`** command creates the **engines** group:

```
# groupadd engines
```

You can delete a group with the **`groupdel`** command. In the next example, the **engines** group is deleted:

```
# groupdel engines
```

You can change the name of a group or its ID using the **`groupmod`** command. Enter **`groupmod-g`** with the new ID number and the group name. To change the name of a group, you use the **`-n`** option. Enter **`groupmod-n`** with the new name of the group, followed by the current name. In the next example, the **engines** group has its name changed to **trains**:

```
# groupmod -n trains engines
```

Disk Quotas

With disk quotas, you can control how much disk space a particular user makes use of on your system. On your Linux system, unused disk space is held as a common resource that each user can access as they need it. As a user creates more files, they take the space they need from the pool of available disk space. In this sense, all the users are sharing this one resource of unused disk space. However, if one user were to use up all the remaining disk space, then none of the other users would be able to create files or even run programs. To counter this problem, you can create disk quotas on particular users, limiting the amount of available disk space they can use.

Note *You can also enable disk quotas using administrative tools like Webmin and Linuxconf.*

Quotas are enabled using the quotacheck and quotaon programs. On Mandrake and Red Hat, they are executed in the **/etc/rc.d/rc.sysinit** script, which is run whenever you start up your system. Each partition then needs to be mounted with the quota options, **`usrquota`** or **`grpquota`**. **`usrquota`** enables quota controls and users, and **`grpquota`** works for groups. These options are usually placed in the mount entry in the **/etc/fstab** file for a particular partition. For example, to mount the **/dev/hda6** hard disk partition mounted to the **/home** directory with support for user and group quotas, you would require a mount entry like the following:

```
/dev/hda6 /home ext2 defaults,usrquota,grpquota 1 1
```

You also need to create **quota.user** and **quota.group** files for each partition for which you enable quotas. These are the quota databases used to hold the quota information for each user and group. You can create these files by running the **`quotacheck`** command with the **`-a`** option or the device name of the file system where you want to enable quotas.

The limit you set for a quota can be hard or soft. A hard limit will deny a user the ability to exceed his or her quota, whereas a soft limit will just issue a warning. For the soft limit, you can designate a grace period during which time the user has the chance to reduce his or her disk space below the limit. If the disk space still exceeds the limit after the grace period expires, the user can be denied access to their account.

You can set disk quotas using the **`edquota`** command. The **`edquota`** command is run from the command line. With it you can access the quota record for a particular user and group, which is maintained in the disk quota database. You can also set default quotas that will be applied to any user or group on the file system for which quotas have not been set. **`edquota`** will open the record in your default editor, and you can use your editor to make any changes. To open the record for a particular user, use the **`-u`** option and the username as an argument for **`edquota`** (see Table 27-2). The following example opens the disk quota record for the user **larisa**:

```
edquota -u larisa
```

edquota	Description
`-u`	Edits the user quota. This is the default.
`-g`	Edits the group quota.
`-p`	Duplicates the quotas of the prototypical user specified for each user specified. This is the normal mechanism used to initialize quotas for groups of users.
`-t`	Edits the soft time limits for each file system.
quota	**Description**
`-g`	Prints group quotas for the group of which the user is a member.
`-u`	Prints the user's quota.
`-v`	Displays quotas on file systems where no storage is allocated.
`-q`	Prints information on file systems where usage is over quota.

Table 27-2. *The Options* **edquota** *and* **quota**

The quota record begins with the hard disk device name and the blocks of memory and inodes in use. The Limits segments have parameters for soft and hard limits. If these entries are 0, there are no limits in place. You can set both hard and soft limits, using the hard limit as a firm restriction. Blocks in Linux are currently about 1,000 bytes. The inodes are used by files to hold information about the memory blocks making up a file. To set the time limit for a soft limit, you use the **edquota** command with the **-t** option. The following example displays the quota record for **larisa**:

```
Quotas for user larisa:
/dev/hda3: blocks in use: 9000, limits (soft = 40000, hard = 60000)
 inodes in use: 321, limits (soft = 0, hard = 0)
```

These records are maintained in the quota database for that partition. Each partition that has quotas enabled will have its own quota database. You can check the validity of your quota database with the **quotacheck** command. You can turn quotas on and off using the **quotaon** and **quotaoff** commands. When you start up your system, **quotacheck** is run to check the quota databases and then **quotaon** is run to turn on quotas.

As the system administrator, you can use the **repquota** command to generate a summary of memory usage, checking to see what users are approaching or exceeding quota limits. Individual users can use the **quota** command to check their memory use and how much disk space they have left in their quota (see Table 27-2).

Lightweight Directory Access Protocol

The Lightweight Directory Access Protocol (LDAP) is designed to implement network-accessible directories of users, providing information about them such as their e-mail address or phone numbers. Such directories can also be used for authentication purposes, identifying that a certain user belongs to a specified network. You can find out more information on LDAP at **www.ldapman.org**. You can think of an LDAP directory as an Internet-accessible phone book, where anyone can look you up to find your e-mail address or other information. In fact, it may be more accurate to refer to such directories as databases. They are databases of user information, accessible over networks like the Internet. Normally, the users on a local network are spread across several different systems. Ordinarily, to obtain information about a user, you would have to know what system the user is on and then query that system. With LDAP, user information for all users on a network is kept in the LDAP server. You only have to query the network's LDAP server to obtain information about a user. For example, Sendmail can use LDAP to look up user addresses.

With LDAP, you can also more carefully control the kind of information given and to whom. Using a PAM module (pam_ldap), LDAP can perform user authentication tasks, providing centralized authentication for users. Login operations that users perform for different services such as mail POP server, system login, and Samba logins can all be carried out through LDAP using a single PAM secured user ID and password.

Note *You can use the GQ (Gnome) and kldap (KDE) clients to query LDAP servers.*

LDAP directories are implemented as clients and servers, where you use an LDAP client to access an LDAP server that manages the LDAP database. Most Linux distributions use OpenLDAP, an open source version of LDAP (you can find out more about OpenLDAP at **www.openldap.org**). This package includes an LDAP server (slapd), an LDAP replication server (slurpd), an LDAP client, and tools. slurpd is used to update other LDAP servers on your network, should you have more than one. Once the LDAP server is installed, you can start, stop, and restart the LDAP server with the **ldap** startup script.

```
service ldap restart
```

An entry in an LDAP database will consist of a name (known as a distinguished name) followed by a set of attributes and their values. For example, a name could be a username and the attribute would be the user's e-mail address, the address being the attribute's value. Allowable attributes are determined by object class sets defined in the **/etc/openldap/schema** directory. To actually make entries in the LDAP database, you use the ldapadd and ldapmodify utilities. With ldapdelete, you can remove entries. Once you have created an LDAP database, you can then query it, through the LDAP server, with ldapsearch. You can also create a text file of LDAP entries using an LDAP Data Interchange Format (LDIF) format. Such text files can then be read in all at once to the LDAP database using the slapadd utility.

Note *You can use the LDAP Browser/Editor or the Gnome Directory Administrator to manage and edit LDAP directories.*

All LDAP configuration files are kept in the **/etc/openldap** directory. These include **sldap.conf**, the LDAP server configuration file, and **ldap**, the LDAP clients and tools configuration file. In the **sldap.conf** file, the suffix entry should be changed to your own network's domain address. This is the network that will be serviced by the LDAP server. You will have to perform the same task for the **ldap.conf** file, to enable use of your LDAP clients and tools like ldapadd. For LDAP authentication, you will need to make the same modifications for **nss_ldap** and **pam_ldap** files. To use LDAP for authentication, you will need to configure PAM to use it, as well as migrate authentication files to the LDAP format. The **/usr/share/openldap/migration** directory holds scripts you can use to translate the old files into LDAP versions.

Pluggable Authentication Modules (PAM)

Pluggable Authentication Modules (PAM) is an authentication service that lets a system determine the method of authentication to be performed for users. In a Linux system, authentication has traditionally been performed by looking up passwords. When a user logs in, the login process will look up their password in the password file. With PAM, users' requests for authentication are directed to PAM, which in turn will use a specified method to authenticate the user. This could be a simple password lookup or a request to an LDAP server. But it is PAM that provides authentication, not a direct password lookup by the user or application. In this respect, authentication becomes centralized and controlled by a specific service, PAM. The actual authentication procedures can be dynamically configured by the system administrator. Authentication is carried out by modules that can vary according to the kind of authentication needed. An administrator can add or replace modules by simply changing the PAM configuration files. See the PAM Web site at **www.kernel.org/pub/linux/libs/pam** for more information and a listing of PAM modules. PAM modules are located in the **/lib/security** directory.

On Red Hat, PAM uses different configuration files for different services that would request authentication. Such configuration files are kept in the **/etc/pam.d** directory. For example, you have a configuration file for logging in to your system (**/etc/pam.d/login**), one for the graphical login (**/etc/pam.d/gdm**), and one for accessing your Samba server (**/etc/pam.d/samba**). A default PAM configuration file, called **/etc/pam.d/other**, is invoked if no services file is present. On Red Hat, the **system-auth** file contains standard authentication modules for system services generated by authconfig and is invoked in many of the other configuration files.

A PAM configuration file contains a list of modules to be used for the authentication. They have the following format:

```
module-type control-flag module-path module-arguments
```

The *module-path* is the module to be run, and *module-arguments* are the parameters you want passed to that module. Though there are a few generic arguments, most modules have their own. The *module-type* refers to different groups of authentication management: account, authentication, session, and password. The account management performs account verification, checking such account aspects as whether the user has access, or whether the password has expired. Authentication (**auth**) verifies who the user is, usually through a password confirmation. Password management performs authentication updates such as password changes. Session management refers to tasks performed before a service is accessed and before it is left. These include tasks like initiating a log of a user's activity or mounting and unmounting home directories.

Note *As an alternative to the **/etc/pam.d** directory, you could create one configuration file called the **/etc/pam.conf** file. Entries in this file have a* service *field, which refers to the application that the module is used for. If the **/etc/pam.d** directory exists, **/etc/pam.conf** is automatically ignored.*

The *control-flag* field indicates how PAM is to respond if the module fails. The control can be a simple directive or a more complicated response that can specify return codes like **open_err** with actions to take. The simple directives are **requisite**, **required**, **sufficient**, and **optional**. The **requisite** directive will end the authentication process immediately if the module fails to authenticate. The **required** directive will only end the authentication after the remaining modules are run. The **sufficient** directive indicates that success of this module is enough to provide authentication unless a previous required module has failed. The **optional** directive indicates the modules success is not needed unless it is the only authentication module for its service. If you specify return codes, you can refine the conditions for authentication failure or success. Return codes can be given values such as **die** or **ok**. The **open_err** return code could be given the action **die**, which would stop all authentication and return failure.

The **/etc/pam.d/ftpwu** configuration file for the FTP server is shown here.

ftpwu
```
#%PAM-1.0
auth   required  /lib/security/pam_listfile.so item=user sense=deny
file=/etc/ftpusers
onerr=succeed
auth     required     /lib/security/pam_stack.so service=system-auth
auth     required     /lib/security/pam_shells.so
account  required     /lib/security/pam_stack.so service=system-auth
session  required     /lib/security/pam_stack.so service=system-auth
```

Chapter 28

Software Management

Installing or updating software packages has always been a simple process in Linux due to the widespread use of the Red Hat Package Manager on major distributions, include SuSE, Caldera, Mandrake, and Red Hat. Instead of using a standard tar archive, software is packaged in special archives (known as RPMs) for use with the Red Hat Package Manager. An RPM archive contains all the program files, configuration files, data files, and even documentation that constitute a software application. With one simple operation, the Red Hat Package Manager installs all these for you from an RPM software package. You can even create your own RPM packages. You can use any of several RPM window-based utilities to manage your RPM packages, installing new ones or uninstalling ones you have. These utilities provide an easy-to-use interface for managing your packages, enabling you to obtain detailed information on a package easily, including a complete listing of the files it installs. Also, as part of their administration tools, distributions like Caldera, SuSE, and Mandrake also provide software management for packages on their CD-ROMs. On Mandrake you can use the Mandrake Software Manager to install and update software and on SuSE you can use the YaST Control Center (see Chapter 4).

Note *The distribution update tools such as the Red Hat Network, the Mandrake Software Manager, and SuSE's Online Update will automatically download and update any RPM packages that are installed on your system and are part of your distribution.*

You can also download source code versions of applications, and then compile and install them on your system. This process was once complex, but it has been significantly streamlined with the addition of configure scripts. Most current source code, including GNU software, is distributed with a configure script. The *configure script* automatically detects your system configuration and generates a **Makefile** with which a binary file is created compatible to your system. With three simple commands, you can compile and install complex source code on any system.

Extensive online sources exist for downloading Linux software. Sites are available for particular kinds of applications, such as Gnome and KDE, as well as for particular distributions, such as SuSE, Mandrake, and Red Hat. As you have seen, an update agent like the Red Hat Network or SuSE's Online Update can automatically download and update software installed from RPM packages that make up the respective distribution (see Chapter 4). Some sites are repositories for RPM packages, such as **rpmfind.net,** while others like **freshmeat.net** refer you to original development sites where you can download software packages. The **freshmeat.net** and **www.linuxapps.com** sites are useful for finding out about new available software. Many of the open source Linux projects can now be found at **sourceforge.net**. Here you will find detailed documentation and recent versions of software packages. For applications designed for the Gnome desktop, you can check **www.gnome.org**, and you can find KDE applications at **apps.kde.com**. For particular database and office applications, you can download software packages directly from the company's Web site, such as **www.sun.com** for the StarOffice office suite and **www.oracle.com** for the Oracle database (see Chapter 17). Table 28-1 lists several popular Linux software sites.

FTP and Web Sites	Applications
ftp.redhat.com	Software packaged in RPM packages for Red Hat. Check the **contrib** directory for contributed software.
freshmeat.net	Linux software, includes RPMs.
linuxapps.com	Linux software, includes RPMs.
rpmfind.net	RPM package repository.
www.sourceforge.net	Linux open source software projects.
www.gnome.org	Gnome software.
apps.kde.com	KDE software.
www.filewatcher.org	Linux FTP site watcher.
www.gnu.org	GNU archive.
www.ximian.com	Ximian Gnome, office applications for Gnome.
koffice.kde.com	The KDE KOffice suite of office applications.
www.xdt.com/ar/linux-snd	Linux MIDI and sound pages.
www.linuxvideo.org	The Linux Video and DVD Project, LiViD.
www.opensound.com	Open Sound System drivers.
metalab.unc.edu	Extensive Linux archive (formerly **sunsite.unc.edu**).
happypenquin.org	Linux Game Tome.
www.linuxgames.com	Linux games.
www.linuxquake.com	Quake.

Table 28-1. *Linux Software Sites*

The software packages on RPM sites like Red Hat and **rpmfind.net** will have the file extension **.rpm**. RPM packages that contain source code have an extension **.src.rpm**. Other packages such as those in the form of source code that you will need to compile come in a variety of compressed archives. These will commonly have the extensions **.tar.gz** or **tar.bz2**. They are explained in detail later in the chapter. Table 28-2 lists several common file extensions that you will find for the great variety of Linux software packages available to you. See Chapter 11 for more details on archives and compression.

Extension	File
.rpm	Software package created with the Red Hat Software Package Manager (RPM), used on Red Hat, Caldera, Mandrake, and SuSE distributions.
.src.rpm	Software packages that are source code versions of applications, created with the Red Hat Software Package Manager (RPM).
.gz	gzip compressed file (use gnunzip to decompress, also **z** option with tar, as in **xvzf**).
.bz2	bzip2 compressed file (use bunzip2 to decompress, also **j** option with tar, as in **xvjf**).
.tar	A tar archive file, use tar with **xvf** to extract.
.tar.gz	gzip compressed tar archive file.
.tar.bz2	bzip2 compressed tar archive file.
.tz	tar archive file compressed with the **compress** command.
.Z	File compressed with the **compress** command (use the **decompress** command to decompress).
.deb	Debian Linux package.

Table 28-2. *Linux Software Package File Extensions*

Red Hat Package Manager (RPM)

Several Linux distributions, including Red Hat, Mandrake, Caldera, and SuSE, use RPM to organize Linux software into packages you can automatically install or remove. An RPM software package operates as its own installation program for a software application. A Linux software application often consists of several files that need to be installed in different directories. The program itself is most likely placed in a directory called **/usr/bin**, online manual files go in another directory, and library files in yet another directory. In addition, the installation may require modification of certain configuration files on your system. The RPM software package performs all these tasks for you. Also, if you later decide you don't want a specific application, you can uninstall packages to remove all the files and configuration information from your system. RPM works similarly to the Windows Install Wizard, automatically installing software, including configuration, documentation, image, sample, and program files, along with any other files an application may use. All are installed in their appropriate directories on your system.

RPM maintains a database of installed software, keeping track of all the files installed. This enables you to use RPM also to uninstall software, automatically removing all files that are part of the application.

To install and uninstall RPM packages, you can use the **rpm** command on a shell command line, a distribution software management tool like the Mandrake Software Manager or SuSE's Yast Control Center, or any available RPM window-based utility, such as Kpackage or GnomeRPM. Although you should download RPM packages from your particular distribution, numerous RPM software packages are designed to run on any Linux system. Many of these will have the term **noarch** in their name. You can learn more about RPM at its Web site at **www.rpm.org**. The site contains up-to-date versions for RPM, documentation, and RPM support programs, such as **rpm2html** and **rpm2cpio**. **rpm2html** takes a directory containing RPM packages and generates Web pages listing those packages as links that can be used to download them. **rpm2cpio** is a Perl script to extract RPMs. You can obtain further documentation from the RPM Documentation Project site at **www.rpmdp.org**.

The naming conventions for RPM packages vary from one distribution to another. On Red Hat the package name includes the package version along with its platform (**i386** for Intel PCs) and the **.rpm** extension. An example of the Red Hat kernel RPM package is shown here.

```
kernel-2.4.18-3.i386.rpm
```

Mandrake uses a slightly different naming format for its RPM packages, which includes the term **mdk**.

```
kernel-2.4.18.13mdk.i686.rpm
```

SuSE uses a much more simple naming format. Packages are located in various subdirectories.

```
k_i386_24.rpm
```

The RPM packages on your DVD-ROM or distribution CD-ROM only represent a small portion of the software packages available for Linux. An extensive repository for RPM packages is also located at **http://rpmfind.net/linux/RPM**. Packages here are indexed according to distribution, group, and name. It includes packages for every distribution, including Red Hat. From **http://rpmfind.net,** you can download the **rpmfind** command that enables you to search for RPM packages, either on your local system or on the RPM repository at **rpmfind.net**. You can even use **rpmfind** to download and update packages. **rpmfind** detects your system's distribution and lists RPM packages for it. Search results also tell you what other packages a given RPM can depend on. With the **--appropos** option, you can use more general terms to locate a package, instead of filename patterns. With the **--upgrade** option, you can download and install newer versions of installed packages. The **rpmfind** command also sets up a **.rpmfind** configuration file, where you can specify such features as a download directory, the remote servers to search, and the location of local RPM packages on your system.

*RPM packages with the term **noarch** are used for architecture-independent packages. This means that they are designed to install on any Linux distribution. Packages without **noarch** may be distribution dependent, designed to install on a particular distribution such as Caldera, Mandrake, or SuSE.*

You could place these packages in a directory on your system, and then use either **rpm** or a GUI RPM utility such as GnomeRPM to install it. Normally, you should always try to use the version of the RPM package set up for your distribution. In many cases, attempting to install an RPM package meant for a different distribution may fail. Popular RPM package managers are listed here:

Kpackage	K Desktop RPM package manager
GnomeRPM	GnomeRPM package manager
rpm	The shell command to manage RPM packages

The K Desktop Package Manager: Kpackage

The KDE desktop provides a powerful and easy-to-use RPM package manager called *Kpackage*. You run Kpackage under any window manager or desktop (including Gnome), as long as you have installed the K Desktop on your system. You can start Kpackage by selecting its entry in the K menu Utility menu or by entering the **kpackage** command in a terminal window.

The right side of Kpackage contains two tabbed panels: one for Properties and the other for the File List. The Properties panel displays information about the software in the currently selected RPM package, including the version number and the authors. The File List panel lists all the files contained in the software package, including **README** files. If you are using Kpackage on the K Desktop, you can click any text file in the File List and it is displayed by the text editor. This is a convenient way to read installation files, such as **README** or **install** files. To uninstall a package, select it and click Uninstall.

GnomeRPM

GnomeRPM provides an effective and easy-to-use interface for managing RPM packages on your Gnome desktop. It runs on any window manager, provided Gnome is installed on your system. The GnomeRPM window displays two panes, the left one showing a tree listing categories of different installed RPM packages. Expand a category to display the packages in the right pane. You can query a package by selecting it and clicking the Uninstall icon in the icon bar, or by right-clicking it and selecting Uninstall from the pop-up menu. You can use the same method for querying packages and for displaying information and file listings. The GnomeRPM package also features a find utility, which you can use to locate RPM packages easily. In the find window, you can then query or uninstall the package. To install new packages with GnomeRPM, click the Install icon. This opens a window that displays the selected packages to install. You then click Add to open a window for locating packages on your system. You can add as many windows as you want to the list. Click Install to install the packages. To upgrade a package that is already installed, click Upgrade and follow the same procedure.

Tip *On Gnome, if you just want to find out what a package is, along with a list of files in that package, you can right-click on the package and select the Show Info entry. A window opens displaying a description of the software and a list of all the files in the package. There are also buttons to let you install or upgrade the software.*

Updating Software

As noted in Chapter 4, you can update your Linux system automatically using a distribution update agent like the Red Hat Network, Mandrake's Software manger, or SuSE's Online Update. You can also manually download packages using an FTP client, Web browser, or the Gnome or KDE file managers, and then use the **rpm** command to install the software. Also, you can use Kpackage or Gnome RPM to access the distribution FTP sites directly, download the package, and automatically install it on your system. Just enter the FTP URL for the site in the Location box.

For the **rpm** command, you use the **-U** option to upgrade packages. In the following example, the **rpm** command with the **-Uvh** option installs an upgrade for emacs:

```
$ rpm -Uvh emacs-21.2-2.i386.rpm
```

With either Webmin or Linuxconf, you can also manage software installations. From the Software Packages page, you can view installed packages or install new ones, as well as search for packages.

Command Line Installation: rpm

If you do not have access to the desktop or you prefer to work from the command line interface, you can use the **rpm** command to manage and install software packages. **rpm** is the command that actually performs installation, removal, and queries of software packages. In fact, GnomeRPM and Kpackage use the **rpm** command to install and remove packages. An RPM package is an archive of software files that include information about how to install those files. The filenames for RPM packages end with **.rpm**, indicating software packages that can be installed by the Red Hat Package Manager.

With the **rpm** command, you can maintain packages, query them, build your own, and verify the ones you have. Maintaining packages involves installing new ones, upgrading to new versions, and uninstalling packages. The **rpm** command uses a set of options to determine what action to take. In addition, certain tasks, such as installing or querying packages, have their own options that further qualify the kind of action they take. For example, the **-q** option queries a package, but when combined with the **-l** option it lists all the files in that package. Table 28-3 lists the set of **rpm** options.

Mode of Operation	Effect
rpm -i*options package-file*	Installs a package; the complete name of the package file is required.
rpm -e*options package-name*	Uninstalls (erases) a package; you only need the name of the package, often one word.
rpm -q*options package-name*	Queries a package. An option can be a package name, a further option and package name, or an option applied to all packages.
rpm -U*options package-name*	Upgrades; same as install, but any previous version is removed.
rpm -bO*options package-specifications*	Builds your own RPM package.
rpm -F*options package-name*	Upgrades, but only if package is currently installed.
rpm -verify*options*	Verifies a package is correctly installed; uses same options as query. You can use **-V** or **-y** in place of **-verify**.
--nodeps	Installs without doing any dependency checks.
--force	Forces installation despite conflicts.
--percent	Displays percentage of package during installation.
--test	Tests installation; does not install, only checks for conflicts.
-h	Displays # symbols as package is installed.
--excludedocs	Excludes documentation files.
Uninstall Options (to be used with -e)	
--test	Tests uninstall. Does not remove, only checks for what is to be removed.
--nodeps	Uninstalls without checking for dependencies.
--allmatches	Removes all versions of package.
Query Options (to be used with -q)	
package-name	Queries package.
-qa	Queries all packages.

Table 28-3. *Red Hat Package Manager (RPM) Options*

Mode of Operation	Effect
Query Options (to be used with `-q`)	
`-qf` *filename*	Queries package that owns *filename*.
`-qR`	List packages on which this package depends.
`-qp` *package-name*	Queries an uninstalled package.
`-qi`	Displays all package information.
`-ql`	Lists files in package.
`-qd`	Lists only documentation files in package.
`-qc`	Lists only configuration files in package.
`-q --dump`	Lists only files with complete details.
General Options (to be used with any option)	
`-vv`	Debugs; displays descriptions of all actions taken.
`--quit`	Displays only error messages.
`--version`	Displays **rpm** version number.
`--help`	Displays detailed use message.
`--root`*directory*	Uses directory as top-level directory for all operations (instead of root).
`--dbpath`*directory*	Uses **RPM** database in the specified directory.
`--dbpath` *cmd*	Pipes output of RPM to the command **cmd**.
`--rebuilddb`	Rebuilds the RPM database; can use with **-root** and **-dbpath** options.
`--initdb`	Builds a new RPM database; **-root** and **-dbpath** options.
Other Sources of Information	
RPM-HOWTO	More detailed information, particularly on how to build your own RPM packages.
Man rpm	Detailed list of options.

Table 28-3. *Red Hat Package Manager (RPM) Options* (continued)

You use the **-i** option to install a new software package and the **-U** option to update a currently installed package with a newer version. With an **-e** option, **rpm** uninstalls the package. The **-q** option tells you if a package is already installed, and the **-qa** option displays a list of all installed packages. Piping this output to a pager utility, such as more, is best.

```
rpm -qa | more
```

In the next example, the user checks to see if Mozilla is already installed on the system. Notice the full filename of the RPM archive is unnecessary. If the package is installed, your system has already registered its name and where it is located.

```
# rpm -q mozilla
mozilla-1.0rc3-0
```

*Keep in mind the distinction between the installed software package name and the package filename. The filename will end in a **.rpm** extension and can only be queried with a **p** option.*

You can combine the **q** options with the **i** or **l** option to display information about the package. The options **-qi** display information about the software, such as the version number or author (**-qpi** queries an uninstalled package file). The option **-ql** displays a listing of all the files in the software package. The --**h** option provides a complete list of **rpm** options. Common query options are shown here:

-q *application*	Checks to see if an application is installed
-qa *application*	Lists all installed RPM applications
-qf *filename*	Queries applications that own *filename*
-qR *application*	Lists applications on which this application depends
-qi *application*	Displays all application information
-ql *application*	Lists files in application
-qd *application*	Lists only documentation files in application
-qc *application*	Lists only configuration files in application

If you want to query an RPM package file, a file ending with **.rpm**, you use the same query options, but with the **p** option added, as shown here:

-qpi *RPM-file*	Displays all package information in the RPM package
-qpl *RPM-file*	Lists files in the RPM package
-qpd *RPM-file*	Lists only documentation files in the RPM package
-qpc *RPM-file*	Lists only configuration files in the RPM package
-qpR *RPM-file*	List packages on which this RPM package depends

If your RPM query outputs a long list of data, like an extensive list of files, you can pipe the output to the **more** command to look at it screen by screen, or even redirect the output to a file.

```
rpm -ql mozilla | more
rpm -qpl openmotif-2.2.2-5.386.rpm  > mytemp
```

The syntax for the **rpm** command is as follows (*rpm-package-name* is the name of the software package you want to install):

```
rpm options rpm-package-name
```

*The software package filename is usually lengthy, including information about version and release in its name. All end with **.rpm**.*

If you are installing from a CD-ROM, you can change to the CD-ROM's **RPMS** directory, which holds the RPM packages (the RPMS directory may be a located within a directory like RedHat on the Red Hat CD-ROM). An **ls** command lists all the software packages. If you know how the name of a package begins, you should include that with the **ls** command and an attached *****. The list of packages is extensive and does not all fit on one screen. This is helpful for displaying the detailed name of the package. The following example lists most X Window System packages:

```
# ls x*
```

You use the **-i** option to install new packages and the **-U** option to update currently installed packages with new versions. If you try to use the **-i** option to install a newer version of an installed package, you receive an error saying the package is already installed. In the next example, the user first installs a new package with the **-i** option, and then updates a package with the **-U** option. Including the **-v** and **-h** options is customary. Here, **-v** is the verbose option that displays all files as they are installed, and **-h** displays a crosshatch symbol periodically to show RPM is still working.

In the following example, the user installs the software package for the XV screen capture program available from **rpmfind.net**. Notice the full filename is entered. To list the full name, you can use the **ls** command with the first few characters and an asterisk, **ls htdig***. The **h** option displays **#** symbols as the installation takes place. The **rpm** command with the **-q** option is then used to check that the software was installed. For installed packages only, the software name needs to be used—in this case, xv-3.10a-23.

```
 [root@turtle mypackages]# ls xv*
xv-3.10a-23.i386.rpm
[root@turtle mypackages]# rpm -ivh xv-3.10a-23.i386.rpm
xv-3.10a-23              ##########################################
```

```
[root@turtle mypackages]# rpm -q xv
xv-3.10a-23
```

To display information about the installed package, use **-qi;**, and **-ql** displays a listing of the files a given RPM package contains.

```
# rpm -qi xv
# rpm -ql xv
```

To display information taken directly from an RPM package, you add the **p** qualifier to the **q** options. The **-qpi** combination displays information about a specific package, and **-qpl** displays a listing of the files a given RPM package contains. In this case, you must specify the entire filename of the RPM package. You can avoid having to enter the entire name simply by entering a unique part of the name and using the ***** filename-matching character to generate the rest.

```
[root@turtle mypackages]# ls proftp*
proftpd-core-1.2.0pre10-1.i386.rpm
[root@turtle mypackages]# rpm -qp proftpd.1.2.5rc1-1.i386.rpm
proftpd-1.2.0pre3-2
[root@turtle mypackages]# rpm -qpi proftpd.1.2*.rpm
Name        : proftpd                    Relocations: (not relocateable)
Version     : 1.2.5rc1-1                      Vendor: (none)
........................................
[root@turtle mypackages]# rpm -qpl proftpd*
/etc/logrotate.d/proftpd
/etc/pam.d/ftp
/etc/proftpd.conf
........................................
```

Remember, if you are installing an upgrade, you need to use the **-U** option instead of the **-i** option. If you try to use **-i** to upgrade a package, you receive an error saying the package is already installed.

```
# rpm -Uvh mozilla-1.0rc3-0.i386.rpm
```

If you are worried that a software package will install on your system incorrectly, you can use the test option (**--test**) in the debut mode (**vv**) to see exactly what actions RPM will take.

```
# rpm -ivv --test xv-3.10a-23.i386.rpm
```

A few RPM packages, like those for OpenOffice, are designed only to extract a subdirectory of install binaries with its own install program. For example, OpenOffice uses its own installation program called setup in its subdirectory. Use **`./setup`** *to run it.*

To remove a software package from your system, first use **`rpm -q`** to make sure it is actually installed. Then use the **`-e`** option to uninstall it. You needn't use the full name of the installed file. You only need the name of the application. For example, if you decide you do not need XV, you can remove it using the **`-e`** option and the software name, as shown here:

```
# rpm  -e  xv
```

If direct conflicts occur with another software package, you may have to uninstall the other package first. This is the case with wu-ftpd and ProFTP on many distributions. Many distributions currently install wu-ftpd as the default FTP server. You must first uninstall wu-ftpd with the **`-e`** option before you can install ProFTP. However, when you try to do this, you receive a dependency error. You can overcome this error by using the **`--nodeps`** option. Once wu-ftpd is removed, you can install ProFTP.

```
[root@turtle mypackages]# rpm -e --nodeps wu-ftpd
[root@turtle mypackages]# rpm -ivh proftpd.1.2*rpm
proftpd       ##############################################
[root@turtle mypackages]# rpm -q proftpd
proftpd-core-1.2.5rc1-1
```

You can use the verify option (**`-V`**) to check to see if any problems occurred with the installation. RPM compares the current attributes of installed files with information about them placed in the RPM database when the package was installed. If no discrepancies exist, RPM outputs nothing. Otherwise, RPM outputs a sequence of eight characters, one for each attribute, for each file in the package that fails. Those that do not differ have a period. Those that do differ have a corresponding character code, as shown here:

5	MD5 checksum
S	File size
L	Symbolic link
T	File modification time
D	Device
U	User
G	Group
M	Mode (includes permissions and file types)

The following example verifies the proftpd package:

```
[root@turtle mypackages]# rpm -V proftpd
```

To compare the installed files directly with the files in an RPM package file, you use the **-Vp** option, much like the **-qp** option. To check all packages, use the **-Va** option as shown here:

```
rpm -Va
```

If you want to verify a package, but only know the name of a file in it, you can combine verify with the **-f** option. The following example verifies the RPM package containing the **ftp** command:

```
rpm -Vf  /bin/ftp
```

A complete description of **rpm** and its capabilities is provided in the online manual.

```
# man rpm
```

RPM maintains a record of the packages it has installed in its **RPM** database. You may, at times, have to rebuild this database to ensure RPM has current information on what is installed and what is not. Use the **--rebuilddb** option to rebuild your database file.

```
rpm --rebuilddb
```

To create a new RPM database, use the **--initdb** option. This can be combined with **--dbpath** to specify a location for the new database.

Note *You can also use the **rpm** command with its build options to build your own RPM packages. See RPM documentation for more details.*

Debian

Among Linux distributions, there are basically two major software packaging methods: the Red Hat Package Manager (RPM) and the Debian package system, used primarily in the Debian distribution. The Debian package system is much more capable than its RPM counterpart. For, example, a Debian package will automatically resolve dependencies, installing any other needed packages instead of simply reporting their absence, like RPM does. Debian also uses a different package naming format than RPM. Packages are named with the software name, the version number, and the **.deb** extension. For example, Kernel packages bear a name like **kernel-image-2.2.19.deb**.

Two basic package managers are available for use with Debian packages: the Advanced Package Tool (apt-get) and the Debian Package tool (dpkg). The apt-get tool is used as the core for a command line version called apt-pkgset and a Gnome-based version called gnome-apt-pkgset. apt-get can even download packages as well as compile source code versions for you. The apt-get tool takes two arguments: the command to perform and the name of the package. Other Debian package tools follow the same format. The command is a term such as **install** for installing packages or **remove** to uninstall a package. To install the kernel image package you would use:

```
apt-get install kernel-image-2.2.19.deb
```

Upgrading is a simple matter of using the **upgrade** command. With no package specified, apt-get with the **upgrade** command will upgrade your entire system, downloading from an FTP site or copying from a CD-ROM, and installing packages as needed. Add the **-u** option to list packages as they are upgraded.

```
apt-get -u upgrade
```

You can even upgrade to a new Debian release with the **dist-upgrade** command.

```
apt-get -u dist-upgrade
```

You can also use the dpkg tool to manage software, though it is used primarily to obtain information about a package. Its more complex version, dpkg-deb, is used to construct Debian packages.

Installing Software from RPM Source Code Files: SRPMs

Red Hat and several other distributors also make available source code versions of their binary RPM packaged software. The source code is packaged into RPM packages that will be automatically installed into designated directories where you can easily compile and install the software. Source code packages are called SRPMs and have added to their names the term **src**. The names for these packages end in the suffix **.src.rpm**. Source code versions for packages in the Red Hat distribution are located on Red Hat releases in the **SRPMS** directory. Many online sites like **rpmfind.net** will also list SRPM packages. Source code versions have the advantage of letting you make your own modifications to the source code, allowing you to generate your own customized versions of RPM packaged software. You still use the **rpm** command with the **-i** option to install source code packages. In the following example, you install the source code for xpuzzles:

```
rpm -i xpuzzles-5.5.2-4.src.rpm
```

SRPM files are installed in various subdirectories in the **/usr/src** directory (On Red Hat these are placed in the **/usr/src/redhat** directory). On Red Hat, when SRPMs are installed, a spec file is placed in the **/usr/src/redhat/SPECS** directory and the compressed archive of the source code files is placed in the **/usr/src/redhat/SOURCES** directory. For xpuzzles, a spec file called **xpuzzles.spec** was placed in **/usr/src/redhat/SPECS**, and a compressed archive called **xpuzzles-5.5.2.tar.gz** was placed in the **/usr/src/redhat/SOURCES** directory. SuSE, Mandrake, and Caldera use comparable SOURCES and SPECS directories for their source code files.

You now need to build the source code files, extracting them and running any patches on them that may be included with the package. You do this with a single **rpm** command run on the SPEC file using the **-bp** option. Change to the **/usr/src/redhat/SPECS** directory and use the **rpm** command again, this time with the **-bp** option, to generate the source code files.

```
cd /usr/src/redhat/SPECS
rpm -bp xpuzzles.spec
```

The resulting source code files are placed in their own subdirectory with the package's name in the **/usr/src/redhat/BUILD** directory. For xpuzzles, the xpuzzle source code is placed in **/usr/src/redhat/BUILD/xpuzzles-5.5.2** directory. In this subdirectory you can then modify the source code, as well as compile and install the application. Check the **README** and **INSTALL** files for details.

Installing Software from Compressed Archives: .tar.gz

Linux software applications in the form of source code are available at different sites on the Internet. You can download any of this software and install it on your system. You download software using an FTP client as described in Chapter 14. Recent releases for software are often available in the form of a compressed archive file. Applications will always be downloadable as compressed archives, if they don't have an RPM version. This is particularly true for the recent versions of Gnome or KDE packages. RPM packages are only intermittently generated. A *compressed archive* is an archive file created with **tar**, and then compressed with **gzip**. To install such a file, you must first decompress it with the gunzip utility, and then use **tar** to extract the files and directories making up the software package. Instead of the gunzip utility, you could also use **gzip -d**. The next example decompresses the **htdig-3.1.6.tar.gz** file, replacing it with a decompressed version called **htdig-3.1.6.tar**:

```
$ ls
 htdig-3.1.6.tar.gz
$ gunzip htdig-3.1.5.tar.gz
$ ls
htdig-3.1.6.tar.gz
```

First, use **tar** with the **t** option to check the contents of the archive. If the first entry is a directory, that directory is created and the extracted files are placed in it. If the first entry is not a directory, you should first create one and then copy the archive file to it. Then extract the archive within that directory. If no directory exists as the first entry, files are extracted to the current directory. You must create a directory yourself to hold these files.

```
$ tar tvf htdig-3.1.6.tar
```

Now you are ready to extract the files from the tar archive. You use **tar** with the **x** option to extract files, the **v** option to display the pathnames of files as they are extracted, and the **f** option, followed by the name of the archive file:

```
$ tar xvf htdig-3.1.6.tar
```

You can combine the decompressing and unpacking operation into one **tar** command by adding a **z** option to the option list, **xzvf**. The following command both decompresses and unpacks the archive:

```
$ tar xzvf htdig-3.1.6.tar.gz
```

The extraction process will create a subdirectory consisting of the name and release of the software. In the previous example, the extraction created a subdirectory called **htdig-3.1.6**. You can then change to that directory to access the software files.

```
$ cd htdig-3.1.6
```

Installation of your software may differ for each package. Instructions are usually provided along with an installation program. See the following section on compiling software for information on how to create and install the application on your system.

Downloading Compressed Archives from Online Sites

Many software packages under development or designed for cross-platform implementation may not be in an RPM format. Instead, they may be archived and compressed (see Chapter 11). The filenames for these files end with the extensions **.tar.gz**, **.tar.bz2**, or **.tar.Z**. The different extensions indicate different decompression methods using different commands: **gunzip** for **gz**, **bunzip2** for **bz2**, and **decompress** for **Z**. In fact, most software with an RPM format also has a corresponding **.tar.gz** format. After you download such a package, you must first decompress it, and then unpack it with the **tar** command. For the **.gz** files, you use **gunzip**, and for **.bz2** files, you can use **bunzip2**. The compressed archives could hold either source code that you then need to compile or, as is the case with Java packages, binaries that are ready to run.

You can download compressed archives from many different sites, including those mentioned previously. Downloads can be accomplished with FTP clients such as ncftp and Gftp, or with any Web browser, such as Mozilla. Once downloaded, any file that ends with **.Z** , **bz2**, **.zip**, or **.gz** is a compressed file that must be decompressed. In the following example, the **gunzip** command is used to decompress the CD-Rchive CD writer downloaded from **apps.kde.com**.

```
# gunzip cdrchive-1.2.2.tar.gz
```

For files ending with **bz2**, you would use the **bunzip2** command. The following example decompresses the Java 2 SDK downloaded through **www.blackdown.org**:

```
# bunzip2 j2sdk-1.3.0-FCS-linux-i386.tar.bz2
```

If the file ends with **.tar**, it is an archived file that must be unpacked using the **tar** command. Before you unpack the archive, move it to the directory where you want it. Source code you intend to compile is usually placed in the **/usr/local/src** directory. Packages that hold binary programs ready to run, like Java, are meant to be extracted in certain directories. Usually this is the **/usr/local** directory. Most archives, when they unpack, create a subdirectory they named with the application name and its release, placing all those files or directories making up the software package into that subdirectory. For example, the file **cdrchive-1.2.2.tar** unpacks to a subdirectory called **cdrchive-1.2.2**. In certain cases, the software package that contains precompiled binaries is designed to unpack directly into the system subdirectory where it will be used. For example, it is recommended that **j2sdk-1.3.0-FCS-linux-i386.tar** be unpacked in the **/usr/local** directory where it will create a subdirectory called **j2sdk-1.3.0**. The **/usr/local/j2sdk-1.3.0/bin** directory will hold the Java binary programs. To check if an archive unpacks to a directory, use **tar** with the **t** option to list its contents and see if the names are prefixed by a directory. If so, that directory is created and the extracted files are placed in it. If no directory name exists, create one and then copy the archive file to it. Then extract the archive within that directory.

```
# tar tf j2sdk-1.3.0-FCS-linux-i386.tar
```

Now you are ready to extract the files from the tar archive (see Chapter 11). You use **tar** with the **x** option to extract files, the **v** option to display the pathnames of files as they are extracted, and the **f** option, followed by the name of the archive file:

```
# tar xvf j2sdk-1.3.0-FCS-linux-i386.tar
```

This will create a subdirectory called **j2sdk-1.3.0**. You can change to this subdirectory and examine its files, such as the **README** and **INSTALL** files.

```
# cd j2sdk-1.3.0
```

The tar utility provides decompression options you can use to have **tar** first decompress a file for you, invoking the specified decompression utility. The **z** options will automatically invoke gunzip to unpack a **.gz** file, and the **j** option will unpack a **.bz2** file. Use the **Z** options for **.Z** files. The next example shows how you can combine decompression and extraction in one step:

```
# tar xvjf j2sdk-1.3.0-FCS-linux-i386.tar.bz2
# tar xvzf cdrchive-1.2.2.tar.gz
```

Installation of your software may differ for each package. Instructions are usually provided, along with an installation program. Downloaded software usually includes **README** files or other documentation. Be sure to consult them.

Compiling Software

Some software may be in the form of source code that you need to compile before you can install it. This is particularly true of programs designed for cross-platform implementations. Programs designed to run on various Unix systems, such as Sun, as well as on Linux, may be distributed as source code that is downloaded and compiled in those different systems. Compiling such software has been greatly simplified in recent years by the use of configuration scripts that automatically detect a given system's configuration and compile the program accordingly. For example, the name of the C compiler on a system could be **gcc** or **cc**. Configurations scripts detect which is present and use it to compile the program.

First change to the directory where the software's source code has been extracted to.

```
# cd /usr/local/src/cdrchive-1.2.2
```

Before you compile software, first read the **README** or **INSTALL** files included with it. These give you detailed instructions on how to compile and install this particular program. If the software uses configuration scripts, compiling and installing usually involves only the following three simple commands:

```
# ./configure
#  make
#  make install
```

Be sure to remember to place the period and slash before the **`configure`** *command.* **`./`** *references a command in the current working directory, rather than another Linux command.*

The **`./configure`** command performs configuration detection. The **`make`** command performs the actual compiling, using a **Makefile** script generated by the **`./configure`** operation. The **`make install`** command installs the program on your system, placing the executable program in a directory, such as **/usr/local/bin,** and any configuration files in **/etc**. Any shared libraries it created may go into **/usr/local/lib**.

Certain software may have specific options set up for the **`./configure`** operation. To find out what these are, you use the **`./configure`** command with the **`--help`** option.

```
./configure --help
```

A useful common option is the **`-prefix`** option, which lets you specify the install directory.

```
./configure -prefix=/usr/bin
```

If you are compiling an X-, Gnome-, or KDE-based program, be sure their development libraries have been installed. For X applications, be sure the xmkmf program is also installed. If you chose a standard install when you installed your distribution system, these most likely were not installed. For distributions using RPM packages, these come in the form of a set of development RPM packages, usually having the word "development" or "develop" in their name. You need to install them using either RPM, Kpackage, or GnomeRPM. Gnome, in particular, has an extensive set of RPM packages for development libraries. Many X applications need special shared libraries. For example, some applications may need the xforms library or the qt library. Some of these you need to obtain from online sites.

Note

You can also use the autoconf tool to build your own source packages, installable with the **`configure`** *command.*

Some older X applications use **xmkmf** directly instead of a configure script to generate the needed **Makefile**. In this case, enter the command **xmkmf** in place of **./configure**. Be sure to consult the **INSTALL** and **README** files for the software. Usually, you only need to issue the following commands within the directory that contains the source code files for the software:

```
xmkmf
make
make install
```

If no configure script exists and the program does not use **xmkmf,** you may have to enter the **make** command, followed by a **make install** operation. Check the **README** or **INSTALL** files for details.

```
make
make install
```

Be sure to check the documentation for such software to see if any changes must be made to the **Makefile**. Only a few changes may be necessary, but more detailed changes require an understanding of C programming and how **make** works with it. If you successfully configure the **Makefile**, you may only have to enter the **make** and **make install** operations. One possible problem is locating the development libraries for C and the X Window System. X libraries are in the **/usr/X11R6/lib** directory. Standard C libraries are located in the **/usr/lib** directory.

Once you have compiled and installed your application, and have checked that it is working properly, you can remove the source code directory that was created when you extracted the software. You can keep the archive file (**tar**) in case you need to extract the software again. Use **rm** with the **-rf** options so all subdirectories will be deleted and you do not have to confirm each deletion.

```
rm -rf cdrchive.1.2.2
```

The Complete Reference

Chapter 29

File System Administration

Files reside on physical storage devices such as hard drives, CD-ROMs, or floppy disks. The files on each storage device are organized into a file system. The storage devices on your Linux system are treated as a collection of file systems that you can manage. When you want to add a new storage device, you will need to format it as a file system and then attach it to your Linux file structure. Hard drives can be divided into separate storage devices called *partitions*, each of which would have its own file system. You can perform administrative tasks on your file systems, such as backing them up, attaching or detaching them from your file structure, formatting new devices or erasing old ones, and checking a file system for problems. This chapter discusses how you can manage file systems on your storage devices.

To access files on a device, you attach its file system to a specified directory. This is called *mounting* the file system. For example, to access files on a floppy disk, you first mount its file system to a particular directory. With Linux, you can mount a number of different types of file systems. You can even access a Windows hard drive partition or tape drive, as well as file systems on a remote server (see Chapter 34).

Recently developed file systems for Linux now support journaling, which allows your system to recover from a crash or interruption easily. Both the ext3 and ReiserFS file systems maintain a record of file and directory changes, called a journal, which can be used to recover files and directories in use when a system suddenly crashes due to unforeseen events such as power interruptions. Most distributions currently use the ext3 file system as their default, though you also have the option of using ReiserFS, an independently developed journaling system.

Linux also supports RAID devices. These are multiple hard drives that are treated as one hard drive. They include recovery information that allows you to restore your files should one of the drives fail. You can use RAID in several ways depending upon the degree of reliability you need.

Your Linux system is capable of handling any number of storage devices that may be connected to it. You can configure your system to access multiple hard drives, partitions on a hard drive, CD-ROM disks, floppy disks, and even tapes. You can elect to attach these storage components manually or have them automatically mount when you boot. For example, the main partition holding your Linux system programs is automatically attached whenever you boot, whereas a floppy disk must be manually attached when you put one in your floppy drive. You can configure this access to different storage devices either by manually editing configuration files, such as **/etc/fstab**, or by using a file system configuration tool such as the Linuxconf's fsconf.

File Systems

Although all the files in your Linux system are connected into one overall directory tree, the files themselves reside on storage devices such as hard drives or CD-ROMs. The Linux files on a particular storage device are organized into what is referred to as a *file system*. Your Linux directory tree may encompass several file systems, each on different storage devices. On a hard drive with several partitions, you would have a file system for each partition. The files themselves are organized into one seamless tree of directories, beginning from the root directory. Although the root may be located in a file system on a hard drive partition, a pathname leads directly to files located on the file system for your CD-ROM.

The files in a file system remain separate from your directory tree until you specifically connect them to it. A file system has its files organized into its own directory tree. You can think of this as a *subtree* that must be attached to the main directory tree. For example, a floppy disk with Linux files has its own tree of directories. You need to attach this subtree to the main tree on your hard drive partition. Until they are attached, you cannot access the files on your floppy disk.

Attaching a file system on a storage device to your main directory tree is called mounting the device. The **mount** operation attaches the directory tree on the storage device to a directory you specify. You can then change to that directory and access those files. The directory in the file structure to which the new file system is attached is referred to as the *mountpoint*. For example, to access files on a CD-ROM, first you have to mount the CD-ROM.

Currently, Linux systems have several ways to mount a file system. You can use Linuxconf to select and mount a file system easily. If you are using either Gnome or the K Desktop, you can use special desktop icons to mount a file system. From a shell command line, you can use the **mount** command. Mounting file systems can only be done as the root user. This is a system administration task and cannot be performed by a regular user. To mount a file system, be sure to log in as the root user (or use the **su** operation). As the root user, you can, however, make a particular device like a CD-ROM user mountable. In this way, any user could put in a CD-ROM and mount it. You could do the same for a floppy drive.

On Gnome, you can use the Disk Management tool on the System menu to mount and unmount file systems, including floppy disks and CD-ROMs. On KDE, you can use the KDiskFree utility, which also lists your mountable file as well as their disk usage.

For a file system to be accessible, it must be mounted. Even the file system on your hard disk partition must be mounted with a **mount** command. When you install your Linux system and create the Linux partition on your hard drive, however, your system is automatically configured to mount your main file system whenever it starts. Floppy disks and CD-ROMs must be explicitly mounted. Remember, when you mount a CD-ROM or floppy disk, you cannot then simply remove it to put in another one. You first have to unmount it. In fact, the CD-ROM drive remains locked until you unmount it. Once you unmount a CD-ROM, you can then take it out and put in another one, which you then must mount before you can access it. When changing several CD-ROMs or floppy disks, you are continually mounting and unmounting them.

The file systems on each storage device are formatted to take up a specified amount of space. For example, you may have formatted your hard drive partition to take up 3GB.

Files installed or created on that file system take up part of the space, while the remainder is available for new files and directories. To find out how much space you have free on a file system, you can use the **df** command or, on Gnome, you can use either the Gnome System Monitor or the Gnome Disk Free utility. For the Gnome System Monitor, click the Filesystems tab to display a bar graph of the free space on your file systems. Gnome DiskFree displays a list of meters showing how much space is used on each partition and how much space you have left. KDiskFree, a KDE utility, provides similar information.

The **df** command lists all your file systems by their device names, how much memory they take up, and the percentage of the memory used, as well as where they are mounted. With the **-h** option, it displays information in a more readable format. The **df** command is also a safe way to obtain a listing of all your partitions, instead of using **fdisk**. **df** only shows mounted partitions, however, whereas **fdisk** shows all partitions.

```
$ df
Filesystem 1024-blocks Used Available Capacity Mounted on
/dev/hda3 297635 169499 112764 60% /
/dev/hda1 205380 182320 23060 89% /mnt/dos
/dev/hdc 637986 637986 0 100% /mnt/cdrom
```

You can also use **df** to tell you to what file system a given directory belongs. Enter **df** with the directory name or **df .** for the current directory.

```
$ df .
Filesystem 1024-blocks Used Available Capacity Mounted on
/dev/hda3 297635 169499 112764 60% /
```

To make sure nothing is wrong with a given file system, you can use the **fsck** command to check it. However, be sure that the file system is unmounted. **fsck** should not be used on mounted file systems. To use **fsck**, enter **fsck** and the device name that references the file system. **fsck** is run automatically on all your file systems when you boot up your system, so your file systems are continually checked. Table 29-1 lists the **fsck** options. The following examples check the disk in the floppy drive and the primary hard drive:

```
# fsck /dev/fd0
# fsck /dev/hda1
```

Note

*Instead of using **fsck**, you can use **e2fsck** to check standard Linux partitions (ext3). In earlier distribution versions, **fsck** was also used to recover file systems after disk crashes or reset-button reboots. With recent releases, journaling capabilities were introduced with the ext3 and ReiserFS file system. Journaling provides for fast and effective recovery in case of disk crashes, instead of using **fsck** or **e2fsck**.*

Options	Description
file-system	Specifies the file system to be checked. Use the file system's device name, such as **/dev/hda3**.
`-A`	Checks all file systems listed in the **/etc/fstab** file.
`-V`	Verbose mode. Lists actions that **`fsck`** takes.
`-t` *file-system-type*	Specifies the type of file system to be checked.
`-a`	Automatically repairs any problems.
`-l`	Lists the names of all files in the file system.
`-r`	Asks for confirmation before repairing file system.
`-s`	Lists superblock before checking file system.

Table 29-1. *The `fsck` Options for Checking and Repairing File Systems*

Journaling

The ext3 and ReiserFS file systems introduced journaling capabilities to Linux systems. Journaling provides for fast and effective recovery in case of disk crashes, instead of using **`fsck`** or **`e2fsck`**. With journaling, a log is kept of all file system actions. These are placed in a journal file. In the event of a crash, Linux only needs to read the journal file to restore the system to its previous state. Files that were in the process of writing to the disk can be restored to their original state. Journaling also avoids lengthy **`fsck`** checks on reboots that occur when your system suddenly loses power or freezes and has to be restarted physically. Your system just reads its journal files to restore the file system, instead of manually checking each file and directory with **`fsck`**.

Journaling is implemented automatically with ext3. The ext3 file system is also fully compatible with the earlier ext2 version it replaces. To create an ext3 file system, you use the **`mk2fs`** command with the **`-j`** option. You can even upgrade ext2 file systems to ext3 versions automatically, with no loss of data or change in partitions. This upgrade just adds a journal file to an ext2 file system and enables journaling on it, using the **`tune2fs`** command. Be sure to change the ext2 file type to ext3 in any corresponding **/etc/fstab** entries. The following example converts the ext2 file system on **/dev/hda3** to an ext3 file system by adding a journal file (**`-j`**).

```
tune2fs -j /dev/hda3
```

There are other kinds of journaling file systems you can use on Linux. These include ReiserFS, JFS, and XFS. ReiserFS is named after Hans Reiser and provides a completely reworked file system structure based on journaling (**www.reiserfs.org**). Most distributions also provide support for ReiserFS file systems. JFS is the IBM version of a journaling file system, designed for use on servers providing high throughput such as e-business enterprise servers (**oss.software.ibm.com/developerworks/opensource/jfs/**). It is freely distributed under the GNU public license. XFS is another high performance journaling system developed by Silicon Graphics (**oss.sgi.com/projects/xfs/**). XFS is compatible with RAID and NFS file systems.

Though journaling is often used to recover from disk crashes, a journal-based file system can do much more. The ext3, JFS, and XFS file systems only provide the logging operations used in recovery, whereas ReiserFS uses journaling techniques to completely rework file system operations. In ReiserFS, journaling is used to read and write data, abandoning the block structure used in traditional Unix and Linux systems. This gives it the capability to access a large number of small files very quickly, as well as use only the amount of disk space they would need. However, efficiency is not that much better with larger files.

Filesystem Hierarchy Standard

Linux organizes its files and directories into one overall interconnected tree, beginning from the root directory and extending down to system and user directories (see Chapter 11). The organization and layout for the system directories is determined by the Filesystem Hierarchy Standard (FHS). The FHS provides a standardized layout that all Linux distributions should follow in setting up their system directories. For example, there must be an **/etc** directory to hold configuration files and a **/dev** directory for device files. You can find out more about FHS, including the official documentation, at **www.pathname.com/fhs**. The current release is FHS 2.1, which is the successor to FSSTND 1.2, a precursor to FHS. Linux distributions, developers, and administrators all follow the FHS to provide a consistent organization to the Linux file system.

Linux uses a number of specifically named directories for specialized administration tasks. All these directories are directories at the very top level of your main Linux file system, the file system root directory represented by a single slash, **/**. For example, the **/dev** directory holds device files, the **/etc** directory holds configuration files, and the **/home** directory holds the user home directories and all their user files. You only have access to these directories and files as the system administrator. You need to log in as the root user, placing you in a special root user administrative directory called **/root**. From here, you can access any directory on the Linux file system, both administrative and user.

The directories held in the root directory, **/**, are listed in Table 29-2, along with other useful subdirectories. Ones that you may commonly access as an administrator are the **/etc** directory that holds configuration files, the **/dev** directory that holds device files, and the **/var** directory that holds server data files for DNS, Web, mail, and FTP servers along with system logs and scheduled tasks. For managing different versions of the kernel, you may need to access the **/boot** and **/lib/modules** directories. The **/boot** directory will hold the kernel image files for any new kernels you install, and the **/lib/modules** directory will hold modules for your different kernels.

Directory	Function
/	Begins the file system structure—called the root.
/boot	Holds the kernel image files and modules loaded when your system boots up.
/home	Contains users' home directories.
/sbin	Holds administration level commands and any used by the root user.
/dev	Holds file interfaces for devices such as the terminal and printer.
/etc	Holds system configuration files and any other system files.
/etc/opt	Holds system configuration files for applications in **/opt**.
/etc/X11	Holds system configuration files for the X Window System and its applications.
/bin	Holds the essential user commands and utility programs.
/lib	Holds essential shared libraries and kernel modules.
/lib/modules	Holds the kernel modules.
/mnt	Used to hold directories for mounting file systems like CD-ROMs or floppy disks that are mounted only temporarily.
/opt	Holds added software applications (for example, KDE on some distributions).
/proc	Process directory, a memory-resident directory containing files used to provide information about the system.
/tmp	Holds temporary files.
/usr	Holds those files and commands used by the system; this directory breaks down into several subdirectories.
/var	Holds files that vary, such as mailbox, Web, and FTP files.

Table 29-2. *Linux File System Directories*

The **/usr** directory contains a multitude of important subdirectories used to support users, providing applications, libraries, and documentation (see Table 29-3). **/usr/bin** holds numerous user-accessible applications and utilities. **/usr/sbin** holds user-accessible administrative utilities. The **/usr/share** directory holds architecture-independent data that includes an extensive number of subdirectories, including those for the documentation such as Man, info, and doc files.

The **/var** directories are designed to hold data that changes with the normal operation of the Linux system (see Table 29-4). For example, spool files for documents that you are printing are kept here. A spool file is created as a temporary printing file and is removed after printing. Other files, like system log files, are changed constantly.

The **/proc** file system is a special file system that is generated in system memory (see Table 29-5). It does not exist on any disk. **/proc** contains files that provide important information about the state of your system. For example, **/proc/cpuinfo** holds information about your computer's CPU processor. **/proc/devices** will list those devices currently configured to run with your kernel. **/proc/filesystems** will list the file systems. **/proc** files are really interfaces to the kernel, obtaining information from the kernel about your system.

Directory	Description
/usr/bin	Holds most user commands and utility programs.
/usr/sbin	Holds nonessential administrative applications.
/usr/lib	Holds libraries for applications, programming languages, desktops, etc.
/usr/games	Games and educational program.
/usr/include	C programming language header files (**.h**).
/usr/doc	Holds Linux documentation.
/usr/local	Directory for locally installed software.
/usr/share	Architecture independent data such as documentation like Man and info pages.
/usr/src	Holds source code, including the kernel source codes.
/usr/X11R6	X Window System–based applications and libraries.

Table 29-3. */usr Directories*

Directory	Description
/var/account	Processes accounting logs.
/var/cache	Application cache data for Man pages, Web proxy data, fonts, or application-specific data.
/var/crash	System crash dumps.
/var/games	Varying games data.
/var/lib	Holds state information for particular applications.
/var/local	Used for data that changes for programs installed in **/usr/local**.
/var/lock	Holds lock files that indicate when a particular program or file is in use.
/var/log	Holds log files such as **/var/log/messages** that contain all kernel and system program messages.
/var/mail	User mailbox files.
/var/opt	Variable data for applications installed in **/opt**.
/var/run	Information about system's running processes.
/var/spool	Holds application's spool data such as that for mail, news, and printer queues as well as cron and at jobs.
/var/tmp	Holds temporary files that should be preserved between system reboots.
/var/yp	Network Information Service (NIS) data files.

Table 29-4. */var Directories*

Files	Description
/proc/*num*	There is a directory for each process labeled by its number. **/proc/1** is the directory for process 1.
/proc/cpuinfo	Contains information about the CPU, such as its type, make, model, and performance.
/proc/devices	List of the device drivers configured for the currently running kernel.
/proc/dma	Displays the DMA channels currently used.
/proc/filesystems	File systems configured into the kernel.

Table 29-5. */proc Directories and Files*

Files	Description
/proc/interrupts	Displays the interrupts in use.
/proc/ioports	Shows the I/O ports are in use.
/proc/kcore	Holds an image of the physical memory of the system.
/proc/kmsg	Messages generated by the kernel.
/proc/ksyms	Symbol table for the kernel.
/proc/loadavg	The system load average.
/proc/meminfo	Memory usage.
/proc/modules	Lists the kernel modules currently loaded.
/proc/net	Status information about network protocols.
/proc/stat	System operating statistics, such as page fault occurrences.
/proc/uptime	The time the system has been up.
/proc/version	The kernel version.

Table 29-5. *\/proc Directories and Files* (continued)

Device Files: /dev

To mount a file system, you have to specify its device name. The interfaces to devices that may be attached to your system are provided by special files known as *device files*. The names of these device files are the device names. Device files are located in the **/dev** directories and usually have abbreviated names ending with the number of the device. For example, **fd0** may reference the first floppy drive attached to your system. On Linux systems operating on PCs, the IDE hard disk partitions have a prefix of **hd,** followed by a character that labels the hard drive, and then a number for the partition. For example, **hda2** references the second partition on the first IDE hard drive. The prefix **sd** references SCSI hard drives, so **sda3** would reference the second partition on the first SCSI hard drive. In most cases, you can use the `man` command with a prefix to obtain more detailed information about this kind of device. For example, `man sd` displays the Man pages for SCSI devices. A complete listing of all device names can be found in the **devices** file located in the **linux/doc/device-list** directory at the **www.kernel.org** Web site. Table 29-6 lists several of the commonly used device names.

The device name for your floppy drive is **fd0** and is located in the directory **/dev**. **/dev/fd0** references your floppy drive. Notice the numeral **0** after **fd**. If you have more than one floppy drive, they are represented by **fd1**, **fd2**, and so on.

IDE hard drives use the prefix **hd**, while SCSI hard drives use the prefix **sd**. RAID devices, on the other hand, will use the prefix **md**. The prefix for a hard disk is followed

Device Name	Description
hd	IDE hard drives; 1–4 are primary partitions, and 5 and up are logical partitions
sd	SCSI hard drives
scd	SCSI CD-ROM drives (used on Mandrake and Red Hat)
sr	SCSI CD-ROM drives (alternative prefix name, used on other distributions)
fd	Floppy disks
st	SCSI tape drives
nst	SCSI tape drives, no rewind
ht	IDE tape drives
tty	Terminals
lp	Printer ports
pty	Pseudoterminals (used for remote logins)
js	Analog joy sticks
midi	Midi ports
ttyS	Serial ports
md	RAID devices
rd/c*n*d*n*	Directory that holds RAID devices is **rd**; **c*n*** is the RAID controller and **d*n*** is the RAID disk for that controller
cdrom	Link to your CD-ROM device file
cdwriter	Link to your CD-R or CD-RW device file
modem	Link to your modem device file
floppy	Link to your floppy device file
tape	Link to your tape device file
scanner	Link to your scanner device file

Table 29-6. *Device Name Prefixes*

by a letter that labels the hard drive and a number for the partition. For example, **hda2** references the second partition on the first IDE hard drive, where the first hard drive is referenced with the letter "a," as in **hda**. The device **sdb3** refers to the third partition on the second SCSI hard drive (**sdb**). RAID devices, however, are numbered from 0, like floppy drives. Device **md0** references the first RAID device and **md1**, the second. To find the device name, you can use **df** to display your hard partitions or examine the **/etc/fstab** file.

The device name for your CD-ROM drive varies depending on the type of CD-ROM you have. The device name for an IDE CD-ROM has the same prefix as an IDE hard disk partition, **hd**, and is identified by a following letter that distinguishes it from other IDE devices. For example, an IDE CD-ROM connected to your secondary IDE port may have the name **hdc**. An IDE CD-ROM connected as a slave to the secondary port may have the name **hdd**. The actual name is determined when the CD-ROM is installed, as happened when you installed your Linux system. SCSI CD-ROM drives use a different nomenclature for their device names. They begin with **scd** for SCSI drive and are followed by a distinguishing number. For example, the name of a SCSI CD-ROM could be **scd0** or **scd1**. The name of your CD-ROM was determined when you installed your system. You can find out what it is either by examining the **/etc/fstab** file or by using Linuxconf on your root user desktop.

Mounting File Systems: /etc/fstab

Although you can mount a file system directly with only a **mount** command, you can simplify the process by placing mount information in the **/etc/fstab** configuration file. Using entries in this file, you can have certain file systems automatically mounted whenever your system boots. For others, you can specify configuration information, such as mountpoints and access permissions, which can be automatically used whenever you mount a file system. You needn't enter this information as arguments to a **mount** command as you otherwise must. This feature is what allows mount utilities on Gnome, KDE, and Linuxconf to enable you to mount a file system simply by clicking a button. All the mount information is already in the **/etc/fstab** file. For example, when adding a new hard disk partition to your Linux system, you most likely want to have it automatically mounted on startup, and then unmounted when you shut down. Otherwise, you must mount and unmount the partition explicitly each time you boot up and shut down your system. To have Linux automatically mount the file system on your new hard disk partition, you only need to add its name to the **fstab** file. You can do this by directly and carefully editing the **/etc/fstab** file to type in a new entry, or you can use Linuxconf, as described in the next section.

An entry in an **fstab** file contains several fields, each separated by a space or tab. These are described as the device, mountpoint, file system type, options, dump, and **fsck** fields, arranged in the sequence shown here:

```
<device> <mountpoint> <filesystemtype> <options> <dump> <fsck>
```

The first field is the name of the file system to be mounted. This usually begins with **/dev**, such as **/dev/hda3** for the third hard disk partition. The next field is the directory in your file structure where you want the file system on this device to be attached. The third field is the type of file system being mounted. Table 29-7 provides a list of all the different types you can mount. The type for a standard Linux hard disk partition is **ext3**. The next example shows an entry for the main Linux hard disk partition. This entry is mounted at the root directory, **/**, and has a file type of **ext3** (earlier distributions use an older version called **ext2**).

```
/dev/hda3 / ext3 defaults 0 1
```

Types	Description
auto	Attempts to automatically detect the file system type.
minux	Minux file systems (filenames are limited to 30 characters).
ext	Earlier version of Linux file system, no longer in use.
ext3	Standard Linux file system supporting large filenames and file sizes. Includes journaling.
ext2	Older standard Linux file system supporting large filenames and file sizes. Does not have journaling.
xiaf	Xiaf file system.
msdos	File system for MS-DOS partitions (16-bit).
vfat	File system for Windows 95, 98, and Millennium partitions (32-bit).
ntfs	Windows NT, Windows XP, and Windows 2000 file systems (read only access).
hpfs	File system for OS/2 high-performance partitions.
proc	Used by operating system for processes.
nfs	NFS file system for mounting partitions from remote systems.
umsdos	UMS-DOS file system.
swap	Linux swap partition or swap file.
sysv	UNIX System V file systems.
iso9660	File system for mounting CD-ROM.

Table 29-7. *File System Types*

The type of file system on a floppy drive could vary often depending on the type of floppy you are trying to mount. For example, you may want to read a Windows-formatted floppy disk at one time and a Linux-formatted floppy disk at another time. For this reason, the file system type specified for the floppy device is **auto**. With this option, the type of file system formatted on the floppy disk will be automatically detected and the appropriate file system type used.

```
/dev/fd0  /mnt/floppy  auto   defaults,noauto   0 0
```

The field after the file system type lists the different options for mounting the file system. You can specify a default set of options by simply entering **defaults**. You can list specific options next to each other separated by a comma (no spaces). The **defaults** option specifies that a device is read/write (**rw**), asynchronous (**async**), a block device (**dev**), cannot be mounted by ordinary users (**nouser**), and that programs can be executed on it (**exec**). By contrast, a CD-ROM only has two options listed for it: **ro** and **noauto**. **ro** specifies this is read-only, and **noauto** specifies this is not automatically mounted. The **noauto** option is used with both CD-ROMs and floppy drives, so they won't automatically mount since you don't know if you have anything in them when you start up. At the same time, the entries for both the CD-ROM and the floppy drive specify where they are to be mounted when you decide to mount them. Table 29-8 lists the options for mounting a file system. The floppy drive entry also has all the **default** options of the hard disk partitions, with the exception that it is not automatically mounted (not mountable with the **-a** option). An example of CD-ROM and floppy drive entries follows. Notice the type for a CD-ROM file system is different from a hard disk partition, **iso9660**.

```
/dev/hdc /mnt/cdrom    iso9660 ro,noauto          0 0
/dev/fd0 /mnt/floppy  auto    defaults,noauto    0 0
```

Options	Description
async	All I/O to the file system should be done asynchronously.
auto	Can be mounted with the **-a** option. A **mount -a** command executed when the system boots, in effect, mounts file systems automatically.
defaults	Uses default options: **rw**, **suid**, **dev**, **exec**, **auto**, **nouser**, and **async**.

Table 29-8. *-o and /etc/fstab*

Options	Description
`dev`	Interprets character or block special devices on the file system.
`noauto`	Can only be mounted explicitly. The **-a** option does not cause the file system to be mounted.
`exec`	Permits execution of binaries.
`nouser`	Forbids an ordinary (that is, nonroot) user to mount the file system.
`remount`	Attempts to remount an already mounted file system. This is commonly used to change the mount flags for a file system, especially to make a read-only file system writable.
`ro`	Mounts the file system as read-only.
`rw`	Mounts the file system as read/write.
`suid`	Allows set-user-identifier or set-group-identifier bits to take effect.
`sync`	All I/O to the file system should be done synchronously.
`user`	Enables an ordinary user to mount the file system. Ordinary users always have the following options activated: **noexec**, **nosuid**, and **nodev**.
`nodev`	Does not interpret character or block special devices on the file system.
`nosuid`	Does not allow set-user-identifier or set-group-identifier bits to take effect.

Table 29-8. *-o and /etc/fstab* (continued)

The last two fields consist of an integer value. The first one is used by the **dump** command to determine if a file system needs to be dumped, backing up the file system. The last one is used by **fsck** to see if a file system should be checked at reboot and in what order. If the field has a value of 1, it indicates a boot partition, and 2 indicates other partitions. The 0 value means **fsck** needn't check the file system.

*You can also configure your **fstab** file with Linuxconf and Webmin. They also let you mount and unmount file systems.*

A copy of an **/etc/fstab** file is shown here. Notice the first line is comment. All comment lines begin with a **#**. The entry for the **/proc** file system is a special entry used by your

Linux operating system for managing its processes, and it is not an actual device. To make an entry in the **/etc/fstab** file, you can either edit the **/etc/fstab** file directly or use Linuxconf, which prompts you for information and then makes the correct entries into your **/etc/fstab** file. You can use the **/etc/fstab** example here as a guide to show how your entries should look. The **/proc** and **swap** partition entries are particularly critical.

/etc/fstab

```
  # <device> <mountpoint> <filesystemtype> <options> <dump><fsck>
/dev/hda3   /             ext3             defaults          0     1
/dev/hdc    /mnt/cdrom    iso9660          ro,noauto         0     0
/dev/fd0    /mnt/floppy   auto             defaults,noauto 0
/proc       /proc         proc             defaults
/dev/hda2   none          swap             sw
/dev/hda1   /mnt/windows vfat              defaults          0     0
```

Mandrake, Red Hat, and SuSE will create entries in the **fstab** file for any CD-ROM and floppy devices you may have. They will also create directories where they can be mounted. For Red Hat and zMandrake, these are **/mnt/cdrom** for your CD-ROM and **/mnt/floppy** for your floppy disk. SuSE just uses **/cdrom** and **/floppy**. Should you have several CD-ROMs or floppy drives, directories are created for them with sequential numbers. So on Mandrake, a second CD-ROM drive will use a directory named **/mnt/cdrom1**.

You can mount either MS-DOS or Windows 95/98/ME partitions used by your MS-DOS or Windows operating system onto your Linux file structure, just as you would mount any Linux file system. You only have to specify the file type of **vfat** for Windows 95/98/ME and **msdos** for MS-DOS. You may find it convenient to have your Windows partitions automatically mounted when you start up your Linux system (the same is true for MS-DOS partitions). To do this, you need to put an entry for your Windows partitions in your **/etc/fstab** file and give it the **defaults** option or be sure to include an **auto** option. You make an entry for each Windows partition you want to mount, and then specify the device name for that partition followed by the directory in which you want to mount it. The **/mnt/windows** directory would be a logical choice (be sure the **windows** directory has already been created in **/mnt**). For the file system type, enter **`vfat`**. The next example shows a standard MS-DOS partition entry for an **/etc/fstab** file. Notice the last entry in the **/etc/fstab** file example was an entry for mounting a Windows partition.

```
/dev/hda1 /mnt/windows vfat defaults 0 0
```

*Linux kernel 2.4 systems currently can only mount **ntfs** file systems (Windows NT, Windows 200, and Windows XP) as read only. They cannot write to these partitions.*

Tip *SuSE automatically detects and mounts any Windows partition in the **/windows** directory, giving each partition a directory named for its drive letter, such as **/windows/C** for a Windows C drive. Mandrake automatically detects and mounts Windows partitions in the **/mnt/windows** directory, giving each partition a directory named for its drive letter, such as **/mnt/windows/C** for a Windows C drive.*

If your **/etc/fstab** file ever becomes corrupt—say, a line gets deleted accidentally or changed—your system will boot into a maintenance mode, giving you read-only access to your partitions. To gain read/write access so you can fix your **/etc/fstab** file, you have to remount your main partition. The following command performs such an operation:

```
# mount -n -o remount,rw /
```

File systems listed in the **/etc/fstab** file are automatically mounted whenever you boot, unless this feature is explicitly turned off with the **noauto** option. Notice the CD-ROM and floppy disks have a **noauto** option. Also, if you issue a **mount -a** command, all the file systems without a **noauto** option are mounted. If you want to make the CD-ROM user-mountable, add the **user** option.

```
/dev/hdc /mnt/cdrom iso9660 ro,noauto,user 0 0
```

Note *The "automatic" mounting of file systems from **/etc/fstab** is actually implemented by executing a **mount -a** command in the **/etc/rc.d/rc.sysinit** file that is run whenever you boot. The **mount -a** command will mount any file system listed in your **/etc/fstab** file that does not have a **noauto** option. The **umount -a** option will unmount the file systems in **/etc/fstab** (which is executed when you shut down your system).*

The mount and umount Commands

You can also mount or unmount any file system using the **mount** and **umount** commands. You enter these commands on a shell command line. In a window manager or desktop, you can open a terminal window and enter the command there, or you can simply use your login shell. The mount operations discussed in the previous sections use the **mount** command to mount a file system. Normally, mounting file systems can only be done as the root user (unless the device is user mountable). This is a system administration task and cannot be performed by a regular user. To mount a file system, be sure to log in as the root user. Table 29-9 lists the different options for the **mount** command.

Mount Options	Description
`-f`	Fakes the mounting of a file system. Use it to check if a file system can be mounted.
`-v`	Verbose mode. Mount displays descriptions of the actions it is taking. Use with `-f` to check for any problems mounting a file system, `-fv`.
`-w`	Mounts the file system with read/write permission.
`-r`	Mounts the file system with read-only permission.
`-n`	Mounts the file system without placing an entry for it in the **mstab** file.
`-t` *type*	Specifies the type of file system to be mounted. See Table 29-7 for valid file system types.
`-a`	Mounts all file systems listed in **/etc/fstab**.
`-o` *option-list*	Mounts the file system using a list of options. This is a comma-separated list of options following `-o`. See Table 29-8 for a list of the options and the Man pages for **mount**.

Table 29-9. *The* `mount` *Command*

The **mount** command takes two arguments: the storage device through which Linux accesses the file system, and the directory in the file structure to which the new file system is attached. The *mountpoint* is the directory on your main directory tree where you want the files on the storage device attached. The *device* is a special device file that connects your system to the hardware device. The syntax for the **mount** command is as follows:

```
# mount device mountpoint
```

Device files are located in the **/dev** directories and usually have abbreviated names ending with the number of the device. For example, **fd0** may reference the first floppy drive attached to your system. On Linux systems operating on PCs, the hard disk partitions have a prefix of **hd,** followed by a letter that labels the hard drive, and then a number for the partition. For example, **hda2** references the second partition on the first hard drive. In most cases, you can use the **man** command with a prefix to obtain more detailed information about that kind of device. For example, **man sd** displays the Man pages for SCSI devices. The following example mounts a floppy disk in the first floppy drive device (**fd0**) to the **/mydir** directory. The mountpoint directory needs to be empty. If you already have a file system mounted there, you will receive a message that another file system is already mounted there and that the directory is busy. If you mount a file system to a directory that already has files and subdirectories in it, those will be bypassed, giving you access only to the files in the mounted file system. Unmounting the file system restores access to the original directory files.

```
# mount /dev/fd0 /mydir
```

For any partition with an entry in the **/etc/fstab** file, you can mount it using only the mount directory specified in its **fstab** entry. You needn't enter the device filename. The **`mount`** command looks up the entry for it in the **fstab** file, using the directory to identify the entry and, in that way, find the device name. For example, to unmount the **/dev/hda1** DOS partition in the previous example, the **`mount`** command only needs to know the directory it is mounted to—in this case, **/mnt/dos**.

```
# mount /mnt/dos
```

If you want to replace one mounted file system with another, you must first explicitly unmount the one already mounted. Say you have mounted a floppy disk, and now you want to take it out and put in a new one. You must unmount that floppy disk before you can put in and mount the new one. You unmount a file system with the **`umount`** command. The **`umount`** command can take as its argument either a device name or the directory where it was mounted. Here is the syntax:

```
# umount device-or-mountpoint
```

The following example unmounts the floppy disk mounted to the **/mydir** directory:

```
# umount /dev/fd0
```

Using the example where the device was mounted on the **/mydir** directory, you could use that directory to unmount the file system:

```
# umount /mydir
```

One important constraint occurs on the **`umount`** command. You can never unmount a file system in which you are currently working. If you change to a directory within a file system that you then try to unmount, you receive an error message saying the file system is busy. For example, suppose you mount the distribution CD-ROM on the **/mnt/cdrom** directory and then change to that **/mnt/cdrom** directory. If you decide to change CD-ROMs, you first have to unmount the current one with the **umount** command. This will fail because you are currently in the directory in which it is mounted. You have to leave that directory before you can unmount the CD-ROM.

```
# mount /dev/hdc /mnt/cdrom
# cd /mnt/cdrom
# umount /mnt/cdrom
umount: /dev/hdd: device is busy
# cd /root
# umount /mnt/cdrom
```

If other users are using a file system you are trying to unmount, you can use the **lsof** or **fuser** command to find out who they are.

If you are unsure as to the type of file system that the floppy disk holds, you can mount it specifying the **auto** file system type with the **-t** option. Given the **auto** file system type, **mount** will attempt to automatically detect the type of file system on the floppy disk.

```
# mount -t auto /dev/fd0 /mydir
```

Mounting Floppy Disks

To access a file on a floppy disk, you first have to mount that disk onto your Linux system. The device name for your floppy drive is **fd0**, and it is located in the directory **/dev**. Entering **/dev/fd0** references your floppy drive. Notice the number **0** after **fd**. If you have more than one floppy drive, they are represented by **fd1**, **fd2**, and so on. You can mount to any directory you want. Many distributions create a convenient directory to use for floppy disks, **/mnt/floppy**. The following example mounts the floppy disk in your floppy drive to the **/mnt/floppy** directory:

```
# mount /dev/fd0 /mnt/floppy
```

Remember, you are mounting a particular floppy disk, not the floppy drive. You cannot simply remove the floppy disk and put in another one. The **mount** command has attached those files to your main directory tree, and your system expects to find those files on a floppy disk in your floppy drive. If you take out the disk and put another one in, you get an error message when you try to access it.

To change disks, you must first unmount the floppy disk already in your disk drive. Then, after putting in the new disk, you must explicitly mount that new disk. To do this, use the **umount** command. Notice that the **umount** command begins with just *u*, not *un*.

```
# umount /dev/fd0
```

For the **umount** operation, you can specify either the directory it is mounted on or the **/dev/fd0** device.

```
# umount /mnt/floppy
```

You can now remove the floppy disk, put in the new one, and then mount it.

```
# mount /mnt/floppy
```

When you shut down your system, any disk you have mounted is automatically unmounted. You do not have to unmount it explicitly.

Mounting CD-ROMs

You can also mount CD-ROM disks to your Linux system using the **mount** command. On many distributions, the directory **/mnt/cdrom** has been reserved for CD-ROM file systems. You see an entry for this in the **/etc/fstab** file. With such an entry, to mount a CD-ROM, all you have to do is enter the command **mount** and the directory **/mnt/cdrom**. You needn't specify the device name. Once mounted, you can access the CD-ROM through the **/mnt/cdrom** directory.

```
# mount /mnt/cdrom
```

As with floppy disks, remember you are mounting a particular CD-ROM, not the CD-ROM drive. You cannot just remove the CD-ROM and put in a new one. The **mount** command has attached those files to your main directory tree, and your system expects to find them on a disc in your CD-ROM drive. To change discs, you must first unmount the CD-ROM already in your CD-ROM drive with the **umount** command. Your CD-ROM drive will not open until you issue this command. Then, after putting in the new disc, you must explicitly mount that new CD-ROM. You can then remove the CD-ROM and put in the new one. Then issue a **mount** command to mount it.

```
# umount /mnt/cdrom
```

If you want to mount a CD-ROM to another directory, you have to include the device name in the **mount** command. The following example mounts the disc in your CD-ROM drive to the **/mydir** directory. The particular device name for the CD-ROM in this example is **/dev/hdc**.

```
# mount /dev/hdc /mydir
```

To change discs, you have to unmount the CD-ROM already in your CD-ROM drive, and then, after putting in the new disc, you must explicitly mount that new CD-ROM.

```
# umount /mydir
```

You can now remove the CD-ROM and put in the new one. Then issue a **`mount`** command to mount it.

```
# mount /dev/hdc /mydir
```

When burning a CD, you may need to create a CD image file. You could access such an image file from your hard drive, mounting it as if it were another file system (even ripped images could be mounted in this way). For this you use the loop option, specifying an open loop device such as **/dev/loop0**. If no loop device is indicated, **`mount`** will try to find an open one. The file system type is iso9660, a CD-ROM iso image file type.

```
# mount -t iso9660 -o loop=/dev/loop0 image-file  mount-directory
```

To mount the image file **mymusic.cdimage** to the **/mnt/mystuff** directory and make it read-only, you would use:

```
# mount -t iso9660 -o ro,loop=/dev/loop0 mymusic.cdimage /mnt/mystuff
```

Once mounted, you can access files on the CD-ROM as you would in any directory.

Note *You use mkisofs to create a CD-ROM image made up from your files or another CD-ROM.*

Mounting Hard Drive Partitions: Linux and Windows

You can mount either Linux or Windows hard drive partitions with the **`mount`** command. However, it is much more practical to have them mounted automatically, using the **/etc/fstab** file as described in the next section. The Linux hard disk partitions you created during installation are already automatically mounted for you. To mount a Linux hard disk partition, enter the **`mount`** command with the device name of the partition and the directory to which you want to mount it. IDE hard drives use the prefix **hd**, and SCSI hard drives use the prefix **sd**. The next example mounts the Linux hard disk partition on **/dev/hda4** to the directory **/mnt/mydata**:

```
# mount -t ext3 /dev/hda4 /mnt/mydata
```

You can also mount a Windows partition and directly access the files on it. As with a Linux partition, you use the **mount** command, but you also have to specify the file system type as Windows. For that, use the **-t** option, and then type **vfat** for Windows 95/98/ME (**msdos** for MS-DOS). For Windows XP, 2000, and NT you would use **ntfs** (limited read-only access). In the next example, the user mounts the Windows hard disk partition **/dev/hda1** to the Linux file structure at directory **/mnt/windows**. The **/mnt/windows** directory is a common designation for Windows file systems, though you can mount it in any directory (**/mnt/dos** for MS-DOS). If you have several Windows partitions, you could create a Windows directory and then a subdirectory for each drive using the drive's label or letter, such as **/mnt/windows/a** or **/mnt/windows/mystuff**. Be sure you have already created the directory.

```
# mount -t vfat /dev/hda1 /mnt/windows
```

Installing IDE CD-R/RW and DVD-R/RW devices

Linux CD writing applications all treat CD-R/RW and DVD-R/RW drives as if they were SCSI drives. This means that IDE CD-R/RW drives have to emulate SCSI drives for them to be recognized and used by CD or DVD writing software. Even if you want to use an IDE CD-ROM or DVD-ROM in a CD writing applications—say, as just the reader to copy a CD disk—that IDE CD-ROM drive would still have to emulate a SCSI CD-ROM drive. Only SCSI drive (CD-R/RW/ROM or DVD-R/RW/ROM) are recognized by Linux CD or DVD writing software. For example, if you have a regular IDE CD-ROM and you want to use it in Linux CD-write software to copy CDs (ripping), you still have to have that IDE CD-ROM emulate a SCSI CD-ROM. Check the CD-Writing HOW-TO at **www.linuxdoc.org** for more details. A brief description is shown here.

Note *SCSI emulation for IDE devices is implemented in the kernel as SCSI Emulation Support in the IDE, ATA, and ATAPI Block Devices entry, located in the ATA/IDE/MFM/RLL Support window opened from the main kernel configuration menu. Normally, it is compiled as a module.*

IDE CD and DVD drives (CD-R/RW/ROM or DVD-R/RW/ROM) will be recognized as IDE devices during installation and installed as such. However, when you start up your system, you need to instruct the Linux kernel to have the IDE CD and DVD drives emulate SCSI CD or DVD drives. This means that a CD-R drive that would be normally recognized as a **/dev/hdc** drive has to be recognized as a **/dev/scd0** device, the first SCSI CD-ROM drive. You do this by loading the **ide-scsi** module, which allows an IDE CD drive to emulate a SCSI CD drive.

You can implement SCSI emulation for IDE CD and DVD drives in one of two ways: either by loading the **ide-scsi** module as a kernel parameter, or specifying the module in the **/etc/modules.conf** file. You will also have to indicate the IDE drives that will be emulated. If the **ide-scsi** module is compiled into the kernel (not as a separate module), then you have to load it as a kernel parameter. An **ide-scsi** module can be loaded either way.

Note *During installation, most distributions, including Mandrake, Caldera, Red Hat, and SuSE, will recognize the IDE CD and DVD drives you have installed on your system, and will include the* ***ide-scsi*** *kernel parameter automatically as part of either your LILO or Grub boot loader configurations. You will not need to perform any of the specific configuration tasks described in this section.*

As a kernel parameter, you can either manually enter the **ide-scsi** parameter at the boot prompt or place it in the **/etc/grub.conf** or **/etc/lilo.conf** files (depending on whether you are using the GRUB or LILO boot loader) to have it automatically entered. The parameter is read when the kernel boots. List each IDE CD or DVD drive that needs to emulate a SCSI drive as using the **ide-scsi** module. You assign the **ide-scsi** module to the device name of the IDE CD drive to be emulated. The following example would load the **ide-scsi** module to have the master IDE drive on the secondary IDE connection (**hdc**) emulate a SCSI drive.

```
hdc=ide-scsi
```

The following example shows how two IDE CD drives are specified at the Linux boot prompt.

```
boot:  linux hdc=ide-scsi hdd=ide-scsi
```

For the **/etc/grub.conf** file, you add these parameters to the Linux kernel line, just as you would to a boot entry.

```
kernel /boot/vmlinuz-2.4.18-3 ro root=/dev/hda3 hdc=ide-scsi
```

For the **/etc/lilo.conf** file, you assign these parameters to an **append** command in the image segment for the Linux kernel. The **append** command is assigned a string listing the parameters for that kernel image. Be sure to enclose the string in double quotes. The following example shows the kernel parameter that configures the **hdc** IDE drive to emulate a SCSI drive, enabling it to operate as a CD-R or CD-RW drive.

```
append="hdc=ide-scsi"
```

For two IDE CD drives, you would use both parameters in the same string.

```
append="hdc=ide-scsi hdd=ide-scsi"
```

Be sure to execute the `lilo` command to effect the changes you make to **/etc/lilo.conf**.

If you are not using LILO, or, for some reason, you do not want to modify the **/etc/lilo.conf** file, you can configure the **/etc/modules.conf** file to load and implement the SCSI emulation for your IDE CD drives. This involves entering several module configuration commands in the **/etc/modules.conf** file. When your system starts up, it will load the modules as specified in that file.

Initially, your IDE CD drives will be recognized and configured as IDE CD-ROMs by the **ide-cd** module. You will need to specify options for the **ide-cd** module to ignore the IDE CD-R and CD-RW drives, as well as any CD-ROM drives you want to use in CD writing applications. You do this with the **`options`** command and the **`ignore`** option. The following example instructs **ide-cd** to ignore an IDE CD-R that has been installed as an IDE CD-ROM at **/dev/hdc**, the secondary IDE master.

```
options ide-cd ignore=hdc
```

You then have to enter alias commands to identify the **scd** SCSI drives as using the SCSI CD module, **sr_mod**. The following example aliases the **/dev/scd0** device as using the **sr_mod** SCSI CD module.

```
alias scd0 sr_mod
```

There are also several preinstall commands that will load the **ide-scsi** module which provides the SCSI emulation, as well as govern the sequence in which SCSI (**sg** and **sr_mod**) and IDE CD (**ide-cd**) modules are loaded.

```
pre-install sg     modprobe ide-scsi # load ide-scsi before sg
pre-install sr_mod modprobe ide-scsi # load ide-scsi before sr_mod
pre-install ide-scsi modprobe ide-cd # load ide-cd   before ide-scsi
```

The following example shows the lines added to the **/etc/modules.conf** file to have two IDE CD drives (**hdc** and **hddd**) emulate SCSI CD drives (**scd0** and **scd1**). Notice the double quotes around the **ide-cd** options on the first line.

```
options ide-cd "ignore=hdc ignore=hdd"
alias scd0 sr_mod
alias scd1 sr_mod
pre-install sg modprobe ide-scsi
pre-install sr_mod modprobe ide-scsi
pre-install ide-scsi modprobe ide-cd
```

Once you have installed your SCSI emulation, you should check that your IDE drives are being recognized as SCSI drives. To do this, you run the **cdrecord** program with the **-scanbus** option (or **dvdrecord** for DVD writers). This example shows two IDE CD drives now emulating SCSI CD drives. One is a Plextor IDE CD-RW drive (**scd0**) and the other is a Toshiba DVD-ROM drive (**scd1**).

```
# cdrecord -scanbus
Cdrecord 1.9 (i686-pc-linux-gnu) Copyright (C) 1995-2000 Jörg Schilling
Linux sg driver version: 3.1.17
Using libscg version 'schily-0.1'
scsibus0:
0,0,0  0) 'PLEXTOR ' 'CD-R   PX-W1210A' '1.02' Removable CD-ROM
0,1,0  1) 'TOSHIBA ' 'DVD-ROM SD-M1402' '1010' Removable CD-ROM
0,2,0  2) *
0,3,0  3) *
0,4,0  4) *
0,5,0  5) *
0,6,0  6) *
0,7,0  7) *
```

You then need to change the device links for any IDE CD drives already installed. Your Linux CD writing software, as well as your **/etc/fstab** entries, are designed to reference **/etc/cdrom** links. Originally, these were set up to link to your IDE device files, such as **/dev/hdc**. You now have to change them to reference the SCSI CD device files, such as **/dev/scd0**. For example, if you have two IDE CD drives, you will have two device links called **/etc/cdrom** and **/etc/cdrom1**. If both IDE CD drives are now emulating SCSI drives, you have to change both the **cdrom** and **cdrom1** links.

First, erase the IDE CD-ROM links in the **/dev** directory. These are currently pointing to the IDE CD-ROM devices such as **hdc** or **hdb**.

```
rm /dev/cdrom
rm /dev/cdrom1
```

Then, create them again to point to the corresponding SCSI devices for these drives. Use the **ln** command with the **-s** option to create symbolic links. These devices begin with the prefix **scd** (SCSI CD) and are numbered from 0, beginning with **scd0**, **scd1**, and so on.

```
ln -s /dev/scd0  /dev/cdrom
ln -s /dev/scd1 /dev/cdrom1
```

As the links are specified in the **/etc/fstab** file, you can now mount and access the drives just using their mountpoint.

```
mount /mnt/cdrom
```

Finally, in the CD-ROM entry for your CD-R or CD-RW drive in the **/etc/fstab** file, you would specify the `rw` (read/write) option instead of the `ro` (read-only) option. In this example, **/dev/cdrom** links to **/dev/scd0**, which is a Plextor IDE CD-RW drive.

```
/dev/cdrom  /mnt/cdrom    iso9660 noauto,owner,kudzu,rw 0 0
```

Formatting File Systems: mkfs, mke2fs, mkswap, and fdisk

If you want to mount a new partition from either a new hard drive or your current drive, you must first create that partition using the Linux fdisk and format it with mkfs. Once created and formatted, you can then mount it on your system. If you need to create a swap partition, you use mkswap. To format Linux ext3 partitions, you can use mke2fs instead of mkfs. And for DOS partitions, you can use mkdosfs. mke2fs has its own set of options geared to technical aspects such as block and fragment sizes. To format standard Linux partitions, it is advisable to simply use mke2fs. The mkisofs tool will create a CD image. This is used primarily for creating CDs. Linux formatting and partition tools are listed in Table 29-10.

Tool	Description
fdisk	Creates and deletes partitions.
cfdisk	Screen-based interface for fdisk.
mkfs	Formats a partition or floppy disk using specified file system type. Front end to format utilities.
mke2fs	Formats an ext2 Linux partition.
mke2fs `-j`	Formats an ext3 Linux partition.
mkswap	Formats a swap partition.
mkdosfs	Formats a DOS partition.
mkisofs	Creates an ISO CD-ROM disk image.
kfloppy	KDE utility to format a floppy disk.

Table 29-10. *Linux Partition and Formatting Tools*

To start fdisk, enter **fdisk** on the command line. This brings up an interactive program you can use to create your Linux partition. Be careful using Linux fdisk. It can literally erase your entire hard disk if you are not careful.. The command **n** creates a new partition, and the command **t** enables you to set its type to that of a Linux type, 83. Table 29-11 lists the fdisk commands.

Hard disk partitions are named with **hd** (IDE drive) or **sd** (SCSI drives), followed by a letter indicating the hard drive, and then a number for the partition on the hard drive. They can belong to any operating system, such as Linux, Unix, MS-DOS, Windows XP, or Windows NT. The first partition created is called **hda1**—the first partition on the first IDE hard drive, A. If you add another partition, it will have the name **hda2**. If you add a new IDE hard drive, its first partition will have the name **hdb1**.

Commands	Description
`a`	Sets and unsets the bootable flag for a partition.
`c`	Sets and unsets the DOS compatibility flag.
`d`	Deletes a partition.
`l`	Lists partition types.
`m`	Displays a listing of fdisk commands.
`n`	Creates a new partition.
`p`	Prints the partition table, listing all the partitions on your disk.
`q`	Quits without saving changes. Use this to abort an fdisk session if you made a mistake.
`y`	Selects the file system type for a partition.
`v`	Verifies the partition table.
`w`	Writes partition table to disk and exits. At this point, the changes are made irrevocably.
`x`	Displays a listing of advanced fdisk commands. With these, you can set the number of cylinders, sectors, and heads; print raw data; and change the location of data in the partition table.

Table 29-11. *The fdisk Commands*

Note *If you want to resize a partition, making it smaller or larger, you can use the GNU Parted utility, **www.gnu.org/software/parted**.*

Once you create your partition, you have to format it. For this, use the **mkfs** command and the name of the hard disk partition. A hard disk partition is a device with its own device name in the **/dev** directory. You must specify its full pathname with the **mkfs** command. For example, the second partition on the first hard drive has the device name **/dev/hda2**. You can now mount your new hard disk partition, attaching it to your file structure. The next example formats that partition:

```
# mkfs -t ext3 /dev/hda2
```

mkfs is a front end that calls other tools to perform the actual formatting operation. For example, to format a Linux partition, mkfs uses mke2fs. For a Windows or DOS partition, it uses mkdosfs. To create an **ext3** Linux partition, you could just as easily use mke2fs with the **-j** option, and not have to specify a type, as shown here (without the **-j** option, it creates an **ext2** file system):

```
# mke2fs -j /dev/hda2
```

To format a floppy disk, use the **mkfs** command. This creates a Linux file system on that disk. Be sure to specify the **ext3** file system type with the **-t ext3** option. Once formatted, you can then mount that file system. The **mkfs** command takes as its arguments the device name and the number of memory blocks on the disk (see Table 29-12). At

Options	Description
Blocks	Number of blocks for the file system. There are 1,440 blocks for a 1.44MB floppy disk.
-t *file-system-type*	Specifies the type of file system to format. The default is the standard Linux file system type, **ext3**.
fs *-options*	Options for the type of file system specified.
-V	Verbose mode. Displays description of each action mkfs takes.

Table 29-12. *The mkfs Options*

Options	Description
`-v`	Instructs the file system builder program that mkfs invokes to show actions it takes.
`-c`	Checks a partition for bad blocks before formatting it (may take some time).
`-l` *file-name*	Reads a list of bad blocks.

Table 29-12. *The mkfs Options* (continued)

1,000 bytes per block, **1400** formats a 1.44MB disk. You do not first mount the blank disk; you simply put it in your floppy drive and enter the **mkfs** command with its arguments. The next example formats a 1.44MB floppy disk:

```
# mkfs -t ext3 /dev/fd0 1400
```

With **mke2fs**, you could use:

```
# mke2fs -j /dev/fd0 1400
```

If you have the K Desktop installed, you can use the kfloppy utility to format your floppy disks. kfloppy enables you to choose an MS-DOS or Linux file system type. For MS-DOS disks, you can choose a quick or full format.

If you want to create a swap partition, you first use fdisk to create the partition if it does not already exist, and then you use the **mkswap** command to format it as a swap partition. **mkswap** will format the entire partition unless otherwise instructed. It takes as its argument the device name for the swap partition.

```
mkswap /dev/hda5
```

CD-ROM Recording

Recording data to CD-ROM disks on Linux involves creating a CD image file of the CD-ROM and then writing that image file to a CD-R or CD-RW disk in your CD-R/RW drive. With the **mkisofs** command, you can create a CD image file, which you can then write to a CD-R/RW write device. Once you create your CD image file, you can write it to a CD-write device, using the **cdrecord** or **cdwrite** applications. The **cdrecord** application is a more powerful application with many options. You can also use Gnome and KDE

CD recording applications such as KOnCD and Gnome Toaster to create your CDs easily. Most are front ends to the **mkisofs** and **cdrecord** tools. To record DVD disks on DVD writers, you can use **dvdrecord** (the counterpart to cdrecord) for DVD-R/RW drives and the dvd+rw tools for DVD+RW/+R drives. If you want to record CD-ROMS on a DVD writer, you can just use **cdrecord**.

Tip ***dvdrecord*** *currently works only on DVD-R/RW drives and is part of the dvdrtools package. If you want to use DVD+RW/+R drives, you would use the dvd+rw tools such as* ***growisofs*** *and* ***dvd+rw-format****. dvd+rw tools is currently included only in the Debian distribution. For Red Hat, SuSE, and others, you have to download and compile dvd+rw tools from DVD+RW/+R for Linux page at* ***http://fy.chalmers.se/~appro/linux/DVD+RW****.*

To create a CD image, you first select the files you want on your CD. Then you can use **mkisofs** to create an ISO CD image of them. You may need to include several important options with **mkisofs** to create a distribution CD properly. The **-o** option is used to specify the name of the CD image file. This can be any name you want to give it. The **-R** option specifies Rockridge CD protocols, and the **-J** option provides for long Windows 95/98/ME or XP names. The **-r** option, in addition to the RockRidge protocols (**-R**), will also set standard global permission for your files, like read access for all users and no write access since the CD-ROM is read only. The **-T** option will create translation tables for file names for use on systems that are not RockRidge compliant. The **-U** option provides for relaxed filenames that are not standard ISO compliant such as long file names, those with more than one period in their name, those that begin with a period like shell configuration files, and ones that use lowercase characters (there are also separate options for each of these features if you just want to use a few of them). Most RPM and source code package names would fall in this category. The **-iso-level**. options lets you remove ISO restrictions such as the length of a file name. The **-V** options set the volume label (name) for the CD. Finally, the **-v** option will display the progress of the image creation.

The last argument is the directory that contains the files for which you want to make the CD image. For this, you can specify a directory. For example, if you are creating a CD-ROM to contain the data files in the **mydocs** directory, you would specify that directory. This top directory will not be included, just the files and subdirectories in it. You can also change to that directory and then use **.** to indicate the current directory.

Here the verbose option will show the creation progress, and the **-V** option lets you specify the CD label. A CD image called **moresongs.iso** is created using the file located in the **newsongs** directory.

```
mkisofs -v -V "Goodsongs" -o moresongs.iso  newsongs
```

If you also wanted to use the CD on a Windows system, you would add the -r (RockRidge with standard global file access) and -J (Joliet) options.

```
mkisofs -v -r -J -V "Goodsongs" -o moresongs.iso  newsongs
```

You need to include certain options if you are using filenames that are not ISO compliant such as ones greater than 31 characters or ones that use lowercase characters. The **-U** option let you use completely unrestricted filenames, whereas certain options like **-L** for the unrestricted length will release specific restrictions only. The following example creates a CD image called **mydocuments.iso** using the files and subdirectories located in the **mydocs** directory and labels the CD image with the name "Greatdocs."

```
mkisofs -v -r -T -J -U -V "Greatdocs" -o mydocuments.iso   mydocs
```

Once you have created your CD image, you can check to see if it is correct by mounting it as a file system on your Linux system. In effect, to test the CD image, you mount it to a directory, and then access it as if it were simply another file system. Mounting a CD image requires the use of a loop device. Specify the loop device with the loop option as shown in the next example. Here, the mydocuments.iso is mounted to the **/mnt/cdrom** directory as a file system of type **iso9660**. Be sure to unmount it when you finish.

```
mount -t iso9660 -o ro,loop=/dev/loop0 mydocuments.iso /mnt/cdrom
```

Once **mkisofs** has created the CD image file, you can use **cdrecord** or **cdwrite** to write it to a CD write disk. Should you have more than one SCSI device, you should specify the CD-R/RW drive to use by indicating its SCSI bus number (recall that even IDE CD-R/RW drives are treated as SCSI devices on Linux). You can use **cdrecord** with the **-scanbus** option to find out the SCSI numbers of your re-writeable devices. In this example, as shown previously in the **-scanbus** example, the device number for the re-writable CD/RW drive is **0,0**. The **dev=** option is used to indicate this drive. The final argument for **cdrecord** is the name of the CD image file. **dvdrecord** works the same way as DVD-R/RW writers, and is in fact an extension of **cdrecord**.

```
cdrecord  dev=0,0  mydocuments.iso
```

If you are creating an audio CD, then you use the **-audio** option, as shown here. This option will use the CD-DA audio format.

```
cdrecord  dev=0,0 -audio moresongs.iso
```

The dummy option for cdrecord will let you test the CD writing operation for a given image.

If you are creating a bootable CD-ROM, you will need to indicate the boot image file to use and the boot catalogue. With the **-c** option, you specify the boot catalogue. With the **-b** option, you specify the boot image. The *boot image* is a boot disk image, like that used to start up an installation procedure. For example, on the Red Hat CD-ROM, the boot image is **images/boot.img**. and the boot catalogue is **boot.cat**. The following example creates a bootable CD-ROM using Red Hat distribution files located in the current directory. (Since Red Hat provides ISO images for their distribution, you will not need to do this.)

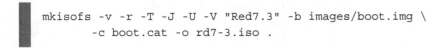

```
mkisofs -v -r -T -J -U -V "Red7.3" -b images/boot.img \
      -c boot.cat -o rd7-3.iso .
```

If you have mounted an MS-DOS or Windows partition, you could copy a CD image file to that partition, and then use Windows CD-write software to create the CD-ROM disk. The **`mkisofs`** *command creates an image of type ISO, and you may need to specify that type.*

Configuring RAID Devices

The redundant array of independent devices (RAID) is a method of storing data across several disks to provide greater efficiency and redundancy. In effect, you can have several hard disks treated as just one hard disk by your operating system. RAID then efficiently stores and retrieves data across all these disks, instead of having the operating system separately access each one as a separate file system. Lower-level details or storage and retrieval are removed from concern of the operating system. This allows greater flexibility in adding or removing hard disks, as well as implementing redundancy in the storage system to provide greater reliability. With RAID, you can have several hard disks that are treated as one virtual disk, where some of the disks are used as real-time mirrors, duplicating data.

RAID can be implemented on a hardware or software level. On a hardware level, you can have hard disks connected to a RAID hardware controller, usually a special PC card . Your operating system then accesses storage through the RAID hardware controller. Alternatively, you can implement RAID as a software controller, letting a software RAID controller program manage access to hard disks treated as RAID devices. The software version lets you use IDE hard disks as RAID disks. Linux uses the MD driver, supported in the 2.4 kernel, to implement a software RAID controller.

Before you can use RAID on your system, make sure it is implemented on your kernel. If not, you will have to reconfigure and install a new version of the kernel (see Chapter 31). Check the Multi-Driver Support component in your kernel configuration. You can specify support of any or all of the RAID levels.

RAID can be implemented at different levels depending on whether you want efficiency, redundancy, or reconstruction capability. For efficiency, RAID stores data using disk stripping, where data is organized into standardized strips that can be stored across the RAID drives for faster access (level 0). Redundancy is implemented with mirroring. With mirroring, the same data is written to each RAID drive (level 1). Each disk has a complete copy of all the data written so that if one or more fails, the others still have your data. Redundancy can be very inefficient and take up a great deal of storage. It is usually implemented on RAID arrays of only two disk drives, where one is used as a real-time backup. As an alternative, data can be reconstructed using parity information in case of a hard drive crash. Parity information is saved instead of full duplication of the data (level 5). Parity information takes up the space equivalent of one drive, leaving most of the space on the RAID drives free for storage. RAID supports three levels as well as a simple linear implementation (see Table 29-13).

Note

Most distributions allow you to create and format RAID drives during installation. At that time, you can create your RAID partitions and devices.

This section will discuss Linux software RAID devices as they are implemented using the RAID tools (see Table 29-14). A RAID device is called an **md** device because it uses the MD driver. These devices are already defined on your Linux system in the **/etc/dev** directory, starting with **md0**. **/dev/md0** is the first RAID device, and **/dev/md1** is the second, and so on. Each RAID device, in turn, will use hard disk partitions,

RAID Levels	Description
0	Implements disk stripping across drives with no redundancy.
1	Implements a high level of redundancy. Each drive is treated as a mirror for all data.
5	Implements a data reconstruction capability using parity information distributed across all drives. The parity information takes up the equivalent of one drive.
linear	Simply treats RAID hard drives as one virtual drive with no stripping, mirroring, or parity reconstruction.

Table 29-13. *RAID Levels*

Tool	Description
mkraid	Creates (configures) RAID devices from a set of block devices, initializing them.
raidstart	Activates RAID devices.
raid0start	Activates older non-persistent linear and RAID 0 RAID devices.
raidstop	Turns off a RAID device, unconfiguring it.

Table 29-14. *RAID Tools*

where each partition contains an entire hard disk. These partitions are usually referred to as RAID disks, whereas a RAID device is an array of the RAID disks its uses.

The term "device" can be confusing as it is also used to refer to the particular hard disk partitions that make up a RAID device. In fact, a RAID device is an array of hard disk partitions, with each partition taking up an entire hard disk. You can think of a RAID device as consisting of a set (array) of hard disks (devices).

If you created your RAID devices and their partitions during the installation process, you should already have working RAID devices. Your RAID devices will be configured in the **/etc/raidtab** file, and the status of your RAID devices will be listed in the **/proc/mdstat** file. You can manually start or stop your RAID devices with the **`raidstart`** and **`raidstop`** commands. The **`-a`** option will operate on all of them, though you can specify particular devices if you want.

Creating and installing a new RAID device involves the following steps:

1. Make sure that your kernel supports the kind of RAID device you are creating.
2. If you have not already done so, create the RAID disks (partitions) you will use for your RAID device.
3. Configure your RAID device (**/dev/md***n*) in the **/etc/raidtab** file, specifying the RAID disks to use.
4. Create your RAID device with **`mkraid`**.
5. Activate the RAID device with **`raidstart`**.
6. Create a file system on the RAID device (**`mke2fs`**) and then mount it.

To add new RAID devices or to create them in the first place, you will need to manually create the hard disk partitions they will use and then configure RAID devices to use those partitions. To create a hard disk partition for use in a RAID array, you use fdisk and specify **fd** as the file system type. You invoke fdisk with the device name of the hard disk you want to create the partition on. Be sure to specify **fd** as the partition type. The following example will invoke fdisk for the hard disk **/dev/hdb** (the second hard disk on the primary IDE connection).

```
fdisk /dev/hdb
```

Though technically partitions, these hard disk devices are referred to as disks in RAID configuration documentation and files, so that is how they will be referred to from this point on.

Once you have your disks, you then need to configure RAID devices to use them. RAID devices are configured in the **/etc/raidtab** file. Here you create a **raiddev** entry for each RAID device and specify which disks they will use. **raiddev** specifies the name of the RAID device you are configuring, such as **/dev/md0** for the first RAID device.

```
raiddev   /dev/md0
```

You then specify the level for the RAID device such as 0, 4, or 5 (**raidlevel**). You then add any options you may need along with the list of disks making up the RAID array. A disk is defined with the **device** entry, and its position in the RAID array with the **raid-disk** option. The configuration directives and options are listed in Table 29-15. A sample entry for the **/etc/raidtab** file is shown here.

```
raiddev /dev/md0
        raid-level             5
        nr-raid-disks          3
        nr-spare-disks         1
        persistent-superblock  1
        chunk-size             4
        parity-algorithm       left-symmetric

        device                 /dev/hdb1
        raid-disk              0
        device                 /dev/hdc1
        raid-disk              1
        device                 /dev/hdd1
        raid-disk              0
```

Directives and Options	Description
raiddev *device*	Starts a configuration section for a particular RAID device.
raid-level *num*	The RAID level for the RAID device, such as 0, 1, 4, 5, and –1 (linear).
device *disk-device*	The disk device (partition) to be added to the RAID array. The number of device entries specified for a RAID device must match that specified by **nr-raid-disk**.
nr-raid-disks *count*	Number of RAID devices in an array. Each RAID device section must have this directive. Maximum limit is 12 (256 experimental).
nr-spare-disks *count*	Number of spare devices in the array. Used only for RAID 4 and RAID 5. Kernel must be configured to allow the automatic addition of new RAID disks as needed. Can add and remove spare disks with **raidhotadd** and **raidhotremove**.
persistent-superblock *0/1*	Specifies whether a newly created RAID array should use a persistent superblock. Used to help the kernel safely detect the RAID array. RAID array information is kept in a superblock on each RAID member.
chunk-size *size*	Sets the stripe size to size bytes, in powers of 2.
device *devpath*	Adds the most recently defined device to the list of devices which make up the RAID system.
raid-disk *index*	Inserts the most recently defined RAID device at the specified position in the RAID array.
spare-disk *index*	Inserts the most recently defined RAID device as a spare device at the specified position in the RAID array.

Table 29-15. *raidtab Options*

Directives and Options	Description
`parity-disk` *index*	The most recently defined device is used as the parity device, placing it at the end of the RAID array.
`parity-algorithm` *algoritm*	For RAID 5 devices, specifies the parity algorithm to use: left-asymmetric, right-asymmetric, left-symmetric, or right-symmetric.
`failed-disk` *index*	The most recently defined device is added to a RAID array as a failed device at the specified position.

Table 29-15. *raidtab Options* (continued)

The previous example configures the RAID device **/dev/md0** as a RAID 5 (**`raid-level`** 5) device. There are three disks (partitions) that make up this RAID array, **/dev/hdb1**, **/dev/hdc1**, and **/dev/hdd1**, of which **/dev/hdb1** is the first and **/dev/hdc1** is the second. There is one spare disk, **/dev/hdd1**. There are three RAID disks altogether (**`nr-raid-disks`**) and one spare partition (**`nr-spare-disks`**). The RAID file system uses persistent superblocks (**`persistent-superblock`**) to hold file system configuration information. The **`parity-algorithm`** option is used for RAID 5 devices to specify the type of parity algorithm to use for parity restoration, in this example, left-symmetric.

Once you have configured your RAID devices in the **/etc/raidtab** file, you then use the **`mkraid`** command to create your RAID devices. **`mkraid`** takes as its argument the name of the RAID device, such as **/dev/md0** for the first RAID device. It then locates its entry in the **/etc/raidtab** file and uses that configuration information to create the RAID file system on that device. You can specify an alternative configuration file with the **`-c`** option, if you wish. **`mkraid`** operates as a kind of **`mkfs`** command for RAID devices, initializing the partitions and creating the RAID file systems. Any data on the partitions making up the RAID array will be erased.

```
mkraid /dev/md0
```

Once you have created your RAID devices, you can then activate them with the **`raidstart`** command. **`raidstart`** makes your RAID file system accessible. **`raidstart`** takes as its argument the name of the RAID device you want to start. The **`-a`** option will activate all RAID devices.

```
raidstart /dev/md0
```

Once the RAID devices are activated, you can then create file systems on the RAID devices and mount those file systems. The following example creates a standard Linux file system on the **/dev/md0** device.

```
mke2fs /dev/md0
```

The user then creates a directory called **/myraid** and mounts the RAID device there.

```
mkdir /myraid
mount /dev/md0 /myraid
```

If you plan to use your RAID device for maintaining your user directories and files, you would mount the RAID device as your **/home** partition. Such a mountpoint might normally be used if you created your RAID devices when you installed your system. To transfer your current home directories to a RAID device, first back them up on another partition, and then mount your RAID device, copying your home directories to it.

If you decide to change your RAID configuration or add new devices, you first have to deactivate your currently active RAID devices. To deactivate a RAID device, you use the **`raidstop`** command. Be sure to close any open files and unmount any file systems on the device first.

```
umount /dev/md0
raidstop /dev/md0
```

The **`raidhotadd`** and **`raidhotremove`** commands are used to add and remove partitions from an active RAID array. You use **`raidhotadd`** to add a spare partition and **`raidhotremove`** to remove any partitions that have failed.

Note *__`raidstop`__, __`raidhotadd`__, and __`raidhotremove`__ are simply links to the `raidstart` command. They run the __`raidstart`__ command with certain options.*

The Complete Reference

Chapter 30

Devices and Printers

All devices, such as printers, terminals, and CD-ROMs, are connected to your Linux operating system through special files called *device files*. Such a file contains all the information your operating system needs to control the specified device. This design introduces great flexibility. The operating system is independent of the specific details for managing a particular device; the specifics are all handled by the device file. The operating system simply informs the device what task it is to perform, and the device file tells it how. If you change devices, you only have to change the device file, not the whole system.

To install a device on your Linux system, you need a device file for it, software configuration such as provided by a configuration tool, and kernel support—usually supplied by a module or already built into the kernel. An extensive number of device files are already set up for different kinds of devices. You usually only need to choose one of these. For kernel support, you may have to load a kernel module or recompile the kernel, both simple procedures. In most cases, support is already built into the kernel. Configuration of your device may be provided by desktop configuration tools such as the Gnome Control Center or distribution configuration tools such as Yast and the Mandrake Control Center.

Printers are one of the most commonly installed devices. Though printer installation is almost automatic on most Linux distributions, it helps to understand the underlying process. In a fairly recent development, the Common Unix Print System (CUPS) offers an alternative to the older Linux line printer software. CUPS aims to run a printer off an independent print server instead of as a device attached to a particular system.

Device Files

The name of a device file is designed to reflect the task of the device. Printer device files begin with **lp** for "line print." Because you could have more than one printer connected to your system, the particular printer device files are distinguished by two or more numbers or letters following the prefix **lp**, such as **lp0**, **lp1**, **lp2**. The same is true for terminal device files. They begin with the prefix **tty**, for "teletype," and are further distinguished by numbers or letters such as **tty0**, **tty1**, **ttyS0**, and so on. You can obtain a complete listing of the current device filenames and the devices for which they are used from the **kernel.org** Web site at **http://www.kernel.org/pub/linux/docs/device-list/devices.txt**.

All of these filenames will be implemented as device files in your **/dev** directory. Here you can find printer, CD-ROM, hard drive, SCSI, and sound device files, along with many others. Certain link files bear common device names that are often linked to the actual device file used. For example, a **/dev/cdrom** symbolic link links to the actual device used for your CD-ROM. If your CD-ROM is an IDE device, it may use the device file **hdc**. In this case, **/dev/cdrom** would be a link to **/dev/hdc**. In effect, **/dev/cdrom** is another name for **/dev/hdc**. You can use **/dev/cdrom** to reference your CD-ROM's device file, instead of **/dev/hdc**. A **/dev/modem** link file also exists for your modem. If your modem is connected to the second serial port, its device file would be **/dev/ttyS1**. In this case, **/dev/modem** would be a link to that device file. Applications can then use **/dev/modem** to access your modem, instead of having to know the actual device file used. A listing of commonly used device links is shown in Table 30-1.

Note *You will notice that there are no entries for the Ethernet devices in the* ***/dev*** *file, such as* ***eth0*** *or* ***eth1****. That is because these are really aliases for kernel modules defined in the* ***/etc/modules.conf*** *file, or devices handled by the kernel directly. They are not device files.*

Two types of devices are implemented in Linux: block and character. A *block device,* such as a hard disk, transmits data a block at a time. A *character device,* such as a printer or modem, transmits data one character at a time, or rather as a continuous stream of data, not as separate blocks. Device driver files for character devices have a *c* as the first character in the permissions segment displayed by the **ls** command. Device driver files for block devices have a *b*. In the next example, **lp0** (the printer) is a character device and **hda1** (the hard disk) is a block device:

```
# ls -l hda1 lp0
brw-rw---- 1 root disk 3, 1 Sep 7 1994 hda1
crw-r----- 1 root daemon 6, 0 Dec 31 1979 lp0
```

Link	Description
/dev/mouse	Current mouse device
/dev/tape	Current tape device
/dev/cdrom	Current CD-ROM device
/dev/cdwriter	Current CD-writer device
/dev/scanner	Current scanner device
/dev/modem	Current dial-out device, modem port
/dev/root	Current root file system
/dev/swap	Current swap device

Table 30-1. *Device Links*

Although most distributions include an extensive set of device files already set up for you, you can create your own. You use the **mknod** command to create a device file, either a character or block type. The **mknod** command has the following syntax:

```
mknod options device device-type major-num minor-num
```

The device type can be either *b*, *c*, *p*, or *u*. As already mentioned, the *b* indicates a block device, and *c* is for a character device. The *u* is for an unbuffered character device, and the *p* is for a FIFO device. Devices of the same type often have the same name, for example, serial interfaces all have the name: **ttyS**. Devices of the same type are then uniquely identified by a number attached to the name. This number has two components: the major number and the minor number. Devices may further have the same major number, but if so, the minor number is always different. This major and minor structure is designed to deal with situations in which several devices may be dependent on one larger device, such as several modems connected to the same I/O card. All would have the same major number that would reference the card, but each modem would have a unique minor number. Both the minor and major numbers are required for block and character devices (*b*, *c*, and *u*). They are not used for FIFO devices, however.

For example, Linux systems usually provide device files for three parallel ports (**lp0–2**). If you need more, you can use the **mknod** command to create a new one. Printer devices are character devices and must be owned by the root and daemon. The permissions for printer devices are read and write for the owner and the group, 660 (see Chapter 11 for a discussion of file permissions). The major device number is set to 6, while the minor device number is set to the port number of the printer, such as 0 for LPT1 and 1 for LPT2. Once the device is created, you use **chown** to change its ownership to **root.daemon**. In the next example, a parallel printer device is made on a fourth parallel port, **/dev/lp3**. The **-m** option specifies the permissions—in this case, 660. The device is a character device, as indicated by the *c* argument following the device name. The major number is 6, and the minor number is 3. If you were making a device at **/dev/lp4**, the major number would still be 6, but the minor number would be 4. Once the device is made, the **chown** command then changes the ownership of the parallel printer device to **root.daemon**. Be sure to check if a spool directory has been created for your device. If not, you need to make one.

```
# mknod -m 660 /dev/lp3 c 6 3
# chown root.daemon /dev/lp3
```

Valid device names along with their major and minor numbers are listed in the **devices.txt** file located in the documentation directory for the kernel source code, **/usr/src/linux**. When creating a device, you use the major and minor numbers as well as the device name prefix for the particular kind of device you are creating. Most of these devices are already created for you and are listed in the **/etc/dev** directory.

Device Information: /proc

The **/proc** file system (see Chapter 29) maintains special information files for your devices. The **/proc/devices** file lists all your installed character and block devices along with their major numbers. IRQs, DMAs, and I/O ports currently used for devices are listed in the **interrupts**, **dma**, and **ioports** files, respectively. Certain files list information covering several devices, such as **pci**, which lists all your PCI devices, and **sound**, which lists all your sound devices. The **sound** file will list detailed information about your sound card. Several subdirectories, such as **net**, **ide**, and **scsi**, contain information files for different devices. Table 30-2 lists several device-related **/proc** files (see Chapter 29 for other entries).

The Line Printer server: LPRng

Printers are installed and managed by print servers. Currently, there are two in common use, the Line Printer, Next Generation (LPRng) and the Common Unix Printing System (CUPS). LPRng is described here. LPRng is an enhanced version of the Berkeley Line Printer Daemon (LPD) **lpd** and associated **lpr** applications. It features a wide range of capabilities that include security measures and access to remote printers. Many of the commands are the same as those used by LPD on a standard Unix system. The Linux printer server program is called **lpd**, the line printer daemon. Printers are installed to run under **lpd**, which then handles print jobs for them both locally and from remote sources. Though **lpd** is called the line printer daemon, it is designed to manage any kind of

File	Description
/proc/devices	List of the device drivers configured for the currently running kernel
/proc/dma	Displays the DMA channels currently used
/proc/interrupts	Displays the IRQs (interrupts) in use
/proc/ioports	Shows the I/O ports in use
/proc/pci	Lists PCI devices
/proc/sound	Lists sound devices
/proc/scsi	Directory for SCSI devices
/proc/ide	Directory for IDE devices
/proc/net	Directory for network devices

Table 30-2. *Proc Device Information Files*

printer, not just line printers. You should think of it as a general-purpose print server capable of handling laser, inkjet, postscript, and dot-matrix printers. You can find out more information about printing in Linux at **www.linuxprinting.org**. LPRng also features a companion IFHP filter package which provides hardware-level support for postscript, PCL, and text printers, among others (**www.astart.com/lprng**).

Printers can be attached directly to your system or attached to other systems on your network. A printer attached directly to your system is referred to as a local printer. For example, a local printer would be a printer connected to your parallel port on your PC. A remote printer would be one connected directly to another system on your network. A remote printer could also be one that is designed to operate as its own host on a network, accessible directly by other systems on the network. You could even have printers connected to a single system operating just as a print server that then manages access to them. Access to both local and remote printers is managed by the **lpd** daemon. Requests are submitted to the **lpd** daemon along with the print job. The **lpd** daemon then spools the print job, making its own copy, and then sends that job to the specified printer.

The **lpd** daemon was installed and configured on your Linux system during installation. **lpd** is run as a standalone process by the **lpd** startup script in the **/etc/rc.d/init.d** directory. You can use the **service** command on this script to start, stop, and restart the daemon.

```
service lpd restart
```

lpd makes use of two configuration files: **lpd.conf** and **lpd.perms**. **lpd.conf** contains general **lpd** configuration commands. You use **lpd.perms** to set up rules by which you can restrict access to the **lpd** server. Here you can deny access by certain hosts, users, or even networks.

Requests to print documents are performed by print clients such as **lpr**. When a document is submitted for printing, it becomes a print job that is placed on a queue for the printer it was sent to. While the job is on the queue waiting to print, you can check its status and even remove it from the queue, canceling the job. The **lpq** client lets you check a print queue, **lpc** allows you to make changes to it, and **lprm** can be used to remove a print job from a queue.

Installing Printers

To use any printer, it first has to be installed on a Linux system that is on your network. A local printer is installed directly on your own system. This involves creating an entry for the printer in the **/etc/printcap** file that defines the kind of printer it is along with other features such as the device file and spool directory it uses. Installing a printer is fairly simple: determine which device file to use for the printer, and place printer configuration entries for it in your **/etc/printcap** file. You can use several configuration tools to enable you to set up and configure your printer easily. Mandrake provides Printerdrake, and Red Hat provides the printconf utility. For most distributions, printer configuration is a part of their centralized configuration utility, such as the Mandrake Control Center and SuSE's Yast Control Center. KDE also provides its own K Printer System utility.

Linux creates three device names for parallel printers automatically during installation: **lp0**, **lp1**, and **lp2**. (Most systems currently use **lp1**.) The number used in these names corresponds to a parallel port on your PC. **lp0** references the LPT1 parallel port, usually located at address 0x03bc, **lp1** references the LPT2 parallel port located at 0x0378, and **lp2** references LPT3 at address 0x0278. If you are unsure at which address your parallel port is located, you can use the **`msd.exe`** command on your DOS system to find it. Serial printers use the serial ports, referenced by the device files **ttyS0**, **ttyS1**, **ttyS2**, and so on. For a detailed explanation of printer installation, see the Printing-HOWTO file in **/usr/share/doc/HOWTO**.

Note *If you cannot find the drivers for your printer, you may be able to download them from www.linuxprinting.org. The site maintains an extensive listing of drivers.*

When your system prints a file, it makes use of special directories called *spool directories.* A print job is a file to be printed. When you print a file to a printer, a copy of it is made and placed in a spool directory set up for that printer. The location of the spool directory is obtained from the printer's entry in the **/etc/printcap** file. On Linux, the spool directory is located at **/var/spool/lpd** under a directory with the name of the printer. For example, the spool directory for the myepson printer would be located at **/var/spool/lpd/myepson**. The spool directory contains several files for managing print jobs. Some will bear as their extension the name of the printer. For example, the myepson printer will have the files **control.myepson** which provides printer queue control, and **active.myepson** for the active print job, as well as **log.myepson** which is the log file.

The **/etc/printcap** file holds entries for each printer connected to your system. A *printcap entry* holds information, such as the pathname for a printer's spool directory and the device name of the printer port the printer uses. The first field in a **printcap** entry is a list of possible names for the printer. These are names you can make up yourself, and you can add others if you want. Each name is separated by a |. You use these names to identify the printer when entering various printer commands or options, such as the **`-P`** option. These names are also used for special shell variables, such as the **PRINTER** variable, used in many initialization scripts.

The fields following the list of names set different fields for your printer. The fields have two-letter names and are usually assigned a value using **=**. These assignments are separated by colons. Three of the more important fields are **lp**, **sd**, and **of**. The **lp** field is set to the device name the printer uses. The **sd** field is set to the pathname of the spool directory, and **of** is set to the particular filter used for this printer. Some have Boolean values and simply list the field name with no assignment for a true value.

You can find a complete listing of the **printcap** fields in the **printcap** Man pages: **`man printcap`**. An example of a **printcap** entry follows.

```
myprinter|myepson:\
        :sh:\
        :ml=0:\
        :mx=0:\
        :sd=/var/spool/lpd/myprinter:\
        :lp=/dev/lp0:\
        :lpd_bounce=true:\
        :if=/usr/share/printconf/mf_wrapper:
```

Instead of making your own entries in the **/etc/printcap** *file, you can use a printer configuration tool such as Mandrake's Printerdrake, SuSE's Yast, Red Hat's printconf, Linuxconf, or Webmin to make them for you automatically.*

To install a remote (network or remote host–attached) printer, you place remote entries for the printer host and device in the printer's **/etc/printcap** file entry. An **:rm** entry identifies the remote host that controls the remote printer, and an **:rp** entry specifies the device name of the remote printer. In the following example, the remote printer is located at **rabbit.mytrek.com** and is called **lp1**:

```
:rm=rabbit.mytrek.com
:rp=lp1
```

Configuring lpd

LPRng allows you to configure your **lpd** server, providing support found in other servers such as secure access or setting global defaults. There are only two configuration files to manage, and both are heavily commented. Your distribution will normally provide basic versions for both. An extensive set of features are available, letting you create servers with powerful and complex capabilities.

General Configuration: lpd.conf

The general configuration for the **lpd** print server is handled in the **/etc/lpd.conf** file. Here you can specify features that apply to all printers and print management. You should think of these more as default features, as any of them can be overridden in a printer's **printcap** entry.

The **lpd.conf** file installed with LPRng will hold an extensive list of configuration parameters. They will all be commented out, using preceding **#** signs. A comment describing the parameter precedes each. The entry itself lists the default value given to the parameters, preceding the entry with the term "default". The entry for the connect_timeout parameter is shown here:

```
# Purpose: connection timeout for remote printers
# default connect_timeout=10 (INTEGER)
```

To create your own timeout entry, it is best to add your own entry below, as shown here. Notice that the preceding **#** and the term "default" are missing from the new entry. The connection timeout for remote printers is now set at 20. This can be overridden by a printer's **printcap** file entry.

```
# Purpose: connection timeout for remote printers
# default connect_timeout=10 (INTEGER)
connect_timeout=20
```

Parameters can also be flags that you can turn on or off. An off flag is noted with an attached **@** sign. In the following example, the allow_user_logging parameter is a flag that will allow users to request login information. By default it is turned off. The following example turns it on:

```
# Purpose: allow users to request logging info using lpr
-mhost%port
# default allow_user_logging@ (FLAG off)
allow_user_logging
```

Printer Security: lpd.perms

LPRng provides access control rules for controlling access your print server, and thereby the printers it controls, by remote users. These are placed in the **lpd.perms** file and can be used to refuse print services to specific hosts or users. Such rules consist of an action and a set of keys (see Table 30-3). The keys specify criteria to be met, and if met, their associated action is taken. In each rule you have one action and one or more keys. If there are several keys, all their criteria must be met for the action to take place. An example of a key would be to specify the IP address of a host. In addition, you have to specify the kind of service that is being requested, such as a printing or connection request. The action is usually either ACCEPT or REJECT. Keys operate as flags or variables. To specify a host you would assign the address to the HOST key, using an assignment operator. For a user, you would use USER, and for IP addresses, IFIP. The kind of service is specified by the SERVICE key. For a printing request, the value you assign is the **lpd** code **P**. The following example specifies a host as the key and will REJECT any request from that address:

```
REJECT SERVICE=P HOST=192.168.0.57
```

A special DEFAULT rule is designed to match any request. You can then specify the default action to take. The following entry accepts any request. A REJECT action would reject any request.

```
DEFAULT ACCEPT
```

Key	Description
SERVICE	Type of service
USER	Users specified in a print job control file
HOST	Hosts specified in a print job control file
IP	IP address specified in a print job control file
IFIP	IP address of requests origin (interface IP address)
GROUP	Checks to see if user is part of specified group
REMOTEHOST	Hostname or IP address of remote host specified in a printer command or derived from network information
REMOTEPORT	Port number of remote connection
REMOTEUSER	Remote user specified in a printer command or derived from network information
SAMEUSER	Checks to see if the user issuing a command for a job (REMOTEUSER) is the same as the user that created it (USER), as listed in the job's control file
SAMEHOST	Checks to see if the host issuing a command for a job (REMOTEHOST) is the same as the host that created it (HOST), as listed in the job's control file
PRINTER	Specified printer
SERVER	Request originated from print server
AUTH	Enable authentication
AUTHTYPE	Type of authentication
AUTHUSER	Authenticated userID
AUTHFROM	Authenticated ID of requestor

Table 30-3. *lpd.perm Keys*

The **lpd.perms** file consists of a set of rules that are sequentially evaluated until a match is found. The DEFAULT action rule should be the last rule and is normally one to accept any requests. In other words, any request that is not matched by the previous rules is accepted. Normally you would set up rules to reject certain requests, such as requests for specific hosts. Most requests would not match these rules and should fall through to the DEFAULT action, which would ACCEPT them.

SERVICE key values differ depending on type of request submitted. These can range from a simple connection request by a remote server to a removal of a print job.

The print clients like **lpr**, **lpq**, **lprm**, and **lpc** will make different kinds of service requests. **lpq** will make a request for queue information that has the key value Q for SERVICE. **lprm** will issue a removal request indicated by a key value M. The different service values for the SERVICE key are shown here:

Key Value	**Service Requests**
X	Connection request
R	Job spool
P	Printing
Q	Queue status information (**lpq**)
M	Removal request (**lprm**)
C	Printer control (**lpc**)
S	Printer status (**lpc**)

A further distinction is made between keys that reference information in a print job's control file and that provided by a print command like `lpc` or `lpq`. For example, the HOST key references hostnames in a print job's control file, allowing you to reject or accept print job requests. The REMOTEHOST key will reference hostnames derived from the remote connection directly for all types of requests except for an **lpr** request. Check the key table in the **lpd.perm** or **lpd** Man page for a detailed breakdown of requests and the type of information they reference. As another example, SAMEUSER will match the user indicated in a print request for a print job, such as status or removal, against the user in the control file for that print job, to make sure they are the same user.

The settings for the **/etc/lpd.perms** file are shown here. The file itself includes detailed documentation as well as several commented recommended entries.

```
# allow root on server to control jobs
ACCEPT SERVICE=C SERVER REMOTEUSER=root
# allow anybody to get server, status, and printcap
ACCEPT SERVICE=C LPC=lpd,status,printcap
# reject all others
REJECT SERVICE=C
#
# allow same user on originating host to remove a job
ACCEPT SERVICE=M SAMEHOST SAMEUSER
# allow root on server to remove a job
ACCEPT SERVICE=M SERVER REMOTEUSER=root
REJECT SERVICE=M
# all other operations allowed
DEFAULT ACCEPT
```

The Print Queue Clients

As noted previously, printing on your system is handled by a print daemon called **lpd**, which is constantly running, waiting for print jobs and then managing their printing procedures. The **lpd** daemon places its print jobs on print queues. Once on the queue, there are several clients you can use to manage print jobs such as **lpq**, which lists a print queue, **lpc**, which can reorder it, and **lprm**, which can remove a print job, effectively canceling it. Documents are initially submitted to **lpd** with the **`lpr`** print command.

The **lpr** client submits a job, and **lpd** then takes it in turn and places it on the appropriate print queue. **lpr** takes as its argument the name of a file. You can also feed data to **lpr** through the standard input, piping in the data to be printed from another operation. The **`-P`** option enables you to specify a particular printer. In the next example, the user first prints the file **preface**, then uses the **`cat`** command to generate combined output of the files **intro** and **digest**. This is piped to the **`lpr`** command, which then prints it. Finally, the user prints the file **report** to the printer with the name myepson.

```
$ lpr preface
$ cat intro digest | lpr
$ lpr -P myepson report
```

If no printer is specified for the **`lpr`** *command, the default printer is used. This is determined by either the default_printer entry in* ***lpd.conf****, the PRINTER environment variable, or the first entry in the* ***/etc/printcap*** *file.*

You can also print directly to the printer by simply redirecting output to the printer's device file. This does not place anything on the print queue. The print operation becomes a command to be immediately executed. However, your system is occupied until the file completes printing. The following example uses this technique to print the **report** file to a printer connected to device **lp1**:

```
$ cat report > /dev/lp1
```

To manage the printing jobs on your printer or printers, you can use either **Klpq** or the LPRng clients **lpc**, **lpq**, and **lprm**. **Klpq** is a KDE desktop utility and labeled the Print Job Administration tool (see Figure 30-1). With **Klpq**, you can list the print jobs for a printer, remove a print job, and move a print job to the top of the queue. You can also disable printing for a printer. To have the print queue listing automatically updated, you can set an update frequency in the Options menu.

You can use **lpc** to enable or disable printers, reorder their print queues, and reexecute configuration files. To use **lpc**, enter the command **`lpc`** at the shell prompt. You are then given an **`LPC>`** prompt at which you can enter **lpc** commands to manage your printers and reorder their jobs. The **`status`** command with the name of the printer displays whether the printer is ready, how many print jobs it has, and so on. The **stop** and **start** commands can stop a printer and start it back up.

```
# lpc
lpc> status hp1
hp1|lp1:
 queuing is enabled
 printing is enabled
 1 entry in spool area
```

You can manage the print queue using the **lpq** and **lprm** commands. The **lpq** command lists the printing jobs currently on the print queue. With the **-P** option and the printer name, you can list the jobs for a particular printer. If you specify a username, you can list the print jobs for that user. With the **-l** option, **lpq** displays detailed information about each job. If you want information on a specific job, simply use that job's ID number with **lpq**. To check the status of a printer you use **lpstat**.

With the **lprm** command, you can remove a printing job from the queue, erasing the job before it can be printed. The **lprm** command takes many of the same options as **lpq**. To remove a specific job, use **lprm** with the job number. To remove all printing jobs for a particular user, enter **lprm** with the username. To remove all printing jobs for a particular printer, use the **-P** option with the printer name.

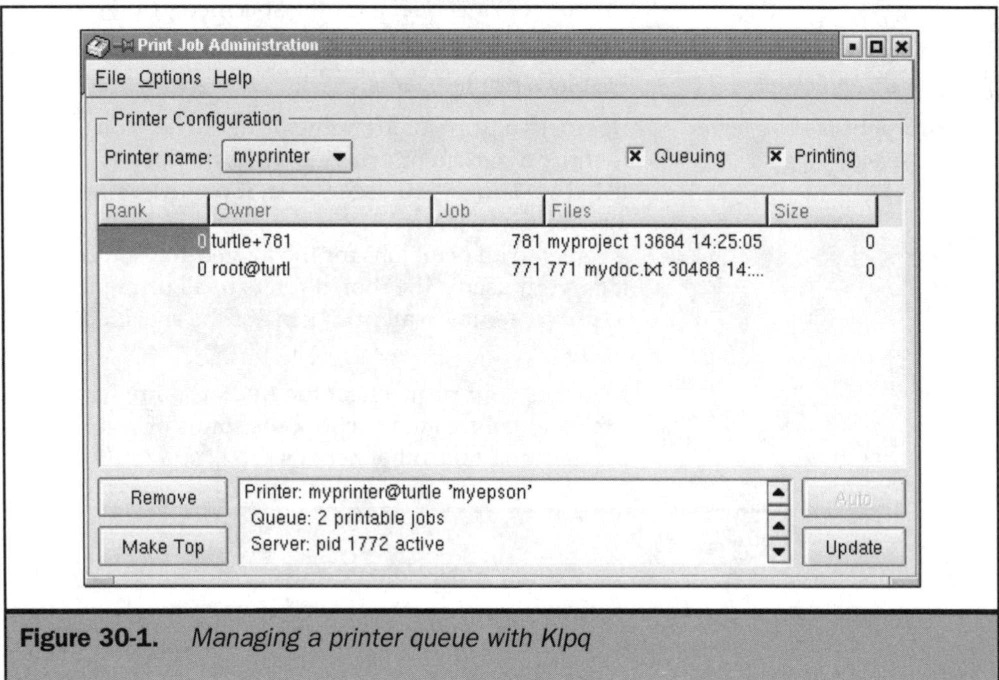

Figure 30-1. *Managing a printer queue with Klpq*

The **lprm** command has a special argument indicated by a hyphen, **-**, that references all print jobs for the user who issues the command. For example, to remove all your own print jobs, enter **lprm -**. If you logged in as the root user, **lprm -** removes all print jobs for all printers and users from the print queue, emptying it completely.

You should not use **lprm** to kill a print job that has already started printing. Instead, you may have to use the **kill** command on the print job process. You can display processes using the **ps -ax** command, and then use **kill** and the number of the process to end it. For a job that is already printing, you see a process for its filter. This is the process to kill. If the process does not end, you can force its termination by using the **-s** option and the kill signal number, 9.

Table 30-4 shows various printer commands; Table 30-5 includes **lpc** commands.

Printer Management	Description
Klpq	KDE print queue management tool.
lpr *options file-list*	Prints a file; copies the file to the printer's spool directory, and places it on the print queue to be printed in turn. **-P***printer* prints the file on the specified printer.
lpq *options*	Displays the print jobs in the print queue. **-P***printer* prints queue for the specified printer. **-l** prints a detailed listing.
lpstat *options*	Displays printer status.
lprm *options Printjob-id* or User-id	Removes a print job from the print queue. You identify a particular print job by its number as listed by **lpq**; if you use *User-id*, it removes all print jobs for that user. **-** refers to all print jobs for the logged-in user. If the logged-in user is the root, it refers to all print jobs. **-P***printer* removes all print jobs for the specified printer.
lpc	Manages your printers. At the **LPC>** prompt, you can enter commands to check the status of your printers and take other actions.

Table 30-4. *Printer Commands*

Commands	Operation
help [*command* ...]	Prints a short description of each command
abort *printers*	Terminates an active spooling daemon on the local host immediately, and then disables printing for the specified printers; use **all** to indicate all printers
clean *printers*	Removes any temporary files, data files, and control files that cannot be printed
disable *printers*	Turns the specified printer queues off; new jobs are not accepted
down *printers message*	Turns the specified printer queue off, disables printing, and puts *message* in the printer status file
enable *printers*	Enables spooling for the listed printers; allows new jobs into the spool queue
quit or **exit**	Exits from **lpc**
restart *printers*	Starts a new printer daemon; used if the printer daemon, **lpd**, dies, leaving jobs yet to be printed
reread	Reads and executes the **lpd.conf** and **lpd.perms** configuration files
start *printers*	Enables printing and starts a spooling daemon for the listed printers
status *printers*	Displays the status of daemons and queues on the local machine
stop *printers*	Stops a spooling daemon after the current job completes and disables printing
topq *printer* [*jobnum* ...] [*user* ...]	Places the jobs in the order listed at the top of the printer queue
up *printers*	Enables everything and starts a new printer daemon; undoes the effects of **down**

Table 30-5. *lpc Commands*

Installing and Managing Printers with CUPS

The Common Unix Printing System (CUPS) is an alternative for LPRng that provides printing services. It is freely available under the GNU Public License. Though now included with most distributions, you can also download the most recent source-code version of CUPS from their Web site at **www.cups.org**. The site also provides detailed documentation on installing and managing printers. Whereas LPRng is derived from the old Berkeley line printer daemon (LPD), CUPS is based on the newer Internet Printing Protocol (IPP). The Internet Printing Protocol is designed to establish a printing standard for the Internet (for more information, see **www.pwg.org/ipp**). Whereas the older LPD-based printing systems focused primarily on line printers, an IPP-based system provides networking, postscript, and Web support. CUPS works like an Internet server and employs a configuration setup much like that of the Apache Web server. Its network support lets clients directly access printers on remote servers, without having to configure the printers themselves. Configuration needs only to be maintained on the print servers.

To install CUPS, you first have to uninstall LPRng. For distributions that use RPM, such as Mandrake, Caldera, and Red Hat, you use the **rpm -e** command to remove those applications. Bear in mind that you will lose your **/etc/printcap** file, so you may want to back up that file before you remove LPRng. You can use the **rpm -i** command to install CUPS.

With the RPM version used by Mandrake and Red Hat, a **cups** startup script is installed in the **/etc/rc.d/init.d** directory. You can start, stop, and restart CUPS using the service command and the **cups** script. When you make changes or install printers, be sure to restart CUPS to have your changes take effect. On Mandrake and Red Hat, you can use the following:

```
service cups restart
```

The easiest way to configure and install printers with CUPS is to use its Web interface. This is a Web browser–based configuration tool like Webmin and SWAT. To start the Web interface, you open a browser like Mozilla and Netscape and enter the following URL:

```
http://localhost:631/admin
```

This displays the initial administration screen where you can manage print jobs and add printers (see Figure 30-2).

You install a printer on CUPS through a series of Web pages, each requesting different information. To install a printer, click the Add Printer button to display a page where you enter the printer name and location. The location is the host to which the printer is connected. In Figure 30-3, the myepson printer is connected to the host **turtle.mytrek.com**.

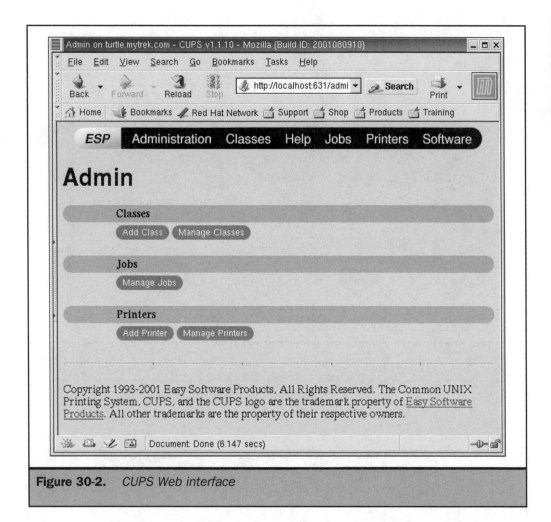

Figure 30-2. *CUPS Web interface*

Subsequent pages will prompt you to enter the model of the printer and driver. These you select from available listings. Once you have added the printer you can configure it. Clicking on the Manage Printers entry in the Administration page will list your installed printers. You can then click on a printer to display a page that will let you control the printer. You can stop the printer, configure its printing, and modify its installation, and even delete the printer. Clicking the Configure Printer button will display a page where you can configure how your printer prints, specifying the resolution or paper size. The printer entry will be displayed as shown in Figure 30-4.

You can perform all administrative tasks from the command line using the **`lpadmin`** *command. See the CUPS documentation for more details.*

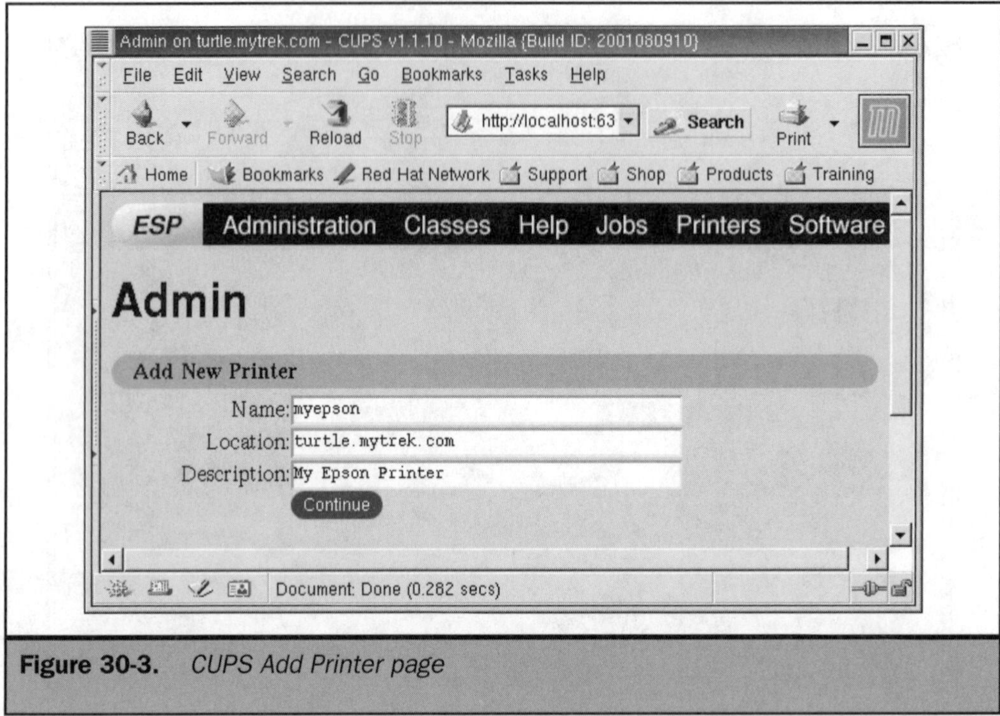

Figure 30-3. *CUPS Add Printer page*

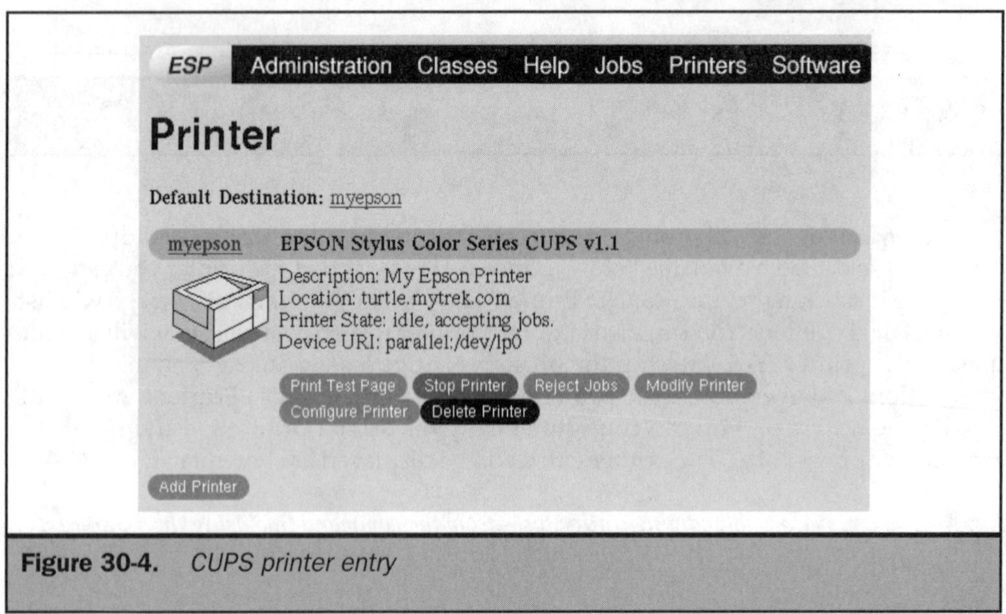

Figure 30-4. *CUPS printer entry*

To install a remote printer that is attached to a Windows system or another Linux system running LPRng or LPD, you specify its location using special URL protocols. For a Windows printer, you will first need to install, configure, and run Samba. CUPS uses Samba to access Windows printers. When you install the Windows printer on CUPS, you specify its location using the URL protocol **smb**. The user allowed to log in to the printer is entered before the hostname and separated by a @ sign. On most configurations this is the **guest** user. The location entry for a Windows printer called myhp attached to a Windows host named **lizard** is shown here. Its Samba share reference would be **//lizard/myhp**.

```
smb://guest@lizard/myhp
```

To enable Samba on CUPS, you will also have to set the printing option in the **/etc/cups/cupsd.conf** file to Samba, as shown here.

```
printing = samba
```

You will also have to link the **smbspool** directory to the CUPS **smb** spool directory.

```
ln -s 'which smbspool`   /usr/cups/backend/smb
```

To access a printer connected to a Linux or Unix system running LPRng, you would use the protocol **lpd** when specifying its location. In the following example, the printer mylaser is connected to the Linux host **rabbit**.

```
lpd://rabbit.mytrek.com/mylaser
```

CUPS features a way to let you select a group of printers to print a job instead of selecting just one. That way, if one printer is busy or down, another printer can be automatically selected to perform the job. Such groupings of printers are called *classes*. Once you have installed your printers you can then group them into different classes. For example, you may want to group all inkjet printers in one class and lasers in another. Or you might want to group printers connected to a printer server in their own class. To create a class, select Classes on the Administration page and enter the name of the class. You can then add printers to it.

CUPS configuration files will be placed in the **/etc/cups** directory. They are listed in Table 30-6. The **classes.conf**, **printers.conf**, and **client.conf** files can be managed by the Web interface. In the **printers.conf** file you will see the configuration information for the different printers you have installed. Any of these files can be edited manually, if you wish.

The CUPS server is configured with the **cupsd.conf** file. Configuration options have to be manually edited. The server is not configured with the Web interface. Your

Filename	Description
classes.conf	Configurations for different printer classes
client.conf	Lists specific option for specified clients
cupsd.conf	Configures the CUPS server, **cupsd**
printers.conf	Printer configurations

Table 30-6. *CUPS Configuration Files*

installation of CUPS will install a commented version of the **cupsd.conf** file, with each option listed, though most commented out. Commented lines are preceded with a # symbol. Each option is documented in detail. The server configuration uses an Apache Web server syntax consisting of a set of directives. As with Apache, several of these directives can group other directives into blocks.

Certain directives allow access controls to be placed on specific locations. These can be printers or resources such as the administrative tool or the spool directories. Location controls are implemented with the Location directive. Allow From and Deny From directives can deny or permit access from specific hosts. CUPS supports both Basic and Digest forms of authentication, specified in the AuthType directive. Basic authentication uses a user and password. For example, to use the Web interface you were prompted to enter the root user and the root user password. Digest authentication makes use of user and password information kept in the CUPS **/etc/cups/passwd.md5** file, using MD5 versions of a user and password for authentication. The AuthClass specifies the class allowed access. The System class includes the root, sys, and system users. The following example shows the Location directive for the **/admin** resource, the administrative tool.

```
<Location /admin>

AuthType Basic
AuthClass System

## Restrict access to local domain
Order Deny,Allow
Deny From All
Allow From 127.0.0.1

#Encryption Required
</Location>
```

Installing and Managing Terminals and Modems

With a multiuser system such as Linux, you might have several users logged in at the same time. Each user would, of course, need their own terminal through which to access the Linux system. The monitor on your PC acts as a special terminal, called the *console,* but you can add other terminals either through the serial ports on your PC or a special multiport card installed on your PC. The other terminals can be standalone terminals or PCs using terminal emulation programs. For a detailed explanation of terminal installation, see the **Term-HOWTO** file in **/usr/share/doc/HOWTO**. A brief explanation is provided here.

The serial ports on your PC are referred to as COM1, COM2, on up to COM4. These serial ports correspond to the terminal devices **/dev/ttyS0** through **/dev/ttyS3**. Note, several of these serial devices may already be used for other input devices such as your mouse, and for communications devices such as your modem. If you have a serial printer, one of these serial devices is already used for that. If you installed a multiport card, you have many more ports from which to choose. For each terminal you add, you must create a character device on your Linux system. As with printers, you use the **mknod** command to create terminal devices. The permissions for a terminal device are 660. *Terminal devices* are character devices with a major number of 4 and minor numbers usually beginning at 64.

Terminal devices are managed by your system using the getty program and a set of configuration files. When your system starts, it reads a list of connected terminals in the **inittab** file and then executes an **/etc/getty** program for each one. The getty program sets up the communication between your Linux system and a specified terminal. It obtains from the **/etc/gettydefs** file certain parameters, such as speed and the login prompt, as well as any special instructions.

```
# Format: <speed># <init flags> # <final flags> #<login
 string>#<next-speed>
# 38400 fixed baud Dumb Terminal entry
DT38400# B38400 CS8 CLOCAL # B38400 SANE -ISTRIP CLOCAL #@S login:
 #DT38400
```

The **/etc/inittab** file holds instructions for your system on how to manage terminal devices. A line in the **/etc/inittab** file has four basic components: an ID, a runlevel, an action, and a process. Terminal devices are identified by ID numbers, beginning with 1 for the first device. The runlevel at which the terminal operates is usually 1. The action is usually *respawn,* which says to run the process continually. The process is a call to **/etc/getty** with the baud rate and terminal device name. The **/etc/ttys** file associates the type of terminal used with a certain device.

The **/etc/termcap** file holds the specifications for different terminal types. These are the different types of terminals users could use to log in to your system. Your **/etc/termcap** file is already filled with specifications for most of the terminals currently produced. An entry in the **/etc/termcap** file consists of various names that can be used for a terminal separated by a | and then a series of parameter specifications, each ending in a colon. You find the name used for a specific terminal type here. You can use more to display your **/etc/termcap** file, and then use a search, `/`, to locate your terminal type. You can set many options for a terminal device. To change these options, use the **`stty`** command instead of changing configuration files directly. The **`stty`** command with no arguments lists the current setting of the terminal.

When a user logs in, having the terminal device initialized using the **`tset`** command is helpful. Usually the **`tset`** command is placed in the user's **.bash_profile** file and is automatically executed whenever the user logs in to the system. You use the **`tset`** command to set the terminal type and any other options the terminal device requires. A common entry of **`tset`** for a **.bash_profile** file follows. The **`-m dialup:`** option prompts the user to enter a terminal type. The type specified here is a default type that is displayed in parentheses. The user presses ENTER to choose the default. The prompt looks like this: **`TERM=(vt100)?`**.

```
eval 'tset -s -Q -m dialup:?vt00'
```

Input Devices

Input devices, such as mice and keyboards, are displayed on several levels. Initial configuration is performed during installation where you select the mouse and keyboard types. You can change that configuration with your administration configuration tools, such as Red Hat Setup or the Mandrake Control Center. Special configurations also exist for mice and keyboard for the X Window System, and for the KDE and Gnome desktops. You select the keyboard layout and language, as well as configure the speed and display of the mouse.

Installing Sound, Network, and Other Cards

For you to install a new card, your kernel must be configured to support it. Support for most cards is provided in the form of modules that can be dynamically loaded in and attached to the kernel, running as its extension. Installing support for a card is usually a simple matter of loading a module that includes the drives for it. For example, drivers for the Sound Blaster sound card are in the module **sb.o**. Loading this module makes your sound card accessible to Linux. Most distributions automatically detect the cards installed on your system and load the needed modules. If you change cards, you may have to load the module you need manually, removing an older conflicting one. For example, if you change your Ethernet card, you may have to unload the module for your previous card and load in the one for your new card. Certain utilities, such as Linuxconf and netcfg, enable you to choose a new Ethernet card and have the module loaded for you. You can, however, load modules manually. The section "Modules" later in this chapter describes this process.

Device files for most cards are already set up for you in the **/dev** directory. For example, the device name for your sound card is **/dev/audio**. The device names for network cards are aliases for network modules instead of device files. For example, the device name for your Ethernet card begins with **eth,** with the numbering starting from 0, as in **eth0** for the first Ethernet card on your system. They will alias the module used for that particular card, for example, a 3Com Etherlink XL card will be the 3c59x network module, whose alias would be **eth0** if it is the first Ethernet card.

Multimedia Devices: Sound, Video, and DVD

Most Linux sound drivers are developed as part of the Open Sound System and freely distributed as OSS/Free. These are installed as part of Linux distributions. The OSS (*Open Sound System*) device drivers are intended to provide a uniform API for all Unix platforms, including Linux. They support Sound Blaster and Windows Sound System compatible sound cards (ISA and PCI). OSS is also available for a nominal fee and features configuration interfaces for device setup. A listing of the different OSS/Free sound devices is provided in Table 30-7. On Red Hat, you can use the sndconfig utility to install most sound cards on Linux. Some sound cards may require more specialized support (see Table 30-8). For sound cards, you can tell what your current sound configuration is by listing the contents of the **/dev/sndstat** file. You can test your card by simply redirecting a sound file to it, as shown here:

```
cat sample.au > /dev/audio.
```

The Linux Musical Instrument Digital Interface (MIDI) and Sound Pages, currently at **www.xdt.com/ar/linux-snd**, hold links to Web and FTP sites for Linux sound drivers for various sound cards. They also include links to sites for Linux MIDI and sound software. Most Linux sound drivers have been developed as part of the Open Sound System and are freely distributed as OSS/Free. These are installed as part of most

Device	Description
/dev/sndstat	Sound driver status
/dev/audio	Audio output device
/dev/dsp	Sound sampling device
/dev/mixer	Control mixer on sound card
/dev/music	High-level sequencer
/dev/sequencer	Low-level sequencer
/dev/midi	Direct MIDI port

Table 30-7. *Sound Devices*

Linux distributions. The OSS device drivers are intended to provide a uniform API for all Unix platforms, including Linux. They support Sound Blaster and Windows Sound System compatible sound cards (ISA and PCI).

The Advanced Linux Sound Architecture (ALSA) project is developing a modular sound driver, API, and configuration manager that aims to be a better alternative to OSS, while maintaining compatibility with it. ALSA is a GNU project and is entirely free; its Web site at **www.alsa-project.org** contains extensive documentation, applications, and drivers. Currently under development are the ALSA sound driver, the ALSA Kernel API, the ALSA library to support application development, and the ALSA manager to provide a configuration interface for the driver. ALSA evolved from the Linux Ultra Sound Project.

The Linux Ultra Sound Project has developed drivers for Gravix Ultrasound sound cards. Although Gravis Ultrasound is supported by OSS/Free, the Linux Ultra Sound Project drivers offer many more features. See Table 30-8 for a listing of sites providing sound drivers. Included are drivers for Turtle Beach sound cards and Sound Blaster AWE native support.

Driver Site	Description
Linux MIDI and Sound Pages	Information and links to Linux Sound projects and site: **www.xdt.com/ar/linux-snd**
Advanced Linux Sound Architecture (ALSA)	The Advanced Linux Sound Architecture project (ALSA) is developed on Linux under the GPL: **www.alsa-project.org**
Open Sound System/Free	The standard Linux sound drivers formerly known as USS/Lite, TASD, and Voxware are now called OSS/Free: **www.opensound.com**
Open Sound System/Linux	OSS/Linux is a commercial version of the Linux sound drivers: **www.opensound.com**
Linux Ultra Sound Project	Drivers for the Gravis Ultrasound: **www.perex.cz/~perex/ultra**
PC Serial Port MIDI Driver	Linux MIDI driver for IBM-PC serial ports: **http://crystal.apana.org.au/ghansper/midiaxis.html**

Table 30-8. *Linux Sound Driver Sites*

Device Name	Type of Device
/dev/video	Video capture interface
/dev/vfx	Video effects interface
/dev/codec	Video codec interface
/dev/vout	Video output interface
/dev/radio	AM/FM radio devices
/dev/vtx	Teletext interface chips
/dev/vbi	Data services interface

Table 30-9. *Video Devices*

Device names used for TV, video, and DVD devices are listed in Table 30-9. Drivers for DVD and TV decoders have been developed (see Table 30-10). mga4linux is developing video support for the Matrox Multimedia cards like the Marvel G200. The General ATI TV and Overlay Software (GATOS) has developed drivers for the currently unsupported features of ATI video cards, specifically TV features. The BTTV Driver

Project	Description
linuxtv.org	Links to video, TV, and DVD sites
video4linux 2	Video for Linux Two
LiViD	The Linux Video and DVD Project **www.linuxvideo.org**
LSDVD	LSDVD Linux Player Project **www.csh.rit.edu/projects/lsdvd/**
mga4linux	Driver for Matrox Multimedia Cards **marvel.sourceforge.net/**
GATOS	The General ATI TV and Overlay Software **gatos.sourceforge.net**
BTTV	BTTV drivers for cards with Booktree video chips **www.sourceforge.net**
DVD DXR2	Drivers for Creative DVD DXR2 decoders **opensource.creative.com**.

Table 30-10. *Video, TV, and DVD Projects and Drivers*

Project has developed drivers for the Booktree video chip. Creative Labs sponsors Linux drivers for the Creative line of DVD DXR2 decoders (**opensource.creative.com**).

Modules

Beginning with Linux kernel 2.0, the Linux kernel adopted a modular structure. In earlier kernel versions, support for specific features and devices had to be included directly into the kernel program. Adding support for a new device—say, a new kind of sound card—required you to create a new version of your kernel program that included the code for supporting that device. This involved a sometimes lengthy configuration, followed by compiling and installing the new kernel program, as well as making sure it was called properly when your system booted up.

As an alternative to this rebuilding of the kernel, Linux now supports the use of modules. *Modules* are components of the Linux kernel that can be loaded and attached to it as needed. To add support for a new device, you can now simply instruct a kernel to load its module. In some cases, you may have to recompile only that module to provide support for your device. The use of modules has the added advantage of reducing the size of the kernel program. The kernel can load modules in memory only as they are needed. For example, the module for the PPP network interface used for a modem only needs to be used when you connect to an ISP.

The modules your system needs are usually determined during installation, based on the kind of configuration information you provided. For example, if your system uses an Ethernet card whose type you specified during installation, the system loads the module for that card. You can, however, manually control what modules are to be loaded for your system. In effect, this enables you to customize your kernel whatever way you want. You can use several commands, configuration tools, and daemons to manage kernel modules. The 2.4 Linux kernel includes the Kernel Module Loader (Kmod), which has the capability to load modules automatically as they are needed. In addition, several tools enable you to load and unload modules manually, if you must. The Kernel Module Loader uses certain kernel commands to perform the task of loading or unloading modules. The **modprobe** command is a general-purpose command that calls **insmod** to load modules and **rmmod** to unload them. These commands are listed in Table 30-11. Options for particular modules, general configuration, and even specific module loading are specified in the **/etc/modules.conf** file. You can use this file to automatically load and configure modules. You can also specify modules to be loaded at the boot prompt or in **lilo.conf** or **grub.conf** (see Chapters 3 and 26).

The filename for a module has the extension **.o**. Modules reside in the **/lib/modules/***version* directory, where *version* is the version number for your current module. The directory for the 2.4 kernel is **/lib/modules/2.4**. As you install new kernels on your system, new module directories are generated for them. One trick to access the directory for the current kernel is to use the **uname -r** command to generate the kernel version number. This command needs to have backquotes.

```
cd /lib/modules/`uname -r`
```

In this directory, modules for the kernel reside in the kernel directory. And within the kernel directory are several subdirectories, including the **drivers** directory that holds subdirectories for modules like the sound drivers or video drivers. These subdirectories serve to categorize your modules, making them easier to locate. For example, the **kernel/drivers/net** directory holds modules for your Ethernet cards, and the **kernel/drivers/sound** directory contains sound card modules.

Managing Modules with /etc/modules.conf

As noted previously, there are several commands you can use to manage modules. The **`lsmod`** command lists the modules currently loaded into your kernel, and **`modinfo`** provides information about particular modules. Though you can use the **`insmod`** and **`rmmod`** commands to load or unload modules, you should only use **`modprobe`** for these tasks. See Table 30-11 for kernel module commands. It is often the case, however, that a given module requires other modules to be loaded. For example, the module for the Sound Blaster sound card, sb.o, requires the sound.o module to be loaded also. Instead of manually trying to determine what modules a given module depends on,

Command	Description
`lsmod`	Lists modules currently loaded.
`insmod`	Loads a module into the kernel. Does not check for dependencies.
`rmmod`	Unloads a module currently loaded. Does not check for dependencies.
`modinfo`	Display information about a module: **`-a`** (author) **`-d`** (description) **`-p`** (module parameters) **`-f`** (module filename) **`-v`** (module version)
`depmod`	Creates a dependency file listing all other modules on which the specified module may rely.
`modprobe`	Loads a module with any dependent modules it may also need. Uses the file of dependency listings generated by **`depmod`**: **`-r`** (unload a module) **`-l`** (list modules)

Table 30-11. *Kernel Module Commands*

you use the **depmod** command to detect the dependencies for you. The **depmod** command generates a file that lists all the modules on which a given module depends. The **depmod** command generates a hierarchical listing, noting what modules should be loaded first and in what order. Then, to load the module, you use the **modprobe** command using that file. **modprobe** reads the file generated by **depmod** and loads any dependent modules in the correct order, along with the module you want. You need to execute **depmod** with the **-a** option once, before you ever use **modprobe**. Entering **depmod -a** creates a complete listing of all module dependencies. This command creates a file called **modules.deb** in the module directory for your current kernel version, **/lib/modules/***version*.

```
depmod -a
```

To install a module manually, you use the **modprobe** command and the module name. You can add any parameters the module may require. The following command installs the Sound Blaster sound module with the I/O, IRQ, and DMA values. **modprobe** also supports the use of the * character to enable you to use a pattern to select several modules.

```
modprobe sb io=0x220 irq=5 dma=1
```

To discover what parameters a module takes, you can use the **modinfo** command with the **-p** option.

```
modinfo -p sb
```

You can use the **-l** option to list modules and the **-t** option to look for modules in a specified subdirectory. In the next example, the user lists all modules in the **sound** directory:

```
# modprobe -l -t sound
/lib/modules/2.4.2-2/kernel/drivers/sound/sb.o
/lib/modules/2.4.2-2/kernel/drivers/sound/sb_lib.o
/lib/modules/2.4.2-2/kernel/drivers/sound/sound.o
/lib/modules/2.4.2-2/kernel/drivers/sound/soundcore.o
```

Options for the **modprobe** command are placed in the **/etc/modules.conf** file. Here, you can enter configuration options, such as default directories and aliases. An alias provides a simple name for a module. For example, the following entry enables you to reference the 3c59x.o Ethernet card module as **eth0** (Kmod will automatically detect the 3Com Ethernet card and load the 3c59x module):

```
alias eth0 3c59x
```

Notice that there is no device name for Ethernet devices in the **/dev** directory. This is because the device name is really an alias for a Ethernet network module that has been defined in the **modules.conf** file. If you were to add another Ethernet card of the same type, you would place an alias for it in the **modules.conf** file. For a second Ethernet card, you would use the device name **eth1** as its alias. This way, the second Ethernet device can be referenced with the name **eth1**. A **modules.conf** entry is shown here:

```
alias eth1 3c59x
```

Note *After making changes to **/etc/modules.conf**, you should run **depmod** again to record any changes in module dependencies.*

The previous entry assumes that the Ethernet card was of the same model. If you had added a different model Ethernet card, you would have to specify the module used for that kind of card. In the following example, the second card is a standard PCI Realteck card. Kmod has already automatically detected the new card and loaded the ne2k-pci module for you. You only need to identify this as the **eth1** card in the **/etc/modules.conf** file.

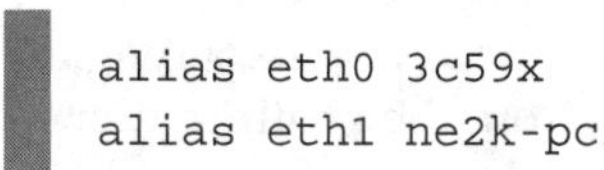

```
alias eth0 3c59x
alias eth1 ne2k-pci
```

A sample **modules.conf** file is shown here. Notice the aliases for the USB controller and the sound card.

modules.conf

```
alias eth0 3c59x
alias eth1 ne2k-pci
alias parport_lowlevel parport_pc
alias usb-controller usb-uhci
alias sound-slot-0 i810_audio
```

Note *In some cases, Kmod may not detect a device in the way you want, and thereby not load the kernel module you would like. This was the case in Chapter 29, where you needed to provide SCSI emulation for IDE CD write devices. In this case, entries in the **/etc/modules.conf** were used to manually load modules, with certain options, overriding the original setup.*

Installing New Modules for the Kernel

The source code for your Linux kernel contains an extensive set of modules, of which only a few are actually used on your system. When you install a new device, you may have to install the kernel module that provides the drivers for it. This involves selecting the module you need from a listing and then regenerating your kernel modules with the new module included. Then the new module is copied into the module library, installing it on your system. You can then enter it in the **/modules.conf** file with any options, or use **`modprobe`** to install it manually.

First, make sure you have installed the kernel source code in the **/usr/src/linux** directory (see Chapter 31). If not, simply use your distribution's installation utility such as rpm or an RPM utility like kpackage or Gnomerpm to install the kernel source RPM packages. If you are using the source code version of the kernel, unpack it and move its contents to the **/usr/src** directory.

Now change to the **usr/src/linux** directory (some distributions, such as Red Hat, will include the version number in the directory name, as in **/usr/src/linux***version*, where *version* is the kernel version). Then use the **`make`** command with the **`xconfig`** or **`menuconfig`** argument to display the kernel configuration menus, invoking them with the following commands. The **`make xconfig`** command starts an X Window System interface that needs to be run on your desktop from a terminal window.

```
make xconfig
make menuconfig
```

Using the menus, as described in Chapter 31, select the modules you need. Make sure each is marked as a module, clicking the Module check box in **xconfig** or typing *m* for **menuconfig**. Once the kernel is configured, save it and exit from the configuration menus. Then you create the modules with the following command:

```
make modules
```

This places the modules in the kernel source modules directory: **/usr/src/linux/**. You can copy the one you want to the kernel modules directory, **/lib/modules/***version***/kernel**, where *version* is the version number of your Linux kernel. A simpler approach is to reinstall all your modules, using the following command. This copies all the compiled modules to the **/lib/modules/***version***/kernel** directory.

```
make modules-install
```

For example, if you want to provide AppleTalk support and your distribution did not create an AppleTalk module or incorporate the support into the kernel directly, you can use this method to create and install the AppleTalk modules. First, check to see if your distribution has already included it. The AppleTalk modules should be in the **/lib/modules/***version***/kernel/drivers/net/appletalk** directory. If not, you can move to the **/usr/src/linux***version* directory, run **make xconfig**, and select AppleTalk as a module. Then generate the modules with the **make modules** command. You could then use the **make modules-install** command to install the new module, along with your other modules. Or you can copy the **appletalk** directory and the modules it holds to the module directory.

The Complete Reference

Chapter 31

Kernel Administration

The *kernel* is the core of the operating system, performing core tasks such as managing memory and disk access, as well as interfacing with the hardware that makes up your system. For example, the kernel makes possible such standard Linux features as multitasking, which allows several users to work on the same system. It also handles communications with devices like your CD-ROM or hard disk. Users send requests for access to these devices through the kernel, which then handles the lower-level task of actually sending instructions to a device. Given the great variety of devices available, the system will vary in the kind of devices connected to a Linux system. These devices are automatically detected and the kernel is appropriately configured when Linux is installed. However, if you add a new device, you may have to enable support for it in the kernel. This would involve creating a modified version of the kernel, often referred to as building or compiling the kernel. In addition, new versions of the kernel are continuously made available that will provide improved support for your devices, as well as a smoother running system. These you can easily download and install on your system. This chapter covers how you can download and install new kernels, as well as modify your current one.

The version number for a Linux kernel consists of three segments: the major, minor, and revision numbers. The *major number* increments with major changes in the kernel. The *minor number* indicates stability. *Even numbers* are used for stable releases, whereas *odd numbers* are reserved for development releases, which may be unstable. New features first appear in the development versions. If stability is a concern, waiting for the stable version is best. The *revision number* refers to the corrected versions. As bugs are discovered and corrected, new revisions of a kernel are released. A development kernel may have numerous revisions. For example, kernel 2.4.18 has a major number of 2 and a minor number of 4, with a revision number of 18. Distributions often add another number that refers to a specific set of patches applied to the kernel. For example, for Red Hat 7.3, the kernel is 2.4.18-3, with 3 being the patch number. Currently, the newest stable kernel is 2.4.19, which also has a major number of 2 and minor number of 4, and a revision number of 19. This is the most recent stable release of the Linux kernel. On distributions that support RPM packages, you can use an RPM query to learn what version is installed, as shown here:

```
rpm -q kernel
```

Note *Unless you are experimenting with kernel development, you should always install a stable version of the kernel. The current stable version is 2.4, whereas 2.5 is the development version.*

The Linux kernel is being worked on constantly, with new versions released when they are ready. Distributions may include different kernel versions. For example, Red Hat includes the most up-to-date kernel in its releases, whereas Caldera will use older and more stable releases. Linux kernels are kept at **www.kernel.org**. Also, RPM packages for a new kernel often are available at distribution update sites. One reason you may need to upgrade your kernel is to provide support for new hardware or for features not supported by the distribution's version. For example, you may need support for a new device not provided in the distribution's version of the kernel. Certain features may not be included in a distribution's version because they are considered experimental or a security risk.

Note *You probably don't need to install a new kernel only to add support for a new device. Kernels provide most device support in the form of modules, of which only those needed are installed with the kernel. Most likely your current kernel has the module you need. You simply have to install it. For this task, see the "Installing New Modules for the Kernel" section in Chapter 30.*

You can learn more about the Linux kernel from **www.kernel.org**, the official repository for the current Linux kernels. The most current source code, as well as documentation, is there. Your distribution Web site will also provide online documentation for installing and compiling the kernel on its systems. Several Linux HOW-TOs also exist on the subject. The kernel source code software packages also include extensive documentation. Kernel source code files are always installed in the **/usr/src/linux** directory. In this directory, you can find a subdirectory named **Documentation,** which contains an extensive set of files and directories documenting kernel features, modules, and commands. See the following listing of kernel resources.

Site	Description
www.kernel.org	The official Linux kernel Web site. All new kernels originate from here.
linuxhq.com	Linux headquarters, kernel sources, and patches.

Precautionary Steps for Modifying Kernels

If you want to modify your current kernel, you should take care to retain your current one. Otherwise, your working kernel will be overwritten with the modified version. If something should go wrong, you will be unable to restore the previous working kernel. You should retain a copy of your current kernel so you can use it again in case something goes wrong with the new one. You do not have to worry about this happening if you are installing a new kernel. New kernels are given different names, so the older one is not overwritten.

To retain a copy of your current kernel, you can either make a backup copy of it, letting the original be overwritten, or modify the kernel source **Makefile** to have your modified version created with a different name. The kernel image file is called **vmlinuz-***version* where *version* is the version number attached, as in **vmlinuz-2.4.18**. It is located in the **/boot** directory. Also, there is a file called **/boot/vmlinuz**, which is only a symbolic link to the actual kernel file. When you generate a modified version of the kernel, the kernel file, here called **vmlinuz-2.4.18**, will be overwritten with the new kernel image.

To edit the **Makefile**, you change to the **/usr/src/linux-2.4** directory and carefully open the **Makefile** with a text editor. Then you locate the line that says EXTRAVERSION = and assign to it a unique name you want appended to the modified kernel to identify it. For example, if you appended a date, you could easily identify the kernel and know when you modified it.

```
EXTRAVERSION = -July2002
```

This would give you two kernels, keeping the original one. Corresponding map files and modules will also be generated. When you install your modified kernel, **/boot/vmlinuz** will link to it, in this case, **vmlinuz-2.4.18-July2002**.

```
/boot/vmlinuz-2.4.18
/boot/vmlinuz-2.4.18-July2002
```

Making a backup copy is a more intuitive process, but takes a few more steps. You would make a copy of the **/boot/mvlinux-2.4.18** file, giving it another name as shown here:

```
cp /boot/vmlinuz2.4.18 /boot/vmlinuz2.4.18.back
```

You could also make a backup of the **System.map** file. This file contains kernel symbols needed by modules to start kernel functions. In the case of kernel 2.4.18, this would be **System.map-2.4.18**. You should also back up your modules located in the **/lib/modules/***version* directory, where *version* is the version number of the kernel. Otherwise, you will lose the modules already set up to work with the original kernel. For version 2.4.18, the libraries are located in **/lib/modules/2.4.18**. If you are compiling a different version, those libraries are placed in a new directory named with the new version number.

If you are using a boot loader, you should create a new entry for the old kernel in the boot loader configuration file (see Chapter 26). You can then make an entry for the new kernel in that configuration file. Leaving the entry for the old kernel is advisable in case something goes wrong with the new kernel. This way, you can always reboot and select the old kernel. For example, in the **grub.conf,** add a new entry, similar to the one for the old kernel, which references the new kernel in its image line. The **grub.conf** entry would look something like the following code. You could then select the entry with the title "Old Linux (2.4.18.back)" at the GRUB menu to launch the old kernel.

```
title Old Linux (2.4.18.back)
        root (hd0,2)
        kernel /boot/vmlinuz-2.4.18.back ro root=/dev/hda3
        initrd /boot/initrd-2.4.18.back.img
```

It's also advisable to have a boot disk ready, just in case something goes wrong with the installation. With a boot disk, you can start your system without using the boot loader. You can create a boot disk using the **mkbootdisk** utility. To create a boot disk, you will need to know the full version number for your kernel. You can, in fact, have several kernels installed, and create boot disks for each one (your **grub.conf** will list your kernel version number). If the kernel version is 2.4.18, use it as the argument to the **mkbootdisk** command to create a boot disk for your system.

```
mkbootdisk 2.4.18
```

If the kernel version includes the patch number, as Red Hat does, the kernel name would be 2.4.18-3. The **mkbootdisk** command would be:

```
mkbootdisk 2.4.18-3
```

Installing Distribution Kernel Binaries and Source: RPM

To install a new kernel, you need to download the software packages for that kernel to your system. If your distribution uses RPM packages, such as Mandrake, SuSE, Caldera, or Red Hat, it is advisable to download the RPM packages for new kernels from your distribution FTP site. Alternatively, you can download the most recent version from **www.kernel.org**. You can install a new kernel either by downloading a binary version from your distribution's Web site and installing it or by downloading the source code, compiling the kernel, and then installing the resulting binary file. For Mandrake, SuSE, Caldera, and Red Hat, the binary version of the kernel is provided in an RPM package. You can install a new kernel, just as you would any other RPM software package.

The easiest way to install a new kernel on most distributions is to use the update agent that most provide. With update agents like Mandrake Software Manager, SuSE's Online Update, and Red Hat Network, you can automatically download, update, and install a new kernel. Some agents, like Red Hat Network, will not automatically select kernel files for download. In this case, though listed, you have to explicitly select them to be downloaded and installed.

The source code version is available for download from distribution FTP sites and is included on distribution CD-ROMs. You can also download the latest source directly from **www.kernel.org**. Wherever you download a kernel version from, it is always the same. The source code downloaded for a particular kernel version from a distribution site is the same as the one for **www.kernel.org**. Patches for that version can be applied to any distribution.

If you want to manually download kernel RPM packages directly from Mandrake for Red Hat, keep in mind that the complete kernel installation usually includes a series of RPM packages, all beginning with the word *kernel*. There are also other packages you may need, which contain updated system configuration files used by the new kernel. As an example, the kernel packages for Red Hat are listed here. Only install one of the **kernel-*version*-ix86** packages and one of the **kernel-smp** packages. Choose the one for your machine—for example, i686 for a Pentium II and up, i586 for a Pentium, and i386 for other PCs.

```
kernel-2.4.18-3.i386.rpm
kernel-2.4.18-3.althion.rpm
kernel-2.4.18-3.i686.rpm
kernel-doc-2.4.18-3.i386.rpm
kernel-enterprise-2.4.18-3.i686.rpm
kernel-headers-2.4.18-3.i386.rpm
kernel-pcmcia-cs-2.4.18-3.i386.rpm
kernel-smp-2.4.18-3.i386.rpm
kernel-smp-2.4.18-3.althion.rpm
kernel-smp-2.4.18-3.i686.rpm
kernel-source-2.4.18-3.i386.rpm
```

Mandrake uses a slightly different naming format for its kernel RPM packages.

```
kernel-2.4.18.13mdk.i686.rpm
kernel-enterprise-2.4.18.13mdk.i686.rpm
kernel-headers-2.4.18-25mdk.i386.rpm
```

SuSE uses still a different naming format. Packages are located in the distribution's **images** directory.

```
k_deflt_24.rpm
k_smp_24.rpm
k_i386_24.rpm
```

To make sure a kernel RPM package was downloaded without any errors, you can use the **rpm** command with the **-K --nopgp** options to check it:

```
rpm -K --nopgp *rpm
```

Note *The Debian Linux distribution uses a different package format than RPM. Packages are installed with the* **apt-get** *command. Packages are named with the software name, the version number, and the* ***.deb*** *extension. Kernel packages bear a name like* ***kernel-image-2.2.19.deb****.*

You are now ready to install the new kernel. First, install updated versions, if any, of other support packages. In Red Hat, these currently include mkinitrd, SysVinit, and initscripts. Use the **-Uvh** option to update those packages:

```
# rpm -Uvh mkinitrd*rpm SysVinit*rpm initscripts*rpm
```

Installing the source code and headers for the kernel is also essential. You use the source code to generate any modules and tailor the kernel to your own needs. For example, you can use the source code to generate modules containing devices drivers for any uncommon devices you may have installed, as shown here:

```
# rpm -Uvh kernel-headers-2.4.18-3.i386.rpm
# rpm -Uvh kernel-source-2.4.18-3.i386.rpm
```

You can now install the kernel. As a safety precaution, it is advisable to preserve your old kernel in case the new one does not work out for some reason. This involves installing with the install (**-i**) option instead of the update (**-U**) option, creating a separate RAM disk for the new kernel, and then modifying **grub.conf** to have GRUB start up using the new kernel.

```
# rpm -Uvh kernel-2.4.18-3.i686.rpm
# rpm -Uvh kernel-pcmcia-cs-2.4.18-3.386.rpm
# rpm -Uvh kernel-smp-2.4.18-3.i686.rpm
```

On most distributions, kernels are installed in the **/boot** directory. Performing an **ls -l** operation on this directory lists all the currently installed kernels. A file for your old kernel and a file for your new one now exist, as well as a link file called **vmlinuz** that links to the new kernel file. If you took the precautions described in the previous section, you may have already renamed the older kernel. If you are using a boot loader such as GRUB, you needn't change its configuration file (**grub.conf**) because the entry to invoke the kernel still references the **/boot/vmlinuz** link, which now points to the new kernel. The kernel boots using the **/boot/vmlinux** link to the kernel file. In your **grub.conf** file, the kernel line for the kernel file references this link.

```
kernel /boot/vmlinuz-2.4.18-3
```

Compiling the Kernel from Source Code

Instead of installing already compiled binary versions of the kernel, you can install the kernel source code on your system and use it to create the kernel binary files yourself. Kernel source code files are compiled with the gcc compiler just as any other source code files are. One advantage to compiling the kernel is that you are able to customize its configuration, selecting particular devices you want supported by the kernel or the kind of networking support you want. You can have more control over exactly what your operating system can support. The 2.4 kernel is described here.

Installing Kernel Sources: Kernel Archives and Patches

You can obtain a recent version of the kernel source code from your distribution. It will have the name **kernel-source**. The **kernel-source** file is usually installed as part of your installation. New versions can be downloaded with your distribution update agent, or by directly accessing the distribution's FTP site. Be sure to download both the kernel headers and the source code RPM files. As noted previously, you simply install them as you would any RPM package.

```
# rpm -Uvh kernel-headers-2.4.18-3.i386.rpm
# rpm -Uvh kernel-source-2.4.18-3.i386.rpm
```

The source files are placed in the **/usr/src** directory, within the subdirectory that will have the prefix *linux* and a suffix consisting of the kernel version, as in **linux-2.4.18** for kernel 2.4, release 2, patch 18. The full directory will be **/usr/src/linux-2.4.18**. When you download and install a new kernel, a separate subdirectory will be created for it. For example, the 2.4.18-3 kernel will be placed in **/usr/src/linux-2.4.18**. A link is created called **/usr/src/linux-2.4** (or just **/usr/src/linux** on Mandrake) that will link to the most recent kernel source directory that you installed. You can use this link to access your most recent kernel source. Originally, this would link to **/usr/src/linux-2.4.18**. If you later installed the 2.4.19 kernel, this would link to **/usr/src/linux2.4.19**. The name of this directory may vary depending on the distribution. On Red Hat this will be called **/usr/src/linux-2.4.18-3** whereas on Mandrake it will be **/usr/src/linux-2.4.18-13mdk**.

You can also obtain the most recent version of the source code from **www.kernel.org**. These versions are normally much more recent than those available on your distribution site, but may not have been thoroughly tested on the distribution platform. The kernel source will be in the form of compressed archives (**.tar.gz**). They will have the prefix **linux** with the version name as the suffix. For example, **linux-2.4.18** is the 2.4 kernel, revision 18. You decompress and extract the archive with the following commands. *vnum* is the version number. First, you change to the **/usr/src** directory and then unpack the archive. It will create a directory called **linux** where the source files are placed. The following example extracts the 2.4.18 kernel:

```
cd /usr/src
gzip -cd linux-2.4.18.tar.gz | tar xvf -
```

Be sure to unpack it in the **/usr/src** directory. The archive extracts a directory named **linux** that holds the source code files. This way, the files are located in the **/usr/src/linux** directory.

Once you have extracted your kernel source, you should download and apply any patches. A *patch* modifies a source code file, making required changes. To install a patch, download the patch file and then execute the following command. The patch file is first decompressed, and then the **patch** command implements the changes.

```
cd /usr/src
gzip -cd patchvnum.gz | patch -p0
```

You can also decompress the patch and then redirect it to the **patch** command. **patch** reads its patches from the standard input.

```
gunzip patch-2.4.18.gz
patch -p0 < patch-2.4.18
```

You may have to implement several patches, depending on how out of date your kernel is. In this case, you must execute a patch operation for each patch file needed. Patches need to be applied in sequence. The latest patch does not include any previous ones. So to apply patch 2.4.18, you would first have to apply patch 2.4.1. Or you can use the patch-kernel script, which determines your kernel version and applies the patches needed.

```
cd /usr/src
linux/scripts/patch-kernel linux
```

Before you can install the kernel, you have to configure and compile it, as discussed in the next section.

Once you have installed a kernel source for a particular revision, you can update it by downloading and installing any patches for it.

Configuring the Kernel

Once the source is installed, you must configure the kernel. Configuration consists of determining the features for which you want to provide kernel-level support. These include drivers for different devices, such as sound cards and SCSI devices. This process is referred to as *configuring the kernel*. You can configure features as directly included in the kernel itself or as modules the kernel can load as needed. You can also specifically exclude features. Features incorporated directly into the kernel make for a larger kernel program. Features set up as separate modules can also be easily updated. Documentation for many devices that provide sound, video, or network support can be found in the **/usr/share/doc** directory. Check the kernel-doc package to find a listing of the documentation provided.

```
rpm -ql kernel-doc
```

If you configured your kernel previously and now want to start over from the default settings, you can use the **make mrproper** *command to restore the default kernel configuration.*

You can configure the kernel using one of several available configuration tools: config, menuconfig, or xconfig. They perform the same configuration tasks, but use different interfaces. The config tool is a simple configure script providing line-based prompts for different configuration options. The menuconfig tool provides a cursor-based menu, which you can still run from the command line. Menu entries exist for different configuration categories, and you can pick and choose the ones you want. To mark a feature for inclusion in the kernel, move to it and press the SPACEBAR. An asterisk appears in the empty parentheses to the left of the entry. If you want to make it a module, press M and an *M* appears in the parentheses. The xconfig tool runs on a window manager and provides a window interface with buttons and menus. You can use your mouse to select entries. A menu consists of configuration categories that are listed as buttons you can click. All these tools save their settings to the **.config** file in the kernel source's directory. If you want to remove a configuration entirely, you can use the **mrproper** option to remove the **.config** file, starting over from scratch.

```
make mrproper
```

You start a configuration tool by preceding it with the **make** command. Be sure you are in the **/usr/src/linux-***version* directory. The process of starting a configuration tool is a **make** operation that uses the Linux kernel **Makefile**. The xconfig tool should be started from a terminal window on your window manager. The menuconfig and config tools are started on a shell command line. The following example lists commands to start xconfig, menuconfig, or config:

```
make xconfig
make menuconfig
make config
```

The xconfig tool opens a Linux Kernel Configuration window listing the different configuration categories. Figure 31-1 shows the configuration categories for the

Linux Kernel Configuration

Code maturity level options	SCSI support	File systems
Loadable module support	Fusion MPT device support	Console drivers
Processor type and features	IEEE 1394 (FireWire) support (EXPERIMENTAL)	Sound
General setup	I2O device support	USB support
Binary emulation of other systems	Network device support	Additional device driver support
Memory Technology Devices (MTD)	Amateur Radio support	Bluetooth support
Parallel port support	IrDA (infrared) support	Kernel hacking
Plug and Play configuration	ISDN subsystem	Library routines
Block devices	Old CD-ROM drivers (not SCSI, not IDE)	
Multi-device support (RAID and LVM)	Input core support	Save and Exit
Networking options	Character devices	Quit Without Saving
Telephony Support	Multimedia devices	Load Configuration from File
ATA/IDE/MFM/RLL support	Crypto Hardware support	Store Configuration to File

Figure 31-1. *The xconfig Linux Kernel Configuration tool*

2.4 kernel. Buttons at the right of the screen are used to save the configuration or to copy it to a file, as well as to quit. Clicking an entry opens a window that lists different features you can include. Three check boxes to the left of each entry enable you to choose to have a feature compiled directly into the kernel, created as a separate module that can be loaded at runtime, or not included at all. As a rule, features in continual use, such as network and file system support, should be compiled directly into the kernel. Features that could easily change, such as sound cards, or features used less frequently, should be compiled as modules. Otherwise, your kernel image file may become too large and slower to run.

If you decide to include a feature directly into the kernel that was previously a module, be sure to check that the old module is removed from the ***/lib/modules/****version directory. Otherwise, conflicts can occur between the module and its corresponding code, which is now directly part of the kernel.*

The xconfig and menuconfig tools provide excellent context-sensitive help for each entry. To the right of an entry is a Help button. Click it to display a detailed explanation of what that feature does and why you would include it either directly or as a module, or even exclude it. When in doubt about a feature, always use the Help button to learn exactly what it does and why you would want to use it. Many of the key features are described here.

- **Loadable Module Support** In most cases, you should make sure your kernel can load modules. Click the Loadable Module Support button to display a listing of several module management options. Make sure Enable Loadable Module Support is marked Yes. This feature allows your kernel to load modules as they are needed. Kernel Module Loader should also be set to Yes, as this allows your daemons, like your Web server, to load any modules they may need. The Set Version Information entry enables you to use any modules set up for previous kernels.
- **Processor Type And Features** The Processor Type And Features window enables you to set up support for your particular system. Here, you select the type of processor you have (486, 586, 686, Pentium III, Pentium IV, and so forth), as well as the amount of maximum memory your system supports (up to 64 gigs with 2.4 kernel).
- **General Setup** The General Setup window enables you to select general features, such as networking, PCI BIOS support, power management, as well as support for ELF and a.out binaries (see Figure 31-2).

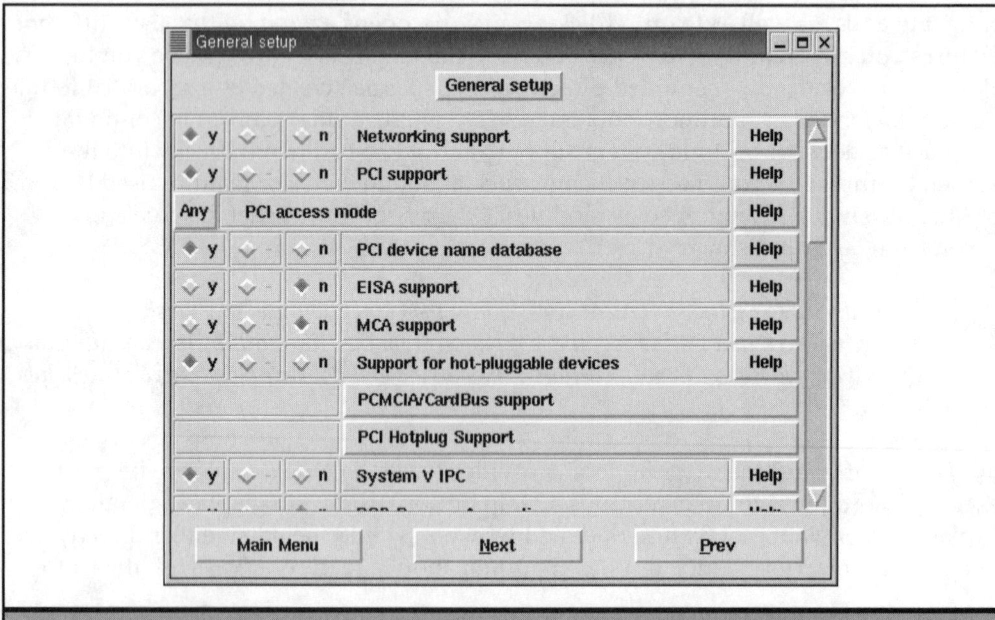

Figure 31-2. *General Setup window*

- **Block Devices** The Block Devices window lists entries that enable support for your IDE, floppy drive, and parallel port devices. Special features, such as RAM disk support and the loopback device for mounting CD-ROM image files, are also there.
- **Multi-Device Support** The Multi-Device Support window lists entries that enable the use of RAID devices. You can choose the level of RAID support you want.
- **Networking Options** The Networking Options window, shown in Figure 31-3, lists an extensive set of networking capabilities. The TCP/IP Networking entry must be set to enable any kind of Internet networking. Here, you can specify features that enable your system to operate as a gateway, firewall, or router. Network Aliasing enables support for IP aliases. Support also exists for other kinds of networks, including AppleTalk and IPX. AppleTalk must be enabled if you want to use NetaTalk to connect to a Macintosh system on your network.
- **ATA/IDE/MFM/RLL Support** In the ATA/IDE/MFM/RLL Support window, you can click on the "IDE, ATA, and ATAPI Block Device" button to open a window where you can select support for IDE ATA hard drives and ATAPI CD-ROMs. Included here are IDE chipsets such as HTP366 used for ATA66 drives.

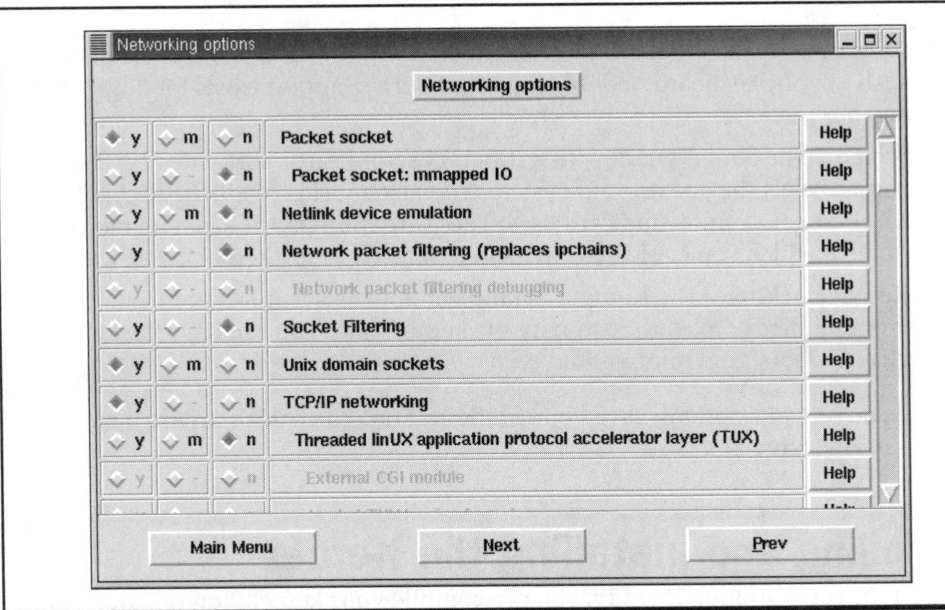

Figure 31-3. *Networking Options window*

- **SCSI Support** If you have any SCSI devices on your system, make sure the entries in the SCSI Support window are set to Yes. You enable support for SCSI disks, tape drives, and CD-ROMs here. The SCSI Low-Level Drivers window displays an extensive list of SCSI devices currently supported by Linux. Be sure the ones you have are selected.
- **Network Device Support** The Network Device Support window lists several general features for network device support. There are entries here for windows that list support for particular types of network devices, including Ethernet (10 or 100Mbit) devices, token ring devices, WAN interfaces, and AppleTalk devices. Many of these devices are created as modules you can load as needed. You can elect to rebuild your kernel with support for any of these devices built directly into the kernel.
- **Multimedia Devices** Multimedia devices provide support for various multimedia cards as well as Video4Linux.
- **File Systems** The File Systems window lists the different types of file systems Linux can support. These include DOS, VFAT (Windows 95/98), and ISO9660 (CD-ROM) file systems. Network file systems—such as NFS, SMB (Samba), and NCP (NetWare)—HFS (Macintosh), and NTFS are also listed. Note, the Linux file system type, **ext3fs**, must be included in the kernel, and is not compiled as a module.
- **Character Devices** The Character Devices window lists features for devices such as your keyboard, mouse, and serial ports. Support exists for both serial and bus mice.
- **Sound** The Sound window lists different sound cards supported by the kernel. Select the one on your system. You also must provide the IRQ, DMA, and Base I/O your sound card uses. These are compiled as separate modules, some of which you could elect to include directly in the kernel if you want.
- **Kernel Hacking** The Kernel Hacking window lists features of interest to programmers who want to modify the kernel code. You can have the kernel include debugging information.

Once you set your options, save your configuration. You can also make a backup copy by clicking Save To File.

Compiling and Installing the Kernel

Now that the configuration is ready, you can compile your kernel. You first need to generate a dependency tree to determine what part of the source code to compile, based on your configuration. Use the following command:

```
make dep
```

You also have to clean up any object and dependency files that may remain from a previous compilation. Use the following command to remove such files:

```
make clean
```

You can use several options to compile the kernel (see Table 31-1). The **bzImage** option simply generates a kernel file called **bzImage** and places it in the **arch** directory. For Intel systems, you find **bzImage** in the **i386/boot** subdirectory, **arch/i386/boot**. For a kernel source, this would be in **/usr/src/linux-2.4/arch/i386/boot**. For a kernel archive source, this would be in **/usr/src/linux/ arch/i386/boot**.

```
make bzImage
```

The **install** option generates both the kernel files and installs them on your system, as **vmlinuz**.

```
make install
```

The **zlilo** option installs the kernel file as well, but also runs **lilo** to update LILO. The **zlilo** option is designed for use with systems that run LILO. If you are booting Linux from DOS using **loadlin**, you will need to copy the **bzImage** file to the **loadlin** directory on the DOS partition where you are starting Linux from.

To install a kernel **bzImage** file manually, copy the **bzImage** file to the directory where the kernel resides and give it the name used on your distribution, such as **vmlinuz**. Remember to first back up the old kernel file. **vmlinuz** is a symbolic link to an actual kernel file that will have the term "vmlinuz" with the version name. So, to manually install a **bzImage** file, you copy it to the **/boot** directory with the name **vmlinuz** and the attached version number such as **vmlinuz-2.4.19**. You then create a symbolic link from **/boot/vmlinuz** to **/boot/vmlinuz-2.4.19**.

```
make bzImage
cp arch/i386/boot/bzImage /boot/vmlinuz-2.4.19
ln -s /boot/vmlinuz /boot/vmlinuz-2.4.19
```

The **bzImage** option and those options that begin with the letter *b*, like **bzlilo**, create a compressed kernel image. This kernel image may not work on older systems. If not, try using the **zImage** option to create a kernel file called **zImage**. Then install the **zImage** file manually. Bear in mind that support for **zImage** will be phased out eventually.

```
make zImage
```

Configuration Tools	Description
config	Line-based interface for kernel configuration.
menuconfig	Screen-based interface for kernel configuration.
xconfig	X Window System interface for kernel configuration.
Maintenance Options	
`checkhelp`	Checks configuration for options not documented.
`checkconfig`	Checks source tree for missing header files.
`clean`	Removes old object files and dependencies.
`mrproper`	Performs a more complete removal of object files, including the kernel configuration file, **.config**. Usually run before a new patch.
Compiling Options	
`zImage`	Creates the kernel file called **zImage** located in the **/usr/src/linux/arch** or **arch/i386/boot** directory.
`install`	Creates the kernel and installs it on your system.
`zlilo`	Creates the kernel, installs it on your system, and runs LILO.
`zdisk`	Creates a kernel file and installs it on a floppy disk (creates a boot disk).
`bzImage`	Creates the kernel file and calls it **bzImage**.
`bzlilo`	Creates and installs the kernel and runs LILO.
`bzdisk`	Creates the kernel and installs it on a floppy disk (creates a boot disk).
Module Options	
`modules`	Creates kernel modules.
`modules-install`	Installs kernel modules in the **/lib/modules** directory.

Table 31-1. *Kernel Compile Options Used as Arguments to the* `make` *Command in /usr/src/linux*

The **bzlilo** option both installs the kernel file on your system and runs LILO. You should use this option if you receive an error saying your kernel is too large. The following command compiles the kernel, installs it on your system, and runs LILO for you. To install and update LILO, use the following:

```
make zlilo
```

If you receive an error saying the kernel is too large, try using a *b* version of the option, such as **bzlilo**, to further reduce its size.

```
make bzlilo
```

If you want to create a boot disk with the new kernel, use the **bzdisk** option. This option will install the kernel on a floppy disk placed in your floppy drive. The kernel will reside on the floppy disk, and to use that kernel, you boot your system from the floppy (the kernel is not installed on your root partition as it is with the install option).

```
make bzdisk
```

The previous options will create the kernel, but not the modules—those features of the kernel to be compiled into separate modules. To compile your modules, use the **make** command with the **modules** argument.

```
make modules
```

To install your modules, use the **make** command with the **modules_install** option. This installs the modules in the **/lib/modules/***version-num* directory, where *version-num* is the version number of the kernel. Making a backup copy of the old modules before you install the new ones may be advisable.

```
make modules_install
```

The commands for a simple compilation and installation are shown here:

```
make dep
make clean
make bzImage
make modules
make modules_install
make install
```

If you want, you could enter these all on just two lines, separating the commands with semicolons, as shown here:

```
make dep; make clean; make bzImage; make modules
make modules_install; make install
```

The following commands show a basic compilation and a manual installation. First, all previous binary files are removed with the **clean** option. Then the kernel is created using the **bzImage** option. This creates a kernel program called bzImage located in the **arch/i386/boot** directory. Copy this kernel file to the **/boot** directory and give it the name **vmlinuz-***version*, where *version* is the kernel version. Then create a symbolic link called **/boot/vmlinuz** to the kernel **vmlinuz-***version* file. Then create the modules and install the modules:

```
make dep
make clean
make bzImage
make modules
make modules_install
cp arch/i386/boot/bzImage /boot/vmlinuz-2.4.18-3
ln -s /boot/vmlinuz /boot/vmlinux-2.4.18-3
```

Instead of installing the kernel on your system, you can simply place it on a boot disk and boot your system from that disk. In that case, you just have to create a boot disk using the **bzdisk** option. Be sure a formatted floppy disk is in the floppy drive. You will still have to create and install your modules. Be sure that the **bzImage** file is small enough to fit on a floppy disk. If not, you will have to reconfigure your kernel, compiling as many features as possible as modules instead of as part of the kernel.

```
make clean
make bzImage
make bzdisk
make modules
make modules_install
```

If you are experimenting with your kernel configurations, it may be safer to put a new kernel version on a boot disk, rather than installing it on your system. If something goes wrong, you can always boot up normally with your original kernel still on your system.

Boot Loader Configurations

If you are using a boot loader such as GRUB or LILO, you can configure your system to enable you to start any of your installed kernels. As seen in the "Precautionary Steps for Modifying Kernels" section, you can create an added entry in the boot loader configuration file for your old kernel. As you install new kernel versions, you could simply add more entries, enabling you to use any of the previous kernels. For example, you could install a developmental version of the kernel, along with a current stable version, while keeping your old version. In the image line for each entry, you would specify the filename of the kernel. Whenever you install the kernel using the RPM kernel package, the **/boot/vmlinuz** link is automatically changed to the new kernel. You can still create another boot loader entry for your older kernel.

In the next example, the **grub.conf** file contains entries for two Linux kernels, one for the kernel installed earlier, 2.4.18, and one for a more recent kernel, 2.4.19. With GRUB, you only have to add an new entry for the new kernel. If you are using LILO, just add a new image segment for the new kernel in the **/etc/lilo.conf** file. Be sure to execute the `lilo` command to update LILO.

/etc/grub.conf

```
# grub.conf generated by anaconda
#
#boot=/dev/hda
default=0
timeout=30
splashimage=(hd0,2)/boot/grub/splash.xpm.gz
title New Linux (2.4.19)
       root (hd0,2)
       kernel /boot/vmlinuz-2.4.19 ro root=/dev/hda3 hdc=ide-scsi
       initrd /boot/initrd-2.4.19.img
title  Old Linux (2.4.18)
       root (hd0,2)
       kernel /boot/vmlinuz-2.4.18 ro root=/dev/hda3 hdc=ide-scsi
       initrd /boot/initrd-2.4.18.img
title Windows XP
       root (hd0,0)
       imakeactive
       chainloader +1
```

Module RAM Disks

If your system requires certain modules to be loaded when you boot, you may have to create a RAM disk for them. For example, if you have a SCSI hard drive or CD-ROMs, the SCSI drivers for them are often held in modules that are loaded whenever you start up your system. These modules are stored in a RAM disk from which the startup process reads. If you create a new kernel that needs to load modules to start up, you must create a new RAM disk for those modules. When you create a new kernel, you also need to create its modules. You place the modules needed for startup, such as SCSI hard drive modules, in a new RAM disk. In the **lilo.conf** file, add an entry to load this RAM disk. You only need to create a new RAM disk if your kernel has to load modules at startup. If, for example, you use a SCSI hard drive, but you incorporated SCSI hard drive and CD-ROM support (including support for the specific model) directly into your kernel, you needn't set up a RAM disk. Support for IDE hard drives and CD-ROMs is already incorporated directly into the kernel.

If you need to create a RAM disk, you can use the **mkinitrd** command to create a RAM disk image file or create a RAM disk device. See the Man pages for **mkinitrd** and RAM disk documentation for more details. **mkinitrd** takes as its arguments the name of the RAM disk image file and the kernel that the modules are taken from. In the following example, a RAM disk image called **initrd-2.4.19.img** is being created in the **/boot** directory using modules from the 2.4.19 kernel. The 2.4.19 kernel needs to already be installed on your system and its modules created.

```
# mkinitrd /boot/initrd-2.4.19.img 2.4.19
```

In the **lilo.conf** segment for the new kernel, you would place an **initrd** entry specifying the new RAM disk.

```
image=/boot/vmlinuz-2.4.19
 label=linux
 root=/dev/hda3
 initrd=/boot/initrd-2.4.19.img
 read-only
```

The Complete Reference

Chapter 32

The X Window System, XFree86, and Display Managers

Linux and Unix systems use the same standard underlying graphics utility known as the X Window System, also known as X or X11. This means that, in most cases, an X-based program can run on any of the window managers and desktops. X-based software is often found at Linux or Unix FTP sites in directories labeled **X11**. You can download these packages and run them on any window manager running on your Linux system. Some may already be in the form of Linux binaries that you can download, install, and run directly. Netscape is an example. Others are in the form of source code that can easily be configured, compiled, and installed on your system with a few simple commands. Some applications, such as Motif applications, may require special libraries.

The X Window System is designed for flexibility—you can configure it in various ways. You can run the X Window System on almost all the video cards currently available. The X Window System is not tied to any specific desktop interface. It provides an underlying set of graphical operations that user interface applications such as window managers, file managers, and even desktops can use. A window manager uses these operations to construct widgets for manipulating windows, such as scroll bars, resize boxes, and close boxes. Different window managers can construct them to appear different, providing interfaces with different appearances. All window managers work on the X Window System. You can choose from a variety of different window managers, and underlying X Window System graphic operations. You can even run X programs without any window or file managers.

To run the X Window System, you need to install an X Window System server. A free version of X Window System server software, known as XFree86, is used on most Linux systems, though commercial versions are available from MetroLink (**www.metrolink.com**) and Xi graphics. Once you install the XFree86 server, you must provide configuration information about your monitor, mouse, and keyboard. This information is then used in a configuration file called **/etc/X11/XF86Config**, which includes technical information best generated by an X Window System configuration program, such as Xconfigurator, xlizard, or XF86Setup. When you configured the X Window System when you installed your system, this file was automatically generated.

You can also configure your own X interface using the **.xinitrc** and **/etc/X11/xinit/xinitrc** configuration files, where window managers, file managers, and initial X applications can be selected and started. And you can use a set of specialized X commands to configure your root window, load fonts, or configure X Window System resources, such as setting the color of window borders. You can also download X utilities from online sources that serve as Linux mirror sites, usually in their **/pub/Linux/X11** directory. If you have to compile an X application, you may have to use special procedures, as well as install support packages. An official source for X Window System news, tools, and window managers is **www.X11.org**. Here you can find detailed information about X Window System features, along with compliant desktops and window managers.

The X Window System was developed and is maintained by The Open Group (TOG), a consortium of over a hundred companies, including Sun, HP, IBM, Motorola, and Intel (**www.opengroup.org**). Development is currently managed by the X.org group (**www.X.org**) on behalf of the TOG. X.org is a nonprofit organization that maintains the existing X Window System code. X.org periodically provides free official Window System update releases to the general public. It controls the development of the X11R6 specifications, working with appropriate groups to revise and release updates to the standard, as required. XFree86 is a free distributed version of X Window System servers used on most Linux systems. You can find out more about XFree86 at **www.xfree86.org**.

The X Protocol

The X protocol was developed for Unix systems in the mid-1980s to provide a network-transparent graphical user interface. The X protocol organizes display operations into a client and server relationship, in which a client submits display requests to a server. The client is known as an X client, and the server as an X server. The client, in this case, is an application, and the server is a display. This relationship separates an application from the server. The application acts as a client sending requests to the server, which then does the actual work of performing the requested display operation. This has the advantage of letting the server interact with the operating system and its devices, whereas the application need know nothing of these details. An application operating as an X client can display on any system that uses an X server. In fact, a remote X client can send requests to have an X server on a local machine perform certain display operations. In effect, the X server/client relationship is inverted from the way we normally think of servers. Usually, several client systems access a single server. In the X server model, you have each system operating as an X server that can access a single system that holds X client programs.

XFree86

The XFree86 Project (**www.xfree86.org**) is a nonprofit organization that provides free X Window System servers and supporting materials for several operating systems on PCs and other microcomputers. The X server, client programs, and documentation supplied by the XFree86 Project are commonly referred to as XFree86. The XFree86 server is available free and includes source code. The project is funded entirely by donations.

In releases 3.3 and earlier, XFree86 organized video card and monitor drivers into separate servers. You had to find the correct one to use and load it. With release 4.0, XFree86 uses only one server, called the XFree86 X server, which includes all video card and monitor drivers. You only need to install the XFree86 X server package along with basic support packages such as those for fonts. The XFree86 X server will have support for given video cards and monitors implemented as static libraries or as modules it can load as needed. The XFree86 X server uses a built-in runtime loader, donated by Metro Link, that is operating system independent, though it is still hardware dependent. Currently, the XFree86 X server supports the Intel, Alpha, PowerPC, and Sparc platforms.

The XFree86 server supports a wide range of video cards and monitors, including monochrome, VGA, and Super VGA, and accelerated video cards. You can find a detailed listing of supported cards by checking the driver status for a particular release. To obtain information about a particular XFree86 release, just attach its release number to the **www.xfree86.org** site address (as in **www.xfree86.org/4.0** for information about release 4.0). To find out the driver status for release 4.2.0, go to **www.xfree86.org/4.2.0** and click the Driver Status link. This will list links for supported video cards. Also, you can consult the Man pages for the different driver types, such as **nv** for Nvidia cards, **mga** for Matrox, and **ati** for ATI graphics cards.

XFree86 configuration tools, such as SuSE's Sax2, Red Hat's Xconfigurator, and XFree86's xf86cfg, make configuring your video card and monitor a simple process. They keep on hand an extensive list of video cards and monitors provided by XFree86, from which you can select your own. If your video card or monitor is quite new, however, it may not be on this list. If this is the case, first check to see if a new release of XFree86 has come out. The new release may have support for your card or monitor. For example, release 4.1 now has support for Nvidia GeForce3 and ATI Radeon cards. If your card is not supported, you will need to enter certain hardware specifications, such as horizontal and vertical sync frequencies for monitors. If you must do this, be careful to enter the correct information. The wrong settings could damage both your card and your monitor.

Be sure to check for new releases of XFree86 servers periodically at the XFree86 Web site. You can download the new releases from there or from your distribution's update sites. It's always preferable to download from your Linux distribution sites, since those packages may be modified to work better with your system. The entire XFree86 software release includes the XFree86 X server and its modules along with several supporting packages such as those for fonts and configuration files. Table 32-1 lists the current XFree86 packages. For downloads from the XFree86 site, it is strongly recommended that you use the Xinstall.sh installer. Xinstall.sh will query for installation information and then download and install all needed XFree86 packages. XFree86 provides versions for different platforms on its FTP site at **ftp.xfree86.org**.

Packages	Description
Xinstall.sh	The installer script
Extract	The utility for extracting tarballs
Xbin.tgz	X clients/utilities and runtime libraries
Xlib.tgz	Some data files required at runtime
Xman.tgz	Manual pages

Table 32-1. *XFree86 Packages*

Packages	Description
Xdoc.tgz	XFree86 documentation
Xfnts.tgz	Base set of fonts
Xfenc.tgz	Base set of font encoding data
Xetc.tgz	Runtime configuration files
Xvar.tgz	Runtime data
Xxserv.tgz	XFree86 X server
Xmod.tgz	XFree86 X server modules
Optional Packages	**Description**
Xfsrv.tgz	Font server
Xnest.tgz	Nested X server
Xprog.tgz	X header files, config files, and compile-time libs
Xprt.tgz	X Print server
Xvfb.tgz	Virtual frame buffer X server
Xf100.tgz	100-dpi fonts
Xfcyr.tgz	Cyrillic fonts
Xflat2.tgz	Latin-2 fonts
Xfnon.tgz	Some large bitmap fonts
Xfscl.tgz	Scalable fonts (Speedo and Type1)
Xhtml.tgz	HTML version of the documentation
Xps.tgz	PostScript version of the documentation
Xjdoc.tgz	Documentation in Japanese

Table 32-1. *XFree86 Packages* (continued)

In addition to the server, XFree86 includes support programs and development libraries. The entire XFree86 collection is installed in various directories, beginning with the pathname **/usr/X11R6**. Directories are here for X programs, development files, libraries, Man pages, and documentation. Configuration files are placed in the **/etc/X11** directory. Applications written to support X usually install in the **/usr/X11R6/bin** directory. You can also find the XFree86 servers and support programs here. Table 32-2 lists XFree86 configuration directories.

*XFree86 now includes Direct Rendering Interface (DRI) and OpenGL support (GLX) for 3D cards like ATI, Matrox, and 3dfx (**dri.sourceforge.net**).*

You can use X servers to run X Window System applications on a remote system. When you access a remote system, you can have the X server on that system generate a new display for you to run the remote X application. Every X server has a display name consisting of a hostname, a display number, and a screen number. These are used by an application to determine how to connect to the server and the screen it should use.

```
hostname:displaynumber.screennumber
```

The hostname is the host where the X server is physically located. The display number is the number of the display being managed by the X server. On a local workstation, there is usually only one display. However, on a multiuser system where several terminals (each with its own keyboard and mouse) are connected to a single system, each terminal is its own display with its own display number. This way, several users can be running X applications at the same time off the same X server. If your system has two or more monitors sharing the same keyboard and mouse, a different screen number would be applied to each monitor, though they would have the same display number.

Directory	Description
/usr/X11R6/bin	Programs (X Window System clients and servers)
/usr/X11R6/include	Development files
/usr/X11R6/lib	Libraries
/usr/X11R6/man	Man pages
/usr/X11R6/lib/X11/doc	Documentation
/etc/X11	Configuration files
/usr/X11R6/lib/X11/	Contains subdirectories for window manager program functions

Table 32-2. *XFree86 Directories*

The display a user is currently using is listed as the DISPLAY environment variable. On a single-user system, you will find that the display entry begins with a colon and is followed by a 0, as shown here. This indicates that the X server is on the local system (not a remote host) and has the display number of 0.

```
$ echo $DISPLAY
:0
```

To use a remote X application, you have to change the display name for the DISPLAY variable. You can do this manually by assigning a new hostname and display number to the variable, or you can use the **xon** script:

```
$ DISPLAY=rabbit.mytrek.com:0
$ export DISPLAY
```

You can also use the **-display** option when invoking an X application to specify the remote X server to use:

```
$ xterm -display rabbit.mytrek.com:0
```

XFree86 Configuration: /etc/X11/XF86Config

The XFree86 servers provide a wide range of hardware support, but it can be challenging to configure. You can consult the XFree86-HOWTO document at **www.linux.org** or in the **/usr/share/doc/HOWTO** directory for most distributions. There are also Man pages for XFree86 and XF86Config, and documentation and FAQs are available at **www.xfree86.org**. The configuration file used for your XFree86 server is called **XF86Config**, located in the **/etc/X11** directory. **XF86Config** contains all the specifications for your graphics card, monitor, keyboard, and mouse. To configure the **XF86Config** file, you need specific information on hand about your hardware. For your monitor, you must know the horizontal and vertical sync frequency ranges and bandwidth. For your graphics card, you have to know the chipset, and you may even need to know the clocks. For your mouse, you should know whether it is Microsoft-compatible or some other brand, such as Logitech. Also, know the port to which your mouse is connected.

Note *XFree86 4.x uses the **/etc/X11/XF86Config-4** file, instead of **/etc/X11/XF86Config**, if it exists. Some distributions, such as Red Hat, will generate both files, but the **/etc/X11/XF86Config-4** file takes precedence and uses XFree86 4.x commands.*

Although you could create and edit the file directly, using a configuration utility such as Xconfigurator or xf86config is better. (Table 32-3 lists these various configuration tools.) With these, you simply answer questions about your hardware or select options

Tool	Description
xf86cfg	XFree86 screen-based X Window System configuration tool
XFree86 -configure	XFree86 X Window System configuration tool that is built into the XFree86 X server
XF86Setup	GUI X Window System configuration tool; use after installation process
Xconfigurator	Screen-based X Window System configuration tool
Sax2	SuSE X Window System configuration tool
xf86config	XFree86 command line X Window System configuration tool; requires no screen-based support
/etc/X11/XF86Config	The X Window System configuration file; edited by the configuration tools

Table 32-3. *X Window System Configuration Tools*

on the dialog window, and the program generates the appropriate **/etc/X11/XF86Config** file. xf86config provides line-mode prompts where you type responses or enter a menu selection, and it provides explanations of each step. You can run it from any shell command line. Xconfigurator uses a cursor-based screen that also operates on a shell command line. You can use arrow keys, TAB, and the ENTER key to make your selections. xf86config also attempts to detect your card automatically, or you can select your monitor from a predetermined list.

If you have problems configuring with a configuration utility, however, you can use the **`XFree86`** command with the **`-configure`** option to generate a version for you. With the **`-configure`** option, XFree86 will probe your video card, keyboard, and mouse, and then generate an XF86Config file automatically, naming it **XF86Config.new**. It will also display a report on the results of its probe. This approach can be helpful if you have difficulty installing a new video card.

```
XFree86 -configure
```

The Complete Reference

Part VII

Network Administration

Chapter 33

Configuring Network Connections

Most distributions enable you to configure your network during installation. If you did so, then your system is ready to go. If you need to change your configuration later, you may find the information in this chapter helpful. Administering and configuring a TCP/IP network on your Linux system is not particularly complicated. Your system uses a set of configuration files to set up and maintain your network. Table 36-5 in Chapter 36 provides a complete listing.

Instead of manually editing configuration files, you can use the GUI or cursor-based configuration tools included in many distributions that prompt you for network information. Many distributions incorporate this kind of network configuration into the installation process. If you chose not to configure your network during configuration or you need to make changes to it, you may find it easier and safer to use a network configuration tool as described in Chapter 5. Red Hat, SuSE, Caldera, Debian, and Mandrake all provide network configuration tools.

Many networks now provide a service that automatically configures a system's network interface. They use a protocol called DHCP (Dynamic Host Configuration Protocol). If your network is configuring your system with DHCP, you will not have to configure it manually. All necessary information will be automatically entered into your network configuration files.

If your system does not have a direct hardware connection to a network, such as an Ethernet connection, and you dial into a network through a modem, you will probably have to set up a PPP connection. Several GUI tools are available for use with Linux that you can use to configure your PPP connection. These include Kppp and Gnomeppp. You can even initiate PPP connections from the command line.

Note *If you just want to dial into a remote network using a simple command line interface, you can use a dial-in terminal program like minicom.*

Network Startup Script

On Mandrake, Red Hat, SuSE, and Caldera distributions, your network interface is started up using the **network** script in the **/etc/rc.d/init.d** directory (**/etc/rc.d** on SuSE). On Red Hat and Mandrake, you can manually shut down and restart your network interface by invoking this script with the **service** command and the **start**, **stop**, or **restart** options. On other distributions you have to use the script directly. The following command shuts down and then starts up your network interface:

```
service network restart
```

To test if your interface is working, use the **ping** command with an IP address of a system on your network, such as your gateway machine. The **ping** command continually repeats until you stop it with CTRL-C. For example, if you have a host on your network with the IP address 192.168.1.42, you could enter

```
ping 192.168.1.42
```

Hardware Specifications

In addition to your configuration files, you may also have to configure support for your networking hardware, such as Ethernet cards and modems. Ethernet cards use different modules. During installation, kmod automatically detects your Ethernet card type and has the appropriate module loaded whenever you boot up, as noted in Chapters 30 and 31. If you change your Ethernet card, it will be detected and the appropriate module loaded. An alias entry for it is entered in the **/etc/modules.conf** file, assigning it an **eth** device name such as **eth0** or **eth1** (if it is a second card). If your card is not correctly detected or if it needs certain parameters set, you will have to make an alias entry for it manually in the **/etc/modules.conf** file.

If you are using a modem, you should make sure a link by the name of **/dev/modem** exists to your modem device, which is usually one of the **/dev/ttyS***num* devices, where *num* is in the range of 0–3. For example, a modem on the second serial port has a device name of **/dev/ttyS1**, and **/dev/modem** is a link to the **/dev/ttyS1** device file (see Chapter 30). On most distributions, this is usually done for you during installation. Many modem programs and PPP configuration programs look for the **/dev/modem** file by default.

Dynamic Host Configuration Protocol

The Dynamic Host Configuration Protocol (DHCP) provides configuration information to systems connected to a TCP/IP network, whether the Internet or an intranet. The machines on the network operate as DHCP clients, obtaining their network configuration information from a DHCP server on their network. A machine on the network runs a DHCP client daemon that automatically downloads its network configuration information from its network's DHCP server. The information includes its IP address, along with the network's name server, gateway, and proxy addresses, including the netmask. Nothing has to be entered manually on the local system. This has the added advantage of centralizing control over network configuration for the different systems on the network. A network administrator can manage the network configurations for all the systems on the network from the DHCP server.

DHCP is based on the BOOTP protocol developed for diskless workstations. Check DHCP documentation for options specific to machines designed to work with BOOTP.

A DHCP server also supports several methods for IP address allocation: automatic, dynamic, and manual. Automatic allocation assigns a permanent IP address for a host. Manual allocation assigns an IP address designated by the network administrator. With dynamic allocation, a DHCP server can allocate an IP address to a host on the network only when the host actually needs to use it. Dynamic allocation takes addresses from a pool of IP addresses that hosts can use when needed and release when they are finished.

Dynamic allocation of IP addresses currently suffers from one major limitation. In its current form, DHCP cannot sync with a DNS server. A DNS server is associating hostnames with particular IP addresses, whereas, in the case of dynamic allocation, the DHCP server is randomly assigning its own IP addresses to different hosts. These may or may not be the same as the IP addresses that the DNS server expects to associate with a hostname. A solution to this problem is being developed called Dynamic DNS. With Dynamic DNS, the DHCP server will be able to automatically update the DNS server with the IP addresses the DHCP server has assigned to different hosts. Until then, if you want to sync your DHCP and DNS server you have to configure DHCP to assign fixed addresses to hosts. You can then have the DHCP server perform a DNS lookup to obtain the IP address it should assign, or you can manually assign the same IP address in the DHCP configuration file. Performing a DNS lookup has the advantage of specifying IP address in one place, the DNS server.

A variety of DHCP servers and clients are available for different operating systems. For Linux, you can obtain DHCP software from the Internet Software Consortium (ISC) at **www.isc.org**. The software package includes a DHCP server, client, and relay agent. Linux includes a DHCP server and client. The DHCP client is called **dhcpcd**, and the server is called **dhcpd**. The network information a DHCP client downloads is kept in its own network configuration files in the **/etc/dhcpc** directory. For example, here you can find a **resolv.conf** file for your network's name servers.

Configuring DHCP Client Hosts

Configuring hosts to use a DHCP server is a simple matter of setting options for the host's network interface device, such as an Ethernet card. For a Linux host, you can use a distribution network tool to set the host to automatically access a DHCP server for network information. On a network tool's panel for configuring the Internet connection, you will normally find a check box for selecting DHCP. Clicking this box will enable DHCP. On Red Hat and Mandrake, this will set the **BOOTPROTO** entry in that interface's network script in the **/etc/sysconfig/network-scripts** directory, such as **ifcfg-eth0** for the first Ethernet card. You could also manually make this entry.

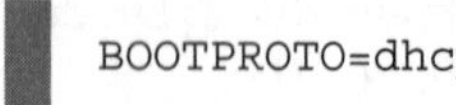

```
BOOTPROTO=dhcp
```

Be sure to restart your network devices with the network script to have the changes take effect.

The information that is being provided to a client by a DHCP server is listed in the client's **/etc/dhcpc** directory. Here you will find information files for the client's specific network device. For example, information provided for the first Ethernet device will be listed in the **/etc/dhcpc/dhcpcd-etho.info** file. You will find information such as the IP address, netmask, broadcast address, the hostname, domain name, and the DNS servers—all assigned by the DHCP server to the client.

On a Windows client, locate the TCP/IP entry for your network interface card, then open its properties window. Click the box labeled Obtain IP Address Automatically. Then locate the Wins panel (usually by clicking the Advanced button) and select DHCP as the protocol you want to use.

On Mandrake Control Center, the Internet Connection Sharing tool (drakgw) will automatically set up a DHCP network configuration for you.

Configuring the DHCP Server

On Mandrake and Red Hat systems, you can stop and start the DHCP server using the **dhcpd** command in the **/etc/rc.d/init.d** directory (on SuSE this is at the **/etc/rc.d directory**). Use the **service** command with the **start**, **restart**, and **stop** options. The following example starts the DHCP server. Use the **stop** option to shut it down, and **restart** will restart it.

```
service dhcpd start
```

Dynamically allocated IP addresses will be assigned for a given time, known as *leases*. When a lease expires, it can be extended or a new one generated. Current leases are listed in the **dhcpd.leases** file located in the **/var/lib/dhcp** directory. A lease entry will specify the IP address and the start and end time of the lease along with the client's hostname.

The configuration file for the DHCP server is **/etc/dhcpd.conf**, where you specify parameters and declarations that define how different DHCP clients on your network are accessed by the DHCP server, along with options that define information passed to the clients by the DHCP server. These parameters, declarations, and options can be defined globally, for certain subnetworks, or for specific hosts. Global parameters, declarations, and options apply to all clients, unless overridden by corresponding declarations and options in subnet or host declarations. Technically, all entries in a **dhcpd.conf** file are statements that can be either declarations or parameters. All statements end with a semicolon. Options are specified in **options** parameter statements. Parameters differ from declarations in that they define if and how to perform tasks, such as how long a lease is allocated. Declarations describe network features like the range of addresses to allocate or the networks that are accessible. See Table 33-1 for a listing of commonly used declarations and options.

Entries	Description
Declarations	
`shared-network` *name*	Used to note if some subnets share the same networks.
`subnet` *subnet-number netmask*	References an entire subnet of addresses.
`range [` *dynamic-bootp* `]` *low-address* `[` *high-address*`] ;`	Provides the highest and lowest range for dynamically allocated IP addresses.
`host` *hostname*	References a particular host.
`group`	Lets you label a group of parameters and declarations, and then use the label to apply them to subnets and hosts.
`allow unknown-clients;` `deny unknown-clients;`	Do not dynamically assign addresses to unknown clients.
`allow bootp; deny bootp;`	Whether to respond to `bootp` queries.
`allow booting; deny booting;`	Whether to respond to client queries.
Parameters	
`default-lease-time` *time*`;`	Length in seconds assigned to a lease.
`max-lease-time` *time*`;`	Maximum length of lease.
`hardware` *hardware-type hardware-address*`;`	Network hardware type (Ethernet or token ring) and address.
`filename` "*filename*"`;`	Name of the initial boot file.
`server-name` "*name*"`;`	Name of the server from which a client is booting.
`next-server` *server-name*`;`	Server that loads the initial boot file specified in the filename.
`fixed-address` *address* `[,` *address* ... `];`	Assigns a fixed address to a client.
`get-lease-hostnames` *flag*`;`	Whether to look up and use IP addresses of clients.

Table 33-1. *DHCP Declarations, Parameters, and Options*

Entries	Description
authoritative; not authoritative;	Denies invalid address requests.
server-identifier hostname;	Specifies the server.
Options	
option subnet-mask *ip-address*;	Client's subnet mask.
option routers *ip-address* [, *ip-address...*];	List of router IP addresses on client's subnet.
option domain-name-servers *ip-address* [, *ip-address...*];	List of domain name servers used by the client.
option log-servers *ip-address* [, *ip-address...*];	List of log servers used by the client.
option host-name *string*;	Client's hostname.
option domain-name *string*;	Client's domain name.
option broadcast-address *ip-address*;	Client's broadcast address.
option nis-domain *string*;	Client's Network Information Service domain.
option nis-servers *ip-address* [, *ip-address...*];	NIS servers the client can use.
option smtp-server *ip-address* [, *ip-address...*];	List of SMTP servers used by the client.
option pop-server *ip-address* [, *ip-address...*];	List of POP servers used by the client.
option nntp-server ip-address [, *ip-address...*];	List of NNTP servers used by the client.
option www-server *ip-address* [, *ip-address...*];	List of Web servers used by the client.

Table 33-1. *DHCP Declarations, Parameters, and Options* (continued)

Declarations provide information for the DHCP server or designate actions it is to perform. For example, the **range** declaration is used to specify the range of IP addresses to be dynamically allocated to hosts.

```
range 192.168.0.5 192.168.0.128;
```

With parameters, you can specify how the server is to treat clients. For example, the **default-lease-time** declaration sets the number of seconds a lease is assigned to a client. The **filename** declaration specifies the boot file to be used by the client. The **server-name** declaration informs the client of the host from which it is booting. The **fixed-address** declaration can be used to assign a static IP address to a client. See the Man page for **dhcpd.conf** for a complete listing.

Options provide information to clients that they may need to access network services, such as the domain name of the network, the domain name servers that clients use, or the broadcast address. See the Man page for **dhcp-options** for a complete listing. This information is provided by **option** parameters as shown here:

```
option broadcast-address 192.168.0.255;
option domain-name-servers 192.168.0.1, 192.168.0.4;
option domain-name "mytrek.com";
```

Your **dhcpd.conf** file will usually begin with declarations, parameters, and options that you define for your network serviced by the DHCP server. The following example provides router (gateway), netmask, domain name, and DNS server information to clients. Additional parameters define the default and maximum lease times for dynamically allocated IP addresses.

```
option routers 192.168.0.1;
option subnet-mask 255.255.255.0;
option domain-name "mytrek.com ";
option domain-name-servers 192.168.0.1;
default-lease-time 21600;
max-lease-time 43200;
```

With the subnet, host, and group declarations, you can reference clients in a specific network, particular clients, or different groupings of clients across networks. Within these declarations you can enter parameters, declarations, or options that will apply only to those clients. Scoped declarations, parameters, and options are enclosed in braces. For example, to define a declaration for a particular host, you use the **host** declaration as shown here:

```
host rabbit {
        declarations, parameters, or options;
        }
```

Dynamic Addresses

Your DHCP server can be configured to select IP addresses from a given range and assign them to different clients. Given a situation where you have many clients that may not always be connected to the network, you could effectively service them with a smaller pool of IP addresses. IP addresses are assigned only when they are needed. With the **range** declaration, you specify a range of addresses that can be dynamically allocated to clients. The declaration takes two arguments, the first and last addresses in the range.

```
range 192.168.1.5 192.168.1.128;
```

For example, if you are setting up your own small home network, you would use a network address beginning with 192.168. The range would specify possible IP addresses with that network. So for a network with the address 192.168.0.0, you would place a **range** declaration along with any other information you want to give to your client hosts. In the following example, a range of IP addresses beginning from 192.168.0.1 to 192.168.0.128 can be allocated to the hosts on that network.

```
range 192.168.0.5 192.168.0.128;
```

You should also define your lease times, both a default and a maximum.

```
default-lease-time 21600;
max-lease-time 43200;
```

For a small, simple home network, you just need to list the **range** declaration along with any global options as shown here. If your DHCP server is managing several subnetworks, you will have to use the **subnet** declarations.

In order to assign dynamic addresses to a network, the DHCP server will require that your network topology be mapped. This means it needs to know what network addresses belong to a given network. Even if you only use one network, you will need to specify the address space for it. You define a network with the **subnet** declaration. Within this **subnet** declaration you can specify any parameters, declarations, or options to use for that network. The **subnet** declaration informs the DHCP server of the possible IP addresses encompassed by a given subnet. This is determined by the network IP address and the netmask for that network. The next example defines a local network with address space from 192.168.0.0 to 192.168.0.255. The **range** declaration allows addresses to be allocated from 192.168.0.5 to 192.168.0.128.

```
subnet 192.168.1.0 netmask 255.255.255.0 {
          range 192.168.0.5 192.168.0.128;
  }
```

Versions of DHCP prior to 3.0 required that you even map connected network interfaces that are not being served by DHCP. So each network interface would have to have a corresponding **subnet** declaration. Those not being serviced by DHCP would have a "not authoritative" parameter as shown here (192.168.2.0 being a network not to be serviced by DHCP). In version 3.0 and later, DHCP simply ignores unmapped network interfaces.

```
subnet 192.168.2.0 netmask 255.255.255.0 {
          not authoritative;
  }
```

The implementation of a very simple DHCP server for dynamic addresses is shown in the sample **dhcpd.conf** file that follows.

/etc/dhcpd.conf

```
option routers 192.168.0.1;
option subnet-mask 255.255.255.0;
option domain-name "mytrek.com ";
option domain-name-servers 192.168.0.1;

subnet 192.168.1.0 netmask 255.255.255.0 {
range 192.168.0.5 192.168.0.128;
default-lease-time 21600;
max-lease-time 43200;
}
```

Subnetworks

If you are dividing your network space in several subnetworks, you could use a single DHCP server to manage them. In that case, you would have a **subnet** declaration for each subnetwork. If you are setting up your own small network, you would use a network address beginning with 192.168. The range would specify possible IP addresses within that network. So for a network with the address 192.168.0.0, you would create a **subnet** declaration with the netmask 255.255.255.0. Within this declaration you would place a **range** declaration along with any other information you want to give to your client hosts. In the following example, a range of IP addresses beginning from 192.168.0.1 to 192.168.0.75 can be allocated to the hosts on that network.

```
subnet 192.168.0.0 netmask 255.255.255.0 {
 range 192.168.0.5 192.168.0.75;
}
```

For each subnetwork you may want to specify different policies such as different lease times. Any entries in a **subnet** declaration will override global settings. So if you already have a global lease time set, a lease setting in a **subnet** declaration will override it for that subnet. The next example sets different lease times for different subnets, as well as different address allocations. The lease times for the first subnet are taken from the global lease time settings, whereas the second subnet defines its own lease times.


```
default-lease-time 21600;
max-lease-time 43200;

subnet 192.168.1.0 netmask 255.255.255.0 {
 range 192.168.0.5 192.168.0.75;
}
subnet 192.168.1.128 netmask 255.255.255.252 {
 range 192.168.0.129 192.168.0.215;
 default-lease-time 56000;
 max-lease-time 62000;
}
```

Fixed Addresses

Instead of using a pool of possible IP addresses for your hosts, you may want to give each one a specific addresses. Using the DHCP server still gives you control over which address will be assigned to a given host. However, to assign an address to a particular host, you need to know the hardware address for that host's network interface card (NIC). In effect, you have to inform the DHCP server that it has to associate a particular network connection device with a specified IP address. To do that, the DHCP server needs to know which network device you are referring to. You can identify a network device by its hardware address, known as its MAC address. To find out a client's hardware address, you log in to the client and use the **ifconfig** command to find out information about your network devices. To list all network devices, use the **-a** option. If you know your network device name, you can use that. The next example will list all information about the first Ethernet device, **eth0**.

```
ifconfig eth0
```

This will list information on all the client's network connection devices. The entry (usually the first) with the term **HWaddr** will display the MAC address. Once you have the MAC address, you can use it on the DHCP server to assign a specific IP address to that device.

In the **dhcpd.conf** file, you use a **host** declaration to set up a fixed address for a client. Within the **host** declaration you place a hardware option in which you list the type of network connection device and its MAC address. Then you use the **fixed-address** parameter to specify the IP address to be assigned to that device. In the following example, the client's network device with a MAC address of 08:00:2b:4c:29:32 is given the IP address 192.168.0.2.

```
host rabbit.mytrek.com {
                    hardware ethernet 08:00:2b:4c:29:32;
                    fixed-address 192.168.0.2;
                    }
```

You can also have the DHCP server perform a DNS lookup to obtain the host's IP address. This has the advantage of letting you manage IP addresses in only one place, the DNS server. Of course, this requires that the DNS server be operating so that the DHCP server can determine the IP address. For example, a proxy server connection (which can provide direct Web access) just needs an IP address, not a DNS hostname to operate. If the DNS server were down, the previous example would still assign an IP address to the host, whereas the following example would not.

```
host rabbit {
                    hardware ethernet 08:00:2b:4c:29:32;
                    fixed-address rabbit.mytrek.com;
                    }
```

You can also use the **host** declaration to define network information for a diskless workstation or terminal. In this case, you add a **filename** parameter specifying the boot file to use for that workstation or terminal. Here the terminal called **myterm** obtains boot information from the server **turtle.mytrek.com**.

```
host myterm {
                    filename "/boot/vmlinuz";
                    hardware ethernet 08:00:2b:4c:29:32;
                    server-name "turtle.mytrek.com";
                    }
```

The implementation of a very simple DHCP server for fixed addresses is shown in the sample **dhcpd.conf** file that follows. In the second **host** declaration, the DHCP will perform a DNS lookup to obtain the IP address of **rabbit.mytrek.com**.

/etc/dhcpd.conf

```
option routers 192.168.0.1;
option subnet-mask 255.255.255.0;
option domain-name "mytrek.com ";
option domain-name-servers 192.168.1.1;

subnet 192.168.1.0 netmask 255.255.255.0 {
host turtle {
            hardware ethernet 08:00:2b:4c:29:32;
            fixed-address 192.168.0.1;
            }
host rabbit {
            hardware ethernet 00:80:AD:30:17:2A;
            fixed-address rabbit.mytrek.com;
            }
host lizard {
            hardware ethernet 00:70:2b:4b:29:14;
            fixed-address 192.168.0.3;
            }
}
```

host declaration can also be placed within **subnet** declaration to provide information about particular hosts in that subnet.

A common candidate for a fixed address is the DNS server for a network. Usually you would want the DNS server located at the same IP address, so that it can be directly accessed. The DHCP server can then provide this IP address to its clients.

Note *With Webmin, you can configure your DHCP server easily, entering parameters, options, and declarations for subnets and hosts as well as globally.*

Wireless Tools

To avoid having different configuration options for each make of wireless device, most wireless devices currently support the Wireless Extensions. These extensions provide a standard format for configuring all wireless devices. With the same set of configuration options, you can configure any wireless device that supports Wireless Extensions. The Wireless Tools package is a set of network configuration and report tools for wireless devices installed on a Linux system. They are currently supported and developed as part of the Linux Wireless Extension and Wireless Tools Project, an open-source project maintained by Hewlett-Packard.

Wireless Tools consists of the configuration and report tools listed here:

Tool	Description
iwconfig	Sets the wireless configuration options basic to most wireless devices
iwlist	Displays the current status information of a device
iwspy	Tests mobile IP support
iwpriv	Lists access configuration options specific to a particular device

The wireless LAN device will have an Ethernet name just like an Ethernet card. kmod will automatically detect and load the appropriate modules, listing its alias in the **/etc/modules.conf** file.

iwconfig works much like ifconfig, configuring a network connection. Added parameters let you set wireless-specific features such as the network name (**`nwid`**), the frequency or channel it uses (**`freq`** or **`channel`**), and the bit rate for transmissions (**`rate`**). See the iwconfig Man page for a complete listing of accepted parameters. Some of the commonly used parameters are listed here:

Parameter	Description
`essid`	A network name
`freq` or **`channel`**	The frequency of the connection or the channel used
`nwid` or **`domain`**	The network ID or domain
`mode`	The operating mode used for the device, such as ad hoc, managed, or auto; determined by the network structure (topology)
`sens`	The sensitivity, the lowest signal level at which data can be received
`key` or **`enc`**	The encryption key used

For example, to set the channel used for the wireless device installed as the first Ethernet device, you would use the following, setting the channel to 2:

```
iwconfig eth0 channel 2
```

You can also use iwconfig to display statistics for your wireless devices, just as ifconfig does. Enter the **iwconfig** command with no arguments or with the name of the device. Information such as the name, frequency, sensitivity, and bit rate are listed. Check also **/proc/net/wireless** for statistics.

iwpriv works in conjunction with iwconfig, allowing you to set options specific to a particular kind of wireless device. With iwpriv, you can also turn on roaming or select the port to use. You use the **private-command** parameter to enter the device-specific options. The following example sets roaming on:

```
iwpriv eth0 roam on
```

Your wireless device can check its connection to another wireless device it is receiving data from, reporting the quality, signal strength, and noise level of the transmissions. Your device can maintain a list of addresses for different devices it may receive data from. You use the iwspy tool to set or add the addresses that you want checked. You can list either IP addresses or the hardware versions. A **+** sign will add the address, instead of replacing the entire list.

```
iwspy eth0 +192.168.2.5
```

To display the quality, signal, and noise levels for your connections, you use the **iwspy** command with just the device name:

```
iwspy eth0
```

To obtain more detailed information about your wireless device, such as all the frequencies or channels available, you use the iwlist tool.

DSL

To connect using DSL, you use the pppoe utility to make your DSL connections. pppoe implements the Point-to-Point-over-Ethernet protocol (PPPoE). PPPoE combines the direct connection capability of PPP (Point-to-Point Protocol) used with dial-up modems, with the Ethernet protocol used in cable and LAN connections. With PPPoE, PPP operations are able to support multiple users like an Ethernet connection does. PPPoE is used by DSL networks to set up direct connections from multiple users to an ISP.

Several Linux distributions use the Roaring Penguin package of pppoe commands (rp-pppoe). Configuration settings are saved to the **/etc/ppp/pppoe.conf** file. Roaring Penguin also includes several configuration tools such as TkPPPoE, which provides a GUI interface for configuring your DSL connection. For a corresponding command line configuration, you can use the **adsl-setup** command. You are prompted to enter your username, password, Ethernet card, and domain name server addresses. You can also specify basic firewall security levels. You can then establish your DSL connection with the **adsl-start** command, and disconnect with the **adsl-stop** command.

You can start up a PPPoE connection directly using the **pppoe** command, or configure your pppd client to use pppoe. The **-I** option is used to indicate the Ethernet device your system will use for your PPPoE connection. To configure pppd to use pppoe, you would add the following line in the **/etc/ppp/options** file.

```
pty "/sbin/pppoe -I eth0"
```

PPP and SLIP

As an alternative to hardwired network connections such as Ethernet, you can use a modem with telephone lines to connect to a network. Two protocols can transmit IP communications across the telephone lines. These are the Serial Line Internet Protocol (SLIP) and the Point-to-Point Protocol (PPP). SLIP is an older protocol, whereas PPP is newer and has become predominant. Most high-speed connections used by current ISPs use PPP. The SLIP and PPP protocols are especially designed for users who connect their systems to the Internet over a modem and a telephone line. Usually, a connection is made to an ISP, which then connects the system to the Internet through its own systems. An ISP supports either SLIP or PPP on a given line. Find out which protocol your ISP supports; you need to use one or the other. Setting up a SLIP or PPP connection can be a complicated process. For more detailed explanations, see the PPP-HOWTO along with other PPP documentation and guides. Go to the PPP Using page under Support and Docs. You can also check the **/usr/share/doc/ppp-***version* directory where *version* is the PPP package version.

There are two PPP tools installed with most distributions, pppd and wvdial. The pppd tool is used widely on many Linux systems. The wvdial tool is a newer PPP tool that is easier to use. Unlike pppd, it does not require the use of an extra chat script to first establish a connection. The wvdial tool was described in Chapter 5. The older pppd tool is described here.

PPP

If you use a modem instead of an Ethernet card to connect to a network, you need to configure a dial-up interface. Many Internet service providers (ISPs) set up connections over a modem using PPP interfaces, providing a dial-up phone number, the modem device, and the login name and password you use to connect to your ISP. For a simple PPP connection, you can use the KDE PPP tool called Kppp, a Gnome PPP tool called Gnomeppp, and several X Window System–based tools such as xisp. All the tools offer the same kind of interface, providing panels for login information, modem configuration, and dial-up connections. Login operations are handled using Expect/Send entries where you specify what password and login prompt to expect. Although their interfaces are somewhat different, Webmin and Linuxconf do perform many of the same tasks.

You can manually create your own PPP connection, invoking the PPP program directly on the command line with chat scripts to make the appropriate dial-up connections. The PPP program is called pppd. The pppd program doesn't make the initial connection nor does it dial up through your modem and provide login and password information. To use pppd, you first must establish the connection to the remote host. You can make such a connection using the chat program, which has its own options and format. The chat program first makes the connection, and then pppd configures it. You needn't call chat first, and then call pppd, however. The pppd program is designed to take as its argument a program that can make the connection—in this case, chat. You simply specify **`chat`** along with its options on the command line with **`pppd`**.

SLIP: dip

Two types of SLIP connections exist: the standard one referred to simply as SLIP, and the newer Compressed SLIP (CSLIP). Be sure you know which type of connection your ISP is giving you. You must specify one or the other as your protocol mode when you connect. Except for specifying the mode, the connection procedure is the same for both. References to SLIP apply to both SLIP and CSLIP, unless specifically noted. You use the dip program to manage and set up your SLIP connection. The dip program operates like an interpreter. In a file called a **dip** script, you specify certain commands needed to log in to the ISP and make the connection. The dip program then reads the commands in this file, executing them one by one. With Linux, not only can you make a SLIP connection to a remote system, but other systems can also make their own SLIP connections to your system. Another system can dial in to your system and make a SLIP connection. If you have provided an account for a user on that remote system, the user could dial in a SLIP connection and log in to that account. Such remote dial-up SLIP connections are managed by **`dip`** with the **`-i`** option. This places dip in a dial-in mode to receive incoming connections. In the dial-in mode, dip prompts a remote user for a user ID and a password, and then makes the SLIP connection.

Chapter 34

NFS, NIS, and AppleTalk

Linux provides several tools for accessing files on remotes systems connected to a network. The Network File System (NFS) enables you to connect to and directly access resources such as files or devices like CD-ROMs that reside on another machine. The Network Information Service (NIS) maintains configuration files for all systems on a network. With Samba, you can connect your Windows clients on a Microsoft Windows network to services such as shared files, systems, and printers controlled by the Linux Samba server (see Chapter 35). Netatalk enables you to connect your Linux systems to an AppleTalk network, enabling you to access remote Macintosh file systems directly, as well as to access any Apple printers such as LaserWriters.

Network File Systems: NFS and /etc/exports

NFS enables you to mount a file system on a remote computer as if it were local to your own system. You can then directly access any of the files on that remote file system. This has the advantage of allowing different systems on a network to access the same files directly, without each having to keep its own copy. Only one copy would be on a remote file system, which each computer could then access. You can find out more about NFS at its Web site at **nfs.sourceforge.net**.

NFS operates over a TCP/IP network. The remote computer that holds the file system makes it available to other computers on the network. It does so by exporting the file system, which entails making entries in an NFS configuration file called **/etc/exports**, as well as by running several daemons to support access by other systems. These include rpc.mountd, rpc.nfsd, and rpc.portmapper. Access to your NFS server can be controlled by the **/etc/hosts.allow** and **/etc/hosts.deny** files. The NFS daemons are listed here:

- **rpc.nfsd** Receives NFS requests from remote systems and translates them into requests for the local system.
- **rpc.mountd** Performs requested mount and unmount operations.
- **rpc.portmapper** Maps remote requests to the appropriate NFS daemon.
- **rpc.rquotad** Provides user disk quote management.
- **rpc.statd** Provides locking services when a remote host reboots.
- **rpc.lockd** Handles lock recovery for systems that have gone down.

Note *It is advisable to use NFS on a local secure network only. If used over the Internet, NFS would open your system up to nonsecure access.*

On Mandrake and Red Hat, you can start up and shut down the NFS daemons using the **/etc/rc.d/init.d/nfs** script (On SuSE you use the **/etc/rc.d/nfs** file). For Mandrake and Red Hat you can also use `service nfs start`. On most distributions, including SuSE, Mandrake, and Red Hat, to have NFS started automatically you can use `chkconfig`, the Service Configuration tool, or a runlevel tool like the Sys V Init

Editor to specify the runlevels at which it will operate (On Mandrake, you can select nfs in the System Services panel in the Mandrake Control Center). The following example will have NFS start up automatically at runlevels 3 and 5 on Red Hat:

```
chkconfig -level 35  nfs on
```

The **nfs** script will start up the portmapper, nfsd, mountd, and rquotad daemons. To enable NFS locking, you use the **nfslock** script. This will start up the statd and lockd daemons. NFS locking provides for better recovery from interrupted operations that can occur from system crashes on remote hosts.

To see if NFS is actually running, you can use the **rpcinfo** command with the **-p** option as shown here. You should see entries for **mountd** and **nfs**. If not, NFS is not running.

```
rpcinfo -p
   program vers proto   port
    100000    2   tcp    111  portmapper
    100000    2   udp    111  portmapper
    100024    1   udp  32768  status
    100024    1   tcp  32768  status
    100011    1   udp    647  rquotad
    100011    2   udp    647  rquotad
    100005    1   udp  32769  mountd
    100005    1   tcp  32769  mountd
    100005    2   udp  32769  mountd
    100005    2   tcp  32769  mountd
    100003    2   udp   2049  nfs
    100003    3   udp   2049  nfs
    100021    1   udp  32770  nlockmgr
    100021    3   udp  32770  nlockmgr
```

Note *The NFS package also includes analytical tools with which you can measure the performance of a NFS server.* ***nhfsstone*** *will generate performance data on specified test directories by generating an artificial load (demand on the server) based on a range of different NFS operations.* ***nhfsrun*** *will run* ***nhfsstone*** *with a variety of loads. You can use* ***nhfsnum*** *to generate a graph of the data, and* ***nhfsgraph*** *for a postscript version.*

NFS Configuration: /etc/exports

An entry in the **/etc/exports** file specifies the file system to be exported and the hosts on the network that can access it. For the file system, enter its *mountpoint,* the directory to which it was mounted on the host system. This is followed by a list of hosts that can access this file system along with options to control that access. A comma-separated list of export options placed within a set of parentheses may follow each host. For example, you might want to give one host read-only access and another read and write access. If the options are preceded by an * symbol, they are applied to any host. A list of options is provided in Table 34-1. The format of an entry in the **/etc/exports** file is shown here:

```
directory-pathname   host-designation(options)
```

General Options	Description
secure	Requires request originate on secure ports, those less than 1024. This is on by default.
insecure	Turns off the **secure** option.
ro	Allows only read-only access. This is the default.
rw	Allows read-write access.
sync	Performs all writes when requested. This is the default.
async	Performs all writes when the server is ready.
no_wdelay	Performs writes immediately, not checking to see if they are related.
wdelay	Checks to see if writes are related, and, if so, waits to perform them together. Can degrade performance. This is the default.
hide	Automatically hides an exported directory that is the subdirectory of another exported directory. The subdirectory has to be explicitly mounted to be accessed. Mounting the parent directory does not allow access. This is the default.
no_hide	Does not hide an exported directory that is the subdirectory of another exported directory (opposite of **hide**). Only works for single hosts and can be unreliable.
subtree_check	Checks parent directories in a file system to validate an exported subdirectory. This is the default.
no_subtree_check	Does not check parent directories in a file system to validate an exported subdirectory.

Table 34-1. *The /etc/exports Options*

General Options	Description
`insecure_locks`	Does not require authentication of locking requests. Used for older NFS versions.
User ID Mapping	**Description**
`all_squash`	Maps all uids and gids to the anonymous user. Useful for NFS-exported public FTP directories, news spool directories, and so forth.
`no_all_squash`	The opposite option to **all_squash**. This is the default setting.
`root_squash`	Maps requests from remote root user to the anonymous uid/gid. This is the default.
`no_root_squash`	Turns off root squashing. Allows the root user to access as the remote root.
`anonuid` `anongid`	Sets explicitly the uid and gid of the anonymous account used for **all_squash** and **root_squash** options. The defaults are nobody and nogroup.

Table 34-1. *The /etc/exports Options* (continued)

You can have several host entries for the same directory, each with access to that directory:

```
directory-pathname   host(options) host(options)  host(options)
```

You have a great deal of flexibility when specifying hosts. For hosts within your domain you can just use the hostname, whereas for those outside you need to use a fully qualified domain name. You could also just use the host's IP address. Instead of just a single host, you can reference all the hosts within a specific domain, allowing access by an entire network. A simple way to do this is to use the * for the host segment, followed by the domain name for the network, such as ***.mytrek.com** for all the hosts in the **mytrek.com** network. Instead of domain names, you could use IP network addresses using a CNDR format where you specify the netmask to indicate a range of IP addresses. You can also use an NIS netgroup name to reference a collection of hosts. The NIS netgroup name is preceded by a @ sign.

```
directory      host(options)
directory      *(options)
```

```
directory        *.domain(options)
directory        192.168.1.0/255.255.255.0(options)
directory        @netgroup(options)
```

Options in **/etc/exports** operate as permissions to control access to exported directories. Read-only access is set with the **ro** option, and read-write with the **rw** option. The **sync** and **async** options specify whether a write operation is performed immediately (**sync**) or when the server is ready to handle it (**async**). By default, write requests are checked to see if they are related, and, if so, are written together (**wdelay**). This can degrade performance. You can override this default with **no_wdelay** and have writes executed as they are requested. If two directories are exported, where one is the subdirectory of another, the subdirectory is not accessible unless it is explicitly mounted (**hide**). In other words, mounting the parent directory does not make the subdirectory accessible. The subdirectory remains hidden until also mounted. You can overcome this restriction with the **no_hide** option (though this can cause problems with some file systems). If an exported directory is actually a subdirectory in a larger file system, its parent directories are checked to make sure that the subdirectory is the valid directory (**subtree_check**). This option works well with read-only file systems, but can cause problems for write-enabled file systems, where filenames and directories can be changed. You can cancel this check with the **no_subtree_check** option.

Along with general options, there are also options that apply to user-level access. As a security measure, the client's root user is treated as an anonymous user by the NFS server. This is known as squashing the user. In the case of the client root user, squashing prevents the client from attempting to appear as the NFS server's root user. Should you want a particular client's root user to have root-level control over the NFS server, you can specify the **no_root_squash** option. To prevent any client user from attempting to appear as a user on the NFS server, you can classify them as anonymous users (the **all_squash** option). Such anonymous users would only have access to directories and files that are part of the anonymous group.

Normally, if a user on a client system has a user account on the NFS server, that user can mount and access his or her files on the NFS server. However, NFS requires the User ID for the user be the same on both systems. If this is not the case, he or she is considered two different users. To overcome this problem, you could use an NIS service, maintaining User ID information in just one place, the NIS password file (see the following section for information on NIS).

Examples of entries in an **/etc/exports** file are shown here. Read-only access is given to all hosts to the file system mounted on the **/pub** directory, a common name used for public access. Users, however, are treated as anonymous users (**all_squash**). Read and write access is given to the **lizard.mytrek.com** computer for the file system mounted on the **/home/foodstuff** directory. The next entry would allow access by **rabbit.mytrek.com** to the NFS server's CD-ROM. The last entry allows anyone secure access to **/home/richlp**.

/etc/exports

```
/pub                *(ro,insecure,all_squash)
/home/foodstuff     lizard.mytrek.com(rw)
/mnt/cdrom          rabbit.mytrek.com(ro)
/home/richlp        *(secure)
```

Note *Instead of editing the* ***/etc/exports*** *file directly, you can use utilities like Webmin Linuxconf.*

Each time your system starts up the NFS server (usually when the system starts up), the **/etc/exports** file will be read and those directories specified will be exported. When a directory is exported, an entry for it is made in the **/var/lib/nfs/xtab** file. It is this file that NFS reads and uses to perform the actual exports. Entries are read from **/etc/exports** and corresponding entries made in **/var/lib/nfs/xtab**. The **xtab** file maintains the list of actual exports.

If you want to export added entries in the **/etc/exports** file immediately, without rebooting, you can use the **exportfs** command with the **-a** option. It is helpful to add the **-v** option to display the actions that NFS is taking. Use the same options to effect any changes you make to the **/etc/exports** file.

```
exportfs -a -v
```

If you later make changes to the **/etc/exports** file, you can use the **-r** option to re-export its entries. The **-r** option will resync the **/var/lib/nfs/xtab** file with the **/etc/exports** entries, removing any other exports or any with different options.

```
exportfs -r -v
```

To both export added entries and re-export changed ones, you can combine the **-r** and **-a** options.

```
exportfs -r -a -v
```

You can also use the **exportfs** command to manually export file systems instead of using an entry for it in the **/etc/exports** file. Export entries will be added to the **/var/lib/nfs/xtab** file directly. With the **-o** option you can list various permissions, and then follow them with the host and file system to export. The host and file system are separated by a colon. For example, to manually export the **/home/myprojects** directory to **golf.mytrek.com** with the permissions **ro** and **insecure**, you would use the following:

```
exportfs -o rw,insecure golf.mytrek.com:/home/myprojects
```

You can also use **exportfs** to unexport a directory that has already been exported, either manually or by the **/etc/exports** file. Just use the **-u** option with the host and the directory exported. The entry for the export will be removed from the **/var/lib/nfs/xtab** file. The following example will unexport the **/home/foodstuff** directory that was exported to **lizard.mytrek.com**:

```
exportfs -u lizard.mytrek.com:/home/foodstuff
```

NFS Security: /etc/hosts.allow and /etc/hosts.deny

The **/etc/hosts.allow** and **/etc/hosts.deny** files are used to restrict access to services provided by your server to hosts on your network or on the Internet (if accessible). For example, you can use the **hosts.allow** file to permit access by certain hosts to your FTP server. Entries in the **hosts.deny** file would explicitly deny access to certain hosts. For NFS, you can provide the same kind of security by controlling access to specific NFS daemons.

You can further secure your NFS transmissions by having them operate over TCP instead of UDP. Use the **tcp** *option to mount your NFS file systems (UDP is the default). However, performance does degrade for NFS when it uses TCP.*

The first line of defense is to control access to the portmapper service. The portmapper tells hosts where the NFS services can be found on the system. Restricting access does not allow a remote host to even locate NFS. For a strong level of security, you should deny access to all hosts except those that are explicitly allowed. In the **hosts.deny** file, you would place the following entry, denying access to all hosts by default. ALL is a special keyword denoting all hosts.

```
portmap:ALL
```

In the **hosts.allow** file, you would then enter the hosts on your network, or any others that you would want to permit access to your NFS server. Again, you would specify the portmapper service, then list the IP addresses of the hosts you are permitting access. You can list specific IP addresses or a network range using a netmask. The following example allows access only by hosts in the local network, 192.168.0.0, and to the host 10.0.0.43. You can separate addresses with commas.

```
portmap: 192.168.0.0/255.255.255.0, 10.0.0.43
```

The portmapper is also used by other services such as NIS. If you close all access to the portmapper in **hosts.deny**, you will also need to allow access to NIS services in **hosts.allow**, if you are running them. These include ypbind and ypserver. In addition, you may have to add entries for remote commands like **ruptime** and **rusers**, if you are supporting them.

In addition, it is also advisable to add the same level of control for specific NFS services. In the **hosts.deny** file you would add entries for each service, as shown here:

```
mountd:ALL
rquotad:ALL
statd:ALL
lockd:ALL
```

Then, in the **hosts.allow** file, you can add entries for each service:

```
mountd: 192.168.0.0/255.255.255.0, 10.0.0.43
rquotad: 192.168.0.0/255.255.255.0, 10.0.0.43
statd: 192.168.0.0/255.255.255.0, 10.0.0.43
lockd: 192.168.0.0/255.255.255.0, 10.0.0.43
```

You can further control access using Netfilter to check transmissions from certain hosts on the ports used by NFS services. See Chapter 37 for an explanation of Netfilter. The portmapper uses port 111 and nfsd uses 2049. Netfilter is helpful if you have a private network that has an Internet connection, and you want to protect it from the Internet. Usually a specific network device, like an Ethernet card, is dedicated to the Internet connection. The following examples assume that device **eth1** is connected to the Internet. Any packets attempting access on ports 111 and 2049 are refused.

```
iptables -A INPUT -i eth1 -p 111 -j DENY
iptables -A INPUT -i eth1 -p 2049 -j DENY
```

To enable NFS for your local network, you will have to allow packet fragments. Assuming that **etho** is the device used for the local network, you could use the following example:

```
iptables -A INPUT -i eth0 -f -j ACCEPT
```

Note *A root user on a remote host can try to access a remote NFS server as a root user with root level permissions. The* **root_squash** *option (a default) will automatically change the remote root user to the nobody (anonymous) user.*

Mounting NFS File Systems: NFS Clients

Once NFS makes directories available to different hosts, those hosts can then mount those directories on their own systems and access them. The host needs to be able to operate as NFS clients. Current Linux kernels all have NFS client capability built in. This means that any NFS client can mount a remote NFS directory that they have access to by performing a simple mount operation.

Mounting NFS Automatically: /etc/fstab

You can mount an NFS directory either by an entry in the **/etc/fstab** file or by an explicit **mount** command. You have your NFS file systems mounted automatically by placing entries for them in **/etc/fstab** file. An NFS entry in the **/etc/fstab** file has a mount type of NFS. An NFS file system name consists of the hostname of the computer it is located on, followed by the pathname of the directory where it is mounted. The two are separated by a colon. For example, **rabbit.trek.com:/home/project** specifies a file system mounted at **/home/project** on the **rabbit.trek.com** computer. The format for an NFS entry in the **/etc/fstab** file follows. Notice that the file type is **nfs**.

```
host:remote-directory    local-directory     nfs   options   0   0
```

You can also include several NFS-specific mount options with your NFS entry. You can specify the size of datagrams sent back and forth, and the amount of time your computer waits for a response from the host system. You can also specify whether a file system is to be hard-mounted or soft-mounted. For a *hard-mounted* file system, your computer continually tries to make contact if for some reason the remote system fails to respond. A *soft-mounted* file system, after a specified interval, gives up trying to make contact and issues an error message. A hard mount is the default. A system making a hard-mount attempt that continues to fail will stop responding to user input as it tries continually to achieve the mount. For this reason, soft mounts may be preferable as they will simply stop attempting a mount that continually fails. Table 34-2 and the Man pages for **mount** contain a listing of these NFS client options. They differ from the NFS server options indicated previously.

An example of an NFS entry follows. The remote system is **rabbit.mytrek.com** and the file system is mounted on **/home/projects**. This file system is to be mounted on the local system as the **/home/dylan/projects** directory. The **/home/dylan/projects** directory must already be created on the local system. The type of system is NFS and the **timeo** option specifies the local system waits up to 20 tenths of a second (two seconds) for a response. The mount is a soft mount and it can be interrupted by NFS.

```
rabbit.mytrek.com:/home/projects /home/dylan/projects  nfs  soft,intr,timeo=20
```

Note *Instead of editing the **/etc/fstab** file directly, you can use Linuxconf or Webmin.*

Options	Description
`rsize=`*n*	The number of bytes NFS uses when reading files from an NFS server. The default is 1,024 bytes. A size of 8,192 can greatly improve performance.
`wsize=`*n*	The number of bytes NFS uses when writing files to an NFS server. The default is 1,024 bytes. A size of 8,192 can greatly improve performance.
`timeo=`*n*	The value in tenths of a second before sending the first retransmission after a timeout. The default value is seven-tenths of a second.
`retry=`*n*	The number of minutes to retry an NFS mount operation before giving up. The default is 10,000 minutes (one week).
`retrans=`*n*	The number of retransmissions or minor timeouts for an NFS mount operation before a major timeout (default is 3). At that time, the connection is cancelled or a "server not responding" message is displayed.
`soft`	Mount system using soft mount.
`hard`	Mount system using hard mount. This is the default.
`intr`	Allow NFS to interrupt the file operation and return to the calling program. The default is not to allow file operations to be interrupted.
`bg`	If the first mount attempt times out, continue trying the mount in the background. The default is to fail without backgrounding.
`tcp`	Mount the NFS file system using the TCP protocol, instead of the default UDP protocol.

Table 34-2. *NFS Options*

Mounting NFS Manually: mount

You can also use the **mount** command with the **-t nfs** option to mount an NFS file system explicitly. To mount the previous entry explicitly, use the following command:

```
# mount -t nfs -o soft,intr,timeo=20   \
        rabbit.mytrek.com:/home/projects   /home/dylan/projects
```

You can, of course, unmount an NFS directory with the **umount** command. You can specify either the local mountpoint or the remote host and directory, as shown here:

```
umount /home/dylan/projects
umount  rabbit.mytrek.com:/home/projects
```

On Mandrake and Red Hat systems, you can also mount and unmount all your NFS file systems at once with the ***/etc/rc.d/init.d/netfs*** *script, which you can invoke with the* **service** *command. This script reads the NFS entries in the* ***/etc/fstab*** *file, using them to mount and unmount NFS remote directories. Using the* **stop** *argument unmounts the file systems, and with the* **start** *argument, you mount them again. The* **restart** *argument first unmounts and then remounts the file systems.*

Mounting NFS on Demand: autofs

You can also mount NFS file systems using the automount service, autofs. This requires added configuration on the client's part. The autofs service will mount a file system only when you try to access it. A directory change operation (**cd**) to a specified directory will trigger the mount operation, mounting the remote file system at that time.

The autofs service is configured using a master file to list map files, which in turn lists the file systems to be mounted. The **/etc/auto.master** file is the autofs master file. The master file will list the root pathnames where file systems can be mounted along with a map file for each of those pathnames. The map file will then list a key (subdirectory), mount options, and the file systems that can be mounted in that root pathname directory. On some distributions, the **/auto** directory is already implemented as the root pathname for files systems automatically mounted. You could add your own in the **/etc/auto.master** file along with your own map files, if you wish. You will find that the **/etc/auto.master** file contains the following entry for the **/auto** directory, listing **auto.misc** as its map file:

```
/auto    auto.misc    --timeout 60
```

Following the map file you can add options, as shown in the previous example. The **timeout** option specifies the number of seconds of inactivity to wait before trying to automatically unmount.

In the map file, you list the key, the mount options, and the file system to be mounted. The key will be the subdirectory on the local system where the file system is mounted. For example, to mount the **/home/projects** directory on the **rabbit.mytrek.com** host to the **/auto/projects** directory, you would use the following entry:

```
projects  soft,intr,timeo=20   rabbit.mytrek.com:/home/projects
```

You could also create a new entry in the master file for an NFS file system, as shown here:

```
/myprojects    auto.myprojects   --timeout 60
```

You would then create an **/etc/auto.myprojects** file and place entries in it for NFS files system mounts, like the following:

```
dylan   soft,intr,rw   rabbit.mytrek.com:/home/projects
newgame   soft,intr,ro   lizard.mytrek.com:/home/supergame
```

Note *The autofs service can be used for any file systems, including floppy disks and CD-ROMs. See Chapter 29.*

Network Information Service: NIS

On networks supporting NFS, many resources and devices are shared by the same systems. Normally, each system would need its own configuration files for each device or resource. Changes would entail updating each system individually. However, NFS provides a special service called Network Information Services (NIS) that maintains such configuration files for the entire network. For changes, you only need to update the NIS files. NIS works for information required for most administrative tasks, such as those relating to users, network access, or devices. For example, you can maintain user and password information with an NIS service, having only to update those NIS password files.

Note *NIS+ is a more advanced form of NIS that provides support for encryption and authentication. However, it is more difficult to administer.*

NIS was developed by Sun Microsystems and was originally known as Sun's Yellow Pages (YP). NIS files are kept on an NIS server (NIS servers are still sometimes referred to as YP servers). Individual systems on a network use NIS clients to make requests from the NIS server. The NIS server maintains its information on special database files called *maps*. Linux versions exist for both NIS clients and servers. Linux NIS clients easily connect to any network using NIS.

The NIS client is installed as part of the initial installation on most Linux distributions. NIS client programs are ypbind (the NIS client daemon), ypwhich, ypcat, yppoll, ypmatch, yppasswd, and ypset. Each has its own Man page with details of its use. The NIS server programs are ypserv, ypinit, yppasswdd, yppush, ypxfr, and netgroup—each also with its own Man page. A detailed NIS HOW-TO document is available in the **/usr/share/doc/HOWTO** directory.

You can use such tools as Linuxconf, Webmin, SuSE's Yast, and Red Hat's authconfig to specify the remote NIS server on your network.

NIS Servers

You have significant flexibility when setting up NIS servers. If you have a small network, you may need only one NIS domain for which you would have one NIS server. For larger networks, you can divide your network into several NIS domains, each with its own server. Even if you only have one domain, you may want several NIS slave servers. For an NIS domain, you can have a master NIS server and several NIS slave servers. The slave servers can act as backups, in case the master server goes down. A slave server only contains copies of the configuration files set up on the NIS master server.

Configuring an NIS server involves several steps, listed here:

1. Define the NIS domain name that the NIS server will work for.
2. Start the ypserv daemon.
3. In the **/var/yp/Makefile** file, set any NIS server options and specify the configuration files to manage.
4. Use ypinit to create the NIS versions of the configuration files.

You first have to define an NIS domain name. You can have the NIS domain defined whenever you start up your system, by defining the NIS_DOMAIN variable in the **/etc/sysconfig/network** file. To this variable, you assign the name you want to give your NIS domain. The following example defines the NIS domain called **myturtles.nis**:

```
NIS_DOMAIN=myturtles.nis
```

When first setting up the server, you may want to define your NIS domain name without having to restart your system. You can do so with the **domainname** command, as shown here:

```
domainname myturtles.nis
```

You can start the NIS server with the ypserv startup script:

```
service ypserv start
```

Instead of the **service** command you could reference the ypserv script directly, as shown here:

```
/etc/rc.d/init.d/ypserv start
```

Then edit the **/var/yp/Makefile** file to select the configuration files that the NIS server will maintain, along with setting any NIS server options. Standard options as well as listed most commonly used configuration files are usually already set up.

NIS server options are listed first. The NOPUSH option will be set to true, indicating that there are no slave NIS servers. If you are setting up any slave NIS servers for this domain, you will have to set this option to no:

```
NOPUSH = true
```

The minimum user and group ids are set to 500. These are set using the MINUID and MINGID variables:

```
MINUID=500
MINGID=500
```

Most distributions use a shadow password and shadow group files to encrypt passwords and groups; the MERGE_PASSWD and MERGE_GROUP settings will be set to true. NIS will merge shadow password information into its password file:

```
MERGE_PASSWD=true
MERGE_GROUP=true
```

The directories where NIS will find password and other configuration files are then defined using the YPSRCDIR and YPPWDIR variables. This is the **/etc** directory:

```
YPSRCDIR = /etc
YPPWDDIR = /etc
```

Then the configuration files that NIS could manage are listed. Here, you will find entries like PASSWD for password, GROUP for your groups, and PRINTCAP for your printers. The current entries are shown here:

```
GROUP       = $(YPPWDDIR)/group
PASSWD      = $(YPPWDDIR)/passwd
SHADOW      = $(YPPWDDIR)/shadow
GSHADOW     = $(YPPWDDIR)/gshadow
ADJUNCT     = $(YPPWDDIR)/passwd.adjunct
#ALIASES     = $(YPSRCDIR)/aliases  # aliases could be in /etc or /etc/mail
ALIASES     = /etc/aliases
ETHERS      = $(YPSRCDIR)/ethers     # ethernet addresses (for rarpd)
BOOTPARAMS  = $(YPSRCDIR)/bootparams # for booting Sun boxes (bootparamd)
HOSTS       = $(YPSRCDIR)/hosts
```

```
NETWORKS     = $(YPSRCDIR)/networks
PRINTCAP     = $(YPSRCDIR)/printcap
PROTOCOLS    = $(YPSRCDIR)/protocols
PUBLICKEYS   = $(YPSRCDIR)/publickey
RPC          = $(YPSRCDIR)/rpc
SERVICES     = $(YPSRCDIR)/services
NETGROUP     = $(YPSRCDIR)/netgroup
NETID        = $(YPSRCDIR)/netid
AMD_HOME     = $(YPSRCDIR)/amd.home
AUTO_MASTER  = $(YPSRCDIR)/auto.master
AUTO_HOME    = $(YPSRCDIR)/auto.home
AUTO_LOCAL   = $(YPSRCDIR)/auto.local
TIMEZONE     = $(YPSRCDIR)/timezone
LOCALE       = $(YPSRCDIR)/locale
NETMASKS     = $(YPSRCDIR)/netmasks
```

The actual files that are shared on the network are listed in the **all:** entry, which follows the list of configuration files. Only some of the files defined are listed as shared, those listed in the first line after **all:**. The remaining lines are automatically commented out (with a preceding **#** sign). You can add files by removing the **#** sign, or moving its entry to the first line.

```
all:  passwd group hosts rpc services netid protocols mail \
      # netgrp shadow publickey networks ethers bootparams printcap \
      # amd.home auto.master auto.home auto.local passwd.adjunct \
      # timezone locale netmasks
```

Be sure not to touch the remainder of the **Makefile**.

You then enter the **ypinit** command with the **-m** option to create the NIS database consisting of the NIS configuration files. Your NIS server will be detected, and then you will be asked to enter the names of any slave NIS servers used on this NIS domain. If there are any, enter them in. When you are finished, press CTRL-D. The NIS database files are then created.

```
/usr/lib/yp/ypinit -m

At this point, we have to construct a list of the hosts which will run NIS
servers.  turtle.mytrek.com is in the list of NIS server hosts.
Please continue to add the names for the other hosts, one per line.
When you are done with the list, type a <control D>.
      next host to add:  turtle.mytrek.com
      next host to add:
The current list of NIS servers looks like this:

turtle.mytrek.com
```

```
Is this correct?  [y/n: y]  y
We need some  minutes to build the databases...
Building /var/yp/myturtles.nis/ypservers...
Running /var/yp/Makefile...
gmake[1]: Entering directory '/var/yp/myturtles.nis'
Updating passwd.byname...
Updating passwd.byuid...
Updating group.byname...
Updating group.bygid...
Updating hosts.byname...
Updating hosts.byaddr...
Updating rpc.byname...
Updating rpc.bynumber...
Updating services.byname...
Updating services.byservicename...
Updating netid.byname...
Updating protocols.bynumber...
Updating protocols.byname...
Updating mail.aliases...
gmake[1]: Leaving directory '/var/yp/myturtles.nis'
```


For an NIS slave server, you would use:

```
ypinit -s masterhost
```

Should you receive the following error, it most likely means that your NIS server was not running. Be sure to start ypserv before you run ypinit.

```
failed to send 'clear' to local ypserv: RPC: Program not registeredUpdating
```

If you later need to update your NIS server files, you would change to the **/var/yp** directory and issue the **make** command.

```
cd /var/yp
make
```

The **/var/yp/securenets** file enables access by hosts to your NIS server. Hosts can be referenced by network or individually. Entries consist of subnet mask and an IP address. For example, you could give access to all the hosts in an local network with the following entry:

```
255.255.255.0  192.168.1.0
```

For individual hosts, you can use the mask 255.255.255.255 or just the term "host", as shown here:

```
host   192.168.1.4
```

Controlling how different hosts access NIS shared data is determined in **/etc/ypserv.conf**.

Netgroups

You can use NIS to set up netgroups, which allows you to create network level groups of users. Whereas normal groups are created locally on separate hosts, an NIS netgroup can be used for network wide services. For example, you can use NIS netgroups to control access to NFS file systems. Netgroups are defined in the **/etc/netgroup** file. Entries consist of a netgroup name followed by member identifiers consisting of three segments: the hosts, the user, and the NIS domain:

```
group    (host, user, NIs-domain) (host, user, NIS-domain) ...
```

For example, in the NIS domain **myturtles.nis**, to define a group called **myprojects** that consists of the user **chris** on the host **rabbit**, and the user **george** on the host **lizard.mytrek.com**, you would use the following:

```
myprojects (rabbit, chris, myturtles.nis) \
                          (lizard.mytrek.com, george, myturtles.nis)
```

A blank segment will match on any value. The following entry includes all users on the host **rabbit**:

```
newgame (rabbit,,myturtles.ni)
```

If your use of a group doesn't need either a user or host segment, you can eliminate the other using a hyphen (-). The following example generates a netgroup consisting just of hostnames, with no usernames:

```
myservers (rabbit,-,) (turtle.mytrek.com,-,)
```

You can then reference different netgroups in various configuration files by prefixing the netgroup name with an **@** sign, as shown here:

```
@newgame
```

NIS Clients

For a host to use NIS on your network, you first need to specify your NIS domain name on that host. In addition, your NIS clients need to know the name of your NIS server. If you installed Linux on a network already running NIS, you may have already entered this information during the installation process.

Note *On Red Hat, you can specify your NIS domain name and server with the Text Mode Setup Tool (setuptool), which you can access from the Gnome system menu or by entering the command* **setup** *at the shell prompt. From the menu, select Authentication. This opens the authconfig window. For NIS, you can enter the name of the NIS domain as well as the NIS server. The setuptool will save the NIS domain in the* ***/etc/sysconfig/network*** *file, and the NIS server in the* ***/etc/yp.conf*** *file.*

Each NIS client host on your network then has to run the ypbind NIS client to access the server. In the client's **/etc/yp.conf** file, you need to specify the NIS server it will use. The following entry would reference the NIS server at 192.168.1.1:

```
ypserver 192.168.1.1
```

Alternatively, you can specify the NIS domain name and the server it uses:

```
domain mydomain.nis  server servername
```

Setuptool will make the following entry in **/etc/yp.conf** for the **myturtle.nis** NIS domain using the **turtle.mytrek.com** server:

```
domain myturtles.nis server turtle.mytrek.com
```

To start the NIS client, you run the ypbind script:

```
service ypbind start
```

Then, to check that all is working, you can use ypcat to try to list the NIS password file:

```
ypcat passwd.
```

You can use ypcat to list any of the NIS configuration files. The **ypwhich** command will display the name of the NIS server your client is using. ypmatch can be used to find a particular entry in a configuration file.

```
ypmatch cecelia passwd.
```

User can change their password in the NIS **passwd** file by using the **yppasswd** command. It works the same as the **passwd** command. You will also have to have the yppasswdd daemon running.

To ensure that the client accesses the NIS server for a particular configuration file, you should specify **nis** in file's entry in the **/etc/nsswitch.conf** file. The **/etc/nsswitch.conf** file specifies where a host should look for certain kinds of information. For example, the following entry says to check the NIS server (**nis**) first and then the local configuration files (**files**) for passwords data:

```
passwd:   nis files
```

The **files** designation says to first use the system's own files, those on the local host. **nis** says to look up entries in the NIS files, accessing the NIS server. **nisplus** says to use NIS+ files maintained by the NIS+ server. **dns** says to perform DNS lookups and can only be used on files like **hosts** that contain hostnames. These are some standard entries:

```
passwd:     files nisplus nis
shadow:     files nisplus nis
group:      files nisplus nis

hosts:      files nisplus nis dns
bootparams: nisplus [NOTFOUND=return] files

ethers:     files
netmasks:   files
networks:   files
protocols:  files nisplus nis
rpc:        files
services:   files nisplus nis
netgroup:   files nisplus nis
publickey:  nisplus
automount:  files nisplus nis
aliases:    files nisplus
```

Netatalk: AppleTalk

To access Apple file systems and printers such as those on Macintosh computers you need to use specialized servers that support the AppleTalk protocol. AppleTalk is the network protocol used for Apple Macintosh computers. AppleTalk supports file sharing and network printing, where different Macs can share each other's file systems and printers. For example, if you have a LaserWriter connected to a Macintosh, you can have other Macintosh systems access it and print on that LaserWriter. You can also access any shared file systems that may be set up on the Macintoshes on the network.

Note *Mac OS X, which is based on BSD Unix, now supports NFS for file sharing.*

To enable Apple systems such as Macintosh to access a Linux system, that Linux system has to emulate the AppleTalk protocols. You can do this with a Netatalk daemon. Netatalk implements the classic AppleTalk and AppleShare IP network protocol on Unix and Linux systems. AppleShare IP implements AppleTalk over an IP network. Netatalk provides support for sharing file systems, accessing printers, and routing AppleTalk. Netatalk allows a Mac machine connected to an AppleTalk network to access a Linux system as if it were an AppleTalk file and print server. Linux systems can also use Netatalk to access Mac machines connected to an AppleTalk network. The current Netatalk Web sites are **www.umich.edu/~rsug/netatalk/** and **netatalk.sourceforge.net**, with links to the FAQ and the HOW-TO sections.

The Netatalk server is called afpd and is used to implement both classic AppleTalk and AppleShare IP connections. Classic AppleTalk further needs the atalkd daemon which sets up interfaces between the kernel AppleTalk module and classic AppleTalk operations. It performs much the same function as routed and ifconfig. Several programs manage printing. The papd program lets Macs spool to a Linux printer. The pap program lets Linux systems print to an AppleTalk printer. The psf program is a PostScript printer filter for pap, and psorder enables you to print PostScript pages in reverse. The apfd program provides an interface to the Linux file system, while the nbplkup program lists all AppleTalk objects on the network. For example, **`nbplkup :LaserWriter`** lists the LaserWriters available. You would use the pap program to access and print to a LaserWriter. To use Linux commands to access a printer, you need to make an entry for the command in the **/etc/printcap** file, and create spool, status, and lock files for it.

Netatalk requires kernel-level support for the AppleTalk Datagram Delivery Protocol (DDP) for classic AppleTalk. If your kernel does not currently support it, you either must rebuild the kernel including AppleTalk support or use a loadable module for AppleTalk, **appletalk.o**. Current kernels for most distributions include AppleTalk support. AppleShare IP only requires TCP/IP support.

Netatalk uses five configuration files, as shown in Table 34-3. The software package includes default versions you can modify. The RPM package includes the **/etc/atalk/config** file that contains documented default entries for use by the **atalk** startup script. Check the variable entries for any parameters you may want to change, such as the maximum number of allowed simultaneous users.

Configuration files are automatically installed for you by the RPM package versions of Netatalk. If you are installing from the source distribution, you need to install these from default files in the source directory. Also, make sure the following lines are in your **/etc/services** file (RPM packages add these automatically):

```
rtmp    1/ddp # Routing Table Maintenance Protocol
nbp     2/ddp # Name Binding Protocol
echo    4/ddp # AppleTalk Echo Protocol
zip     6/ddp # Zone Information Protocol
```

```
afpovertcp 548/tcp # AFP over TCP
afpovertcp 548/udp
```

Netatalk is started using a startup script called **atalk**. You can also use a System V Init runlevel editor to manage startup and shutdown operations. A link is set up to start the **atalk** script when you boot. You can also use **start** and **stop** arguments directly with **atalk**:

```
service atalk  start
```

The afpd server will implement both classic AppleTalk and AppleShare IP, though classic AppleTalk also requires that the atalkd server be running. Once apfd is started, you can then use your Macintosh client to access your shared Linux directories or printers. On your Macintosh, select AppleShare under the Chooser. Your Netatalk server should appear. For AppleShare IP, select the AppleShareIP button and enter your Netatalk server's IP address. You can then log in to the server and access shared files.

If you want to use Netatalk to mount Apple file systems locally—say, like an Apple CD-ROM disk—you need to have HFS support in your kernel. HFS (Hierarchical File System) is the Apple file system format. You can then use the **fork=netatalk** option to use Netatalk to access an Apple CD-ROM disk.

Note *Currently under development is the afpfs daemon, which allows Linux systems to mount Apple file systems.*

Filename	Description
AppleVolumes.default	List of shared directories, including optional names
AppleVolumes.system	Maps of file extensions to Mac OS types
afpd.conf	Configuration file for afpd daemon that implements both classic AppleTalk and AppleShare IP (AppleTalk File system and printer daemon)
atalkd.conf	Controls the interfaces for classic AppleTalk to which Netatalk binds, enabling you to specify network numbers or zones; if empty, Netatalk detects the interfaces itself
papd.conf	Provides AppleTalk access to Linux print queues; if empty, uses **/etc/printcap**

Table 34-3. *Netatalk Configuration Files*

Chapter 35

Samba

With Samba, you can connect your Windows clients on a Microsoft Windows network to services such as shared files, systems, and printers controlled by the Linux Samba server. Whereas most Unix and Linux systems use the TCP/IP protocol for networking, Microsoft networking with Windows uses a different protocol, called the Server Message Block (SMB) protocol, that implements a local area network (LAN) of PCs running Windows. SMB makes use of a network interface called Network Basic Input Output System (NetBIOS) that allows Windows PCs to share resources, such as printers and disk space. One Windows PC on such a network can access part of another Windows PC's disk drive as if it were its own. SMB was originally designed for small LANs. To connect it to larger networks, including those with Unix systems, Microsoft developed the Common Internet File System (CIFS). CIFS still uses SMB and NetBIOS for Windows networking. Wanting to connect his Linux system to a Windows PC, Andrew Tridgell wrote a SMB client and server that he called Samba. Samba allows Unix and Linux systems to connect to such a Windows network, as if they were Windows PCs. Unix systems can share resources on Windows systems as if they were just another Windows PC. Windows PCs can also access resources on Unix systems as if they were Windows systems. Samba, in effect, has become a professional level, open source, and free version of CIFS. It also runs much faster than CIFS. Samba effectively enables you to use a Linux or Unix server as a network server for a group of Windows machines operating on a Windows network. You can also use it to share files on your Linux system with other Windows PCs, or to access files on a Windows PC from your Linux system, as well as between Windows PCs. On Linux systems, an **smbfs** file system enables you, in effect, to mount a remote SMB-shared directory on to your own file system. You can then access it as if it were a directory on your local system.

You can obtain extensive documentation and current releases from the Samba Web and FTP sites at **www.samba.org** and **ftp.samba.org**. RPM packages can be obtained from respective distribution FTP sites, such as **ftp.redhat.com**. Samba is also included on most Linux distributions. Other information can be obtained from the SMB newsgroup, **comp.protocols.smb**. Extensive documentation is provided with the software package and installed on your system, usually in the **/usr/share/doc** directory under a subdirectory bearing the name of the Samba release. Here, you can find extensive documentation in HTML and text format, as well as numerous examples and the current FAQs. Samba HOW-TO documentation is also available at **www.linuxdoc.org**. The examples include sample **smb.conf** files for different kinds of configuration. The home page of the SWAT configuration utility also provides Web page–based Samba documentation, as well as context-level help for different features.

The Samba software package consists of two server daemons and several utility programs (see Table 35-1). One daemon, **smbd**, provides file and printer services to SMB clients and other systems, such as Windows, that support SMB. The nmbd utility is a daemon that provides NetBIOS name resolution and service browser support. The smbclient utility provides FTP-like access by Linux clients to Samba services. smbmount and smbumount enable Linux clients to mount and unmount Samba shared directories. The smbstatus utility displays the current status of the smb server and who is using it.

Application	Description
smbd	Samba server daemon that provides file and printer services to SMD clients
nmbd	Samba daemon that provides NetBIOS name resolution and service browser support
smbclient	Provides FTP-like access by Linux clients to Samba services
smbmount	Mounts Samba share directories on Linux clients
smbumount	Unmounts Samba share directories mounted on Linux clients
smbpasswd	Changes SMB-encrypted passwords on Samba servers
smbstatus	Displays the current status of the SMB network connections
smbrun	Interface program between smbd and external programs
testparm	Tests the Samba configuration file, **smb.conf**
smbtar	Backs up SMB/CIFS-shared resources directly to a Unix tape drive
nmblookup	Maps the NetBIOS name of a Windows PC to its IP address
SWAT	Samba Web administration tool for configuring **smb.conf** with a Web browser; enables you to use a Web page interface to create and maintain your Samba configuration file, **smb.conf**
windbind	Uses authentication services provided by Windows domain

Table 35-1. *Samba Applications*

You use testparm to test your Samba configuration. **smbtar** is a shell script that backs up SMB/CIFS-shared resources directly to a Unix tape drive. You use nmblookup to map the NetBIOS name of a Windows PC to its IP address. Also included with the package is the Samba Web administration tool (SWAT). This enables you to use a Web page interface to create and maintain your Samba configuration file, **/etc/samba/smb.conf**. Samba configuration files are kept in the **/etc/samba** directory.

Samba provides four main services: file and printer services, authentication and authorization, name resolution, and service announcement. The SMB daemon, **smbd**, provides the file and printer services, as well as authentication and authorization for those services. This means users on the network can share files and printers. You can control access to these services by requiring users to provide a password. When users try to access a shared directory, they are prompted for a password. Control can be implemented in share mode or user mode. The *share* mode sets up one password for the shared resource, and then enables any user who has that password to access it. The *user* mode provides a different password for each user. Samba maintains its own password file for this purpose: **/etc/samba/smbpasswd**.

Name resolution and service announcements are handled by the nmbd server. Name resolution essentially resolves NetBIOS names with IP addresses. Service announcement, also known as *browsing*, is the way a list of services available on the network is made known to the connected Windows PCs (and Linux PCs connected through Samba).

Samba also includes the **windbind** daemon, which allows Samba servers to use authentication services provided by a Windows domain. Instead of a Samba server maintaining its own set of users to allow access, it can make use of a Windows domain authentication service to authenticate users.

Note *If you want to download source code or binaries in compressed archives (**.tar.gz**) from **www.samba.org**, the archive will extract to its own **samba** subdirectory. To use it, extract the archive in a software directory like **/usr/local**. Be sure to add **/usr/local/samba/bin** in your PATH. Alternatively, you could copy the **samba/bin** files to **/usr/bin**, except for nmb and smbd, which should be copied to **/usr/sbin**.*

Setting Up Samba

For a simple Samba setup, you should be able to use the default **smb.conf** file installed with the Linux distribution package of Samba. If you need to make changes, however, you must restart the Samba server to have the changes take effect. Starting, stopping, and restarting the Samba server is managed by the **/etc/rc.d/init.d/smb** script using the options start, stop, and restart (**/etc/rc.d/smb** on SuSE). On Mandrake and Red Hat, you can run the **smb** script directly as shown here:

```
service smb restart
```

On Red Hat, you can also use the desktop Service Configuration tool (serviceconf) to start and stop Samba, and on Mandrake you can use the System Services panel in the Mandrake Control Center (on SuSE use YaST).

To ensure name resolution, you can enter the name of your host and its IP address in the **/etc/lmhosts** file. On Windows systems, **lmhosts** entries consist of an IP address and the system's NetBIOS name, the name it is known by on a Microsoft network. For your Linux system, you can enter the IP address and the Linux system's hostname.

To test your connection from a Linux system, you can use the **`smbclient`** command to query the Samba server. To access the home directory of a user on the Samba server, use the IP or hostname address of the Samba server, along with the **homes** section. With the **`-U`** option, specify a user to connect to on the system, as shown here:

```
smbclient //turtle.mytrek.com/homes -U dylan
```

You are then prompted for a password. If the client password is different from the server password, use the server password. Once connected, you are presented with the smb client prompt as shown here. You can then access the files on the user's home directory:

```
smb: \>
```

To set up a connection for a Windows client, you need to specify the Windows workgroup name and configure the password. The workgroup name is the name that appears in the Entire Network window in the Network Neighborhood on the Windows desktop (My Network Places on Windows 2000, NT, and XP). In the **smb.conf** file, you specify the workgroup name in the **workgroup=** entry in the **global** section. The workgroup name should be uppercase, no more than eight characters, and with no spaces.

You can then restart the Samba server. On a Windows client, you see the workgroup name in the Entire Network folder in your Network Neighborhood. Within the workgroup is an icon for the Samba server, and within that is an icon for the user directory, as specified in the **homes** section of the **smb.conf** file.

Samba configuration options are kept in the **/etc/samba/smb.conf** file. You edit this file to make changes to the configuration. Once you finish making any changes, you should test your **smb.conf** file using the testparm program. The testparm program checks the validity of your configuration entries. By default, testparm uses the **/etc/samba/smb.conf** file, although you can supply a different configuration file as an argument:

```
testparm
```

To check your network connections, use the **smbstatus** command. This command returns a listing of all active smb connections.

*The **/etc/samba/smbusers** file associates Windows network usernames with corresponding users on your Linux Samba server. For example, admin and administrator are made equivalent to the Linux root user.*

Passwords

Connections between Windows clients and Samba servers have been further complicated by the implementation of password encryption on Microsoft networks. Current versions of Windows operating systems, including upgraded versions of Windows NT, 2000, 98, and 95, now require the use of encrypted passwords by default. Samba, on the other hand, uses unencrypted passwords by default. To enable communication between Samba servers and Windows clients, you have to either change Windows clients to use unencrypted passwords or change the Samba server to use encrypted passwords. The more secure course is to implement encrypted passwords on Samba servers, though this entails more administrative work. Though not distributed by default, Samba can be built with SSL support. This SSL-enabled Samba provides support for encrypted SSL network communications. SSL-enabled Samba includes several SSL specific configuration options, each preceded by the term **ssl**. For example **ssl cipher** lets you determine the ciphers that can be used, and **ssl CA certFile** specifies the certificates file.

Samba also provides its own Samba password PAM module, **pam_smbpass.o**. With this module, you provide PAM authentication support for Samba passwords, enabling the use of Windows hosts on a PAM-controlled network. The module could be used for authentication and password management in your PAM samba file. The following entries in the PAM samba file would implement PAM authentication and passwords using the Samba password database:

```
auth required pam_smbpass.so nodelay
password required pam_smbpass.so nodelay
```

Be sure to enable PAM in the **smb.conf** file:

```
obey pam restrictions = yes
```

Samba Encrypted Passwords: smbpasswd

Encrypted passwords come into play if you are using a user-level security instead of share-level security. With user-level security, access to Samba server resources by a Windows client is allowed only to users on that client. Each user on the Windows client has to have a corresponding user account on the Samba server. A user logs in to their Windows account, and can then log in to their Samba server account. Users have to log in providing their username and password. Their username and password have to be registered with the Samba server in the **/etc/samba/smbpasswd** file. You use the **smbpasswd** command to add these passwords.

To implement encrypted passwords on Samba, the Samba server then needs to maintain an encrypted version of user passwords that can be used by Windows clients. This file of encrypted passwords is **/etc/samba/smbpasswd**. Samba passwords can be added or changed for different users with the **smbpasswd** command. Initially, you should generate the Samba password file so it will have entries for all your current Samba users. For this task, you use the **mksmbpasswd.sh** script. You input to this script the contents of the Samba server's **/etc/passwd** file, and it generates entries that can be used for encrypted passwords. You use redirection (**>**) to create the encrypted file. In the following example, an **/etc/samba/smbpasswd** file is initially generated by the **mksmbpasswd** script. The **cat** command with a pipe operation is used to input the contents of the **/etc/passwd** file to the **mksmbpasswd.sh** script:

```
cat /etc/passwd | mksmbpasswd.sh > /etc/samba/smbpasswd
```

If your users and their passwords are being managed by NIS, you would use the **ypcat** command to access the user passwords, as shown here:

```
ypcat passwd | mksmbpasswd.sh > /etc/samba/smbpasswd
```

You then need to change the permissions on this file to protect it from unauthorized access. The 600 option allows only read and write access by the root user:

```
chmod 600 /etc/samba/smbpasswd
```

At this point, **/etc/samba/smbpasswd** will contain entries for all your current users with dummy fields for the passwords. You then use the **smbpasswd** command to add, or later change, encrypted passwords. To add a password for a particular user, you use the **smbpasswd** command with the user's name:

```
# smbpasswd dylan
New SMB Password: new-password
Repeat New SMB Password: new-password
```

Users can use **smbpasswd** to change their own password. The following example shows how you would use **smbpasswd** to change your Samba password. If the user has no Samba password, they can just press the ENTER key.

```
$ smbpasswd
Old SMB password: old-password
New SMB Password: new-password
Repeat New SMB Password: new-password
```

You also have to make sure that Samba is configured to use encrypted passwords. Set the **encrypt passwords** option to **yes** and specify the smb password file. These options are already set in the **/etc/samba/smb.conf** file (described in the following section), but they are commented with a preceding **;** symbol. Just locate the lines and remove the **;** symbols at the beginning of the lines:

```
encrypt passwords = yes
smb passwd file = /etc/samba/smbpasswd
```

You can also use SWAT to make this change. In the GLOBALS page, select Yes from the pop-up menu for the Encrypt Password entry. Then save your changes by clicking the Commit Changes button.

Be sure to restart the Samba server with the following command:

```
service smb restart
```

Clear-Text Passwords on Windows Clients

If you want to use clear-text passwords for Samba, you must manually edit the Windows registry of each Windows client. This is a much riskier approach, because passwords will be transmitted across the network in clear text. On the other hand, you do not need to maintain a separate Samba password file (**/etc/samba/smbpasswd**).

For all Windows clients, you need to add an entry in the Windows registry for **EnablePlainTextPassword** and set the entry to 1:

- For Windows 95 and 98, the **EnablePlainTextPassword** entry is located in **HKEY_LOCAL_MACHINES\System\CurrentControlSet\Services\VxD\VNETSUP**. If this entry is not there, you must make one. Select Edit | New | DWORD Value from the regedit menu bar and rename the entry from New Value #1 to EnablePlainTextPassword.
- For Windows NT, you create a registry entry in **HKEY_LOCAL_MACHINE\System\CurrentControlSet\Services\Rdr\Parameters**. Select Edit | New | DWORD Value to create the entry EnablePlainTextPassword Data: 0x01.
- For Windows 2000, you create a registry entry in **HKEY_LOCAL_MACHINE\SYSTEM\CurrentControlSet\Services\LanmanWorkStation\Parameters**. Select Edit | New | DWORD Value to create the entry EnablePlainTextPassword Data: 0x01.

Make sure Samba is not using encrypted passwords. The encrypt passwords entry in **smb.conf** needs to be commented out or turned off.

Samba Configuration: smb.conf

You configure the Samba daemon using the **smb.conf** file located in the **/etc/samba** directory. The file is separated into two basic parts: one for global options and the other for shared services. A shared service, also known as *shares,* can either be filespace services (used by clients as an extension of their native file systems) or printable services (used by clients to access print services on the host running the server). The filespace service is a directory to which clients are given access and can use the space in it as an extension of their local file system. A printable service provides access by clients to print services, such as printers managed by the Samba server.

The **/etc/samba/smb.conf** file holds the configuration for the various shared resources, as well as global options that apply to all resources. Linux installs an **smb.conf** file in your **/etc/samba** directory. The file contains default settings used for your distribution. You can edit the file to customize your configuration to your own needs. Many entries are commented with either a semicolon or a **#** sign, and you can remove the initial comment symbol to make them effective. Instead of editing the file directly, you may want to use the SWAT configuration utility, which provides an easy-to-use, full-screen Web page interface for entering configurations for shared resources. The SWAT configuration utility also provides extensive help features and documentation. For a complete listing of the Samba configuration parameters, check the Man page for **smb.conf**. An extensive set of sample **smb.conf** files is located in the **/usr/share/doc/samba*** directory in the **examples** subdirectory.

In the **smb.conf** file, global options are set first, followed by each shared resource's configuration. The basic organizing component of the **smb.conf** file is a section. Each resource has its own section that holds its service name and definitions of its attributes. Even global options are placed in a section of their own, labeled **global**. For example, each section for a filespace share consists of the directory and the access rights allowed to users of the filespace. The section of each share is labeled with the name of the shared resource. Special sections, called **printers** and **homes**, provide default descriptions for user directories and printers accessible on the Samba server. Following the special sections, sections are entered for specific services, namely access to specific directories or printers.

A section begins with a section label consisting of the name of the shared resource encased in brackets. Other than the special sections, the section label can be any name you want to give it. Following the section label, on separate lines, different parameters for this service are entered. The parameters define the access rights to be granted to the user of the service. For example, for a directory, you may want it to be browsable, but read-only, and to use a certain printer. Parameters are entered in the format *parameter name = value*. You can enter a comment by placing a semicolon at the beginning of the comment line.

A simple example of a section configuration follows. The section label is encased in brackets and followed by two parameter entries. The **`path`** parameter specifies the directory to which access is allowed. The **`writable`** parameter specifies whether the user has write access to this directory and its filespace.

```
[mysection]
path = /home/chris
writable = true
```

A printer service has the same format, but requires certain other parameters. The **`path`** parameters specify the location of the printer spool directory. The **`read-only`** and **`printable`** parameters are set to true, indicating the service is read-only and printable. **`public`** indicates anyone can access it.

```
[myprinter]
path = /var/spool/samba
read only = true
printable = true
public = true
```

Parameter entries are often synonymous but different entries that have the same meaning. For example, **`read only = no`**, **`writable = yes`**, and **`write ok = yes`**, all mean the same thing, providing write access to the user.

NETWORK ADMINISTRATION

SWAT and smb.conf

SWAT is a network-based Samba configuration tool that uses a Web page interface to enable you to configure your **smb.conf** file. SWAT is, by far, the easiest and simplest way to configure your Samba server. SWAT provides a simple-to-use Web page interface with buttons, menus, and text boxes for entering values. A simple button bar across the top enables you to select the sections you want to configure. A button bar is even there to add passwords. To see the contents of the **smb.conf** file as SWAT changes it, click the View button. The initial screen (HOME) displays the index for Samba documentation (see Figure 35-1). One of SWAT's more helpful features is its context-sensitive help. For each parameter and option SWAT displays, you can click a Help button to display a detailed explanation of the option and examples of its use.

SWAT is normally installed with Samba. SWAT is an xinetd service. As an xinetd service, it will be listed in the **/etc/services** and **/etc/xinetd.d/swat** files. The SWAT program uses port 901, as designated in the **/etc/services** file and shown here:

```
swat 901/tcp # Samba Web Administration Tool
```

As an xinetd service, SWAT will have its own xinetd file in the **/etc/xinetd.d** directory, **/etc/xinetd.d/swat**. SWAT is turned off by default, and its **`disable`** option is set to **`yes`**. To use SWAT, you will have to change the **`disable`** option to **`no`** as shown here:

```
# default: off
# description: SWAT is the Samba Web Admin Tool. Use swat \
#       to configure your Samba server. To use SWAT, \
#       connect to port 901 with your favorite web browser.
service swat
{
      disable = no
      port = 901
      socket_type = stream
      wait = no
      only_from = 127.0.0.1
      user = root
      server = /usr/sbin/swat
      log_on_failure += USERID
}
```

You can do this by either using chkconfig or the Service Configuration tool to turn on the SWAT service or by manually editing the **/etc/xinetd.d/swat** file and changing the **`disable`** option to **`no`**. chkconfig will edit the **/etc/xinetd.d/swat** file for you, making this change (see Chapter 19 for more information about chkconfig).

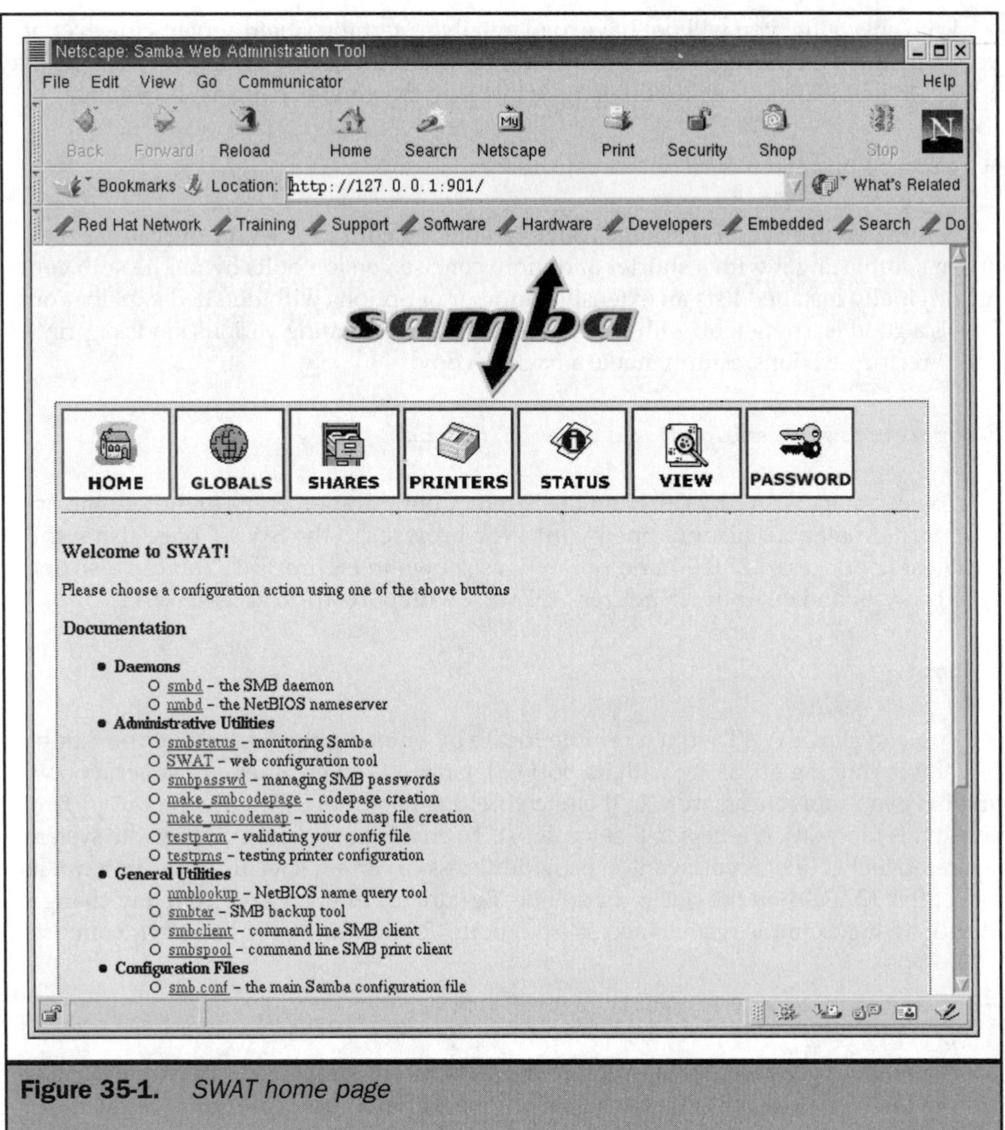

Figure 35-1. *SWAT home page*

The following example shows how you would enable SWAT with the **chkconfig** command:

```
chkconfig swat on
```

With chkconfig, you will not have to manually restart the xinetd server. However, if you manually edit the file, you will also have to restart the server to have the change take effect. On Red Hat, you can do this simply by using the **xinetd** script, as shown here:

```
service xinetd restart
```

Before you use SWAT, back up your current **smb.conf** file. SWAT overwrites the original, replacing it with a shorter and more concise version of its own. The **smb.conf** file originally installed lists an extensive number of options with detailed explanations. This is a good learning tool, with excellent examples for creating various kinds of printer and directory sections. Simply make a backup copy:

```
cp /etc/samba/smb.conf /etc/samba/smb.bk
```

You can start SWAT by selecting the Samba Configuration entry in the Gnome or KDE System menu. This will open your Web browser to the SWAT page using the localhost IP address, 127.0.0.1 and port 901, as shown in Figure 35-1. You can also open your browser and enter the IP address 127.0.0.1 with port 901 to access SWAT.

```
http://127.0.0.1:901
```

You can start SWAT from a remote locate by entering the address of the Samba server it is running on, along with its port (901) into a Web browser. However, you will first have to enable this feature in the **/etc/xinetd.d/swat** file. Currently the **`only_from`** line in this file restricts access to just localhost. To enable access from any remote system, just remove this line. If you want to provide access to certain specific hosts, you can list them after 127.0.0.1 on the **`only_from`** line. Be sure to restart SWAT after any changes. The following example enables access from both 127.0.0.1 and **rabbit.mytrek.com**:

```
only_from 127.0.0.1 rabbit.mytrek.com
```

The following URL entered into a Web browser on a remote system would then display the Web page interface for SWAT on the **turtle.mytrek.com** Samba server:

```
http://turtle.mytrek.com:901
```

You are first asked to enter a username and a password. To configure Samba, you need to enter **`root`** and the root password. (If you are connecting from a remote system, it is *not* advisable to enter the root password in clear text—see Chapter 27.) The main SWAT page is displayed with a button bar, with buttons for links for HOME, GLOBAL,

SHARES, PRINTERS, STATUS, VIEW, and PASSWORD (see Table 35-2). You can use STATUS to list your active SMB network connections.

For the various sections, SWAT can display either a basic or advanced version. The basic version shows only those entries needed for a simple configuration, whereas the advanced version shows all the possible entries for that type of section. A button—labeled Advanced View and Basic View, respectively—is at the top of the section page for toggling between the advanced or basic versions (see Figure 35-2). Section pages for printers and shares have added buttons and a menu for selecting the particular printer or share you want to configure. The term "share," as it's used here, refers to directories you want to make available through Samba. When you click the SHARES button, you initially see only a few buttons displayed at the top of the SHARES page. You use these buttons to create new sections or to edit sections already set up for shares. For setting up a new Share section, you enter its name in the box next to the Create Share button and then click that button. The new share name appears in the drop-down menu next to the Choose Share button. Initially, this button is blank. Click it to display the list of current Share sections. Select the one you want, and then click the Choose Share button. The page then displays the entries for configuring a share. For a new share, these are either blank or default values. For example, to select the Homes section that configures the default setting for user home directories, click the drop-down menu where you find a Homes entry. Select it, and then click the Choose Share button. The entries for the Homes section are displayed. The same process works for the Printers page, where you can select either the Printers section or Create sections for particular printers.

Page	Description
HOME	SWAT home page listing documentation resources.
GLOBALS	Configure the global section for Samba.
SHARES	Select and configure directories to be shared (shares).
PRINTERS	Set up access to printers.
STATUS	Check the status of the Samba server, both smbd and nmbd; list clients currently active and the actions they are performing. You can restart, stop, or start the Samba server from this page.
VIEW	Display the **smb.conf** configuration file.
PASSWORD	Set up password access for the server and users that have access.

Table 35-2. *SWAT Configuration Pages*

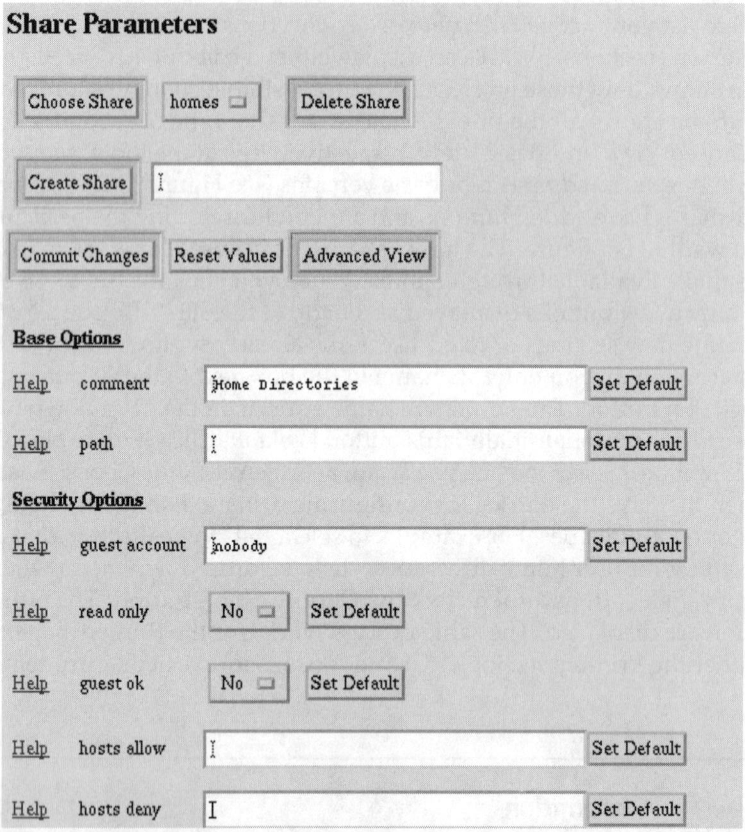

Figure 35-2. *SWAT Share page showing Homes section*

Note

*Samba automatically creates entries for any printer already configured for use on your system or network. It reads these from your **/etc/printcap** file. You will need to edit the printer entries to control access to your printers. For Samba to use a printer, it first has to be configured on your system as either a local or network printer (see printconf in Chapter 4). Keep in mind that a network printer could be a printer connected to a Windows system.*

In Figure 35-2, notice the Help links next to each entry. Such a link displays a Web page showing the Samba documentation for **smb.conf**, positioned at the appropriate entry. In this figure, the Guest OK part of the documentation is displayed after the user clicks the Help link next to the Guest OK entry.

When you finish working on a section, click the Commit Changes button on its page to save your changes. Do this for each separate page you work on, including the GLOBALS page. Clicking the Commit Changes button generates a new version of the **smb.conf** file. To have the Samba server read these changes, you then have to restart it. You can do this by clicking on the Restart smb button on the Status page.

The basic procedures for creating a new share using SWAT include the following steps:

1. Select the Share page and, in the Create Share text box, enter the name of the new share.
2. Click the Create Share button to open a configuration page for the new share. The name of the new share will appear in the pop-up menu next to the Choose Share button.
3. Enter various options. For the Basic Options, you will have to specify the directory for the share in the Path text box. In the Comment text box, you enter the label that will appear on Windows for the share.
4. Click the Commit Changes button to save your share entry to the Samba configuration file, **smb.conf**. Then restart the Samba server to effect your changes (click the Restart smb button on the Status page).

You can follow a similar procedure to add a new printer, but make sure the printer is also configured on the system with the Samba server.

You can, of course, edit the **/etc/samba/smb.conf** file directly. This is a simple text file you can edit with any text editor. You still must restart the smb server to have the changes take effect, which you can do manually on Mandrake and Red Hat with the following command:

```
service smb restart
```

The following example shows an **smb.conf** file generated by SWAT for a simple configuration. This is much smaller than the comment-intensive versions originally installed with Samba. In this configuration, share-level security is implemented and password encryption is enabled. A share called myprojects is defined which has guest access and is writeable. A printer share called myhp is also defined that also supports guest access.

```
# Samba config file created using SWAT
# from localhost.localdomain (127.0.0.1)
# Date: 2001/09/09 01:09:07

# Global parameters
[global]
```

```
            server string = Samba Server
            security = SHARE
            encrypt passwords = Yes
            ssl CA certFile = /usr/share/ssl/certs/ca-bundle.crt
            log file = /var/log/samba/%m.log
            max log size = 0
            socket options = TCP_NODELAY SO_RCVBUF=8192
SO_SNDBUF=8192
            dns proxy = No
            printing = lprng

[homes]
            comment = Home Directories
            path = /home
            writeable = Yes
            guest ok = Yes

[printers]
            comment = All Printers
            path = /var/spool/samba
            guest ok = Yes
            printable = Yes
            browseable = No

[myprojects]
            path = /myprojects
            writeable = Yes
            guest ok = Yes

[myhp]
            path = /var/spool/samba
            writeable = Yes
            guest ok = Yes
            printable = Yes
            printer = myhp
            oplocks = No
            share modes = No
```

Global Section

The Global section determines configuration for the entire server, as well as specifying default entries to be used in the home and directory segments. In this section, you find entries for the workgroup name, password configuration, and directory settings. Several of the more important entries are discussed here. Figure 35-3 shows the Global Variables

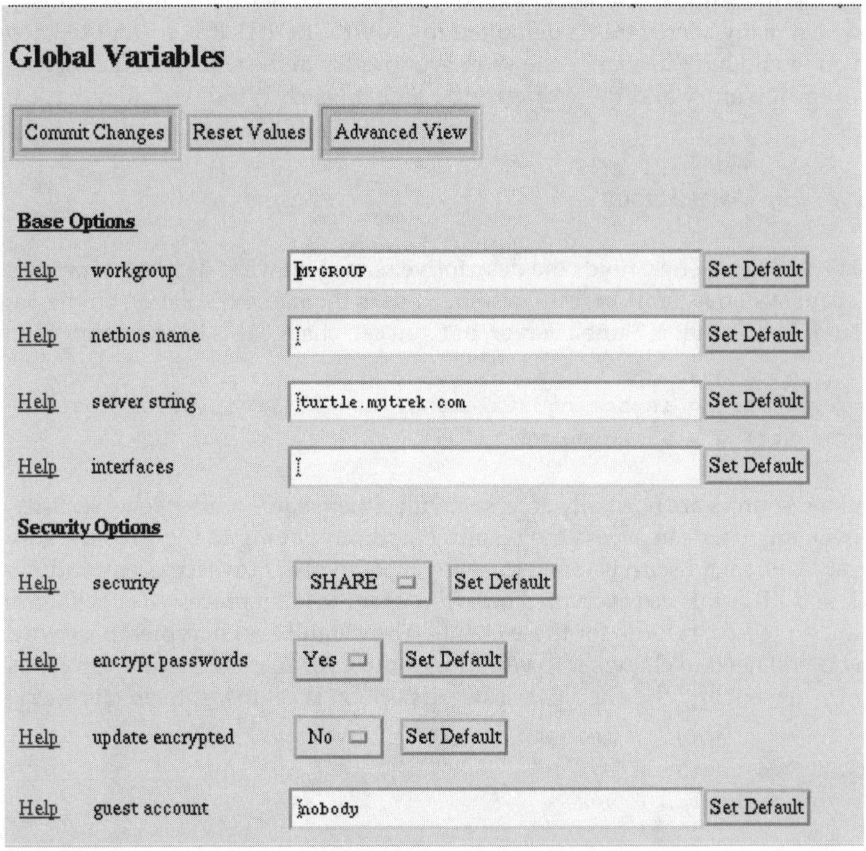

Global Variables

Commit Changes | Reset Values | Advanced View

Base Options

Help	workgroup	MYGROUP	Set Default
Help	netbios name		Set Default
Help	server string	turtle.mytrek.com	Set Default
Help	interfaces		Set Default

Security Options

Help	security	SHARE	Set Default
Help	encrypt passwords	Yes	Set Default
Help	update encrypted	No	Set Default
Help	guest account	nobody	Set Default

Figure 35-3. *SWAT Global Variables page*

page on the SWAT that you can use to set global options. The Basic View of this page lists the options you would most likely need.

The Workgroup entry specifies the workgroup name you want to give to your network. This is the workgroup name that appears on the Windows client's Network Neighborhood window. The default Workgroup entry in the **smb.conf** file is shown here:

```
[global]

# workgroup = NT-Domain-Name or Workgroup-Name
 workgroup = MYGROUP
```

The workgroup name has to be the same for each Windows client that the Samba server supports. On a Windows client, the workgroup name is usually found on the

Network Identification or General panel in the System tool located in the Control Panel window. On many clients this is defaulted to WORKGROUP. If you want to keep this name, you would have to change the Workgroup entry in the **smb.conf** file accordingly. The Workgroup entry and the workgroup name on each Windows client have to be the same.

```
workgroup = WORKGROUP
```

The server string entry holds the descriptive name you want displayed for the server on the client systems. On Windows systems, this is the name displayed on the Samba server icon. The default is Samba Server, but you can change this to any name you want.

```
# server string is the equivalent of the NT Description field
server string = Samba Server
```

Samba resources are normally accessed with either share- or user-level security. On a share level, any user can access the resource without having to log in to the server. On a user level, each user has to log in, using a password. Furthermore, Windows 98, ME, NT, and XP clients use encrypted passwords for the login process. You will have to enable encrypted passwords for these clients. The default for encrypted passwords is no, so you will need to change it to yes. In the **smb.conf** file, the security option is set to the level you want and the encrypt passwords option is set to yes to enable encryption.

```
security = user
encrypt passwords = yes
```

If you want share-level security, specify share as the security option.

```
security = share
```

On the SWAT GLOBALS page, select the security level from the pop-up menu, either user or share. Then select Yes for the encrypt passwords entry.

As a security measure, you can restrict access to SMB services to certain specified local networks. On the host's network, type the network addresses of the local networks for which you want to permit access. The localhost (127) is always automatically included. The next example allows access to two local networks:

```
hosts allow = 192.168.1. 192.168.2.
```

To enable printing, allow Samba to load the printer descriptions from your **printcap** file. Although you can specify a particular print system type with the printing entry, this usually is unnecessary.

```
printcap name = /etc/printcap
load printers = yes
```

You can use a guest user to make resources available to anyone without requiring a password. A guest user login would handle any users who log in without a specific account. On Linux systems, by default Samba will use the **nobody** user as the guest user. Alternatively, you can set up and designate a specific user to use as the guest user. You designate the guest user with the Guest Account entry in the **smb.conf** file. The commented **smb.conf** file provided with Samba currently lists a commented entry for setting up a guest user called **pcguest**. You can make this the user you want to be used as the guest user. Be sure to add the guest user to the password file:

```
guest account = pcguest
```

On SWAT you can specify a guest account entry on the GLOBALS page. By default this is already set to the **nobody** user.

Passwords

As noted previously, user-level security requires that each user log in to the Samba server using passwords. Samba can use either clear text or encrypted passwords, though current Windows clients support encrypted passwords. You can use the **smbpasswd** command to add and change Samba passwords. On SWAT, you enable password encryption on the Globals page and manage passwords on the Passwords page. In the Server Password Management section, you can add, change, remove, enable, or disable users. To add a new user, enter the username and password, then click Add New User. As the root user on the Samba server, you can add new passwords as well as enable or disable current ones. Normal users can use the Client/Server Password Management section to change their own passwords.

Homes Section

The Homes section specifies default controls for accessing a user home directory through the SMB protocols by remote users. Setting the Browseable entry to no prevents the client from listing the files with the browser, such as that used by a file manager to display files and directories (for example, Explorer on Windows). The Writable entry specifies whether users have read and write control over files in their home directories. On SWAT, you simply select the SHARES page, select the Homes entry from the drop-down menu, and click Choose Share (see Figure 35-2).

```
[homes]
 comment = Home Directories
 browseable = no
 writable = yes
```

Printers Section

The Printers section specifies the default controls for accessing printers. These are used for printers for which no specific sections exist. In this case, Samba uses printers defined in the server's **printcap** file.

In this context, setting Browesable to no simply hides the Printers section from the client, not the printers. The path entry specifies the location of the spool directory Samba will use for printer files. To enable printing at all, the printable entry must be set to yes. To allow guest users to print, set the Guest OK entry to yes. The Writable entry set to no prevents any kind of write access, other than the printer's management of spool files. On SWAT, select the PRINTER page and the Printers entry in the drop-down menu, and then select Choose Printers. A standard implementation of the Printers section is shown here:

```
[printers]
comment = All Printers
path = /var/spool/samba
browseable = No
guest ok = Yes
writable = No
printable = Yes
```

If you can't print, be sure to check the Default Print entry. This specifies the command the server actually uses to print documents.

Shares

Sections for specific shared resources, such as directories on your system, are usually placed after the Homes and Printers sections. For a section defining a shared directory, enter a label for the system. Then, on separate lines, enter options for its pathname and the different permissions you want to set. In the **`path`** = option, specify the full pathname for the directory. The **`comment`** = option holds the label to be given the share. You can make a directory writable, public, or read-only. You can control access to the directory with the Valid Users entry. With this entry, you can list those users permitted access. For those options not set, the defaults entered in the Global, Homes, and Printers segments are used.

On SWAT, you use the SHARES page to create and edit shared directories. Select the one you want to edit from the drop-down menu and click Choose Share. The Basic View shows the commonly used entries. For entries such as Valid Users, you need to select the Advanced View. Be sure to click Commit Changes before you move on to another Share or Printer section (see Figure 35-4).

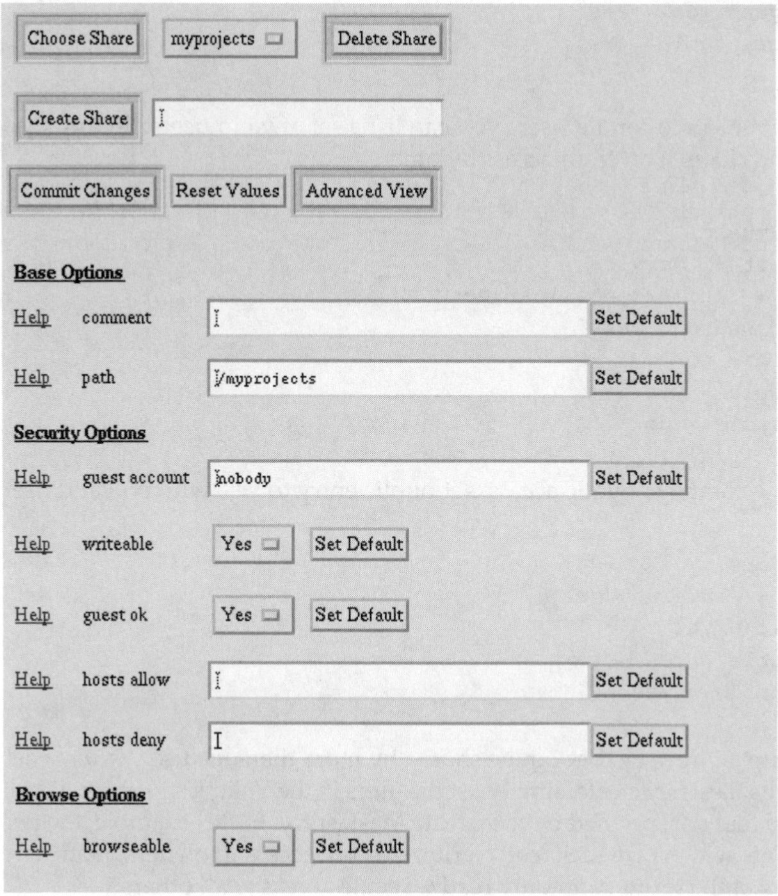

Figure 35-4. *SWAT Samba shares*

The following example is the myprojects share generated by SWAT from the share page shown in Figure 35-4. Here the **/myprojects** directory is defined as a share resource that is open to any user with guest access.

```
[myprojects]
     comment = Great Project Ideas
     path = /myprojects
     writeable = Yes
```

```
      guest ok = Yes
      printable = Yes
```

To limit access to certain users you can list a set of valid users. Setting the public option to no closes it off from access by others.

```
[mynewmusic]
 comment =  Service
 path = //home/specialprojects
 valid users = mark
 public = no
 writable = yes
 printable = no
```

To allow complete public access, set public entry to yes, with no valid user's entry.

```
 [newdocs]
 path = /home/newdocs
 public = yes
 writable = yes
 printable = yes
```

To set up a directory that can be shared by more than one user, where each user has control of the files they create, simply list the users in the Valid Users entry. Permissions for any created files are specified by the Create Mask entry. In this example, the permissions are set to 765, which provides read/write/execute access to owners, read/write access to members of the group, and only read/execute access to all others:

```
[myshare]
 comment = Writer's projects
 path = /usr/local/drafts
 valid users = justin chris dylan
 public = no
 writable = yes
 printable = no
 create mask = 0765
```

For more examples, check those in the original **smb.conf** file that shows a Shares section for a directory **fredsdir**.

Printers

Access to specific printers is defined in the Printers section of the **smb.conf** file. You can also configure printers in the SWAT Printers page. For a printer, you need to include the Printer and Printable entries. With the Printer entry, you name the printer, and by setting the Printable entry to yes, you allow it to print. You can control access to specific users with the valid users entry and by setting the Public entry to no. For public access, set the Public entry to yes. On SWAT, you can create individual Printer sections on the Printers page. Default entries are already set up for you.

The following example sets up a printer accessible to guest users. This opens the printer to use by any user on the network. Users need to have write access to the printer's spool directory, located in **/var/spool/samba**. Keep in mind that any printer has to first be installed on your system. The following printer was already installed as myhp and has an **/etc/printcap** entry with that name. On Red Hat, you can use printconf to install your printer, giving it a name and selecting its driver (see Chapter 4).


```
[myhp]
      path = /var/spool/samba
      writeable = Yes
      guest ok = Yes
      printable = Yes
      printer = myhp
      oplocks = No
      share modes = No
```

As with shares, you can restrict printer use to certain users, denying it from public access. The following example sets up a printer accessible only by the users **larisa** and **aleina** (you could add other users if you want). Users need to have write access to the printer's spool directory.

```
[larisalaser]
      path = /var/spool/samba
      writeable = Yes
      valid users = larisa aleina
      public = no
      printable = Yes
      printer = myhp
      oplocks = No

      share modes = No
```

Though SWAT is preferred, you can also use Linuxconf and Webmin to configure Samba.

Variable Substitutions

For string values assigned to parameters, you can incorporate substitution operators. This provides greater flexibility in designating values that may be context-dependent, such as usernames. For example, suppose a service needs to use a separate directory for each user who logs in. The path for such directories could be specified using the **%u** variable that substitutes in the name of the current user. The string **path = /tmp/%u** would become **path = /tmp/justin** for the **justin** user and **/tmp/dylan** for the **dylan** user. Table 35-3 lists several of the more common substitution variables.

Variable	Description
%S	Name of the current service
%P	Root directory of the current service
%u	Username of the current service
%g	Primary group name of the user
%U	Session username (the username the client wanted)
%G	Primary group name of session user
%H	Home directory of the user
%v	Samba version
%h	Internet hostname on which Samba is running
%m	NetBIOS name of the client machine
%L	NetBIOS name of the server
%M	Internet name of the client machine
%N	Name of your NIS home directory server
%p	Path of the service's home directory
%d	Process ID of the current server process
%a	Architecture of the remote machine
%I	IP address of the client machine
%T	Current date and time

Table 35-3. *Samba Substitution Variables*

Testing the Samba Configuration

After you make your changes to the **smb.conf** file, you can then use the testparm program to see if the entries are correctly entered. testparm checks the syntax and validity of Samba entries. By default, testparm checks the **/etc/samba/smb.conf** file. If you are using a different file as your configuration file, you can specify it as an argument to testparm. You can also have testparm check to see if a particular host has access to the service set up by the configuration file.

With SWAT, the Status page will list your connections and shares. From the command line, you can use the **smbstatus** command to check on current Samba connections on your network.

To check the real-time operation of your Samba server, you can log in to a user account on the Linux system running the Samba server and connect to the server.

Domain Logons

Samba also supports domain logons whereby a user can log on to the network. Logon scripts can be set up for individual users. To configure such netlogon capability, you need to set up a netlogon share in the **smb.conf file**. The following sample is taken from the original **smb.conf file.** This share holds the **netlogon** scripts—in this case, the **/home/netlogon** directory—which should not be writable, but it should be accessible by all users (Guest OK).

```
[netlogon]
 comment = Network Logon Service
 path = /home/netlogon
 guest ok = yes
 writeable = no
 share modes = no
```

The Global section would have the following parameters enabled:

```
domain logons = yes
```

With netlogon, you can configure Samba as an authentication server for both Linux and Windows hosts. A Samba username and password need to be set up for each host. In the Global section of the **smb.conf** file, be sure to enable encrypted passwords, user-level security, and domain logons, as well as an operating system level of 33 or more:

```
[global]
encrypt passwords = Yes
```

```
security = user
domain logons = Yes
os level = 33
```

You can also configure Samba to be a Primary Domain Controller (PDC) for Windows NT networks. As a PDC, Samba can handle domain logons, retrieve lists of users and groups, and provide user-level security.

Accessing Samba Services with Clients

Client systems connected to the SMB network can access the shared services provided by the Samba server. Windows clients should be able to access shared directories and services automatically through the Network Neighborhood and the Entire Network icons on a Windows desktop. For other Linux systems connected to the same network, Samba services can be accessed using special Samba client programs. With smbclient, a local Linux system can connect to a shared directory on the Samba server and transfer files, as well as run shell programs. With smbmount, directories on the Samba server can be mounted to local directories on the Linux client.

Note

Several Samba browser clients are available for Gnome and KDE. For KDE, you can use Komba2 (downloadable from ***apps.kde.com****). For Gnome, you can use Gnomba.*

smbclient

smbclient operates like FTP to access systems using the SMB protocols. Whereas with an FTP client you can access other FTP servers or Unix systems, with smbclient you can access SMB-shared services, either on the Samba server or on Windows systems. Many smbclient commands are similar to FTP, such as **mget** to transfer a file or **del** to delete a file. The smbclient program has several options for querying a remote system, as well as connecting to it (see Table 35-4). See the smbclient Man page for a complete list of options and commands. The smbclient program takes as its argument a server name and the service you want to access on that server. A double slash precedes the server name and a single slash separates it from the service. The service can be any shared resource, such as a directory or a printer. The server name is its NetBIOS name, which may or may not be the same as its IP name. For example, to specify the **myreports** shared directory on the server named **turtle.mytrek.com**, use **//turtle.mytrek.com/myreports**. If you must specify a pathname, use backslashes for Windows files and forward slashes for Unix/Linux files:

```
//server-name/service
```

Option	Description
password	The password required to access the specified service on the server. If no password is supplied, the user is prompted to enter one.
-s *smb.conf*	Specify the pathname to **smb.conf** file.
-B *IP_address*	Specify the broadcast IP address.
-O *socket_options*	List the socket options.
-R *name resolve order*	Use these name resolution services only.
-M *host*	Send a winpopup message to the host.
-i *scope*	Use this NetBIOS scope.
-N	Don't ask for a password.
-n *netbios name*	Use this name as my NetBIOS name.
-d *debuglevel*	Set the debug level.
-P	Connect to the service as a printer.
-p *port*	Connect to the specified port.
-l *log basename*	Base name for log/debug files.
-h	Print this help message.
-I *IP_address*	Specify the IP address to connect to.
-E	Write messages to stderr instead of stdout.
-U *username*	Specify the user to login as on the remote system.
-L *host*	List the shares available on the specified host.
-t *terminal code*	Terminal i/o code used {sjis | euc | jis7 | jis8 | junet | hex}.
-m *max protocol*	Set the max protocol level.
-W *workgroup*	Set the workgroup name.
-T<c | x>	Command line **tar** operation.
-D *directory*	Start from this directory.
-c *command_string*	Execute semicolon-separated commands.
-b *xmit/send buffer*	Changes the transmit/send buffer (default: 65520).

Table 35-4. *smbclient Options*

You can also supply the password for accessing the service. Enter it as an argument following the service name. If you do not supply the password, you are prompted to enter it.

You can then add several options, such as the remote username or the list of services available. With the **-I** option, you can specify the system using its IP address. You use the **-U** option and a login name for the remote login name you want to use on the remote system. Attach **%** with the password if a password is required. With the **-L** option, you can obtain a list of the services provided on a server, such as shared directories or printers. The following command will list the shares available on the host **turtle.mytrek.com**:

```
smbclient -L turtle.mytrek.com
```

To access a particular directory on a remote system, enter the directory as an argument to the **smbclient** command, followed by any options. For Windows files, you use backslashes for the pathnames, and for Unix/Linux files you use forward slashes. Once connected, an smb prompt is displayed and you can use smbclient commands such as **get** and **put** to transfer files. The **quit** or **exit** commands quit the smbclient program. In the following example, smbclient accesses the directory **myreports** on the **turtle.mytrek.com** system, using the **dylan** login name:

```
smbclient //turtle.mytrek.com/myreports -I 192.168.0.1 -U dylan
```

In most cases, you can simply use the server name to reference the server, as shown here:

```
smbclient //turtle.mytrek.com/myreports -U dylan
```

If you are accessing the home directory of a particular account on the Samba server, you can simply specify the **homes** service. In the next example, the user accesses the home directory of the **aleina** account on the Samba server, after being prompted to enter that account's password:

```
smbclient //turtle.mytrek.com/homes -U aleina
```

You can also use smbclient to access shared resources located on Windows clients. Specify the computer name of the Windows client along with its shared folder. In the next example, the user accesses the **windata** folder on the Windows client named **lizard**. The folder is configured to allow access by anyone, so the user just presses the ENTER key at the password prompt.

```
$ smbclient //lizard/windata
added interface ip=192.168.0.2 bcast=192.168.0.255 nmask=255.255.255.0
Got a positive name query response from 192.168.0.3 ( 192.168.0.3 )
Password:
```

```
Domain=[WORKGROUP] OS=[Windows 5.1] Server=[Windows 2000 LAN Manager]
smb: \> ls
  .                                  D        0  Sat Sep  8 17:29:19 2001
  ..                                 D        0  Sat Sep  8 17:29:19 2001
  hi                                 A       10  Sat Sep  8 17:29:27 2001
  mynewdoc.doc                       A        0  Sat Sep  8 16:59:13 2001
        39997 blocks of size 1048576. 39930 blocks available
smb: \> mget hi
Get file hi? y
getting file hi of size 10 as hi (1.22069 kb/s) (average 1.2207 kb/s)
smb: \> quit
```


Once logged in, you can execute smbclient commands to manage files and change directories. The smbclient commands are listed in Table 35-5. Shell commands can be

Command	Description
? *[command]*	With no command argument, lists of all available commands are displayed. Use command argument to display information about a particular command.
! *[shell command]*	With no shell command argument, runs a local shell. If a shell command is provided, it executes that command.
cd *[directory name]*	Change directory on server. With no directory specified, the name of the current working directory is displayed.
del *mask*	Request the server delete all files matching mask from the current working directory on the server.
dir *mask*	A list of the files matching the mask in the current working directory on the server is retrieved from the server and displayed.
exit	Terminate the connection with the server and exit from the program.
get *remote filename [local filename]*	Copy a file from the server to the local system. You can rename the local system copy. Transfer is binary.
help *[command]*	With no command argument, lists of all available commands are displayed. Use command argument to display information about a particular command. Same as **!**.
lcd *[directory name]*	Change directories on the local system. With no argument, the local directory name is displayed.

Table 35-5. *smbclient Commands*

Command	Description
`lowercase`	Toggle lowercasing of filenames for the **`get`** and **`mget`** commands. When lowercasing is toggled on, local filenames are converted to lowercase when using the **`get`** and **`mget`** commands. This is often useful when copying, say, MS-DOS files from a server because lowercase filenames are the norm on Unix systems.
`ls` *mask*	A list of the files matching the mask in the current working directory on the server is retrieved from the server and displayed. Same as **`dir`**.
`mask` *mask*	This command enables the user to set up a mask that is used during recursive operation of the **`mget`** and **`mput`** commands. The masks specified to the **`mget`** and **`mput`** commands act as filters for directories, rather than files when recursion is toggled on. The value for mask defaults to blank (equivalent to `*`) and remains so until the **`mask`** command is used to change it.
`md` *directory name*	Create a new directory on the server (user access privileges permitting) with the specified name. Same as **`mkdir`**.
`mget` *mask*	Copy all files matching *mask* from the server to the machine running the client. Note, *mask* is interpreted differently during recursive operation and nonrecursive operation—refer to the **`recurse`** and **`mask`** commands for more information. Transfers are binary.
`mkdir` *directory name*	Create a new directory on the server (user access privileges permitting) with the specified name.
`mput` *mask*	Copy all files matching mask in the current working directory on the local system to the current working directory on the server. Transfers in are binary.
`print` *filename*	Print the specified file from the local machine through a printable service on the server.
`printmode` *graphics or text*	Set the print mode for either binary data (graphics) or text. Subsequent print commands use the currently set print mode.
`prompt`	Toggle prompting for filenames during operation of the **`mget`** and **`mput`** commands.

Table 35-5. *smbclient Commands* (continued)

Command	Description
put *local filename [remote filename]*	Copy a file on the local system to the server. You can rename the server copy. Transfers are binary.
queue	Displays the print queue, showing the job ID, name, size, and current status.
quit	Terminate the connection with the server and exit from the program. Same as **exit** command.
rd *directory name*	Delete the specified directory (user access privileges permitting) from the server. Same as **rmdir** command.
recurse	Toggle directory recursion for the commands **mget** and **mput**. When toggled on, the **mget** and **mput** commands will copy any subdirectories and files. Files can be selected by a mask specified with the **mget** and **mput** commands. The mask for directories is specified with the **mask** command. When toggled off, only files from the current working directory are copied.
rm *mask*	Delete all files matching mask from the current working directory on the server.
rmdir *directory name*	Delete the specified directory (user access privileges permitting) from the server.
tar *c | x [IXbgNa]*	Performs a **tar** operation. Behavior may be affected by the **tarmode** command.
blocksize *blocksize*	Specify block size. Must be followed by a valid (greater than zero) block size. Causes **tar** file to be written out in blocksize*TBLOCK (usually 512-byte) blocks.
tarmode *full | inc | reset | noreset*	Changes **tar**'s behavior regarding archive bits. In full mode, **tar** backs up everything, regardless of the archive bit setting (this is the default mode). In incremental mode, **tar** only backs up files with the archive bit set. In reset mode, **tar** resets the archive bit on all files it backs up (implies read/write share).
setmode *filename perm=[+ | \-]rsha*	A version of the DOS **attrib** command to set file permissions. For example: **setmode myfile +r** would make **myfile** read-only.

Table 35-5. *smbclient Commands* (continued)

executed with the **!** operator. To transfer files, you can use the **mget** and **mput** commands, much as they are used in the FTP program. The **recurse** command enables you to turn on recursion to copy whole subdirectories at a time. You can use file-matching operators, referred to here as *masks*, to select a certain collection of files. The file-matching (mask) operators are *****, **[]**, and **?** (see Chapter 10). The default mask is *****, which matches everything. The following example uses **mget** to copy all files with a **.c** suffix, as in **myprog.c**:

```
smb> mget *.c
```

During transfers, you can have smbclient either prompt you for each individual file or simply transfer all the selected ones. The **prompt** command toggles this file, prompting on and off.

To access a particular printer on a remote system, enter the printer name as an argument to the **smbclient** command, followed by any options. In the following example, smbclient accesses the myepson printer on the **turtle.mytrek.com** system, using the **dylan** login name:

```
smbclient //turtle.mytrek.com/myepson -U dylan
```

Once connected, an smb prompt is displayed and you can use smbclient commands such as **print** to print files and **printmode** to specify graphics or text. In the next example, the user prints a file called **myfile**, after having accessed the myepson printer on **turtle.mytrek.com**:

```
smb> print myfile
```

smbmount

With the **smbmount** command, a Linux or Unix client can mount a shared directory onto its local system. The syntax for the **smbmount** command is similar to the **smbclient** command, with many corresponding options. The **smbmount** command takes as its arguments the Samba server and shared directory, followed by the local directory where you want to mount the directory. The following example mounts the **myreports** directory onto the **/mnt/myreps** directory on the local system:

```
smbmount //turtle.mytrek.com/myreports /mnt/myreps -U dylan
```

To unmount the directory, use the **smbumount** command with the local directory name, as shown here:

```
smbumount /mnt/myreps
```

To mount the home directory of a particular user on the server, specify the **homes** service and the user's login name. The following example mounts the home directory of the user **larisa** to the **/home/chris/larisastuff** directory on the local system:

```
smbmount //turtle.mytrek.com/homes /home/chris/larisastuff -U larisa
```

You can also use smbmount to mount shared folders on Windows clients. Just specify the computer name of the Windows client along with its folder. If the folder name contains spaces, enclose it in single quotes. In the following example, the user mounts the **windata** folder on **lizard** as the **/mylinux** directory. For a folder with access to anyone, just press ENTER at the password prompt.

```
$ smbmount //lizard/windata  /mylinux
Password:
$ ls /mylinux
_hi_mynewdoc.doc_myreport.txt
```

To unmount the shared folder when you are finished with it, use the **smbumount** command.

```
smbumount /mylinux
```

Instead of using **smbmount** explicitly, you can use the **mount** command with the file system type **smbfs**. **mount** will then run the **/sbin/mount.smbfs** command, which will invoke smbclient to mount the file system:

```
mount -t smbfs //lizard/windata  /mylinux
```

You could also specify a username and password as options, if user-level access is required:

```
mount -t smbfs -o username=chris passwd=mypass //lizard/windata /mylinux
```

You can also use the smbfs type in an **/etc/fstab** entry to have a Samba file system mounted automatically:

```
//lizard/windata /mylinux smbfs defaults 0 0
```

Windows Clients

To access Samba resources from a Windows system, you will need to make sure that your Windows system has enabled TCP/IP networking. This may already be the case if your Windows client is connected to a Microsoft network. If you need to connect a Windows system directly to a TCP/IP network that your Linux Samba server is running on, you should check that TCP/IP networking is enabled on that Windows system. This involves making sure that the Microsoft Network client and the TCP/IP protocol are installed, and that your network interface card (NIC adapter) is configured to use TCP/IP. The procedures differ slightly on Windows 2000 and XP, and Windows 95, 98, and ME.

Once connected, your Samba shares and printers will appear in the Windows network window. If you are going to use a share frequently, you can assign it a disk label. Right-click on the share and select Map Network Drive, and select the drive label you want to use. On XP you can further select whether you want the drive automatically mounted when you log in.

Windows 95, 98, and ME

For Windows 95, 98, and ME, you click on a Network icon in the Control Panel window. Here you will see the network components loaded for your system. Check to make sure that Client For Microsoft Networks and TCP/IP protocol are installed. If not, click the Add button, select Client or Protocol, and then select the needed client or protocol. For example, to add the TCP/IP protocol, click Add, then click Protocol, and then select TCP/IP from the list of protocols. You can also allow the Windows system to share its own files and printers by selecting File And Print Sharing.

Next, check the computer's name and workgroup by selecting the Identification panel. Make sure your Samba entry for the workgroup matches it. Select the kind of access control for sharing you set up for Samba, either user level or share level. Click on the Access Control tab and select either Share-level or User-level access.

Now open the Network Neighborhood icon on your desktop. This will list your Samba server. If it's not listed, open Entire Network and then Workgroups to find it. When you open your Samba server icon, the shared printers and directories set up on your Samba server should be displayed.

Windows 2000 and XP

On Windows 2000, open the Network And Dialup Connections window in the Control Panel. In Windows XP, open the Network Connections window, also in the Control Panel. If you do not already have a LAN connection, create one with the Make New Connection tool. Each NIC card will have its own Local Area Connections file (you probably have only one). Right-click on the one for the NIC adapter connected to the TCP/IP network that your Linux Samba server is on. Select Properties from the pop-up menu. The General tab will show the NIC card's name (adapter) and the components loaded and checked in support for this connection. Make sure the following are listed and checked:

- Client for Microsoft Networks
- File and Printer Sharing for Microsoft Networks
- Internet Protocol (TCP/IP)

Should any of these be missing, you can click the Install button to install them. From a dialog box listing Client, Service, and Protocol, select the type of component you want to install. A list of components is displayed. For example, to install TCP/IP, click the Install button, and then the Protocol entry in the Component Type window, and finally the TCP/IP protocol listed in the Select Network Protocol window.

File and printer sharing enables access to the directories and printers on the Windows client. It is not essential for accessing shares and printers on the Samba server. However, if you want a user to be able to access, through Samba, a printer on a Windows client, this feature has to be enabled on that Windows client.

Make sure that the IP address for this adapter is entered. This is the IP address for your Windows host. Click on the TCP/IP entry and then click the Properties button. This displays a window for entering the IP address for this NIC adapter. Click the Advanced button and then click on the WINS tab. Also, make sure that the Enable LMHOSTS Lookup and the Enable NetBIOS Over TCP/IP entries are checked.

Next, check to make sure that the computer name and workgroup are the same as that used in your Samba **smb.conf** file. Click on System in the Control Panel and click on the Network Identification tab. The computer name and workgroup for the Windows system will be displayed. If none are given, or if you want to change it, click the Properties button to open a window where you can enter a computer name and workgroup.

To access your Samba server, click on the My Network Places icon, and then the Computers Near Me icon. On Windows XP, you can open the My Computer window and select the Computers Near Me entry on the left panel. A listing for your Samba server will then appear. Double-click on it to display the shares available on your Samba server. You can also click on the Entire Network icon and choose to show the entire contents. Click on the Microsoft Windows Network icon and then your Workgroup icon. Your Samba server will be listed along with your Windows client.

If you specified share-level security in your **smb.conf** file (or on the Globals page of SWAT), the shares available to you will be displayed. Normally, you would use share-level security if you are supporting resources such as printers that you do not want to require users to log in for each time they use them.

If you specified user-level security in the **smb.conf** file or the SWAT Globals page, a dialog box will first appear that will prompt you for a username and password. You need to be logged in on Windows as the same user that you will be using to access the Samba server. If you want to access the Samba server as the **aleina** user, you need to be logged in as the **aleina** user on your Windows system.

To see what resources on your Windows client can be shared, double-click on the icon for your client in the Workgroup or Computers Near Me window. Any resources that you specified should be shared, such as printers or folders, will be listed.

To use a printer connected to the Samba server, the Windows client first has to connect to it. Click on the printer's icon in the Samba server's window and select Connect. The first time you do this, you will be prompted to configure the printer for use on your Windows system. A window will let you select the driver needed for that printer. Now when you print in an application, you can choose the remote Linux printer from your list of available printers. For example, to use a printer on a Samba server named myhp, click on the myhp icon in the Samba server window and select Connect. The first time you will be asked to specify the driver to use for this printer. If it is an HP printer, select its model. The appropriate Windows driver for that printer will be installed on the Windows client. Now when you print, you can select the myhp printer and have your document printed on that Linux printer. For example, if the Samba server's name is rabbit and the printer's name is myhp, you will see an entry like that below among your list of printers.

```
\\rabbit\myhp
```

Mounting Linux Shares and Printers on Windows Clients

Your Samba shares and printers will appear in your Windows network window. You can access them here. You could also mount a share as a disk on your Windows system. The share will appear with a disk label, just as your other disks are listed. You can mount shares either with a **net** command entered in a command window or by right-clicking on the share and selecting Map Network Drive. As noted previously, selecting Map Network Drive will open a window where you can choose a disk label to use for the share. You can also specify if you want to have the share automatically mounted as that disk whenever you log in.

With the **net** command, you give a share a disk label with which you can reference it on your Windows system. The syntax for the command is as follows (notice that backslashes are used on Windows instead of the forward slashes used on Linux):

```
net use label: \\server\service
```

For example, to mount the **myprojects** directory on the Samba server **turtle.mytrek.com** as the h: disk, you would use the following command.

```
net use h: \\turtle.mytrek.com\myprojects
```

To print, you would specify the remote printer and the local port to use it as follows:

```
net use lpt1: \\turtle.trek.com\myhp
```

Then use the **print** command to print a file:

```
print filename
```

Sharing Windows Directories and Printers

To manage directory shares, open the Computer Management tool in the Administrative window in the Control Panel. Click on Shared Folders and there you can see the Shares, Sessions, and Open folders. To add a new share, click on the Shares folder and then click on the Action menu and select New File Share. The Sessions and Open folders' Action menus let you disconnect active sessions and folders.

To allow share-level open access by users on other clients or on the Samba server, be sure to enable the guest user on your Windows client. It is not enabled by default. Access the Users and Passwords tool in the Control Panel to a set up the guest user. Guest access is particularly important for providing access to a printer connected to a Windows client. The Linux system that wants to access a printer on a Windows's system will configure the printer on its own system as a remote Samba printer. The user normally entered to access the printer is **guest**. For the Linux system to access the Windows printer, that Windows system has to have a guest user.

To share a printer, locate the printer in the Printers window and right-click on it, selecting the Sharing As option. This opens the Sharing panel where you can click the Shared As button and enter the name under which the printer will be known by other hosts. For example, on the Windows client named lizard, to have a printer called Epson Stylus Color shared as myepson, the Sharing panel for this printer would have the Shared As button selected and the name myepson entered. Then when the user double-clicks on the lizard icon in the Computers Near Me window, the printer icon labeled myepson will appear.

For a Linux system to use this printer, it will have be first configured as a remote Windows printer on that Linux system. You can do this easily with printconf. You give the printer a name by which it is known on your Linux system. Then you will enter the Windows client computer name, the name of the printer as it is accessed on the Windows client, along with the username for access (usually **guest**). Once configured, your printing commands can access it using just the printer name, as they would any other printer. For example, the myepson printer installed on the Windows client has to also be installed on the Linux system operating as the Samba server (see Figure 35-5). On Red Hat, using printconf, you can give the printer the same name, if you wish, and then in the Queue Type panel select Windows Printer (SMB Share). For the Share, you enter **//lizard/ myepson**; for User, enter **guest**; and for Workgroup, enter the Windows client's workgroup (usually **WORKGROUP**).

Once installed, you can restart the lpd server. Then an `lpr` command can access the remote Windows printer directly. The next example prints the **mydoc** file on the Windows client's Epson printer.

```
lpr -P myepson mydoc
```

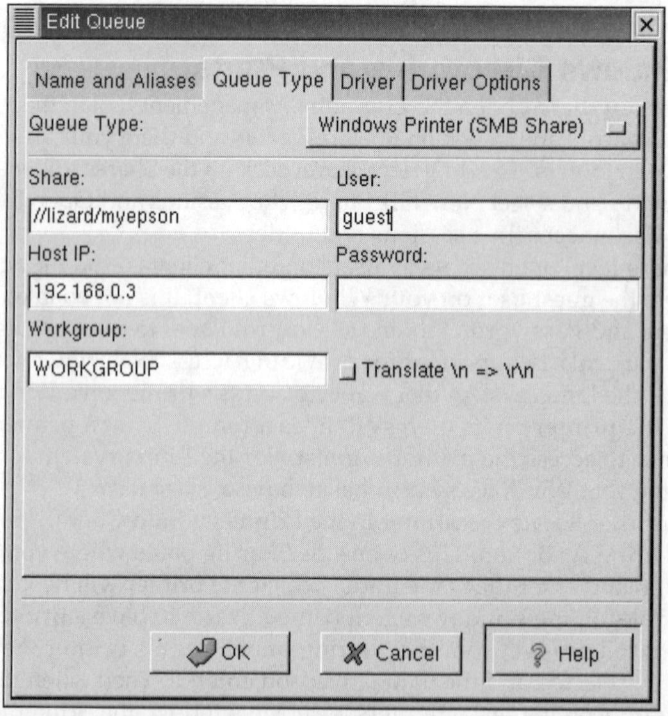

Figure 35-5. *A Windows printer on Linux, printconf*

To share a directory, right-click on the directory and select Sharing from the pop-up menu (Sharing And Security on Windows XP). Click on Share This Folder and then enter the share name, the name by which the directory will be known by Samba. You can specify whether you want to allow others to change files on the share. You can also specify a user limit (maximum allowed is the default). You can further click the Permissions button to control access by users. Here, you can specify which users will have access, as well as the type of access. For example, you could allow only read access to the directory.

The Complete Reference

Chapter 36

Administering TCP/IP Networks

Linux systems are configured to connect into networks that use the TCP/IP protocols. These are the same protocols that the Internet uses, as do many local area networks (LANs). In Chapter 22, you were introduced to TCP/IP, a robust set of protocols designed to provide communications among systems with different operating systems and hardware. The TCP/IP protocols were developed in the 1970s as a special DARPA project to enhance communications between universities and research centers. These protocols were originally developed on Unix systems, with much of the research carried out at the University of California, Berkeley. Linux, as a version of Unix, benefits from much of this original focus on Unix. Currently, the TCP/IP protocol development is managed by the Internet Engineering Task Force (IETF), which, in turn, is supervised by the Internet Society (ISOC). The ISOC oversees several groups responsible for different areas of Internet development, such as the Internet Assigned Numbers Authority (IANA), which is responsible for Internet addressing (see Table 36-1). Over the years, TCP/IP protocol standards and documentation have been issued in the form of Requests for Comments (RFC) documents. Check the most recent ones for current developments at the IETF Web site at **www.ietf.org**.

The TCP/IP protocol suite actually consists of different protocols, each designed for a specific task in a TCP/IP network. The three basic protocols are the Transmission

Group	Title	Description
ISOC	Internet Society	Professional membership organization of Internet experts that oversees boards and task forces dealing with network policy issues **www.isoc.org**
IESG	The Internet Engineering Steering Group	Responsible for technical management of IETF activities and the Internet standards process **www.ietf.org/iesg.html**
IANA	Internet Assigned Numbers Authority	Responsible for Internet Protocol (IP) addresses **www.iana.org**
IAB	Internet Architecture Board	Defines the overall architecture of the Internet, providing guidance and broad direction to the IETF **www.iab.org**
IETF	Internet Engineering Task Force	Protocol engineering and development arm of the Internet **www.ietf.org**

Table 36-1. *TCP/IP Protocol Development Groups*

Control Protocol (TCP), which handles receiving and sending out communications, the Internet Protocol (IP), which handles the actual transmissions, and the User Datagram Protocol (UDP), which also handles receiving and sending packets. The IP protocol, which is the base protocol that all others use, handles the actual transmissions, handling the packets of data with sender and receiver information in each. The TCP protocol is designed to work with cohesive messages or data. This protocol checks received packets and sorts them into their designated order, forming the original message. For data sent out, the TCP protocol breaks the data into separate packets, designating their order. The UDP protocol, meant to work on a much more raw level, also breaks down data into packets, but does not check their order. The TCP/IP protocol is designed to provide stable and reliable connections that ensure that all data is received and reorganized into its original order. UDP, on the other hand, is designed to simply send as much data as possible, with no guarantee that packets will all be received or placed in the proper order. UDP is often used for transmitting very large amounts of data of the type that can survive the loss of a few packets—for example, temporary images, video, and banners displayed on the Internet.

Other protocols provide various network and user services. The Domain Name Service (DNS) provides address resolution. The File Transfer Protocol (FTP) provides file transmission, and Network File System (NFS) provides access to remote file systems. Table 36-2 lists the different protocols in the TCP/IP protocol suite. These protocols make use of either the TCP or UDP protocol to send and receive packets, which, in turn, uses the IP protocol for actually transmitting the packets.

In a TCP/IP network, messages are broken into small components, called *datagrams*, which are then transmitted through various interlocking routes and delivered to their destination computers. Once received, the datagrams are reassembled into the original message. Datagrams themselves can be broken down into smaller packets. The *packet* is

Transport	**Description**
TCP	Transmission Control Protocol; places systems in direct communication
UDP	User Datagram Protocol
IP	Internet Protocol; transmits data
ICMP	Internet Control Message Protocol; status messages for IP
Routing	**Description**
RIP	Routing Information Protocol; determines routing
OSPF	Open Shortest Path First; determines routing

Table 36-2. *TCP/IP Protocol Suite*

Network Addresses	Description
ARP	Address Resolution Protocol; determines unique IP address of systems
DNS	Domain Name Service; translates hostnames into IP addresses
RARP	Reverse Address Resolution Protocol; determines addresses of systems
User Services	**Description**
FTP	File Transfer Protocol; transmits files from one system to another using TCP
TFTP	Trivial File Transfer Protocol; transfers files using UDP
TELNET	Remote login to another system on the network
SMTP	Simple Mail Transfer Protocol; transfers e-mail between systems
RPC	Remote Procedure Call; allows programs on remote systems to communicate
Gateway	**Description**
EGP	Exterior Gateway Protocol; provides routing for external networks
GGP	Gateway-to-Gateway Protocol; provides routing between Internet gateways
IGP	Interior Gateway Protocol; provides routing for internal networks
Network Services	**Description**
NFS	Network File System; allows mounting of file systems on remote machines
NIS	Network Information Service; maintains user accounts across a network
BOOTP	Boot Protocol; starts system using boot information on server for network
SNMP	Simple Network Management Protocol; provides status messages on TCP/IP configuration
DHCP	Dynamic Host Configuration Protocol; automatically provides network configuration information to host systems

Table 36-2. *TCP/IP Protocol Suite* (continued)

the physical message unit actually transmitted among networks. Sending messages as small components has proved to be far more reliable and faster than sending them as one large, bulky transmission. With small components, if one is lost or damaged, only that component must be resent, whereas if any part of a large transmission is corrupted or lost, the entire message has to be resent.

The configuration of a TCP/IP network on your Linux system is implemented using a set of network configuration files. Many of these can be managed using administrative programs, such as provided by Mandrake, Red Hat, and SuSE control centers as well as third-party tools like Webmin and Linuxconf, on your root user desktop (see Chapter 33). You can also use the more specialized programs, such as netstat, ifconfig, and route. Some configuration files are easy to modify yourself using a text editor.

TCP/IP networks are configured and managed with a set of utilities: ifconfig, route, and netstat. The ifconfig utility operates from your root user desktop and enables you to configure your network interfaces fully, adding new ones and modifying others. The ifconfig and route utilities are lower-level programs that require more specific knowledge of your network to use effectively. The netstat utility provides you with information about the status of your network connections.

IPv4 and IPv6

Traditionally, a TCP/IP address is organized into four segments, consisting of numbers separated by periods. This is called the *IP address.* The IP address actually represents a 32-bit integer whose binary values identify the network and host. This form of IP addressing adheres to Internet Protocol, version 4, also known as IPv4. IPv4, the kind of IP addressing described here, is still in wide use.

Currently, a new version of the IP protocol called Internet Protocol, version 6 (IPv6) is gradually replacing the older IPv4 version. IPv6 expands the number of possible IP addresses using a 128-bit address. It is fully compatible with systems still using IPv4. IPv6 addresses are represented differently, using a set of eight 16-bit segments, each separated by a colon. Each segment is represented by a hexadecimal number. A sample address would be:

```
FEDC:0:0:200C:800:BA98:7654:3210
```

IPv6 features simplified headers that allow for faster processing. It also provides support for encryption and authentication. Its most significant advantage is extending the address space to cover 2 to the power of 128 possible hosts (billions of billions). This extends far beyond the 4.2 billion supported by IPv4.

TCP/IP Network Addresses

As noted previously, the traditional IPv4 TCP/IP address is organized into four segments, consisting of numbers separated by periods. This kind of address is still in wide use and is what people commonly refer to as an *IP address.* Part of an IP address is used for the network address, and the other part is used to identify a particular interface on a host in that network. You should realize that IP addresses are assigned to interfaces—such as Ethernet cards or modems—and not to the host computer. Usually a computer has only one interface and is accessed using only that interface's IP address. In that regard, an IP address can be thought of as identifying a particular host system on a network, and so the IP address is usually referred to as the *host address.*

In fact, though, a host system could have several interfaces, each with its own IP address. This is the case for computers that operate as gateways and firewalls from the local network to the Internet. One interface usually connects to the LAN and another to the Internet, as by two Ethernet cards. Each interface (such as an Ethernet card) has its own IP address. For example, when you use Red Hat Configuration Tool to specify an IP address for an Ethernet card on your system, the Devices panel lists an entry for each Ethernet card installed on your computer, beginning with eth0 for the first. Opening up a Device window you can select the TCP protocol in the Protocols panel to open a TCP/IP setting window where you can enter the card's IP address. Other Ethernet cards have their own IP addresses. Currently, the Linux kernel can support up to four network adapters. If you use a modem to connect to an ISP, you would set up a PPP interface that would also have its own IP address (usually dynamically assigned by the ISP). Remembering this distinction is important if you plan to use Linux to set up a local or home network, using Linux as your gateway machine to the Internet (see the section "IP Masquerading" later in Chapter 37).

Network Addresses

The IP address is divided into two parts: one part identifies the network, and the other part identifies a particular host. The network address identifies the network of which a particular interface on a host is a part. Two methods exist for implementing the network and host parts of an IP address: the original class-based IP addressing and the current Classless Interdomain Routing (CIDR) addressing. Class-based IP addressing designates officially predetermined parts of the address for the network and host addresses, whereas CIDR addressing allows the parts to be determined dynamically using a netmask.

Class-Based IP Addressing

Originally, IP addresses were organized according to classes. On the Internet, networks are organized into three classes depending on their size—classes A, B, and C. A class A network uses only the first segment for the network address and the remaining three for the host, allowing a great many computers to be connected to the same network. Most IP addresses reference smaller, class C, networks. For a class C network, the first three segments are used to identify the network, and only the last segment identifies the host. Altogether, this forms a unique address with which to identify any network interface on computers in a TCP/IP network. For example, in the IP address 192.168.1.72, the network part is 192.168.1 and the interface/host part is 72. The interface/host is a part of a network whose own address is 192.168.1.0.

In a class C network, the first three numbers identify the network part of the IP address. This part is divided into three network numbers, each identifying a subnet. Networks on the Internet are organized into subnets, beginning with the largest and narrowing to small subnetworks. The last number is used to identify a particular computer, referred to as a *host*. You can think of the Internet as a series of networks with subnetworks; these subnetworks have their own subnetworks. The rightmost number identifies the host computer, and the number preceding it identifies the subnetwork of which the computer is a part. The number to the left of that identifies the network the subnetwork is part of, and so on. The Internet address 192.168.187.4 references the fourth computer connected to the network identified by the number 187. Network 187 is a subnet to a larger network identified as 168. This larger network is itself a subnet of the network identified as 192. Here's how it breaks down:

192.168.187.4	IP address
192.168.187	Network identification
4	Host identification

Netmask

Systems derive the network address from the host address using the netmask. You can think of an IP address as a series of 32 binary bits, some of which are used for the network and the remainder for the host. The *netmask* has the network set of bits set to 1s, with the host bits set to 0s (see Figure 36-1). In a standard class-based IP address, all the numbers in the network part of your host address are set to 255, and the host part is set to 0. This has the effect of setting all the binary bits making up the network address to 1s. This, then, is your netmask. So, the netmask for the host address 192.168.1.72 is 255.255.255.0. The network part, 192.168.1, has been set to 255.255.255, and the host part, 72, has been set to 0. Systems can then use your netmask to derive your network address from your host address. They can determine what part of your host address makes up your network address and what those numbers are.

For those familiar with computer programming, a bitwise AND operation on the netmask and the host address results in zeroing the host part, leaving you with the network part of the host address. You can think of the address as being implemented as a 4-byte integer with each byte corresponding to a segment of the address. In a class C address, the three network segments correspond to the first three bytes and the host segment corresponds to the fourth byte. A netmask is designed to mask out the host part of the address, leaving the network segments alone. In the netmask for a standard class C network, the first three bytes are all 1s and the last byte consists of 0s. The 0s in the last byte mask out the host part of the address, and the 1s in the first three bytes leave the network part of the address alone. Figure 36-1 shows the bitwise operation of the netmask

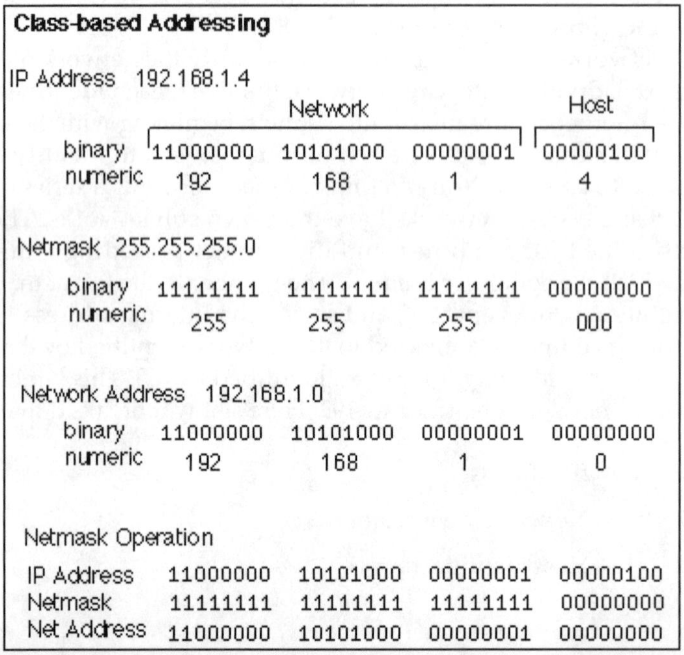

Class-based Addressing

```
IP Address   192.168.1.4
                         Network                        Host
     binary    11000000   10101000   00000001     00000100
     numeric     192        168         1            4

Netmask 255.255.255.0
     binary    11111111   11111111   11111111   00000000
     numeric     255        255        255        000

Network Address   192.168.1.0
     binary    11000000   10101000   00000001   00000000
     numeric     192        168         1          0

Netmask Operation
IP Address     11000000   10101000   00000001   00000100
Netmask        11111111   11111111   11111111   00000000
Net Address    11000000   10101000   00000001   00000000
```

Figure 36-1. *Class-based netmask operations*

on the address 192.168.1.4. This is a class C address to the mask, which consists of twenty-four 1s making up the first three bytes and eight 0s making up the last byte. When it is applied to the address 192.168.1.4, the network address remains (192.168.1) and the host address is masked out (4), giving you 192.168.1.0 as the network address.

The netmask as used in Classless Interdomain Routing (CIDR) is much more flexible. Instead of having the size of the network address and its mask determined by the network class, it is determined by a number attached to the end of the IP address. This number simply specifies the size of the network address, how many bits in the address it takes up. For example, in an IP address whose network part takes up the first three bytes (segments), the number of bits used for that network part is 24—eight bits to a byte (segment). Instead of using a netmask to determine the network address, the number for the network size is attached to the end of the address with a slash, as shown here:

```
192.168.1.72/24
```

CIDR gives you the advantage of specifying networks that are any size bits, instead of only three possible segments. You could have a network whose address takes up 14 bits, 22 bits, or even 25 bits. The host address can use whatever bits are left over. An IP address with 21 bits for the network can cover host addresses using the remaining 11 bits, 0 to 2,047.

Classless Interdomain Routing (CIDR)

Currently, the class-based organization of IP addresses is being replaced by the CIDR format. CIDR was designed for midsized networks, those between a class C and classes with numbers of hosts greater than 256 and smaller than 65,534. A class C network–based IP address using only one segment for hosts uses only one segment, an 8-bit integer, with a maximum value of 256. A class B network–based IP address uses two segments, which make up a 16-bit integer whose maximum value is 65,534. You can think of an address as a 32-bit integer taking up 4 bytes, where each byte is 8 bits. Each segment conforms to one of the 4 bytes. A class C network uses three segments, or 24 bits, to make up its network address. A class B network, in turn, uses two segments, or 16 bits, for its address. With this scheme, allowable host and network addresses are changed an entire byte at a time, segment to segment. With CIDR addressing, you can define host and network addresses by bits, instead of whole segments. For example, you can use CIDR addressing to expand the host segment from 8 bits to 9, rather than having to jump it to a class B 16 bits (two segments).

CIDR addressing notation achieves this by incorporating netmask information in the IP address (the netmask is applied to an IP address to determine the network part of the address). In the CIDR notation, the number of bits making up the network address is placed after the IP address, following a slash. For example, the CIDR form of the class C 192.168.187.4 IP address is:

```
192.168.187.4/24
```

Figure 36-2 shows an example of a CIDR address and its network mask. The IP address is 192.168.1.6 with a network mask of 22 bits, 192.168.1.6/22. The network address takes up the first 22 bits of the IP address and the remaining 10 bits are used

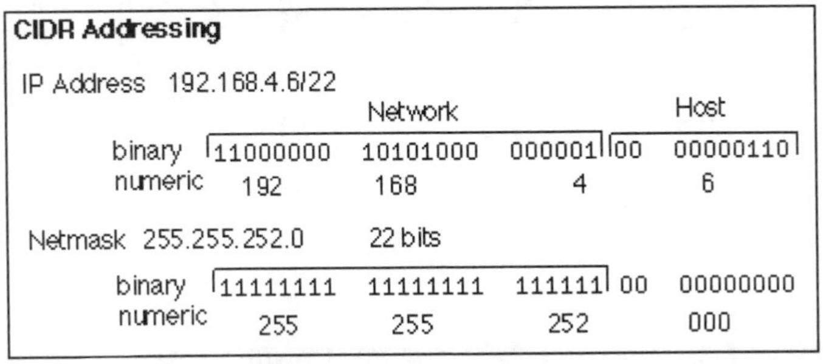

CIDR Addressing

IP Address 192.168.4.6/22

	Network			Host
binary	11000000	10101000	000001 00	00000110
numeric	192	168	4	6

Netmask 255.255.252.0 22 bits

binary	11111111	11111111	111111 00	00000000
numeric	255	255	252	000

Figure 36-2. *CIDR addressing*

for the host address. The host address is taking up the equivalent of a class-based IP address's fourth segment (8 bits) and 2 bits from the third segment.

Table 36-3 lists the different CIDR network masks available along with the maximum number of hosts. Both the short form and the full forms of the netmask are listed.

The network address for any standard class C IP address takes up the first three segments, 24 bits. If you want to create a network with a maximum of 512 hosts, you can give them IP addresses where the network address is 23 bits and the host address takes up 9 bits (0–511). The IP address notation remains the same, however, using the four 8-bit segments. This means a given segment's number could be used for both a network address and a host address. Segments are no longer wholly part of either the host address or the network address. Assigning a 23-bit network address and a 9-bit host address means that the number in the third segment is part of both the network address and the host address, the first 7 bits for the network and the last bit for the host. In this

Short Form	Full Form	Maximum Number of Hosts
/8	/255.0.0.0	16,777,215 (A class)
/16	/255.255.0.0	65,535 (B class)
/17	/255.255.128.0	32,767
/18	/255.255.192.0	16,383
/19	/255.255.224.0	8,191
/20	/255.255.240.0	4,095
/21	/255.255.248.0	2,047
/22	/255.255.252.0	1,023
/23	/255.255.254.0	511
/24	/255.255.255.0	255 (C class)
/25	/255.255.255.128	127
/26	/255.255.255.192	63
/27	/255.255.255.224	31
/28	/255.255.255.240	15
/29	/255.255.255.248	7
/30	/255.255.255.252	3

Table 36-3. *CIDR Network Masks*

following example, the third number, 145, is used as the end of the network address and as the beginning of the host address:

```
192.168.145.67/23
```

This situation complicates CIDR addressing, and in some cases the only way to represent the address is to specify two or more network addresses. Check RFC 1520 at **www.ietf.org** for more details.

Note

A simple way to calculate the number of hosts a network can address is to take the number of bits in its host segment as a power of 2, then subtract 2—that is, 2 to the number of host bits, minus 2. For example, an 8-bit host segment would be 2 to the power of 8, which equals 256. Subtract 2 (1 for the broadcast address, 255, and 1 for the zero value, 000) to leave you with 254 possible hosts.

CIDR also allows a network administrator to take what is officially the host part of an IP address and break it up into subnetworks with fewer hosts. This is referred to as *subnetting*. A given network will have its official IP network address recognized on the Internet or by a larger network. The network administrator for that network could, in turn, create several smaller networks within it using CIDR network masking. A classic example is to take a standard class C network with 254 hosts and break it up into two smaller networks, each with 64 hosts. You do this by using a CIDR netmask to take a bit from the host part of the IP address and use it for the subnetworks. Numbers within the range of the original 254 addresses whose first bit would be set to 1 would represent one subnet, and the others, whose first bit would be set to 0, would constitute the remaining network. In the network whose network address is 192.168.187.0, where the last segment is used for the hostnames, that last host segment could be further split into two subnets, each with its own hosts. For two subnets, you would use the first bit in the last 8-bit segment for the network. The remaining 7 bits could then be used for host addresses, giving you a range of 127 hosts per network. The subnet whose bit is set to 0 would have a range of 1 to 127, with a CIDR netmask of 25. The 8-bit segment for the first host would be 00000001. So the host with the address of 1 in that network would have this IP address:

```
192.168.187.1/25
```

For the subnet where the first bit is 1, the first host would have an address of 129, with the CIDR netmask of 25, as shown here. The 8-bit sequence for the first host would be 10000001.

```
192.168.187.129/25
```

Each subnet would have a set of 126 addresses, the first from 1 to 126, and the second from 129 to 254; 127 is the broadcast address for the first subnet, and 128 is the network address for the second subnet. The possible subnets and their masks that you could use are shown here.

Subnetworks	CIDR Address	Binary Mask
First subnet network address	.0/25	00000000
Second subnet network address	.128/25	10000000
First subnet broadcast address	.127/25	01111111
Second subnet broadcast address	.255/25	11111111
First address in first subnet	.1/25	00000001
First address in second subnet	.129/25	10000001
Last address in first subnet	.126/25	01111110
Last address in second subnet	.254/25	11111110

Obtaining an IP Address

IP addresses are officially allocated by IANA, which manages all aspects of Internet addressing (**www.iana.org**). IANA oversees Internet Registries (IRs), which, in turn, maintain Internet addresses on regional and local levels. The Internet Registry for the Americas is the American Registry for Internet Numbers (ARIN), whose Web site is at **www.arin.net.** These addresses are provided to users by Internet service providers (ISPs). You can obtain your own Internet address from an ISP, or if you are on a network already connected to the Internet, your network administrator can assign you one. If you are using an ISP, the ISP may temporarily assign one from a pool it has on hand with each use.

Certain numbers are reserved. The numbers 127, 0, or 255 cannot be part of an official IP address. The number 127 is used to designate the network address for the loopback interface on your system. The loopback interface enables users on your system to communicate with each other within the system without having to route through a network connection. Its network address would be 127.0.0.0 and its IP address is 127.0.0.1. For class-based IP addressing, the number 255 is a special broadcast identifier you can use to broadcast messages to all sites on a network. Using 255 for any part of the IP address references all nodes connected at that level. For example, 192.168.255.255 broadcasts a message to all computers on network 192.168, all its subnetworks, and their hosts. The address 192.168.187.255 broadcasts to every computer on the local network. If you use 0 for the network part of the address, the host number references a computer within your local network. For example, 0.0.0.6 references the sixth computer in your local network. If you want to broadcast to all computers on your local network, you can use the number 0.0.0.255. For CIDR IP addressing, the broadcast address may appear much like a normal IP address. As indicated in the previous section, CIDR addressing allows the use of any number of bits to make up the IP address for either the network or the host part. For a broadcast address, the host part must have all its bits set to 1 (see Figure 36-3).

A special set of numbers is reserved for use on non-Internet LANs (RFC 1918). These are numbers that begin with the special network number 192.168 (for class C networks), as used in these examples. If you are setting up a LAN, such as a small business or a home network, you are free to use these numbers for your local machines. You can set up an intranet using network cards, such as Ethernet cards and Ethernet hubs, and then configure your machines with IP addresses starting from 192.168.1.1. The host segment can go up to 256. If you have three machines on your home network, you could give them the addresses 192.168.1.1, 192.168.1.2, and 192.168.1.3. You can implement Internet services, such as FTP, Web, and mail services, on your local machines and use any of the Internet tools to make use of those services. They all use the same TCP/IP protocols used on the Internet. For example, with FTP tools, you can transfer files among the machines on your network. With mail tools, you can send messages from one machine to another, and with a Web browser, you can access local Web sites that may be installed on a machine running its own Web servers. If you want to have one of your machines connected to the Internet or some other network, you can set it up to be a gateway machine. By convention, the gateway machine is usually given the address 192.168.1.1. With a method called *IP masquerading,* you can have any of the non-Internet machines use a gateway to connect to the Internet.

Numbers are also reserved for class A and class B non-Internet local networks. Table 36-4 lists these addresses. The possible addresses available span from 0 to 255 in the host segment of the address. For example, class B network addresses range from 172.16.0.0 to 172.31.255.255, giving you a total of 32,356 possible hosts. The class C network

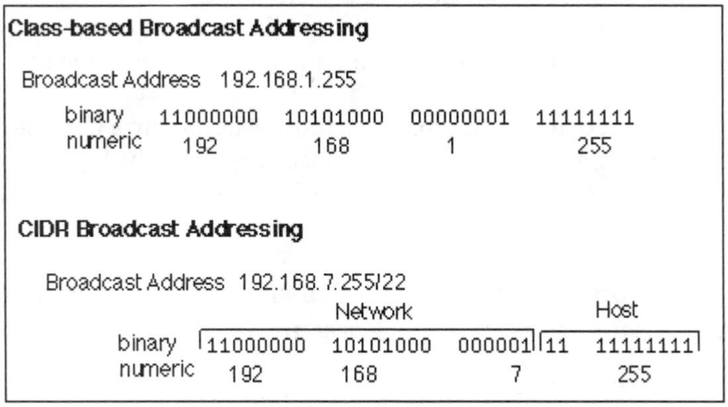

Class-based Broadcast Addressing

Broadcast Address 192.168.1.255

binary	11000000	10101000	00000001	11111111
numeric	192	168	1	255

CIDR Broadcast Addressing

Broadcast Address 192.168.7.255/22

	Network			Host	
binary	11000000	10101000	000001	11	11111111
numeric	192	168	7		255

Figure 36-3. *Class-based and CIDR broadcast addressing*

Private Network Address	Network Classes
10.0.0.0	Class A network
172.16.0.0 to 172.31.255.255	Class B network
192.168.0.0	Class C network
127.0.0.0	Loopback network (for system self-communication)

Table 36-4. *Non-Internet Local Network IP Addresses*

ranges from 192.168.0.0 to 192.168.255.255, giving you 256 possible subnetworks, each with 256 possible hosts. The network address 127.0.0.0 is reserved for a system's loopback interface, which allows it to communicate with itself, enabling users on the same system to send messages to each other.

Broadcast Addresses

The broadcast address allows a system to send the same message to all systems on your network at once. With class-based IP addressing, you can easily determine the broadcast address using your host address: the broadcast address has the host part of your address set to 255. The network part remains untouched. So the broadcast address for the host address 192.168.1.72 is 192.168.1.255 (you combine the network part of the address with 255 in the host part). For CIDR IP addressing, you need to know the number of bits in the netmask. The remaining bits are set to 1 (see Figure 36-3). For example, an IP address of 192.168.4.6/22 has a broadcast address of 192.168.7.255/22. In this case, the first 22 bits are the network address and the last 10 bits are the host part set to the broadcast value (all 1s).

In fact, you can think of a class C broadcast address as merely a CIDR address using 24 bits (the first three segments) for the network address, and the last 8 bits (the fourth segment) as the broadcast address. The value 255 expressed in binary terms is simply 8 bits that are all 1s. 255 is the same as 11111111.

IP Address	Broadcast Address	IP Broadcast Number	Binary Equivalent
192.168.1.72	192.168.1.255	255	11111111
192.168.4.6/22	192.168.7.255/22	7.255 (last 2 bits in 7)	1111111111

Gateway Addresses

Some networks have a computer designated as the gateway to other networks. Every connection to and from a network to other networks passes through this gateway computer. Most local networks use gateways to establish a connection to the Internet. If you are on this type of network, you must provide the gateway address. If your network does not have a connection to the Internet, or a larger network, you may not need a gateway address. The gateway address is the address of the host system providing the gateway service to the network. On many networks, this host is given a host ID of 1: the gateway address for a network with the address 192.168.1 would be 192.168.1.1, but this is only a convention. To be sure of your gateway address, ask your network administrator.

Name Server Addresses

Many networks, including the Internet, have computers that provide a Domain Name Service (DNS) that translates the domain names of networks and hosts into IP addresses. These are known as the network's *domain name servers*. The DNS makes your computer identifiable on a network, using only your domain name, rather than your IP address. You can also use the domain names of other systems to reference them, so you needn't know their IP addresses. You must know the IP addresses of any domain name servers for your network, however. You can obtain the addresses from your system administrator (often more than one exists). Even if you are using an ISP, you must know the address of the domain name servers your ISP operates for the Internet.

TCP/IP Configuration Files

A set of configuration files in the **/etc** directory, shown in Table 36-5, are used to set up and manage your TCP/IP network. These configuration files specify such network information as host and domain names, IP addresses, and interface options. The IP addresses and domain names of other Internet hosts you want to access are entered in these files. If you configured your network during installation, you can already find that information in these files.

Identifying Hostnames: /etc/hosts

Without the unique IP address the TCP/IP network uses to identify computers, a particular computer cannot be located. Because IP addresses are difficult to use or remember, domain names are used instead. For each IP address, a domain name exists. When you use a domain name to reference a computer on the network, your system translates it into its associated IP address. This address can then be used by your network to locate that computer.

Address	Description
Host address	IP address of your system; it has a network part to identify the network you are on and a host part to identify your own system
Network address	IP address of your network
Broadcast address	IP address for sending messages to all hosts on your network at once
Gateway address	IP address of your gateway system, if you have one (usually the network part of your host IP address with the host part set to 1)
Domain name server addresses	IP addresses of domain name servers your network uses
Netmask	Used to determine the network and host parts of your IP address
Files	**Description**
/etc/hosts	Associates hostnames with IP addresses
/etc/networks	Associates domain names with network addresses
/etc/host.conf	Lists resolver options
/etc/nsswitch.conf	Lists resolver options
/etc/hosts	Lists domain names for remote hosts with their IP addresses
/etc/resolv.conf	Lists domain name server names, IP addresses (nameserver), and domain names where remote hosts may be located (search)
/etc/protocols	Lists protocols available on your system
/etc/services	Lists available network services, such as FTP and Telnet, and the ports they use
/etc/HOSTNAME	Holds the name of your system
/etc/sysconfig/network	Network configuration information

Table 36-5. *TCP/IP Configuration Addresses and Files*

Originally, every computer on the network was responsible for maintaining a list of the hostnames and their IP addresses. This list is still kept in the **/etc/hosts** file. When you use a domain name, your system looks up its IP address in the **hosts** file. The system administrator is responsible for maintaining this list. Because of the explosive growth of the Internet and the development of more and more large networks, the responsibility for associating domain names and IP addresses has been taken over by domain name servers. The **hosts** file is still used to hold the domain names and IP addresses of frequently accessed hosts, however. Your system normally checks your **hosts** file for the IP address of a domain name before taking the added step of accessing a name server.

The format of a domain name entry in the **hosts** file is the IP address followed by the domain name, separated by a space. You can then add aliases for the hostname. After the entry, on the same line, you can enter a comment. A comment is always preceded by a # symbol. You can already find an entry in your **hosts** file for localhost with the IP address 127.0.0.1. Localhost is a special identification used by your computer to enable users on your system to communicate locally with each other. The IP address 127.0.0.1 is a special reserved address used by every computer for this purpose. It identifies what is technically referred to as a *loopback device*. A sample **/etc/hosts** file is shown here.

/etc/hosts

```
127.0.0.1       turtle.mytrek.com localhost
192.168.0.1       turtle.mytrek.com
192.168.0.2       rabbit.mytrek.com
192.168.34.56       pangol.mytrain.com
202.211.234.1       rose.berkeley.edu
```

Network Name: /etc/networks

The **/etc/networks** file holds the domain names and IP addresses of networks you are connected to, not the domain names of particular computers. Networks have shortened IP addresses. Depending on the type of network, they use one, two, or three numbers for their IP addresses. You also have your localhost network IP address 127.0.0.0. This is the network address used for the loopback device.

The IP addresses are entered, followed by the network domain names. Recall that an IP address consists of a network part and a host part. The network part is the network address you find in the **networks** file. You always have an entry in this file for the network portion of your computer's IP address. This is the network address of the network to which your computer is connected. A sample **/etc/networks** file is shown here with an entry for the **mytrek.com** network.

/etc/networks

```
loopback 127.0.0.0
mytrek.com 192.168.1.0
```

/etc/HOSTNAME

The **/etc/HOSTNAME** file holds your system's hostname. To change your hostname, you change this entry. The netcfg program enables you to change your hostname and places the new name in **/etc/HOSTNAME**. Instead of displaying this file to find your hostname, you can use the **hostname** command:

```
$ hostname
turtle.mytrek.com
```

/etc/services

The **/etc/services** file lists network services available on your system, such as FTP and Telnet, and associates each with a particular port. Here, you can find out what port your Web server is checking or what port is used for your FTP server. You can give a service an alias, which you specify after the port number. You can then reference the service using the alias.

/etc/protocols

The **/etc/protocols** file lists the TCP/IP protocols currently supported by your system.

/etc/sysconfig/network

The **/etc/sysconfig/network** file contains system definitions for your network configuration. These include definitions for your domain name, gateway, and hostname, as shown here:

```
NETWORKING=yes
HOSTNAME=turtle.mytrek.com
GATEWAY=192.168.0.1
```

Domain Name Service (DNS)

Each computer connected to a TCP/IP network, such as the Internet, is identified by its own IP address. IP addresses are difficult to remember, so a domain name version of each IP address is also used to identify a host. As described in Chapter 10, a domain name consists of two parts, the hostname and the domain. The hostname is the computer's specific name, and the domain identifies the network of which the computer is a part. The domains used for the United States usually have extensions that identify the type of host. For example, **.edu** is used for educational institutions and **.com** is used for businesses. International domains usually have extensions that indicate the country they are located in, such as **.de** for Germany or **.au** for Australia. The combination of a hostname, domain, and extension forms a unique name by which a computer can be referenced. The domain can, in turn, be split into further subdomains.

As you know, a computer on a network can still only be identified by its IP address, even if it has a hostname. You can use a hostname to reference a computer on a network, but this involves using the hostname to look up the corresponding IP address in a database. The network then uses the IP address, not the hostname, to access the computer. Before the advent of large TCP/IP networks, such as the Internet, it was feasible for each computer on a network to maintain a file with a list of all the hostnames and IP addresses of the computers connected on its network. Whenever a hostname was used, it was looked up in this file and the corresponding IP address was located. You can still do this on your own system for remote systems you access frequently.

As networks became larger, it became impractical—and, in the case of the Internet, impossible—for each computer to maintain its own list of all the domain names and IP addresses. To provide the service of translating domain addresses to IP addresses, databases of domain names were developed and placed on their own servers. To find the IP address of a domain name, you send a query to a name server, which then looks up the IP address for you and sends it back. In a large network, several name servers can cover different parts of the network. If a name server cannot find a particular IP address, it sends the query on to another name server that is more likely to have it.

If you are administering a network and you need to set up a name server for it, you can configure a Linux system to operate as a name server. To do so, you must start up a name server daemon and then wait for domain name queries. A name server makes use of several configuration files that enable it to answer requests. The name server software used on Linux systems is the Berkeley Internet Name Domain (BIND) server distributed by the Internet Software Consortium (**www.isc.org**). Chapter 22 describes the process of setting up a domain name server in detail.

Name servers are queried by resolvers. These are programs specially designed to obtain addresses from name servers. To use domain names on your system, you must configure your own resolver. Your local resolver is configured with your **/etc/host.conf** and **/etc/resolv.conf** files. You can use **/etc/nsswitch** in place of **/etc/host.conf**.

host.conf

Your **host.conf** file lists resolver options (shown in Table 36-6). Each option can have several fields, separated by spaces or tabs. You can use a **#** at the beginning of a line to enter a comment. The options tell the resolver what services to use. The order of the list is important. The resolver begins with the first option listed and moves on to the next ones in turn. You can find the **host.conf** file in your **/etc** directory, along with other configuration files.

In the next example of a **host.conf** file, the `order` option instructs your resolver first to look up names in your local **/etc/hosts** file, and then, if that fails, to query domain name servers. The system does not have multiple addresses.

/etc/host.conf

```
# host.conf file
# Lookup names in host file and then check DNS
order bind host
# There are no multiple addresses
multi off
```

/etc/nsswitch.conf: Name Service Switch

Different functions in the standard C Library must be configured to operate on your Linux system. Previously, database-like services, such as password support and name

Options	Description
`order`	Specifies sequence of name resolution methods: `hosts` Checks for name in the local **/etc/host** file `bind` Queries a DNS name server for address `nis` Uses Network Information Service protocol to obtain address
`alert`	Checks addresses of remote sites attempting to access your system; you turn it on or off with the `on` and `off` options
`nospoof`	Confirms addresses of remote sites attempting to access your system
`trim`	Checks your local host's file; removes the domain name and checks only for the hostname; enables you to use only a hostname in your host file for an IP address
`multi`	Checks your local hosts file; allows a host to have several IP addresses; you turn it on or off with the `on` and `off` options

Table 36-6. *Resolver options, host.conf*

services like NIS or DNS, directly accessed these functions, using a fixed search order. For GNU C Library 2.*x*, used on current versions of Linux, this configuration is carried out by a scheme called the Name Service Switch (NSS), which is based on the method of the same name used by Sun Microsystems Solaris 2 OS. The database sources and their lookup order are listed in the **/etc/nsswitch.conf** file.

The **/etc/nsswitch.conf** file holds entries for the different configuration files that can be controlled by NSS. The system configuration files that NSS supports are listed in Table 36-7. An entry consists of two fields: the service and the configuration specification. The service consists of the configuration file followed by a colon. The second field is the configuration specification for that file, which holds instructions on how the lookup procedure will work. The configuration specification can contain service specifications and action items. Service specifications are the services to search. Currently, valid service specifications are nis, nis-plus, files, db, dns, and compat (see Table 36-8). Not all are valid for each configuration file. For example, the dns service is only valid for the **hosts** file, whereas nis is valid for all files. An action item specifies the action to take for a specific service. An action item is placed within brackets after a service. A configuration specification can list several services, each with its own action item. In the following example, the entry for the network file has a configuration specification that says to check the NIS service and, if not found, to check the **/etc/networks** file:

```
networks: nis [NOTFOUND=return] files
```

Files	Description
aliases	Mail aliases, used by Sendmail
ethers	Ethernet numbers
group	Groups of users
hosts	Hostnames and numbers
netgroup	Network-wide list of hosts and users, used for access rules; C libraries before glibc 2.1 only support netgroups over NIS
network	Network names and numbers
passwd	User passwords
protocols	Network protocols
publickey	Public and secret keys for SecureRPC used by NFS and NIS+
rpc	Remote procedure call names and numbers
services	Network services
shadow	Shadow user passwords

Table 36-7. *NSS Supported Files*

Service	Description
files	Checks corresponding **/etc** file for the configuration (for example, **/etc/hosts** for hosts); this service is valid for all files
db	Checks corresponding **/var/db** databases for the configuration; valid for all files except **netgroup**
compat	Valid only for **passwd**, **group**, and **shadow** files
dns	Checks the DNS service; valid only for **hosts** file
nis	Checks the NIS service; valid for all files
nisplus	NIS version 3
hesoid	Uses Hesoid for lookup

Table 36-8. *NSS Configuration Services*

An action item consists of a status and an action. The status holds a possible result of a service lookup, and the action is the action to take if the status is true. Currently, the possible status values are SUCCESS, NOTFOUND, UNAVAIL, and TRYAGAIN (service temporarily unavailable). The possible actions are return and continue: return stops the lookup process for the configuration file, whereas continue continues on to the next listed service. In the previous example, if the record is not found in NIS, the lookup process ends.

Shown here is a copy of the current Red Hat **/etc/nsswitch.conf** file which lists commonly used entries. Comments and commented-out entries begin with a **#** sign.

/etc/nsswitch.conf

```
#
# /etc/nsswitch.conf
#
# An example Name Service Switch config file. This file should be
# sorted with the most-used services at the beginning.
#
# The entry '[NOTFOUND=return]' means that the search for an
# entry should stop if the search in the previous entry turned
# up nothing. Note that if the search failed due to some other reason
# (like no NIS server responding) then the search continues with the
# next entry.
#
# Legal entries are:
#
# nisplus or nis+ Use NIS+ (NIS version 3)
# nis or yp Use NIS (NIS version 2), also called YP
# dns Use DNS (Domain Name Service)
# files Use the local files
# db Use the local database (.db) files
# compat Use NIS on compat mode
# hesoid Use Hesoid for user lookups
# [NOTFOUND=return] Stop searching if not found so far
#

# To use db, put the "db" in front of "files" for entries you want to
# be looked up first in the databases
#
# Example:
#passwd: db files nisplus nis
#shadow: db files nisplus nis
#group: db files nisplus nis

passwd: files nisplus nis
shadow: files nisplus nis
group: files nisplus nis

hosts: files nisplus nis dns

# Example - obey only what nisplus tells us...
```

```
#services: nisplus [NOTFOUND=return] files
#networks: nisplus [NOTFOUND=return] files
#protocols: nisplus [NOTFOUND=return] files
#rpc: nisplus [NOTFOUND=return] files
#ethers: nisplus [NOTFOUND=return] files
#netmasks: nisplus [NOTFOUND=return] files

bootparams: nisplus [NOTFOUND=return] files

ethers: files
netmasks: files
networks: files
protocols: files
rpc: files
services: files

netgroup: nisplus

publickey: nisplus
automount: files nisplus
aliases: files nisplus
```


Network Interfaces and Routes: ifconfig and route

Your connection to a network is made by your system through a particular hardware interface, such as an Ethernet card or a modem. Data passing through this interface is then routed to your network. The **ifconfig** command configures your network interfaces, and the **route** command sets up network connections accordingly. If you configure an interface with a network configuration tool, such as the Mandrake, Red Hat, or SuSE network configuration tools, you needn't use **ifconfig** or **route**. If you are using another Linux system, the netconfig utility also performs the same configuration as netcfg. However, you can directly configure interfaces using **ifconfig** and **route**, if you want. Every time you start your system, the network interfaces and their routes must be established. This is done automatically for you when you boot up by **ifconfig** and **route** commands executed for each interface by the **/etc/rc.d/init.d/network** initialization file, which is executed whenever you start your system. If you are manually adding your own interfaces, you must set up the network script to perform the **ifconfig** and **route** operations for your new interfaces.

Network Startup Script: /etc/rc.d/init.d/network and /etc/sysconfig/network-scripts

On Red Hat and Caldera distributions, your network interface is started up using the **network** script in the **/etc/rc.d/init.d** directory. This script will activate your network interface cards (NIC) as well as implement configuration information such as gateway, host, and name server identities. You can manually shut down and start your network interface using this script and the **restart**, **start**, or **stop** options. You can run the script on Red Hat with the **service** command. The following commands shut down and then start up your network interface:

```
service network stop
service network start
```

If you are changing network configuration, you will have to restart your network interface for the changes to take effect:

```
service network restart
```

To test if your interface is working, use the **ping** command with an IP address of a system on your network, such as your gateway machine. The **ping** command continually repeats until you stop it with a CTRL-C.

```
ping 192.168.0.1
```

The **/etc/rc.d/init.d/network** file performs the startup operations by executing several specialized scripts located in the **/etc/sysconfig/network-scripts** directory. The **network** script uses a script in that directory called **ifup** to activate a network connection, and **ifdown** to shut it down. **ifup** and **ifdown** will invoke other scripts tailored to the kind of device being worked on, such as **ifup-ppp** for modems using the PPP protocol, or **ifup-ipv6** for network devices that use IP Protocol version 6 addressing.

The **ifup** and **ifdown** scripts make use of interface configuration files that bear the names of the network interfaces currently configured, such as **ifcfg-eth0** for the first Ethernet device. These files define shell variables that hold information on the interface, such as whether to start them at boot time. For example, the **ifcfg-eth0** file holds definitions for NETWORK, BROADCAST, and IPADDR, which are assigned the network, broadcast, and IP addresses that the device uses.

The **ifdown** and **ifup** scripts, in turn, hold the **ifconfig** and **route** commands to activate scripts using these variables defined in the interface configuration files. If you want to manually start up an interface with **ifup**, you simply use the interface configuration file as its argument. The following command starts up the second Ethernet card:

```
cd /etc/sysconfig/network-scripts
ifup ifcfg-eth1
```

Interface configuration files are automatically generated when you configure your network connections, such as with a distribution's network administrative tool or third-party tools like Webmin. You can also manually edit these interface configuration files, making changes such as whether to start up the interface at boot or not (though using a configuration tool like netcfg is easier). A sample **ifcfg-eth0** file is shown here.

/etc/sysconfig/network-scripts/ifcfg-eth0

```
DEVICE=eth0
BOOTPROTO=static
BROADCAST=192.168.0.255
IPADDR=192.168.0.1
NETMASK=255.255.255.0
NETWORK=192.168.0.0
ONBOOT=yes
```


ifconfig

The **ifconfig** command takes as its arguments the name of an interface and an IP address, as well as options. The **ifconfig** command then assigns the IP address to the interface. Your system now knows that such an interface exists and that it references a particular IP address. In addition, you can specify whether the IP address is a host address or a network address. You can use a domain name for the IP address, provided the domain name is listed along with its IP address in the **/etc/hosts** file. The syntax for the **ifconfig** command is as follows:

```
# ifconfig interface -host_net_flag address options
```

The *host_net_flag* can be either **-host** or **-net** to indicate a host or network IP address. The **-host** flag is the default. The **ifconfig** command can have several options, which set different features of the interface, such as the maximum number of bytes it can transfer (**mtu**) or the broadcast address. The **up** and **down** options activate and deactivate the interface. In the next example, the **ifconfig** command configures an Ethernet interface:

```
# ifconfig eth0 192.168.0.1
```

For a simple configuration such as this, **ifconfig** automatically generates a standard broadcast address and netmask. The standard broadcast address is the network address with the number 255 for the host address. For a class C network, the standard netmask is 255.255.255.0, whereas for a class A network, the standard netmask is 255.0.0.0. If you are connected to a network with a particular netmask and broadcast address, however, you must specify them when you use **ifconfig**. The option for specifying the broadcast address is **broadcast**; for the network mask, it is **netmask**. Table 36-9 lists the different **ifconfig** options. In the next example, **ifconfig** includes the netmask and broadcast address:

```
# ifconfig eth0 192.168.0.1 broadcast 192.168.0.255 netmask
255.255.255.0
```

Option	Description
Interface	Name of the network interface, such as **eth0** for the first Ethernet device or **ppp0** for the first PPP device (modem)
`aftype`	Address family for decoding protocol addresses; default is inet, currently used by Linux
`up`	Activates an interface; implied if IP address is specified
`down`	Deactivates an interface
`arp`	Turns ARP on or off; preceding hyphen (-) turns it off
`trailers`	Turns on or off trailers in Ethernet frames; preceding hyphen (-) turns it off
`allmulti`	Turns on or off the promiscuous mode; preceding hyphen (-) turns it off; this allows network monitoring
`metric` *n*	Cost for interface routing (not currently supported)
`mtu` *n*	Maximum number of bytes that can be sent on this interface per transmission
`dstaddr` *address*	Destination IP address on a point-to-point connection
`netmask` *address*	IP network mask; preceding hyphen (-) turns it off
`broadcast` *address*	Broadcast address; preceding hyphen (-) turns it off
`point-to-point` *address*	Point-to-point mode for interface; if address is included, it is assigned to remote system
`hw`	Sets hardware address of interface
Address	IP address assigned to interface

Table 36-9. *The* `ifconfig` *Options*

Once you configure your interface, you can use **`ifconfig`** with the **`up`** option to activate it and with the **`down`** option to deactivate it. If you specify an IP address in an **`ifconfig`** operation, as in the previous example, the **`up`** option is implied.

```
# ifconfig eth0 up
```

Point-to-point interfaces such as Parallel IP (PLIP), Serial Line IP (SLIP), and Point-to-Point Protocol (PPP) require you to include the **pointopoint** option. A PLIP interface name is identified with the name **plip** with an attached number. For example, **plip0** is the first PLIP interface. SLIP interfaces use **slip0**. PPP interfaces start with **ppp0**. Point-to-point interfaces are those that usually operate between only two hosts, such as two computers connected over a modem. When you specify the **pointopoint** option, you need to include the IP address of the host. In the next example, a PLIP interface is configured that connects the computer at IP address 192.168.1.72 with one at 204.166.254.14. If domain addresses were listed for these systems in **/etc/hosts**, those domain names could be used in place of the IP addresses.

```
# ifconfig plip0 192.168.1.72 pointopoint 204.166.254.14
```

If you need to, you can also use **ifconfig** to configure your loopback device. The name of the loopback device is **lo**, and its IP address is the special address 127.0.0.1. The following example shows the configuration:

```
# ifconfig lo 127.0.0.1
```

The **ifconfig** command is useful for checking on the status of an interface. If you enter the **ifconfig** command along with the name of the interface, information about that interface is displayed:

```
# ifconfig eth0
```

To see if your loopback interface is configured, you can use **ifconfig** with the loopback interface name, **lo**:

```
# ifconfig lo

lo Link encap:Local Loopback
 inet addr:127.0.0.1 Bcast:127.255.255.255 Mask:255.0.0.0
 UP BROADCAST LOOPBACK RUNNING MTU:2000 Metric:1
 RX packets:0 errors:0 dropped:0 overruns:0
 TX packets:12 errors:0 dropped:0 overruns:0
```

Routing

A packet that is part of a transmission takes a certain *route* to reach its destination. On a large network, packets are transmitted from one computer to another until the destination computer is reached. The route determines where the process starts and to what computer your system needs to send the packet for it to reach its destination. On small networks, routing may be static—that is, the route from one system to another is fixed. One system knows how to reach another, moving through fixed paths. On larger networks and on the Internet, however, routing is dynamic. Your system knows the first computer to send its packet off to, and then that computer takes the packet from there, passing it on to another computer, which then determines where to pass it on. For dynamic routing, your system needs to know little. Static routing, however, can become complex because you have to keep track of all the network connections.

Your routes are listed in your routing table in the **/proc/net/route** file. To display the routing table, enter **`route`** with no arguments (the **`netstat -r`** command will also display the routing table):

```
# route
Kernel routing table
Destination Gateway Genmask Flags Metric Ref Use Iface
loopback * 255.0.0.0 U 0 0 12 lo
pangol.train.com * 255.255.255.0 U 0 0 0 eth0
```

Each entry in the routing table has several fields, providing information such as the route destination and the type of interface used. The different fields are listed in the Table 36-10.

Field	Description
Destination	Destination IP address of the route
Gateway	IP address or hostname of the gateway the route uses; * indicates no gateway is used
Genmask	The netmask for the route
Flags	Type of route: U = up, H = host, G = gateway, D = dynamic, M = modified
Metric	Metric cost of route
Ref	Number of routes that depend on this one
Window	TCP window for AX.25 networks
Use	Number of times used
Iface	Type of interface this route uses

Table 36-10. *Routing Table Entries*

You should have at least one entry in the routing table for the loopback interface. If not, you must route the loopback interface using the **route** command. The IP address for an interface has to be added to the routing table before you can use that interface. You add an address with the **route** command and the **add** option:

```
route add address
```

The next example adds the IP address for the loopback interface to the routing table:

```
route add 127.0.0.1
```

With the **add** argument, you can add routes either for networks with the **-net** option or with the **-host** option for IP interfaces (hosts). The **-host** option is the default. In addition, you can then specify several parameters for information, such as the netmask (**netmask**), the gateway (**gw**), the interface device (**dev**), and the default route (**default**). If you have more than one IP interface on your system, such as several Ethernet cards, you must specify the name of the interface using the **dev** parameter. If your network has a gateway host, you use the **gw** parameter to specify it. If your system is connected to a network, at least one entry should be in your routing table that specifies the default route. This is the route taken by a message packet when no other route entry leads to its destination. The following example is the routing of an Ethernet interface:

```
# route add 192.168.1.2 dev eth0
```

If your system has only the single Ethernet device as your IP interface, you could leave out the **dev eth0** parameter:

```
# route add 192.168.1.2
```

You can delete any route you establish by invoking **ifconfig** with the **del** argument and the IP address of that route, as in this example:

```
# route del 192.168.1.2
```

You also need to add routes for networks that an IP interface can access. For this, you use the **-net** option. In this example, a route is set up for a system's LAN at 192.168.1.0:

```
# route add -net 192.168.1.0 dev eth0
```

For a gateway, you first add a route to the gateway interface, and then add a route specifying that it is a gateway. The address of the gateway interface in this example is 192.168.1.1:

```
# route add 192.168.1.1
# route add default gw 192.168.1.1
```

If you are using the gateway to access a subnet, add the network address for that network (in this example, 192.168.23.0):

```
# route add -net 192.168.23.0 gw dev eth1
```

To add another IP address to a different network interface on your system, use the **ifconfig** and **route** commands with the new IP address. The following command configures a second Ethernet card (eth1) with the IP address 192.168.1.3:

```
ifconfig eth1 192.168.1.3
route add 192.168.1.3 dev eth1
```

Monitoring Your Network: ping and netstat

With the ping program, you can check to see if you can actually access another host on your network. The ping program sends a request to the host for a reply. The host then sends a reply back, and it is displayed on your screen. The ping program continually sends such a request until you stop it with a **break** command, CTRL-C. You see one reply after another scroll by on your screen until you stop the program. If ping cannot access a host, it issues a message saying the host is unreachable. If ping fails, this may be an indication that your network connection is not working. It may only be the particular interface, a basic configuration problem, or a bad physical connection. ping uses the Internet Control Message Protocol (ICMP), discussed in Chapter 37. Networks may block these protocols as a security measure, also preventing ping from working. A ping failure may simply indicate a security precaution on the part of the queried network.

To use ping, enter **ping** and the name of the host. You can also use the KDE network utilities on the KDE desktop and gfinger on the Gnome desktop.

```
$ ping ftp.redhat.com
```

The netstat program provides real-time information on the status of your network connections, as well as network statistics and the routing table. The netstat program has several options you can use to bring up different sorts of information about your network (see Table 36-11):

```
# netstat
Active Internet connections
Proto Recv-Q Send-Q Local Address Foreign Address (State) User
tcp 0 0 turtle.mytrek.com:01 pango1.mytrain.com.:ftp ESTABLISHED dylan
Active UNIX domain sockets
Proto RefCnt Flags Type State Path
unix 1 [ ACC ] SOCK_STREAM LISTENING /dev/printer
unix 2 [ ] SOCK_STREAM CONNECTED /dev/log
unix 1 [ ACC ] SOCK_STREAM LISTENING /dev/nwapi
unix 2 [ ] SOCK_STREAM CONNECTED /dev/log
unix 2 [ ] SOCK_STREAM CONNECTED
unix 1 [ ACC ] SOCK_STREAM LISTENING /dev/log
```


The **netstat** command with no options lists the network connections on your system. First, active TCP connections are listed, and then the active domain sockets are listed. The domain sockets contain processes used to set up communications among your

Option	Description
-a	Displays information about all Internet sockets, including those sockets that are only listening
-i	Displays statistics for all network devices
-c	Displays network status continually every second until the program is interrupted
-n	Displays remote and local addresses as IP addresses
-o	Displays timer states, expiration times, and backoff state for network connections
-r	Displays the kernel routing table
-t	Displays information about TCP sockets only, including those that are listening
-u	Displays information about UDP sockets only
-v	Displays version information
-w	Displays information about raw sockets only
-x	Displays information about Unix domain sockets

Table 36-11. *The* **netstat** *Options*

system and other systems. The various fields are described in Table 36-11. You can use **netstat** with the **-r** option to display the routing table, and **netstat** with the **-i** option displays the uses of the different network interfaces.

IP Aliasing

In some cases, you may want to assign a single Linux system that has only one network interface to two or more IP addresses. For example, you may want to run different Web sites that can be accessed with separate IP addresses on this same system. In effect, you are setting up an alias for your system, another address by which it can be accessed. In fact, you are assigning two IP addresses to the same network interface—for example, assigning a single Ethernet card two IP addresses. This procedure is referred to as *IP aliasing* and is used to set up multiple IP-based virtual hosts for Internet servers. This method enables you to run several Web servers on the same machine using a single interface (or more than one on each of several interfaces). See Chapters 23 and 24 for FTP and Web server information about virtual hosts, and Chapter 22 for Domain Name Service configuration.

Setting up an IP alias is a simple matter of configuring a network interface on your system to listen for the added IP address. Your system needs to know what IP addresses it should listen for and on what network interface. You set up IP aliases using the **ifconfig** and **route** commands, or a network administrative tool.

To add another address to the same interface, you need to qualify the interface by adding a colon and a number. For example, if you are adding another IP address to the first Ethernet card (**eth0**), you would add a **:0** to its interface name, **eth0:0**. The following example shows the **ifconfig** and **route** commands for the Ethernet interface 192.168.1.2 and two IP aliases added to it: 192.168.1.100 and 192.168.1.101. To add yet another IP address to this same interface, you would use **eth0:1**, incrementing the qualifier, and so on. The first **ifconfig** command assigns the main IP address, 192.168.1.2, to the first Ethernet device, **eth0**. Then, two other IP addresses are assigned to that same device. In the first **route** command, the network route is set up for the Ethernet device, and then routes are set up for each IP interface. The interfaces for the two aliases are indicated with **eth0:0** and **eth0:1**:

```
ifconfig eth0 192.168.1.2
ifconfig eth0:0 192.168.1.100
ifconfig eth0:1 192.168.1.101
route add -net 192.168.1.0 dev eth0
route add -host 192.168.1.2 dev eth0
route add -host 192.168.1.100 dev eth0:0
route add -host 192.168.1.101 dev eth0:1
```

IP aliasing must be supported by the kernel before you can use it. If your kernel does not support it, you may have to rebuild the kernel (including IP aliasing support), or use loadable modules to add IP aliasing.

Chapter 37

Network Security: Firewalls, Encryption, and Authentication

Most systems currently connected to the Internet are open to attempts by outside users to gain unauthorized access. Outside users can try to gain access directly by setting up an illegal connection, by intercepting valid communications from users remotely connected to the system, or by pretending to be a valid user. Firewalls, encryption, and authentication procedures are ways of protecting against such attacks. A *firewall* prevents any direct unauthorized attempts at access, *encryption* protects transmissions from authorized remote users, and *authentication* verifies that a user requesting access has the right to do so. The current Linux kernel incorporates support for firewalls using the Netfilter (iptables) packet filtering package (the previous version, ipchains, is used on older systems). To implement a firewall, you simply provide a series of rules to govern what kind of access you want to allow on your system. If that system is also a gateway for a private network, the system's firewall capability can effectively help protect the network from outside attacks. To provide protection for remote communications, transmission can be simply encrypted. For Linux systems, you can use the Secure Shell (SSH) suite of programs to encrypt any transmissions, preventing them from being read by anyone else. The SSH programs are meant to replace the remote tools such as rsh and rcp (see Chapter 15), which perform no encryption and include security risks such as transmitting passwords in clear text. In addition, Kerberos authentication provides another level of security whereby individual services can be protected, allowing use of a service only to users who are cleared for access. Table 37-1 lists several network security applications commonly used on Linux.

Outside users may also try to gain unauthorized access through any Internet services you may be hosting, such as a Web site. In such a case, you can set up a proxy to protect your site from attack. For Linux systems, use Squid proxy software to set up a proxy to protect your Web server (see Chapter 24).

Web Site	Security Application
netfilter.samba.org	Netfilter project, iptables, and NAT
netfilter.samba.org/ipchains	IP-Chains firewall
www.openssh.org	Secure Shell encryption
www.squid.org	Squid Web Proxy server
web.mit.edu/kerberos	Kerberos network authentication

Table 37-1. *Network Security Applications*

Firewalls: iptables and NAT

A good foundation for your network's security is to set up a Linux system to operate as a firewall for your network, protecting it from unauthorized access. You can use a firewall to implement either packet filtering or proxies. *Packet filtering* is simply the process of deciding whether a packet received by the firewall host should be passed on into the local network. The packet-filtering software checks the source and destination addresses of the packet and sends the packet on, if it's allowed. Even if your system is not part of a network but connects directly to the Internet, you can still use the firewall feature to control access to your system. Of course, this also provides you with much more security.

With proxies, you can control access to specific services, such as Web or FTP servers. You need a proxy for each service you want to control. The Web server has its own Web proxy, while an FTP server has an FTP proxy. Proxies can also be used to cache commonly used data, such as Web pages, so that users needn't constantly access the originating site. The proxy software commonly used on Linux systems is Squid, discussed in Chapter 24.

An additional task performed by firewalls is network address translation (NAT). Network address translation redirects packets to appropriate destinations. It performs tasks such as redirecting packets to certain hosts, forwarding packets to other networks, and changing the host source of packets to implement IP masquerading.

Note *ipchains was used to implement packet filtering and NAT tasks on firewalls for the Linux 2.2 kernel and earlier.*

The Netfilter software package implements both packet filtering and NAT tasks for the Linux 2.4 kernel and above. The Netfilter software is developed by the Netfilter Project, which you can find out more about at **netfilter.samba.org**. The command used to execute packet filtering and NAT tasks is **`iptables`**, and the software is commonly referred to as simply iptables. However, Netfilter implements packet filtering and NAT tasks separately using different tables and commands. A table will hold the set of commands for its application. This approach streamlines the packet-filtering task, letting iptables perform packet-filtering checks without the overhead of also having to address translations. NAT operations are also freed from being mixed in with packet-filtering checks. You use the **`iptables`** command for both packet filtering and NAT tasks, but for NAT you add the **`-nat`** option.

The iptables software can be built directly into the 2.4 kernel or loaded as a kernel module, iptable_filter.o. Unlike its predecessor, ipchains, Netfilter is designed to be modularized and extensible. Capabilities can be added in the form of modules such as the state module, which adds connection tracking.

iptables includes backward-compatible modules for both ipfwadm and ipchains. In fact, iptables is very similar to ipchains. You can still use ipchains and the earlier ipfwadm commands by loading the ipchains.o or ipfwadm.o modules provided with the Netfilter software. These provide full backward compatibility. For the sake of older systems, ipchains is also discussed here.

Packet Filtering

Netfilter is essentially a framework for packet management that can check packets for particular network protocols and notify parts of the kernel listening for them. Built on the Netfilter framework is the packet selection system implemented by IP tables. With IP tables, different tables of rules can be set up to select packets according to differing criteria. Packet filtering is implemented using a filter table that holds rules for dropping or accepting packets. Network address translation operations such as IP masquerading are implemented using the NAT table that holds IP masquerading rules. Preroute packet mangling uses the mangle table. This structure is extensible in that new modules can define their own tables with their own rules. It also greatly improves efficiency. Instead of all packets checking one large table, they only access the table of rules they need to.

IP table rules are managed using the **iptables** command. For this command, you will need to specify the table you want to manage. The default is the filter table, which need not be specified. You can list the rules you have added at any time with the **-L** and **-n** options, as shown here. The **-n** option says to use only numeric output for both IP addresses and ports, avoiding a DNS lookup for hostnames. You could, however, just use the **-L** option to see the port labels and hostnames:

```
iptables -L -n
```

In iptables commands, chain names have to be entered in uppercase, as with the chain names INPUT, OUTPUT, and FORWARD.

Packet-filtering rules are very similar to those used in ipchains with few exceptions. Rules are combined into different chains. The kernel uses chains to manage packets it receives and sends out. A *chain* is simply a checklist of rules. These rules specify what action to take for packets containing certain headers. The rules operate with an if-then-else structure. If a packet does not match the first rule, the next rule is then checked, and so on. If the packet does not match any rules, the kernel consults chain policy. Usually, at this point the packet is rejected. If the packet does match a rule, it is passed to its target, which determines what to do with the packet. The standard targets are listed in Table 37-2. If a packet does not match any of the rules, it is passed to the chain's default target.

A *target* could, in turn, be another chain of rules, even a chain of user-defined rules. A packet could be passed through several chains before finally reaching a target. In the case of user-defined chains, the default target is always the next rule in the chains from which it was called. This sets up a procedure or function call—like flow of control found in programming languages. When a rule has a user-defined chain as its target, when activated, that user-defined chain is executed. If no rules are matched, execution returns to the next rule in the originating chain.

Target	Function
ACCEPT	Allow packet to pass through the firewall
DROP	Deny access by the packet (same as DENY in ipchains)
REJECT	Deny access and notify the sender
QUEUE	Send packets to user space
RETURN	Jump to the end of the chain and let the default target process it

Table 37-2. *iptables Targets*

Tip *Specialized targets and options can be added by means of kernel patches provided by the Netfilter site. For example, the SAME patch returns the same address for all connections. A patch-o-matic option for the Netfilter make file will patch your kernel source code, adding support for the new target and options. You can then rebuild and install your kernel as described in Chapter 31.*

The kernel uses three firewall chains: INPUT, OUTPUT, and FORWARD. When a packet is received through an interface, the INPUT chain is used to determine what to do with it. The kernel then uses its routing information to decide where to send it. If the kernel sends the packet to another host, the FORWARD chain is checked. Before the packet is actually sent, the OUTPUT chain is also checked. In addition, two NAT table chains, POSTROUTING and PREROUTING, are implemented to handle masquerading and packet address modifications. The built-in Netfilter chains are listed in Table 37-3.

Chain	Description
INPUT	Rules for incoming packets
OUTPUT	Rules for outgoing packets
FORWARD	Rules for forwarded packets
PREROUTING	Rules for redirecting or modifying incoming packets, NAT table only
POSTROUTING	Rules for redirecting or modifying outgoing packets, NAT table only

Table 37-3. *Netfilter Built-in Chains*

You add and modify chain rules using the **iptables** commands. An **iptables** command consists of the keyword **iptables**, followed by an argument denoting the command to execute. For example, **iptables -A** is the command to add a new rule, whereas **iptables -D** is the command to delete a rule. The **iptables** commands are listed in Table 37-4. The following command simply lists the chains along with their rules currently defined for your system. The output shows the default values created by **iptables** commands.

```
iptables -L -n
Chain input (policy ACCEPT):
Chain forward (policy ACCEPT):
Chain output (policy ACCEPT):
```

To add a new rule to a chain, you use **-A**. Use **-D** to remove it, and **-R** to replace it. Following the command, list the chain to which the rule applies, such as the INPUT, OUTPUT, or FORWARD chain, or a user-defined chain. Next, you list different options that specify the actions you want taken. Most are the same as those used for ipchains, with a few exceptions. The **-s** option specifies the source address attached to the

Option	Function
-A *chain*	Appends a rule to a chain.
-D *chain*	Deletes matching rule from a chain.
-D *chain rulenum*	Deletes rule *rulenum* (1 = first) from *chain*.
-I *chain* [*rulenum*]	Inserts in *chain* as *rulenum* (default 1 = first).
-R *chain rulenum*	Replaces rule *rulenum* (1 = first) in *chain*.
-L [*chain*]	Lists the rules in *chain* or all chains.
-E [*chain*]	Renames a chain.
-F [*chain*]	Deletes (flushes) all rules in *chain* or all chains.
-R *chain*	Replaces a rule; rules are numbered from 1.
-Z [*chain*]	Zero counters in *chain* or all chains.
-N *chain*	Creates a new user-defined chain.
-X *chain*	Deletes a user-defined chain.
-P *chain target*	Changes policy on *chain* to *target*.

Table 37-4. *iptables Commands*

packet, **-d** specifies the destination address, and the **-j** option specifies the target. The ACCEPT target will allow a packet to pass. The **-i** option now indicates the input device and can only be used with the INPUT and FORWARD chains. The **-o** option indicates the output device and can only be used for OUTPUT and FORWARD chains. Table 37-5 lists several basic options. Many are similar to the ipchains options, but some, like **-i**, are different and others are missing (like **-y**).

Option	Function
-p [!] *proto*	Specifies a protocol, such as TCP, UDP, ICMP, or ALL.
-s [!] *address* **[/***mask***] [!] [***port* **[:***port***]]**	Source address to match. With the *port* argument, you can specify the port.
--sport [!] [*port* **[:***port***]]**	Source port specification. You can specify a range of ports using the colon, *port:port*.
-d [!] *address* **[/***mask***] [!] [***port* **[:***port***]]**	Destination address to match. With the *port* argument, you can specify the port.
--dport [!] [*port* **[:***port***]]**	Destination port specification.
--icmp-type [!] *typename*	Specifies ICMP type.
-i [!] *name* **[+]**	Specifies an input network interface using its name (for example, **eth0**). The + symbol functions as a wildcard. The + attached to the end of the name matches all interfaces with that prefix (**eth+** matches all Ethernet interfaces). Can only be used with the INPUT chain.
-j *target* **[port]**	Specifies the target for a rule (specify **[port]** for REDIRECT target).
--to-source < *ipaddr*> **[-**< *ipaddr*>**] [:** *port* **-** *port***]**	Used with the SNAT target, rewrites packets with new source IP address.
--to-destination < *ipaddr*> **[-**< *ipaddr*>**] [:** *port* **-** *port***]**	Used with the DNAT target, rewrites packets with new destination IP address.
-n	Numeric output of addresses and ports, used with **-L**.

Table 37-5. *iptables Options*

Option	Function
`-o [!]` *name* `[+]`	Specifies an output network interface using its name (for example, **eth0**). Can only be used with FORWARD and OUTPUT chains.
`-t` *table*	Specifies a table to use, as in **-t nat** for the NAT table.
`-v`	Verbose mode, shows rule details, used with **-L**.
`-x`	Expands numbers (displays exact values), used with **-L**.
`[!] -f`	Matches second through last fragments of a fragmented packet.
`[!] -V`	Prints package version.
`!`	Negates an option or address.
`-m`	Specifies a module to use, such as state.
--state	Specifies options for the state module such as NEW, INVALID, RELATED, and ESTABLISHED. Used to detect packet's state. NEW references SYN packets (new connections).
--syn	SYN packets, new connections.
--tcp-flags	TCP flags: SYN, ACK, FIN, RST, URG, PS, and ALL for all flags.
--limit	Option for the limit module (**-m limit**). Used to control the rate of matches, matching a given number of times per second.
--limit-burst	Option for the limit module (**-m limit**). Specifies maximum burst before the limit kicks in. Used to control denial-of-service attacks.

Table 37-5. *iptables Options* (continued)

iptables is designed to be extensible, and there are number of options with selection criteria that can be included with iptables. For example, the TCP extension includes the **--syn** option that checks for SYN packets. The ICMP extension provides the **--icmp-type** option for specifying ICMP packets as those used in ping operations. The limit extension includes the **--limit** option with which you can limit the maximum number of matching packets in a specified time period, such as a second.

In the following example, the user adds a rule to the INPUT chain to accept all packets originating from the address 192.168.0.55. Any packets that are received (**INPUT**) whose source address (**-s**) matches 192.168.0.55 are accepted and passed through (**-j ACCEPT**).

```
iptables -A INPUT -s 192.168.0.55 -j ACCEPT
```

There are two built-in targets, DROP and ACCEPT. DROP is the same as the ipchains DENY target. Other targets can be either user-defined chains or extensions added on, such as REJECT. There are two special targets used to manage chains, RETURN and QUEUE. RETURN indicates the end of a chain and returns to the chain it started from. QUEUE is used to send packets to userspace (replaces **-o** in ipchains).

```
iptables -A INPUT -s www.myjunk.com -j DROP
```

You can turn a rule into its inverse with an **!** symbol. For example, to accept all incoming packets except those from a specific address, place an **!** symbol before the **-s** option and that address. The following example will accept all packets except those from the IP address 192.168.0.45:

```
iptables -A INPUT -j ACCEPT ! -s 192.168.0.45
```

You can specify an individual address using its domain name or its IP number. For a range of addresses, you can use the IP number of their network and the network IP mask. The IP mask can be an IP number or simply the number of bits making up the mask. For example, all of the addresses in network 192.168.0 can be represented by 192.168.0.0/225.255.255.0 or by 192.168.0.0/24. To specify any address, you can use 0.0.0.0/0.0.0.0 or simply 0/0. By default, rules reference any address if no **-s** or **-d** specification exists. The following example accepts messages coming in that are from (source) any host in the 192.168.0.0 network and that are going (destination) anywhere at all (the **-d** option is left out or could be written as **-d 0/0**):

```
iptables -A INPUT -s 192.168.0.0/24  -j ACCEPT
```

The iptables rules are usually applied to a specific network interface such as the Ethernet interface used to connect to the Internet. For a single system connected to the Internet, you will have two interfaces, one that is your Internet connection and a localhost interface (**lo**) for internal connections between users on your system. The network interface for the Internet is referenced using the device name for the interface. For example, an Ethernet card with the device name **/dev/eth0** would be referenced by the name **eth0**. A modem using PPP protocols with the device name **/dev/ppp0** would have the name **ppp0**. In iptables rules, you use the `-i` option to indicate the input device; it can only be used with the INPUT and FORWARD chains. The `-o` option indicates the output device and can only be used for OUTPUT and FORWARD chains. Rules can then be applied to packets arriving and leaving on particular network devices. In the following examples, the first rule references the Ethernet device **eth0**, and the second, the localhost:

```
iptables -A INPUT -j DROP -i eth0 -s 192.168.0.45
iptables -A INPUT -j ACCEPT  -i lo
```

User-Defined Chains

With iptables, the FORWARD and INPUT chains are evaluated separately. One does not feed into the other. This means that if you want to completely block certain addresses from passing through your system, you will need to add both a FORWARD and an INPUT rule for them.

```
iptables -A INPUT -j DROP -i eth0 -s 192.168.0.45
iptables -A FORWARD -j DROP -i eth0 -s 192.168.0.45
```

A common method for reducing repeated INPUT and FORWARD rules is to create a user chain that both the INPUT and FORWARD chains feed into. You define a user chain with the `-N` option. The next example shows the basic format for this arrangement. A new chain is created called incoming (it can be any name you choose). The rules you would define for your FORWARD and INPUT chains are now defined for the incoming chain. The INPUT and FORWARD chains then use the incoming chain as a target, jumping directly to it and using its rules to process any packets they receive.

```
iptables -N incoming

iptables -A incoming -j DROP -i eth0 -s 192.168.0.45
iptables -A incoming -j ACCEPT  -i lo

iptables -A FORWARD -j incoming
iptables -A INPUT -j incoming
```

ICMP Packets

Firewalls often block certain Internet Control Message Protocol (ICMP) messages. ICMP redirect messages, in particular, can take control of your routing tasks. You need to enable some ICMP messages, however, such as those needed for ping, traceroute, and particularly destination-unreachable operations. In most cases, you always need to make sure destination-unreachable packets are allowed, otherwise, domain name queries could hang. Some of the more common ICMP packet types are listed in Table 37-6. You can enable an ICMP type of packet with the **-icmp-type** option, which takes as its argument a number or a name representing the message. The following examples enable the use of echo-reply, echo-request, and destination-unreachable messages, which have the numbers 0, 8, and 3.

```
iptables -A INPUT -j ACCEPT  -p icmp -i eth0 --icmp-type  echo-reply -d 10.0.0.1
iptables -A INPUT -j ACCEPT  -p icmp -i eth0 --icmp-type  echo-request -d 10.0.0.1
iptables -A INPUT -j ACCEPT -p icmp -i eth0 --icmp-type  destination-unreachable -
d 10.0.0.1
```

Their rule listing will look like this:

```
ACCEPT     icmp --   0.0.0.0/0              10.0.0.1            icmp type 0
ACCEPT     icmp --   0.0.0.0/0              10.0.0.1            icmp type 8
ACCEPT     icmp --   0.0.0.0/0              10.0.0.1            icmp type 3
```

Ping operations need to be further controlled to avoid the ping-of-death security threat. You can do this several ways. One way is to deny any ping fragments. Ping packets are normally very small. You can block ping-of-death attacks by denying any ICMP packet that is a fragment. Use the **-f** option to indicate fragments.

```
iptables -A INPUT -p icmp -j DROP -f
```

Another way is to limit the number of matches received for ping packets. You use the limit module to control the number of matches on the ICMP ping operation. Use

Number	Name	Required by
0	echo-reply	ping
3	destination-unreachable	Any TCP/UDP traffic
5	redirect	Routing if not running routing daemon
8	echo-request	ping
11	time-exceeded	traceroute

Table 37-6. *Common ICMP Packets*

-m limit to use the limit module, and **--limit** to specify the number of allowed matches. **1/s** will allow one match per second.

```
iptables -A FORWARD -p icmp --icmp-type echo-request -m limit --limit 1/s -j
ACCEPT
```

Ports

If your system is hosting an Internet service, such as a Web or FTP server, you can use iptables to control access to it. You can specify a particular service by using the source port (**--sport**) or destination port (**--dport**) options with the port that the service uses. iptables lets you use names for ports such as **www** for the Web server port. The names of services and the ports they use are listed in the **/etc/services** file, which maps ports to particular services. For a domain name server, the port would be **domain**. You can also use the port number if you want, preceding the number with a colon. The following example accepts all messages to the Web server located at 192.168.0.43:

```
iptables -A INPUT -d 192.168.0.43 --dport www -j ACCEPT
```

You can also use port references to protect certain services and deny others. This approach is often used if you are designing a firewall that is much more open to the Internet, letting users make freer use of Internet connections. Certain services you know can be harmful, such as Telnet and NTP, can be denied selectively. For example, to deny any kind of Telnet operation on your firewall, you can drop all packets coming in on the Telnet port, 23. To protect NFS operations, you can deny access to the port used for the portmapper, 111. You can use either the port number or the port name.

```
# deny outside access to portmapper port on firewall.
iptables -A arriving  -j DROP -p tcp -i eth0  --dport 111
# deny outside access to telnet port on firewall.
iptables -A arriving  -j DROP -p tcp -i eth0  --dport telnet
```

The rule listing will look like this:

```
DROP      tcp  --  0.0.0.0/0     0.0.0.0/0      tcp dpt:111
DROP      tcp  --  0.0.0.0/0     0.0.0.0/0      tcp dpt:23
```

One port-related security problem is access to your X server on the XFree86 ports that range from 6000 to 6009. On a relatively open firewall, these ports could be used to illegally access your system through your X server. A range of ports can be specified with a colon, as in 6000:6009. You can also use x11 for the first port, x11:6009. Sessions on the X server can be secured by using SSH, which normally accesses the X server on port 6010.

```
iptables -A arriving  -j DROP -p tcp -i eth0  --dport 6000:6009
```

Common ports checked and their labels are shown here:

Service	Port Number	Port Label
Auth	113	auth
Finger	79	finger
FTP	21	ftp
NTP	123	ntp
Portmapper	111	sunrpc
Telnet	23	telnet
Web server	80	www
XFree86	6000:6009	x11:6009

States

One of the more useful extensions is the state extension, which can easily detect tracking information for a packet. You need to specify the state module first with **-m state**. Then you can use the **--state** option. Here you can specify any of the following states:

State	Description
NEW	A packet that creates a new connection
ESTABLISHED	A packet that belongs to an existing connection
RELATED	A packet that is related to, but not part of, an existing connection, such as an ICMP error or a packet establishing an FTP data connection
INVALID	A packet that could not be identified for some reason
RELATED+REPLY	A packet that is related to an established connection, but not part of one directly

If you are designing a firewall that is meant to protect your local network from any attempts to penetrate it from an outside network, you may want to restrict packets coming in. Simply denying access by all packets is unfeasible because users connected to outside servers—say, on the Internet—must receive information from them. You can, instead, deny access by a particular kind of packet used to initiate a connection. The idea is that an attacker must initiate a connection from the outside. The headers of these kinds of packets have their SYN bit set on and their FIN and ACK bits empty. The state module's NEW state matches on any such SYN packet. By specifying a DROP target for such packets, you deny access by any packet that is part of an attempt to make a connection with your system. Anyone trying to connect to your system from the outside is unable to do so. Users on your local system who have initiated connections with outside hosts can still communicate with them. The following example will drop any packets trying to create a new connection on the **eth0** interface, though they will be accepted on any other interface:

```
iptables -A INPUT -m state --state NEW -i eth0 -j DROP
```

You can use the **!** operator on the **eth0** device combined with an ACCEPT target to compose a rule that will accept any new packets except those on the **eth0** device. If the **eth0** device is the only one that connects to the Internet, this still effectively blocks outside access. At the same time, input operation for other devices such as your localhost are free to make new connections. This kind of conditional INPUT rule is used to allow access overall with exceptions. It usually assumes that a later rule such as a chain policy will drop remaining packets.

```
iptables -A INPUT -m state --state NEW ! -i eth0 -j ACCEPT
```

The next example will accept any packets that are part of an established connection or related to such a connection on the **eth0** interface:

```
iptables -A INPUT -m state --state ESTABLISHED,RELATED -j ACCEPT
```

Network Address Translation (NAT)

Network address translation (NAT) is the process whereby a system will change the destination or source of packets as they pass through the system. A packet will traverse several linked systems on a network before it reaches its final destination. Normally, they will simply pass the packet on. However, if one of these systems performs a NAT on a packet, it can change the source or destination. A packet sent to a particular destination could have its destination address changed. To make this work, the system also needs to remember such changes so that the source and destination for any reply packets are altered back to the original addresses of the packet being replied to.

NAT is often used to provide access to systems that may be connected to the Internet through only one IP address. Such is the case with networking features such as IP masquerading, support for multiple servers, and transparent proxying. With IP masquerading, NAT operations will change the destination and source of a packet moving through a firewall/gateway linking the Internet to computers on a local network. The gateway has a single IP address that the other local computers can use through NAT operations. If you have multiple servers but only one IP address, you can use NAT operations to send packets to the alternate servers. You can also use NAT operations to have your IP address reference a particular server application such as a Web server (transparent proxy).

Packet selection rules for NAT operations are added to the NAT table managed by the **iptables** command. To add rules to the NAT table, you have to specify the NAT table with the **-t** option. Thus to add a rule to the NAT table, you would have to specify the NAT table with the **-t nat** option as shown here:

```
iptables -t nat
```

With the **-L** option, you can list the rules you have added to the NAT table:

```
iptables -t nat -L -n
```

Adding the **-n** option will list IP addresses and ports in numeric form. This will speed up the listing as iptables will not attempt to do a DNS lookup to determine the hostname for the IP address.

In addition, there are two types of NAT operations: source NAT, specified as SNAT target, and destination NAT, specified as DNAT target. SNAT target is used for rules that alter source addresses, and DNAT target for those that alter destination addresses.

Three chains in the NAT table are used by the kernel for NAT operations. These are PREROUTING, POSTROUTING, and OUTPUT. PREROUTING is used for destination NAT (DNAT) rules. These are packets that are arriving. POSTROUTING is used for source NAT (SNAT) rules. These are for packets leaving. OUTPUT is used for destination NAT rules for locally generated packets.

As with packet filtering, you can specify source (**-s**) and destination (**-d**) addresses, as well as the input (**-i**) and output (**-o**) devices. The **-j** option will specify a target such as MASQUERADE. You would implement IP masquerading by adding a MASQUERADE rule to the POSTROUTING chain:

```
# iptables -t nat -A POSTROUTING -o eth0 -j MASQUERADE
```

To change the source address of a packet leaving your system, you would use the POSTROUTING rule with the SNAT target. For the SNAT target, you use the **--to-source** option to specify the source address:

```
# iptables -t nat -A POSTROUTING -o eth0 -j SNAT --to-source
192.168.0.4
```

To change the destination address of packets arriving on your system, you would use the PREROUTING rule with the DNAT target and the **--to-destination** option:

```
# iptables -t nat -A PRETROUTING -i eth0 \
          -j DNAT --to-destination 192.168.0.3
```

To redirect a packet, you use the REDIRECT target on the PREROUTING chain:

```
# iptables -t nat -A PREROUTING -i eth1 --dport 80 -j REDIRECT --to-port 3128
```

With the TOS and MARK targets, you can mangle the packet to control its routing or priority. A TOS target sets the type of service for a packet, which can set the priority using criteria such as normal-service, minimize-cost, maximize-throughput, among others.

The targets only valid for the NAT table are shown here:

SNAT	Modify source address, use **--to-source** option to specify new source address
DNAT	Modify destination address, use **--to-destination** option to specify new destination address
REDIRECT	Redirect a packet
MASQUERADE	IP masquerading
MIRROR	Reverse source and destination and send back to sender
MARK	Modify the Mark field to control message routing
TOS	Modify the Type of Service field to manage the priority of the packet

IP Tables Scripts

Though you can enter iptables rules from the shell command line, when you shut down your system, these commands will be lost. On Mandrake and Red Hat, you can make use of the built-in support for saving and reading iptables rules using the iptables service script. Alternatively, you can manage the process yourself, saving to files of your own choosing. In either event, you will most likely need to place your iptables rules in a script that can then be executed directly. This way you can edit and manage a complex set of rules, adding comments and maintaining their ordering.

Mandrake and Red Hat iptables Support

Mandrake and Red Hat provide support for iptables as part of their system configuration. When you install the RPM package for iptables, an iptables service script in installed that will read and save iptables commands using the **/etc/sysconfig/iptables** file. If you have set iptables to be started up automatically when you boot your system, this file will be checked to see if it exists and is not empty. If so, iptables will automatically read the iptables commands that it holds. This helps to integrate iptables more smoothly into the system setup process.

You can sidestep this automatic iptables setup by simply deleting the **/etc/sysconfig/iptables** file (running lokkit and choosing No Firewall will do the same). Be sure you back it up first in case it has important commands.

It is possible to edit the **/etc/sysconfig/iptables** file directly and enter iptables commands, but it is not recommended. Mandrake and Red Hat add some notation of their own, such as a colon at the beginning of each line, and using the notation to detect commands. Instead, you should think of this file as holding a final installation of your iptables commands.

You should think of the iptables service script that Mandrake and Red Hat provide as a versatile management tool, not as a service startup script. The use of the **`service`** command for this script can be confusing. The iptables script only manages iptables rules, flushing, adding, or reporting them. It does not start and stop the iptables service. If Netfilter is not running, you will need to instruct that it be started up when your system boots. For this, you can use setuptool (setup or Text Mode Setup Tool) to select System Services (ntsysv), then select ipchains from the list of services (press SPACEBAR). Make sure that ipchains is not selected. ipchains and iptables cannot run at the same time.

The service script **/etc/rc.d/init.d/iptables** supports several options with which to manage your rules. The **`status`** option displays a listing of all your current rules. The **`stop`** option will flush your current rules. Unlike **`stop`** and **`status`**, the **`start`** and **`save`** options are tied directly to the **/etc/sysconfig/iptables** file. The **`start`** option will flush your current iptables rules and add those in the **/etc/sysconfig/iptables** file. The **`save`** option will save your current rules to the **/etc/sysconfig/iptables** file. Keep in mind that the **`stop`** and **`status`** operations work on the current iptables rules, no matter if they were added manually on the command line, added by your own script, or added by the **`start`** option from **/etc/sysconfig/iptables**. The following command will list your current rules:

```
service iptables status
```

Perhaps the most effective way to think of the iptables service script is as an iptables development tool. When creating firewall rules, you should first create a script and place your rules in them, as described later in the iptables script example. Make the script executable. Any changes you need to make as you debug your firewall, you make to this script. Before you run it, run the iptables service script with the **`stop`** option to clear out any previous rules:

```
service iptables stop
```

Then run your script, as shown here for the myfilters script:

```
./myfilters
```

To see how the commands have been interpreted by iptables, use the service script with the **status** option:

```
service iptables status
```

For any changes, edit your iptables script. Then run the service script again to clear out the old rules. Run the iptables script again, and use the **status** option with the service script to see how they were implemented:

```
service iptables stop
./myfilters
service iptables status
```

Once you are satisfied that your iptables rules are working correctly, you can save your rules to the **/etc/sysconfig/iptables** file. Use the iptables service script with the **save** option. Now your rules will be read automatically when your system starts up. You can think of the save operation as installing your iptables rules on your system, making them part of your system setup whenever you start your system.

```
service iptables save
```

To make changes, modify your iptables script, run the service script with **stop** to clear out the old rules, run the iptables script, and then use the service script with the **save** option to generate a new **/etc/sysconfig/iptables** file.

Manually Saving and Reading Rules

Instead of using the service script, you can save your rules to a file of your choosing using the **iptables-save** script. The recommended file to use is **/etc/iptables.rules**. The **iptables-save** command outputs rules to the standard output. To save them in a file, you must redirect the output to a file with the redirection operator, **>**, as shown here:

```
iptables-save > /etc/iptables.rules
```

Then, to restore the rules, use the **iptables-restore** script to read the iptables commands from that saved file:

```
iptables-restore < /etc/iptables.rules
```

You could then place the **iptables-restore** operation in the **/etc/rc.d/rc.local** script to have it run automatically.

An iptables Script Example

You now have enough information to create a simple iptables script that will provide basic protection for a single system connected to the Internet. The following script provides an IP tables filtering process to protect a local network and a Web site from outside attacks. It configures a simple firewall for a private network (check the ipchains HOWTO for a more complex example). If you have a local network, you could adapt this script to it. In this configuration, all remote access initiated from the outside is blocked, but two-way communication is allowed for connections that users in the network make with outside systems. In this example, the firewall system functions as a gateway for a private network whose network address is 192.168.0.0 (see Figure 37-1). The Internet address is, for the sake of this example, 10.0.0.1. The system has two Ethernet devices: one for the private network (**eth1**) and one for the Internet (**eth0**). The gateway firewall system also supports a Web server at address 10.0.0.2. Entries in this example that are too large to fit on one line are continued on a second line, with the newline quoted with a backslash.

The basic rules as they apply to different parts of the network are illustrated in Figure 37-2.

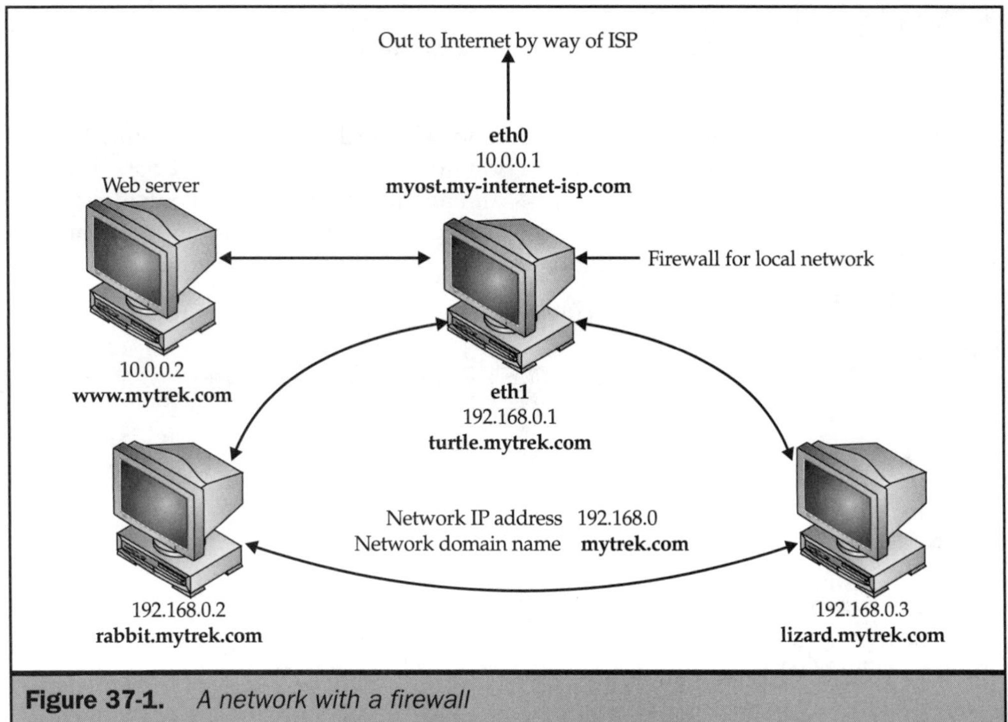

Figure 37-1. *A network with a firewall*

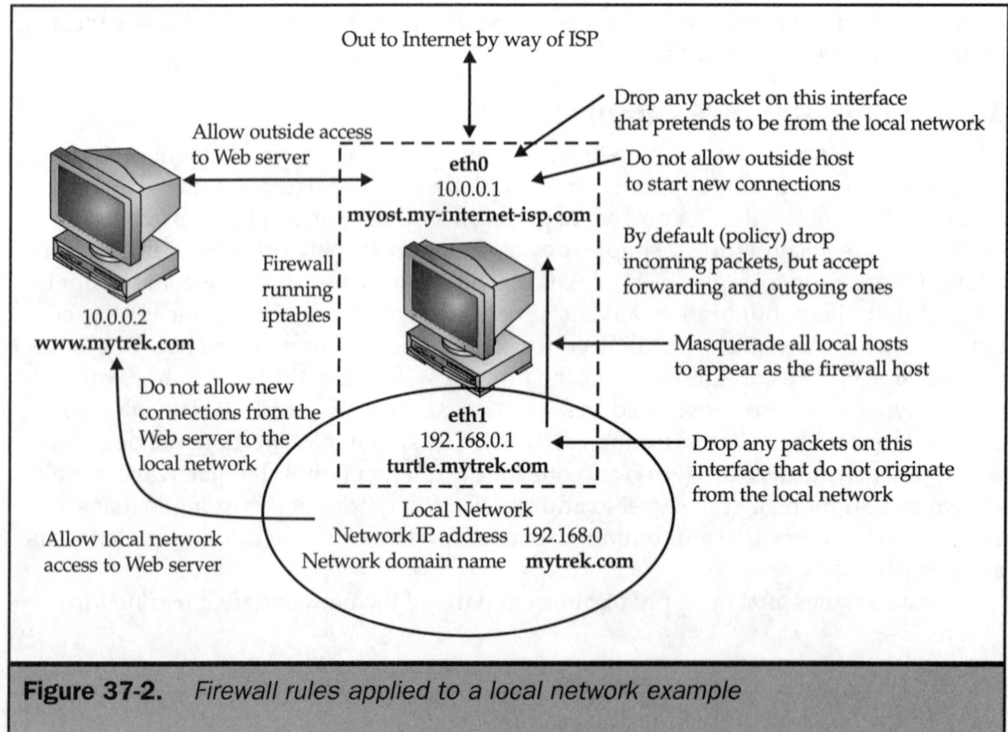

Figure 37-2. *Firewall rules applied to a local network example*

First, a DROP policy is set up for INPUT and FORWARD built-in IP chains. This means that if a packet does not meet a criterion in any of the rules to let it pass, it will be dropped. Then both IP spoofing attacks and any attempts from the outside to initiate connections (SYN packets) are rejected. Outside connection attempts are also logged. This is a very basic configuration that can easily be refined to your own needs by adding iptables rules.

myfilter

```
# Firewall Gateway system IP address is 10.0.0.1 using Ethernet device eth0
# Private network address is 192.168.0.0 using Ethernet device eth1
# Web site address is 10.0.0.2

# modprobe iptable_filter
# turn off IP forwarding
echo 0 > /proc/sys/net/ipv4/ip_forward

# Flush chain rules
iptables -F INPUT
iptables -F OUTPUT
iptables -F FORWARD

# set default (policy) rules
iptables -P INPUT DROP
iptables -P OUTPUT ACCEPT
iptables -P FORWARD ACCEPT
```

```
# IP spoofing, deny any packets on the internal network that has an external source
address.
iptables -A INPUT -j LOG  -i eth1 \! -s 192.168.0.0/24
iptables -A INPUT -j DROP  -i eth1 \! -s 192.168.0.0/24
iptables -A FORWARD -j DROP  -i eth1 \! -s 192.168.0.0/24
# IP spoofing, deny any outside packets (any not on eth1) that have the source address of
the internal network
iptables -A INPUT -j DROP \! -i eth1 -s 192.168.0.0/24
iptables -A FORWARD -j DROP \! -i eth1 -s 192.168.0.0/24
# IP spoofing, deny any outside packets with localhost address
# (packets not on the lo interface (any on eth0 or eth1) that have the source address of
localhost)
iptables -A INPUT -j DROP  -i \! lo  -s  127.0.0.0/255.0.0.0
iptables -A FORWARD -j DROP  -i \! lo  -s  127.0.0.0/255.0.0.0

# allow all incoming messages for users on your firewall system
iptables -A INPUT -j ACCEPT  -i lo

# allow  communication to the Web server (address 10.0.0.2), port www
iptables -A INPUT  -j ACCEPT -p tcp -i eth0  --dport www -s 10.0.0.2
# Allow  established connections from Web servers to internal network
iptables -A INPUT -m state --state ESTABLISHED,RELATED -i eth0 -p tcp  --sport www
-s 10.0.0.2 -d 192.168.0.0/24  -j ACCEPT
# Prevent new  connections from Web servers to internal network
iptables -A OUTPUT -m state --state  NEW -o eth0 -p tcp  --sport www -d 192.168.0.0/24  -j
DROP

# allow established and related outside communication to your system
# allow outside communication to the firewall, except for ICMP packets
iptables -A INPUT -m state --state ESTABLISHED,RELATED -i eth0 -p \! icmp -j
ACCEPT
# prevent outside initiated connections
iptables -A INPUT -m state --state NEW -i eth0 -j DROP
iptables -A FORWARD -m state --state NEW -i eth0 -j DROP

# allow all local communication to and from the firewall on eth1  from the local network
iptables -A INPUT -j ACCEPT -p all -i eth1 -s 192.168.0.0/24

# Set up masquerading to allow internal machines access to outside network
iptables -t nat -A POSTROUTING -o eth0 -j MASQUERADE

# Accept ICMP Ping (0 and 8) and Destination unreachable (3)  messages
# Others will be rejected by INPUT and OUTPUT DROP policy
iptables -A INPUT -j ACCEPT  -p icmp -i eth0 --icmp-type  echo-reply -d 10.0.0.1
iptables -A INPUT -j ACCEPT  -p icmp -i eth0 --icmp-type  echo-request -d 10.0.0.1
iptables -A INPUT -j ACCEPT -p icmp -i eth0 --icmp-type  destination-unreachable -d
10.0.0.1

 # Turn on IP Forwarding
echo 1 > /proc/sys/net/ipv4/ip_forward
```

Initially, in the script you would clear your current iptables with the flush option (**-F**), and then set the policies (default targets) for the non-user-defined rules. IP forwarding should also be turned off while the chain rules are being set:

```
echo 0 > /proc/sys/net/ipv4/ip_forward
```

One way to protect the private network from IP spoofing any packets is to check for any outside addresses on the Ethernet device dedicated to the private network. In this example, any packet on device **eth1** (dedicated to the private network) whose source address is not that of the private network (`! -s 192.168.0.0`) is denied. Also, check to see if any packets coming from the outside are designating the private network as their source. In this example, any packets with the source address of the private network on any Ethernet device other than for the private network (**eth1**) are denied. The same strategy can be applied to the local host.

```
# IP spoofing, deny any packets on the internal network
# that has an external source address.
iptables -A INPUT -j LOG  -i eth1 \! -s 192.168.0.0/24
iptables -A INPUT -j DROP  -i eth1 \! -s 192.168.0.0/24
iptables -A FORWARD -j DROP  -i eth1 \! -s 192.168.0.0/24
# IP spoofing, deny any outside packets (any not on eth1)
# that have the source address of the internal network
iptables -A INPUT -j DROP \! -i eth1 -s 192.168.0.0/24
iptables -A FORWARD -j DROP \! -i eth1 -s 192.168.0.0/24
# IP spoofing, deny any outside packets with localhost address
# (packets not on the lo interface (any on eth0 or eth1)
# that have the source address of localhost)
iptables -A INPUT -j DROP   -i \! lo  -s  127.0.0.0/255.0.0.0
iptables -A FORWARD -j DROP  -i \! lo  -s  127.0.0.0/255.0.0.0
```

Then, you would set up rules to allow all packets sent and received within your system (localhost) to pass:

```
iptables -A INPUT -j ACCEPT  -i lo
```

For the Web server, you want to allow access by outside users, but block access by anyone attempting to initiate a connection from the Web server into the private network. In the next example, all messages are accepted to the Web server, but the Web server cannot initiate contact with the private network. This prevents anyone from breaking into the local network through the Web server, which is open to outside access. Established connections are allowed, permitting the private network to use the Web server.

```
# allow  communication to the Web server (address 10.0.0.2), port www
iptables -A INPUT  -j ACCEPT -p tcp -i eth0  --dport www -s 10.0.0.2
# Allow  established connections from Web servers to internal network
iptables -A INPUT -m state --state ESTABLISHED,RELATED -i eth0 \
   -p tcp  --sport www -s 10.0.0.2 -d 192.168.0.0/24  -j ACCEPT
# Prevent new  connections from Web servers to internal network
iptables -A OUTPUT -m state --state  NEW -o eth0 -p tcp \
  --sport www -d 192.168.0.1.0/24  -j DROP
```

To allow access by the firewall to outside networks, you allow input by all packets except for ICMP packets. These are handled later. The firewall is specified by the firewall device, **eth0**. First, allow established and related connections to proceed:

```
# allow outside communication to the firewall,
# except for ICMP packets
iptables -A INPUT -m state --state ESTABLISHED,RELATED \
        -i eth0 -p \! icmp -j ACCEPT
```

To prevent outsiders from initiating any access to your system, create a rule to block access by SYN packets from the outside using the **state** option with NEW. Drop any new connections on the **eth0** connection (assumes only **eth0** is connected to the Internet or outside network).

```
# prevent outside initiated connections
iptables -A INPUT -m state --state NEW -i eth0 -j DROP
iptables -A FORWARD -m state --state NEW -i eth0 -j DROP
```

To allow interaction by the internal network with the firewall, you allow input by all packets on the internal Ethernet connection, **eth1**. The valid internal network addresses are designated as the input source:

```
iptables -A INPUT -j ACCEPT -p all -i eth1 -s 192.168.0.0/24
```

To implement masquerading, where systems on the private network can use the gateway's Internet address to connect to Internet hosts, you create a NAT table (**-t nat**) POSTROUTING rule with a MASQUERADE target:

```
iptables -t nat -A POSTROUTING -o eth0 -j MASQUERADE
```

In addition, to allow ping and destination-reachable ICMP packets, you enter INPUT rules with the firewall as the destination. To enable ping operations, you use both echo-reply and echo-request ICMP types, and for destination unreachable, you use the destination-unreachable type:

```
iptables -A INPUT -j ACCEPT  -p icmp -i eth0 --icmp-type \
   echo-reply -d 10.0.0.1
iptables -A INPUT -j ACCEPT  -p icmp -i eth0 --icmp-type \
   echo-request -d 10.0.0.1
iptables -A INPUT -j ACCEPT -p icmp -i eth0 --icmp-type \
   destination-unreachable -d 10.0.0.1
```

At the end, IP forwarding is turned on again:

```
echo 1 > /proc/sys/net/ipv4/ip_forward
```

A listing of these iptables options shows the different rules for each option, as shown here:

```
# iptables -L
Chain INPUT (policy DROP)
target     prot opt source             destination
LOG        all  -- !192.168.0.0/24    anywhere           LOG level warning
DROP       all  -- !192.168.0.0/24    anywhere
DROP       all  --  192.168.0.0/24    anywhere
DROP       all  --  127.0.0.0/8       anywhere
ACCEPT     all  --  anywhere          anywhere
ACCEPT     tcp  --  10.0.0.2          anywhere           tcp dpt:http
ACCEPT     tcp  --  10.0.0.2          192.168.0.0/24     state RELATED,ESTABLISHED
                                                               tcp spt:http
ACCEPT    !icmp --  anywhere          anywhere           state RELATED,ESTABLISHED
DROP       all  --  anywhere          anywhere           state NEW
ACCEPT     all  --  192.168.0.0/24    anywhere
ACCEPT     icmp --  anywhere          10.0.0.1           icmp echo-reply
ACCEPT     icmp --  anywhere          10.0.0.1           icmp echo-request
ACCEPT     icmp --  anywhere          10.0.0.1           icmp
destination-unreachable

Chain FORWARD (policy ACCEPT)
target     prot opt source             destination
DROP       all  -- !192.168.0.0/24    anywhere
DROP       all  --  192.168.0.0/24    anywhere
DROP       all  --  127.0.0.0/8       anywhere
DROP       all  --  anywhere          anywhere           state NEW

Chain OUTPUT (policy ACCEPT)
target     prot opt source          destination
DROP          tcp  --  anywhere        192.168.0.0/24  state NEW tcp spt:http
# iptables -t nat -L
Chain PREROUTING (policy ACCEPT)
target         prot opt source          destination

Chain POSTROUTING (policy ACCEPT)
target         prot opt source          destination
MASQUERADE  all  --  anywhere          anywhere

Chain OUTPUT (policy ACCEPT)
target       prot opt source          destination
```

For more complex rules, you may want to create your own chain to reduce repetition. A common method is to define a user chain for both INPUT and FORWARD chains, so that you do not have to repeat DROP operations for each. Instead you would have only one user chain that both FORWARD and INPUT chains would feed into for DROP operations. Keep in mind that both FORWARD and INPUT operations may have separate rules in addition to the ones they share. In the next example, the **myfilter** script has been rewritten, as **myfilter2**, with a user-defined chain called arriving. The chain is defined with the **-N** option at the top of the script:

```
iptables -N arriving
```

A user chain has to be defined before it can be used as a target in other rules. So you have to first define and add all the rules for that chain, and then use it as a target. In the **myfilter2** script, the arriving chain is defined and its rules added. Then, at the end of the file, it is used as a target for both the INPUT and FORWARD chains. The INPUT chain lists rules for accepting packets, whereas the FORWARD chain has an ACCEPT policy which will accept them by default.

myfilter2

```
# )# Firewall Gateway system IP address is 10.0.0.1 using Ethernet device eth0
# Private network address is 192.168.0.0 using Ethernet device eth1
# Web site address is 10.0.0.2

# modprobe iptable_filter
# turn off IP forwarding
echo 0 > /proc/sys/net/ipv4/ip_forward

iptables -N arriving

# Flush chain rules
iptables -F INPUT
iptables -F OUTPUT
iptables -F FORWARD
iptables -F arriving

# set default (policy) rules
iptables -P INPUT DROP
iptables -P OUTPUT ACCEPT
iptables -P FORWARD ACCEPT

# IP spoofing, deny any packets on the internal network that has an external source
address.
iptables -A arriving -j LOG  -i eth1 \! -s 192.168.0.0/24
iptables -A arriving -j DROP  -i eth1 \! -s 192.168.0.0/24
# IP spoofing, deny any outside packets (any not on eth1) that have the source address of
the internal network
iptables -A arriving -j DROP \! -i eth1 -s 192.168.0.0/24
# IP spoofing, deny any outside packets with localhost address
```

```
# (packets not on the lo interface (any on eth0 or eth1) that have the source address of
localhost)
iptables -A arriving -j DROP  -i \! lo  -s  127.0.0.0/255.0.0.0

# allow all incoming messages for users on your firewall system
iptables -A arriving -j ACCEPT  -i lo

# allow  communication to the Web server (address 10.0.0.2), port www
iptables -A arriving  -j ACCEPT -p tcp -i eth0  --dport www -s 10.0.0.2
# Allow  established connections from Web servers to internal network
iptables -A arriving -m state --state ESTABLISHED,RELATED -i eth0 -p tcp  --sport www
-s 10.0.0.2 -d 192.168.0.0/24  -j ACCEPT
# Prevent new  connections from Web servers to internal network
iptables -A OUTPUT -m state --state  NEW -o eth0 -p tcp  --sport www -d 192.168.0.0/24  -j
DROP

# allow established and related outside communication to your system
# allow outside communication to the firewall, except for ICMP packets
iptables -A arriving -m state --state ESTABLISHED,RELATED -i eth0 -p \! icmp -j
ACCEPT
# prevent outside initiated connections
iptables -A arriving -m state --state NEW -i eth0 -j DROP

# allow all local communication to and from the firewall on eth1  from the local network
iptables -A arriving -j ACCEPT -p all -i eth1 -s 192.168.0.0/24

# Set up masquerading to allow internal machines access to outside network
iptables -t nat -A POSTROUTING -o eth0 -j MASQUERADE

# Accept ICMP Ping (0 and 8) and Destination unreachable (3)  messages
# Others will be rejected by INPUT and OUTPUT DROP policy
iptables -A arriving -j ACCEPT  -p icmp -i eth0 --icmp-type  echo-reply -d 10.0.0.1
iptables -A arriving -j ACCEPT  -p icmp -i eth0 --icmp-type  echo-request -d 10.0.0.1
iptables -A arriving -j ACCEPT -p icmp -i eth0 --icmp-type  destination-unreachable -d
10.0.0.1

iptables -A INPUT -j arriving
iptables -A FORWARD -j arriving

# Turn on IP Forwarding
echo 1 > /proc/sys/net/ipv4/ip_forward
```

A listing of the rules is shown here:

```
# iptables -L -n
Chain INPUT (policy DROP)
target     prot opt source            destination
arriving  all  --  0.0.0.0/0           0.0.0.0/0

Chain FORWARD (policy ACCEPT)
```

```
target     prot opt source             destination
arriving   all  --  0.0.0.0/0           0.0.0.0/0

Chain OUTPUT (policy ACCEPT)
target     prot opt source             destination
DROP       tcp  --  0.0.0.0/0           192.168.0.0/24   state NEW tcp spt:80

Chain arriving (2 references)
target     prot opt source             destination
LOG        all  -- !192.168.0.0/24    0.0.0.0/0        LOG flags 0 level 4
DROP       all  -- !192.168.0.0/24    0.0.0.0/0
DROP       all  --  192.168.0.0/24    0.0.0.0/0
DROP       all  --  127.0.0.0/8       0.0.0.0/0
ACCEPT     all  --  0.0.0.0/0         0.0.0.0/0
ACCEPT     tcp  --  10.0.0.2          0.0.0.0/0        tcp dpt:80
ACCEPT     tcp  --  10.0.0.2          192.168.0.0/24   state RELATED,ESTABLISHED
                                                                tcp spt:80
ACCEPT    !icmp --  0.0.0.0/0         0.0.0.0/0        state RELATED,ESTABLISHED
DROP       all  --  0.0.0.0/0         0.0.0.0/0        state NEW
ACCEPT     all  --  192.168.0.0/24    0.0.0.0/0
ACCEPT     icmp --  0.0.0.0/0         10.0.0.1         icmp type 0
ACCEPT     icmp --  0.0.0.0/0         10.0.0.1         icmp type 8
ACCEPT     icmp --  0.0.0.0/0         10.0.0.1         icmp type 3
```

For rules where chains may differ, you will still need to enter separate rules. In the **myfilter2** script, the FORWARD chain has an ACCEPT policy, allowing all forwarded packets to the local network to pass through the firewall. If the FORWARD chain had a DROP policy, like the INPUT chain, then you may need to define separate rules under which the FORWARD chain could accept packets. In this example, the FORWARD and INPUT chains have different rules for accepting packets on the **eth1** device. The INPUT rule is more restrictive. To enable the local network to receive forwarded packets through the firewall, you could enable forwarding on its device using a separate FORWARD rule, as shown here.

```
iptables -A FORWARD -j ACCEPT -p all -i eth1
```

The INPUT chain would accept packets only from those in the local network.

```
iptables -A INPUT -j ACCEPT -p all -i eth1 -s 192.168.0.0/24
```

IP Masquerading

On Linux systems, you can set up a network in which you can have one connection to the Internet, which several systems on your network can use. This way, using only one IP address, several different systems can connect to the Internet. This method is called *IP masquerading*, where a system masquerades as another system, using that system's IP address. In such a network, one system is connected to the Internet with its own IP address, while the other systems are connected on a local area network (LAN) to this system. When a local system wants to access the network, it masquerades as the Internet-connected system, borrowing its IP address.

IP masquerading is implemented on Linux using the ipchains firewalling tool. In effect, you set up a firewall, which you then configure to do IP masquerading. Currently, IP masquerading supports all the common network services—as does ipchains firewalling—such as Web browsing, Telnet, ping, and Gopher. Other services, such as IRC, FTP, and Real Audio, require the use of certain modules. Any services you want local systems to access must also be on the firewall system because request and response actually are handled by services on that system.

You can find out more information on IP masquerading at the IP Masquerade Resource Web site at **ipmasq.cjb.net**. In particular, the Linux IP Masquerade mini-HOWTO provides a detailed, step-by-step guide to setting up IP masquerading on your system. IP masquerading must be supported by the kernel before you can use it. If your kernel does not support it, you may have to rebuild the kernel, including IP masquerade support, or use loadable modules to add it. See the IP Masquerade mini-HOWTO for more information.

With IP masquerading, as implemented on Linux systems, the machine with the Internet address is also the firewall and gateway for the LAN of machines that use the firewall's Internet address to connect to the Internet. Firewalls that also implement IP masquerading are sometimes referred to as *MASQ gates*. With IP masquerading, the Internet-connected system (the firewall) listens for Internet requests from hosts on its LAN. When it receives one, it replaces the requesting local host's IP address with the Internet IP address of the firewall and then passes the request out to the Internet, as if the request were its own. Replies from the Internet are then sent to the firewall system. The replies the firewall receives are addressed to the firewall using its Internet address. The firewall then determines the local system to whose request the reply is responding. It then strips off its IP address and sends the response on to the local host across the LAN. The connection is transparent from the perspective of the local machines. They appear to be connected directly to the Internet.

IP masquerading is often used to allow machines on a private network to access the Internet. These could be machines in a home network or a small LAN, such as for a small business. Such a network might have only one machine with Internet access, and as such, only the one Internet address. The local private network would have IP addresses chosen from the private network allocations (10., 172.16., or 192.168.). Ideally, the firewall has two Ethernet cards: one for an interface to the LAN (for example, **eth1**) and one for an interface to the Internet, such as **eth0** (for dial-up ISPs, this would be **ppp0** for the modem). The card for the Internet connection (**eth0**) would be assigned the Internet IP address. The Ethernet interface for the local network (**eth1**, in this example) is the firewall Ethernet interface. Your private LAN would have a network address like 192.168.0. Its Ethernet firewall interface (**eth1**) would be assigned the IP address 192.168.0.1. In effect, the firewall interface lets the firewall operate as the local network's gateway. The firewall is then configured to masquerade any packets coming from the private network. Your LAN needs to have its own domain name server, identifying the machines on your network, including your firewall. Each local machine needs to have the firewall specified as its gateway. Try not to use IP aliasing to assign both the firewall and Internet IP addresses to the same physical interface. Use separate interfaces for them, such as two Ethernet cards, or an Ethernet card and a modem (**ppp0**).

Certain services such as FTP and IRC can conflict with the IP masquerading setup where your firewall denies new connections. FTP operations use two ports, one to set up the connection and one to handle the data transfer. Connecting on the second port can appear to an IP masqueraded firewall as a new connection attempt, and it will deny it. To overcome this problem, special Netfilter modules are used for specific services. For the FTP service you use ip_masq_ftp, and for IRC you use ip_masq_irc. There are also modules for quake, Real Audio (raudio), and VDO live (vdolive).

IP Masquerading with Netfilter (NAT and iptables)

In Netfilter, IP masquerading is a NAT operation and is no longer integrated with packet filtering as in ipchains. IP masquerading commands are placed on the NAT table and treated separately from the packet-filtering commands. To implement IP masquerading with Netfilter, first make sure that the iptable_nat module is loaded (you can have this operation built into the kernel). Normally it is loaded by default.

```
modprobe iptable_nat
```

Then use iptables to place a masquerade rule on the NAT table. First reference the NAT table with the **-t nat** option. Then add a rule to the POSTROUTING chain with the **-o** option specifying the output device and the **-j** option with the MASQUERADE command:

```
iptables -t nat -A POSTROUTING -o eth0 -j MASQUERADE
```

Then turn on IP forwarding as you normally would:

```
echo 1 > /proc/sys/net/ipv4/ip_forward
```

Instead of masquerading all local hosts as the single IP address of the firewall/gateway host, you could use the NAT table to rewrite addresses for a few selected hosts. Such an approach is often applied to setups where you want several local hosts to appear as Internet servers. Using the DNAT and SNAT targets, you can direct packets to specific local hosts. You would use rules on the PREROUTING and POSTROUTING chains to direct input and output packets.

For example, the Web server described in the previous example could have been configured as a local host to which a DNAT target could redirect any packets originally received for 10.0.0.2. Say the Web server was set up on 192.168.0.5. It could appear as having the address 10.0.0.2 on the Internet. Packets sent to 10.0.0.2 would be rewritten and directed to 192.168.0.5 by the NAT table. You would use the PREROUTING chain with the `-d` option to handle incoming packets and POSTROUTING with the `-s` option for outgoing packets.

```
iptables -t nat -A PREROUTING -d 10.0.0.2   \
            --to-destination 192.168.0.5 -j DNAT
iptables -t nat -A POSTROUTING -s 192.168.0.5 \
            --to-source 10.0.0.2 -j SNAT
```

Bear in mind that with iptables, masquerading is no longer combined with the FORWARD chain, as it is with ipchains. So, if you specify a DROP policy for the FORWARD chain, you will also have to specifically enable FORWARD operation for the network that is being masqueraded. You will need both a POSTROUTING rule and FORWARD rule.

IP Masquerading with ipchains

You need to specify forwarding rules for use by ipchains to implement IP masquerading. (See the **mychains** file in the previous section for another example of an ipchains masquerade entry.) The following example assumes the Internet connection host, the firewall, uses its first Ethernet device to connect to the Internet, **eth0**. If you are using a modem to dial up a connection to an ISP, the interface used would probably be the first PPP interface, **ppp0**. The second command appends (`-A`) the forward rule to the target (`-j`) MASQ (masquerade) for the interface (`-i`) **eth0**. The host machines on the LAN must specify the connected system as their gateway machine. The last command enables IP forwarding. To enable IP masquerading using Linuxconf's firewalling entries, select Forward Firewalling and click the Do Masquerade check box for any firewall forwarding rules you add that you want to apply to IP masquerading.

```
ipchains -P forward DENY
ipchains -A forward -i eth0 -j MASQ
echo 1 > /proc/sys/net/ipv4/ip_forward
```

ipchains (Kernel 2.2)

ipchains is the precursor to iptables that was used on Linux systems running the 2.2 kernel. It is still in use on many Linux systems. The Linux Web site for ipchains, which is the successor to ipfwadm used on older versions of Linux, is currently **netfilter.samba.org/ipchains/**. Support for ipchains is already implemented on the Linux 2.2

kernel. For earlier versions, you must enable support in the kernel, rebuilding it with network firewalls and IP firewalling features (see Chapter 31). The IP chains HOWTO, located in your **/usr/doc/ipchains** directory, provides an excellent introduction and tutorial for ipchains and how you use it to implement a firewall. The HOWTO is in Web page format and can be viewed with any Web browser. The HOWTO features specific examples on how to guard against several standard attacks, such as IP spoofing, the ping of death, and teardrop.

Like iptables, ipchains organizes its rules into chains. A *chain* is simply a checklist of rules. These rules specify what action to take for packets containing certain headers. If the packet does match a rule, it is passed to its target, which determines what to do with the packet. If a packet does not match any of the rules, it is passed to the chain's default target. The standard targets are listed in Table 37-7. Unlike iptables, ipchains has both a MASQ and DENY target. A major difference between iptables and ipchains is that ipchains does not treat masquerading as a separate process. It is just another ipchains rule, not a separate process as in iptables.

A *target* could, in turn, be another chain of rules, even a chain of user-defined rules. A packet could be passed through several chains before finally reaching a target. In the case of user-defined chains, the default target is always the next rule in the chain from which it was called. This sets up a procedure or function call—like flow of control found in programming languages. When a rule has a user-defined chain as its target, then, when activated, that user-defined chain is executed. If no rules are matched, execution returns to the next rule in the originating chain.

Target	Function
ACCEPT	Allow packet to pass through the firewall
DENY	Deny access by the packet (changed to DROP in iptables)
REJECT	Deny access and notify the sender
MASQ	Masquerade the packet. Used only in the forward chain or chains called from the forward chain. Replaces sender's address with firewall host address (changed to MASQUERADE in iptables and made a NAT task)
REDIRECT	Redirect the packet to a local socket or process on the firewall. Used only in the input chain or chains called from the forward chain (changed to a NAT task in iptables)
RETURN	Jump to the end of the chain and let the default target process it

Table 37-7. *ipchains Targets*

The kernel uses three firewall chains: input, output, and forward. Unlike iptables, in ipchains these chains are written in lowercase. When a packet is received through an interface, the input chain is used to determine what to do with it. The kernel then uses its routing information to decide where to send it. If the kernel sends the packet to another host, the forward chain is checked. Before the packet is actually sent, the output chain is also checked.

You add and modify chain rules using the **ipchains** commands. An **ipchains** command consists of the keyword **ipchains**, followed by an argument denoting the command to execute. For example, **ipchains -A** is the command to add a new rule, whereas **ipchains -D** is the command to delete a rule. The **ipchains** options are listed in Table 37-8. Except for the masquerading options, they are much the same as those used in iptables. The following command simply lists the chains along with their

Option	Function
-A *chain*	Appends a rule to a chain
-D *chain*	Deletes matching rule from *chain*
-D *chain rulenum*	Deletes rule *rulenum* (1 = first) from *chain*
-I *chain* [*rulenum*]	Inserts in *chain* as *rulenum* (default 1 = first)
-R *chain rulenum*	Replaces rule *rulenum* (1 = first) in *chain*
-L [*chain*]	Lists the rules in *chain* or all chains
-F [*chain*]	Deletes (flushes) all rules in *chain* or all chains
-Z [*chain*]	Zero counters in *chain* or all chains
-C *chain*	Tests this packet on *chain*
-N *chain*	Creates a new user-defined chain
-X *chain*	Deletes a user-defined chain
-P *chain target*	Changes policy on *chain* to *target*
-M -L	Lists current masquerading connections (not valid for iptables)
-M -S *tcp tcpfin udp*	Sets masquerading timeout values (not valid for iptables)
-h	Displays list of commands
--*version*	Displays version

Table 37-8. *ipchains Options*

rules currently defined for your system. The output shows the default values created by **ipchains** commands.

```
ipchains -L
Chain input (policy ACCEPT):
Chain forward (policy ACCEPT):
Chain output (policy ACCEPT):
```

Following the command, list the chain to which the rule applies, such as the input, output, or forward chain, or else a user-defined chain. Next, list different options that specify the actions you want taken. Options exist to specify the address a rule is to match on (**-s, -d**) and to specify the target the rule is to execute (**-j**). The **-s** option specifies the source address attached to the packet, while the **-d** option specifies the destination address attached to the packet (where it is coming from and where it is going). The **-j** option, which stands for *jump*, is used to specify the target to jump to and execute. This is the target that is executed if the packet in a chain matches all the options. The standard targets used for a firewall are ACCEPT and DENY. The ACCEPT target will allow a packet to pass, whereas a DENY target will refuse access. Table 37-8 lists the available options.

In the following example, the user adds a rule to the input chain to accept all packets originating from the address 192.168.0.55. Any packets that are received (input) whose source address (**-s**) matches 192.168.0.55 are accepted and passed through as specified by the ACCEPT target, **-j ACCEPT**.

```
ipchains -A input -s 192.168.0.55 -j ACCEPT
```

To deny access from a particular site, simply specify the DENY target (in iptables, this was changed to DROP). Alternatively, you can send a packet back to where it came from using the REJECT target instead of the DENY target. In the following example, any packet received from **www.myjunk.com** is rejected:

```
ipchains -A input -s www.myjunk.com -j DENY
```

You can specify an individual address using its domain name or its IP number. For a range of addresses, you can use the IP number of their network and the network IP mask. The IP mask can be an IP number or simply the number of bits making up the mask. For example, all of the addresses in network 192.168.0 can be represented by 192.168.0.0/225.255.255.0 or by 192.168.0.0/24. To specify any address, you can use 0.0.0.0/0.0.0.0 or simply 0/0. By default, rules reference any address if no **-s** or **-d** specification exists. The following example accepts messages coming in that are from (source) any host in the 192.168.0.0 network and that are going (destination) anywhere at all (the **-d** option is left out or could be written as **-d 0/0**):

```
ipchains -A input -s 192.168.0.0/24  -j ACCEPT
```

If your system is hosting an Internet service, such as a Web or FTP server, you can use ipchains to control access to it. You can specify a particular service by specifying the port it uses. For a Web server, the port would be www. The names of services and the ports they use are listed in the **/etc/services** file, which maps ports to particular services. For a domain name server, the port would be domain. You can also use the port number if you want, preceding the number with a colon. The following example accepts all messages to the Web server located at 192.168.0.43:

```
ipchains -A input -d 192.168.0.43 www -j ACCEPT
```

With the **!** operator, you can change the effect of a rule to its inverse. The **!** operator works like a "not" logical operator in programming languages. Placing an **!** operator before a **-s** entry matches on any address that is not the specified address: **! -s 192.168.0.66** matches on any packet whose address is not 192.168.0.66. The operator is helpful if you want to restrict by only a few selected sites. The following example restricts access to 192.168.0.66, denying access to all others:

```
ipchains -A input ! -s 192.168.0.66 -j DENY
```

The inverse can apply also to ports, protocols, and devices. For example, to allow access to any port except the Ethernet device **eth2**, you would use

```
ipchains -A input ! eth2 -j ACCEPT
```

The following example denies access to any port except the Web server:

```
ipchains -A input ! www -j DENY
```

You can enter **ipchains** commands from the shell command line. When you shut down your system, however, these commands will be lost. To save your commands, you can use the **ipchains-save** script to save them to a file. The recommended file to use is **/etc/ipchains.rules**. The **ipchains-save** command outputs rules to the standard output. To save them in a file, you must redirect the output to a file with the redirection operator, **>**.

Secure Shell (SSH)

Although a firewall can protect a network from attempts to break into it from the outside, the problem of securing legitimate communications to the network from outside sources still exists. A particular problem is one of users who want to connect to your network remotely. Such connections could be monitored, and information such as passwords and user IDs used when the user logs in to your network could be copied and used later to break in. One solution is to use a Secure Shell (SSH) tool like slogin for remote logins. SSH encrypts any communications between the remote user and a system on your network. The SSH programs are meant to replace remote tools such as rsh and rcp (see Chapter 15), which perform no encryption and introduce security risks such as transmitting passwords in clear text. You can also use SSH to encode X server sessions as well as FTP transmissions (sftp).

Two different implementations of SSH currently use what are, in effect, two different and incompatible protocols. The first version of SSH, known as SSH1, uses the original SSH protocol. Version 2.0, known as SSH2, uses a completely rewritten version of the SSH protocol. Encryption is performed in different ways, encrypting different parts of a packet. SSH1 uses server and host keys to authenticate systems, whereas SSH2 only uses host keys. Furthermore, certain functions, such as sftp, are only supported by SSH2.

SSH secures connections by both authenticating users and encrypting their transmissions. The authentication process is handled with public key encryption, described in Chapter 6. Once authenticated, transmissions are encrypted by a cipher agreed upon by the SSH server and client for use in a particular session. SSH supports multiple ciphers, as listed in Table 37-14. Authentication is applied to both hosts and users. SSH first authenticates a particular host, verifying that it is a valid SSH host that can be securely communicated with. Then the user is authenticated, verifying that the user is who they say they are.

The public key encryption used in SSH authentication makes use of two keys: a public key and a private key. The *public key* is used to encrypt data, while the *private key* decrypts it. Each host or user has their own public and private keys. The public key is distributed to other hosts, who can then use it to encrypt data that only the host's private key can decrypt. For example, when a host sends data to a user on another system, the host encrypts the data with a public key, which it previously received from that user. The data can only be decrypted by the user's corresponding private key. The public key can safely be sent in the open from one host to another, allowing it to be installed safely on different hosts. You can think of the process as taking place between a client and a server. When the client sends data to the server, it first encrypts the data using the server's public key. The server can then decrypt the data using its own private key.

The mechanics of authentication in SSH version 1 and version 2 differ slightly. However, the procedure on the part of users is the same. Essentially, a user creates both public and private keys. For this you use the **ssh-keygen** command. The user's public key then has to be distributed to those users that the original user wants access to. Often this is an account a user has on another host. A passphrase further protects access. The original user will need to know the other user's passphrase to access it.

SSH Version 1 uses RSA authentication. When a remote user tries to log in to an account, that account is checked to see if it has the remote user's public key. That public key is then used to encrypt a challenge (usually a random number) that can only be decrypted by the remote user's private key. When the remote user receives the encrypted challenge, that user decrypts the challenge with its private key. SSH Version 2 can use either RSA or

DSA authentication. The remote user will first encrypt a session identifier using its private key, signing it. The encrypted session identifier is then decrypted by the account using the remote user's public key. The session identifier has been previously set up by SSH for that session.

SSH authentication is first carried out with the host, and then with users. Each host has its own host keys, public and private keys used for authentication. Once the host is authenticated, the user is queried. Each user has their own public and private keys. Users on an SSH server who want to receive connections from remote users will have to keep a list of those remote user's public keys. Similarly, an SSH host will maintain a list of public keys for other SSH hosts.

SSH uses strong encryption methods, and their export from the United States may be restricted. Currently, SSH can deal with the following kinds of attacks:

- IP spoofing, where a remote host sends out packets that pretend to come from another, trusted host
- IP source routing, where a host can pretend an IP packet comes from another, trusted host
- DNS spoofing, where an attacker forges name server records
- Interception of clear text passwords and other data by intermediate hosts
- Manipulation of data by people in control of intermediate hosts
- Attacks based on listening to X authentication data and spoofed connections to the X11 server

Note *A commercial version of SSH is available from SSH Communications Security, whose Web site is **www.ssh.com**. SSH Communications Security provides SSH free for noncommercial use and sells SSH for commercial use through Datafellows.*

The SSH protocol has become an official Internet Engineering Task Force (IETF) standard. A free and open source version is developed and maintained by the OpenSSH project, currently supported by the OpenBSD project. OpenSSH is the version supplied with most Linux distributions, including Red Hat, Mandrake, Caldera, SUSE, and Debian. You can find out more about OpenSSH at **www.openssh.org**, where you can download the most recent version, though your distribution will provide current RPM versions.

SSH Applications

The full set of OpenSSH packages include the general OpenSSH package (openssh), the OpenSSH server (openssh-server), and the OpenSSH clients (openssh-clients). These packages also require OpenSSL (openssl), which installs the cryptographic libraries that SSH uses. You can easily update them from distribution FTP.

The SSH applications are listed in Table 37-9. They include several client programs and the ssh server. The ssh server (sshd) provides secure connections to anyone from the outside using the ssh client to connect. With ssh, users can remotely log in and execute commands using encrypted transmissions. In the same way, with scp, users can copy files from one host to another securely. The ssh server can also invoke the sftp-server to provide encrypted FTP transmissions to those using the sftp client. This client, which only works with ssh version 2, operates much like ftp, with many of the same commands (see Chapter 20). Several configuration utilities are also included, such as ssh-add, which adds valid hosts to the authentication agent, and ssh-keygen, which generates the keys used for encryption.

On Mandrake and Red Hat you can start, restart, and stop the sshd server with the **service** command:

```
service sshd restart
```

SSH was originally designed to replace remote access operations, such as rlogin, rcp, and Telnet, as well as FTP (see Chapter 15). The ssh-clients package contains corresponding SSH clients to replace these applications. With slogin or ssh, you can log in from a remote host to execute commands and run applications, much as you can with rlogin and rsh. With scp, you can copy files between the remote host and a network host, just as with rcp. scftp lets you make secure FTP connections.

For version 2, names of the actual applications have a 2 suffix. Version 1 applications have a 1 as their suffix. During installation, however, links are set for each application to use only the name with the suffix. For example, if you have installed version 2, there is a link called scp to the scp2 application. You can then use the link to invoke the application. Using scp starts scp2. Table 37-9 specifies only the link names, as these are the same for each version. Remember, though, some applications, such as sftp, are only available with version 2.

SSH Setup

Using SSH involves creating your own public and private keys and then distributing your public key to other users you want to access. These can be different users or simply user accounts of your own that you have on remote systems. Often people remotely log in from a local client into an account on a remote server, perhaps from a home computer to a company computer. Your home computer would be your client account and the account on your company computer would be your server account. On your client account you would need to generate your public and private keys. Then you would have to place a copy of your public key in the server account. You can do this by simply e-mailing the key file or copying the file from a floppy disk. Once the account on your server has a copy of your client user's public key, you can access the server account from your client account. You will be also prompted for the server

Application	Description
ssh	ssh client.
sshd	ssh server (daemon).
sftp	sftp client. Version 2 only. Use **?** to list sftp commands.
sftp-server	sftp server. Version 2 only.
scp	scp client.
ssh-keygen	Utility for generating keys. **-h** for help.
ssh-add	Adds identities to the authentication agent.
ssh-agent	SSH authentication agent.
ssh-askpass	X Window System utility for querying passwords.
ssh-askpass-gnome	Gnome utility for querying passwords.
ssh-signer	Signs host-based authentication packets. Version 2 only. Must be suid root (performed by installation).
slogin	Remote login (version 1).

Table 37-9. *SSH Applications*

account's passphrase. You will have to know this to access that account. Figure 37-3 illustrates the SSH setup that allows a user **george** to access the account **cecelia**.

The following steps are needed to allow you to use SSH to access other accounts:

- Create public and private keys on your account along with a passphrase. You will need to use this passphrase to access your account from another account.
- Distribute your public key to other accounts you want to access, placing them in the **.ssh/authorized_keys** or **.ssh/authorized_keys2** file.
- Other accounts also have to set up a public and private key along with a passphrase.
- You will need to also know the other account's passphrase to access it.

You create your public and private keys using the **ssh-keygen** command. The **ssh-keygen** command prompts you for a passphrase, which it will use as a kind of password to protect your private key. The passphrase should be several words long. You are also prompted to enter a filename for the keys. If you do not enter one, SSH will use its defaults. The public key will be given the extension **.pub**. For SSH version 1, the **ssh-keygen** command generates the public key and places it in your **.ssh/identity.pub**

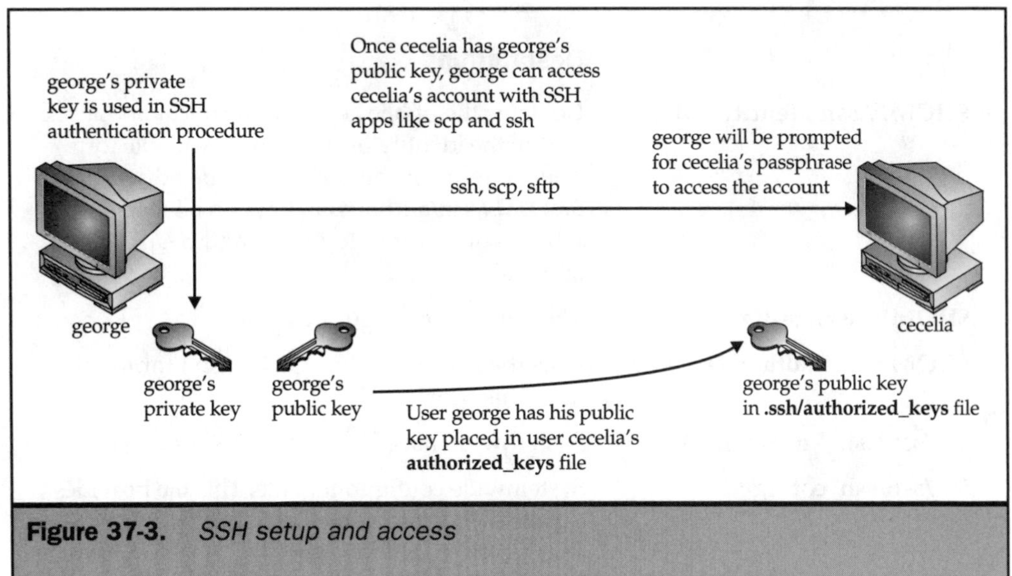

Figure 37-3. *SSH setup and access*

file; it places the private key in the **.ssh/identity** file. For SSH version 2, the **`ssh-keygen`** command generates the public key and places it in your **.ssh/id_dsa.pub** file; it places the private key in the **.ssh/id_dsa** file.

If you need to change your passphrase, you can do so with the **`ssh-keygen`** command and the **`-p`** option. Each user will have their own SSH configuration directory, called **.ssh**, located in their own home directory. The public and private keys, as well as SSH configuration files, are placed here. If you build from the source code, the **`make install`** operation will automatically run **`ssh-keygen`**. Table 37-10 lists the SSH configuration files.

File	Description
$HOME/.ssh/known_hosts	Records host keys for all hosts the user has logged in to (that are not in **/etc/ssh/ssh_known_hosts**).
$HOME/.ssh/random_seed	Used for seeding the random number generator.
$HOME/.ssh/identity	Contains the RSA authentication identity of the user.

Table 37-10. *SSH Configuration Files (SSH2 Files Are Placed in /etc/ssh2 and .ssh2 Directories)*

File	Description
$HOME/.ssh/identity.pub	Contains the public key for authentication (public part of the identity file in human-readable form). The contents of this file should be added to **$HOME/.ssh/authorized_keys** on all machines where you want to log in using RSA authentication.
$HOME/.ssh/config	The per-user configuration file.
$HOME/.ssh/authorized_keys	Lists the RSA keys that can be used for logging in as this user.
/etc/ssh/ssh_known_hosts	Systemwide list of known host keys.
/etc/ssh/ssh_config	Systemwide configuration file. This file provides defaults for those values not specified in the user's configuration file.
/etc/ssh/sshd_config	SSH server configuration file.
$HOME/.rhosts	This file is used in **.rhosts** authentication to list the host/user pairs permitted to log in. Note, this file is also used by rlogin and rsh, which makes using this file insecure.
$HOME/.shosts	This file is used exactly the same way as **.rhosts**. The purpose for having this file is to use rhosts authentication with ssh without permitting login with rlogin or rsh.
/etc/hosts.equiv	This file is used during **.rhosts** authentication. It contains canonical hostnames, one per line. If the client host is found in this file, login is automatically permitted, provided client and server usernames are the same.
/etc/ssh/shosts.equiv	This file is processed exactly as **/etc/hosts.equiv**. This file may be useful to permit logins using ssh, but not using rsh/rlogin.

Table 37-10. *SSH Configuration Files (SSH2 Files Are Placed in /etc/ssh2 and .ssh2 Directories)* (continued)

File	Description
/etc/ssh/sshrc	System default. Commands in this file are executed by ssh when the user logs in just before the user's shell (or command) is started.
$HOME/.ssh/rc	Commands in this file are executed by ssh when the user logs in just before the user's shell (or command) is started.

Table 37-10. *SSH Configuration Files (SSH2 Files Are Placed in /etc/ssh2 and .ssh2 Directories)* (continued)

A public key is used to authenticate a user and its host. You use the public key on a remote system to allow that user access. In SSH version 2, the public key is placed in the remote user account's **.ssh/authorized_keys2** file. Recall that the public key is held in the **.ssh/id_dsa.pub** file. If a user wants to log in remotely from a local account to an account on a remote system, they would first place their public key in the **.ssh/authorized_keys2** file in the account on the remote system they want to access. If the user **larisa** on **turtle.mytrek.com** wants to access the **aleina** account on **rabbit.mytrek.com, larisa**'s public key from **/home/larisa/.ssh/id_dsa.pub** first must be placed in **aleina**'s **authorized_keys2** file, **/home/aleina/.ssh/authorized_keys2. larisa** could send the key or have it copied over. A simple cat operation can append a key to the authorized key file. In the next example, the user adds the public key for **aleina** in the **larisa.pub** file to the authorized key file. The **larisa.pub** file is a copy of the **/home/larisa/.ssh/id_dsa.pub** file that the user received earlier.

```
cat larisa.pub >>  .ssh/authorized_keys2
```

For SSH version 1, the default name for the authorized key file is simply **.ssh/authorized_keys.**

If you regularly make connections to a variety of remote hosts, you can use the **ssh-agent** command to place private keys in memory where they can be accessed quickly to decrypt received transmissions. The **ssh-agent** command is intended for use at the beginning of a login session. If you are using a shell in your work, use that shell as the argument for the **ssh-agent** command. If you are using the X Window System (Gnome or KDE), use the **startx** command as your argument. That way, any applications you start inherit a connection to **ssh-agent**. For a graphical login, such as GDM, place the **ssh-agent** command in your **.Xclients** file. For Gnome, you can use the openssh-askpass-gnome utility, which allows you to enter a password when you log in to Gnome. Gnome will automatically supply that password whenever you use an SSH client.

Although the **ssh-agent** command enables you to use private keys in memory, you also must specifically load your private keys into memory using the **ssh-add** command. **ssh-add** with no arguments loads your private key from your **.ssh/identity** file. You are prompted for your passphrase for this private key. To remove the key from memory, use **ssh-add** with the **-d** option. If you have several private keys, you can load them all into memory. **ssh-add** with the **-l** option lists those currently loaded.

SSH also supports the original rhosts form of authentication where hosts and users that are permitted access are placed in an **.rhosts** or **.shosts** file. However, this method is not considered secure.

To use SSH in scripts that run in the background or when you are not logged in, you need to either create a key that has no passphrase or allow automatic access with **.shosts**. To create a key with no passphrase, you run **ssh-keygen** and then press ENTER for the passphrase. Give the key a separate filename. Then, when you invoke SSH, use the **-i** option to designate that key. Make sure that the remote user you are accessing has the public key for this key pair. Alternatively, you can use **.shosts**. Make sure that the remote user you want to automatically access has your public key. In the remote user's **.shosts** file, add an entry for your host and username.

ssh

With ssh, you can remotely log in from a local client to a remote system on your network operating as the SSH server. The term *local client* here refers to one outside the network, such as your home computer, and the term *remote* refers to a host system on the network to which you are connecting. In effect, you connect from your local system to the remote network host. It is designed to replace rlogin, which performs remote logins, and rsh, which executes remote commands. With ssh, you can log in from a local site to a remote host on your network and then send commands to be executed on that host. ssh is also capable of supporting X Window System connections. This feature is automatically enabled if you make an ssh connection from an X Window System environment, such as Gnome or KDE. A connection is set up for you between the local X server and the remote X server. The remote host sets up a dummy X server and sends any X Window System data through it to your local system to be processed by your own local X server.

The ssh login operation function is much like the **rlogin** command. You enter the **ssh** command with the address of the remote host, followed by a **-l** option and the login name (username) of the remote account you are logging into. The following example logs into the **aleina** user account on the **rabbit.mytrek.com** host:

```
ssh rabbit.mytrek.com -l aleina
```

You can also use the username in an address format with ssh, as in:

```
ssh aleian@rabbit.mytrek.com
```

The following listing shows how the user **george** accesses the **cecelia** account on **turtle.mytrek.com**.

```
[george@turtle george]$ ssh turtle.mytrek.com -l cecelia
cecelia@turtle.mytrek.com's password:
Last login: Wed Sep 19 15:13:05 2001 from turtle.mytrek.com
[cecelia@turtle cecelia]$
```

A variety of options are available to enable you to configure your connection (see Table 37-11). Most have corresponding configuration options that can be set in the configuration file. For example, with the **-c** option, you can designate which encryption method you want to use. With the **-i** option, you can select a particular private key to use. The **-C** option enables you to have transmissions compressed at specified levels.

Option	Description
-a	Disables forwarding of the authentication agent connection.
-c idea|des|3des|blowfish|]arcfour|none	Selects the cipher to use for encrypting the session. **idea** is used by default and is believed to be secure. **none** disables encryption entirely; it is only intended for debugging and renders the connection insecure.
-e *ch*|^*ch*|**none**	Sets the escape character for sessions with a pty (default: ~). The escape character is only recognized at the beginning of a line. The escape character followed by a dot (.) closes the connection, followed by CTRL-Z suspends the connection, and followed by itself sends the escape character once. Setting the character to "none" disables any escapes and makes the session fully transparent.
-f	Requests ssh to go to background after authentication is done and forwardings are established.
-i *identity_file*	Selects the file from which the identity (private key) for RSA authentication is read. Default is **.ssh/identity** in the user's home directory.
-k	Disables forwarding of the Kerberos tickets.
-l *login_name*	Specifies the user to log in as on the remote machine.

Table 37-11. *ssh Command Options*

Option	Description
`-n`	Redirects stdin from **/dev/null** (actually, prevents reading from stdin). Used when ssh is run in the background. Used to run X11 programs in a remote machine.
`-o` *option*	Specifies options.
`-p` *port*	Port to connect to on the remote host.
`-q`	Quiet mode, suppresses warning and diagnostic messages.
`-P`	Uses nonprivileged port.
`-t`	Forces pseudo-tty allocation.
`-v`	Verbose mode.
`-V`	Displays version number.
`-g`	Allows remote hosts to connect local port-forwarding ports.
`-x`	Disables X11 forwarding.
`-C`	Requests compression of all data. The compression algorithm is the same used by gzip and the level can be controlled by the CompressionLevel option.
`-L` *port*`:`*host*`:`*hostport*	Specifies that the given port on the local (client) host is to be forwarded to the given host and port on the remote side.
`-R` *port*`:`*host*`:`*hostport*	Specifies that the given port on the remote (server) host is to be forwarded to the given host and port on the local side.

Table 37-11. *ssh Command Options* (continued)

scp

You use scp to copy files from one host to another on a network. Designed to replace rcp, scp actually uses ssh to transfer data and employs the same authentication and encryption (see Table 37-12). If authentication requires it, scp requests a password or passphrase. scp operates much like rcp. Directories and files on remote hosts are specified using the username and the host address before the filename or directory.

Option	Description
`-q`	Turns off statistics display
`-Q`	Turns on statistics display
`-r`	Recursively copies entire directories.
`-v`	Verbose mode
`-B`	Selects batch mode (prevents asking for passwords or passphrases)
`-C`	Compression-enabled
`-P` *port*	Specifies the port to connect to on the remote host
`-S` *path-to-ssh*	Specifies the path to sch program

Table 37-12. *scp Options*

The username specifies the remote user account that scp is accessing, and the host is the remote system where that account is located. You separate the user from the host address with an @, and you separate the host address from the file or directory name with a colon. The following example copies the file party from a user current directory to the user **aleina**'s **birthday** directory, located on the **rabbit.mytrek.com** host:

```
scp party aleina@rabbit.mytrek.com:/birthday/party
```

Of particular interest is the `-r` option (recursive), which enables you to copy whole directories. In the next example, the user copies the entire **reports** directory to the user **justin**'s **projects** directory:

```
scp -r reports justin@rabbit.mytrek.com:/projects
```

In the next example, the user **george** copies the **mydoc1** file from the user **cecelia**'s home directory.

```
[george@turtle george]$ scp cecelia@turtle.mytrek.com:mydoc1  .
cecelia@turtle.mytrek.com's password:
mydoc1      0% |                                  |   0 --:--
ETA
mydoc1    100% |*****************************|  17 00:00
[george@turtle george]$
```

From a Windows system, you can also use scp clients such as winscp which will interact with Linux scp-enabled systems.

Port Forwarding (Tunneling)

If, for some reason, you can only connect to a secure host by going through an insecure host, ssh provides a feature called port forwarding. With *port forwarding*, you can secure the insecure segment of your connection. This involves simply specifying the port at which the insecure host is to connect to the secure one. This sets up a direct connection between the local host and the remote host, through the intermediary insecure host. Encrypted data is passed through directly. This process is referred to as tunneling, creating a secure tunnel of encrypted data through connected servers.

You can set up port forwarding to a port on the remote system or your local system. To forward a port on the remote system to a port on your local system, use the **ssh -R** option, followed by an argument holding the local port, the remote host address, and the remote port to be forwarded, each separated by a colon. This works by allocating a socket to listen to the port on the remote side. Whenever a connection is made to this port, the connection is forwarded over the secure channel, and a connection is made to a remote port from the local machine. In the following example, port 22 on the local system is connected to port 23 on the **rabbit.mytrek.com** remote system:

```
ssh -R 22:rabbit.mytrek.com:23
```

To forward a port on your local system to a port on a remote system, use the **ssh -L** option, followed by an argument holding the local port, the remote host address, and the remote port to be forwarded, each two arguments separated by a colon. A socket is allocated to listen to port on the local side. Whenever a connection is made to this port, the connection is forwarded over the secure channel and a connection is made to the remote port on the remote machine. In the following example, port 22 on the local system is connected to port 23 on the **rabbit.mytrek.com** remote system:

```
ssh -L 22:rabbit.mytrek.com:23
```

You can use the LocalForward and RemoteForward options in your **.ssh/config** file to set up port forwarding for particular hosts or to specify a default for all hosts you connect to.

SSH Session

An SSH session can be implemented as a pseudoterminal, much like a Telnet connection, or it can be transparent, as is the case with X server connections. With a pseudoterminal, the user can control the connection with a set of escape characters, each beginning with a tilde (~). To end the connection, use a tilde-dot (~.) escape sequence. Using ~CTRL-Z suspends the session. The escape sequence must be entered in a line of its own. Using **~?** lists the available escape sequences you can use.

If no pseudoterminal is set up, the session is transparent. Usually, setting the escape character to "none" makes the session transparent. Binary data can safely be transmitted during transparent sessions. A transparent session ends when the shell or command on the remote system ends and all connections have been closed. X Window System connections are automatically set up as transparent connections. SSH sets up a proxy X server on the remote system.

SSH Configuration

The SSH configuration file for each user is in their **.ssh/config** file. The **/etc/ssh/sys_config** file is used to set sitewide defaults. In the configuration file, you can set various options, as listed in Table 37-13. The configuration file is designed to specify options for different remote hosts to which you might connect. It is organized into segments where each segment begins with the keyword **HOST**, followed by the IP address of the host. The following lines hold the options you have set for that host. A segment ends at the next **HOST** entry. Of particular interest are the **User** and **Cipher** options. Use the **User** option to specify the names of users on the remote system who are allowed access. With the **Cipher** option, you can select which encryption method to use for a particular host (see Table 37-14). The following example allows access from **larisa** at **turtle.mytrek.com** and uses Blowfish encryption for transmissions:

```
Host turtle.mytrek.com
     User larisa
     Compression no
     Cipher blowfish
```

Option	Description
Host *hostname*	Specifies the host to which the following options apply. All options apply to this host until the next **Host** entry. You can specify a range of hosts by using the ***** and **?** pattern-matching wildcard symbols. A host specified as only ***** matches on all hosts and can be used to specify global options.

Table 37-13. *SSH Configuration Options*

Option	Description
BatchMode (yes | no)	If set to yes, passphrase/password querying is disabled. This option is useful in scripts and other batch jobs where you have no user to supply the password. The argument must be yes or no.
Cipher *cipher*	Specifies the cipher to use for encrypting the session, such as idea, des, 3des, blowfish, arcfour, and none. The default is idea (or 3des if idea is not supported by both hosts). Using "none" (no encryption) renders the connection insecure and is intended only for debugging.
ClearAllForwardings (yes | no)	Clears all forwardings after reading all config files and parsing the command line. This is useful to disable forwardings in config files when you want to make a second connection to the host having forwardings in the config file. scp sets this to yes by default, so it does not fail, even if you have some forwardings set in a config file.
Compression (yes | no)	Specifies whether to use compression.
CompressionLevel (*1–9*)	Specifies the compression level. The argument must be an integer from 1 (fast) to 9 (slow, best). The default level is 6.
ConnectionAttempts *num*	Specifies the number of tries (one per second) to make.
EscapeChar	Sets the escape character (default: ~). The argument should be a single character, ^, followed by a letter or "none" to disable the escape character entirely (making the connection transparent for binary data).
FallBackToRsh (yes | no)	Specifies if connecting with ssh fails because no sshd is on the remote host, rsh should automatically be used instead.

Table 37-13. *SSH Configuration Options* (continued)

Option	Description
`ForwardAgent` (yes | no)	Specifies whether the connection to the authentication agent should be forwarded to the remote machine.
`ForwardX11` (yes | no)	Specifies whether X11 connections should be automatically redirected over the secure channel and DISPLAY set.
`GatewayPorts` (yes | no)	Specifies that remote hosts may connect to locally forwarded ports.
`GlobalKnownHostsFile` *file*	Specifies a file to use instead of **/etc/ssh/ssh_known_hosts**.
`HostName` *hostname*	Specifies the real hostname to log in to. This can be used to specify nicknames or abbreviations for hosts.
`IdentityFile` *file*	Specifies the file from which the user's RSA authentication identity is read (default **.ssh/identity** in the user's home directory).
`KeepAlive` (yes | no)	Specifies whether the system should send keepalive messages to the other side. Used to detect if connection fails.
`KerberosAuthentication` (yes | no)	Specifies whether Kerberos V5 authentication should be used.
`KerberosTgtPassing` (yes | no)	Specifies whether a Kerberos V5 TGT is to be forwarded to the server.
`LocalForward` *host host*`:`*port*	Specifies a TCP/IP port on the local machine be forwarded over the secure channel to given host:port from the remote machine. The first argument must be a port number, and the second must be host:port.
`NumberOfPasswordPrompts` *num*	Specifies the number of password prompts before giving up.
`PasswordAuthentication` (yes | no)	Specifies whether to use password authentication.
`PasswordPromptHost` (yes | no)	Specifies whether to include the remote hostname in the password prompt.

Table 37-13. *SSH Configuration Options* (continued)

Option	Description
`PasswordPromptLogin` (yes | no)	Specifies whether to include the remote login name in the password prompt.
`Port`	Specifies the port number to connect on the remote host. Default is 22.
`ProxyCommand` *command*	Specifies the command to use to connect to the server.
`RemoteForward` *host host:port*	Specifies a TCP/IP port on the remote machine be forwarded over the secure channel to given host:port from the local machine. The first argument must be a port number, and the second must be host:port.
`RhostsAuthentication` (yes | no)	Specifies whether to try rhosts-based authentication.
`RhostsRSAAuthentication` (yes | no)	Specifies whether to try rhosts-based authentication with RSA host authentication.
`RSAAuthentication` (yes | no)	Specifies whether to try RSA authentication.
`StrictHostKeyChecking` (yes | no | *ask*)	If this flag is set to yes, ssh never automatically adds host keys to the **$HOME/.ssh/known_hosts** file and refuses to connect hosts whose host key has changed.
`TISAuthentication` (yes | no)	Specifies whether to try TIS authentication.
`UsePrivilegedPort` (yes | no)	Specifies whether to use a privileged port when connecting to other end.
`User` *username*	Specifies the user login name.
`UserKnownHostsFile` *file*	Specifies a file to use instead of **$HOME/.ssh/known_hosts**.
`UseRsh` (yes | no)	Specifies rlogin/rsh should be used for this host if it does not support the ssh protocol.
`XAuthLocation` *path*	Specifies the path to xauth program.

Table 37-13. *SSH Configuration Options* (continued)

Method	Description
idea	Believed to be secure.
Des	The data encryption standard, but this is breakable by governments, large corporations, and major criminal organizations.
3des (triple-des)	Encrypt-decrypt-encrypt triple with three different keys. Presumably more secure than DES and used as the default if both sites do not support IDEA.
blowfish	128-bit key encryption algorithm invented by Bruce Schneier.
arcfour	Equivalent with the RC4 cipher from RSA Data Security (RC4 is a trademark of RSA Data Security). This is the fastest algorithm currently supported. Version 2 only
twofish	Version 2 only.
cast128-cbc	Version 2 only.

Table 37-14. *SSH2 Encryption Methods*

To specify global options that apply to any host you connect to, create a **HOST** entry with the asterisk as its host, **HOST ***. This entry must be placed at the end of the configuration file because an option is changed only the first time it is set. Any subsequent entries for an option are ignored. Because a host matches on both its own entry and the global one, its specific entry should come before the global entry. The asterisk, *****, and the question mark, **?**, are both wildcard matching operators that enable you to specify a group of hosts with the same suffix or prefix.

```
Host *
  FallBackToRsh yes
  KeepAlive no
  Cipher idea
```

Kerberos Authentication and Encryption

Kerberos is a network authentication protocol that provides encrypted authentication to connections between a client and a server. As an authentication protocol, Kerberos requires a client to prove their identity using encryption methods before they can access a server. Once authenticated, the client and server can conduct all communications using encryption. Whereas firewalls only protect from outside attacks, Kerberos is designed to also protect from attacks from those inside the network. Users already within a network could try to break into local servers. Kerberos places protection around the servers themselves, rather than an entire network or computer. A free version is available from the Massachusetts Institute of Technology at **web.mit.edu/kerberos** under the MIT Public License, which is similar to the GNU Public License. The name *Kerberos* comes from Greek mythology and is the name of the three-headed watchdog for Hades. Be sure to check the **web.mit.edu/kerberos** site for recent upgrades and detailed documentation, including FAQs, manuals, and tutorials.

The Kerberos V5 package includes its own versions of network tools such as Telnet, RCP, FTP, and RSH. These provide secure authenticated access by remote users. The tools operate in the same way as their original counterparts described in Chapter 15. The package also contains a Kerberos version of the **su** *administrative login command,* **ksu**.

The key to Kerberos is a Kerberos server through which all requests for any server services are channeled. The Kerberos server then authenticates a client, identifying the client and validating the client's right to use a particular server. The server maintains a database of authorized users. Kerberos then issues the client an encrypted ticket that the client can use to gain access to the server. For example, if a user needs to check their mail, a request for use of the mail server is sent to the Kerberos server, which then authenticates the user and issues a ticket that is then used to access the mail server. Without a Kerberos-issued ticket, no one can access any of the servers. Originally, this process required that users undergo a separate authentication procedure for each server they wanted to access. However, users now only need to perform an initial authentication that is valid for all servers.

This process actually involves the use of two servers, an authentication server (AS) and a ticket-granting server (TGS). Together they make up what is known as the key distribution center (KDC). In effect, they distribute keys used to unlock access to services. The authentication server first validates a user's identity. The AS issues a ticket called the ticket-granting ticket (TGT) that allows the user to access the ticket-granting server. The TGS then issues the user another ticket to actually access a service. This way, the user never has any direct access of any kind to a server during the authentication process. The process is somewhat more complex than described. An authenticator using information such as the current time, a checksum, and an optional encryption key is sent along with the ticket and is decrypted with the session key. This authenticator is used by a service to verify your identity.

Note

You can view your list of current tickets with the **klist** *command.*

The authentication server validates a user using information in its user database. Each user needs to be registered in the authentication server's database. The database will include a user password and other user information. To access the authentication server, the user provides the username and the password. The password is used to generate a user key with which communication between the AS and the user is encrypted. The user will have their own copy of the user key with which to decrypt communications. The authentication process is illustrated in Figure 37-4.

Accessing a service with Kerberos involves the following steps:

1. The user has to be validated by the authentication server and granted access to the ticket-granting server with a ticket access key. You do this by issuing the **kinit** command, which will ask you enter your Kerberos username and then send it on to the authentication server (the Kerberos username is usually the same as your username).

   ```
   kinit
   ```

2. The AS generates a ticket-granting ticket with which to access the ticket-granting server. This ticket will include a session key that will be used to let you access the TGS. The TGT is sent back to you encrypted with your user key (password).
3. The kinit program then prompts you to enter your Kerberos password, which it then uses to decrypt the TGT. You can manage your Kerberos password with the **kpasswd** command.
4. Now you can use a client program such as a mail client program to access the mail server, for instance. When you do so, the TGT is used to access the TGS, which then will generate a ticket for accessing the mail server. The TGS will generate a new session key for use with just the mail server. This will be provided in the ticket sent to you for accessing the mail server. In effect, there is a TGT sessions key used for accessing the TGS, and a mail session key used for accessing the mail server. The ticket for the mail server is sent to you encrypted with the TGS session key.
5. The client then uses the mail ticket received from the TGS to access the mail server.
6. If you want to use another service such as FTP, when your FTP client sends a request to the TGS for a ticket, the TGS will automatically obtain authorization from the authentication server and issue an FTP ticket with an FTP session key. This kind of support remains in effect for a limited period of time, usually several hours, after which you again have to use **kinit** to undergo the authentication process and access the TGS. You can manually destroy any tickets you have with the **kdestroy** command.

Note *With Kerberos V5 (version 5), a Kerberos login utility is provided whereby users are automatically granted ticket-granting tickets when they log in normally. This avoids the need to use* **kinit** *to manually obtain a TGT.*

Setting up a particular service to use Kerberos (known as Kerberizing) can be a complicated process. A Kerberized service needs to check the user's identity and credentials, check for a ticket for the service, and, if one is not present, obtain one. Once

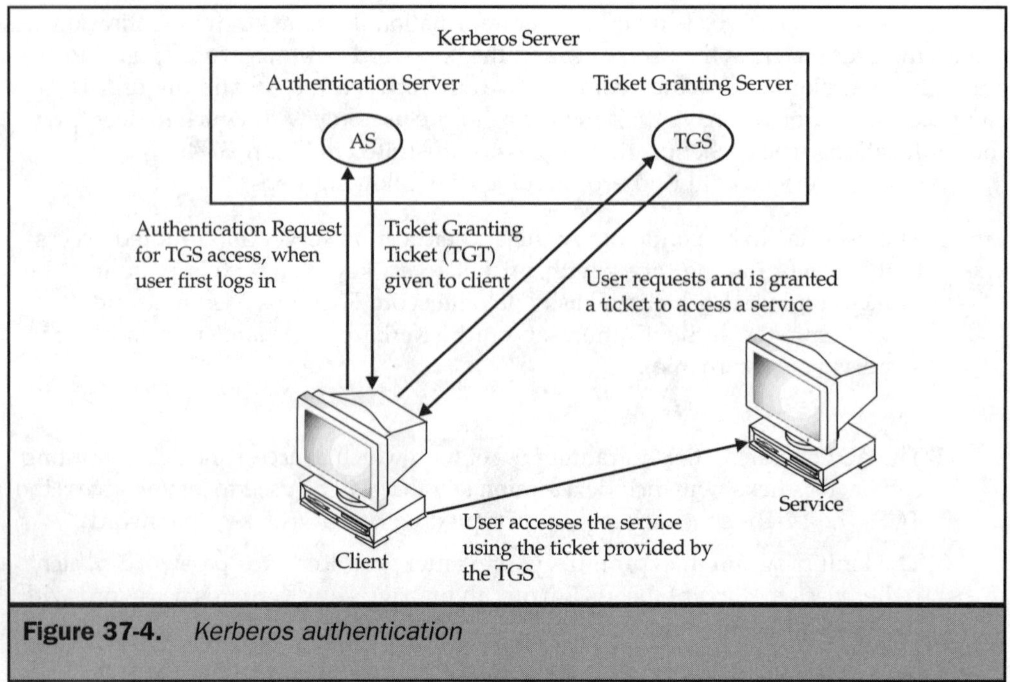

Figure 37-4. *Kerberos authentication*

they are set up, use of Kerberized services is nearly transparent to the user. Tickets are automatically issued and authentication carried out without any extra effort by the user.

Installing and configuring a Kerberos server is also a complex process. Carefully check the documentation for installing the current versions. Some of the key areas are listed here. In the Kerberos configuration file, **krb5.conf**, you can set such features as the encryption method used and the database name. When installing Kerberos, be sure to carefully follow the instructions for providing administrative access. The **/etc/services** file should contain a listing of all Kerberized services. These are services such as kftp or klogin that provide Kerberos FTP and login services. To run Kerberos, you start the Kerberos server with the **`krb5kdc`** and **`kadmin`** commands.

On Gnome, you can use the krb5 tool to manage Kerberos tickets, and the gkadmin tool to manage Kerberos realms. These are part of the Gnome-Kerberos package on Red Hat distributions.

Check your distribution's Reference Manual for more detailed instructions on setting up Kerberos servers and clients on your system.

The Complete Reference

Appendix

About the DVD-ROM

The Linux distribution DVD-ROM, Red Hat Linux 7.3, is included in this book, featuring the complete five CD-ROM set for the entire Red Hat distributions. The Red Hat Linux distribution installs a professional-level and very stable Linux system along with the KDE and Gnome GUI interfaces, flexible and easy-to-use system configuration tools, an extensive set of Internet servers, a variety of different multimedia applications, and more than 1,500 Linux applications of all kinds. The DVD also includes the complete set of source code files for all the Linux software provided, making up over 3GB of software overall. You can find recent information about Red Hat at **www.redhat.com**.

The DVD-ROM and the Red Hat Web site (**www.redhat.com**) include extensive documentation, including HOW-TO documents, tutorials in Web page format, and online manuals. Four very helpful Red Hat guides are the *Red Hat Installation Guide*, the *Red Hat Getting Started Guide*, the *Red Hat Linux Reference Guide*, and the *Red Hat Customization Guide*. All are in Web page format and can be viewed with any Web browser on any system. The *Red Hat Installation Guide* provides a detailed walk-through of the installation procedure with graphics and helpful suggestions. It is best to check it before you install Red Hat. The *Red Hat Getting Started Guide* provides an overview of basic Red Hat operations such as working with Gnome and basic configuration. The *Red Hat Linux Reference Guide* covers administration and configuration tasks in detail. The *Red Hat Linux Customization Guide* covers specialized administration tasks such as DNS, NFS, and Samba configuration, along with using encryption and the Red Hat Package manager.

The DVD includes a comprehensive set of Linux software applications, including the GNU software packages (graphics, communications, publishing, editing, programming, games), as well as development tools, and Internet servers (FTP, Web, mail, news, and DNS). Both Gnome and the K Desktop Environment (KDE) GUI user interfaces, along with an extensive number of Gnome and KDE applications, are included. It also installs a complete set of Internet clients such as mail, news, FTP, and Web browsers. There are clients for both the Gnome and KDE desktops, as well as for shell and window manager interfaces. With your installation, you are entitled to join the Red Hat Network, which provides you with automatic updates for your installed software and system. You can check periodically for updates. The needed software updates will be detected, downloaded, and installed for you. For added functionality, you can download numerous software applications for various sites. Some of the more popular software sites are listed here.

Linux Applications	Internet Site
Linux applications and development sites	**www.sourceforge.net**
Red Hat FTP site	**ftp.redhat.com** (for updates)
Linux Documentation Project	**www.linuxdoc.org**
Java Development Kit	**www.blackdown.org**

Linux Applications	Internet Site
Gnome applications	**www.gnome.org**
KDE applications	**apps.kde.com**
Linux applications in RPM packages	**www.rpmfind.net**
Window manager and desktop themes	**www.themes.org**
New Linux applications	**www.freshmeat.net**

*You will need a DVD-ROM drive on your computer to read the DVD-ROM disk, and a floppy drive to install Red Hat from the DVD-ROM. On either a Windows, DOS, or Linux system you will need to create an install floppy disk with the **images/boot.img** file on the DVD-ROM (unless you are performing a network or hard disk installation).*

To install Red Hat, you first have to create a floppy install disk using the rawrite or rawritewin application in the **/dosutils** directory on the DVD-ROM, and the **boot.img** image file in the **/images directory** (see Chapter 2 for more details). Booting from the floppy install disk, you install Red Hat from the DVD-ROM (the DVD-ROM is not bootable itself). At two points, the installation process will eject the DVD-ROM and ask you to insert the next CD-ROM. Just reinsert the same DVD-ROM. All the Red Hat CD-ROM disks are on the DVD-ROM.

You create the install disk from either Windows, DOS, or Linux. On Windows, you can use either the Windows **`rawritewin`** or the MS-DOS **`rawrite`** program. On MS-DOS, you use **`rawrite`**. The install disk has to be created on a computer that runs Windows or DOS. Install disk images exist for CD/DVD-ROM installation (**boot.img**), installing from a network source such as a Web site (**netimage.img**), and installing with PCMCIA support (**pcmcia.img**).

To use the **`rawritewin`** program to create a floppy install disk on Windows, first insert the DVD-ROM into your DVD-ROM drive. Change to your DVD-ROM drive. Once you have changed to the DVD-ROM drive, you then need to change to the **\dosutils\rawritewin** directory. The **`rawritewin`** command is in the **dosutils\rawritewin** directory. Just double-click to start it. It is very easy to create a boot disk with **`rawritewin`**. Just run it from within Windows and use its interface to select the floppy disk image you want. On the DVD-ROM included with this book, the install disk images are **boot.img**, **pcmia.img**, and **netboot.img**. The image file you want for a DVD-ROM installation is the **boot.img** file located on your DVD-ROM in the images directory**, images/boot.img**. Be sure that your floppy drive is correctly listed. The default will be drive A. Then, place a blank floppy in your floppy drive and click Write. If you need to create a network boot disk, use **netimage.img** instead. For PCMCIA support, use **pcmcia.img**.

For **`rawrite`**, which you have to use on MS-DOS, at your DOS prompt, change to your DVD-ROM drive, using whatever the letter that drive may be. For example, if your DVD-ROM drive is the E drive, just type **e:** and press ENTER. Once you have changed to the DVD-ROM drive, you then need to change to the **\images** directory. On the DVD-ROM included with this book, the install disk images are **boot.img**, **pcmia.img**, and **netboot.img**. The **rawritewin** command is in the **dosutils** directory.

The **rawrite** command has to be run at a DOS prompt. Enter the full path for the **rawrite** command including the DVD-ROM drive letter such as **e:\dosutils\rawrite**. The **rawrite** command first prompts you for the name of the disk image file you want to copy. Enter the full name of the install image file (in this example, **boot.img**). The command then asks you to enter the letter of the floppy drive where you put your floppy disk. On many systems, this is the A drive.

```
E:\> cd images
E:\col\launch\floppy > e:\dosutils\rawrite
Enter source file name: boot.img
Enter destination drive (A or B) and press ENTER: a
```

Press ENTER to confirm that you have a blank floppy disk in the drive. **rawrite** will then copy the image file to your floppy disk, creating your install disk. When it finishes, remove your disk from the floppy drive.

To create floppy disks on a Linux or Unix system, use the **dd** command and specify the boot image file to use along with the name of the floppy device and the size of the floppy disk. You will first need to mount the DVD-ROM, then change to its mount directory. On most Linux systems, the first floppy disk drive is at **/dev/fd0** and its size is usually 1400 for a 1.4 floppy disk. With the **if** option you specify the image file to use, the **of** option indicates the floppy device name, and the **bs** option specifies the block size.

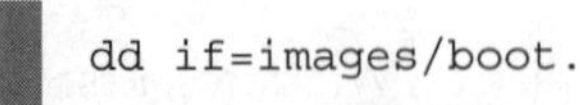

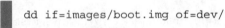

```
dd if=images/boot.img of=dev/fd0  bs=1440k
```

Note

During the software package installation phase with the DVD-ROM, you will be prompted to insert the second and later, possibly, the third CD-ROM. Just reinsert the same DVD-ROM disk. The single Red Hat DVD-ROM with this book is recognized as all three Red Hat CD-ROMs in the Red Hat distribution. The disk will be automatically ejected; just reinsert it.

Index

References to figures and illustrations are in italics.

B

E

F

G

H

K

L

N

O

P

Q

R

S

Z

INTERNATIONAL CONTACT INFORMATION

AUSTRALIA
McGraw-Hill Book Company Australia Pty. Ltd.
TEL +61-2-9415-9899
FAX +61-2-9415-5687
http://www.mcgraw-hill.com.au
books-it_sydney@mcgraw-hill.com

CANADA
McGraw-Hill Ryerson Ltd.
TEL +905-430-5000
FAX +905-430-5020
http://www.mcgrawhill.ca

GREECE, MIDDLE EAST, NORTHERN AFRICA
McGraw-Hill Hellas
TEL +30-1-656-0990-3-4
FAX +30-1-654-5525

MEXICO (Also serving Latin America)
McGraw-Hill Interamericana Editores S.A. de C.V.
TEL +525-117-1583
FAX +525-117-1589
http://www.mcgraw-hill.com.mx
fernando_castellanos@mcgraw-hill.com

SINGAPORE (Serving Asia)
McGraw-Hill Book Company
TEL +65-863-1580
FAX +65-862-3354
http://www.mcgraw-hill.com.sg
mghasia@mcgraw-hill.com

SOUTH AFRICA
McGraw-Hill South Africa
TEL +27-11-622-7512
FAX +27-11-622-9045
robyn_swanepoel@mcgraw-hill.com

UNITED KINGDOM & EUROPE (Excluding Southern Europe)
McGraw-Hill Education Europe
TEL +44-1-628-502500
FAX +44-1-628-770224
http://www.mcgraw-hill.co.uk
computing_neurope@mcgraw-hill.com

ALL OTHER INQUIRIES Contact:
Osborne/McGraw-Hill
TEL +1-510-549-6600
FAX +1-510-883-7600
http://www.osborne.com
omg_international@mcgraw-hill.com